Moreton Morrell Site

POVERTY AND DEVELOPMENT
INTO THE 21ST CENTURY

This book is the first in a series published by Oxford University Press
in association with The Open University

Poverty and Development into the 21st Century
edited by Tim Allen and Alan Thomas

Industrialization and Development
edited by Tom Hewitt, Hazel Johnson and David Wield

Rural Livelihoods: crises and responses
edited by Henry Bernstein, Ben Crow and Hazel Johnson

Development Policy and Public Action
edited by Marc Wuyts, Maureen Mackintosh and Tom Hewitt

The books are one component of the Open University course U208 *Third World Development*. Details of this and other Open University courses can be obtained from the Course Reservations Centre, PO Box 724, The Open University, Milton Keynes MK7 6ZS, United Kingdom: tel. +44 (0)1908 653231, e-mail ces-gen@open.ac.uk

Alternatively, you may visit the Open University website at http://www.open.ac.uk where you can learn more about the wide range of courses and packs offered at all levels by the Open University.

For information about the purchase of Open University course components, contact Open University Worldwide Ltd, The Berrill Building, Walton Hall, Milton Keynes MK7 6AA, United Kingdom: tel. +44 (0)1908 858785; fax +44 (0)1908 858787; e-mail ouwenq@open.ac.uk; website http://www.ouw.co.uk

POVERTY AND DEVELOPMENT
INTO THE 21ST CENTURY

EDITED BY TIM ALLEN AND ALAN THOMAS

The Open
University

in association with

OXFORD
UNIVERSITY PRESS

2000

This book has been printed on 115 gsm Precision Matt paper produced in Sweden from wood from managed forests using an elemental chlorine free bleaching process. It has been checked as being environmentally friendly by the Swedish Association for the Protection of Nature

OXFORD
UNIVERSITY PRESS

Great Clarendon Street, Oxford OX2 6DP

Oxford University Press is a department of the University of Oxford.
It furthers the University's objective of excellence in research, scholarship, and education by publishing wordwide in

Oxford New York Athens Auckland Bangkok Bogotá Buenos Aires Calcutta
Cape Town Channai Dar es Salaam Delhi Florence Hong Kong Istanbul
Karachi Kuala Lumpur Madrid Melbourne Mexico City Mumbai
Nairobi Paris São Paulo Singapore Taipei Tokyo Toronto Warsaw
with associated companies in Berlin Ibadan

Oxford is a registered trade mark of Oxford University Press in the UK
and certain other countries

Published in the United States by Oxford University Press Inc., New York

Published in association with The Open University

The Open University, Walton Hall, Milton Keynes MK7 6AA

First published 1992 as *Poverty and Development in the 1990s*

This completely revised edition first published 2000. Reprinted 2001, 2002, 2003, 2004.

Edited, designed and typeset by The Open University

Printed and bound by The Bath Press, Glasgow

British Library Cataloguing in Publication Data
Data available

Library of Congress Cataloguing in Publication Data
Data available

ISBN 0 19 877626 8

2.4

CONTENTS

List of authors and book production team *vi*

Preface
Tim Allen and Alan Thomas *vii*

Map of countries and major cities of the world *x*

CONCEPTIONS OF POVERTY AND DEVELOPMENT

1 Poverty and the 'end of development'
Alan Thomas **3**

2 Meanings and views of development
Alan Thomas **23**

A WORLD OF PROBLEMS?

3 Understanding famine and hunger
Ben Crow **51**

4 Diseases of poverty
Melissa Parker and Gordon Wilson **75**

5 Unemployment and making a living
David Wield and Joanna Chataway **99**

6 Is the world overpopulated?
Tom Hewitt and Ines Smyth **125**

7 Environmental degradation and sustainability
Philip Woodhouse **141**

8 A world at war
Tim Allen **163**

9 Agencies of development
Alan Thomas and Tim Allen **189**

THE GREAT TRANSFORMATION?

10 Diversity in pre-capitalist societies
Janet Bujra **219**

11 Colonialism, capitalism, development
Henry Bernstein **241**

12 The power of colonial states
David Potter **271**

13 Half a century of development
Tom Hewitt **289**

14 Socialist models of development
Andrew Kilmister **309**

15 The second 'great transformation'? Capitalism at the end of the twentieth century
John Harriss **325**

UNDERSTANDING DEVELOPMENT NOW

16 Sustainable globalization? The global politics of development and exclusion in the new world order
Anthony McGrew **345**

17 Democratization, 'good governance' and development
David Potter **365**

18 Rethinking gender matters in development
Ruth Pearson **383**

19 Technology, poverty and development
Gordon Wilson and Richard Heeks **403**

20 Life in the cities
Jo Beall **425**

21 Taking culture seriously
Tim Allen **443**

THE FUTURE OF DEVELOPMENT

22 Genetic engineering of development? Myths and possibilities
Joanna Chataway, Les Levidow and Susan Carr **469**

23 The new politics of identity
Tim Allen and John Eade **485**

24 Industrialization and development: prospects and dilemmas
Joanna Chataway and Tim Allen **509**

References **533**

Acknowledgements **553**

List of acronyms, abbreviations and organizations **556**

Index **558**

AUTHORS AND BOOK PRODUCTION TEAM

Tim Allen, Lecturer in the Development Studies Institute, London School of Economics

Jo Beall, Lecturer in Social Policy and Planning in Developing Countries, Department of Social Policy, London School of Economics

Sylvan Bentley, Picture Researcher, The Open University

Henry Bernstein, Professor of Development Studies at the School of Oriental and African Studies, University of London

Philippa Broadbent, Print Buying Controller, The Open University

Janet Bujra, Senior Lecturer and Director of Post-graduate Research, Department of Peace Studies, University of Bradford

Susan Carr, Lecturer in Systems, The Open University

Joanna Chataway, Lecturer in Development Management, The Open University

Daphne Cross, Print Buying Co-ordinator, The Open University

Ben Crow, Assistant Professor of Sociology, University of California, Santa Cruz

Sue Dobson, Graphic Artist, The Open University

Tony Duggan, Project Control, The Open University

John Eade, Reader in Sociology and Anthropology, Roehampton Institute, London

Sarah Gamman, Rights Editor, The Open University

John Harriss, Reader in the Development Studies Institute, London School of Economics

Richard Heeks, Senior Lecturer in Information Systems and Development, Institute for Development Policy and Management, University of Manchester

Tom Hewitt, Senior Lecturer in Development Policy and Practice, The Open University

Zoë Hoult, Course Manager, The Open University

Andrew Kilmister, Senior Lecturer in Economics, School of Business, Oxford Brookes University

Les Levidow, Research Fellow, Faculty of Technology, The Open University

Anthony McGrew, Professor of International Relations, Southampton University

June McGowan, Secretary, The Open University

Ray Munns, Cartographer, The Open University

Melissa Parker, Lecturer in Social Anthropology in the Department of Human Sciences, Brunel University

Ruth Pearson, Professor of Development Studies, University of Leeds

David Potter, Professor of Political Science, The Open University

Janice Robertson, Editor, The Open University

Jane Sheppard, Graphic Designer, The Open University

Ines Smyth, Policy Advisor, Gender and Learning Team, Oxfam GB

John Taylor, Copublishing Manager, The Open University

Alan Thomas, Senior Lecturer in Development Policy and Practice, The Open University

David Wield, Professor of Innovation and Development, The Open University

Gordon Wilson, Senior Lecturer in Development Policy and Practice, The Open University

Philip Woodhouse, Senior Lecturer in Environment and Rural Development at the Institute for Development Policy and Management, University of Manchester.

PREFACE

This is a completely revised edition of an ambitious book. As with the previous version, it is about huge topics which have implications for the whole future of humanity. In an important sense it is much too big for us, the editors, and for any of the authors. We do not know what is going on with any certainty, and despite the future-oriented title we certainly do not know what current trends will lead to. Still, this is no reason not to try to make sense of world affairs, and our aim is to help readers find ways of understanding and analysing events and actions around poverty and development as we move into the twenty-first century.

The original book aimed to introduce poverty and development in the 1990s, so it clearly had a limited shelf life. However, the work of revising the book for the first decade of the new century was much more than a simple updating. Much has changed in the world and in the study of development. The Cold War has receded into history and it has become clear that our previous concentration on development as a post-world-war phenomenon taking place in the 'third world' was a limited view shaped by Cold War thinking.

One of the implications is that the term 'third world' should be dropped, since it perpetuates a negative view of part of the world which is somehow to be thought of as separate from the part which really matters. As far as possible we have not used it in this second edition of the book. We now treat both poverty and development as concepts relevant anywhere and at all levels from the local to the global, and development in particular as having a 200-year history which parallels that of industrial capitalism, rather than one of only 50 years.

There is still at times a need for language to denote groups of countries. In this book, authors use different terms to refer to the poorer countries of the world as a group. Note, however, that whatever language is chosen and whatever definitions are used they are bound to contain an implicit view of the world. The World Bank classifies economies as 'low-income', 'middle-income' and 'high-income' (see world map, p.x). One can talk in terms of 'developing' and 'developed' countries or 'less developed countries' (LDCs) and 'advanced industrial countries' (AICs). Those who want to emphasize the common ground and the scope for political and economic solidarity that arises from being in a common position in relation to global capital might prefer the term 'the South' to refer to the mostly non-industrialized countries of Africa, Asia and Latin America on one side, and 'the North' for the industrialized, high-income countries on the other.

In the period since the first book was published the post-development school has utilized post-modern discourse analysis to make some trenchant criticisms of the whole concept of development and its historical and political pedigree. We would reply, however, that global poverty and the related problems which development addresses remain of vital importance, and the criticisms offer useful insights within a discussion of different forms of development rather than providing reason to abandon the idea.

Moreover, the demise of Soviet-style Communism, and also the shift away from simple neoliberal ideologies in western countries, has opened up more room for discussion and for potential action. Enthusiasm for market-driven strategies has waned, and there has been new interest in possible roles for the state – even if there remains little enthusiasm for old-style structuralist approaches – as well as a growing recognition of the importance of various non-governmental agencies. The main debate is no longer between grand theories of social transformation, but about degrees and forms of intervention.

This new edition takes all these changes on board. Still, in many respects our approach is the same. Although we expect many readers to be motivated by seeking to know what can be done about global poverty, the book is not mainly about policy. It is mostly about explanations and different ways of analysing and viewing the world, including the actions of development agencies. The explanations are generally in terms of livelihoods and social relations on the one hand and large-scale structural changes on the other.

This is still the first book in a series produced for an Open University course on development. The other books will also be replaced within two years, when there will be a completely revised course, concentrating on themes of development, globalization and sustainability. In the meantime the present book offers a self-contained introduction to issues and ways of thinking around poverty and development. Partly for this reason, it is longer than *Poverty and Development in the 1990s* and is even broader in scope (although it still cannot hope to be fully comprehensive).

We now deal directly with conceptions of poverty in Chapter 1 and have included several new chapters: on war, development agencies, the recent history of capitalism, urbanization, biotechnology. What is left out? Education, human rights, religion, nationalism, and information technology are all touched on, but, as we said in the previous edition about all these except the last, they could each have warranted a chapter to themselves. Information technology, in particular, could turn out to underlie a complete change in the global structure of society to what has been dubbed a 'knowledge society'.

Because of the remarkable Jubilee 2000 Campaign, debt cancellation is an issue in many people's minds at the turn of the millennium. We have not allocated a whole chapter to this, although international debt is discussed in several places in the book. Our own view is that although debt cancellation is of high importance for certain poor countries, it is unlikely to be the elixir some enthusiasts have suggested. The underlying problems, which are treated at length, will remain.

The book is arranged in five parts. The first introduces the concepts of poverty and development. Chapter 1 discusses how development is thought of differently since the end of the Cold War, introduces a variety of conceptions of poverty and deals with the suggestion from the post-development school that there is an 'end of development'. Chapter 2 sets out in some detail the different senses in which 'development' is used, in all their ambiguity, and the main theoretical views on development, all in relation to global capitalism.

The second part presents the idea of 'a world of problems'. Chapters 3 to 8 deal in turn with hunger and famine, diseases, unemployment, population, environmental degradation and war – each of which relates to an aspect of poverty and may be seen as one of the world's 'problems'. Then Chapter 9 looks at the question from the other side, suggesting that maybe the 'problem' is the inability to deal with these issues and hence focusing on the agencies of development which attempt to do so.

The third part takes its title from Karl Polanyi's idea of the 'great transformation' to an industrial market society which occurred from the early nineteenth century. It analyses the historical 'development' of capitalism, alongside which the history of development was also unfolding. Chapter 10 looks at pre-capitalist diversity; Chapters 11 and 12 consider European colonialism in relation to the development of capitalism on a world scale; Chapter 13 presents the history of development in the last 50 years; while Chapters 14 and 15 discuss the opposing socialist models of development and changes in late capitalism which have also shaped development as it is thought of today.

The fourth part explains further some current issues and concepts useful for understanding development as we enter the twenty-first century. Chapter 16 sets the scene with a critical exposition on globalization and Chapter 17 relates development to the current trend towards democratization and 'good governance'. Chapters 18, 19, 20 and 21 underline the necessity of including consideration, respectively, of technology, gender relations, urbanization, and wider aspects of culture in any assessment of development.

The final part, on the future of development, is more speculative but still concentrates on how to understand the issues that may dominate development in the early decades of the twenty-first century, rather than engaging in crystal-ball gazing. Will genetic engineering help feed the world (Chapter 22)? Will international politics be dominated by questions of ethnicity (Chapter 23)? The concluding chapter returns to the discussion of what general options are feasible for development into the twenty-first century, and in particular whether any such options are at all viable unless based, like previously dominant models of development, on large-scale industrialization.

By the end of the book you should be in a better position to begin to analyse or at least to ask the right kind of questions about any given example of 'development' in the coming years.

Throughout the book various devices are used to help you in your reading and study. Within the first introductory paragraphs of each chapter there is an emphasized Question or Questions, to which the rest of the chapter should provide some sort of answer. Each chapter ends with a Summary or Conclusion which you should be able to link back to the chapter Question(s). Key concepts are emphasized in bold lettering and have a boxed summary discussion of their meaning nearby. Numbered Boxes are used for long examples, cases, illustrations or specific explanations that can be taken separately from the main flow of the argument. Photographs and cartoons may be used not just to illustrate the text but to give additional examples, so you should look carefully at the captions. Tables are used to provide data to back up arguments in the text; note that different authors may have used different sources so that not all the tables are precisely compatible with each other.

Concepts may be mentioned without definition that are discussed more fully later. You should find that the Index emphasizes the place in the text where a concept is explained or where the boxed summary discussion of a concept occurs.

Apart from the Index, other points of reference are the World Map which follows this Preface and the List of Acronyms, Abbreviations and Organizations at the end of the book.

Sometimes the text asks you to make some calculations on a table, look carefully for certain features of an argument in an extract, consider your own views on a subject before going on, etc. Of course, you can simply read on and treat such questions as rhetorical – but in general you will gain more understanding through stopping briefly to try to answer the question posed.

Finally, please note that although the editors have endeavoured to arrange this book so that conceptual material is explained and built on throughout, it is written by a variety of authors with differing expertise as well as differing views. Not all the disagreements, points of overlap, possible cross-references, and so on, have been pointed out, though we hope there are not too many places where one author actually contradicts another! You should find it useful to try to make as many links for yourself as you can between the arguments in different chapters, so that you get as rounded a picture as possible of the complexity of poverty and development into the twenty-first century.

Tim Allen, London
Alan Thomas, Milton Keynes
July 1999

Map of countries and major cities of the world

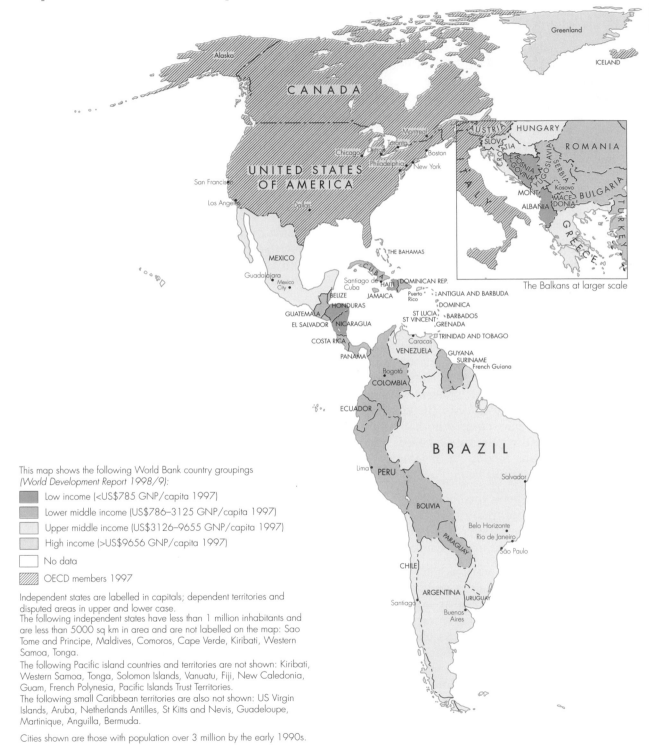

The Balkans at larger scale

This map shows the following World Bank country groupings (*World Development Report 1998/9*):

- Low income (<US$785 GNP/capita 1997)
- Lower middle income (US$786–3125 GNP/capita 1997)
- Upper middle income (US$3126–9655 GNP/capita 1997)
- High income (>US$9656 GNP/capita 1997)
- No data
- OECD members 1997

Independent states are labelled in capitals; dependent territories and disputed areas in upper and lower case.

The following independent states have less than 1 million inhabitants and are less than 5000 sq km in area and are not labelled on the map: Sao Tome and Principe, Maldives, Comoros, Cape Verde, Kiribati, Western Samoa, Tonga.

The following Pacific island countries and territories are not shown: Kiribati, Western Samoa, Tonga, Solomon Islands, Vanuatu, Fiji, New Caledonia, Guam, French Polynesia, Pacific Islands Trust Territories.

The following small Caribbean territories are also not shown: US Virgin Islands, Aruba, Netherlands Antilles, St Kitts and Nevis, Guadeloupe, Martinique, Anguilla, Bermuda.

Cities shown are those with population over 3 million by the early 1990s.

RUSSIAN FEDERATION

NORWAY
SWEDEN
FINLAND
ESTONIA
St Petersburg
UNITED
KINGDOM
LATVIA
LITHUANIA
DENMARK
Moscow
IRELAND
NETHERLANDS
BELARUS
GERMANY
POLAND
KAZAKSTAN
MONGOLIA
BELGIUM
LUX.
CZECH
SLOV.
UKRAINE
Beijing
Shenyang
AUSTRIA
HUNG.
MOLDOVA
UZBEKISTAN
KYRGYZ
REP.
NORTH KOREA
Tianjin
Seoul
JAPAN
FRANCE
SWITZ.
Milan
ROMANIA
GEORGIA
TAJIKISTAN
SOUTH
KOREA
Pusan
Tokyo/
Yokohama
Barcelona
Rome
BULGARIA
Istanbul
ARMENIA
AZERBAIJAN
CHINA
Osaka
PORTUGAL
Madrid
SPAIN
Naples
ALBANIA
GREECE
Ankara
TURKEY
TURKMENISTAN
Wuhan
Shanghai
Athens
AFGHANISTAN
Tehran
TUNISIA
MALTA
CYPRUS
LEBANON
SYRIA
IRAN
Tibet
BHUTAN
Guangzhou
TAIWAN
Western
Sahara
MOROCCO
ALGERIA
LIBYA
EGYPT
Alexandria
ISRAEL
Palestine
JORDAN
Baghdad
IRAQ
KUWAIT
Lahore
Kashmir
New
Delhi
NEPAL
MYANMAR
LAO
PDR
Hanoi
Hong
Kong
BAHRAIN
UNITED
ARAB
EMIRATES
PAKISTAN
Karachi
Ahmedabad
Calcutta
Dhaka
BANGLADESH
MAURITANIA
MALI
NIGER
CHAD
SUDAN
ERITREA
YEMEN
OMAN
QATAR
SAUDI
ARABIA
INDIA
Bombay
Hyderabad
THAILAND
Bangkok
VIETNAM
Manila
PHILIPPINES
SENEGAL
THE
GAMBIA
GUINEA-
BISSAU
GUINEA
SIERRA LEONE
LIBERIA
COTE
D'IVOIRE
BURKINA
FASO
BENIN
GHANA
TOGO
NIGERIA
CAMEROON
CENTRAL
AFRICAN REP.
DJIBOUTI
ETHIOPIA
SOMALIA
Bangalore
Madras
SRI
LANKA
MALDIVES
CAMBODIA
Ho Chi Minh
City (Saigon)
BRUNEI
MALAYSIA
Lagos
EQUATORIAL
GUINEA
GABON
CONGO
DEM. REP.
of
CONGO
Kinshasa
RWANDA
UGANDA
BURUNDI
KENYA
TANZANIA
SEYCHELLES
SINGAPORE
INDONESIA
Jakarta
Cabinda
ANGOLA
ZAMBIA
MALAWI
MOZAMBIQUE
ZIMBABWE
MADAGASCAR
MAURITIUS
East Timor
NAMIBIA
BOTSWANA
Johannesburg
SWAZILAND
LESOTHO
SOUTH
AFRICA
PAPUA NEW
GUINEA

AUSTRALIA

Melbourne
Sydney

NEW
ZEALAND

CONCEPTIONS OF POVERTY AND DEVELOPMENT

1

POVERTY AND THE 'END OF DEVELOPMENT'

ALAN THOMAS

This book is about poverty and development. Poverty is an age-old concern, but 'development' has only become an important concept in the last 200 years, and especially in the 50 years or so since the end of the Second World War. Alternative meanings of 'development' are hotly contested and indeed the very idea of development is under challenge to an extent not foreseen even a few years ago. Voices from the 'post-development' school claim that, at best, development has failed, or at worst it was always a 'hoax', designed to cover up violent damage being done to the so-called 'developing' world and its peoples. On the other hand, governments and inter-governmental organizations continue to adopt ambitious development targets: for example the aim agreed at the United Nations World Summit on Social Development in Copenhagen in 1995 to reduce by half by 2015 the proportion of people living in extreme poverty.

So a book introducing poverty and development *into the twenty-first century* is a great challenge. In many ways, extrapolating from the experience of the past 200 or 50 years is likely to be a very poor guide to the next decade, and no guide at all to the coming century. But the past is all we have to go on. We have to find modes of analysis that will help in understanding and assessing future experience in different parts of the world, however new and unexpected they may be.

One crucial area for analysis is the relationship between poverty and development. It might at first appear that the two are virtually opposites: surely poverty means a lack of development, whereas development implies moving towards getting rid of poverty, as in the Copenhagen Summit's target noted above. However, in practice it has proved quite possible historically for development to occur without alleviating poverty. Some even argue that development necessarily entails worsening poverty. For example, Karl Polanyi, writing in 1944, quotes an official British government document of 1607 which:

> "set out the problem of change in one powerful phrase: 'The poor man shall be satisfied in his end: Habitation; and the gentleman not hindered in his desire: Improvement.' This formula appears to take for granted the essence of purely economic progress, which is to achieve improvement at the price of social dislocation. But it also hints at the tragic necessity by which the poor man clings to his hovel, doomed by the rich man's desire for a public improvement which profits him privately."
>
> (Polanyi, 1944, p.34)

These days the debate is about 'development' rather than 'improvement', but it is still about whether there is any alternative to the kind of 'purely economic progress' which is achieved at great social cost. It is also still the rich and powerful who are in the position to be able to promote development. They are likely to do so in ways which benefit themselves, and although they will try to avoid 'social dislocation' at least when that dislocation affects them, it is by no means a foregone conclusion that such development will also benefit the poor.

Polanyi has been one of the influences on the revision of this book for its second edition, with his insistence on viewing historical change in relation to the 'great transformation' to industrial capitalism and a global market society, and what he saw as the 'inevitable self-destruction' (ibid., p.4) of that society. Polanyi was analysing the development of capitalism through the nineteenth century and the huge disruptions of the first part of the twentieth. As we enter the next century the idea of 'globalization' is dominating thinking about development. The implication is once again a 'great transformation' to a global market society, and questions about the contradictions, constraints and possibilities in such a context arise which are quite similar to those which exercised Polanyi.

In this new era of globalization, the question of the appalling poverty of large numbers of the world's people, with continuing enormous inequities between rich and poor, remains as potent as ever. Over the past decades, the increasing inequality in wealth between different parts of the world, the spread of localized wars, and the new importance of issues such as environmental degradation, international debt, religious fundamentalism and other forms of competing collective identity, all demonstrate the potential for 'social dislocation' turning into worldwide chaos. Thus it is ever more urgent to address such issues, and declarations such as that at Copenhagen are to be expected. Indeed, since 1995 development goals and targets have been reiterated in several areas related to poverty alleviation. The goals listed in Box 1.1 have been agreed at a series of OECD, United Nations and World Bank conferences. Nevertheless, national governments and international agencies remain apparently unable to mount a concerted and successful 'development' effort to remedy the situation.

> **Box 1.1 The World Bank's development goals**
>
> Six social goals to be monitored by the development community as part of a new international development strategy:
>
> *Poverty*. Reducing by one half the proportion of people in extreme poverty by 2015.
>
> *Mortality*. Reducing by two-thirds the mortality rates for infants and children under 5 and by three-fourths the mortality rates for mothers by 2015.
>
> *Education*. Achieving universal primary education in all countries by 2015.
>
> *Health*. Providing access to reproductive health services for all individuals of appropriate age no later than 2015.
>
> *Gender*. Demonstrating progress toward gender equality and the empowerment of women by eliminating gender disparities in primary and secondary education by 2015.
>
> *Environment*. Implementing national strategies for sustainable development by 2005 to ensure that the current loss of environmental resources is reversed globally and nationally by 2015.
>
> (Source: http://www.worldbank.org/data/ dev/devgoals.html)

You may well be motivated to read this book by a wish to answer the very practical question: 'What can be done?' There are of course no easy prescriptions, not least because of the wide variety of interests (often conflicting) at stake, and the great range of agencies that might potentially be involved in 'doing something' about any one of the varied issues that make up the field of development.

By whom is development being done? To whom? These are also potent questions. They should particularly be asked when 'solutions' are put forward that start 'We should...' without making it clear who 'We' are and what interests 'We' represent. In fact, rather than pursue the impossible aim of giving 'solutions' to development 'problems', the overall aim of this book is to provide you with means to begin *analysing* and *assessing answers* to the questions 'What can be done about world poverty?', 'What form should development take?' and 'What role can development play in reducing poverty?'

By the end of the book, questions will have been raised as to how far development in the twenty-first century is likely to involve new and different issues from those thought of previously as most important, and particularly whether the shift in the range of agencies involved in world development is marking a significant change in global governance. To put it another way, will the new century, following close on the end of the Cold War, see the world and its institutions transformed by the impact of globalization combined with other changes? Or, is the current highly turbulent state of affairs simply a transition to a new phase of development in which more or less the same concerns, the same theoretical frameworks, the same analytical tools, will continue?

In this first chapter we will consider in particular the following questions:

Q Has development failed, is it continuing in the same way, or does it mean something new as we enter the twenty-first century?

Q What are the dimensions of poverty, how do they relate to other global problems, and is there a sense in which this constitutes a 'global crisis'?

1.1 The 'era of development'

The second half of the twentieth century has been called the era of development. According to Sachs, writing in 1992 about the preceding forty years:

"Like a towering lighthouse guiding sailors towards the coast, 'development' stood as *the* idea which oriented emerging nations in their journey through post-war history. No matter whether democracies or dictatorships, the countries of the South proclaimed development as their primary aspiration, after they had been freed from colonial domination."

(Sachs, 1992, p.1)

The beginning of this era of development has been traced to January 20, 1949, when Harry S. Truman took office as President of the United States, declaring in his inaugural address that:

"We must embark on a bold new program for making the benefits of our scientific advances and industrial progress available for the improvement and growth of underdeveloped areas.

The old imperialism – exploitation for foreign profit – has no place in our plans. What we envisage is a program of development based on the concepts of democratic fair dealing."

(Truman, 1949, quoted in Esteva, 1992, p.6)

While claiming that the 'era of development' began at this point, Esteva does not suggest that the concept of development was new, recognizing that it had already been used and debated in many ways for 200 years. What was new, according to Esteva, was to define development in terms of escaping from underdevelopment. Since the latter referred to two-thirds of the world, this meant that most of the world had to define themselves as having fallen into the 'undignified condition called underdevelopment' (Esteva, 1992, p.7) and to look outside their own cultures for salvation. Development was now a 'euphemism' used to refer to United States hegemony, and it was ideals and 'programs' from the United States and its (Western) European allies which would form the basis of development everywhere.

Sachs and Esteva are leading members of the 'post-development school' and argue that development was always unjust, never worked, and has now clearly failed. According to Sachs, 'The idea of development stands like a ruin in the intellectual landscape' and 'it is time to dismantle this mental structure' (1992, p.1). For others, however, including the authors of this book, the idea of development has been of leading importance over the past half century and remains salient today. While there have been recurrent disappointments, it can be claimed that there have also been successes. In economic terms, for example, despite the setbacks of the

Asian financial crisis of late 1997, it remains the case that the four 'Asian Tigers' (Hong Kong, Singapore, South Korea and Taiwan) have industrialized and joined the ranks of the 'high-income economies' in terms of the World Bank's classification, with the implication that others might follow the same path, while China, the world's most populous country, has sustained an economic growth rate of over 10% for the last 20 years, with manufacturing now accounting for 40% of its gross domestic product (GDP – see below). In terms of human development, there have been general improvements such as reductions in mortality and increases in literacy and also specific cases of countries where socially oriented development policies have brought clear benefits (see below).

By contrast, many countries in Latin America, Central Asia and sub-Saharan Africa have sustained very low or even negative economic growth rates for the same twenty years and Africa in particular has seen a spread of civil war and in some cases the effective collapse of state administrations. There is plenty of evidence of what David Korten (1995) calls the 'global threefold human crisis' of 'deepening poverty, social disintegration and environmental destruction' (p.21). Indeed, the main reason to uphold the continuing importance of the idea of development is the vital need to address these issues. Thus the results of half a century of development efforts should perhaps be seen in terms of a 'balance sheet' of advances and setbacks (Table 1.1) rather than as outright failure.

The Cold War and the 'third world'

Truman's speech was mostly about how to respond to what was perceived in the United States as the threat of communism. If he could be said to have inaugurated an 'era of development', it was part of this response. Indeed, most of this 'era of development' has also been the era of the Cold War. The two superpowers, the USA and the USSR, vied with each other for influence over the newly independent, ex-colonial countries of the South. As we shall see in Chapter 14, the model of state-led socialist development exemplified by the USSR proved quite attractive to many of these countries, especially once China began to follow a similar path after the Chinese Communist Party took power in 1949.

Throughout this period too, development has been specifically applied to one part of the world, which became known as the 'third world'. This term came into use in the post-war period of the Cold War, at the same time as the growth of international institutions surrounding the United Nations. It was originally a political or ideological concept, a positive alternative to identification with poverty or underdevelopment. Roughly it denoted the search for a different approach from either capitalist (first world') or communist ('second world') – not necessarily a *middle* way, but certainly a distinctive, positive force.

Many sought a new form of democratic participation; neither the capitalist parties nor the organized communist parties on the Eastern European model provided for the sort of direct democracy they were after. In 1956 the Suez crisis provoked great disillusionment with the capitalist countries, but the Soviet invasion of Hungary in the same year generated a similar disillusion with Eastern European state socialism. This double crisis also gave Nasser, of Egypt, and Tito, of Yugoslavia, independent stature, and with India's Nehru they became the driving force behind the non-aligned movement (NAM).

In the words of Peter Worsley, author of *The Third World* (first published in 1964):

> "What the Third World originally was, then, is clear: it was the non-aligned world. It was also a world of poor countries. Their poverty was the outcome of a more fundamental identity: that they had all been colonized."
>
> (Worsley, 1979, p.102)

Non-aligned conferences have brought together the leaders of most of the countries of the 'developing' world every four years since 1961. By 1970 there was a clear 'non-aligned philosophy',

Table 1.1 'Balance sheet' of human development in the last third of the twentieth century

Indicator	Development	Deprivation
Health	Over the last 36 years life expectancy at birth for developing countries has increased (by over a third) from 46 to 62 years (p.20).	In 1997 31 million people were living with HIV, up from 22.3 million the year before (p.34).
	Four out of five people in the developing countries have access to health services (p.22).	880 million people worldwide have no access to health services (p.49).
Children	Nearly 90% of one-year-olds in developing countries are now immunized against tuberculosis (p.22).	109 million primary-school-age children (22%) are out of school (p.49).
Education	Between 1970 and 1995 the adult literacy rate in developing countries increased from 48% to 70% (p.23).	885 million adults (age 15 or more) worldwide are illiterate (p.49).
Women	Between 1970 and 1992 the female education enrolment ratio in developing countries rose from 38% to 68%.	6–8 hours a day spent by rural women in the South in fetching fuelwood and water (p.49).
Food and nutrition	Between 1970 and 1995 the index of daily calorie supply per capita in the South increased from 71 to 82 (i.e. reached 82% of the rate in the North) (p.151).	841 million people worldwide malnourished (p.49).
Income and poverty	From 1960 to 1995, the average GDP per capita for all developing countries rose from $330 to $867 (in 1987 US dollars) (p.142).	The three richest people in the world have assets that exceed the combined GDP of the 48 least developed countries (p.30).
	Global energy consumption is growing faster than population (p.46).	In the second half of the 1990s 1.3 billion people in developing countries live on less than $1 a day; 32% in the transition economies on less than $4 a day; and 11% in industrial countries on less than $14.40 a day (p.49).
Politics and conflict	In the 1990s two-thirds of the world's people live under fairly democratic regimes (p.23).	13.2 million people worldwide are refugees (p.49).
	Between 1996 and 1997 alone the number of conflicts worldwide fell from 21 to 18 (p.36).	In 1994 100 000 land mines were removed but an additional 2 million were planted (p.35).
Environment	In international conventions (like in Kyoto, Japan) governments agreed to take steps towards protecting the environment.	Desertification and drought affect 1.5 billion people worldwide (p.98).

Source: UNDP (1998a) *Human Development Report 1998*, United Nations Development Programme and Oxford University Press, New York.

emphasizing three basic principles: *peaceful co-existence*, *anti-colonialism* and the struggle for *economic independence*. In recent years the NAM has become much less prominent, though many of its members are also in the 'Group of Seventy-Seven' (G77), which continues to function as a political, and to some extent economic, pressure group, for example at the United Nations (see Chapter 16).

There were also movements towards creating a new, positive identity to counter what was seen as the alienating character of Westernized industrial culture. The extract in Box 1.2 is by Frantz Fanon, who was born in Martinique but spent many years helping in the fight for Algerian independence from France, and published several books aimed at countering 'the colonization of the personality'.

Box 1.2 Extract from *The Wretched of the Earth*

The Third World today faces Europe like a colossal mass whose aim should be to try to resolve the problems to which Europe has not been able to find the answers.

But let us be clear: what matters is to stop talking about output, and intensification, and the rhythm of work.

No, there is no question of a return to Nature. It is simply a very concrete question of not dragging men to mutilation, of not imposing upon the brain rhythms which very quickly obliterate it and wreck it. The pretext of catching up must not be used to push a man around, to tear him away from himself or his privacy, to break and kill him...

So, Comrades, let us not pay tribute to Europe by creating states, institutions and societies which draw their inspiration from her.

Humanity is waiting for something from us other than such an imitation, which would be almost an obscene caricature.

If we want to turn Africa into a new Europe, and America into a new Europe, then let us leave the destiny of our countries to the Europeans. They will know how to do it better than the most gifted among us.

But if we want humanity to advance a step further, if we want to bring it up to a different level than that which Europe has shown it, then we must invent and we must make discoveries...

For Europe, for ourselves and for humanity, Comrades, we must turn over a new leaf, we must work out new concepts, we must set foot a new man.

(Fanon, 1961, pp.253–5)

However, as time went on, both economic differentiation and political polarization tended to break up the rather fragile unity among third world countries and destroyed the original idea of the third world as the non-aligned world. In economic terms there were enormous and growing differences between the 'newly industrializing countries' (NICs), including the four 'Asian Tigers' and some others such as Brazil and Mexico, and the continuing poor agrarian countries such as most of those of sub-Saharan Africa. In political terms, Worsley points out that from the beginning 'Third World countries were overwhelmingly a sub-set of capitalist countries'. Nevertheless, by 1979: 'The choice has become, increasingly, polarized between capitalism and some variant of communism. In the wake of the US defeat [in Vietnam], a few countries have crossed into the other camp. But the choice has been between the two camps, not in some 'Third' direction' (Worsley, 1979, p.108).

Into the twenty-first century

Throughout the 1980s, these divisions if anything became even more pronounced. Also, neoliberalism, with its emphasis on market mechanisms, became the dominant way of thinking about development. New issues came to the forefront, notably the environment, international debt, and the question of gender relations. Then at the end of that decade came the sudden end of the Cold War (Figure 1.1). First, there were changes in Eastern Europe linked to the slogan of 'democratization', and the reunification of Germany in October 1990. It looked briefly as though there was a possibility of the new forms of democratic participation envisaged by those whose ideas gave rise to the 'third world' label back in the 1950s. However, what was happening was the collapse of the Soviet model of state socialism in Europe. The world now had the USA as its sole superpower, a fact underlined by the Gulf War which followed the crisis precipitated by the Iraqi invasion of Kuwait in August 1990. These events were closely followed by the dissolution of the Soviet Union itself. One of the two 'camps' that previously polarized the world effectively disappeared. Although China, Cuba and some other countries continued with state socialism in various forms, they either instituted market-oriented reforms or were so constrained by the global market and the United States' political superiority that they no longer constituted a viable alternative development model (Chapter 14).

*Figure 1.1   The end of the Cold War, 1990. (top) Presidents
Bush and Gorbachev at the signing of the CSCE joint
declaration; (above) demolishing the Berlin wall.*

The United States in particular saw an outbreak of triumphalism. In the words of Henry Kissinger: 'There has been a war between capitalism and socialism and capitalism has won!' American commentators referred to 'the new world order', using phrases such as 'Pax Americana' and 'the coming American century'.

The essay 'The End of History', by US State Department analyst Francis Fukuyama (1989), had already come to epitomize this popular feel-ing. In it Fukuyama put forward a grand view of history as the working out of struggles between great ideological principles. He caught the mood of the moment in the West by arguing that the fusion of liberal democracy and industrial capitalism now represented the only viable basis for modern human society.

The notion that liberal capitalism is now the only basis for development remains strong. However, many would quarrel with this proposition, not least because of continuing problems within global capitalism itself, as evinced by the East Asian financial crisis of 1997–98, as well as its inability to deal with Korten's 'global threefold human crisis'. There is a continuing need to ask 'Is there an alternative?' As Galbraith (1990) argued in a reply to Fukuyama, a concerted attack on poverty cannot be mounted within a pure capitalist framework. In a free market system, public resources are not likely to be mobilized in support of policies aimed directly at improving health, providing employment or protecting the environments which enable people to make their living.

In fact, an alternative is being pursued, though in rather a weak sense. The strict insistence on pure market relations emphasized by neoliberalism in the 1980s has softened. Attempts to achieve development targets such as those in Box 1.1 can be seen as invoking 'development' to ameliorate problems which would otherwise threaten mounting chaos at a global level, thus safeguarding the most important features of capitalist industrialization while allowing some modifications. There may be strong grounds for continuing to seek a more thoroughgoing alternative, but few in positions of power are thinking or acting on these lines.

Thus there are several ways in which development means something different as we enter the twenty-first century from what it has meant for most of the second half of the twentieth.

First, it can no longer be seen in terms of competing capitalist and communist models (with the possibility of searching for a third alternative), since 'capitalism has won'. And the notion that it refers specifically to part of the world, the 'underdeveloped' or 'third' world, which was common throughout this period, is clearly revealed as unhelpful or illusory. Development, if it continues to have meaning as we enter the twenty-first century, surely applies to processes which occur, or fail to occur, at all levels anywhere in the world, from the individual up to the global.

This means that development has to be analysed in relation to capitalism. This has always been the case, but the demise of the state socialist model of development makes it even more es-

sential. Possibilities for development now have to be related to the current realities of global capitalism, and the history of development should be viewed over the whole period of the domination of the industrial capitalist system, rather than only in relation to the polarized post-war world political order of the 'Cold War'.

Finally, since liberal capitalism is accepted as the dominant mode of social organization and the basis for globalization, it can be argued that development is now thought of mostly in terms of ameliorating problems rather than searching for alternative modes of wholesale social transformation. The importance of seeking an alternative remains, but is not manifest in the activities of any major development agencies.

1.2 Conceptions of poverty

Of the problems to be ameliorated, poverty is perhaps the most basic. Indeed, despite the huge differences surrounding the idea of development, what exactly it means and how it is to be achieved, there is general agreement (except from the post-development school – see Section 1.3 below) that it must include tackling poverty. The World Bank, for example, has endorsed this view for the last ten years, since it stated in its *World Development Report 1990* that 'Reducing poverty is the fundamental objective of economic development' (p.24). This commitment has now translated into targets like that in Box 1.1.

Income measures of poverty and development

Note that poverty applies to individuals and households, whereas development also refers to large-scale processes of change at societal level (see Chapter 2). The World Bank target of 'Reducing by one half the proportion of people in extreme poverty by 2015' requires a criterion for deciding if an individual or household is poor. The World Bank does this in economic terms, by measuring a person's income and establishing a 'poverty line' which represents an income level below which a person is held to be in extreme poverty. The global target for reducing poverty uses a single poverty line for the whole world, so that those in extreme poverty are those whose income is less than US$1 per day (measured in '1985 PPP dollars' – i.e. adjusted for 'purchasing power parity' – see Box 1.3 below). It is then possible to think of measuring the proportion of the population of a country below that poverty line – or estimating it, since there are enormous difficulties associated with direct measurement of individuals' incomes on a large scale.

The corresponding indicator used by the World Bank as a measure of the development of different countries is **gross national product (GNP)**. GNP uses market valuations, and is in practice a measure of national income; GNP per capita gives an indication of the average material living standard of a nation's people.

An increase in GNP per capita could mean development in that it implies an increase in prosperity or economic well-being and hence less poverty. However, as will be discussed further

Gross national product (GNP) and **gross domestic product (GDP):** GNP is the total income available for private and public spending in a country, while GDP measures the size of the economy. However, both are defined technically in terms of output. GDP is clearly and simply an *output* measure, defined by the World Bank as the 'total final output of goods and services produced by an economy'. In the case of GNP, output is used to define a measure of *income*. Thus GNP is 'the total domestic and foreign output claimed by residents of a country' in one year. What they 'claim' is also their income; thus GNP is a measure of national income and GNP per capita is a measure of the average income of each member of the population, including what they may earn or receive from abroad. GNP and GDP are of course closely related. The GNP of Nigeria, for example, is the output produced in Nigeria (its GDP), less whatever is 'claimed' by foreigners (repatriated profits, migrant workers' earnings, etc.), plus what Nigerians earn outside the country (remittances from abroad, returns on investments abroad).

in Chapter 3 (on the approach to poverty via the idea of *entitlement*), a measure such as GNP per capita has limitations in this regard (see also Box 1.3). GNP per capita is a measure of *average income* based on *market valuations*, and hence there are several ways in which the measure fails to give a full indication of the incidence of poverty. Being an average, GNP per capita says nothing about the distribution of wealth between rich and poor. Also, in general, GNP as an indicator underestimates both subsistence and collective goods, whereas it overvalues whatever is commercialized, individualized and organized.

Note that the idea of who is poor is different in different societies, and is likely to depend on value systems as well as economic factors. As Rahnema explains:

> "For long, and in many cultures of the world, poor was not always the opposite of rich. Other considerations such as falling from one's station in life, being deprived of one's instruments of labour, the loss of one's status or the marks of one's profession..., lack of protection, exclusion from one's community, abandonment, infirmity, or public humiliation defined the poor.
>
> (Rahnema, 1992, p.158)

Rahnema also points out that '*Global* poverty is an entirely new and modern construct' (ibid., p.161; my emphasis). The idea of measuring poverty at the level of entire nations and hence labelling certain countries as poor on the basis of their GNP per capita is also quite new. Rahnema suggests that while in many pre-industrial societies poverty applied to certain individuals and generally did not carry any implication of personal inadequacy, with the advent of global consumer society 'entire nations and continents were led to believe that they were poor, and in need of assistance, only because their per capita income was below a universally established minimum (ibid., p.162).

We can already see some of the inadequacies of using income as the sole way of measuring poverty (or development). One point is that what is regarded as poverty may differ relative to the

Box 1.3 Limitations of GNP per capita as a measure of prosperity or poverty

First, as an average measure, GNP per capita tells us nothing about income distribution within a country. Income distribution is notoriously difficult to measure, both for political and for technical reasons. Where statistics can be found, however, they indicate that many less developed countries have greater inequalities in income than industrialized countries. A few rich individuals may so distort the picture that the GNP per capita figure corresponds neither to the low standards of the masses nor to the wealth of these few.

Also, even where income distribution figures exist, they will generally be based on surveys carried out using the household as a unit rather than individuals. This leads to two further difficulties. Since larger households may also tend to be poorer, income per head may be even more unevenly distributed than income per household. And inequalities within households will be completely invisible. For example, if men get the meat, if boys get better educated, or if girl babies tend to be weaned earlier, then statistics based on households will not give a correct impression of individuals in absolute poverty.

Second, using market valuations for measuring income per capita gives rise to at least two different problems with relating this measure to poverty levels. GNP is a measure of production and its value is given in currency which can be freely converted internationally, for example into US dollars. However, the wage represented by the average GNP per capita in a

local currency does not have the same purchasing power for commodities at local prices. In fact, real purchasing power in poor countries may be relatively higher, so that, for example, a Sudanese on an annual income the equivalent of US$365 (one US dollar per day) might subsist somewhat better than a US citizen with only a dollar a day in the USA, so long as local Sudanese prices for basic foodstuffs etc. were lower than international prices. (GNP per capita figures – and measures of individual or household income – are often converted to US dollars in such as way as to allow for this factor. When this is done the result is given in 'purchasing power parity dollars' or 'PPP dollars'.)

The final point is that well-being is not entirely a matter of purchasing power. The most obvious example of this may be production for use (i.e. subsistence or 'direct entitlement'; see Chapter 3) by peasants or petty commodity producers. One might be able to measure the potential market value of such items, but what about less concrete items or collective goods? Education and health, for example, are much less tangible but no less basic needs. Education could be considered an inseparable part of life, with no price put on it; or it might be considered a commodity, with school fees charged and salaries paid to teachers, in which case it will form part of a country's GNP. Another, ironic, example, often quoted, is how a polluting industry with added pollution control could contribute more to GNP than a less polluting alternative.

---

norms of each particular society. A second is that income measures only one dimension of well-being, so that a broader view would take it to form only part of any definition of poverty (or vision of development). This latter point may be broadened further to consider poverty itself as only one aspect of the problems confronting humanity, but one which cannot be separated from the others. Below, I discuss each of these three points in turn. There are, however, a number of other dimensions to the debate on how to characterize and measure poverty, which are summarized in Box 1.4.

Relative poverty and social exclusion

One of the best known discussions of the notion of *relative* poverty comes from a work on poverty in Britain at the end of the 1970s by Peter Townsend:

"Individuals, families and groups in the population can be said to be in poverty when they lack the resources to obtain the types of diets, participate in the activities and have the living conditions and amenities which are customary, or at least widely accepted and approved, in the societies to

---

Box 1.4 Dimensions of the poverty debate

The conceptual complexity can be understood as a series of fault lines in the debate about poverty. There are nine of these:

Individual or household measures. Early measurement of poverty…was at the household level, and much still is. Other analysis disaggregates to the individual level, so as to capture intrahousehold factors and different types and causes of deprivation affecting men, women, children, old people, etc.

Private consumption only or private consumption plus publicly provided goods. Poverty can be defined in terms of private income or consumption (usually consumption rather than income, in order to allow for consumption smoothing over time, e.g. by managing savings), or to include the value of goods and services provided publicly, the social wage.

Monetary or monetary plus non-monetary components of poverty. So-called money-metric measures are often used, because they are either regarded as sufficient on their own or seen as an adequate proxy for poverty. However, there is a clear fault line between definitions of poverty which are restricted to income (or consumption) and those which incorporate such factors as autonomy, self-esteem or participation. […]

Snapshot or timeline. Many surveys and poverty assessments report the incidence of poverty at a point in time. However, there is a long history of thinking about poverty in terms of life cycle experience…, seasonal stress, and shocks (illness, drought, war). In both North and South, there has been increasing attention to understanding movement in and out of poverty…

Actual or potential poverty. Some analysts include as poor those who are highly sensitive to shocks, or not resilient. Small-scale pastoralists exposed to the risk of drought are a common example: current income may be adequate, but vulnerability is high…

Stock or flow measures of poverty. The definition of poverty as income focuses on the flow of material goods and services. An alternative is to examine the stock of resources a household controls. This may be measured in terms of physical or monetary assets (land, jewellery, cash), or in terms of social capital (social contacts, networks, reciprocal relationships, community membership…[E]ntitlements may derive not just from current income, but also from past investments, stores or social claims on others (including the State).

Input or output measures. …[P]overty measured as a shortfall in income essentially captures an input to an individual's capability and functioning rather than a direct measure of well-being. Writing about poverty has often assumed, wrongly, an automatic link between income and participation, or functioning, in the life of a community.

Absolute or relative poverty. The World Bank currently uses a figure of $US 1 per day (in 1985 purchasing power parity dollars) for absolute poverty. The alternative has been to define poverty as relative deprivation, for example as half mean income, or as exclusion from participation in society…

Objective or subjective perceptions of poverty. The use of participatory methods has greatly encouraged an epistemology of poverty which relies on local understanding and perceptions. For example, exposure to domestic violence may be seen as important in one community, dependency on traditional structures in another.

(Extracted from Maxwell, 1999)

---

which they belong. Their resources are so seriously below those commanded by the average individual or family that they are, in effect, excluded from ordinary living patterns, customs and activities."

(Townsend, 1979, p.31)

This notion has been attacked by those who argue that people in industrialized countries should not be regarded as poor if, for example, they are unable to afford a television or refrigerator or a few toys for their children, so long as they are able to maintain a minimum level of nutrition. Conversely, there may be objections to setting a poverty line at a higher level in industrialized countries so as to take account of the fact that a minimum of consumer goods is necessary to take part in 'ordinary living patterns' in those countries compared with less developed countries, on the grounds that this downgrades the needs of those living in poorer countries.

Nevertheless, this notion of relative poverty has gained widespread acceptance. Thus the World Bank uses a figure of US$14.40 per day (in 1985 PPP dollars) to calculate the numbers in poverty in industrialized countries (rather than the $1 per day for the world as a whole). This figure was the official United States income poverty line, calculated in terms of the minimum required to obtain what is needed to participate in the everyday life of US society. Another common measure is the percentage whose income is below half the median income level in a particular country.

It is also possible to interpret Townsend's ideas in terms of a broader notion of the 'resources' 'commanded' by a person or household than just income. Thus Amartya Sen puts forward a view of poverty which derives from the idea of failure to be able to take a full part in human society but which sees this as a matter of lack of choice or capability rather than simply material living standards (see e.g. Sen, 1983, 1985; see also Chapter 3 for an expansion of Sen's arguments into the notion of entitlements).

A particularly graphic description of what is meant by poverty as lack of choice (see also Figure 1.2) was given almost thirty years ago by Denis Goulet:

"The prevalent emotion of underdevelopment is a sense of personal and societal impotence in the face of disease and death, of confusion and ignorance as one gropes to understand change, of servility towards men whose decisions govern the course of events, of hopelessness before hunger and natural catastrophe. Chronic poverty is a cruel kind of hell, and one cannot understand how cruel that hell is merely by gazing upon poverty as an object."

(Goulet, 1971, p.23)

A related idea is that of **social exclusion**. This concept originated in France but is now applied throughout the industrialized North and its applicability for the South is a matter of debate (see e.g. de Haan, 1998). De Haan argues that social exclusion is a useful concept for two main reasons. First, it points up the multi-dimensional character of deprivation in that exclusion can have various causes (which often reinforce each other), such as unreliable employment, gender, ethnicity, disability or ill health, and lack of opportunities for participation, as well as low income. Second, it focuses on processes: on 'the mechanisms and institutions that exclude people' (de Haan, 1998, p.10). This makes it clear that deprivation is not simply an attribute of particular people but that different societies have their own ways of defining people out.

> **Social exclusion:** "the process through which individuals or groups are wholly or partially excluded from full participation in the society in which they live" (European Foundation, 1995, p.4).

Bauman discusses the way 'the poor' are defined in similar vein, as follows:

"No society we know of was ever free of a category of people who were seen by the rest as incapable, for whatever reason, of eking out a living by their own efforts; of living as the rest do. It is a social decision to classify people in such a way. Since it has little to do with who those people are, or even what they do, the expectation that 'the poor will always be with us' can hardly be faulted. Each society constitutes and perpetuates itself through setting and prompting certain standards it expects every member to follow, and those standards can only be made visible if some people are seen to fail to meet them. Such people can then be declared a 'problem' which the rest of society must and should cope with.

Figure 1.2   Are these people 'poor'? Labourers in the open-cast Serra Pelada gold mines in northern Brazil have a regular though very low income, working a 12-hour day carrying 120-lb sacks up 200-foot ladders with considerable risk of injury or work-induced illness. How much choice do they have?

The poor of different times and places differ between themselves in virtually every aspect of their condition, just like the societies of which they are part. Who is cast in this way depends not on how the poor live, but on the way society as a whole lives...The treatment reserved for the poor, the way in which pity and condemnation are mixed, is a matter for society at large rather than for the poor themselves; a reflection of the standards a given community holds dear and is bent on cultivating."

(Bauman, 1999, p.20)

Many studies of social exclusion in the North concur with previous discussions of poverty in attributing it mainly to unemployment, so that solutions concentrate on job creation (or the

French term 'insertion' in the sense of insertion into the labour market and hence into the community). However, Bauman argues that modern industrial society is essentially a consumer society and that those unable to contribute to market demand are increasingly blamed, 'accused of flaunting the values by which 'decent' people live', with the result of 'shifting the people living below the poverty line from the realm of moral responsibility to that of law and order' (Bauman, 1999, p.21).

How the concept of social exclusion applies in different cases in the South clearly depends on what defines participation in particular societies. 'The poor' are those unable to participate in whatever way, and although they 'differ between themselves' they may still be regarded as a threat to social order as much as an object of humanitarian concern.

Dimensions of deprivation and of development

As the idea of social exclusion begins to suggest, poor people exhibit a variety of problems which go well beyond low income and which tend to feed off each other. The same can be said for poor neighbourhoods or regions, or even poor countries, though as noted above to define the whole of a country as poor is problematic in many ways. Boxes 1.5 and 1.6 give contrasting vignettes describing a 'poor' neighbourhood in a Northern city and a 'poor' city in a Southern country. Note that both are journalistic accounts rather than the results of academic studies. Both are very different from the traditional Northern image of the poverty of the unemployed, as in the Depression of the 1930s, and from the rural poverty of the mass of the populations of Africa and South Asia. Still, it is clear that in all these cases the poor suffer from a variety of deprivations which reinforce each other.

An alternative approach to the characterization of poverty is to concentrate on measuring the various dimensions of deprivation separately and then put them together. The United Nations Development Programme (UNDP) has followed this approach to develop a series of composite measures.

On the one hand it has produced the Human Development Index (HDI) and a number of variants. The basic HDI is an average of indices of what the UNDP considers to be the three most important aspects of human development: the health of a population, measured by life expectancy; its educational attainment; and its material standard of living, measured by GDP per capita (in PPP dollars; see Box 1.3 above).

More recently the UNDP has also produced a Human Poverty Index (HPI), again with variants. In a similar way, the HPI is an average of three (or four) measures of deprivation: vulnerability to death at a relatively early age, deprivation in knowledge, and lack of decent living standards. Interestingly, the UNDP has developed two different HPIs, one for industrialized countries and one for developing countries. Different standards for what constitutes deprivation are used in the two cases; thus for developing countries the first index is based on the proportion of the population not living beyond the age of 40, whereas for industrialized countries the age of 60 is substituted; for developing countries poor living standards are measured by lack of access to health services and to safe drinking water, whereas for industrialized countries an income measure is used. In addition, for industrialized countries a fourth measure, of social exclusion, as indicated by the level of unemployment, is also included.

There is a clear contrast between the main indicators of poverty and of development used by the World Bank and the UNDP. While the former concentrates on income measures, the latter has a broader view of poverty (and development) as multi-dimensional. The policy implications of the two are also different. Whereas the Bank stresses labour-intensive economic activities, the UNDP would give more emphasis to developments in the social services like education and health.

Poverty as part of the global 'crisis'

You may have noticed that the deprivations suffered by the inhabitants of the locations depicted in Boxes 1.5 and 1.6 go beyond the dimensions

Box 1.5   Poverty in the UK

The 1980s and early 1990s saw the birth of a poverty in this country (UK) which was not simply on a scale that had not been seen for more than 40 years but which was also of a kind that simply had never been seen here at all. This new poverty is complex…

Those communities live under immense pressure, and it is for that reason that significant numbers of those who live there have been shovelled into crime and prostitution and drugs and alcoholism and child abuse, into a life of ruthless self-interest. How else do you survive?…

So what has changed? At its simplest the poor are buried under layers of aggravations. The first layer is the historically familiar one; they suffer material hardship. During the 1980s they were forced out of work and their benefits were cut, over and over again; those who clung on to unskilled or part-time work saw legal safety nets removed so that their low pay fell even lower.

But that is traditional poverty. The other layers under which they are being crushed are new.

The most damaging of these is the war against drugs, which is inflicting enormous harm on the very people it pretends to be protecting…The key point now is not so much the narcotic effect of the drugs black market but its economic importance. If you are a 16-year-old school-leaver on one of those estates with no qualifications and no hope of a decent job, and if you want life to provide you with the income and the status and stimulus which other adolescents will find in college and career, there is an obvious way forward…[Y]ou get on your bike and start dealing and you slip into a vortex of criminality and violence.

Consider, also, what has happened to the classic escape route offered to the poor by state education. Ask social workers how they get on nowadays when they call headteachers to plead for a place for difficult children on their books. The doors to the escape route are shut.

There are still residents' groups and community leaders bravely struggling to hold things together but they are trying to turn a tidal wave with a teaspoon. It is not just that neighbours may no longer help each other; frequently, they do not even know each other. It is not just that

the physical fabric of the estates is collapsing into a mess of brambles and broken windows, there is effectively no one there any more to reverse the decline. The old stability has gone and, with it, the familiar faces and the bonds between them. More than that, they have been replaced by absentee landlords who have only the slightest interest in the physical condition of the houses and in the community around them.

The point of all this is that poverty is not just about being short of money. Take material hardship, combine it with the black market in drugs, close the door on education, kill off the community, add a dozen different other aggravations and you end up with a recipe for deep damage – physical, emotional, social, spiritual damage. When the government looks at the notorious single mother and thinks that the answer is to offer her a job and to threaten her benefit, it ignores the obstacle course of other problems that lie in her path. She may be clinically depressed, simply unable to find the emotional will to cope and/or she may be a heroin addict and/or she has no one to look after her child, who is probably asthmatic and/or she may be terrified to leave her house because she knows it will be burgled (some of the estate gangs specialize in "total burglaries" where they take everything, even the carpets and the hot-water tank) and/or she is scared of being assaulted by some neighbour she fell out with and/or she has unpaid fines and she knows the courts will take whatever extra she earns and/or, and/or. Take the 18-year-old boy who is told that he will lose his welfare if he does not accept the dead-end work he is offered. Why should he play that game when there is a crack cocaine supermarket offering ready, steady career prospects on his doorstep? Take any of those men, women or children who have become so alienated and angry and self-destructive and bad that they may not want to behave in a rational, self-interested way. It does not matter how much you manipulate benefits or rewrite regulations, it's like curing cancer with Elastoplast. The damage is deep, much more complicated than it appears at first sight, much more difficult to reverse.

(Extracts from 'There is nothing natural about poverty', Nick Davies, *New Statesman*, 6 November 1998)

Box 1.6 Poverty in a Brazilian city

Since the second world war the Brazilian Amazon has been the destination of one of the largest migratory waves anywhere this century. Twenty years ago 6 million people lived there; now the figure is 19 million, and growing…

"It is total chaos," said Gilberto Siqueira, a former planning officer of Rio Branco, Acre's capital. "In 1991, when the last census was taken, 40% of urban homes were without running water and 88% had no sewage pipes – more than twice the national average."

Acre, a densely forested region bordering Bolivia and Peru, is the most remote Amazon state and its social problems the most acute. In 1970 Rio Branco was a town of 36,000. Now it is an ugly urban sprawl housing more than 250,000. The roads are full of potholes and you are never far from the stench of sewage.

Bishop Moacyr Grechi, who has served in the diocese for 26 years, said: "When I got here I would leave all the windows of my house open. I could walk through any neighbourhood, no problem. People would be playing dominoes on the street. There were no beggars. Now a family doesn't go out at night for fear of getting robbed."

The city – the 25th largest in Brazil – has the 10th highest violent crime rate. "Proportionately, Rio Branco is the most dangerous city in the Amazon. If the other cities don't manage themselves properly, they will become like us," warned Gercino da Silva, Acre's chief justice.

Mr Da Silva's efforts to crush the three death squads blamed for more than 100 murders in recent years have put a price on his head. The federal government pays for 24-hour armed protection.

"The death squads are run by policemen and taxi drivers. They kill in the shanty towns and think they are doing society a favour," he said.

The medical statistics are chilling: more than 10 per cent of Rio Brancans have the hepatitis virus and the public health services are so poor that not even half the children are vaccinated against it.

Perinatal mortality is the second highest cause of death in the state. In several towns blood transfusions are done without testing the blood. And it has the highest number of leprosy cases in Brazil – about one per thousand – close to levels in India.

The delinquent gangs in the shanty towns kill fewer people than the health service, said Tiao Viana, one of Acre's most eminent doctors. "You can't expand a city without expanding the public health services," he said. "You need to develop everything together – infrastructure, health, education."

Acre's proximity to Peru and Bolivia has put it on the drug trafficking route. Dr Donald de Fernandes, who works with addicts in Rio Branco, estimates that half the adolescents use cocaine.

[One] neighbourhood, Montanhaes, was rainforest until a year ago, when homeless people chopped down the trees to build huts.

Most of them have little chance of securing work. Many can barely sign their name – the illiteracy rate is 49 per cent, way above the national average. Most of the shantytowns have no running water, no tarred roads and no sewerage, and the only way to get electricity is to wire the shack up illegally to a nearby pylon.

(Extracts from 'Seed of hope in Amazon's urban jungle', Alex Bellos, *The Guardian*, 4 December 1998)

of ill health, poor educational attainment and low material standards included in the UNDP's HDI. For example, their neighbourhoods are subject to a high degree of violence and to dangerous levels of pollution. It is unclear whether these should be included as aspects of poverty. What is incontrovertible is that many of the world's poorest people also suffer directly from the consequences of social disintegration and environmental destruction, which together with poverty itself form the 'threefold human crisis' which according to Korten (1995) is affecting the world more and more deeply.

Korten's description of this 'crisis', written in 1995, depicts the three elements as reinforcing each other and spiralling out of control. The following brief extracts give a flavour of his view of the situation, which he argues requires radically new approaches not least from private corporations, not noted for their development activity:

"Even in the world's most affluent countries, high levels of unemployment, corporate downsizing, falling real wages, greater dependence on part-time temporary jobs without benefits, and the weakening of unions are creating a growing sense of insecurity…The world is increasingly divided between those who enjoy opulent affluence and those who live in dehumanizing poverty, servitude and economic insecurity…

Evidence of the resulting social stress is everywhere: in rising rates of crime, drug abuse, divorce, teenage suicide, and domestic violence; growing numbers of political, economic and environmental refugees; and even the changing nature of organized armed conflict…

Environmentally, although there have been important gains in selected localities in reducing air pollution and cleaning up polluted rivers, the deeper reality is one of growing ecological crisis…The younger generation lives with the question of whether they may be turned into environmental refugees by climate changes that

threaten to melt the polar ice caps, flood vast coastal areas, and turn fertile agricultural areas into deserts."

(Korten, 1995, pp.19–21)

You may wonder whether Korten is portraying only one side of the picture. As noted in Table 1.1, there are considerable development achievements to balance against continuing deprivation and the other aspects of Korten's global 'crisis'. Certainly, this 'crisis' is continuing at the same time as high rates of GDP growth and optimism in capital markets. Whether, by the time you read this, these trends will be continuing, or will have been interrupted by a global economic downturn or new financial crisis, remains to be seen. Still, whether they add up to a global 'crisis' or not, it is clear that social dislocation and environmental degradation should be considered alongside poverty, if not as aspects of poverty, when assessing the problems which development has to address as we enter the twenty-first century.

1.3   The end of development?

At the start of this chapter I cited thinkers of the post-development school who regard development as having failed and the 'era of development' as being over. If the 'global threefold crisis' is as serious as Korten suggests, then, given that development has been such a dominant concept during the very period when the crisis has been building up, there is some force to the suggestion that development has failed. Alternatively, as several of the post-development school suggest, development was a 'hoax', never designed to deal with humanitarian and environmental problems, but simply a way of allowing the industrialized North, particularly the USA, to continue its dominance of the rest of the world in order to maintain its own high standards of living.

Some use stronger language still. Alvares (1994) argues that 'development' is 'a label for plunder and violence, a mechanism of triage' (p.1). Using the metaphor of triage, with its implication of dividing a damaged population into those well enough to benefit from assistance and those to be left to their fate, Alvares suggests that industrial development is deliberate 'triage' in that it is known that only some can benefit. In some cases people are simply excluded ('passive triage') or in others those who benefit do so directly at the expense of others ('active triage'). The latter can occur when resources which were used for subsistence are commandeered to feed industry, when markets for industrial goods destroy previous modes of livelihood, or when industrial pollution renders common resources unusable.

Still, does not this simply underline the intractability of the 'threefold crisis', which surely requires some concerted action? If action is not to be in the name of development then would not another concept have to be put forward with probably just as many contradictions?

Some post-development writing seems to imply there is no need for action. Romantic views are put forward of pre-industrial societies where people 'have few possessions, *but they are not poor*' (Sahlins, 1997, p.19, emphasis in original). Sahlins goes on:

> "Poverty is not a certain small amount of goods, nor is it just a relation between means and ends; above all, it is a relation between people. Poverty is a social status. As such, it is the invention of civilization. It has grown with civilization, at once as an invidious distinction between classes and more importantly as a tributary relation – that can render agrarian peasants more susceptible to natural catastrophes than any camp of Alaskan Eskimo."
>
> (Sahlins, 1997, p.19)

It is certainly important to recognize that what is regarded as poverty is not absolute but depends on the value system of a particular society. In my discussion of poverty above I quoted some similar useful insights from Rahnema, another post-development writer. Still, there are two problems with the implication that no action should be taken. First, there may have been a few examples of rural idylls with co-operative

values, but many pre-industrial societies contained their own inequities as well as suffering objectively low standards of living. Second, in today's world industrialization is global so virtually all poor people and communities are not pre-industrial but exist in some relation to global industrial capitalism. There can be no question of foregoing development in order to leave people in a state of pre-industrial grace.

So some kind of action is required. Should it be called development? Post-development thinking is based on post-modern discourse analysis and has a lot of useful insights into the derivation of terms and the politics of the way they are used. Is there not some force in the argument that 'development' is too contaminated a term to be of use? If it is used to denote the type of exploitative capitalist development that is accompanied by extreme negative consequences for many, then how can the same term be used for attempts by other capitalists or by state agencies to ameliorate these consequences in order to avoid social unrest, or for attempts to find radical 'people-centred' alternatives? As we will see in Chapter 2, 'development' is actually used to mean all these things. It may be ambiguous, but common usage cannot be argued away.

What do post-development writers themselves say about what should be done? In fact, despite their romanticizing of pre-industrial societies, they do not deny the need for change. What they argue is that in order for change to be undertaken differently, it needs to be conceived literally in different terms. Here is part of the conclusion to the entry by Arturo Escobar on 'Planning' in Sachs' *Development Dictionary* (1992):

> "While social change has probably always been part of the human experience, it was only within European modernity that 'society', i.e. the whole way of life of a people, was open to empirical analysis and made the subject of planned change. And while communities in the Third World may find that there is a need for some sort of organized or directed change – in part to reverse the damage done by development – this

undoubtedly will not take the form of 'designing life' or social engineering. In the long run, this means that categories and meanings have to be redefined; through their innovative political practice, new social movements of various kinds are already embarked on this process of redefining the social, and knowledge itself."

(Escobar, 1992, p.144)

Majid Rahnema addresses the question of what is to be done directly in his conclusion to *The Post Development Reader* (1997). He admits that "it may be true that the majority of people whose standard of life has in fact greatly deteriorated do want change" (p.388). But the answer he suggests is not development but 'the end of development':

"The end of development should not be seen as an end to the search for new possibilities of change, for a relational world of friendship, or for genuine processes of regeneration able to give birth to new forms of solidarity. It should only mean that the binary, the mechanistic, the reductionist, the inhumane and the ultimately self-destructive approach to change is over. It should represent a call to the 'good people' everywhere to think and work together."

(Rahnema, 1997, p.391)

Rahnema even allows for the possibility of 'intervention', as long as it is done in a spirit of self-criticism:

"The case is different with a *project of intervention*, which is prepared and developed somewhere, often in an institutional framework, with a view to changing the lives of other people, in a manner useful or beneficial to the intervener. Hence the need for the latter to be aware that he or she is launched on an adventure fraught with considerable danger. Such awareness makes it necessary for interveners to start examining the whys and wherefores of their actions. Exceptional personal qualities are needed to prevent 'well intentioned' interventions producing results contrary to those planned – as has been the case in most 'developmental' and many 'humanitarian' instances."

(Rahnema, 1997, p.397)

These are extremely important points. But to me – and to most if not all the authors in this book – they are points *about* development from a radical position, not arguments for abandoning the concept. Deciding not to use the term would not do away with real problems to do with poverty and powerlessness, environmental degradation, and social disorder, or with practical dilemmas such as that posed by the fact that to date there are no examples of large-scale improvements in living standards without industrialization and the huge dislocations it brings. This book is written in the belief that it is useful to help readers understand the issues surrounding poverty and development. The powerful development agencies of the world certainly do not recognize any 'end of development'. It is important to be able to analyse what they are doing as well as alternative positions. However, insisting on the continuing importance of development does not mean endorsing any particular approach.

Let me conclude this introductory chapter by quoting the response of Robert Chambers to Sachs' image of development as a 'ruin in the intellectual landscape':

"That is no grounds for pessimism. Much can grow on and out of a ruin. Past errors as well achievements contribute to current learning."

(Chambers, 1997, p.9)

Summary

1   Some have called the second half of the twentieth century the 'era of development'. That period was also the era of the Cold War and anti-communism in the West, which is now over and 'capitalism has won'.

2   As we enter the twenty-first century, development can no longer be seen as it has been for the past half-century in terms of competing capitalist and communist models, applied specifically to the 'third world'. Development has to be considered in relation to global industrial capitalism, with a history, like industrial capitalism, of 200 years rather than just 50. As a concept, development also applies to processes occurring at all levels anywhere, from the local to the global. In addition, development may now be more about ameliorating problems than wholesale social transformation, though seeking alternatives is still important.

3   Development must include tackling poverty. Poverty can be conceived in different ways, notably: through income measures (GNP per capita, numbers below a poverty line); as relative poverty or social exclusion; as incorporating multiple dimensions of deprivation; as part of a broader 'global crisis'.

4   The post-development school regards development as having failed and as a 'hoax'. There are improvements to balance against the continuing deprivation in many areas, so development is not a total failure. Also, although the post-development arguments give some useful insights, these are effectively arguments about development from a radical position. There is still a need for action to tackle poverty. Thus this book uses the accepted concepts of poverty and development, with all their ambiguities, and attempts to help readers understand issues around poverty and development rather than look for new language.

2

MEANINGS AND VIEWS OF DEVELOPMENT

ALAN THOMAS

Perhaps the simplest definition of development is that given by Chambers (1997), for whom development means just 'good change'. As such, 'development' is a positive word that in everyday parlance is virtually synonymous with 'progress' (Figure 2.1) – although we should note the importance of distinguishing the two concepts (see below). Development may entail disruption of established patterns of living, and there are huge disagreements about how it is obtained or whether it is occurring. Nevertheless, over the long term it implies increased living standards, improved health and well-being for all, and the achievement of whatever is regarded as a general good for society at large.

However, the two words 'good change' already combine quite different ideas which can cause confusion between different senses in which the term 'development' is used. 'Good' implies a vision of a desirable society ('well-being for all'); something to aim at, a state of being with certain positive attributes which can be measured so that we can talk of 'more' or 'less' development. 'Change', on the other hand, is a process, which 'may entail disruption' and which it may or may not be possible to direct.

Thus it is important to be clear about the different senses in which the term 'development' is used. In addition, whichever sense is in use, the term 'development' also embodies competing political aims and social values and contrasting theories of social change. In particular, there are

Of course we have progressed a great deal, first they were coming by bullock-cart , then by jeep — and now this!

Figure 2.1

strongly conflicting views about the relationship of development to capitalism. In the rest of this chapter we take a closer look at the different meanings and views of development. We will consider the following questions, which you should bear in mind as you read through the chapter:

Q What are the different senses in which the term 'development' is used?

Q What are the main views of development and how does it relate to capitalism?

2.1 The ambiguity of development and its relation to capitalism

There are several important general points about the idea of development which go beyond simply 'good change' and which together show it to be an inherently ambiguous concept. First, development generally implies an all-encompassing change, not just an improvement in one aspect. Second, development is not just a question of a one-off process of change to something better, but implies a process which builds on itself, where change is continuous and where improvements build on previous improvements. Third, development is a matter of changes occurring at the level of social change and of the individual human being at one and the same time. Changes in society have implications for the people who live in that society and, conversely, changes in how people think, interact, make their livings and perceive themselves form the basis for changes in society. Finally, development is not always seen positively. These points often go together, in that what some see as a general improvement may have losers as well as winners, and if social change is all-encompassing and continuous then the implication is that previous ways of life may be swept away, with the loss of positive as well as negative features.

One intriguing metaphor which combines all these points comes from Marshall Berman, who writes of 'The Tragedy of Development' and of Goethe's Faust as 'the first developer'. He describes the 'development' that this Faust wants as follows:

"Earlier incarnations of Faust have sold their souls in exchange for certain clearly defined and universally desired good things of life: money, sex, power over others, fame and glory. Goethe's Faust...wants these things, but these things aren't in themselves what he wants...what this Faust wants for himself is a dynamic process that will include every mode of human experience, joy and misery alike, and assimilate them all into his self's unending growth..."

(Berman, 1997, p.73)

Faust plans to:

"draw on nature's own energy and organize that energy into the fuel for new collective human purposes and projects...He outlines great reclamation projects to harness the sea...; man-made harbours and canals that can move ships full of goods and men; dams for large-scale irrigation; green fields and forests, pastures and gardens, a vast and intensive agriculture; waterpower to attract and support emerging industries; thriving settlements, new towns and cities to come – and all this to be created out of a barren wasteland..."

(Berman, 1997, p.75)

Berman points out that this vision of development also entails the self-development of Faust himself; he is becoming a new kind of man: 'the consummate wrecker and creator, the dark and deeply ambiguous figure that our age has come to call 'the developer'' (Berman, 1997, p.75).

Although the story of Faust is a myth, there are lessons to be learnt, not least about the ambiguity of the notion of development. It may be impossible to achieve 'good change' on a continuous basis without destroying something previously held dear, such as traditional values and forms of livelihood, or a sense of control over day-to-day life. For some this may indeed amount to losing one's soul.

I think that you can begin to see how it is impossible to avoid the contradictions behind the idea of development by laying down a single, simple definition of one's own. As Cowen and Shenton point out (1996, p.4): 'Development comes to be defined in a multiplicity of ways because there are a multiplicity of 'developers' who are entrusted with the task of development.'

Capitalism and development

The growth of industrial capitalism as a global system from the first half of the nineteenth century provides a real example of a process of social change which has built on itself and which went alongside the creation of new kinds of human being – or at least new forms of livelihood and of motivation. According to Cowen and Shenton (1996) in their discussion of the history of the idea of development, the era of industrial capitalism has also been the period of the 'modern doctrine of development'. They suggest that the latter was invented in the first half of the nineteenth century precisely to control the social disruptions caused by the unchecked 'development' of capitalism.

Here we run up against an immediate difficulty with different uses of the term 'development'. Capitalism had been 'developing' for several centuries up to this point (see Chapter 11), continues to 'develop' to this day, and can be expected to 'develop' into the future. Indeed, an absolutely crucial aspect of capitalism is that it is intrinsically dynamic; it tends to build on itself and grow or 'develop' from within. This is **immanent development**, and should be clearly differentiated from the **intentional development** which forms the deliberate policy and actions of states and development agencies. Cowen and Shenton also argue that development should be conceptually differentiated from **progress**. They point out that in the preceding centuries progress had been thought of as an immanent process, in that human society was conceived as moving inexorably to a higher and higher stage of civilization. There had always been casualties of this 'progress', as with those agricultural producers dispossessed by the 'enclosures' of the early seventeenth century in Britain. Only when this 'progress' moved to the stage of industrial capitalism did the poverty, unemployment and human misery caused threaten to bring about social disorder on a scale which necessitated 'intentional constructive activity' (Cowen & Shenton, 1996). This was when intentional development was invented.

> "Industrial production and organization was accepted...to be a historically given part of the movement towards an organic, positive or natural stage of society in Europe. The burden of development was to compensate for the negative propensities of capitalism through the reconstruction of social order. To develop, then, was to ameliorate the social misery which arose out of the immanent process of capitalist growth."
>
> (Cowen & Shenton, 1996, p.116)

Progress, **immanent development** and **intentional development:** *Progress* implies continual improvement reaching higher and higher levels perhaps without limit, whereas *development*, as an analogy from the development of living organisms, implies moving towards the fulfilment of a potential. *Immanent* development means a spontaneous and unconscious ('natural'?) process of development from within, which may entail destruction of the old in order to achieve the new. *Intentional* development implies deliberate efforts to achieve higher levels in terms of set objectives.

By the early nineteenth century capitalism had 'developed' into what could be described as a 'market society' (Polanyi, 1957). In other words, not merely the economic aspects but the whole of human existence was governed by the principles of 'a self-regulating system of markets'; 'an industrial system [which] was in full swing over the major part of the planet' (ibid., pp.43–4).

Markets have always been a part of all human societies (Figure 2.2), and all societies have been limited by economic factors. What was new in civilization based on the self-regulating market, according to Polanyi, was that it:

> "...was economic in a different and distinctive sense, for it chose to base itself on a motive only rarely acknowledged as valid in the history of human societies, and certainly never before raised to the level of a justification of action and behavior in everyday life, namely, gain."
>
> (Polanyi, 1957, p.30)

In order for the whole of life to be governed by self-regulating markets, it is necessary not only for what is produced to be bought and sold, i.e. to become a commodity, but for the factors of production – land, labour power and productive organization itself – to become commodities as well. Indeed, one way of characterizing

Figure 2.2   The self-regulating market. The working of markets like this large grain market in north-west India sets prices for commodities. Such markets can exist within or outside capitalism; capitalism requires the combination of regulation through the market with other elements, notably production for profit and accumulation.

capitalism is to call it a system of *generalized commodity production* (see Box 2.1; also Chapter 11). Polanyi argued that the movement towards commodification of the factors of production gave rise to tremendous negative consequences for 'man', 'nature' and productive organization, and hence to movements to 'protect' each of these. Eventually the conflict between these movements and those which tried to promote capitalism would lead to the latter's downfall. Polanyi thought that the events of the first half of the twentieth century (two world wars, the Depression, the growth of Fascism and authoritarian communism) showed that the capitalist market system was indeed self-destructing, but in fact it has regained and increased its strength and become more fully a global system. However, as we will see in Section 2.3 below, Polanyi's conflicting movements can still be recognized today.

Development *of, alongside,* or *against* capitalism

We can already see the makings of the most basic disagreements between different views on development. These are differences in how development is seen to relate to capitalism. At one extreme there is *neoliberalism*, for which the immanent development of capitalism is sufficient. A number of essentially different views, concerned with underlying social and economic structures and which see development as involving changes in these structures, are grouped under the heading *structuralism*. These views tend to be associated with advocating state planning and are generally out of favour as far as development practice is concerned, though as with the views of Polanyi they may still contain useful analytical insights.

Then there is what we may call *interventionism*, which sees the need for intentional development

Box 2.1 The elements of global capitalism

Capitalism can be characterized as a system of production of goods and services for market exchange in order to make a profit. Capitalism has certain basic elements as an ideal system which, taken together, distinguish it from other systems: private ownership; regulation via self-regulating markets (commoditization and competition); distribution of welfare through the market determination of wages; and enterprise management for profit and accumulation. And these elements act together to promote development and growth in the system and to legitimate it as a whole.

Ownership. Capitalism means *private ownership*: the ownership of the means of production is private and individual. The archetypal capitalist owns his or her land, buildings, tools, and equipment, and hires in labour and buys raw materials in order to use these means of production to produce goods and services for sale. In the case of large corporations, there are many owners, but they still hold shares as individuals. Of course, not all individuals own means of production, either directly or through holding shares in productive enterprises. The important point is that the main form of ownership is not a collective form, and in particular is not state ownership.

Regulation. Capitalism means *self-regulating markets*, not state planning or intervention. In this context, regulation refers to how decisions are made about what is produced, how much of each product, at what price and what quality, and so on. Under capitalism, such regulation is effectively imposed through the impersonal mechanism of the self-regulating market, via *commoditization* and *competition*. All goods and services are in principle turned into commodities for exchange rather than for the producer's own use (see Chapter 5 for more on the distinction between commodity and subsistence production). Individual producers and firms can then produce what they like, decide on quality and set what prices they like, but the assumption is that competition between firms, together with consumer choice between competitive versions of the same commodity, will force them to set the 'right' prices and produce what is actually required.

Distribution. Under capitalism the allocation of resources and the distribution of welfare are done through the market determination of wages. In principle, there is no universal provision or rationing even of basic goods or welfare services. How much a person gets (i.e. his or her entitlement, in the terms explained in Chapter 3) depends entirely on personal income, or on how a household's income is divided between income generators and dependants when it comes to consumption. For the majority of the population who work as wage labourers, this in turn depends on how much of the surplus derived from the sale of the products comes to them as wages, rather than going to the capitalist owners as profit. The level of wages is determined through the labour market, and competition for employment will tend to keep wage rates down. Thus workers' labour power is another commodity. This is an important part of characterizing capitalism as a system of *generalized commodity production*, implying that labour power as well as land, means of production and all goods and services are commoditized (see also Chapter 11).

Wages are not the only source of income under capitalism. Those who are capitalists, large or small, get income through dividends on shares or taking profit directly. Chapters 3, 5 and 11 discuss different forms of livelihood and 'labour régime'. We will see that while the division into capitalists and workers may be basic to the notion of capitalism, there are many other groups only partially linked into the overall system but whose welfare is still determined mainly through market mechanisms. Peasants and craft producers, for example, may combine petty commodity production, deriving income from the sale of their produce, with a certain amount of direct production for own use (in other words, to use the language of entitlements explained in Chapter 3, they combine trade with exchange entitlements).

At an international level, markets determine general income levels through their effects on a country's international earnings and liabilities. Market principles apply at international level to set the interest rates and conditions on the servicing of international debts. Markets also regulate the changes in world commodity prices (and the generally adverse movement of the terms of trade from the point of view of the less developed countries, as noted in Chapters 7 and 13).

Enterprise management. Production under capitalism is run with the aim of making a profit in order to accumulate (see below). In the case of small-scale agriculture, trying to achieve a profit leads to a different régime from that which attempts to safeguard all livelihoods against risk. It implies a polarization into a relatively small number of 'rich peasant' or capitalist farmer households and a larger number of landless wage labourers. In general, management is undertaken by or on behalf of the capitalist owners and in their interests, rather than directed primarily towards the interests of the workers in the enterprise, or of the local community or the state. Even if the state itself, or collective institutions such as pension funds, owns shares in productive enterprises, the management of such enterprises still treats these owners as individuals whose prime interest is to maximize the return on their investment.

Development and growth. Capitalism has an inbuilt dynamic tendency to grow and develop. Individual owners aim to accumulate profits and are led, through the necessity to compete, to invest these in technology which is ever more efficient, for example in its use of labour, and in product innovations which substitute for older products. Less efficient production units fail and are taken over by the more efficient and innovative.

Legitimation. All these elements fit together to form a global system that also functions in an ideological fashion to legitimate actions taken in particular ways. In this system *gain* has become a valid justification for actions and behaviour at all levels, from the individual's dealings with others to the activities of transnational corporations. There are many examples where international and Northern agencies have advocated new practices in line with capitalist principles, even where these involved dismantling previous welfare-oriented policies. The idea that the system works as a whole to promote efficiency and wealth creation is very powerful, and acts to legitimate actions which would otherwise appear simply to be favouring the interests of capitalists themselves.

alongside capitalism in order to 'ameliorate the disorded faults of progress' (Cowen & Shenton, 1996, p.7). Since the demise of state socialism and the softening of neo-liberalism in the 1990s, it might appear that those with a degree of power in various development agencies today are all interventionists of some description. Thus subdivisions within interventionism may be the most important divisions in terms of current practical policy debates. Most simply, interventionists may be subdivided into those who intend their interventions to make the market regulate itself better and become more efficient, and those for whom the intention is to achieve social and humanitarian aims directly and to govern the market from outside as part of doing so.

These are not the only possibilities, however. Many still reject capitalism and look for alternatives in different models of development: there are large movements searching for new forms of socialism which do not depend on the state, as well as for what is variously termed *another development*, *alternative development*, or *people-centred development*. Finally there is the *post-development* school, mentioned in Chapter 1 (and of which Berman is a member) which rejects the whole notion of development.

Table 2.1 lays out these views of development schematically. In Section 2.5 below, I explore the dimensions of debate which give rise to the differences between them, and develop the table further (see Table 2.2 below). First, however, it will be useful to disentangle the different *senses* in which the word 'development' is used, often, and confusingly, at one and the same time.

Different senses of 'development'

At the very start of this chapter we noted the potential for confusion arising from the different senses of the term 'development'. Even the simple definition 'good change' combines two different meanings of development (as a vision and as a process). Taking the two together can often have the effect, as Cowen and Shenton point out, that 'the question 'What is intended by development?' is confused with the question 'What is development?'' (1996, p.viii). Most of

Table 2.1 The main views of development and how they relate to capitalism

Development of capitalism	Development alongside capitalism		Development against capitalism		Rejection of development
Neoliberalism	Interventionism		Structuralism	'Alternative' (people-centred) development	'Post-development'
	Intervening to improve 'market efficiency'	Achieving social goals by 'governing the market'			

the rest of this chapter is devoted to distinguishing the main senses in which the term 'development' is used, and exploring each in terms of the alternative political and theoretical views already noted.

'Development' as an idea can of course apply to any field, from crop breeding and child psychology to aesthetics, and holds similar contradictory tendencies within it in each case. In this book we are primarily concerned with the development of societies, although within that the development of individuals and of localities is also important. What people learn from their experiences may be regarded as 'personal development', and one of the most influential attempts at defining what is meant by development is based on the idea of creating the conditions for 'the realization of the potential of human personality' (Seers, 1969; see below). Also, particular building projects may be called 'developments', and development as building is an important idea when considering *how* development occurs or may be brought about. The relationship between development at local levels and at national or societal levels also brings in the idea of equity between various localities or between different social groups or classes. These are useful subsidiary considerations, but our main focus remains at the broad level of development in relation to poverty throughout the world.

Bearing this focus in mind, we can distinguish three main senses in which the term 'development' is used:

1 as a vision, description or measure of the state of being of a desirable society;

2 as an historical process of social change in which societies are transformed over long periods;

3 as consisting of deliberate efforts aimed at improvement on the part of various agencies, including governments, all kinds of organizations and social movements.

We should realize that the term 'development' may still be used when what is referred to does not actually live up to the ideals espoused. Thus, measures of development may be used to analyse lack of development or underdevelopment. As already noted, development as an historical process is certainly not necessarily positive. For their part, development efforts do not all succeed.

The three senses in which 'development' is used are of course related. The state of being a desirable society is supposedly the result of the historical process of development; and the vision of a desirable society may form an aim towards which to direct efforts at improvement. The idea of development as historical social change does not negate the importance of 'doing development'. Historical processes incorporate millions of deliberate actions. Conversely, one's view of what efforts are likely to succeed in leading to 'improvement' is bound to be coloured by one's view of history and of how social change occurs.

In the next three sections we look a little more closely at each of the three senses of 'development' in turn.

2.2 Development as a state of being

The first sense of the word 'development', that of a vision or description of a desirable society, already hides a number of debates. Different political ideals clearly lead to different visions of what is desirable, and one person's utopia could be a nightmare for another. For example, what aspects should be included when considering development, and how should it be measured? Is it primarily an economic concept? Or should social aspects be of equal or even of greater importance? Should questions about what is politically feasible be allowed to constrain one's vision of a desirable, 'developed' society? If, for example, ideals such as equity, political participation and so on may be in conflict with the achievement of development in an economic sense, should the former be included in a *definition* of development – or regarded as additional desirable elements?

Development as a vision can be translated into goals for development efforts (see Box 1.1 in Chapter 1), while development as a state of being lends itself to measurement. Thus one can speak of being more or less developed, and tables are drawn up showing how developed the countries of the world are on various criteria, and even ranking them on different development indicators.

One problem with trying to distinguish between development as a vision or a (desirable) state of being from development as a process is that many visions of development include the idea of constant improvement or growth as part of what constitutes a desirable state. So for many proponents of development as economic well-being, for example, a developed society is a modern industrial society, and this is not just one which has reached certain levels of wealth, but one which is continually growing in economic terms and thus 'improving' further. GNP per capita (see Chapter 1) should not just be high, but always increasing.

To some extent the same is true of those who base their visions more on social factors or on human needs. For example, proponents of 'people-centred development' may argue not that development means a state where everyone's needs are met but one where conditions exist for all to 'develop' themselves to their full potential.

I have now mentioned two very different visions of development: that of a modern industrial society and that of a society where every individual's potential can be realized. A third, rather more prosaic, 'vision' could be of amelioration of poverty and other problems via measurable improvements in a number of indicators (possibly including GNP per capita, but certainly not only that). I will explain each a little further in turn.

Modern industrial society

In a world dominated by advanced capitalist economies, all aspects of modern industrial society are elevated to represent the ideal of what development is trying to achieve. This may be encapsulated in the idea of development as 'following in the footsteps of the West', which, in effect, is to say 'If you want what we have (and have achieved), then you must become like us, and do as we did (and continue to do)' (Bernstein, 1983).

This view of development as *modernization* comes particularly from the 1950s and 1960s. For example:

> "Historically, modernization is the process of change toward those types of social, economic and political systems that have developed in Western Europe and North America from the seventeenth century to the nineteenth and have then spread to other European countries and in the nineteenth and twentieth centuries to the South American, Asian and African continents."
>
> (Eisenstadt, 1966, p.1)

Another modernization theorist lists the following inter-related technical, economic and ecological processes:

> "(1) in the realm of technology, the change *from* simple and traditionalized techniques *towards* the application of scientific knowledge;

(2) in agriculture, the evolution *from* subsistence farming *towards* commercial production of agricultural goods. This means specialization in cash crops, purchase of non-agricultural products in the market, and often agricultural wage labour;

(3) in industry, the transition *from* the use of human and animal power *towards* industrialization proper, or 'men aggregated at power-driven machines, working for monetary return with the products of the manufacturing process entering into a market based on a network of exchange relations';

(4) in ecological arrangements, the movement *from* farm and village *towards* urban centres."

(Smelser, 1968, p.126)

The most obvious distinguishing feature of those Western countries which are thoroughly modernized and developed is that they have undergone industrial revolutions which have led to **economic development** (an increase in productive capacity and labour productivity) and hence **economic growth** (an increasing GNP – or, more precisely, increasing GDP). As a result they now enjoy high per capita income.

> **Economic growth:** A continued increase in the size of an economy (its GDP), i.e. a sustained increase in output over a period.
>
> **Economic development:** 'Raising the *productive capacities of societies*, in terms of their technologies (more efficient tools and machines), technical cultures (knowledge of nature, research and capacity to develop improved technologies), and the physical, technical and organizational capacities and skills of those engaged in production. This can also be expressed in terms of raising the productivity of labour: using the labour available to society in more productive and efficient ways to produce a greater quantity and a more diverse range of goods and services' (Bernstein, 1983, p.59).

Thus, modernization (Figure 2.3) implies complete transformations in many aspects of life, brought about by economic development through **industry** and **industrialization**. The industrial revolution in Britain has been described as a process of 'total' change: 'a change of social structure, of ownership and economic power in society; as well as a change of scale' (Kitching, 1982, p.11). In general, industrialization means an increased percentage of GDP from industrial sector outputs, and, more fundamentally, a general change of social structure, organization, scale, concentration and ways of thinking towards giving primacy to productivity, efficiency and instrumentality.

Figure 2.3

> **Industry:** Can be defined in two different ways. The first divides all economic activity into sectors and defines industry as the production of all material goods not derived directly from the land. Industry thus comprises the mining, energy and manufacturing sectors, and does not include agriculture or services. The second definition emphasizes technical and social change: an industrial production process is one that uses advanced technology and a complex technical division of labour, and is linked to other forms of production through combining a wide range of raw materials, skills and sources of energy.

Industrialization: The process by which production in the industrial sector becomes increasingly important compared with agricultural production; more fundamentally, it means a general change towards the use of advanced technology and a complex division of labour in production with associated changes in social structure and organization.

For Smelser, capitalism itself was an aspect of becoming modern and developed inseparable from industrialization. One might argue that, in principle, industrialization, along with many aspects of modernization, does not necessarily imply a capitalist system. State socialist models of planned development, for example (see Chapter 14), generally included plans for industrialization. Indeed, when Kitching used the phrase 'the old orthodoxy' to describe the idea that 'If you want to develop you must industrialize' (Kitching, 1982, p.6), he was clearly pointing out how both capitalist and state socialist ideas of development take it to mean industrialization. However, in practice, since the collapse of the Soviet Union, modernization, industrialization and capitalism have always gone together.

One further feature in common is that these Western countries are liberal democracies: they combine the prosperity associated with industrialized economies with political systems based on parliamentary representative democracy. Those countries which modernize successfully may then be seen as those where political institutions develop which allow people to give voice to their new aspirations, and which allow at least some of the wealth accumulated by the capitalist entrepreneurs to trickle down to other sections of society. Liberal democracy as a political form allows for 'freedom' in electing representatives to match 'freedom' in the market.

Those few countries which have joined the ranks of 'advanced capitalist economies' in the last thirty years are all from East Asia. This might throw doubt on the cultural specificity of

Bernstein's statement above, with its emphasis on 'the West'. It is also unclear that in all cases they are fully democratic, although it is argued that this is the only one direction in which they can travel, politically speaking.

Thus the combination of capitalist industrialization with liberal democracy is seen by many as now the only viable model for development. Fukuyama (1995), for example, writes,

"Today virtually all advanced countries have adopted, or are trying to adopt, liberal democratic political institutions, and a great number have simultaneously moved in the direction of market-oriented economics and integration into the global capitalist division of labour.

...As modern technology unfolds, it shapes modern economies in a coherent fashion, interlocking them in a vast global economy. The increasing complexity and information intensity of modern life at the same time renders centralized economic planning extremely difficult. The enormous prosperity created by technology-driven capitalism, in turn, serves as an incubator for a liberal regime of universal and equal rights, in which the struggle for recognition of human dignity culminates...[T]he world's advanced countries have no alternative model of political and economic organization other than democratic capitalism to which they can aspire."

(Fukuyama, 1995, pp.3–4)

The realization of human potential

Another vision of development starts not from production but from people and from human needs. David Korten, for example, one of the leading proponents of 'alternative development', contrasts 'growth-centred' with 'people-centred' visions of development. He describes the basis of the latter as follows:

"The survival of our civilization, and perhaps our very lives, depends on committing ourselves to an alternative development practice guided by the three basic principles of authentic development:

justice, sustainability and inclusiveness – each of which is routinely and systematically violated by current practice.

● *Justice:* Priority must be given to assuring a decent human existence for all people;

● *Sustainability:* Earth's resources must be used in ways that assure the well-being of future generations.

● *Inclusiveness:* Every person must have the opportunity to be a recognized and respected contributor to family, community and society.

(Korten, 1995b)

Such an approach was partly foreshadowed in Dudley Seers' (1979) article 'The meaning of development' (first published 1969) which pointed out the importance of value judgements in deciding what is or is not 'development'. Seers suggested that 'the realization of the potential of human personality…is a universally acceptable aim', and development must therefore entail ensuring the conditions for achieving this aim.

The first three conditions were (Seers, 1979, pp.10–11):

● the capacity to obtain physical necessities (particularly food);

● a job (not necessarily paid employment, but including studying, working on a family farm or keeping house); and

● equality, which should be considered an objective in its own right.

Seers (1979, p.12) also recognized the political dimension and suggested further conditions for development in addition to those mentioned above:

● participation in government;

● belonging to a nation that is truly independent, both economically and politically (Figure 2.4);

● adequate educational levels (especially literacy).

Seers' formulation was designed to challenge the economic basis of the type of vision of development outlined above, with its emphasis on productivity, growth, and increasing GNP per capita. Economic development of this type does not necessarily reduce the numbers in poverty, let alone meet other human needs such as those pointed to by Seers. However, Seers was an economist arguing for an emphasis on human needs and equity alongside economic growth, and as such did not go far enough for many seeking an alternative which would provide a clearer break from economistic development thinking.

For example, three further aspects of importance that have gained recognition since Seers wrote his article (in 1969) are the position of women, safeguarding the environment, and human security. Thus we might now add three further items to Seers' six:

● relatively equal status for and participation by women in society (Figure 2.5);

'Here, Señor Carter, is the statue of Simón Bolivar, who liberated Latin America from foreign domination!'

Figure 2.4 'True' national independence: a condition for development?

Figure 2.5   Women's status and political participation: conditions for development? 1986 Muslim women's demonstration in India against divorce bill making concessions to fundamentalists.

- 'meeting the needs of the present without compromising the ability of future generations to meet their own needs' (definition of sustainable development by the Brundtland Commission);

- freedom from social dislocation, violence and war.

This makes nine conditions for what we might call **human-needs centred development**.

Another strand of thinking on what is desirable for development starts with non-economic factors in building a vision of development. One such approach (identified in Chapters 1 and 3 with Amartya Sen) views poverty in terms not of poor material living standards but of lack of choice or of capability: poverty meaning the failure to be able to take a full part in human society. In these terms, development means not just combating or ameliorating poverty but restoring or enhancing basic human capabilities and freedoms. This is often seen in terms of participation and **empowerment**, particularly by non-governmental organizations (NGOs)

Human-needs centred development: A term for development where the level of satisfaction of various dimensions of human needs is considered to have improved. Extending Seers' conditions for development to a list of nine gives:

1 low levels of material poverty;

2 low level of unemployment;

3 relative equality;

4 democratization of political life;

5 'true' national independence;

6 good literacy and educational levels;

7 relatively equal status for women and participation by women;

8 sustainable ability to meet future needs;

9 human security.

that promote participative development at a local level.

> **Empowerment:** A desired process by which individuals, typically including the 'poorest of the poor', are to take direct control over their lives. Once 'empowered' to do so, poor people will then (hopefully) be able to be the agents of their own development.

Here one vision is that people should be enabled (or 'empowered') to take direct action to meet their own needs. In material terms this vision is clear and simple. It accords, for example, with how Schumacher (1973) discusses development in his famous book *Small is Beautiful*, when he comments that 'The really helpful things will not be done from the centre; they cannot be done by big organizations; but they can be done by the people themselves… [I]t is the most natural thing for every person born into this world to use his [sic] hands in a productive way and…it is not beyond the wit of man [sic] to make this possible…' (pp.205–6). This can be conceived in terms of localized or community-based production for material needs. Kitching (1982), tracing the long history of similar ideas arising as a reaction to capitalist development and industrialization, suggests that many have in common a 'populist' vision:

> "A world of 'humanized' production, based on a small scale but modern and scientific technology, a world of co-operation in villages and small towns, a world of enriched social relationships growing out of a process of production and exchange that is under human control rather than 'alienated'…"
>
> (Kitching, 1982, p.179)

One has to ask why it so often does prove 'beyond the wit of man' for production and exchange to be 'under human control'. Clearly a successful process of empowerment must also involve changes in power structures both at local and at broader, national and international, levels. As Korten puts it:

> "Some NGOs have equated people-centred development with participatory village development interventions. Such interventions are important, but in themselves are generally inconsequential…
>
> People-centred development…attributes poverty to a concentration and misuse of power and resources – especially ecological resources – in a finite world. It calls for an equality-led transformation of institutions and values to restore community, redistribute power, and reallocate earth's natural wealth to uses that contribute to sustainable improvements in human well-being."
>
> (Korten, 1995b, pp.178–9)

Empowerment, then, implies redistributing power and transforming institutions. These are aspects of *democracy*, or democratization – a subject discussed further in Chapter 17. Thus, although empowerment in the sense of becoming able to take direct control over one's life appears at first to be a far cry from Seers' 'participation in government', they are arguably closely linked.

It is not certain whether the list of nine 'conditions for human-needs centred development' given above is sufficient to describe the essence of the vision of 'people-centred' or 'alternative' development. Perhaps, for many who conceive a comprehensive vision of development of this type in holistic terms, the very idea of a number of conditions or dimensions is an inadequate way of representing something based on supposedly universal values. There is also the specific point that the nine conditions are formulated in terms of the needs and aspirations of *individuals* and of *nations*, whereas people-centred development also considers development for groups, local communities, and social classes, as well as an international dimension.

A final important aspect of the alternative development vision is cultural diversity. If people and communities are empowered to develop themselves, it follows that they will do so in distinctively different ways which will be affected by a whole variety of cultural variables. There is then a question of the relationship between specific cultural preferences and the presentation of the nine 'conditions for human-needs centred development' or Korten's three 'principles of authentic development' as having universal validity. Thus, while the elements of the alternative development vision may not form one specific cohesive whole, they certainly do form an alternative to the vision of modern, industrial society as the unique goal for the development of all human society.

'Ameliorating the disordered faults of progress'

A third type of vision for development is less thoroughgoing in its value basis than the two discussed so far. Here development means ameliorating poverty, improving the health of populations, mitigating environmental degradation, promoting democratization, and so on. It may be recognized by positive changes in a number of indicators corresponding to the whole range of different dimensions of human existence.

In one way this vision could combine aspects of the other two. Thus modern industrial society could be accepted as a global reality even though it might not be thought of as an ideal since the progress that achieved it also brought enormous problems. The rather minimal 'vision' for development, in this case, would be to make sufficient small improvements to keep these problems manageable and prevent degeneration into chaos. The nine conditions for 'human-needs centred development' given above could then be one way of providing a checklist of areas in which these small improvements would have to be made.

2.3   Development as historical process

The social change which occurs over long periods may or may not be towards closer conformity with one or other of the visions which constitute development in the first sense. Indeed, many argue that the very processes which led to development in some parts of the world were also the cause of *under*development in other parts. These historical processes have to be seen in re-

lation to the 'development' of industrial capitalism. Just as there are very different visions of the desirable 'developed' society, so there are different views of this historical relationship.

Here the distinction made above between *immanent* and *intentional* development is of key importance. As already noted, capitalism includes an internal dynamic which tends to lead to a kind of *immanent* development. The vision of development which I characterized as 'modern industrial society', which we noted is argued to be possible only within liberal capitalism, includes within it the notion of continuous economic growth. There is also room for the idea of intentional development alongside the growth of capitalism, as in the ideas which I have been relaying from Cowen and Shenton, where development is aimed at maintaining order in the face of capitalism's tendency to create social dislocation as well as internal growth.

The alternative vision, based on the realization of human potential in diverse ways, allows for the idea of immanent development at the level of individuals and communities, which should become 'empowered' to develop themselves to their full capacities. However, there is no clear model for how development of this kind might build on itself to create a self-reproducing process of social change throughout a whole society over a long period. It is easier to conceptualize 'alternative development' in terms of development agencies (both individuals and organizations) continually making new efforts to promote their own vision of development. This is dealt with in the next subsection 'doing development' (and in Chapter 9) – rather than here.

However, those who look for an alternative to the notion that liberal capitalism and global market society constitute the only future for humanity tend also to dispute the idea that the development of capitalism accords to some kind of natural historical law. Although its internal dynamics tend towards growth once it is established, industrial capitalism cannot come about or spread to new areas through its own internal logic. Polanyi, for example, argued that the conditions for global capitalism have constantly to be promoted by those political forces which favour them. He characterized the historical processes by which global capitalism has been established not in terms of the immanent development of capitalism itself but as a struggle between two 'movements': one trying to achieve the commoditization of land, labour and economic organization by force; the other attempting to 'protect' these three elements.

Thus there are two distinct views of the historical 'development' of capitalism and its relationship to development as an historical process. The first emphasizes the internal dynamics of capitalist economic growth as the engine of 'development' but has room for intentional development, while the second sees a political struggle between the promotion of a self-regulating market society and its regulation from outside. Let us consider each of these in turn in a little more detail.

The dynamics of capitalist growth

Within the internal logic of the self-regulating market, the owners of the means of production are assumed to be acting rationally in accordance with their own material interests. In turn this is assumed to mean maximizing profit or return on investment in order to accumulate and reinvest. Here market competition is seen as the main force towards economic progress. David McLelland, an American psychologist who claimed to have isolated the vital motivational factor necessary for economic development, suggested the following metaphor for market competition: 'The free enterprise system…may be compared to a garden in which all plants are allowed to grow until some crowd the others out' (McLelland, 1963, p.90).

Faced with market competition, the best ways to ensure continued profits are to grow and innovate. These both lead to increased labour productivity: growth does so through economies of scale, and innovation through capital investment in improved production processes. Thus successful capitalists are able to enter a positively reinforcing cycle: profit – accumulation – reinvestment – growth – innovation – increased

productivity – increased profits; and then can use those increased profits to continue the cycle. This system is seen as progressive because it allows enterprising individuals to thrive, and their innovations and increased productivity will eventually be benefits for all. This argument goes back to the famous phrases of Adam Smith: the 'hidden hand of the market' converts individual interests into 'the wealth of nations'.

However, it also depends on a particular kind of individualist motivation: a drive for achievement which will not only aim at personal gain but also convert this gain into productive investment which may eventually benefit society generally. Some have argued that capitalism took root first in Western Europe and North America because of the kind of individualist motivation found in a culture pervaded by 'the Protestant ethic' (see Chapter 21). More recently it has been suggested (see e.g. Fukuyama, 1995) that another crucial cultural factor is a propensity to associate, or **social capital**. The winners in the competition need to be able to organize others into large corporations or networks and to have confidence that the others can be relied upon to play their organized role. Only then can the winners benefit from economies of scale while remaining flexible. Thus without a combination of social

> **Social capital:** 'The ability of people to work together for common purposes in groups and organizations' (Coleman, 1988). If capital in general is thought of in terms of accumulated resources which allow for productive activity, then social capital is an aspect of human capital; that is, capital which is embodied less in land, factories and buildings and more in human beings, their knowledge and skills. Part of that human capital is to do with the ability of human beings to associate, which in turn comes from shared values and the subordination of individual interests. Out of shared values comes trust, which has 'a large and measurable economic value' (Fukuyama, 1995, p.10).

capital and individual profit motive the reinforcing cycle of reinvestment and increasing productivity will not get going to create economic development.

To extend this argument to a national level, economic growth cannot take place without investment of capital to obtain additional means of production. This implies that a proportion of the total output must be set aside from consumption as *savings*, which can then be channelled into investment. The simplest model of economic growth shows that if a high rate of growth is to be achieved, either a high rate of savings (and thus of foregone consumption) is necessary, or else investment will have to be obtained from elsewhere, e.g. foreign investment or borrowing.

However, this does not tell us which social groups will be going without. Those who are foregoing their consumption may have no choice in the matter. The term 'savings' does not get at this so well as the notions of the **appropriation** of **surplus** and surplus **accumulation**. Also, although there can be no economic growth without investment, by itself investment is not sufficient to guarantee growth. As you will see in Chapter 5, in addition to social capital, some aspects of the organization of production, both technical and social, will have a big effect on how productively any investment can be utilized.

Economic growth may do no more than keep pace with population growth, but where the growth in output is greater than that of population – that is, labour productivity (see Chapter 5) has increased – then economic development in its simplest sense may be said to have occurred (see above). However, for most economists development is more than this. Whereas growth means more of the same type of output, development implies more thoroughgoing changes, changes in the social and technical relations of production (see Chapter 5 again). Thus the productive capacity of a society as a whole has to increase, rather than just increasing productivity within its productive enterprises.

Thus, the dynamic for the 'development' of capitalism is provided by individual entrepreneurs linked through the market. However,

Surplus, appropriation, accumulation: That portion of what is produced at any given time that is not required for immediate consumption, including reproduction, is called the *surplus product* or simply the *surplus*. It may be preserved as a store of produce or implements, or converted through market relations into a sum of cash. There are three main possible uses for the surplus product. It can be kept as a reserve against future needs. It can be taken by dominant social groups or classes and used for 'luxury' or 'conspicuous' consumption and for maintaining their power (e.g. building palaces or temples, keeping armies). Or it can be used as a means of investment in expanding production and/or increasing its efficiency by improving productivity. In the second case the surplus is said to be *appropriated* by the dominant groups or classes concerned. The surplus may also be appropriated by dominant groups in the last case; the difference is that they then use it for what is termed productive accumulation, or simply *accumulation*.

growth is almost always achieved at the cost of inequity. The argument essentially is that the best way to achieve significant growth is by increasing the scale of production and concentrating capital investment in the larger and more productive enterprises. This also means industrializing. In the short run at least, the savings required to increase industrial productivity and output may have to come from the agricultural sector; in other words, part of the agricultural surplus will have to be appropriated for accumulation in the industrial sector. Trying to spread investment equitably in improving productivity everywhere at once may mean its impact is so diluted as to have no real effect anywhere.

Thus the same process which depends on winners also creates losers – for example, agricultural producers who can no longer make a living and who migrate to cities or overseas in search of productive opportunities for their labour. It is in order to harness their talents to increase the productive capacity of society rather than allowing their disaffection to endanger societal order that development was 'invented'. Cowen and Shenton give several detailed examples of intentional development – for example, in Australia and Canada in the mid-nineteenth century and in Kenya in the 1950s – and note that in each case:

"The problem of development was the same – the emergence of a surplus population which was officially recognized to be a national problem because it prompted the fear of social disorder and the loss of a population with the potential for productive force."

(Cowen & Shenton, 1996, p.190)

Although the problem was the same, the solutions proposed could be very different, including the promotion of manufacturing industry via what would now be called a flexible labour market, protection of 'infant industries', state promotion of agricultural colonization and settlement, programmes of public works, and state banks making loans to the poor. Interestingly, policies aimed in a similar way at making 'surplus' populations productive are the substance of many development programmes to this day, including, for example, the recent preoccupation with small-scale credit to promote 'microenterprise' among the poor (see Chapter 5).

In the end, the immanent processes of capitalist growth brought about as the sum of gradual changes initiated by many enterprising individuals combine with these ameliorative programmes of intentional development and lead to a total change in social structure, political systems and culture; in other words, to *modernization* as the term was used in the 1950s and 1960s (see above and Chapter 13).

A struggle between pro-market and protectionist movements

One of Polanyi's main arguments was against the suggestion of Adam Smith and others that the economic motive of personal gain is a basic human characteristic so that markets will tend to 'develop' as soon as they are free from outside regulation. On the contrary, Polanyi argued that while market exchange has generally been an element in the economic organization of human societies, it has tended to be subordinated to other principles such as those of *reciprocity* and *redistribution*. Only with the coming of industrial capitalism in Europe from the early nineteenth century has the principle of the self-regulating market become the organizing feature of society as a whole, and this only because it has actively been promoted.

Polanyi summarized his argument as follows:

"Economic history reveals that the emergence of national markets was in no way the result of the gradual and spontaneous emancipation of the economic sphere from government control. On the contrary, the market has been the outcome of a conscious and often violent intervention on the part of government which imposed the market organization on society for non-economic ends."

(Polanyi, 1957, p.250)

As noted in Section 2.1 above, Polanyi pointed out that the market could not be truly self-regulating unless not only the goods and services produced but the factors of production – land, labour and productive organization – became commodities to be bought and sold. This could not happen 'naturally', not least because it would be so disruptive that powerful forces would arise to 'protect' society from its effects.

"Our thesis is that the idea of a self-adjusting market implied a stark utopia. Such an institution could not exist for any length of time without annihilating the human and natural substance of society; it would have physically destroyed man and transformed his surroundings into a wilderness. Inevitably, society took measures to protect itself, but whatever measures it took impaired the self-regulation of the market, disorganized industrial life, and thus endangered society in yet another way."

(Polanyi, 1957, pp.3–4)

Thus Polanyi interpreted the history of the nineteenth century as a struggle between two 'movements': on the one hand, pro-market forces; on the other, **protectionism**. It was not a question of the 'natural' workings of the market against government, but two competing movements, representing capitalist interests and those adversely affected by capitalism respectively, struggling for influence within government.

> **Protectionism:** In broad terms this refers to any of the movements to 'protect' the elements of production (land, labour, productive organization) from what are seen as the destructive effects of capitalist 'development' – in other words, from becoming fully commoditized and subject to the self-regulating market. It is also used in a more specific sense to refer to state policies to protect 'infant industries' from international competition through tax concessions, restrictions on imports, etc.

It is instructive to attempt to interpret some recent history of development in similar terms. For example, trade unions have long been engaged in trying to protect the collective interests of workers and up to the 1960s and 1970s were increasingly successful in doing so. Up to that time also, in less developed countries (LDCs) there were a large number of state interventions regulating the relation between the national economy and the international. LDCs typically maintained exchange rate and credit controls, tariffs, and import controls. States commonly imposed direct price controls and quality standards; they also employed different types of incentives such as preferential tax treatment for reinvestment in certain areas of production. Not only in LDCs but in advanced capitalist countries as well, many public goods and especially public services were, and are, supplied directly by state agencies. Also, almost all countries have at least some services provided universally, as with the National Health Service and basic educational provision in the UK, and the basic food provisioning policies of the Sri Lankan governments since independence. These can all

be seen as the result of interests outside and within governments restricting the force and scope of capitalism.

In contrast, particularly since the early 1980s, pro-market interests have made headway. Many Southern states compete to attract investment from transnational corporations by making a virtue of their tough anti-union legislation. Structural adjustment programmes, promoted by the World Bank and the International Monetary Fund (IMF), have obliged many LDCs to become almost completely open to overseas ownership of enterprises through foreign investment. Under the so-called 'Washington consensus' both these multilateral agencies and others such as the United States Agency for International Development (USAID) agreed on a range of policies such as minimizing state intervention in the economy, privatization of previously state-owned industries, and a reduction in state provision of services. These policies were not only followed at home but pushed on to LDCs. Rather than being an inevitable consequence of global market forces, they can be seen as the result of a political movement advancing the conditions for capitalism to 'develop' further at the global level.

2.4 'Doing development'

In the third sense of the term, development means not a desired state or the process of social change which might achieve it, but whatever is done in the name of development. In this sense, it appears that as we enter the twenty-first century development has become less about the transformation of the economic and social basis of societies than in previous periods. What are visible as 'development agencies' are mostly engaged either in attempts to reduce poverty (and improve health, education, gender equality and environmental protection – see Box 1.1 in Chapter 1) or in humanitarian relief to mitigate the effects of internal wars and other disasters.

If development is simply what development agencies do, then we must ask what are development agencies and what entitles them to the name. 'Agency' simply means an individual, organization, group, or other source of action and 'development agencies' are those whose actions aim at development. But whose development? Cowen and Shenton suggest that there is a basic 'problem of development' which arises because development as a process of improvement which builds on itself also causes destruction, and those adversely affected are generally powerless to help themselves. As a response to this problem, at the same time as the invention of 'intentional development' the concept of **trusteeship** was also brought into use. Trusteeship means that one agency is 'entrusted' with acting on behalf of another, in this case to try to ensure the 'development' of the other. Trusteeship may be taken on by an agency on another's behalf without 'the other' asking to 'be developed' or even being aware of the intention to 'develop' them.

> **Trusteeship:** 'The intent which is expressed, by one source of agency, to develop the capacities of another. It is what binds the process of development to the intent of development' (Cowen & Shenton, 1996, p.x).

Originally trusteeship was generally exercised by states on behalf of their societies or by colonial states on behalf of the colonized (Chapters 11 and 12). Since attaining independence, many ex-colonial states continued to assume trusteeship over the development of their peoples, and until the 1970s the idea of the state as the sole legitimate agency of development retained strong currency. More recently a variety of agencies can be seen as claiming trusteeship over the development of others, or even over the development of global society as a whole, including a variety of local, national and international NGOs as well as international organizations such as the World Bank, the IMF, and the United Nations and its agencies.

Two questions have to be asked about any agency which claims trusteeship for the development of others. Does it have legitimacy to act on their behalf? And does it have the power and capacity to do so? For almost the whole of the period since the 'invention' of intentional development, the state has claimed both the right and the might to develop its people. However, it can be argued that the idea of the 'developmental state' is now discredited on both counts, or at least that the state is no longer the *sole* source of development action (see Chapter 9). Hence the current crisis in development, evident from the failure to deal with the threefold global crisis, is also a crisis of legitimacy and capacity. Despite the variety of agencies claiming trusteeship in some form, there is no clear successor to the developmental state, certainly not when one starts to think in terms of world development rather than development within the boundaries of nation states.

A third question about trusteeship asks which interests are represented by a development agency. Can the interests of those being developed be represented through the actions of an agency 'entrusted' with acting on their behalf? The very notion of trusteeship depends on being able to answer 'Yes' to this question. However, there are those, particularly those seeking 'alternative development' who see this answer as impossible. Banuri, for example writes that if development means 'what 'we' can do for 'them'' then it is just a 'licence' for imperial intervention (1990, p.96). For these the answer is to reject the notion of trusteeship; people should become the agents of their own development.

We saw above that for people to become their own development agents is the aim of empowerment, and that for this to succeed implies radical changes to power structures and institutional arrangements. How this is to be achieved raises enormous questions about political feasibility as well as the question of whether it is really possible to avoid the notion of trusteeship in this way. Surely empowerment cannot be achieved without being promoted by some powerful agent allied with those to be empowered? Perhaps some form of people's movement might fill the role of this agent, but even then the leadership of that movement would be taking on a trusteeship role in a way. Still, despite these difficulties, the notion of people developing themselves is clearly an alternative to the idea of different kinds of development agencies undertaking trusteeship for development.

2.5 Competing views on development and social change

In the above discussions of the three senses of the term 'development' it was clear in each case that there is no single agreed version of what is meant or implied by 'development'. In an area of debate such as development, definitions and explanations are not cut and dried. They carry implications about one's view of the world that can lead into wide-ranging political, moral and theoretical disputes.

There are a number of competing approaches which entail different visions of what is a desirable 'developed' state, different views of history, how social change occurs and the process of development in relation to the global capitalist system, and different prescriptions for how to achieve development and who should be the agents of it. At the end of Section 2.1 above, these competing views of development were characterized as development *of*, *alongside* or *against* capitalism (Table 2.1). We can now expand that table to include a summary of some of the points made in the above discussions on the competing visions, different theories used to explain social change, and alternative views about the role of 'doing development'. The result is Table 2.2.

As you read the rest of the book you should consider how the views put forward at any point fit in with those outlined in Table 2.2.

It would be useful, and neat, to be able to write that each of the columns in Table 2.2 constitutes a coherent theory of development. In this case, like coherent views on any aspect of society, they would each have both **analytical** and **normative** aspects: i.e. attempt both to explain how development *does* occur and to suggest how it *should* occur. However, in practice things are less clear cut than that. First, the dividing lines between the columns represent my attempt to simplify and to bring out the most important differences between views. In fact some of the views identified overlap, labels are not agreed and the some of the protagonists might distinguish their views from others in quite different ways. Second, not all the views represented in Table 2.2 are complete theories of development.

For example, the 'alternative development' school is strong on vision (the normative aspect) but weak on any theory of social change for how this vision might be achieved (the analytic aspect). Conversely, certain structuralist views concentrate on explaining social change but fail to offer any clear prescriptions.

This fuzziness has led me to organize the following discussion not in terms of a description of each 'view' in turn, but by exploring a number of dimensions of debate.

Neoliberalism versus structuralism

We have noted that *neoliberalism* (or market liberalism) was the dominant view of development in the 1980s. This was so not only in the industrialized North and with the main international agencies such as the World Bank but also with increasing numbers of Southern governments. To a large extent this was a reaction against the *structuralist* views which were concerned with underlying social and economic structures and saw development as involving changes in these structures, and which had achieved widespread credence in the 1960s and 1970s. Thus a major debate in development thinking has been between these two views.

Those who promoted *neoliberalism* were the direct descendants of the proponents of 'free enterprise' in the 1950s and earlier, and traced their theoretical ideas back to the classical econ-

Analytical: Such a view or theory attempts to explain or analyse some aspect of society, perhaps putting forward a conceptual framework for understanding.

Normative: Such a view or theory brings in value judgements and suggests how things should be rather than just explaining how they are and why.

In practice, any view or theory contains both analytical and normative aspects. The use of certain concepts rather than others implies certain values, and conversely value judgements cannot be made without some view about how things work.

Table 2.2 Expanded summary of the main views of development

	Development of capitalism	Development alongside capitalism		Development against capitalism		Rejection of development
	Neoliberalism	Interventionism		Structuralism	'Alternative' (people-centred) development	'Post-development'
		'Market efficiency'	'Governing the market'			
Vision: desirable 'developed' state	Liberal capitalism (modern industrial society and liberal democracy)	(plus achieving basic social/ environmental goals)		Modern industrial society (but not capitalist)	All people and groups realize their potential	['development' is not desirable]
Theory of social change	Internal dynamic of capitalism	Need to remove 'barriers' to modernization	Change can be deliberately directed	Struggle between classes (and other interests)	[not clear]	[not clear]
Role of 'development'	Immanent process within capitalism	To 'ameliorate the disordered faults of [capitalist] progress'		Comprehensive planning/ transformation of society	Process of individual and group empowerment	A 'hoax' which strengthened US hegemony
Agents of development	Individual entrepreneurs	Development agencies or 'trustees' of development (states, NGOs, international organizations)		Collective action (generally through the state)	Individuals, social movements	Development agencies

omics of Adam Smith in the late eighteenth century. In this view the purest form of the system of capitalism outlined in Box 2.1 above is the best. It is said to be both efficient and fair – and these two statements correspond to the analytical and normative aspects respectively of this theoretical view.

Neoliberals viewed the process of capitalist 'development' described above as leading inexorably to the desired result of modernization, with no need for any kind of intentional development. Indeed most actions taken in the name of development were likely to be seen as creating 'obstacles' to the proper working of the market. Neoliberals looked to this idea of obstacles to explain why not all parts of the world had developed to the same extent. Three main kinds of obstacle were put forward to explain different cases of lack of development:

1 *Tradition*. The continuation of non-market social relations and systems of obligation were seen as preventing production for own use from being commoditized.

2 *Monopoly*. Under capitalism, the protagonists naturally try to minimize the regulatory effects of the market as a whole by finding a small market or market segment which they can completely monopolize or at least partly dominate. Two sorts of monopoly can act as obstacles to the self-regulation of the market: monopolies of capital, i.e. industrial monopolies; and monopolies of labour, i.e. trade unions.

3 *State regulation*. In general, any kind of collective or state action was seen as interfering with the proper working of the market. In the neoliberal view, the role of the state should be a minimal one: guaranteeing political order, ensuring the conditions for capitalism (keeping a

'level playing field'), and 'policing' the casualties of the competitive system.

There was a real dilemma here for neoliberal thinkers. While they favoured 'rolling back the state' as far as possible, they also required its policing function, which in practice tended to be considerable. The dilemma was how to guarantee that this policing was done fairly, since it is necessarily done outside the market and hence outside the mechanism which this theory argues is the means of fair regulation.

The main normative aspects of neoliberalism were the positive values put on individual achievement and competition. The most important obstacle was usually seen as that of state intervention. We have noted how states commonly engaged in various policies such as controlling exchange rates, food subsidies, imposing tariffs and quotas, which could all be regarded as 'distorting the price signals' that allow competition to work. Such policies were seen as counter-productive; for example, it was argued that without food subsidies there would be more incentive for farmers to invest in greater productivity and to produce more, and more production would in turn lead to cheaper prices through competition and hence obviate the need for the subsidies.

Structuralism, by contrast, denotes several related but distinct strands of thought, in which development involves changes in underlying social and economic structures. Boxes 2.2 and 2.3 outline two of the most important of these strands (Marxism and the dependency school).

In general, structuralist views differ fundamentally from neoliberalism both in their view of history and in their approach to capitalism. Thus, whereas to neoliberals history is the sum of individuals' actions, and those of individual governments, firms and other organizations, structuralists see history in terms of political and economic struggles between large social groups, particularly classes, as new structures and systems replace old ones across the globe.

There is in fact a structural aspect to some of the views discussed above under 'neoliberalism',

particularly those of the modernization theorists. However, much structuralist thinking on development, including the Marxist and dependency schools emphasized here, has in common a fundamentally critical view of capitalism. While global capitalism is seen as having a quality of dynamism that may be necessary for economic development, it is regarded mainly as a system of *exploitation* which should in the long run be radically altered.

Although the neoliberal and structuralist views were largely opposed, there are two important areas of commonality between them. First, both viewed development mainly in terms of broad historical social change. As theories, though they had their normative aspects, they did not offer detailed prescriptions for what development agencies should do. Second, both looked favourably on industrialization as the only realistic way to the economic growth required to achieve massive improvements in the living standards of the poor. This was seen as a prerequisite for any other aspect of development.

The main area of disagreement and conflict was between the neoliberal insistence on the materialist motivations of individuals and the self-regulating market and the structuralist view of the importance of social solidarity, class and collective forms of action. Since the only examples of large-scale collective action for development have occurred through the state, this opposition tended to be represented as *market versus state* or *profit versus planning*.

In the 1990s, with the demise of the Soviet Union and the general discrediting of comprehensive state planning as a vehicle for development, both Marxism and dependency thinking went out of favour. However, although the model of development associated with Marxism in particular is seen as having failed, this is no reason to reject the analytical insights which can come from structuralist thinking. Karl Polanyi, for example, belongs in the structuralist camp with his insistence that the 'development' of capitalism is better explained by reference to a struggle between 'movements' representing pro-market and protectionist interests than by its own internal dynamics.

Despite the triumphalist cry that 'capitalism has won', neoliberalism too is now largely discredited. The evident chaos caused by the attempt to let capitalism 'develop' itself in the ex-Soviet Union, together with the increases in inequity, poverty, environmental degradation and wars, has led the World Bank and other agencies to modify their position considerably. They now see a major role for 'intentional development', including intervention by the state and actions by other development agencies, including the World Bank itself, which go well beyond simply ensuring the conditions for market competition.

Thus the main area of debate in what may be called 'mainstream' development circles is no longer 'market versus state' but about the form and degree of intervention.

How much, and what kind of intervention?

As we enter the twenty-first century the consensus among the world's decision-makers and academics regards global industrial capitalism broadly positively but at the same time a need is perceived for non-market intervention – or 'intentional development' to 'ameliorate' its 'disordered faults'. Historically, what I am calling *interventionism* has had a lot in common with structuralism, in that the structural inequalities and contradictions inherent in capitalism are to some extent admitted, and the main vehicle for regulating the market has been state intervention. However, instead of hoping to replace the market, this approach could have been said to *combine* state and market. Now, however, the state is only one of a number of agencies with a role to play in intervention.

Box 2.2 Marxism

Karl Marx viewed capitalism as a particular type of *class society*, one constituted by antagonistic relations between different social classes, of which the most important are capitalists and workers.

Any class system is based on particular relations of production, and in the capitalist system those who own the means of production have the power to appropriate surplus, whereas those do not own means of production have to sell their labour power. However, one can also argue that the contradictions inherent in capitalism tend to bring about or accentuate other divisions as well, such as those based on gender, ethnicity, nationality, and so on.

Marx believed that industrial capitalism, in particular, represented a massive advance in the progress of society, particularly in the impetus it gave to the systematic application of science to methods of production. He also saw as very positive the way that capitalism brings people together in an ever-increasing scale of co-operation, with integrated production processes organized on the basis of socialized labour, as opposed to the small-scale 'privatized' labour of household production.

On the other hand, Marx saw class exploitation and oppression as essential features of capitalism. He vehemently condemned the conditions of life of the industrial working class in Victorian Britain and the Europe of the time,

and the brutality perpetrated by British colonial rule in India.

In short, for Marx capitalism was profoundly contradictory, at two levels. First, the development of productive capacities under capitalism represents an enormous potential force for human emancipation and freedom from want, at the same time as the class relations through which the productive forces have developed deny their promise to the majority of people. Second, these class relations embody a contradiction between *private* ownership and control and increasingly *socialized* labour. Marx thought that in time private ownership would begin to obstruct the further development of productive capacities. Then conditions would be ripe for the overthrow of capitalism. This would not be automatic, but result from class struggle between capitalists and workers. The latter would organize in a political movement to dispossess the former and then utilize the productive capacities made available by capitalism to go on and form a different kind of society, i.e. communism.

As for the role of the state, during the class struggle it could be seen as both an enabling structure for capitalist development and a structural obstacle to development that would benefit the workers (Chapter 9). Then, once in the hands of the workers, the state could be used to promote socialist development (see Chapter 14) in the transition to communism.

Box 2.3 The dependency view

The dependency school was prominent in the 1970s. As with Marxism, capitalism was still seen primarily as a system of exploitation (indeed, many dependency thinkers could be called neo-Marxists) but the important point was its international nature. In this view, the historical process which resulted in the development of the industrialized world was the same process in which the South did not become developed. In simple terms, Northern capitalist industrialization created structures in which Southern economies were dependent and which tended to lead to and maintain underdevelopment.

In its most crude version, dependency thinking simply substituted countries for classes so that capitalism was not so much a system of class exploitation as one of exploitation of Southern countries by the North. In less crude versions, the international capitalist class, together with allies from the ruling élites of Southern countries, is able to exploit workers and peasants in the South, at the same time as 'buying off' its own working class with a mixture of material rewards and racist ideology.

As in classical Marxism, capitalism was viewed as having positive as well as negative aspects. For example, dependency thinkers tended to favour industrialization and to note the positive aspects of the dynamism of capitalism in raising productive capacities. However, the dependency view was not clear on how the contradictions of capitalism as an international system might be overcome. Various development strategies were worked out, which differed in the extent to which they rejected or tried to work with international capitalism, but which were all deliberate efforts to improve living standards by changing the structural relationship with international capitalism. This generally meant development was to be achieved through the actions of Southern states.

If we look at development from the perspective of the government of a Southern country, the implication of dependency thinking could be to advocate withdrawal from the international capitalist system, or at least strong local state controls on it. This might be in order to build up national capital or to institute some form of planned development, 'socialist' or otherwise. It might entail a kind of solo self-reliance, or could be in solidarity with other countries of the South.

However, such thinking hardly offered solutions. For one thing, it tended to be uncritical of Southern states, and to make the unwarranted assumption that they are unified organizations with the power and the will to implement anti-capitalist policies. Again, without overseas involvement, where is the investment needed for economic development to come from? (Figure 2.6) The only possibility would seem to be from the savings of that country's own people; in other words, by squeezing surplus out of the same already poor population that may supply the state's political support base.

It is instructive to look at four historically important arguments for intervention. First, in the *Keynesian* view, developed in the context of the great depression of the 1930s, periodic booms and slumps are inherent problems of capitalism, which has no inbuilt mechanism for ensuring a balance between supply and demand as economies grow. John Maynard Keynes proposed state spending to create employment and increase incomes, thus stimulating demand and restoring business confidence.

Second, there is the view first propounded by the nineteenth-century German thinker List, who advanced the case for protecting the 'infant industries' of newly industrializing countries (NICs) from competition by well-established industries elsewhere. List was thinking at the time of protecting German industries from British competition; but his arguments for *protectionism* have been taken up by contemporary Southern governments. Today's NICs are facing competition in global markets from powerful industrial countries and from transnational corporations whose resources and sales may be greater than the annual incomes of many countries. This kind of state 'protection' generally operates through tax concessions and other incentives, as well as restricting imports through the use of tariffs and quotas to ensure less foreign competition in the national market.

A third kind of argument may be labelled *welfarism*. Although capitalist 'development'

It's only some foreign aid mission members, sir. I told them we wanted to be self-reliant and didn't want to depend on any country and sent them away!

Figure 2.6

increases economic output, policies are needed to ensure that this is used to meet basic human needs, particularly since these are not all well mirrored by market valuations. This would require development planning to link investment with the creation of jobs, the eradication of poverty, improved health for all, an improved status for women and so on. These are the type of development objectives that you will recall are now agreed between states at conferences like the Copenhagen Summit and taken up at global level by international organizations such as the World Bank (see Box 1.1 in Chapter 1).

Finally, there is *global environmentalism*. Concern for the environment is often a rather separate motivation for state intervention – and intervention by means of agreements between states, since the problems of managing the global commons necessarily require concerted international action. Following the Rio 'Earth Summit' of 1992, more international agreements are being negotiated to regulate the excesses of global capitalism in this respect.

There are debates about whether intervention should be minimal or far-reaching. These are not simply about how much intervention but hide an important difference about the role of intervention with respect to captialism. On the one hand there are those for whom poverty, pollution, violence and so on are only problems in so far as they threaten the proper working of

the capitalist system. However, they recognize that the answer is not simply to try remove all obstacles to the self-regulation of the market, but that these problems need dealing with at least to the extent that they are kept under control. On the other hand, others see capitalism as dynamic and productive but dangerous if it is not controlled. From this point of view social goals need to be addressed directly and the market must be stringently regulated in order for development goals to be achieved. Kaplinsky (1998) has referred to the former as the *market efficiency* view of intervention, and the latter as *governing the market*.

In either way of thinking, famine, war, and environmental catastrophe are all potentially linked as overriding dangers to humanity, though there might be disagreement as to whether they constitute a 'global threefold *crisis*' (Korten's phrase in Chapter 1). There is wide agreement on the importance of trying to eliminate poverty, and that this at least is an area where both international and state intervention is required. Galbraith (1990), for example, not only sees poverty as an inhumanity in itself but also as 'the source of oppression and conflict'. Thus he advocates economic assistance to achieve economic improvement in the poor countries, not only for the direct benefits of material progress but also to lessen the dangers of war and of violent repression of internal populations.

The most obvious problem with the interventionist approach at the global level is that there is no international state to co-ordinate the implementation of any policies that may be suggested. One possibility is a combination of the activities of different kinds of development agencies with co-ordination through international agreements, but the question remains of how such agreements are to be policed.

'Mainstream' versus 'alternative' development

All the versions of interventionism, as well as neoliberalism and structuralism, envision industrialization as the way to provide the resources to meet human needs or meet the 'global crisis'. The interventionists also see the state and other development agencies as taking on the job of intentional development required. Despite the debates about state versus market or the form and degree of intervention, these may all be termed 'mainstream' views of development. The set of ideas grouped together under the labels 'alternative development', 'another development' or 'people-centred development' are a reaction against this 'mainstream' development. In particular they are a reaction against the 'alienation' of large-scale industrialization and they reject the notion of trusteeship by which others determine what is required for people's development. This current of thought favours small-scale individual and co-operative enterprise both in industry and agriculture. It also places emphasis on people themselves as agents of development, solving their own problems individually or through local organizations and networks.

It has to be admitted that there is little if any theory as to how such dreams could be replicated on a large scale, and how the kind of social change could be brought about that would safeguard them for the future. However, throughout the 1990s there has been a growing consensus on the need to look more closely at the potential for local groups and individuals to be involved as their own development agents, if only because of the manifest failure of the main theoretical perspectives on development to deliver major improvements in living conditions to the world's poorest individuals and communities.

Summary

1 Development means not only 'good change' but also all-encompassing change, which builds on itself, occurs at both societal and individual levels, and may be destructive as well as creative.

2 Development as an 'immanent' process, as with the intrinsic dynamism of capitalism, needs to be distinguished from development as an intentional activity, often designed to 'ameliorate the faults' of capitalist growth.

3 'Development' is used in three main senses: a vision or measure of a desirable society; an historical process of social change; deliberate efforts at improvement by development agencies.

4 Two very different visions for development are that of modern industrial society, usually combined with liberal democracy, and that of a society where every individual's potential can be realized.

5 Two distinct views of development as an historical process are: capitalism creating the engine of growth with some room for intentional development to 'ameliorate the faults'; or a struggle between pro-market and protectionist movements.

6 Consideration of development agencies brings in questions of trusteeship, whether agencies have legitimacy and capacity to 'do development', and what interests they represent.

7 There are several competing overall views on development, each of which combines its own vision, version of history and ideas on development agencies. The debate between *neoliberalism* and *structuralism* has been superseded as both are largely discredited. Instead, the main question within 'mainstream' development is about the degree and form of *interventionism*. *People-centred development* may provide an alternative.

A WORLD OF PROBLEMS?

3

UNDERSTANDING FAMINE AND HUNGER

BEN CROW

"Nourishment is fundamental. The story of human history, reduced to essentials, revolves around the basic requirements for life."

(Rotberg, 1983)

The question of hunger is one of the most pressing problems facing the world at the turn of the millennium. This chapter introduces some ways of understanding famine and hunger, and attempts to explore these questions:

Q What processes lead to famine?

How can famine be prevented?

How many people are hungry?

How can hunger be reduced?

The chapter begins by distinguishing, in Section 3.1, between famine and chronic hunger, and introducing the meanings and measurement of undernutrition. Section 3.2 is about the analysis of famine. It starts by examining the phases of social change which often precede famine mortality. This section goes on to provide a description of a famine which occurred in the Ethiopian province of Wollo in 1984–85, and uses that description and others to explain approaches to the analysis of famine. This section on famine ends with a discussion of the political preconditions for the prevention of famine.

Section 3.3 examines the global scale of chronic hunger, its relationship to poverty and some differences in hunger, poverty and mortality between men and women. Section 3.4 explores how some common-sense ideas about the causes of hunger link to broader themes in the study of

social change. The final section examines some principles for action on famine and hunger.

3.1 Famine and hunger – some starting points

An important distinction

Analysis of hunger, and what to do about it, has been advanced by making a distinction between famine and chronic undernutrition (Figure 3.1). The work of Amartya Sen has been particularly influential. In 1998, his work was recognized by the award of the Nobel Prize for Economics (though it was for his theoretical work on welfare economics, rather than his work on famine,

You don't have to promise them anything, sir. This is not what has been declared famine area — it is further up

Figure 3.1

which is more widely known). This chapter is particularly indebted to two of Sen's books: Sen (1981) and Drèze & Sen (1989).

In the last part of the twentieth century, people in the industrialized world were made aware of famine, particularly in Africa, through television and newspaper reports of starvation. These were accounts of the most acute manifestation of hunger. **Famine** is a crisis in which starvation from insufficient intake of food, combined with high rates of disease, is associated with sharply increased death rates.

Famine is not the only form of hunger. In many parts of the world where famine has not occurred for several decades, sustained nutritional deprivation is, nevertheless, experienced by a significant proportion of the population. This long-term condition of **chronic hunger** is rarely given international media coverage but it may kill more people globally than the acute crisis of famine does.

> **Famine:** A sharp increase in mortality arising from acute starvation and starvation-related disease.
>
> **Chronic hunger:** Sustained nutritional deprivation (i.e. undernutrition).

The terms 'famine' and 'hunger' have broader meanings in other contexts. An early English dictionary defines famine as 'a scarcity of food' (Johnson, 1810), and the term is sometimes also used as a general term for shortage. The same dictionary explains hunger as 'desire of food [and] the pain felt from fasting'. These general usages are inadequate for analysis because they imply connections (food shortage in the case of famine, and desire or pain in the definition of hunger) which may not further our understanding of the causes of famine and hunger. Later in this chapter, I will explain why the notion of food shortage is often not the best place to start the analysis of famine.

One contrast between the industrialized and non-industrialized worlds at the turn of the millennium is that nutritional problems in the former focus on obesity and malnutrition, whereas small body size and poor nutrition are more prevalent in the latter. There is a paradox, notes Garrow (1994, p.63) 'that, in affluent countries such as the UK, where choice of food for the majority of the population is not constrained by availability or economic factors, so many important diseases are largely attributable to diet' (see also Chapter 4).

The abundant and varied food supply available to most people in industrial countries, and relatively inactive modes of making a living, have led to new problems. These problems of abundance do not outweigh the achievements of agricultural plenty: 'it would be folly to suggest that we should revert to the monotonous, uncertain and unsafe food supply of the poor peasant' (Garrow, 1994, pp.72–3). Nevertheless, there is, in affluent countries, both overconsumption of energy, leading to rising prevalence of obesity, and underconsumption of fruits and vegetables, leading to some degenerative diseases. These problems of abundance are thought to arise partly because human bodies lack physiological signals of overeating; conscious regulation of diet is required in conditions of plenty (Garrow, 1994). This chapter is not about these problems of abundance. I will be concentrating on undernutrition, rather than malnutrition or obesity.

It is surprisingly difficult to measure undernutrition, for three reasons:

1 There is no single medical test which will unequivocally indicate the level of nutrition or undernutrition in an individual.

2 This difficulty is compounded by uncertainty about the minimum dietary energy supply below which life and activity may be jeopardized. Box 3.1 describes the main approaches to measurement, and current estimates of minimum required nutrition.

3 Because there is no one test of undernutrition, many indirect measures are used to estimate the prevalence of hunger in a region or country. I will describe some of these indirect measures of hunger in Section 3.3.

Box 3.1 Measuring undernutrition

It is surprisingly difficult to measure undernutrition. There are two general approaches at the individual level, focusing on nutritional or medical indications.

1 Measures of *nutritional intake* estimate how much food a person is eating and assess the adequacy of that quantity of dietary energy supply. In practice, however, it is difficult and expensive to measure what people eat. As a result it is only feasible to measure the nutritional intake of small numbers of people. In addition, doubts arise because the measurement and constant observation required to watch each item of food throughout the day is intrusive and likely to influence eating behaviour. One nutritionist writes that measuring nutritional intake is 'the most difficult, expensive and probably the least satisfactory way of identifying malnourished people' (Payne, 1990, p.16).

2 Measures of *nutritional status* use some physiological characteristic to determine whether an individual appears to be undernourished. Undernourished children tend to be small for their age so a comparison of the height of one individual against the average height for a well-nourished child of that age will provide an indication of undernutrition. Similarly, comparison of upper-arm circumference with typical measurements for well-fed children will provide another indication of undernutrition. Some body measurements, including the overall size of an adult, may provide indications of past levels of nutrition (undernutrition in early childhood is associated with smaller body size), whereas other measurements (such as arm circumference) may provide a better guide to current nutrition.

In order to establish undernutrition, levels of nutritional intake are compared with minimum dietary energy requirements, measured in kilocalories of energy. Accepted standards have been revised downwards from 2830 kcal/day in 1957, and 2450 kcal/day in 1985, to more recent figures of 2200 kcal/day for someone undertaking little activity and a 'survival requirement' of 1550 kcal/day (Payne, 1990, p.15). One reason given for the reduction in accepted standards of dietary energy requirements has been recognition of the small average body size prevailing in many developing countries, even though small body size may itself be a consequence of previous undernutrition.

Severe undernutrition is commonly termed *malnutrition*. This is usually asociated with specific, observable symptoms, such as a very swollen abdomen and clear signs of wasting.

3.2 Famine

"Famine is the closing scene of a drama whose most important and decisive acts have been played out behind closed doors."

(Dessalegn Rahmato, 1987)

The causes of famine are complex. The final crisis which may gain international attention and response frequently has a long and untold history of social disintegration and livelihood collapse behind it. There are often interacting causes, including war, conflict over resources, or other social tensions, ecological decline, changes in market conditions, and climatic stress.

Famine processes

One way of understanding famine is through the description of the phases of social change and response which may lead up to a famine. This way of approaching the problem highlights some of the connections between chronic hunger and starvation, the important role of war and violence, and helps us to distinguish the interacting causes of decline, and the possibilities for response, at different stages of crisis. Four phases can be distinguished in the months and years leading to crisis:

1 dearth: immediate causes of famine leading to austerity;

2 privation and coping strategies: temporary migration in search of work or food; selling of possessions and productive assets;

3 social collapse: exhaustion, dispersal, mass migration;

4 arrival at relief, refugee camps or food distribution centres.

Figure 3.2   International Committee of the Red Cross 'feeding centre' at Tonj, southern Sudan.

International coverage of famine is usually restricted to the final stages when the victims have abandoned their livelihoods and embarked on mass migration in a desperate search for food. If governments and international agencies have established relief camps where food is supplied, the migration may end at these camps (Figure 3.2). The victims have become refugees from their homes, fields, social networks and productive assets.

It is in the camps and distribution centres and during migration that very high mortality rates can be recorded. Death in famine is frequently due to the interaction between disease and undernutrition. Camps for relief, refugees and food distribution, where large populations gather in close quarters, and suffer from inadequate sanitation and clean water supplies, provide conditions for the spread of infectious diseases. A report (Toole & Waldman, *c*.1988) on refugee populations in Thailand in the late 1970s, and in Sudan and Somalia in the early 1980s, described the causes of mortality as follows:

"The main reported causes of mortality were undernutrition, measles, diarrhea, malaria and acute respiratory infections. Measles was a major cause of death in Somalia and Sudan; in Thailand, an early immunization program probably prevented measles mortality. Diarrhea and measles alone accounted for 80% of the deaths in the Sudan camps during the first three months. Other reported causes of death included cholera, tuberculosis, typhus, relapsing fever, meningitis, and hepatitis. Several large epidemics of cholera have occurred in Somali and Sudanese camps since early 1985."

(Toole & Waldman, *c*.1988, p.ii)

Payne (1994) notes that disease and undernutrition reinforce one another, and it is often impossible to distinguish between them as a cause of physiological stress or death:

"An infection can result in loss of appetite and hence initiate undernutrition; it can also result in the depletion of body stores of specific nutrients and hence malnutrition. Dietary deficiencies on the other hand, can reduce the effectiveness of response of the body's immune system, making infection more likely and increasing its severity."

(Payne, 1994, pp.83–4)

Since mortality is particularly high in camps, optimal intervention needs to precede the stage of migration. At the final stage, once such a migration has been embarked upon, mortality can only be avoided by the provision of food and medical support under extreme conditions of overcrowding and poor sanitation. Before mass migration it may be possible to protect livelihoods, productive assets, and social collapse, thus avoiding the problems of mass camps.

What is it that turns the second phase of desperate attempts to cope with privation (Figure 3.3) into the third phase of mass migration (Figure 3.4)? De Waal (1990) terms the third and fourth phases 'social collapse' and argues that the shift from privation to collapse, usually caused by war, raiding or some other form of violence, is what brings mass starvation. He describes the second phase of privation and social disruption as follows (note that the term 'entitlements' is defined below):

> "Faced with a shortage of food and other necessities, people migrate to find work, scour the bush for wild foods, seek out kin and patrons, and travel to market to sell their assets. The population movements these strategies involve may serve to precipitate health crises, for instance by crowding people into inadequate housing with poor sanitation and water supplies. The migration may also…erode the food entitlements of host populations, by bringing down wage rates and the returns on casual low-status trades, and by inflating the price of food. It may also have adverse effects on the entitlements of the migrants. Some of their assets (houses, land, and other immovable property) will be temporarily abandoned and thus irredeemable for cash, and also exposed to the risk of theft or damage. Movable assets such as animals may die on the road…However, in such migration, the gains to the migrant are almost always greater than the losses; conditions were worse at home."

(De Waal, 1990, pp.484–5)

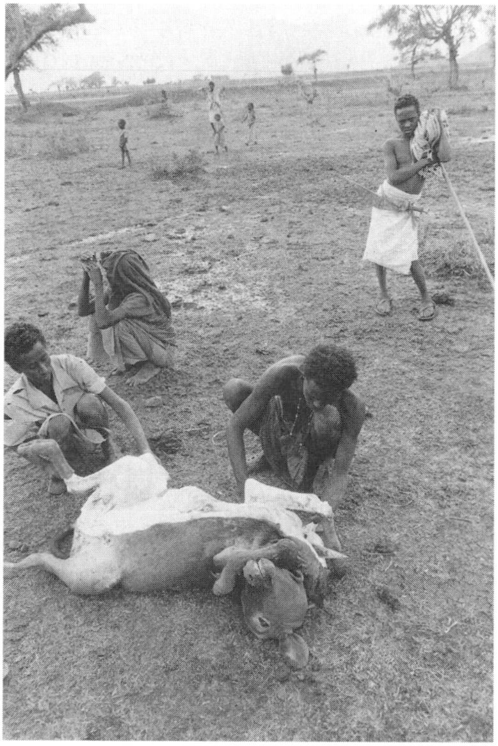

Figure 3.3 Still coping? Afar pastoralists skin a calf during the 1974 drought in Ethiopia. They would try to sell the skin on a glutted market.

Figure 3.4 Social collapse. Families leaving home: collecting water to go to Korem relief camp, Wollo, Ethiopia, 1984.

This is how De Waal describes the turning point from privation to collapse:

> "Social collapse occurs when such coping strategies break down...[which] occurs when they no longer believe that it is possible to preserve [their] way of life...In practice, in Africa at least, this coping capacity does not break down: it is broken. Under peaceable conditions, African populations are not reduced to frank starvation by economic depression and natural disaster alone."
>
> (De Waal, 1990, pp.485–6)

Mass migrations resulting from civil war have been frequent in central and southern Africa in the 1990s and have resulted in unprecedented mortality rates. The severity of disasters has in recent years been measured by the crude mortality rate (CMR). This is the number of deaths per 10 000 persons per day. In the absence of famine and war, there is less than one death every two days in a population of 10 000, or a rate of less than 0.5. In situations of great distress, this figure can rise to 2 or 3 per day per 10 000 people.

In mass migrations of refugees from genocide in Rwanda, and civil war in Congo/Zaïre, crude mortality rates have reached new highs. In refugee camps in Goma, former Zaïre, in 1994, cholera and dysentery killed Rwandan refugees at a rate of 60 per day (Stockton, 1998). In 1997, attempts to forcibly repatriate refugees to Rwanda led tens of thousands of people to flee west into Congo/Zaïre pursued by military forces from Rwanda and Congo. Oxfam estimated that the CMR reached 300 per day. The Emergencies Director of Oxfam wrote that this set 'a public health disaster record that Oxfam has not encountered elsewhere' (Stockton, 1998, p.353).

These are extreme situations, and are clearly linked to their immediate political context. However, recent advances in the understanding of famine have focused on what might be termed its pre-history. In later sections, I will be looking at two arguments about the pre-history of famine. One suggests that war and famine are rooted in pre-existing social tensions and relationships. A second suggests that long-established relationships between vulnerable groups and government may prevent famine.

Before that, I want to examine one of the worst and most publicized famines of the 1980s, the famine in Ethiopia in 1984 and 1985.

Famine in Wollo 1984–85

Wollo was one of the provinces of Ethiopia hardest hit in 1984–85. Some of the most harrowing images of the 1984–85 Ethiopian famine came from the town of Korem in Wollo, where large numbers of peasants and pastoralists gathered to seek relief in the final stages of the crisis (Figure 3.5).

At this stage, when television pictures portrayed an open plain filled with huddled figures waiting for relief food and medicine, famine victims expressed an image of helplessness. In earlier stages of the crisis, this helplessness had been preceded by feverish activity:

> "Neighbours and friends decide to pool their resources the better to withstand the hardship; agreements are reached between relatives or friends to dispose of assets in turns, and to support each other in the meantime; measures are taken to remove livestock to...other areas less exposed to the crisis; arrangements are made to sell livestock to peasants in one's own community or a neighbouring one with the understanding that in the end the sellers will rent the animals for farming purposes; markets both in neighbouring communities and in distant ones, especially those reported to be free from social or ecological stress, are frequently monitored, and the information disseminated widely; distress signals are sent out to relatives living in urban areas or in other provinces..."
>
> (Dessalegn Rahmato, 1987, p.23)

Dessalegn Rahmato notes that 'the Wollo peasantry is diligent, frugal and highly skilled, and yet this same peasantry has been the victim of all the major famines that have occurred in this

Figure 3.5   Korem relief camp, Wollo, Ethiopia, 1984.

country in the last one hundred years.' Why should skilled, hard-working farmers be subject to crisis so often?

The explanation that was widely accepted for this famine is one that is commonly given for many famines: it was a famine caused by drought. This explanation of causation through climatic abnormality, be it flood, drought, frost or cyclone, is probably the explanation of famine most widely accepted. In its simplest version this sort of explanation is sometimes extended to make a distinction between 'man-made' and 'natural' famines. Man-made famines would include those connected with war or displaced populations.

From this distinction an implication is often drawn that 'natural' famines are unavoidable but those caused by human intervention arise from some human failing. However, this distinction can be deeply misleading because:

"Famine is, by its very nature, a social phenomenon (it involves the inability of large groups of people to establish com-

mand over food in the society in which they live), but the forces influencing such occurrences may well include, *inter alia,* developments in physical nature in addition to social processes…[I]t has to be recognized that even when the prime mover in a famine is a natural occurrence such as a flood or a drought, what its impact will be on the population will depend on how society is organized."

(Drèze & Sen, 1989, p.46)

In general, the natural disaster explanation of famine posits a direct sequence of causes starting with climatic abnormality, leading to failure of harvests and a reduction in food available and the amount that people have to eat. However, drought, flood, frost and cyclones occur frequently and persistently all over the world and are only associated with famine on rare occasions. On those occasions the weather is generally only one precipitating factor among several, such as war, social disruption and disturbance of exchange, and these precipitating factors act upon a deeper vulnerability of livelihoods.

Figure 3.6 Drought by itself does not necessarily cause famine. The Shawata Project in central Tigray, in the middle of a drought area, harnessed irregular and light rainfall so that the irrigated land could yield two good harvests a year. The project was, however, bombed by Ethiopian government forces during the civil war.

Almost all recent famines in Africa have been associated with the social disruption of war as well as climatic abnormality (Figure 3.6).

In Wollo, persistent drought (combined with unusual frosts) was one of the factors precipitating the crisis among the peasantry, but the origins of the crisis are to be found in social conditions and economic and political changes unrelated to the drought.

Dessalegn Rahmato writes of 'famine hiding behind the mountains', alluding to the hidden factors contributing to famine vulnerability. He does not claim to understand the full story of the famine among the peasantry in Wollo but he identifies three critical factors behind the long-standing and deepening vulnerability of agricultural livelihoods there.

1   *A stagnant form of production,* discouraging innovation and unresponsive to growing population and deteriorating soil conditions. Agriculture in Wollo is the cultivation of cereals and pulses and the keeping of livestock, primarily for direct consumption (subsistence). There is little connection between agriculture and urban economic activity, and little that is produced in agriculture is exchanged. There are few economic activities other than agriculture and few opportunities for employment. Because agriculture is not integrated with other economic activity, and focused on subsistence, there is little opportunity to incorporate new technologies. A low standard of living is socially accepted and there is little support for innovation. 'Peasants in the Northeast region as a whole are, even in normal conditions, and in times free of environmental and social stress, not too far removed from the precipice of starvation and death' (Dessalegn Rahmato, 1987, p.102).

2   *The rise in the external obligations,* in food, money and labour, of the peasantry over the preceding ten years. Like governments in many non-industrialized countries, the government of Ethiopia obtained food for the cities partly by purchasing it at fixed prices from the peasants. Each peasant household had to deliver a predetermined quota of grain. The price given by the government for this quota was substantially below, and for some crops only a third of, the price available in local markets. These government quotas were not lifted during the famine (but were reduced after it). Some peasants were forced to sell livestock in order to buy food to deliver to the government. Taxes were also

exacted throughout the famine period. In fact, with cruel irony, the victims of the famine were required to pay a special famine levy. This levy was established to help victims of the famine after the crisis was recognized in October 1984, and it was collected in Wollo as in other parts of Ethiopia. One further burden on the peasantry was that they had to contribute labour to communal and state projects. This work included large-scale soil conservation projects, work on the land of those assigned to fight in the civil war, and work on state plantations. This unpaid labour took up at least one day per week. All these obligations had arisen since the change of government in 1974, and they subtracted from the basic necessities of peasant consumption.

3 The third critical factor contributing to the profound vulnerability of peasant livelihoods arose from the preceding two factors. With a dead-end form of production and increasing external obligations, much of the Wollo peasantry was reduced to *acute poverty*. Households had little reserve with which to resist periodic crisis.

These three factors provide a brief summary account of the main causes of famine vulnerability among peasants in one province of Ethiopia in 1984–85. Related but distinct factors are associated with famine among pastoralists. What should already be clear is that the explanation of famine involves several complex and interacting factors, with the organization of production and exchange at the centre of the picture.

The vulnerability of peasant livelihoods in Wollo has to do with all three elements of **production**. Dessalegn Rahmato's account particularly focuses on the stagnation, or lack of development, in the form of production, its inability to respond to deteriorating natural conditions (environmental stress) and growing population. There is not space in this chapter to explore why this form of subsistence production, and the technical skills and social relationships which sustain it, is not generating change. Chapters 6 and 7 begin to examine the social factors contributing to population change and to ecological deterioration.

If we now turn from production to **exchange**, much of the feverish activity leading up to the famine was focused on a new involvement with market exchange. As subsistence activity fails, and as a wide range of survival strategies are exhausted, peasants attempt to sell their assets and their labour power:

"Crisis survival brings sudden and dramatic changes in peasants' economic thinking for a brief period. In this phase of the crisis we see the peasant desperately trying to break out of the subsistence system, and plunge into the cash economy and the exchange system. The market now assumes greater importance than before as the peasant becomes aware that survival depends on acquiring cash to purchase food…However, the food deficit peasant is at a disadvantage in these circumstances

Production: An interaction between people and nature in which human energy is used to transform natural products into goods for human use and consumption. The simplest production process has three elements: (1) the work done by people; (2) the subject of that work, the raw materials of nature and of previous production; (3) the tools and skills used in the work. Thus, agriculture, or production on the land, requires, at its simplest, (a) people to provide labour power; (b) adequately fertile land, rainfall and seeds of the crop to be grown; and (c) a hoe or a plough for tilling the soil and the skills and practices of cultivation.

Exchange: This is required for production to transcend the simplest forms. Most familiarly, exchange involves the buying and selling of goods. It also includes the paying of wages, rents and interest. Exchange is the process through which goods and services are distributed among a population. Exchange enables *specialization*, concentration on the production of one type of good, which is a step to higher levels of productivity.

because what he has to offer [labour power and saleable assets] is not in demand, while what he wishes to acquire, i.e. food, is both relatively scarce and in high demand. On the other hand, the peasant with surplus food and the rural trader stand to gain in the exchange process."

(Dessalegn Rahmato, 1987, pp.167–9)

Approaches to analysing famine

There have been two general categories of approach to famine in recent times. One asks: what reduced the availability of food per person? The second asks: what changed command over food? These two approaches are termed respectively the *food availability decline* approach and the *entitlement* approach. I will describe each of these approaches before turning to some new leads to a wider understanding of famine.

The *food availability decline* approach highlights the supply of food compared with the numbers of people. The supply of food, or food availability, in a country is usually measured in this approach as the total production of food, plus imports and minus exports. This food availability decline thesis lies behind ideas that a flood or a drought, or a harvest failure for some other reason, leads to a reduction in the food available in a region or a country and directly from that to famine. The problem with this approach is that it ignores the ways in which people actually get food.

The *entitlement* approach, by contrast, focuses on the social relations through which people gain command, or entitlement, over food. This approach, suggested by Amartya Sen, identifies two basic characteristics, **endowments** and **entitlements**, which give access to livelihoods and food:

"For example, a peasant has his land, labour power and a few other resources which together make up his endowment. Starting from this endowment, he can produce a bundle of food that will be his. Or by selling his labour power, he can get a wage and with that buy commodities including food. Or, he can grow some cash crops and sell them to buy food and other commodities. There are many other possibilities."

(Sen, 1981, p.46)

The above quotation could be read to imply that all peasants are men, and that it is only the entitlements of men which matter. Such a reading would be misleading. Sen's work (Sen, 1990a; Drèze & Sen, 1989, ch.4) has been influential in the analysis of hunger and gender relations, a question to which I will return in Section 3.4 below.

> **Endowment:** The owned assets and personal capacities which an individual or household can use to establish entitlement to food.
>
> **Entitlement:** The relationships, established by trade, direct production or sale of labour power, through which an individual or household gains access to food. *Direct entitlement* is access to food gained through own production and consumption. *Exchange entitlement* is that command over food which is achieved by selling labour power in order to buy food. *Trade entitlement* is the sale of produce to buy food.

The entitlement approach has been most helpful in the analysis of non-war famines. Amartya Sen (1981) analysed four important famines in this century: the 1943 Bengal famine, the 1973 famine in Wollo, Ethiopia, and two 1974 famines, one in Bangladesh and one in Harerghe province of Ethiopia. Table 3.1 provides a summary of Sen's findings on these four famines.

In his analysis of four famines, Sen showed that particular occupation groups, or **classes** of the population, were more vulnerable than others. In the two South Asian cases, he found that rural labourers, those making a living by working for a wage, were overrepresented in those seeking relief or dying in the famines. Farmers or peasants with access to land on which to grow their own food for consumption or sale were less vulnerable. By contrast, the most vulnerable in the Wollo famine were farmers and in the Harerghe famine they were pastoralists, depending on the products of livestock for their food.

Table 3.1 Comparative analysis of four famines

Which famine?	Was there a food availability collapse?	Which occupation group provided the largest number of famine victims?	Did that group suffer substantial endowment loss?	Did that group suffer exchange entitlement shifts?	Did that group suffer direct entitlement failure?	Did that group suffer trade entitlement failure?
Bengal 1943	No	Rural labour	No	Yes	No	Yes
Ethiopia (Wollo) 1973	No	Farmer	A little, yes	Yes	Yes	No
Ethiopia (Harerghe) 1974	Yes	Pastoralist	Yes	Yes	Yes	Yes
Bangladesh 1974	No	Rural labour	Earlier, yes	Yes	No	Yes

Source: Sen, A. (1981) *Poverty and Famines: an essay on entitlement and deprivation*, p.163, Oxford University Press, Oxford.

Social class: The distinction between different social groups according to the ways in which they make their living, particularly between those who own means of production (land, factories, machines) and those who do not (who sell their labour power to cultivate the land or work in the factories). Important distinctions for this chapter are those between peasants (those who produce on the land, using family labour, partly for their own consumption and partly for sale), wage labourers (those who sell their labour power to make a living as agricultural and industrial workers), and pastoralists (who tend livestock, often nomadically, to produce meat and milk for consumption and exchange).

With this information about the most vulnerable groups, Sen worked back to understand how these classes gained command over food, through wages, sale of goods, or direct production of food. Then he was able to examine how social, political, economic and environmental events had undermined that command or entitlement.

As Vaughan (1985, p.178) notes:

"Sen's entitlement theory is primarily concerned with understanding how different sections of the community obtain their entitlement to food in normal times, and how and to what degree these entitlements might be affected by changes in the market economy. His analysis of access to food thus relates directly to the ownership structure of any given society, and the...class basis of suffering in any famine."

In the case of the Wollo famine among peasant agricultural producers, we can identify the failure of two different kinds of entitlement to food. There was a failure of direct entitlement, i.e. a failure of direct production for own consumption (subsistence). It is in this aspect of the crisis that drought played an important precipitating role. As we have seen, the explanation of this failure of direct entitlement requires an understanding of the organization of production and its ability to cope with changing conditions.

In the later stages of the crisis, the peasants were also engulfed by the failure of their attempt to establish exchange entitlements. One of the advances in the recent understanding of famine has been a recognition of the way that the operation of market exchange may exacerbate or initiate famine. We will look briefly at instances of this below. For the Wollo peasantry, their 'plunge into the cash economy' could not bring adequate command over food. Many people were seeking paid work from an economy which generated little employment at the best of times. Many households were also trying to sell livestock, tools, utensils, houses and jewellery, and prices were reduced to fractions of those expected in more normal times. Those able to sell assets or find employment found that the relative scarcity of food had pushed prices much higher than normal. These two price movements (prices of saleable assets down, prices of food up) interacted with one another. As a result, the proceeds of the sale of livestock, for example, could buy only a fraction of the food that could have been realized by a similar transaction previously.

While the entitlement approach draws our attention to the livelihoods (and the vulnerability of those livelihoods) with which individuals gain command over food, it distracts us from other factors. In the case of Wollo, the Ethiopian government exacerbated famine through increased taxation and obligations to undertake work on state projects. We need to know much more about what governments, and other powerful groups, do to cause as well as to prevent famine. The focus on livelihoods also distracts us from the contemporary importance of war as a proximate condition for famine. 'The role of war', argues Keen (1994, p.12), 'has to a large extent been marginalized in the theoretical literature on famine which for the most part addresses itself to peacetime famines.'

These are new leads to the understanding of famine: identifying the causation of famine in longer term social processes; understanding how political action may both cause and prevent famine.

In a study of famine in Sudan between 1983 and 1989, Keen (1994) has argued that famine brought benefits to some groups:

> "The 1980s famine arose from a combination of four processes: the loss of assets and production (primarily because of raiding); the failure of market strategies; the failure of nonmarket survival strategies; and the inadequacy of relief...All these processes...yielded important benefits for a loose and shifting coalition of politically powerful groups within Sudan, who helped to promote these processes."
>
> (Keen, 1994, p.13)

Keen also criticizes the conceptual separation of famine and war from the long-standing processes in which they are embedded. He writes that it is important to 'avoid a common tendency to dissociate war from economic and political relationships existing in 'normal times'; both war and famine reflect an acceleration of existing processes of exploitation' (Box 3.2).

The struggle against famine

India and China, the two great Asian countries whose citizens constitute some 40% of world

---

Box 3.2 War and famine in Sudan 1983–89

"Commonly, war, even civil war, has been portrayed as something superimposed on society, rather than something that emerges from relationships and conflicts within society. War has frequently been seen...as an essentially senseless outbreak of violence with a number of innocent victims but no clear beneficiaries or functions. The same misleading dislocation is found in many portrayals of famine, which sever famines from normal social relations and from the historical intervals between famines, while at the same time concentrating exclusively on the victims and ignoring the possibility that there may be beneficiaries. In contrast to such portrayals, the civil wars in Sudan and associated famines can usefully be seen as a deepening of exploitative processes already existing in 'normal' times, a continuation and exaggeration of long-standing conflicts over resources (ivory, slaves, cattle, grain, land, oil) and a means – for certain groups – of maximizing the benefits of economic transactions through the exercise of various kinds of force against groups depicted as fair game in the context of civil (or holy) war. Winning the war was not the sole, or even the most important objective of many of those engaging in violence or blocking relief; and famine was more than a weapon of war. The primary goal for many was to manipulate war, violence, famine, and relief in ways that achieved economic goals."

(Keen, 1994, pp.13–14)

population, have had contrasting experiences of famine and hunger. Since the revolution of 1949, China has made progress in reducing chronic hunger, but during the Great Leap Forward, between 1958 and 1961, the largest famine of the twentieth century was allowed to occur, in which some 16–30 million people died. By contrast, there has been no major famine in India since independence from British rule in 1947, but chronic hunger remains widespread. This paradox raises two questions: (a) why did famine occur in China but not in India? (b) How has chronic hunger been reduced in China and not in India? I will briefly tackle the first of these questions here, and will return to the second in Section 3.3.

Drèze and Sen argue that India's better record on famine prevention can be explained primarily by the existence of a governmental system of famine prevention in India, and social processes associated with democracy and a free press which 'trigger' the famine prevention system (Box 3.3).

China had a system of public food distribution but lacked a tradition of adversarial journalism and forms of direct representation which might have provided a political 'trigger' for governmental response:

"…China did not lack a delivery and redistribution mechanism to deal with food shortages as famine threatened in 1958 and later. Despite the size of the decline of food output and the loss of entitlements of large sections of the population, China could have done a much better job of protecting the vulnerable by sharing the shortage in a bearable way.

What was lacking when the famine threatened China was a political system of adversarial journalism and opposition. The Chinese famine raged on for three years without it being even admitted in public that such a thing was occurring, and without there being an adequate policy response to the threat."

(Drèze & Sen, 1989, p.212)

Box 3.3 The Indian system of famine prevention

The Indian system of famine prevention… [has]…two different features…One is a worked-out procedure for entitlement protection through employment creation (usually paying wages in cash), supplemented by direct transfers to the unemployable. The origins of this procedure go back to the 1880s and the Famine Codes of the late nineteenth century…The other part is a political 'triggering mechanism' which brings the protection system into play and indeed which keeps the public support system in a state of preparedness…[In] the political system of post-independence India, it is extremely hard for any government in office…to get away with neglecting prompt and extensive anti-famine measures at the first signs of famine. And these signs are themselves more easily transmitted given India's relatively free media and newspapers, and the active and investigative role that journalists as well as opposition politicians can and do play in this field. […]

After [Indian] Independence, the political incentives to recognize emergencies, and to take action against the threat of famine, had to assume a new form [compared with British rule]. The vigour of political opposition has now made it impossible for the government to remain passive without major political risks, and the fear of losing elections reinforces the general sensitivity to political embarrassment in the state assembly and in the central parliament. In the process of making the facts known and forcing the hands of the respective state and central governments, the press too plays a leading role. The affected populations themselves have a much greater ability than in the past to make their demands felt and to galvanize the authorities into action (especially in view of the importance of winning the rural vote). This is one positive aspect of Indian democracy.

(Drèze & Sen, 1989, pp.212,126)

This analysis suggests that a free press and democracy, plus a governmental system for protecting or replacing entitlements are necessary. De Waal (1997) has taken the analysis further. He says that a free press and democracy may be necessary but not sufficient. This 'triggering mechanism' will not work unless a 'political contract' has been established between government and famine-vulnerable people. De Waal suggests that famine is rare in those countries in which starvation has been made a public or national issue, and there is some form of popular representation for those most vulnerable to starvation. These two political conditions may provide the beginnings of government accountability for famine. In other words, if famine occurs, that government may fall.

> "The right to be free from famine is socially and historically determined and politically negotiated...Empirical guarantees of liberal civil and political rights assist freedom from famine. Once people have the right to assemble [and] freedom of information, and can remove a government by democratic means, it is probable that they will then guarantee that their basic interests are looked after. But it is not certain: famine must be politicized, minorities must be represented, and technical capacity must exist."

> (De Waal, 1997, p.214)

De Waal uses lessons from India and from some countries in Africa to illustrate how political struggle may lead to a 'political contract' against famine. His account of Indian experience traces the rise of famine as a national concern. Under the British *raj*, until the middle of the nineteenth century, relief was denied on the Malthusian grounds that population growth unchecked by famine would create worse impoverishment. The 1857 Mutiny and the growth of the nationalist movement 'led the Raj to the conclusion that mitigating hardship and preventing political unrest were two sides of the same coin.' Famine 'codes' were established which recognized an obligation for the state to prevent famine, primarily through the creation of public employment. In the words of the 1905 Madras Famine Code, the 'State is bound to protect the people from starvation in times of distress.' When the state broke this promise and allowed famine in Bengal in 1943, the broken promise spurred the nationalist movement against British rule. Governments of independent India followed and expanded the 'political contract' against famine, by extending and implementing the famine codes.

In Tigray and Eritrea in the 1980s, where war between liberation movements and the then government of Ethiopia created zones freed from the control of the government, the liberation fronts recognized that what distinguished their rule from that of the government was their concern to ensure the survival of peasant populations. They recognized their obligation to prevent famine, and established relief organizations which brought food from outside Ethiopia. This is another example of a contract against famine, established over a much shorter period.

De Waal also argues that elements of a governmental obligation to prevent famine have been established in Botswana and Zimbabwe. Elsewhere, in Sudan (as we saw in Box 3.2), Ethiopia, Somalia and Zaïre, governments made few promises to the famine vulnerable.

Dilemmas of humanitarian intervention

> "For relief agencies [responding to crises like famine], the media present both unparalleled opportunities to raise money and acute ethical dilemmas when fundraising priorities, developmental strategies and educational values conflict."

> (Benthall, 1993, jacket blurb)

There is growing criticism of international humanitarian action in crises like famine. One fear, which De Waal articulates, is that international agencies may undermine local political processes which could create a political contract against famine.

De Waal suggests that the international response to famine tends to ride roughshod over local organizing. Both non-government relief agencies and UN agencies tend to use news media to present famine as a non-political issue. Relief agencies, such as Oxfam or Save the Children, need to present a simple message to their supporters in order to raise funds (Figure 3.7). UN agencies need to maintain good relations with the government of the country where famine is occurring and with the member governments of the United Nations. Both of these objectives can be most easily realized if a famine is presented as a technical issue, best solved by global professionals.

If it is true, by contrast, that political struggle provides the most effective prevention for famine, the imperatives of UN and non-government relief agencies to present the crisis as a techni-

cal, non-political issue could constitute an obstacle to the conquest of famine. De Waal has suggested (Box 3.4) rules which should guide international humanitarian intervention so as to build the conditions for preventing future famines.

> **Box 3.4   Rules for international humanitarian intervention**
>
> Where there is a political struggle against famine:
>
> 1   support locally accountable organization.
>
> 2   be prepared to work in a political manner.
>
> And in regions where there is no political contract between the state and vulnerable people:
>
> 1   do not obscure power relations
>
> 2   do not claim long term solutions
>
> 3   do not seek media limelight.
>
> (De Waal, 1997, pp.217–21)

3.3   Hunger: chronic undernutrition and poverty

'The phenomenon of endemic hunger is much more pervasive, it affects many times the number of people who are threatened by famine', note Drèze and Sen (1989, p.267). Whereas the catastrophe of famine may occur through the widespread *breakdown* of livelihoods for specific social classes or occupational groups, chronic hunger arises through a *continuous failure* to generate sufficient livelihoods.

There are varying estimates of the global scale of chronic hunger. Payne (1994, p.80) summarizes seven estimates made by the World Bank and the UN Food and Agriculture Organization (FAO) between 1963 and 1980. These estimates of the proportion of the global population that is hungry range from 10–15% (1963, FAO) and 15% (1980, FAO) to 55% (1965, World Bank) and 40% (1970, World Bank), with no evident pattern of change.

Figure 3.7   A simple message? 'Tonj: drinking a cup of milk to survive' (Red Cross photo and caption).

There are two main reasons why estimates vary. One relates to uncertainty about minimum dietary energy requirements (see Box 3.1). The capacity of humans to adapt to different levels of consumption may have been underestimated (Payne, 1994). A second reason relates to differences in methods of estimation.

Overall estimates of global hunger are generally made in one of two ways:

1 Measures of *national food availability* compare average availability of food per head with a minimum necessary dietary energy supply. An estimate for 1984–86, using this method, suggested that 1570 million people (31% of world population) had a 'dietary energy supply less than nutritional requirements' (Chen, 1990).

2 *Income measures* of hunger estimate the average income of poor households and compare that income with the cost of the food necessary to provide a minimum level of nutrition. The World Bank used this method to estimate that in 1985 between 340 million and 730 million people 'did not have enough income to obtain enough energy from their diet' (World Bank, 1986, p.1).

One of the most recent estimates of global hunger (FAO, 1996) uses some elements of both methods. Table 3.2 summarizes the results of this estimate.

These figures are calculated from national food availability and estimates of the distribution of food intake or income across the population. Let me explain. First, an estimate is made of dietary energy supply per head by dividing national food availability by the population of the country. Then, for each country an estimate of the statistical distribution of food across the population is made. This is an estimate of the food intake of different percentiles of the population, the food intake of the top 10%, the next 10% and so on down to the bottom 10%. For 18 countries this estimate is based on sur-

Table 3.2 Regional trends in number and proportion of undernourished people

Region	Year	Proportion of undernourished (%)	Number of undernourished (millions)
Sub-Saharan Africa	1969–71	38	103
	1979–81	41	148
	1990–92	43	215
Near East and North Africa	1969–71	27	48
	1979–81	12	27
	1990–92	12	37
East and South-east Asia	1969–71	41	476
	1979–81	27	379
	1990–92	16	269
South Asia	1969–71	33	238
	1979–81	34	303
	1990–92	22	255
Latin America and Caribbean	1969–71	19	53
	1979–81	14	48
	1990–92	15	64

Source: FAO (1996) *The Sixth World Food Survey*, UN Food and Agriculture Organization, Rome.

vey data on the distribution of household food intakes. For other countries, the distribution of food is estimated from the distribution of income or from the income distribution in neighbouring countries (FAO, 1996, pp.40–1). With these two estimates (per capita food availability and distribution of food intake), the number of people falling below a minimum nutritional level can be estimated.

This method probably provides the best current estimate of the numbers of people in the world facing hunger. In Africa, Asia and Latin America, there were 918 million undernourished people in 1969–71, 905 million in 1979–80, and 840 million in 1990–92. The trend is encouraging even if the numbers remain large. (Note that the FAO's *Sixth World Food Survey* does not estimate the number of people undernourished in the industrialized world. In the USA, for example, in the 1990s, between 20 and 30 million people used Food Stamps giving access to subsidized food.)

One clear regional conclusion can also be drawn from Table 3.2. There has been a rapid decline in hunger in East and South-east Asia. At the end of the 1960s, 41% of people in this region were undernourished. Two decades later, this proportion had fallen to 16%. This region includes both the newly industrializing countries of East Asia, where land reform and vigorous industrial growth have equalized rural landholdings and created urban employment, and China, where the generation of livelihoods and an extensive system of public support, including food distribution, reduced chronic hunger (see below).

Is the counting of the numbers of undernourished people important? Payne (1994) suggests that the issue which should concern us is poverty, rather than chronic hunger:

"If the concern is to reduce differences in the underlying causes of the risk of hunger, then nutritional science gives us no easy escape from the conclusion that differences in poverty will have to be reduced."

(Payne, 1994, p.96)

Pankhurst (1989, p.513) makes a parallel argument in relation to famine:

"Where famine is seen as the outcome and end result of many factors which make people poor and make them vulnerable to changes in their systems of production and reproduction (such as drought and war), then we can avoid seeking solutions to famine, or plans to ensure its prevention, separately from all other analysis of how people come to be so vulnerable."

Chronic hunger is one aspect of a wider set of deprivations understood as *poverty* – one of the two phenomena that concern this whole book. Chapters 2 and 4 have already introduced some of the ways in which poverty has been defined and measured. Chronic hunger and poverty are closely related. It is rare for wealthy households to go hungry, even in a famine.

We can understand a little more about chronic hunger and how it has been reduced by examining the experience of China after the revolution in 1949.

Over a 30-year period, the Chinese revolution made great strides in the reduction of poverty and hunger through (1) effective provision of jobs within production brigades; (2) provision of health services throughout the countryside; (3) effective distribution of food to both cities and countryside; and (4) in total establishing a level of social security.

The key indicators of China's success in hunger reduction compared with India's are the level of life expectancy (the number of years newborn children would live if subject to prevailing mortality risks; see Chapter 4) and the level of mortality among children. These measures of social well-being do not measure chronic undernutrition alone. An increase in life expectancy and a reduction of the level of childhood deaths may be caused both by nutritional improvements and by improvements in health and sanitation (as is discussed in more detail in the next chapter). In the case of China, analysis of nutritional status and mortality patterns confirms that 'China achieved a remarkable transition in health and nutrition' (Drèze & Sen, 1989, p.204).

Starting from similarly low levels at independence for India (in 1947) and the revolution in China (1949), China has begun to approach the levels of life expectancy and under-five mortality achieved in industrialized countries. Thus, in China, life expectancy at birth is in the upper 60s, compared with the mid- to upper 50s in India. The under-five mortality in China in 1996 was 39 per thousand (i.e. 39 children out of every thousand die before they reach the age of five) compared with 85 in India (World Bank, 1998).

We thus arrive at the paradox, identified by Drèze and Sen, of Chinese and Indian experience of famine and hunger. In China there has been some success in the reduction of chronic hunger but the great famine of 1958–61 was not prevented. By contrast, there has been some success in preventing famine in India, but less progress in the reduction of chronic hunger. Drèze and Sen attribute Indian success in famine prevention to relatively effective popular representation which enforces government response to distress. They identify Chinese success in reducing hunger with a large-scale transformation of social organization, providing the capacity for livelihood generation and effective public action to ensure access to nutrition, health facilities and social support.

3.4 Women and men, hunger and famine

Meghan Vaughan describes the victims of a 1949 famine in what is now Malawi as follows:

"The group which emerges as most disadvantaged...is that consisting of households which even in a normal year are not self-sufficient in food, who are short of land, and who make up their food deficit performing casual labour for other peasant farmers...The oral evidence, however, shows that there are added dimensions to the pattern of suffering...Firstly...both young children and the old suffered more than other age groups...[N]ot only were they physically less able to withstand food shortage, but they were also the first

groups to be abandoned by their kin. Secondly... there were large numbers of women who were without the economic support of a husband even before the famine, and many more who found themselves in this position in the course of the famine. Again, the poorer the household, the more likely a husband was to abandon it..."

(Vaughan, 1985, p.204)

Vaughan's account emphasizes the importance of social divisions other than those of entitlement or class, notably age and gender. In my discussion of famine and hunger, I have written as if it is only the deterioration of collective household entitlements that matters. Thus, my description of the entitlement approach implies that households have only one form of entitlement and the food collected through that claim is divided equally among members of the household. As Vaughan's account suggests, the reality is more complicated.

Food coming into a household may not be divided evenly; some members, notably the elderly, children and women, may get less than adult men. The household itself may also change under the stress of the crisis. Children and the elderly may be abandoned. Some members of the household may seek work elsewhere, leaving remaining household members without claims to food. The household may collapse.

Women, children and the elderly may face hunger because the collective entitlements of the household deteriorate. They may also go hungry because the household, and their claims on its resources, may change. In addition, the physical capacity of individuals to withstand nutritional deprivation varies.

The legitimacy of women's and children's claims to food, particularly in South Asia, may rest on the continuation of the household, and be undermined by its breakdown (Kabeer 1991). By contrast, '[m]ost African women have always done, and still do, independent work. They are not expected to rely economically on their husbands or families but to have a separate sphere of their own work' (Whitehead, 1990, p.59).

Thus, Naila Kabeer describes the threats to women's basic needs, including food, in South Asia:

> "Powerful beliefs and practices, sanctioned by the norms of religion and community, produce a highly unequal division of social and economic space. Women's…claims to the means by which they meet their basic needs are embedded…within contractual relations of family and kinship…[Women] can become poorer with the rest of the family-based household through a deterioration in its collective entitlements… Alternatively, they can become poorer with the breakdown of the family unit itself…"

> (Kabeer, 1994, p.141)

The more independent livelihoods of women in Africa do not, however, guarantee freedom from hunger. Women's autonomy is being undermined by increasing market integration and by increasing poverty, itself expressed as conflict between men and women:

> "Economic change and associated food crises have been accompanied by intensified gender conflict. The sex war in rural areas [of Africa] is a response to economic stress and poverty, and it takes its form and seriousness from the deteriorating economic conditions faced by a majority of peasant producers…Consider, for example, the growing number of female-headed households. Abandoned by their husbands and sons, women blame modern men's low standards of personal responsibility, while men argue that women drive them away with unacceptable sexual or domestic conduct and their new desires for personal freedom. The mutually expressed anger and disappointment obscure poverty as a source of crisis."

> (Whitehead, 1990, p.66)

In South Asia, women appear to be nutritionally disadvantaged:

> "It is generally regarded as improper for men to eat in the immediate company of women. Women eat after their husbands,

and last. In some areas "prestigious" foods are never eaten by women…[and women eat] the portions of food left when the men have been served."

> (Whitehead, 1994, p.122)

From fieldwork in Bangladesh, Naila Kabeer quotes how poor women described and justified differential feeding patterns, and the violence with which those differences interacted (Box 3.5).

Nevertheless, Kabeer notes that the most pressing reason for hunger in Bangladesh is not discrimination by age or gender, but that poor people do not have enough food. An extensive examination of household level studies (Harriss, 1991, summarized in Whitehead, 1994, p.123) found 'no confirmed general finding that adult women in South Asia are nutritionally disadvantaged more than men, despite family food practices in which they are treated as inferior.'

The issues of gender relations in famine and hunger raise wider questions about the subordination of women and the causes of poverty which are taken up in later chapters of this book.

Box 3.5 Quotes from poor women in Bangladesh

'When I can, I give my husband and sons more. Men don't understand if food runs short, so I wait till they have eaten.'

'A good wife is one who makes sure her husband has enough to eat.'

'If a woman eats before her husband, she shortens his life.'

'Men work harder than women, they need to eat more.'

'How can you explain to children that there is not enough food…? When my son cries, I feed him. It is easier to make my daughter understand.'

'If there is less, I eat less. You have to feed the men more or they beat you. Even my son beats me if there is not enough food.'

(Kabeer, 1994, pp.143–4)

3.5 Hunger and social change – issues for the analysis of development

In most of this chapter, I have focused primarily on production and livelihoods as the central topic of analysis. I have mentioned only in passing some of the other questions which are frequently raised when people in the industrialized world discuss hunger. As an example of these, I reproduce as Figure 3.8 an advertisement from the early 1990s for the *New Internationalist,* a British magazine which reports on development issues.

Even in this brief cartoon, which contains only a few sentences telling potential readers what they might expect to read about in the *New Internationalist,* some broad explanations for hunger and famine are suggested. Studies of the causes of hunger and poverty cover a very wide ground. However, a basic understanding of prod-uction and livelihoods is essential if the broader arguments about historical, political and international causation are to be evaluated and put to use.

We can take two of the points made in the cartoon to illustrate this.

1   The view that changes made by colonial rule laid the foundation for hunger is not confined to the *New Internationalist*. Much analysis of hunger (e.g. Warnock, 1988) has taken a similar view. However, the generality of the argument has to be restricted. It does not provide much purchase, for example, upon the cases of famine in either Ethiopia or China because the experience of colonial rule in those countries was either brief or indirect. Nevertheless, this view about hunger raises important questions. How did the expansion of European influence and rule change economic activity in different parts of the world? This question is addressed in Chapter 11 of this volume.

2   The idea that the introduction of cash crop production led to hunger is also not confined to

Figure 3.8   Advertisement for the New Internationalist, *early 1990s.*

the *New Internationalist*. There is a considerable body of writing (e.g. George, 1976; Buchanan, 1982) which suggests that the growing of crops for sale may displace food crop cultivation, resulting in a decline of food output and reduced household command over food. This view also raises important questions, though we need to be cautious about trying to apply it as a universal explanation of famine or hunger. The example of peasant production in Wollo highlighted limitations of 'self-sufficient' or 'traditional' forms of livelihood. It is not necessarily the case that food self-sufficiency ensures stable and sufficient command over food.

The cash crop view of hunger causation calls attention to a wider set of social changes which play an important role in hunger and poverty, sometimes exacerbating vulnerabilities at the same time as they hold out the potential for overcoming those vulnerabilities. The cash crop view of hunger refers only to a part of a wider process of commercialization or commoditization. As peasant production becomes integrated with wider economic activity, it is not just the output of that agriculture which is bought and sold as a commodity. As noted in Chapter 1, land, tools and labour power (the work of people) are also increasingly bought and sold. These are fundamental changes in social organization and can lead to increased vulnerabilities. For example:

> "Poor people who possess no means of production excepting their own labour power, which they try to sell for a wage in order to buy enough food, are particularly vulnerable to labour market conditions. A decline in wages *vis-à-vis* food prices, or an increase in unemployment, can spell disaster for this class...The class of landless wage labourers has indeed recurrently produced famine victims in modern times...The importance of the vulnerability of wage labourers can be particularly acute in the intermediate phase in which the class of wage labourers has become large...but a system of social security has not yet developed."
>
> (Drèze & Sen, 1989, pp.5–6)

The general point about both the colonialism view and the cash crop view is that they raise important questions which cannot be adequately assessed without an understanding of employment and production.

The concerns highlighted by the cartoon lead to two of the central questions of development studies: What is the role of (colonial) government? How does economic integration change livelihoods?

In order to try to understand all the diverse causes of poverty and hunger, and even more so if we hope to make suggestions about what can be done, we need to ask about the nature of industrialization, what sorts of livelihoods it provides, and what sorts it destroys, and the rate at which it does so. We will also need to investigate the rate and pattern of economic growth and the nature of social support and social security (provided by local collective action as well as by government).

The causes and responses to hunger also take us into the great questions of social and political organization, the great struggles between capitalist forms of economic organization and its alternatives. These issues all come up again throughout this book. In fact, sooner or later, the subject of hunger is raised in almost every debate in the study of development. To reverse the meaning of the quotation with which I started this chapter, the explanation of hunger raises questions about all aspects of human history.

3.6 Current debate on famine prevention and amelioration

In this final section, I want to summarize the current state of debate about the prevention and amelioration of famine.

In each of the four phases leading up to famine (dearth, privation, dispersal and camp-living) there are actions which can be taken. During dearth and privation, entitlements or livelihoods need to be protected if social collapse is to be prevented. Protection of livelihoods is likely to be much less costly than a response to mass migration and camp living. But this turning point is usually passed before international media coverage is mobilized. Both national and international sensitivity to the stages of dearth and privation preceding famine need to be raised. This is no easy task. Much work has been done on famine early-warning systems relying on technical indicators (particularly climatic but also price information). Approaches focused on social indicators, such as perceptions of livelihoods and threats to livelihood, could conceivably provide better information.

Once dispersal has started, new forms of entitlement have to be created. And, once the turning point of social collapse has been passed and the terrible conditions of camp living are unavoidable, then the massive re-creation of sanitation, water supply, and healthcare is required, as well as food distribution. The scale of response required to meet the overwhelming threats to human life in the final phase of relief camp living is often underestimated (Figure 3.9.)

But perhaps the most fundamental preventive measures precede these four phases of decline, and concern the preconditions for a social response to dearth and privation. Famine prevention, as described in Box 3.3, involves both institutional procedures for protecting or replacing livelihoods, and the political preconditions for ensuring that those procedures are initiated when dire conditions of dearth and privation are experienced. Of what do those political preconditions consist? Amartya Sen says, adversarial democracy and an investigative press. Alex De Waal says, a history of struggle which has produced a 'political contract' against famine. These two views are not incompatible.

Both writers are searching for ways of describing a set of social and political preconditions which another Indian economist named Sen, Gita Sen, has termed social needs, responsibilities and accountability. In her explanation of the striking progress in life and death indicators made in the Indian state of Kerala, Gita Sen (1992) describes the protracted political strug-

Figure 3.9   Kibeho camp for internally displaced persons, Rwanda, 1994: relief camps need large amounts of wood for cooking meals and building shelters, which can lead to the rapid destruction of natural vegetation, especially trees.

gles of workers, the poor, women and men, in particular historical conditions, which have led to an organized populace making government respond to social needs which have been defined in struggle. There is a strong parallel in the prevention of famine.

We can use Gita Sen's terms to identify three preconditions for the prevention of famine: representation, social need, and accountability. Firstly, poor and famine-vulnerable people need *influential representation*, whether through an investigative press and adversarial democracy, or through other forms of representation. Secondly, a history of struggle around the issue of famine is required to establish the prevention of famine as a *social need* for which government may be held responsible. Thirdly, some form of *accountability* is required to ensure that governments which fail to respond to this social need will fall.

Neither popular representation, nor institutional procedures for replacing entitlements will be sufficient if the most vulnerable groups have no voice, and if the society recognizes no obligation to prevent mass starvation. Giving voice to vulnerable groups may be the most important next step in the struggle against famine, but it is no easy step. The struggle for Indian independence was a political movement lasting many decades and involving many millions of people in great sacrifices.

But these preconditions leave two sets of questions unresolved. Both questions relate to public action. Firstly, what can be done to prevent the use of famine in war, and the use of famine by government or influential sections of society (Box 3.2). What, in Keen's words, can prevent the 'manipulat[ion of] war, violence, famine and relief' to achieve economic goals? Reliance on government response is misplaced when government is complicit or government has collapsed.

Secondly, there is a debate about what international action can do. Can international humanitarian action address the failures and complicities of national governments?

At the end of the twentieth century, these questions are unresolved. Thus, Alex De Waal writes 'famine in Africa can be defeated by Africans and only by Africans' (De Waal, 1997, p.214). He is very sceptical of international humanitarianism: 'The future of famine prevention does *not* lie with today's international relief agencies, until they have been radically reformed. On the contrary, while fighting famine remains entrusted to today's humanitarian international, famine will continue' (De Waal, 1997, p.217). He thinks an expansion of the work of international war crimes tribunals to cover famine crimes could be a step toward prevention (De Waal, 1997, p.215).

Others, such as Nicholas Stockton, Emergencies Director of Oxfam, argue that the prevention of famine is an international question as well as a national one and that humanitarian intervention may be problematic but can play a role:

> "…humanitarian demand seems to be outstripping the supply of official and private compassion. But when contrasted with the failures of an international political culture that fails to get to grips with war-crime impunity, the illegal arms trade and those macro-economic processes that sustain the iceberg of poverty and inequality that lies beneath the surface of most violent conflicts, then the humanitarian system… sometimes look[s] like a…beleaguered beacon of hope. This must not be extinguished. A public engagement with the human tragedies of poverty and violence must be renewed, no matter how distant these may seem geographically or politically."

(Stockton, 1998, p.359)

More is known about famine and hunger than was the case thirty years ago. But the urgency and scale of the challenge remain. Perhaps the most important advance to have been made in the last ten years is a recognition that the challenge is not a question of technical expertise, nutritional or economic, but requires political action, giving voice to poor and vulnerable people.

Summary

1 There is a useful practical distinction to be made between famine (a sharp increase in mortality associated with starvation and starvation-related disease) and chronic hunger (chronic undernourishment due to inadequate food consumption). Famines are extreme events demanding identifiable kinds of public action both for prevention and amelioration. Chronic hunger does not necessarily lead to famine but kills larger numbers of people.

2 Examination of the social relationships which provide different classes or occupational groups with command over food (i.e. entitlements) illuminates both chronic hunger and famine more effectively than the level of food availability in a country or region.

3 Famines occur because entitlements, or livelihoods, are made vulnerable by social, economic and climatic change. In recent times, war has been the most common antecedent of famine.

4 Chronic hunger is related to poverty and a persistent failure to generate sufficient entitlements in a society. Egalitarian social and economic development, rather than the provision of food, is likely to be required for sustained, extensive reductions in chronic hunger.

5 Current estimates suggest that over 800 million people worldwide, about 16% of the population, face chronic undernourishment, and this figure does not include the substantial numbers in the industrialized world who go hungry. Over the last twenty years, the numbers have been falling worldwide. In East and South-east Asia the numbers of hungry people have been falling rapidly. In sub-Saharan Africa both the absolute numbers and the proportion of the population facing chronic hunger appear to have been rising over the last twenty years.

6 A key element in the prevention of famine is the protection and creation of livelihoods, which can in principle be achieved through public action. Public action could also reduce chronic hunger through providing jobs, health care, education and elements of social security; this raises questions about development in general.

7 Public action to prevent famine is most likely to be taken when vulnerable people have been empowered by political movements which establish a governmental obligation to prevent mass starvation.

4

DISEASES OF POVERTY

MELISSA PARKER AND GORDON WILSON

The United Nations World Health Organization (WHO) defines health as 'a state of complete physical, mental and social well-being and not just the absence of disease'. Most public health programmes in low-income countries (including those supported by the WHO itself) do not, however, promote this conception of health. Instead they focus almost exclusively on strategies seeking to control or eradicate diseases (Figure 4.1).

There are several reasons for this state of affairs, including the fact that most people in low-income countries simply do not have access to the necessary resources to achieve anything approaching 'a state of complete physical, mental and social well-being'. Diseases afflict poor people in a multitude of ways and it is both sad and shocking to note that many of the diseases responsible for high mortality (notably measles

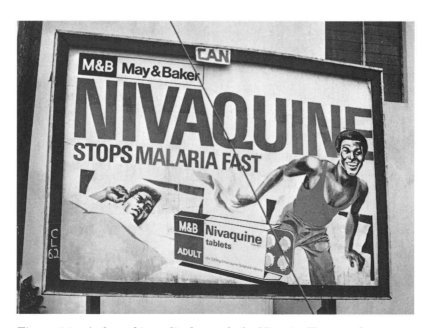

Figure 4.1 A cheap biomedical remedy for Nigeria. However, huge quantities of chloroquine-based drugs (like Nivaquine) have been distributed throughout Africa without wiping out malaria. It remains a major killer, and there are now resistant strains. The signs are that malaria is on the increase.

and diarrhoeal diseases) ought to be easy to cure. It is thus hardly surprising that public health professionals use the limited resources available to prevent and/or treat them directly. The most appropriate strategies to employ are, however, a matter of considerable debate.

With this in mind, the chapter focuses on the following questions:

Q What are the diseases of poverty?

Q How and why does the prevalence of disease vary within and between countries?

Q To what extent can curative, hospital-based care and selective biomedical interventions alleviate the burden of disease in low-income countries, and to what extent can wide-ranging public health programmes tackle the problem more effectively?

Q What are the implications of a new and fatal infection, HIV, for the health of people in low-income countries?

This chapter seeks to engage with these questions. It is divided into four sections. Section 1 introduces some basic statistics that deal with the distribution and incidence of disease in the world. Section 2 sets about examining some of the causes – both immediate and underlying – of diseases in low-income countries. Section 3 examines various strategies for combating disease, and includes a specific consideration of HIV and AIDS. Finally, Section 4 compares two countries with somewhat different disease profiles and uses the comparison to throw greater light on some of our questions.

4.1 Patterns of disease between countries

In order to examine patterns of disease in society we need generalizable evidence in the form of data. In studies of health, the collection and study of data related to health matters form part of that well-established branch of medicine we call epidemiology. Thus, typically, tables of data

are published and analysed showing the incidence of individual diseases among defined populations. Frequently, instead of examining individual diseases, we examine the rate of death in a population in a given year. Death is not a measure of disease directly (after all, most people recover from disease rather than die from it!), but is clearly related to it, particularly when applied to young populations. We can, therefore, call a death rate a *proxy* for how generally prone a given population is to disease and, in this section, we are mainly going to study death (or mortality) rate data.

Before we start, however, we must give voice to some words of caution. In western society especially, numbers are very persuasive and we use them all the time – in our shopping, in our travelling, when we play or watch sport, etc. Numbers, or data, are often synonymous with 'the facts' and 'the facts don't lie'. There is, however, another saying that should make us wary of accepting this: 'There are lies, damned lies and statistics!'.

When examining mortality rate or other data related to disease there are three main problem areas with respect to accepting the numbers at their face value.

Problem area 1 concerns the accuracy of the data. Collection of accurate data is always fraught with difficulty, and nowhere is this more so than in the field of health where practical difficulties for collectors (how, for example, can you collect accurate data within a country bedevilled by civil war?) combine with pressures to supply false information due to the stigmas often attached to disease and death. At regional or country level, figures may even be deliberately manipulated, perhaps to exaggerate a problem in order to gain resources, or to 'prove' that a particular 'health' programme is working effectively.

Problem area 2 concerns the assumptions that lie behind the data, assumptions that are effectively hidden by numbers. For example, some 'health' data tell us how many people there are in a country per qualified doctor or per hospital bed, the implied assumption being that the fewer people there are for each doctor or hospital bed the greater the state of health. Yet it might be that number of doctors or hospital beds bears little direct relation to the health of the country. What might be more important is the number of rural health centres providing basic services or the number of paramedics serving geographically isolated areas. Other assumptions relate to the aggregation of the data. The national death rate in a country tells us nothing about the difference between rural and urban areas, between men and women, between rich and poor.

Problem area 3 concerns interpretation of the data with respect to cause and effect. In the following pages, we shall be examining various patterns, such as the association between low death rates and high literacy or high income. But none of these associations *proves* that one causes the other (no matter what our own common sense or values indicate). They may provide evidence in support of hypotheses (e.g. that education helps combat disease), but we have to look more closely at a range of cases before we can say one way or the other with any certainty. And examining cases in detail is almost certain to complicate matters, meaning at least that we have to qualify the hypothesis (e.g. education helps combat disease in this circumstance, but less so in that).

Having said that, we are not arguing that data are worthless; in fact they are very powerful aids to us. It's simply that we have to be careful with them and not read too much into them. In other words, read them with a broad brush for really significant patterns.

Comparing low- and high-income countries

This chapter focuses on disease within the low-income countries of the world. An underlying reason for this is that it is frequently suggested in various fora that the problems are so much more stark in those countries. Let us start by examining this assertion by comparing both child mortality and how long people are expected to live for a range of countries (Table 4.1; Box 4.1).

Table 4.1 Estimates of under-five mortality rate (U5MR) and life expectancy for selected countries (1997)

Country	World Bank income category	U5MR	Life expectancy at birth (years)
Africa			
Niger	Low	320	48
Angola	Low	292	47
Malawi	Low	215	41
Ethiopia	Low	175	50
Tanzania	Low	143	51
Ghana	Low	107	58
Kenya	Low	87	69
America			
Bolivia	Lower-middle	96	61
Peru	Lower-middle	56	68
Brazil	Upper-middle	44	67
Mexico	Upper-middle	35	72
Jamaica	Lower-middle	11	75
Cuba	Lower-middle	8	76
USA	High	8	77
Asia			
Pakistan	Low	136	64
Bangladesh	Low	109	58
India	Low	108	62
Nepal	Low	104	57
China	Low	47	70
Sri Lanka	Low	19	73
Japan	High	6	80
Europe			
Albania	Low	40	71
Poland	Lower-middle	11	71
Greece	Higher-middle	8	78
UK	High	7	77
Sweden	High	4	78

Sources: UNICEF (1998) *The State of the World's Children 1997*, UNICEF, New York; World Bank (1995) *World Development Report 1995*, Oxford University Press, New York.

Box 4.1 Mortality rates and life expectancy

The *infant* mortality rate is the number of deaths in the first year of life per 1000 live births. The *under-five* (or *child*) mortality rate is the number of children who die before the age of five for every 1000 live births. Life expectancy, measured in years, is the average length of life or the expectation of life at birth in a population. Infant and child mortality rates are strongly correlated with adult mortality. If infant or child mortality is high, adult mortality is likely to be high and life expectancy low. They can, therefore, be useful indicators of susceptibility to diseases. Also, health care policies in low-income countries are often directed at children and changes in infant or child mortality rates are a way that is used to assess these policies.

Table 4.1 shows a fairly obvious pattern. Countries which are conventionally thought of as rich – USA, Japan, Greece, UK, Sweden – all have under-five mortality rates in single figures. Most of the others, mainly the poor countries of the world, have at least double-figure under-five mortality rates, and all of the countries listed in Africa bar one, plus four of the seven countries listed in Asia have triple-figure under-five mortality rates. The country listed with the worst rate (Niger) is 80 times higher than that with the best (Sweden). A similar pattern emerges if we examine the life expectancy data.

In general, therefore, the data support the assertion and give justification for the focus of the chapter! There are exceptions to the general rule, however, and this should remind us to read the data with caution. Cuba (a lower-middle income country), for example, also has an under-five mortality rate in single figures (the same as the USA in fact) and a relatively high life expectancy (Figure 4.2). Jamaica (a lower-middle income country) and Sri Lanka (a low-income country) also stand out with under-five mortality rates of 11 and 19 respectively, and then there is a wide gap before the next country, Mexico, at 35 (almost double that of Sri Lanka and over three times that of Jamaica). We shall return to one of these exceptions to the general trend at the end of the chapter. Their more detailed study is worthwhile precisely because they are exceptions and they can perhaps help us examine some of the complex causal factors behind disease.

Table 4.1 provides a snapshot of disease prevalence in certain countries for the latest year (1997) that data are available at the time of writing. We also need, however, a sense of change, particularly a sense of whether things are improving, especially for those countries with high under-five mortality rates and low life

Figure 4.2 An exception to the rule: pensioners exercising at a street corner of Havana, Cuba.

expectancies in Table 4.1. Table 4.2 provides a crude comparison for the years 1960 and 1997 for the same selected countries.

At first glance, Table 4.2 is good news. All countries bar one (Niger, which seems to have had a stubbornly consistent and high under-five mortality rate over 37 years) have improved their records, many dramatically so. But how does the improvement shown in low- and middle-income countries compare with that in a rich country, such as the UK? Figure 4.3 shows

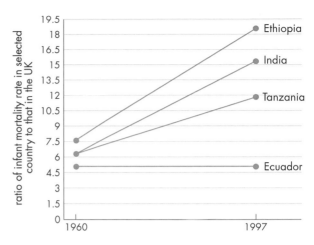

Figure 4.3 Changes in infant mortality relative to the UK in selected countries.

the changes in the infant mortality rate for six countries compared with that of the UK over the period 1960–97.

Apart from Ecuador, Figure 4.3 suggests that the UK's improvement has been even more dramatic. In other words, low- and middle-income countries are not catching up with the rich and, indeed, on this limited evidence the gap is widening for many countries. We would, however, caution against reading too much into these ratios. In terms of absolute reductions, those of low-income countries have been generally impressive. Because the UK's infant mortality rate is low, small absolute changes mean big percentage reductions. For most low-income countries the opposite is the case – their infant mortality rates are high and therefore large absolute changes are needed to produce significant percentage changes.

4.2 Patterns of disease within low-income countries and reasons for its prevalence

We have seen that there are wide variations between countries in the prevalence of diseases as measured by the under-five mortality rate, but generally the high-income countries fare much better than low- and middle-income ones. There are significant exceptions to this pattern, however.

Table 4.2 Changes in under-five mortality rate since 1960 for selected countries

Country	Under-five mortality rate	
	1960	1997
Africa		
Niger	320	320
Angola	345	292
Malawi	361	215
Ethiopia	280	175
Tanzania	240	143
Ghana	215	107
Kenya	205	87
America		
Bolivia	255	96
Peru	234	56
Brazil	177	44
Mexico	134	35
Jamaica	76	11
Cuba	54	8
USA	30	8
Asia		
Pakistan	226	136
Bangladesh	247	109
India	236	108
Nepal	297	104
China	209	47
Sri Lanka	133	19
Japan	40	6
Europe		
Albania	151	40
Poland	70	11
Greece	64	8
UK	27	7
Sweden	20	4

Source: UNICEF (1998) *The State of the World's Children 1997*, UNICEF, New York.

We have already counselled against taking the mortality or life expectancy statistics for a given country as being 'typical' for that country, as if health and ill-health is evenly spread across it. There are in fact many variations within countries and the patterns that these variations form can throw more light on the underlying reasons for disease.

Age

Table 4.3 compares the death rates by age for what the WHO calls 'least developed countries' with those of 'developed market economies'. These statistics are, of course, highly aggregated and tell us nothing of patterns within individual countries, but they do illustrate a trend that is difficult to ignore. Up until the age of 64, a higher percentage die in the least developed countries. The difference is most marked, however, in the early years of life. Then, from the age of 65 onwards, the situation is dramatically reversed: after all, those in the developed market economies have to die at some point. To put it another way, 40% of people in the least developed countries die before they reach the age of 5 and 84% before they reach 65, compared with only 0.7% and 23% respectively in the developed market economies.

This pattern points particularly to diseases that attack the young as being the major killers in developing countries, especially infectious and parasitic diseases, something to which we return below.

Table 4.3 Age structure of deaths 1995

Age	Percentage of deaths occurring in each age range	
	Least developed countries	Developed market economies
<5	40	0.7
5 to 19	15	0.4
20 to 64	29	21
65+	16	77

Source: WHO (1998) *The World Health Report*, World Health Organization, Geneva.

Urban and rural

Collecting and interpreting statistics based on where people live presents numerous problems. For a start, how do we define such things as 'urban' and 'rural'? What size does a town have to be before its inhabitants are classified as urban? How are people classified who depend on cities for their livelihoods and are within easy reach of their services but live outside them? In particular, hospitals are more likely to be situated in cities than rural areas. If seriously ill rural dwellers are sent to these urban hospitals and subsequently die in them, whose death statistics – rural or urban – are they?

Secondly, death registration records are probably more complete for urban areas, which makes the rural populations appear less susceptible to diseases by comparison. Thirdly, the statistics may not be a true reflection of differing conditions in the countryside and towns. If, for example, young healthy adults from the country migrate to the towns to seek work, they leave behind a population that is comparatively more vulnerable to disease. This has the effect of improving the urban statistics and making worse the rural ones.

Table 4.4 gives data on rural and urban mortality for a sample of countries. Generally, infant mortality is higher in rural areas, and in some cases (e.g. India and Peru) significantly so.

Obviously, a multitude of factors combine and it is impossible to predict what the precise urban–rural split will be in each instance. Factors which might make urban populations less susceptible to disease are:

- greater access to medical services;
- greater access to clean water and sanitation, where this is not negated by other factors (see below);
- better educational opportunities;
- generally higher incomes, enhancing the above factors; higher incomes also mean better nutrition.

Factors which might make urban populations more susceptible to diseases include:

Table 4.4 Infant mortality rate and urban/rural residence for selected countries

Country	Infant mortality rate		
	Rural	Urban	Rural/urban ratio
Africa			
Zimbabwe	61.1	48.5	1.3
Mauritius	20.1	19	1.1
Egypt	38.1	32.5	1.2
Asia			
India	80	52	1.5
Tajikistan	50.8	39.9	1.3
Japan	4.5	4.2	1.1
America			
Peru	91.7	64.9	1.4
Chile	13.8	10.7	1.3
Cuba	10.9	10.7	1.0
Europe			
Greece	7.9	8.3	0.96
Romania	23.9	18.2	1.3
Switzerland	5.3	4.9	1.1

Source: United Nations (1998) *Demographic Yearbook 1996*, United Nations, New York.

- overcrowding, enhancing the transmission of infectious diseases;
- insanitary conditions in slums and shanty towns.

In addition, urban populations in many countries are likely to experience greater incidence of accidents and violence.

Gender

The first column of Table 4.5 compares the life expectancy of women with that of men for the same countries as in Tables 4.1 and 4.2. (Figures greater than 100 indicate a greater life expectancy for women compared with men; exactly 100 indicates that women and men in that country have the same life expectancy; and less than 100 – although there aren't any in our sample – would indicate lower life expectancy for women.) It illustrates a general pattern throughout the world: that is, that women tend to live longer than men on average.

Further investigation of the column also reveals, although less clear cut, that this 'female

Table 4.5 Life expectancy and education of women relative to that of men in selected countries

Country	Life expectancy: females as a percentage of males (1997)	Adult literacy rate: females as a percentage of males (1995)	Secondary school enrolment ratio: females as a percentage of males (1990–96)
Africa			
Niger	100	34	51
Angola	107	52*	no data
Malawi	103	58	57
Ethiopia	106	54	83
Tanzania	106	72	83
Ghana	107	71	64
Kenya	108	81	85
America			
Bolivia	105	84	91
Peru	108	87	97
Brazil	113	100	116*
Mexico	109	95	102
Jamaica	107	110	113
Cuba	105	99	105
USA	110	no data	101
Asia			
Pakistan	103	48	52
Bangladesh	100	53	50
India	100	58	62
Nepal	100	34	51
China	106	81	90
Sri Lanka	106	94	110
Japan	108	no data	102
Europe			
Albania	109	no data	100
Poland	113	no data	101
Greece	108	97	91
UK	108	no data	118
Sweden	107	no data	101

* Indicates data that refer to years or periods other than those specified in the column heading, differ from the standard definition, or refer only to part of a country.

Source: UNICEF (1998) *State of the World's Children 1997*, UNICEF, New York.

advantage' in terms of life expectancy is generally less for low-income countries than it is for high-income countries. Indeed, all four countries that show no female advantage (Niger, Bangladesh, India and Nepal) are low-income countries.

The smaller difference in favour of women in low-income countries has been interpreted as women having particular disadvantages in those countries, compared with their rich-country counterparts, which offsets any general life expectancy advantage they may have. This may be due to unequal access to medical care between men and women or unequal distribution of food in households; to the amount and nature of work that women do; or because they experience more pregnancies than do rich-country women, with associated higher risk.

There have been many studies on the particular difficulties experienced by women with respect to health in low-income countries which support the above observations. In 1993, the annual report from the World Bank, *World Development Report*, was devoted to health and, mainly in response to the consistent messages emanating from these studies, it provided two broad proposals of its own (World Bank, 1993, p.6):

- expand investment in schooling, particularly for girls;
- promote the rights and status of women through political and economic empowerment and legal protection against abuse.

Education

The first of the World Bank messages above is about education, and this is another factor that has long been associated with good health. Note also that we suggested earlier that greater educational opportunities might promote good health in urban areas, other things being equal. This shows the interconnectedness of many of these factors, with education being an important contributory element.

Back in 1985, the World Bank report commented generally on 'the extremely powerful role of literacy in determining a population's level of mortality' and suggested that the factor carries far more weight than many others, including income

growth (World Bank, 1985, p.120). This association is supported by the negative correlation between adult literacy level and child mortality in the scatter diagram shown in Figure 4.4.

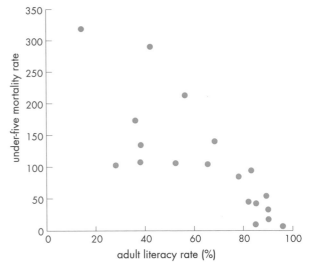

Figure 4.4   Adult literacy and child mortality in selected countries (data from UNICEF, 1998).

Much emphasis has been on the role of female education in promoting good health. Thus, in 1983 a World Bank publication on child mortality in urban Brazil concluded: 'increased maternal education accounted for a larger share (34%) of the mortality decline between 1970 and 1976 than any other single factor, including access to piped water' (World Bank, 1983, abstract). The World Bank repeated the same message ten years later:

> "Education greatly strengthens women's ability to perform their vital role in creating healthy households. It increases their ability to benefit from health information and to make good use of health services; it increases their access to income and enables them to live healthier lives. It is not surprising, therefore, that a child's health is affected more by the mother's schooling than by the father's schooling."
>
> (World Bank, 1993, p.42)

Table 4.5 also bears out the message. Note again the countries that have no 'female advantage' in life expectancy – Niger, Bangladesh, India and

Nepal. For each of these countries the adult literacy of women is poor compared with that of men, and a far lower proportion of females have secondary school education.

Poverty

The preceding sections have alluded to several factors in a person's 'environment' that affect health directly: education, nutrition, income, living conditions, and access to medical services and safe water. The sections have also pointed to some of the interconnections between factors. In fact, many commentators bring these factors together under one umbrella by pointing out that they are all aspects of poverty, and this is why our chapter is entitled 'Diseases of poverty'.

While the influence of poverty on the prevalence of diseases worldwide is well-established, illustrating it with data is very difficult. This is precisely because poverty is multi-faceted and cannot be associated with any one measurable indicator (Chapter 1). A favourite measure for the World Bank is the percentage of people living below an income of one US dollar per day. As discussed in Chapter 1, one problem with this definition is that it does not allow for differences between countries regarding how much one US dollar will buy, and that, in low-income countries especially, many people do not buy all of their food directly with cash, but grow at least some of it for direct consumption or for direct exchange with other goods. The World Bank has tried to get around this by adjusting for different purchasing powers in different countries, which it calls 'adjustment for purchasing power parity' (World Bank, 1998, p.236). The measure of poverty in Figure 4.5 is based on this adjustment, but note that it is still an income-based definition of poverty and therefore rather limited as a measure.

Notwithstanding these difficulties and issues, Figure 4.5 is a scatter diagram of poverty against child mortality and shows a positive correlation, thus supporting the association.

One extremely important facet of poverty in low-income countries is undernutrition. Many children, especially, die directly of undernutrition but many more die of diseases that are linked

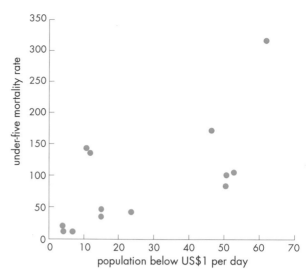

Figure 4.5 Poverty and child mortality in selected countries (data from World Bank, 1998).

Table 4.6 Main causes of death among children under age 5 in the developing world (1995)

Disease	Number of deaths (millions)	Undernutrition-associated deaths (%)
Acute lower respiratory infection	2.1	40
Diarrhoea	2	70
Measles	1.1	65
Prematurity	1	40
Birth asphyxia	0.9	35
Malaria	0.7	40
Congenital anomalies	0.5	30
Neonatal tetanus	0.4	20
Birth trauma	0.4	20
Neonatal sepsis and meningitis	0.4	30
Pertussis	0.4	50
Undernutrition	0.3	100
Tuberculosis	0.1	60

Source: WHO (1998) *The World Health Report*, World Health Organization, Geneva.

to it, as Table 4.6 illustrates. Thus 70% of the 2 million child deaths in what the WHO calls the developing world resulting from diarrhoea in 1995 were associated with undernutrition. The diarrhoea–undernutrition link is a strong one, but so is measles–undernutrition and tuberculosis–undernutrition in Table 4.6, and none of the associations is insignificant. This is because undernutrition both weakens resistance to acquiring disease and lowers the ability to fight it off once it does occur.

Table 4.6 also shows that undernutrition is associated with particular forms of death in children and infants, forms that are related to low body resistance: infectious (e.g. measles), parasitic (e.g. malaria) and respiratory (e.g. tuberculosis) diseases, plus those associated with childbirth. These are what we call the *diseases of poverty* and Figure 4.6 illustrates the point in general terms. Note that, while not insignificant in low-income countries, diseases of the circulatory system (e.g. heart attacks and strokes) and cancers dominate the deaths in the developed (or high-income) world. These are diseases that primarily afflict older people rather than children and, although also associated with poverty in high-income countries (e.g. poor people tend to have diets and lifestyles that contribute to cancers and diseases of the circulatory system), they are also symptomatic of a certain level of affluence. They certainly don't normally result from undernutrition!

4.3 Strategies for controlling infectious diseases

The introduction to this chapter raised the following important questions: to what extent can curative hospital-based care and selective biomedical interventions at a population level alleviate the burden of disease in low-income countries? In a world of limited resources, would it be more appropriate to develop wide-ranging public health programmes at the expense of improving hospital-based care and implementing a series of interventions?

These questions have concerned policy-makers and academics alike for many decades. They remain extremely relevant to low-income countries today and it is often suggested that it is helpful to answer them by drawing upon the experiences of nineteenth-century Britain. The diseases prevalent in nineteenth-century Britain were not, of course, exactly the same as those prevalent in many low-income countries today. Scarlet fever, for example, was far more prevalent in nineteenth-century Britain than figures currently suggest for any of the low-income countries. Nevertheless, there were many similarities as the majority of diseases

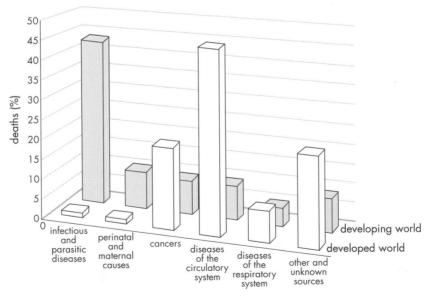

Figure 4.6   Causes of death: distribution of deaths by main causes and by level of development (1997).

were infectious diseases and, in common with low-income countries, these included diarrhoeal diseases and respiratory infections.

With the exception of measles and diphtheria, these infectious diseases all declined massively in Britain over the latter part of the century. In his book *The Role of Medicine*, Thomas McKeown raised the following important question:

"Are the improvements in health with which medicine is commonly credited determined essentially by medical science, or are they due largely to fortuitous changes in which biomedical research has played little part?"

(McKeown, 1979, p.156)

Answering his own question, McKeown argued that the decline in mortality from infectious diseases in the latter part of the nineteenth century in Britain was due, not so much to the development of medical science, but to:

- improvements in nutrition;
- improvements in hygiene, which were 'the predominant reasons for the decline of water and food-borne diseases';

- the change in reproductive behaviour, which led to the decline in the birth rate. If this had not happened, the beneficial effects of improved diet would have been wiped out by runaway population growth.

Smallpox, for which a simple vaccine was developed, is the obvious exception, but McKeown's overall thesis is now widely accepted. The implication is that lasting improvements to health in low-income countries will not come about as a result of medicines or public health interventions seeking to control one or two diseases. Instead they will come about by developing wide-ranging public health programmes promoting clean water (Figure 4.7), sanitation and improved nutrition.

The question which follows is whether the governments of low-income countries and international agencies should pool all their resources and develop wide-ranging public health programmes at the expense of developing hospital-based care and supporting selective biomedical interventions. This is a difficult question to answer as research undertaken in different parts of the world has drawn attention to a diverse

Figure 4.7   Collecting water in Lagos, Nigeria. The rapid growth of the city has made it difficult for the authorities to provide sufficient clean water.

range of issues and generated different results. The following two subsections address this question by examining the strengths and limitations of selective biomedical interventions and comprehensive primary health care in turn.

Selective biomedical interventions

Selective biomedical interventions take many forms (see Box 4.2) and in the 1980s and 1990s they typically included vaccination programmes to prevent deaths from measles, neonatal tetanus and whooping cough; the distribution of oral rehydration salts to prevent deaths from diarrhoeal diseases; the distribution of vitamin A supplements to prevent deaths from diarrhoeal diseases, measles and pneumonia; and the distribution of bed nets impregnated with insecticides to prevent deaths from malaria. More often than not, these interventions have enabled substantial reductions in infant and/or child mortality to be recorded.

With respect to malaria, for example, governments and international agencies such as the World Health Organization and USAID have invested considerable resources into monitoring the effects of bed nets and curtains impregnated

with insecticides on neonatal and child mortality. In sub-Saharan Africa, for example, reductions ranging from 15% to 60% have been recorded in parts of Burkina Faso, Ghana, Kenya and the Gambia (Lengeler, 1998; Habluetzel *et al.*, 1997). Similarly, research documenting the effects of supplementing children's diets with vitamin A capsules has shown that child mortality can be reduced by between 6% and 54% in parts of Asia (Sommer *et al.*, 1986; Muhilal *et al.*,1988; Rahmathullah *et al.*, 1990; West *et al.*,1991) and research undertaken in northern Ghana has documented a reduction of 19% in child mortality (Ghana VAST, 1993). Vaccination programmes (Figure 4.8) have also been shown to be effective. For example, Clemens *et al.* (1988) monitored the effect of a measles vaccination programme on child mortality in Bangladesh and he documented a 57% reduction in the rate of deaths directly attributed to measles and a 36% reduction in overall mortality among children.

These reductions have all been achieved over a period of one to two years and the speed and scale of the reductions is impressive. However, these achievements have to be balanced against the limits of selective interventions. These include

---

Box 4.2 Selective biomedical interventions

Selective biomedical interventions entail a circumscribed number of diseases being targeted for prevention in a clearly defined population. Walsh and Warren (1979) argued that international agencies should focus on selective biomedical interventions (at least as an interim strategy until comprehensive primary health care could be made available to all) on the grounds that they could have a major role in reducing the child mortality rate. Responding to this argument, UNICEF developed a child survival strategy in the early 1980s. This strategy was initially known as GOBI-FFF and included the promotion of Growth monitoring at health centres, the use of Oral rehydration salts to treat diarrhoeal infections among children, the promotion of Breastfeeding among mothers and widespread Immunization programmes. The three 'F's' stood for Food supplements, Fam-

ily planning and Female education. Within a few years, the programme was revised and referred to as the Child Survival Development Revolution. It focused on the control of diarrhoeal disease and an expanded programme of immunization and growth monitoring, and, later, the prevention and treatment of acute respiratory infections. All these interventions focused on women and children at the expense of taking a community-wide perspective. They also focused on exporting simple, low-cost medical technologies to low-income countries (such as oral rehydration salts). By the mid 1990s UNICEF was placing increasing emphasis on the expanded programme of immunization at the expense of the other interventions and this, in large part, reflects the political and economic constraints of having to prioritize interventions deemed to be 'cost effective'.

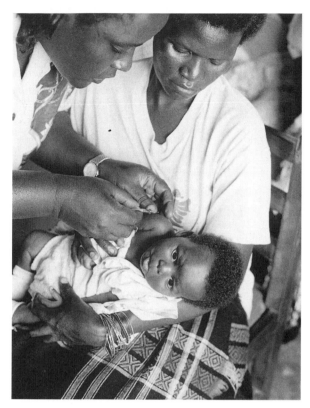

Figure 4.8   Inoculation, Uganda, 1996.

the following. First, it is one thing to reduce infant and child mortality while undertaking a meticulously planned and well-resourced research project and quite another to sustain the reduction over time. The health sector of most low-income countries is notoriously underfunded and it is extremely difficult, if not impossible, for ministries of health to maintain a continuous supply of bed nets, vaccines, vitamin A supplements, oral rehydration salts, etc. A poor infrastructure adds to the problems of sustaining the scale of reductions achieved during research projects as it is often difficult to ensure the widespread distribution of these items.

A second major shortcoming often associated with selective biomedical interventions is that while it may be possible to alter the behaviour of a particular population in such a way as to embrace a 'new' intervention (in the short term), it is often difficult to sustain this response. Indeed, it is increasingly acknowledged that selective interventions cannot achieve sustained

reductions in infant and child mortality unless biomedical practitioners acquire a detailed understanding of the beliefs and behaviours of the local population and develop an ability to present the intervention in ways which embrace, rather than counter, lay perceptions of treatment and prevention. Frankel and Lehmann's research (1984) among the Huli of Papua New Guinea illustrates some of these points. They monitored the success of a health programme promoting the use of oral rehydration salts for the treatment of diarrhoeal diseases among infants and children, and their findings may be summarized as follows. First, mortality from diarrhoeal disease in the under-fives fell from 3.3/1000 per annum before the intervention promoting oral rehydration salts in 1977 to 1.3/1000 per annum after the programme had become established in 1980. Second, Frankel and Lehmann showed that, over time, mothers became increasingly reluctant for their children's diarrhoeal infections to be treated with oral rehydration salts. Consequently, attendance at nearby health centres began to drop and child mortality began to rise. They explained these findings by drawing upon information and insights emerging from anthropological research investigating local understandings of the causes and responses to diarrhoeal diseases. In particular, they found that the willingness of Huli mothers to give their children oral rehydration salts when they had diarrhoea initially reflected their deference to the proven value of health workers past recommendations. As time progressed, however, they became increasingly uninterested in this treatment and this reflected the fact that the benefits of oral rehydration salts had not been explained within the framework of Huli concepts of physiology. Briefly, the purpose of oral rehydration salts, from a biomedical perspective, is to prevent dehydration rather than block the flow of diarrhoea. But this approach is entirely different from that typically employed by Huli mothers and carers. Their treatments involve attempts to withhold fluids in order to dry the stool. In other words, the concept of rehydration was not embraced in the treatment of diarrhoea among the Huli. It has thus been argued that child mortality will continue to rise until the benefits of oral rehydration salts are explained within the framework of Huli concepts of physiology.

A third major difficulty with selective biomedical interventions is that it is often difficult to sustain reductions in mortality and morbidity for biological reasons alone. With respect to malaria, for example, researchers such as Snow *et al.* (1994) and Trape and Rogier (1996) have suggested that the reductions in neonatal and child mortality may be transient. These authors have argued that while the use of bed nets and curtains impregnated with insecticides may reduce transmission and hence, initially, mortality, they also delay the acquisition of immunity. In other words, this kind of intervention only serves to delay rather than prevent mortality from malaria.

Finally, research undertaken by the Kasongo Project Team (1981) in former Zaïre, and others more recently, has suggested that it could be folly to assume that an intervention seeking to prevent the transmission of any one particular disease will necessarily reduce overall mortality. A large number of infectious diseases tend to be endemic in particular environments at any one time and a reduction in child mortality from a disease such as measles may only mean that children who would otherwise have died from measles go on to die from some other infectious disease such as malaria or meningitis. Unfortunately, research documenting the long-term effects of disease-specific interventions on infant and child mortality has been minimal and it is thus difficult to know whether research findings generated by the Kasongo Project Team in Zaïre are generalizable to other parts of the world.

This issue aside, it is often suggested that selective biomedical interventions have so many shortcomings that they should not be thought of as a long-term solution to enhancing the health and well-being of economically poor and vulnerable populations. Indeed, some critics have suggested that the 'benefits' of selective interventions are so transient that allocating resources to this type of health care at best amounts to wastage and, at worst, undermines locally sustainable health-care structures. This

brings us back to a question raised at the beginning of this section: to what extent can wide-ranging public health programmes make a more lasting contribution to the alleviation of poverty and, therefore, the burden of disease in low-income countries?

Comprehensive primary health care

There is no doubt that strategies seeking to reduce the burden of disease on a permanent basis have to go beyond the administration of medicines in hospital settings. Indeed, it has been argued that the most effective way to alleviate the burden of disease is to develop a comprehensive system of primary health care. The World Health Organization defined comprehensive primary health care at a conference held in Alma Ata in 1978 as:

> "The attainment by all peoples of the world by the year 2000 of a level of health that will permit them to lead a socially and economically productive life. Primary health care includes at least: education concerning prevailing health problems and the methods of preventing and controlling them; promotion of food supply and proper nutrition, an adequate supply of safe water and basic sanitation; maternal and child health care, including family planning; immunization against the major infectious diseases; prevention and control of locally endemic diseases; appropriate treatment of common diseases and injuries; and provision of essential drugs."
>
> (World Health Organization conference,
> Alma Ata, 1978)

The plan to develop a comprehensive system of primary health care represented an explicit move away from the curative, hospital-based model towards a more preventive, decentralized and community-based strategy. China is an example of a country which has seen dramatic improvements in health that have been widely attributed to the establishment of comprehensive primary health care. The World Bank's 1990 *World Development Report*, for example, drew attention to the fact that in the previous 25 to 30 years life expectancy in China increased from

52.7 to 69.5 years and the infant mortality rate dropped from 90 to 32 per thousand live births. The report adds:

"China's remarkable performance owes as much to safe drinking water, improved sewage disposal, and other sanitation measures as to broad immunization coverage and mass campaigns against parasitic diseases. It has much to do with the provision of basic health care and affordable drugs to even the most remote parts of the country. It reflects the successful drive to reduce fertility and to increase, through legislation, the age of first delivery, as well as great efforts to provide education on health and nutrition. And it would probably have been impossible without a safety net that, among other things, guaranteed food rations to even the poorest rural people.

China's performance...teaches an important general lesson: large improvements in the health of the population can be achieved if there is a broad and lasting political commitment, with a consistent emphasis on preventive measures and basic curative care. In other words, social progress is not merely a by-product of economic development. Policies matter."

(World Bank, 1990, p.74)

Endeavours to develop comprehensive primary health care programmes elsewhere have been less successful. Werner (1977), for example, shows that in Mexico, as with so many other countries, attempts to develop a primary health care system were hindered by the fact that the government remained authoritarian and paternalistic and, in practice, was only willing to pay lip service to community involvement. In a later article (1983) he suggests that while Cuba has witnessed considerable improvements in health care, the system remains highly centralized and dependent on physicians.

Heggenhougen (1984) has drawn attention to rather different problems. He attributed the failure of many primary health care programmes to the fact that governments have lacked the political will to support them adequately. There are several reasons for this including the fact that physicians often dominate the formation of health policy and, in many low-income countries, they have not been convinced by the arguments for comprehensive primary health care. In particular, many physicians feel they are being asked to develop a second class health care system. It has also been suggested by Davis (1988) that the level of community organization required for the development of primary health care poses a threat to many governments as they run the risk of losing control to a newly militant peasantry.

In sum, most attempts to develop comprehensive primary health care programmes have been far from successful. The reasons vary but more often than not they include a dearth of resources, personnel and political willpower. Against this background, it is not surprising that many international agencies would rather intervene with a series of selective biomedical interventions than do nothing at all. As far as many of their employees are concerned it is surely better to delay the moment of death than to stand by and do nothing at all, and it is not as if there are any major alternatives. This line of argument assumes, of course, that selective biomedical interventions do not do any long-term damage. It is an assumption that is increasingly being questioned.

HIV and AIDS

So far, this chapter has said very little about the impact of a relatively new and fatal virus for low-income countries: the human immuno-deficiency virus. Human immuno-deficiency virus, otherwise known as HIV, was first identified as the cause of acquired immuno-deficiency syndrome (AIDS) in 1983. It accounts for considerable mortality and morbidity and the UN programme UNAIDS recently estimated that by the end of 1996 more than 23 million people worldwide were infected with HIV and more than 6 million people had died with AIDS (World Bank, 1997a). It has also been estimated that approximately 800 000 children are living with HIV in low-income countries.

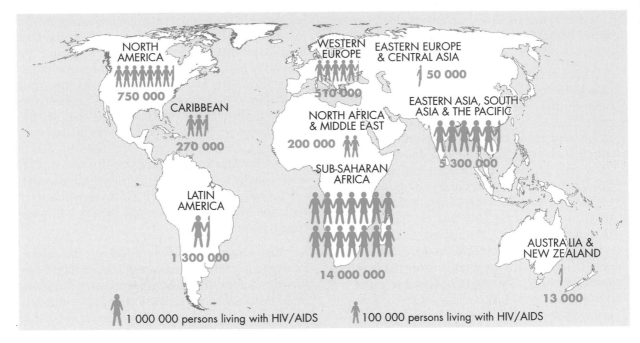

Figure 4.9   Estimated number of adults with HIV/AIDS, by world region, 1997.

The distribution of HIV infection worldwide is shown in Figure 4.9. This figure shows that the majority of infections occur in low-income countries. Sub-Saharan Africa has the largest number – 14 million – followed by Eastern Asia, South Asia and the Pacific with 5.3 million. Figure 4.10 estimates the number of new adult infections by region over time and shows that the speed with which HIV is transmitted varies between regions. In particular, it suggests that the number of new infections is levelling off in sub-Saharan Africa as a whole, whereas infection is spreading rapidly in Asia. The figure also shows that the only region to experience a fall in the number of new infections is North America and Western Europe, but it is far from clear whether this downward trend will continue as infection is increasingly spreading there to low-income populations whose education and access to health care resemble those of low-income countries.

HIV is primarily transmitted from one person to another through sexual intercourse, transfusions of contaminated blood or blood products, and the sharing of contaminated needles and syringes by injecting drug users. It can also be

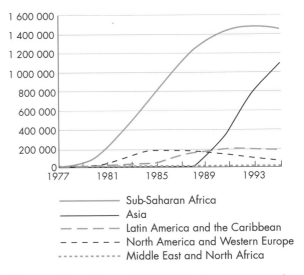

Figure 4.10   New adult HIV infections per year, by world region, 1977–95.

transmitted by infected women to their infants during pregnancy, at delivery and during breastfeeding.

Research currently suggests that three-quarters of HIV transmission worldwide occurs through sex and particularly heterosexual sex. In sub-Saharan Africa, Asia and the Caribbean, for

Figure 4.11   In many families AIDS has killed mothers and fathers.
(top) AIDS orphans at a Christian community centre in Uganda;
(below) grandmother with her two granddaughters whom she has
cared for since their parents died of AIDS, Thailand.

example, sexual transmission primarily occurs between men and women with as little as 1% being attributed to sex between men. It is interesting to note, however, that the transmission of HIV by infected mothers to their children is becoming increasingly common in places where considerable heterosexual transmission already occurs. In Francistown in Botswana and Harare in Zimbabwe, for example, more than 40% women attending antenatal clinics are infected with HIV and the World Bank (1997a) have recently estimated that 15–20% of all HIV infections in Africa now occur in infants that have been infected by their mothers.

Several questions arise from these data: What are the economic and social consequences of this relatively 'new' and fatal infection for low-income countries (Figure 4.11)? What type of links exist between HIV, poverty and inequality? How can our understanding of these links usefully inform strategies seeking to prevent the transmission of HIV? With respect to the first question, there is every indication to suggest that HIV and AIDS have had, and will continue to have, a detrimental impact on general well-being. This can be partially illustrated with reference to the Human Development Index (HDI) which was introduced by the UNDP in 1990. The

HDI measures three basic components of human development: life expectancy, standard of living and knowledge (for example, literacy and education; see Chapter 1). These indicators are combined to form a rank – the more 'developed' the country, the lower the rank.

Table 4.7 shows changes in how the UNDP estimates life expectancy and overall HDI rank in four African countries. These countries all have a high prevalence of HIV and AIDS and the table draws attention to the extent to which the virus has reduced life expectancy and impaired overall development.

Table 4.8 is based on data produced by the Population Division of the US Bureau of the Census. This table suggests that the impact of HIV is even greater than that indicated in Table 4.7. In Zimbabwe, for example, life expectancy has fallen by more than one-third and population growth has declined by more than 50%. It is also interesting to note that in South Africa life expectancy has decreased by almost ten years even though the prevalence of HIV was in single figures as little as seven years ago. The approach reflected in these two tables is, of course, limited. Nevertheless, it provides an indication of the extent to which HIV and AIDS impair general well-being.

It is also important to note that just as HIV and AIDS exacerbate poverty and inequality, so poverty and inequality facilitate the transmission of HIV. For example, the absolute level of poverty increases the susceptibility of the poor to infection from HIV due to a lack of disposable income for purchasing condoms, and poor access to health facilities and HIV prevention programmes. In situations where the disparity between 'rich' and 'poor' is particularly great, there are also data to suggest that the poor and socially most disadvantaged are more vulner-

Table 4.7 Changes in the Human Development Index for four African countries

Country	Rank		Life expectancy	
	1997	1996	1997	1996
Botswana	97	71	52.3	65.2
Zambia	143	136	42.6	48.6
Zimbabwe	129	124	49	53.4
Togo	147	140	50.6	55.2

Source: Whiteside, A. (1998) 'A global pandemic', *The Health Exchange*, August, pp.4–5.

Table 4.8 Life expectancy and population growth 1998, selected African countries

Country	Life expectancy			Population growth rates	
	Without AIDS	With AIDS	Years lost	Without AIDS	With AIDS
Zimbabwe	64.9	39.2	25.7	2.5	1.1
Namibia	65.3	41.5	23.8	2.9	1.6
Botswana	61.5	40.1	21.4	2.4	1.1
Swaziland	58.1	38.5	19.6	3.2	2.0
Zambia	56.2	37.1	19.1	3.3	2.1
Kenya	65.6	47.6	18.0	2.5	1.7
Malawi	51.1	36.6	14.5	2.7	1.7
South Africa	65.4	55.7	9.7	3.2	2.0

Source: Whiteside, A. (1998) 'A global pandemic', *The Health Exchange*, August, pp.4–5.

able to HIV infection. For example, it has been noted in a number of African and Indian cities that the lower social and economic status of many women has reduced their ability to negotiate safer sex and, in some situations, has led women to provide unprotected sex for money, lodging, food or other necessities. Consequently, many more women than men face situations in which they cannot protect themselves from acquiring this infection.

Finally, it is important to note that HIV and AIDS facilitates the transmission of other infectious diseases such as tuberculosis (TB). Many people infected with HIV are at an increased risk of developing active TB through living in poor and overcrowded conditions and they, in turn, are likely to pass on their infection to others – irrespective of their HIV status. In fact, TB is now one of the leading causes of death among adults in many low-income countries and it is estimated that it kills about three million people a year. The increase in fatal cases parallels the AIDS epidemic in many countries.

This trend is worrying. The World Health Organization estimates that 30–50% of adults in most low-income countries have latent TB infection. That is, they have been infected with mycobacterium tuberculosis at some point in their lives but have not developed active TB. The increasing occurrence of active TB (initially through HIV infection) now presents a major public health problem, especially as there is so much resistance to the drugs on offer.

Strategies for preventing transmission of HIV

The links between poverty, inequality, ill-health and the transmission of HIV are numerous and complex. The implications of these links for prevention strategies are wide ranging and this subsection provides a brief outline of some of the most important themes to emerge in the literature. First, there is little doubt that poverty reduces the ability of individuals to purchase condoms and thereby protect themselves from HIV. The cost of purchasing and distributing condoms is often prohibitive for governments

too. Hooper *et al.* (1990), for instance, noted that sexually active males between the ages of 15 to 50 years comprised 15% of the Zimbabwean population. Working on the assumption that each Zimbabwean man needed two condoms a week, they estimated that the total number of condoms required for this group of men would be 130 million per year. However, the Zimbabwean government only distributes 26 million condoms per year. These condoms are all imported and it is currently unclear how adequate foreign exchange will be found to purchase the shortfall.

Second, it has also been noted in many studies that it is one thing to ensure that condoms are widely available and quite another to persuade people to use them. Taylor (1990), for example, investigated the reluctance of certain groups to use condoms in Rwanda. At the time of his study, condoms were widely available and there was widespread understanding that HIV could be sexually transmitted. However, condoms were rarely used as they threatened commonly held ideas about the links between individual and collective health and well-being and fertility. In particular, conception was believed to occur when male semen was mixed with female blood. Condoms inevitably prevent this mixing and thus were deemed to present a major threat to the fertility and well-being of that society. Indeed, it has been suggested that in such a setting condoms are perceived to present a greater threat than that of the HIV infection itself.

In spite of the difficulties mentioned above, there are still reasons to be cautiously optimistic about the possibility of reducing the rate of transmission in low-income countries. Box 4.3 shows, for example, that the overall prevalence of HIV is falling in Uganda (Mulder *et al.*, 1995) and it is possible that at least part of this decline can be attributed to the availability and use of condoms. Other strategies have also been shown to be effective, albeit under well-resourced and carefully monitored research conditions. For example, Grosskurth *et al.* (1995) reported the findings of a study monitoring the effects of

---

Box 4.3 Declining prevalence of HIV in Uganda

Research undertaken in Uganda has documented a decline in the prevalence of HIV, particularly among young adults. In rural Masaka, for example, Mulder *et al.* (1995) recorded a fall in the overall prevalence of HIV from 8.2% in 1989 to 7.6% in 1994. The fall was particularly marked among young adults: the prevalence of HIV fell from 3.4% to 1% among males and 9.9% to 7.3% among females aged 13–24 years. It is important to note, however, that the prevalence of HIV increased among men and women aged over 25 years. Serwadda *et al.* (1995) also recorded a fall in the overall prevalence of HIV in Rakai District. They showed that the prevalence of HIV fell from 23.4% in 1990 to 20.9% in 1992 among adults aged 15–59 years. In common with Masaka District, the fall was particularly marked among young adults: the prevalence of HIV fell from 17.3% to 12.6% among men and women aged 13–24 years.

It is heartening to note that the prevalence of HIV has also fallen among pregnant women attending antenatal clinics in Uganda. Bagenda *et al.* (1995), for example, showed that the prevalence of HIV fell from 28% in 1989 to 16% in 1993 among pregnant women attending a major teaching hospital in Kampala, Uganda.

Explanations for the overall decline in the prevalence of HIV vary. Serwadda *et al.* (1995) suggest that the declines recorded in Masaka and Rakai district can be explained by rising mortality, with no change in the number of new infections. However, Mulder *et al.* (1995) suggest that interventions promoting reductions in the number of sexual contacts, the distribution and use of condoms and the treatment of other sexually transmitted infections may also be important.

---

treating sexually transmitted infections (such as gonorrhoea, chlamydia, genital herpes, etc.) at primary health care clinics in rural Tanzania on the number of new cases of HIV infection among adults. The results were impressive: the number of new cases was reduced by 40%.

We must remember, however, that governments and international agencies seeking to prevent the transmission of HIV often face acute dilemmas about how to proceed. For example, many policy-makers are currently grappling with the extremely difficult question of how to prevent HIV transmission without promoting the transmission of infectious diseases such as diarrhoeal diseases and acute respiratory infections.

You will recall that HIV can be transmitted by infected women to their infants during breastfeeding. Indeed, a UNAIDS report recently estimated that half of all mother-to-child HIV transmission in low-income countries occurs during breastfeeding (UNAIDS, 1998). The dilemma which emerges, therefore, is whether mothers should continue to be encouraged to breastfeed their infants. On the one hand, breastfeeding is known to be protective against a large number of infectious diseases (including diarrhoeal diseases and pneumonia) which have a high mortality and morbidity rate among infants in low-income countries. It also enhances maternal health as it often helps to prevent an early second pregnancy and thereby ensures more appropriate spacing between births. On the other hand, it is clear that the only way to prevent the transmission of HIV from infected mothers to infants in breast milk is to promote the use of formula milks. This is problematic as formula milks are expensive and their preparation requires a certain degree of literacy as well as access to clean water if they are to be appropriately administered. Money, clean water and literacy are, of course, often in scarce supply in low-income countries. Not surprisingly, governments and international agencies have been reluctant to promote their use when they know how easily their abuse can facilitate the spread of diarrhoeal diseases and other serious and often fatal infections.

Opinions are split about how best to proceed and it is interesting to note that, until very recently, the World Health Organization advised governments and international agencies to promote breastfeeding and to discourage the promotion of formula milks. Indeed, this policy was only reversed in October 1998.

4.4 Wealth, disease and public policy: contrasting circumstances in Sri Lanka and Brazil

We end this chapter by examining two countries – Sri Lanka and Brazil – in a little more detail. Sri Lanka is interesting because you will remember that, at the start of this chapter, we pointed out its low child mortality rate relative to most other low-income countries. Sri Lanka also becomes significant if we generate a scatter diagram of under-five mortality rate against average income, as measured by gross national product (GNP) per capita for selected countries (Figure 4.12).

Although there is a broadly negative correlation in that, as average income per capita increases, child mortality declines (as we might expect), Sri Lanka stands outside the general trend. In particular, its under-five mortality rate is very low for such a poor country as measured by GNP per capita. Sri Lanka is, therefore, an outlier on the scatter diagram and challenges the general hypothesis that 'wealth means health'. Brazil, on the other hand, is a comparatively rich country, with a GNP per capita approximately six times higher than that of Sri Lanka, yet its under-five mortality rate is almost double.

These examples serve to illustrate the limitations of generalized data evidence, which we noted in Section 4.1. They can only tell us so much and more detailed studies and comparisons of particular cases have to be carried out in order to further our understanding. Thus, generalized data evidence is good at indicating general patterns (and possible hypotheses to explain these patterns). It can also indicate the exceptions (or outliers) to these patterns, but then these have to be studied in more detail in order to try and find out what is really going on.

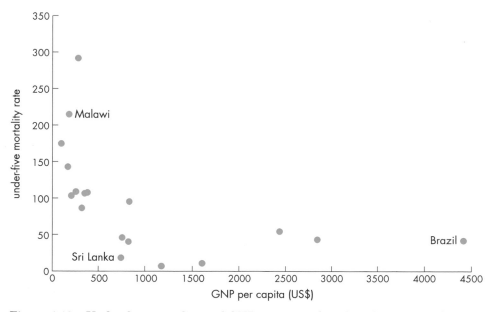

Figure 4.12   Under-five mortality and GNP per capita for selected countries (data from World Bank, 1998).

Table 4.9 Comparative indicators for Brazil and Sri Lanka

Indicator	Brazil	Sri Lanka
GNP per capita (US$) 1997	4400	740
U5MR 1997	44	19
Adult literacy rate (%) 1995	85	90
Gross enrolment at primary school 1990–96	112	113
Primary school entrants reaching grade 5 (%; 1990–95)	71	98
Gross secondary school enrolment ratio (1990–96) male/female	31/36	71/78
Prevalence of child malnutrition (% of children under 5; 1990–96)	7	38
Access to safe water (%; total/urban/rural; 1990–97)	76/88/25	57/88/52
Share of household income of top 20% (1997)	64.2	39.3
Government expenditure (%):		
on education (1995)	no data	2.7
on health (1990–95)	2.7	1.4

Sources: UNICEF (1998) *The State of the World's Children 1997*, UNICEF, New York; World Bank (1998) *World Development Report 1998/99*, Oxford University Press, New York.

Table 4.9 provides a more detailed data comparison of Sri Lanka and Brazil and it's worth while spending a little time studying it. Note immediately that the distribution of income is markedly different between the two countries. In Brazil the wealthiest 20% of the population have over 64% of the income, whereas in Sri Lanka the wealthiest 20% have less than 40%. This points to much greater inequality in income distribution in Brazil than Sri Lanka. Thus, although the former has a much greater *average* income, it is concentrated in relatively few hands.

Examining other indicators also reveals more important differences. Thus, Sri Lanka seems to have a higher level of education than Brazil. On the other hand, there is a greater prevalence of child malnutrition, a lower access to safe water and a lower percentage expenditure on health in Sri Lanka.

These sometimes contradictory data suggest that even more detailed studies are necessary, which we do not have the space to go into here. Certainly two key indicators, distribution of income and level of education, seem to help explain why Sri Lanka has a much lower child mortality than Brazil (Figure 4.13).

Figure 4.13   Slums in Brazil. The poorest live in grinding poverty.

We need, however, to step back further and look for even deeper causes of the differences, and these are not easily captured by data. For example, active promotion of primary education started in Sri Lanka in the early decades of the twentieth century, and a sharp increase in public health measures began in the 1940s. A radically innovative scheme of providing free or heavily subsidized rice to all was introduced in 1942 (Drèze & Sen, 1989, pp.227–9). Brazil, however, emerges as a country where public services have persistently been secondary to economic growth strategies, with Drèze and Sen using the term 'unaimed opulence' to describe the country and its wealth (ibid., p.188).

Perhaps one underlying reason for the difference between the two countries is that Sri Lanka has historically had a long democratic tradition involving widespread popular participation that has held governments accountable. This has not only helped ensure money is spent on public services, but that it has been well-spent too (Wuyts, 1992, p.27). Brazil's history, however, shows periods of military dictatorship punctuating interludes of democratic rule.

But things are changing for both countries. Shifts in the emphasis of government policy in Sri Lanka stemming from the 1980s have led to more economic growth-oriented strategies, with less available for public provisioning. One result has been a scaling-down of the food distribution programme. There has also been an escalating civil war which has not only been a direct drain on the economy, but has eroded democratic rights and meant less public pressure for social provisioning.

Brazil, on the other hand, has enjoyed a period of democracy since 1985. Social reforms designed to tackle health, education and inequality were promised in the Government of Fernando Henrique Cardoso who started his first term of President in 1994. However, economic crisis and austerity measures at the start of his second term, late 1998 and early 1999, have again led to these becoming de-prioritized.

The point of this discussion is that decisions concerning health policy are ultimately a political matter, where choices have to be made concerning limited resources. Although there have been great strides made in the latter half of the twentieth century in fighting diseases of poverty and in reducing mortality rates, they still represent a major challenge. This is especially so in the low-income countries, where most of the world's population lives, and one can make clear arguments for governments directing resources to meet this challenge. The allocation of resource by government is not, however, a technical matter. It involves political decisions about priorities, as resources directed to health mean that they cannot be directed elsewhere. But it also needs to be understood that decisions of government are not simply prescriptions of what is to be done, but are, in large measure, the outcome of pressure applied by many, often conflicting, interests in civil society. If the gains of the late 1990s are to be sustained, therefore, public participation in democratic processes, and the consequent ability to apply pressure, is crucial to ensure that not only is money spent on combating disease and on linked, wider social provisioning, but that it is also spent wisely in order to deliver the goods.

Summary

1   The under-five mortality rate has been steadily decreasing in almost all low-income countries of the world, but it is still considerably higher than in high-income countries. Nor does the gap between low-income and high-income countries seem to be closing. Some ways of measuring the gap suggest that it is widening.

2   There are considerable variations in patterns of disease prevalence within a country which the national statistics can mask. The poor and the very young in low-income countries seem particularly vulnerable to disease and there is evidence to suggest that in many countries the position of women in society relative to that of men makes them more prone to disease.

3   Infectious diseases, many of which are relatively easy to cure, remain the major killers in low income countries. Poverty is clearly connected with vulnerability to these infections, and undernutrition is often a major contributing factor.

4   There are disagreements about the best ways of combating diseases of poverty. In particular, there is a long-standing debate about whether selective biomedical interventions should be the main focus of public health programmes or whether the most effective way forward is to deal with the underlying problem of poverty itself. The debate has been significant in the planning and implementation of primary health care programmes.

5   Over the last two decades there has been great concern about the transmission of HIV/AIDS. It has become apparent that AIDS too is primarily a disease of poverty. HIV/AIDS also raises serious problems with prevalent approaches to primary health care.

6   A comparison of Sri Lanka with Brazil reveals the degree to which health policy is a political matter, and not merely one of biomedical health service delivery.

5

UNEMPLOYMENT AND MAKING A LIVING

DAVID WIELD AND JOANNA CHATAWAY

The issue of unemployment, like famine, poverty and disease, seems simple but conceals confusion and debate. Unemployment was considered important enough to be one of the key theme areas of the 1995 World Summit for Social Development in Copenhagen. There is complexity in the different understandings of the meaning of unemployment, as well as in the different views about what should be done about it. Here are simple statements of four views about the causes of unemployment. Which of them corresponds most closely to your own opinion?

- Overpopulation – too many people in the world (see the next chapter). The world cannot provide enough jobs to absorb the increased numbers seeking work.

- Overurbanization – too many people in the cities. If only people would move back to the land, problems of unemployment would decrease.

- Inappropriate technology – overinvestment in large scale capital-intensive industry that requires few workers, instead of small labour-intensive enterprises.

- Inappropriate education – too many school leavers with high expectations who shun lower level, casual and manual work and thus 'make themselves unemployed'.

You may not agree with any of the above. For example, you may think that unemployment is not such a serious problem – employment over time has risen and there must be a natural balance between supply and demand for employment. You may suggest that problems to do with lack of paid employment are a 'red herring' and that the official statistics overemphasize paid and full-time employment at the expense of the myriad means by which people manage to make their livelihoods. Alternatively, you may argue that the problem is much worse than the statistics suggest since much of the poorer quality and worse-paid work is not registered (principally the work of women). Whichever view you take now, I hope that by the end of this chapter you will understand better the assumptions behind such different views and will have the basis for a much more informed opinion.

Q How do the characteristics and perceptions of employment differ in different parts of the world? To what extent do the ways people make a living differ around the world and to what extent are they similar?

Q What are the special characteristics of unemployment in different parts of the world? Is there a sense in which people can be unemployed, or fully engaged in work?

Q How can we use an understanding of work and unemployment to assess policies designed to improve the work situation of people, locally and globally?

The rest of this chapter is structured in three sections aimed at engaging with these questions. In the course of the chapter the focus moves from unemployment and social exclusion to the issue of human capacities, since attempts to increase human capacities to make a living lie at the heart of issues of economic development.

5.1 What is unemployment? And what are work and employment?

First Person: Ah looking work, mam.

Second Person: I have no work for you.

First: Ah can wash your car, mam.

Second: My husband has that done downtown.

First: Ah can tek care of the garden.

Second: We have a service for …

First: Ah can do anyt'ing, anyt'ing, mam.

Second: There is nothing you can do for me, nothing.

First: Well den, beg you a ten cent, mam.

Second: I don't believe in young healthy boys begging – that's what's ruining this country. Beg. Beg. Beg. You should be ashamed. Go try to make something of yourself.

(Thelwell, 1982, p.109)

There are strong perceptions that less economically developed parts of the world are zones of high **unemployment** and low **employment**. In practice, the situation is more complex. In much of the North, unemployment has come to mean not having paid work. The vast majority of those with paid employment work for others for wages, though in ways that are constantly changing in their 'flexibility' (Figure 5.1). Others, the 'self-employed', are also likely to take a salary out of their businesses. But all over the world, there has been a trend from the classic conception of employment as single-job wage work towards a more diverse portfolio of ways of 'making a living'. At the same time, not having a 'proper' job (meaning a full-time paid job) has become an increasing concern to individuals to governments and to regions – including, for example, the European Union.

The notion of employment being for money is fairly basic. Being unemployed is less simple; it is normally understood as lacking the means of earning a living – but this discounts the fact that unemployed people have to keep themselves (and their dependants) alive somehow.

Unemployment: A concept generally restricted to the wage economy. It means being without work, i.e. not in paid employment, nor in self-employment (performing 'some work for profit or family gain') but currently available for employment and seeking it. This is the official meaning used in statistics.

Employment: Either (1) paid employment for others, or (2) self-employment performing 'some work for profit or family gain'. There are three major attributes of employment (the income aspect; the production aspect; and the recognition/identity aspect).

The *unemployment ratio* is the number of unemployed people expressed as a proportion (usually as a percentage) of the total employed and unemployed population.

But unemployment has a more general meaning than that. We can get a sense of this from the quotation above, which is clearly about someone looking for work from someone else. We do not actually know whether the person is unemployed – but it seems likely. Any type of work will do for him, it seems, providing it brings money. Money, we can safely assume, is needed to survive in this environment (actually Kingston, Jamaica). The second person neither holds out any hope of employment, nor seems sympathetic to the fact that the first person needs to get paid work to earn his living. There seems to be an assumption that work can quite easily be found – blame is attached to the unemployed person for his predicament.

Two dimensions of unemployment are apparent here. The first is the economic, the second social and cultural. To be unemployed is generally to lose self-esteem, and often to be judged as not wanting to work, to be lazy.

The official usage of the concepts 'employment' and 'unemployment', important as it is, does not cover all key ideas associated with making a living. In particular, these concepts focus on work

Figure 5.1   Images of work and employment : (top left) breaking bricks to make gravel on a food-for-work scheme in Bangladesh; (above) goldminers coming off shift, Ghana; (left) workers at a pharmaceutical factory, Bombay, India.

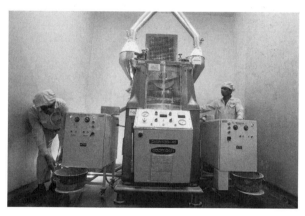

for wages. The gap is an issue even in the rich North – some work is not paid for. Examples are domestic work and voluntary work. But in other parts of the world, especially where non-market (particularly agricultural) production is significant, the polarization between paid work and unemployment is nothing like as straight-forward. The idea of livelihoods put forward in Chapter 3, for example, is much broader and more diverse than the official usage of the terms 'employment' and 'self-employment.

Data on unemployment

One way of unpacking the conceptual problems is by looking at available statistical information (see Chapter 2). Statistics on unemployment show remarkable variations from country to country. Table 5.1 shows the overall unemployment rate for a selection of 15 countries. You can see that it varies from 2.5% in Bangladesh to 12.4% in France. The figures do not seem as high as expected, to me at any rate.

Table 5.1   Incidence of unemployment in selected countries

Country	Year	Age of population	Unemployment (%)		
			Male	Female	Total
Africa					
Egypt	1995	12+	7.6	24.1	11.3
Mauritius	1995	12+	7.8	13.9	9.8
America					
Canada	1996	15+	9.9	9.4	9.7
Chile	1996	15+	4.8	6.7	5.4
Mexico	1996	12+	3.5	5.0	3.7
USA	1996	16+	5.4	5.4	5.4
Asia					
Bangladesh	1996	10+	2.7	2.3	2.5
Indonesia	1996	10+	3.3	5.1	4.0
Western Europe					
Austria	1996	15+	6.9	7.3	7.0
France	1996	15+	10.7	14.4	12.4
Eastern Europe					
Estonia	1995	15+	9.6	7.7	8.7
Poland	1996	15+	11.0	13.9	12.3
Romania	1996	15+	6.3	7.4	6.7
Oceania					
Australia	1996	15+	8.8	8.3	8.6
New Zealand	1996	15+	6.2	6.1	6.1

Source: ILO (1997) Year Book of Labour Statistics 1997, International Labour Organization, Geneva.

It is quite difficult, even with these relatively sophisticated data, to get a clear sense of the meaning of unemployment. Can it really be, for example, that in a country as poor as Bangladesh, there is such a low rate of unemployment as one in 40? Is there any significance that in Bangladesh and Indonesia unemployment is registered for people aged over ten years whereas in other countries it is for those over 15, or in the case of the USA, over 16?

There are a number of possible explanations. It could be that the statistics 'lie'. To be registered unemployed, for example, one first needs to be counted. If there are no labour offices in the rural areas or in the shanty urban areas there may well be a zero or low count in those locations. Also, to be counted as unemployed one usually has to be without employment, currently available for it, and 'seeking' it. There are good reasons why many people may not bother to 'seek' employment. If there are few jobs to be had then it is well known that the number of people seeking them goes down. If employment rises then more people 'come out' to find it. If at the same time there are few jobs and no social security or unemployment benefit, then there is little reason why anyone should register. It is specifically the case that most countries have little or nothing in the way of social security systems. There are no benefits for most who lose their waged jobs, quite apart from those without waged work in the first place. The unemployment rate may well be very low in poor, predominantly rural countries precisely because the poorest cannot afford to be without work of some sort.

The age figures in Table 5.1 are also suspect. Statistics over long historical periods show increased national income associated with lower use of child labour (Figure 5.2). So India, Bangladesh and Indonesia, some of the poorest countries measured in terms of national income, have large numbers of child workers.

All in all, unemployment statistics by themselves do not allow us to get a good picture of how people do make a living nor (crucially if we want to avoid hunger, ill-health and famine) how people stop being able to sustain themselves.

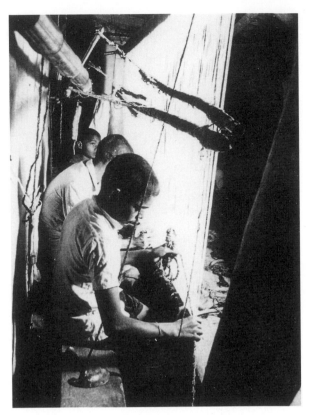

Figure 5.2   Child labour: carpet weaving for export is promoted in India as a 'village industry'.

Data on employment

Can we get any further by looking at data on employment, instead of unemployment? Table 5.2 compares total employment and total population for a selection of countries. Crude though such data are, they again give a striking sense of diversity. Employment as a source of livelihood seems much more important in some countries than in others. Do any patterns emerge?

Paid employment is clearly important all over the world, including the South. For those who think of countries of the South as predominantly peasant societies made up of those producing mainly for themselves (subsistence producers – see below and Chapter 3), Table 5.2 is quite a surprise. In some of these countries paid employment is the dominant activity of men. Such countries, in the main, are those with a high level of urbanization (proportion of the population living in towns). Thus Latin America and

Table 5.2 Employment as a proportion of population, selected countries

Country	Employment (millions, 1996 unless noted)	Population (millions, mid-1995)	Employment as proportion of population (%)
Africa			
Algeria	4.5[a]	28.0	15.9
Botswana	0.2a	1.5	15.5
Egypt	15.3a	57.8	26.5
Mauritius	0.4a	1.1	39.6
America			
Bolivia	1.4	7.4	18.3
Costa Rica	1.2	3.4	33.7
Chile	5.3	14.2	37.3
Mexico	35.2	91.8	38.4
USA	126.7	263.1	48.2
Asia			
China	614.7[a]	1200.2	51.2
Indonesia	85.7	193.3	44.3
Malaysia	8.4	20.1	41.3
Sri Lanka	5.6	18.1	30.9
Philippines	27.4	68.6	40.0
Western Europe			
Germany	36.0	81.9	43.9
Netherlands	7.0	15.5	45.0
Portugal	4.5	9.9	45.1
Sweden	4.0	8.8	45.0
United Kingdom	26.2	58.5	44.8
Eastern Europe and Central Asia			
Azerbaijan	2.9	7.5	38.5
Bulgaria	1.9	8.4	22.0
Czech Republic	5.0	10.3	48.3
Russia	66.0	148.2	44.5
Slovenia	0.9	2.0	43.9
Oceania			
Australia	8.3	18.1	46.1
New Zealand	1.7	3.6	46.9

[a]Reference year for the African countries, 1995; for China, 1994.

Sources: International Labour Organization (1997), *Year Book of Labour Statistics*, ILO, Geneva; World Bank (1997) *World Development Report 1997*, Oxford University Press, New York.

some countries of Asia (see Chile, Mexico, China and Indonesia) had, in 1996, a higher proportion of paid work than Africa. Indeed, some countries in Asia have a relatively high level of paid labour: for example, the newly industrializing countries of Taiwan, South Korea, Hong Kong and Singapore, which are not shown on the table, as well as China.

But Table 5.2, because the data are not available, does not show those countries that more closely fit the stereotype of having predominantly non-waged producers. Many countries in Africa still have relatively lower paid work proportions (see Botswana in the table but there are many others) so that most work is not waged work, even for males.

Data on male and female economic activity

To get at the idea of **work** and 'making a living' more broadly, we can try looking at another set of statistics, on **economic activity** (Figure 5.3). Table 5.3 gives data on the economically active population for a range of countries. What can be seen from the table?

Table 5.3 Total economic activity rates, recent years (%)

Country	Year	Men	Women
Africa			
Chad	1993	47.2	40.8
Egypt	1995	45.9	13.4
Ethiopia	1997	50.8	36.5
Gambia	1993	39.9	26.6
America			
Brazil	1995	59.2	38.5
Colombia	1996	55.5	37.3
Mexico	1996	54.7	25.3
Venezuela	1995	52.0	26.5
Asia			
Bangladesh	1995–96	55.8	35.7
Japan	1996	64.9	42.4
Pakistan	1994–95	45.9	7.6
Sri Lanka	1996	54.9	26.0
Western Europe			
Finland	1996	53.6	45.4
Ireland	1996	51.1	31.6
Italy	1996	51.5	29.6
Spain	1996	51.4	30.8
Eastern Europe and Central Asia			
Czech Republic	1996	58.0	43.3
Lithuania	1996	58.0	52.0
Romania	1996	57.5	46.4
Ukraine	1996	53.7	46.5
Oceania			
New Zealand	1997	56.5	43.9
Tonga	1993–94	43.9	27.8

Source: ILO (1997) *Yearbook of Labour Statistics*, International Labour Organization, Geneva.

First, one sees immediately that the economic activity rates are higher for men than for women everywhere although, in the main, differences are gradually lessening. Overall, the reported activity rates for women are a little over two-thirds those of men. Countries where female

Figure 5.3 Men's work tends to be counted in economic activity statistics whether it is formal waged work or not: (top) worker in the steam-hammer forging workshop of a locomotive factory, Tbilisi, Georgia; (above) radio repair workshop, Ouagadougou, Burkina Faso.

Work: Expenditure of energy for a purpose. Thus work includes both paid work (employment) and unpaid work, so-called 'formal' as well as 'informal' work, and domestic work, work done in kind, even voluntary work.

Economic activity: The *economically active* population includes 'All persons of either sex who furnish the supply of labour for the production of economic goods and services... [The] production of economic goods and services should include all production and processing of primary products whether for market, for barter or for own consumption, the production of all other goods for the market and, in the case of households which produce such goods and services for the market, the corresponding production for own consumption' (ILO, 1989–90).

activity rates approach those of men include much of western Europe – but note that eastern European countries also have high female activity rates and that Ireland and Spain have rather lower rates.

Second, the activity rates for men are rather similar across all countries even between developed and less developed countries. But take a look at exceptions like Japan and Brazil.

Third, although the unequal division of domestic work could perhaps help explain differences between male and female activity rates, it cannot easily explain the widely differing activity rates of women. Compare Egypt with Chad, Pakistan with Bangladesh, Mexico with Brazil, Italy with Finland (see Table 5.3, and for the service sector see Figure 5.4). Why should women's activity rates be so different and apparently so low? Some time ago, Beneria (1982) queried the low female activity rates reported in several parts of the world, including Arab countries as well as Africa and Latin America:

"In a survey in the Andean region, it was found that the proportion of women participating in agricultural work was 21% instead of the 3% officially reported. This type of underestimation is very common across countries, and especially in agricultural areas. To the extent that the amount of agricultural work performed by women is greater in the poorer strata of the peasantry it implies that this underestimation differs according to class background and affects women from the poorer strata to a higher degree."

(Beneria, 1982, p.125)

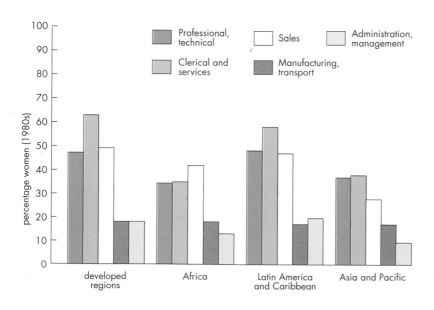

Figure 5.4   Women as a percentage of the labour force by type of employment in services.

Figure 5.5   Much women's work is statistically invisible. (top) Formal waged work for women does get counted, as with these garment workers in Bangladesh; (above) but much work may be done at home and is probably not counted, even though it is often for sale as well as for domestic use: as shown here, husking rice for paddy, also in Bangladesh.

Beneria gave three main reasons for the under-estimation of women's work. First, the problem of defining who is an unpaid family worker.

> "Given that involvement in home production is not considered as being part of the labour force, and to the extent that women's unpaid family work is highly integrated with domestic activities, the line between the conventional classifications of unpaid family worker and domestic worker becomes very thin and difficult to draw."
>
> (Beneria, 1982, p.123)

She was referring here to the difficulty of differentiating between 'domestic work' (such as preparing food for the household) and unpaid work done 'helping the head of the family' in their occupation such as agriculture. Although there has been some improvement, her observations still hold true for many countries.

Second, most censuses classify workers according to their main occupation. This will exclude women who are classified as 'housewife' but who are also working outside the household. In India it was estimated that this single exclusion lowered the female activity rate from 23% to 13%. There are various reasons for under-reporting of women's 'secondary occupations', according to Beneria.

"They range from the relative irregularity of women's work outside the household – that is, the greater incidence among women of seasonal and marginal work – to the deeply ingrained view that woman's place is in the household. In many countries it is considered prestigious to keep women from participating in non-household production; when asked whether women engage in such production, both men and women tend to reply negatively even if that is not the case."

(Beneria, 1982, p.124)

Third, some activities are performed by women at home even though they are clearly tied to the market, as when they produce food and drink for sale, make handicrafts and clothes inside the household for sale outside, and so on. The integration of these activities with domestic labour makes them highly invisible (Figure 5.5).

The limited picture from statistics

So, in summary, what can we deduce from the statistics?

1 Unemployment statistics do not give a reliable estimate of much other than the numbers of people who expect paid work and are without it. The statistics are thus particularly problematic in those countries with low numbers of wage workers, mostly in Africa and Asia.

2 Employment rates do give an idea of the level and extent of payment for work (commoditization of labour power, as Chapter 1 describes it).

3 Economic activity rate statistics do give a better idea of the extent of unpaid work. These data, even though they exhibit significant underreporting, illustrate how important such work is to the ability of most households to make a living.

In what ways are these statistics *not* able to help?

Much economic activity cannot easily be counted – that in the 'hidden economy' of second jobs, cash payment for work to avoid tax, and so on. The very nature of much work as being outside 'formal' wage work makes it difficult to count. More generally, the issue of work and economic activity goes beyond the problem of measuring it, to the questioning of perceptions and social conditioning.

Examples of the kinds of work not adequately described by the statistics include:

1 Work in the **informal sector** (see definition below and Box 5.1). The UN's International Labour Organization has tried to estimate the share of the urban labour force that works in the informal sector. It suggests that the percentages vary from 20% to 70% with an average of 50%. Table 5.4 gives the data from studies carried out in the South. Less formal work is increasing around the world.

Informal sector: A term which is commonly used to encompass petty trading, self-employment, casual and irregular wage work, employment in personal services or in very small 'micro' enterprises in manufacturing and services. Those unable to find or retain full-time regular wage employment swell the ranks of the informal sector, characterized by its relative ease of entry with low capital investment requirements, and by being relatively labour intensive and unregulated. By contrast, work in the 'formal' or 'modern' sector refers to larger scale enterprises and employers with relatively stable employment, higher wages and more regulation of work conditions, and where workers can organize themselves more easily. Informal sector enterprises are not officially registered businesses and exist largely outside the tax system. They are often illegal.

Box 5.1 The informal sector: examples and problems of using the concept

Examples from around the world

Africa
Nearly 75% of the labour force in sub-Saharan Africa...still work outside of the formal economy often in subsistence agriculture or in badly paid 'informal' activities such as small-scale manufacturing, street peddling and the provision of small services (*World of Work*, 1997).

In the United Republic of Tanzania, 'children below 15 years of age now constitute about half of the workforce in the growing urban informal sector' (ILO, 1997b).

Latin America
In Latin America, the informal sector 'accounted for 83% of the 10.1 million jobs created between 1990 and 1993' (Maldonado, 1995).

Eastern Europe
'Four million Hungarians – nearly half of the country's population of 10.5 million – take part in the underground economy. The money generated from this activity makes up 24% of the country's gross national product' (Bruner, 1993).

North America
In the United States...the value of the informal work has been estimated as well over $60 billion per year (Ayres, 1996).

The concepts
The concept of the informal sector is almost 30 years old. During this time, as one would expect, it has been used in various ways by different authors and institutions and its meaning and application has been widely debated and contested. Increasingly, other terms, such as 'micro-enterprise' or 'jua kali' in Kenya have replaced the term (although it should be noted that the terms 'micro' and 'small' enterprises can refer to firms in both the formal and informal sectors). The most widely used limitations of the term include the following:

The term tends to imply the urban sector exclusively. Although early defining studies of the informal sector, such as those carried out by the International Labour Organization (ILO), did not theoretically exclude rural enterprises, they were rarely discussed.

Another problem relates to using the informal sector in development policy. The main problem here is the 'missing middle'. Projects which support informal sector activity have often done so on the supposition that informal sector firms will go on to become registered firms which will eventually be incorporated into the formal sector. However, in many countries, there seems to be a gap between a very dynamic informal/micro-enterprise sector and large-scale 'modern' firms. In other words support for the informal sector may encourage more informal sector enterprises to be set up, but does not necessarily prompt well-established formal sector enterprises. Support for the informal sector may still be favoured because of its beneficial poverty reduction and income generation effects. However, promoting informal sector activity can aggravate the urban employment by attracting more labour than either the informal or the formal sector could absorb. There is also concern over pollution and congestion (e.g. pedi-cabs) and the impact of policies which effectively undermine the state's role in regulating and organizing market activity (Allen, 1998a).

For this reason, a number of authors and policy thinkers favour the conceptual framework built upon the idea of 'real economies'. Janet MacGaffey and Jean-Marie Cour, a senior economist from the World Bank, have both written about the concept of a 'real economy' which includes: the recorded economy, i.e. all economic activities that are recordable and reported and that are gathered by statistics; the non-monetized economy, i.e. all activities concerned with non-monetized production for self-consumption; and all the remainder, which is monetized (though operating with a variety of currencies and also through barter), unrecorded and, because it is more or less illegal, inadmissible (MacGaffey, 1991, p.10).

Estimates of the real economy may differ considerably from official versions; for example, some African economies may not have shrunk as dramatically as official statistics suggest. Policy based on 'real economy' analysis is based on a broader understanding of the political economy of the country or region. Thus, the problem of the missing middle does not reflect a distinction between informal and formal sectors but is more likely to be related to specific class or ethnic divisions, or the imposition of unpredictable regulations, such as arbitrary legislation and a regressive taxation system.

Table 5.4 Estimated share of the urban labour force in the informal sector

	Share (%)
Abidjan, Côte d'Ivoire	31
Lagos, Nigeria	50
Kumasi, Ghana	60–70
Nairobi, Kenya	44
Calcutta, India	40–50
Jakarta, Indonesia	45
Colombo, Sri Lanka	19
São Paulo, Brazil	43
Caracas, Venezuela	40

Source: S.U. Sethuraman, *The Urban Sector in Developing Countries*, ILO, Geneva, quoted in Todaro, (1997, p.270).

2 Women's work, some of which can, of course, be categorized as informal. Time spent in unpaid labour in the industrialized countries of Europe has been estimated approximately to equal the time spent in paid work. In countries of the South the ratio of unpaid to paid work is likely to be considerably higher, given the time spent on agricultural activities (Ginwala *et al.*, 1991, p.7).

3 Agricultural work, which is considerably underestimated in most calculations of its contribution to national wealth.

4 Perhaps most important, the relationship between different types of work. For example, the statistics cannot give an idea of the varied ways in which households (and societies) combine activities to make their livings.

Non-formal work has increased rapidly in much of the world. Table 5.5 gives data on the employment situation in Bogotà, Colombia.

Examples of making a living

If statistics cannot deal with all types of work done, are there other ways we can understand what is going on? Detailed research at a micro level can throw considerable light on the myriad ways in which people make their livings and relate to each other while doing so.

Shahanara is a member of Lucky Mohila Samity, a women's group organized to improve living conditions in the Dhaka, Bangladesh, slum where they live and work. Lucky Mohila Samity was organized by Proshika Manobik Unnayon Kendra (known as Proshika), a large Bangladeshi non-government organization with over 840 000 members. Shahanara is also the joint

Table 5.5 Bogotà: formal and informal employment, 1976–95

	1976	1984	1990	1994	1995
Population (000s)	3168	4034	4375	5620	5850
Occupied population (000s)	1120	1523	1805	2436	2625
Formal workers (000s)	na	696	912	1196	na
Informal workers (000s)	na	787	842	1240	na
Percentage informal	na	46.9	48.0	50.9	na
Permanent workers (000s)	935	1237	1419	1975	2113
Temporary workers (000s)	185	286	386	461	512
Percentage temporary	16.5	18.7	21.4[a]	18.9	19.5
Percentage with no social security	na	na	48.0	47.0	na

[a]Figure for 1991; na, not available.

Source: Mision Siglo XXI (undated), quoted in Gilbert, A. (1997) 'Employment and poverty during economic restructuring: the case of Bogotà, Colombia', *Urban Studies*, 34(7), pp.1047–70.

secretary in her slum federation co-ordination committee (with eight women and nine men). She is married with two daughters and two sons.

"Shahanara's Day

Before Shahanara began doing group work, she spent about seven hours each day getting water because there was only one water source in the vicinity. The remainder of her day was spent on cooking, cleaning, and other household tasks. For a couple of hours each evening, however, she had some time to rest while she oversaw her children's studies. She had to be up by 6 a.m. and went to sleep after 11 p.m.

Shahanara still rises at 6 a.m. but does not get to sleep until around 1 a.m. Since there are now tubewells and wells within the slum, Shahanara spends only two hours getting water each day. She also spends only one hour cooking as she uses an electric cooker instead of firewood because there is electricity in the slum now. The time it takes for her to go marketing for food has also gone down fourfold as there is now a bazaar much closer to the slum. However, this saving in time has been replaced with the three to four hours she spends on group work and income generation – her total workload has actually increased. Early on, she had spent much time organizing women and persuading them to form a group, and now as a leader she provides assistance and advice to her own group, and other groups in the slum, as well as the slum federation and arbitrations.

Shahanara spends six to eight hours per day doing or overseeing embroidery work with her two sons. Before she began her embroidery work, Shahanara took a loan of Tk.30 000 from Proshika to start a shop selling pots, pans, and other metal goods. Several months later the slum was razed, and the entire shop was destroyed. Shahanara spent more than two years repaying the loan. Now, she does embroidery for ten months of the year, and during off-months she does whatever work she can find, such as selling vegetables at the market or hand-sewing designs on clothing. [...]

Shahanara, her husband, and her sons typically manage to earn about Tk.4230 per month which they use to pay expenses (food, Proshika loan repayments, electricity, group savings, clothing, medicine and other items), sometimes saving a small amount for months when household income is less. Shahanara hopes to take another loan from Proshika to open a small shop or buy a rickshaw which she will rent. She would like to save her earnings to pay for training her children in tailoring and driving so that they are able to find jobs in the future."

(Carr *et al.*, 1996)

It is possible to count the number of different types of work that Shahanara did. It is clear that there were other sources of household income – that of her husband and sons. The example illustrates that low levels of wage employment do not equate with a simple life. Making a living here involves a complex and exhausting series of interactions, inside and outside Shahanara's family. The implications are enormous. To give just one example, earlier we found that employment statistics give a better idea of those 'earning a living' (through paid work) than those 'making' a living without regular wages. In fact, it seems impossible to divide 'paid' workers from 'unpaid' in this way, given the ways in which they interact.

At the household level, mixed and complex work arrangements are common. The archetypal peasant household, with enough land and tools to produce for its own consumption and to market crops for those goods it cannot produce itself, is even less of a generalizable family than the proverbial two-parent, two-child household in Europe.

Below are some more descriptions of working situations. In what ways do people relate to each other through work? The first description is from a study of male-headed and female-headed families.

"In nuclear (male-headed) families, especially those with young children, in 55 per cent of the cases housework is carried out single-handedly by the women. When they are aided, help is solicited from daughters and not sons. The key issue here, however, is that there is a full-time houseworker. The fact that women in single-parent families have to take on both the role of wage-earner as well as housewife may mean, therefore, that the housework may not get done so efficiently…Women who are employed effectively work a 'double day' of labour in order to carry out household chores. What is more important, however, in the single-parent units is that both boy and girl children participate actively in sharing the task of running the household. The fact that boys participate as well as girls contains important implications for the socialization of children."

(Chant, 1997)

The above description is from a poor urban settlement in Mexico. To what extent would you expect the situation to be generally applicable around the world?

The second description concerns changing work practices in Tanzania from 1974 to 1988, as a result of the world economic recession of the late 1970s followed by economic restructuring programmes.

"For workers, the process of de-industrialization meant sharply declining real wages and layoffs. There had been an 83% decline in the real income of wage earners between 1974 and 1988. For a low income household food expenditure alone exceeded the minimum salary eight times As real incomes dropped for men, women were more likely to initiate income-generating activities, frequently making them the main bread-winner in the family. The women, who in the past had contributed very little to the urban household income, were now critical to the very survival of the household through their involvement in projects. For low-income women these projects ranged from making and selling pastries, beer, paper bags, and crafts, to tailoring, hair braiding and even urban farming. By the late 1980s it was women themselves who were often rejecting wage employment and seeking more beneficial incomes from self-employment."

(Tripp, 1997)

Overall, such examples show that we need to be concerned not just with 'earning a living' but also with 'making a living'. Conceptual distinctions are required over and above employment and unemployment. Two fundamental distinctions (see also Figure 5.7 below) are:

1 between paid (i.e. waged) and unpaid (i.e. unwaged) work;

2 between work which is remunerated (either indirectly through wages or directly through marketing the product) and work which is un-remunerated (i.e. non-market-oriented subsistence or domestic work).

Although these are important distinctions, it is a mistake to regard different types of work as completely separate. For this reason, the idea of *duality* or *dual economy* (in which the typical 'developing' economy is seen as comprising two separate sectors, the modern/formal and the traditional/informal) is not very useful. It is certainly the case that large-scale modern industries and government bureaucracies offer formal paid employment alongside traditional and informal economic activities of all kinds, but in practice the sectors are connected. The modern sector tends to depend on the informal and traditional for various inputs, and the majority of individuals and households combine work in the two sectors. The study of development profoundly includes understanding of the diversity of ways of making a living. Thus there are also conceptual issues surrounding the relationship between different types of work and different types of production. Much work is not done alone. Production necessarily involves relations with others.

5.2 Unemployment and making a living: processes and concepts

In this section, I shall delve into some of the conceptual difficulties surrounding unemployment, employment and work. I begin with processes that may lead to unemployment, and then introduce concepts of production through which emerge the surprising diversity of ways of making a living.

What causes unemployment?

Unemployment is not a single process. It can be caused by a range of different phenomena that affect the nature of unemployment.

Closing down socio-economic activity
Perhaps the clearest mechanism is the closure of an organization, whether a factory or a whole company, office, school, or hospital. Closure may not necessarily cause unemployment because, in principle, employees can be moved from one site to another, but it usually does. Unemployment can also be caused by the closure of part of a unit – a hospital ward, part of a factory.

In the period 1950s to 1970s, rapid industrial growth (see Chapter 13) meant few closures. Even so, closures dramatically affected some industrial regions. Closures and rationalizations increased from the 1980s.

In contexts where large-scale social and economic change is occurring, the effects on employment can be dramatic. In Central and Eastern Europe, drastically reduced subsidies in the early 1990s, combined with liberalization policies, resulted in large-scale labour shedding or falling real wages, forcing people into informal sector activity, or some combination of the two. For example, between 1989 and 1993, the largest 150–200 firms in the Czech Republic, Hungary and Poland reduced their workforces by 32%, 47% and 33% respectively (World Bank, 1996, p.45).

In Russia the process of firm closures associated with the transition process took longer. The Russian government tried to keep operational as many firms as possible, even though they were not economically viable, primarily because the unemployment consequences threatened to be so severe. This was particularly worrying because in Russia health and education provision were often linked to the enterprise; when the firm collapsed people's access to these services was also threatened. However, people's working lives changed dramatically in any case. Although people still officially had jobs, wages were often paid very late or not at all and the structure of work altered significantly. The 1996 *World Development Report* reported 'Formal layoffs have been fewer. Employees remain on the books and continue to draw benefits, but they have accepted large cuts in hours and cash compensation and progressively shifted to informal activities' (World Bank, 1996, p.45).

By 1998, particularly after the economic collapse during the summer months, the Russian economy began to look dramatically different from the industrial monolith which had existed up to the 1990s. Informal activities became the basis of survival for many people, including the home production of agricultural products. A study of three regions in western Russia suggested that about 20% of Russian households were food and income poor. Moreover, indications were that people in rural areas, because of the greater opportunities for domestic food production, whilst still poor, suffered less. 'The home production of agricultural products has shifted the income equality in Russia between rural and urban areas toward a relatively more favourable situation of rural households, but not actually prevented poverty' (Seeth *et al.*, 1998, p.1623).

Relocating socio-economic activity
The relocation of activity can cause unemployment. Although there may not be an overall global decrease in employment, this is hardly any comfort to those made redundant. Companies can threaten to move from one part of the country to another in search of cheaper costs. They can also threaten to move to another country. Although we have heard more about relocation from 'North' to 'South', threats to relocate from one country of the South to another have

become more common as companies look for cheaper labour, better terms from governments, and so on. However, there are examples of multinationally owned production units relocating from 'higher wage' newly industrializing countries (NICs) to lower wage NICs.

Intensification of labour

So far, the processes we have described as causing unemployment have been straightforward. But 'intensification' is more complicated. Unemployment can be caused by changing the organization of work without increasing investment – for example, by getting employees to work harder. By this means, output can be maintained with fewer workers, or increased with the same workforce. Thus **labour productivity** is increased, perhaps causing unemployment. Labour intensification has been historically important both in industrializing capitalist countries (Chapter 15) and in the South (see Chapter 11 on colonial labour regimes).

> **Labour productivity:** The quantity of goods and services that someone can produce with a given expenditure of effort, usually measured or averaged out in terms of time spent working or labour time. It is the ratio of the amount produced to the amount of labour put in, measured as product per person-hour or person-year.

Contracting out

Another rapidly increasing process is the outsourcing of work from in-house to another company or individuals. This process is often associated with lowering the quantity and quality of employment, by lowering the number of staff and by moving to part-time and to a temporary casual workforce. This is happening all over the world but particularly where formal labour regimes give good conditions to employees, as in much of Europe. Silicon Valley in California, also, has a massive 'contingent' workforce of all types, cleaners, secretaries, data processors as well as programmers and systems people.

'Casualization'

A major feature of labour market policies in many countries since the early 1980s, but in the United Kingdom and the United States in particular, has been an emphasis on making the labour market more 'flexible' through casualization. That is, deregulating work so that the structure and terms of work become increasingly negotiable between employer and employee. This has contributed to a shift in the way that many people worked and the kinds of jobs on offer. By 1996, part-time work had risen to significant levels of 23% of total employment in England, 21% in Japan and 24% in Australia. Women in particular are heavily represented in the part-time workforce; in 1996 61% of part-time workers in Greece and 88% of workers in Germany were female.

Another feature of a more flexible work environment is increasing disparity in wage levels. Data from the OECD confirms this trend, showing that wage dispersion has risen most dramatically in the US, UK, New Zealand, Australia and Canada since the mid-1980s (*OECD Economic Outlook*, 1996, quoted in Posthuma, 1998).

Technical change

An increase in unemployment (and the unemployment problem for those who were employees) does not necessarily correlate with problems for employers. The productivity of labour can depend to a great extent on the tools or technology that the producer uses. Unemployment can result from increased capital investment – investment in new ways of making things or doing things that increases labour productivity and thus requires fewer workers per unit of output (Figure 5.6).

Technical change can occur at the level of one factory, and also more generally. Sometimes a new investment by one company can result in new jobs in that company, while wiping out a whole other way of producing the same goods or services. One major historical example was the introduction of the weaving machine that was estimated to put half a million handloom weavers out of work at the beginning of the industrial revolution. There are many such

Figure 5.6   Work in capital-intensive industry: (top) workers at the press machine, car factory, Shanghai, China; (above) women workers at micro-chip factory, Taiwan.

contemporary processes. For example, the increase in production and sale of plastic footwear has destroyed local leather industries in some countries. Similarly, plastic household wear has lowered the demand for metal pots and pans. Infrastructural technical change can make a major impact. It is estimated in Britain that on average each new out-of-town supermarket causes the loss of 270 more jobs than it creates, particularly in urban centres and villages. Negative reactions against 'technology' have been important in some political movements – Gandhi-ism in India is a well-known example since it served as a model for the appropriate technology movement (see Chapter 19).

Demographic forces
The mechanisms mentioned so far are examples of social processes that can be important causes of job loss. But there are other processes that have been very important in explanations of unemployment in the South, though they may not lead to job loss *per se*.

For example, a major cause of unemployment in many countries is a growth in the number of young people needing employment at a faster rate than employment possibilities for them. There are at least two policy implications. One is that policies are required to stop populations growing so fast (see Chapter 6). The other is that other types of work creation could be prioritized over permanent paid employment, for example the hand-over of land for people to make their own living in rural areas rather than having to migrate to the city. The Government in South Africa faces just such an issue since the level of unemployment is high but much of the population retains a link, albeit a tenuous one, with the rural areas.

Land alienation
But policy and practice do not always converge. In practice, the opposite trend is more common – namely the privatization and enclosure of common lands, concentration of land ownership in fewer hands, and loss of land by many peasant producers.

The alienation of land was an early act of most colonizers of territory in what became the South.

This act of land alienation is not exclusive to the South – on the contrary. However, what is different is the extent to which the contemporary history of the South has been shaped by colonial land alienation, and by continuing land alienation after the colonial period.

In Tanzania, for example, the first few decades of colonialism structured the colony into three main zones: (1) areas where agriculture changed towards the production of cash crops for export, together with food crops for subsistence; (2) areas requiring wage labour (towns, plantations); and (3) labour reserve areas from where most males travelled as migrants to the areas requiring wage labour, leaving the rest of the household remaining on the land they owned or worked. The processes in each area were different, but together they added up to a new labour regime linked to the new colonial economy: some people without land needed to earn wages and became 'proletarianized' (see Chapter 11); others without sufficient land to produce all their needs became partly proletarianized, working for a part of the year, or on contract for a part of their lives; and some were able to make a living mainly from their agricultural production for the market as well as for themselves.

Even in a country like Tanzania, with relatively low colonial investment and industry, the process of proletarianization, slow and incomplete though it was, was under way, bringing an 'unemployment problem' with it.

Some concepts

Analysis of the causes of unemployment leads us to the nature of work itself and thus to basic notions of production and reproduction.

Production
Production at its simplest involves interaction between people and nature. At one extreme, raw materials can appear 'ready made', as in the gathering of natural products. More typically, the raw materials used in a particular production process are the product of another production process. For example, the cotton used in the manufacture of textiles first has to be grown and harvested, then the harvested cotton has to be

processed to separate the fibre from the other parts of the plant, and finally the cotton fibre has to be spun into thread before it can be used in making textiles. Then the textiles need to be sold, a process requiring several steps – the whole set of linked production and marketing process is called a *value-chain*.

A general definition of production is a process in which human energy is expended in changing nature (through various means) to produce goods for consumption (see Chapter 3).

I emphasized earlier the idea of productivity of labour – and how it depends on the capital invested. A farmer in the United States using a tractor and a combine harvester can produce a ton of wheat with much less expenditure of time and human effort than a farmer in India using an ox-plough. In turn the latter can produce a ton of wheat using less time and physical effort than a farmer in Africa who lacks a plough and has to cultivate with a hoe.

This example contrasts different tools and machines, but one crucial 'input' to production is human labour in the shape of those engaged in production. Human labour consists of a variety of physical and mental capacities and skills. We can think of the 'quality' of labour in terms of its possession of the capacities demanded by certain kinds of tasks. If those capacities are not fully available, this affects the productivity of labour adversely; for example, a producer might lack the training or experience to use a complex piece of machinery or a computer efficiently.

The division of labour

It is an obvious assumption that American farmers like the one above do not make their own tractors, and also a realistic assumption that farmers in India and Africa use factory-produced ploughs and hoes. They have to obtain them from somewhere – ultimately from others whose work is to produce and sell these different kinds of tools. This provides a simple example of the **social division of labour**, meaning that there are producers of different kinds of goods and services whose activities are complementary, and who are related to each other through the

exchange of their products (even if the producers do not meet each other directly). As the social division of labour increases in complexity, it makes available a more diverse range of goods and services.

We can still assume for the moment that the three farmers are working alone on their own farms (even though they depend on tools produced by others). Such an assumption would be nonsensical, however, in the case of a car factory, which is a very different kind of *unit of production*. A car factory gives a good example of a **technical division of labour:** the combination of different operations and tasks performed by a number of waged workers in the manufacture of a single product.

> **Social division of labour:** The degree of specialization between different units of production, and how they are related through the exchange of their products.
>
> **Technical division of labour:** The degree of specialization and combination of activities *within* any single unit of production or production process.

Work, then, is more than what one individual does. The work of one individual affects that of others. This simple fact has important implications. For example, policies to improve the quality and quantity of jobs will affect a wide range of related types of labour.

Reproduction

It has been implied that the various elements or 'inputs' of the production process first have to be produced. Even the land used in agriculture, while originally a 'gift' of nature, is changed through people's interaction with it – its fertility can deteriorate, be maintained or be enriched. Tools and machines used in production become worn out after a time; raw materials tend to be used up more quickly – for example, stocks of seeds and fertilizers used in each cycle of agricultural production. Many hybrid seeds cannot be used again, including those of genetically modified crops, so new seeds must be bought. These elements of production have to be replaced: that is, they require **reproduction** for production to continue in future. In the case of land, tools, seeds, etc., this is called social reproduction. It is also the case that the most vital element of the whole process – namely the producer – needs reproducing.

> **Reproduction:** All the processes by which the inputs of production are themselves produced. *Social reproduction* replaces the inert elements of the process. The 'production of the producer' involves biological reproduction (childbearing), generational reproduction (childrearing) and daily reproduction or maintenance (provision of human needs like food, shelter, etc.).

So far we have discussed production without using the 'gendered' terms 'he' or 'she', 'his' or 'hers'. I have signalled gender because we are entering an area of what many people think of as self-evidently 'women's work'.

> "The first and indispensable step, and also the most obvious, in the 'production of the producer' is that of *biological reproduction*. People have to be born for society to continue, and biology determines that only women can bear children. But this is only the first step. A child has to be cared for and raised until it reaches that stage of maturity when it can become independent, economically and in other ways. A third aspect of reproduction is *daily reproduction* or *maintenance*. Adults as well as children need to replace or restore the physical and mental energies that they use up in the course of their daily lives. They have to eat and to rest, which requires the provision and preparation of food and drink, the maintenance of somewhere to live, clothes to wear which have to be washed, and so on."

> (Bernstein, 1988, p.60)

Even childbearing is a social practice, conditioned by social relations and ideologies. While it is 'ordained by nature' that *only* women can bear children, there is nothing 'natural' about *whether* all women bear children, *when* they bear them, *how many* children they bear, nor that in many cultures there is a particular pressure on women to bear sons (see Chapter 6). There is nothing 'natural' about the fact that responsibility for bringing up children devolves on their mothers (or grandmothers, or aunts, or older sisters, or female servants, in different societies and social groups). Nor is there any 'natural' necessity that women should carry out the task of maintaining the current generation of producers as well as their children, who will provide the next generation. Earlier, I have called these tasks *domestic work*. In so far as domestic work is practised as 'women's work', it provides a special case of the division of labour – a *sexual division of labour*.

The specific ways in which the labour associated with generational reproduction is women's work clearly have significant implications for employment policies. In particular, it involves 'double' or even 'triple' days for many women. We have seen that women often have longer working days on average than men, they do different types of work, and often their remuneration is low or zero.

The sexual division of labour extends beyond the domestic sphere. In many areas of Africa and elsewhere the process of agricultural production is divided into tasks by gender, with men tilling the soil and women performing the work of weeding and harvesting. Generally, sexual divisions of labour are accompanied and justified by ideologies of men's 'place' and women's 'place' in society, which go beyond the different kinds of work regarded as fitting for them. The private or domestic domain tends to be seen as the province of women, and the public domain that of men. The latter may include wage employment outside the home (though in practice women also do wage work) and participation in public affairs more generally, whether particular religious and ceremonial roles and activities, deliberations of village councils, holding office in a co-operative, or active membership of a trade union. What do you think are the implications of sexual divisions of labour for a society's or a group's productive capacity? Chapter 18 gives a more detailed answer. For the moment, note how, at the very least, if a particular sexual division of labour restricts a whole category of people to certain kinds of work and disqualifies them from acquiring other kinds of knowledge and skills which enhance their productive capacities, then this is likely to inhibit economic development.

Subsistence and commodity production
You have already encountered the next (and my final) key concepts. **Subsistence production** is production for direct consumption; **commodity production** is for sale and consumption by other than the producer. The distinction here is not in the physical properties of what is produced (tea, sugar, maize) but in the social relations of its production, distribution and consumption.

Subsistence production: Production for the producer's own (or household) use.

Commodity production: Production for sale through the market and consumption by other than the producer. *Full (capitalist) commodity production* is completely integrated into the market. Producers buy all inputs, including waged labour, and sell all the output. *Small (petty) commodity production* is only partly integrated into the market and is based on family not waged labour (see Chapters 1 and 11).

Subsistence production makes up a more significant proportion of goods and services in the South than elsewhere. In agriculture, for example, a higher proportion of crops produced are consumed in the household. There are important implications for work:

1   Subsistence production is both unwaged and unremunerated.

2   Although it should count as 'economic activity', such work is likely to be underestimated in statistics, and thus its importance 'hidden' from policy-makers.

3   In general, more such work is likely to be undertaken by women and children.

However, the use of the term 'subsistence production' can be confusing because it is often assumed that all peasant production is subsistence production. This is far from the case (see Chapter 3): some household members must either sell some product or work at least temporarily for wages in order to buy any basic essentials not produced in the household itself – tools, fuel, school fees, certain foods. Thus, there may be no completely 'subsistence household' in practice, even though a significant proportion of agricultural producers in the South engage in some subsistence production, together with production for markets or paid work.

Production for the market takes two major forms: *small (petty)* and *full (capitalist) commodity production*. The latter is defined simply as production which is completely integrated into the market – producers must buy all their inputs (including labour) and sell all their output. It is called capitalist because it involves as the key social relationship that between owners and wage workers (Figure 5.7).

It is the in-between category of small (petty) commodity production that corresponds most closely to those most difficult categories of work: those that are unwaged but remunerated through marketing (Figure 5.8).

Petty commodity producers (see Chapter 11):

1   have access to means of production (land, tools, technologies);

2   operate on a small scale;

3   use household labour;

4   produce to satisfy basic needs;

5   have links to markets (they buy and sell) and thus operate in a wider social division of labour.

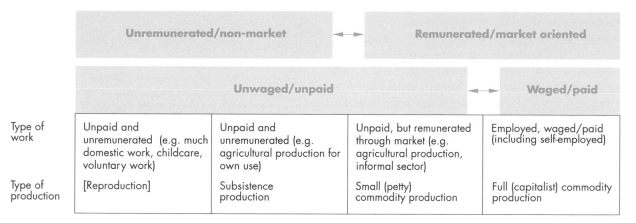

	Unremunerated/non-market		Remunerated/market oriented	
	Unwaged/unpaid			Waged/paid
Type of work	Unpaid and unremunerated (e.g. much domestic work, childcare, voluntary work)	Unpaid and unremunerated (e.g. agricultural production for own use)	Unpaid, but remunerated through market (e.g. agricultural production, informal sector)	Employed, waged/paid (including self-employed)
Type of production	[Reproduction]	Subsistence production	Small (petty) commodity production	Full (capitalist) commodity production

Figure 5.7   Work and production: how they fit together.

Some petty commodity producers have, overall, rather more control and ability to manoeuvre than others, or than wage workers. For example, a peasant household that produces food crops can make decisions on the proportion to sell. Alternatively, peasant households producing predominantly a permanent 'cash' crop of tea or coffee will be much more reliant on the market, since they cannot just tear up their bushes. Some petty commodity producers are able to 'get by' on this mixture of production forms. Others cannot, and may need to sell land or increasingly undertake wage work.

In terms of the question about whether 'employment' and 'making a living' differ around the world, not only do we find a diversity of ways of making a living, but the linkage and mix between different types of work can, and does, change. It can be a very dynamic system: some households 'getting by'; others 'more than getting by'; and others gradually losing their ability to 'get by'. Small commodity production plays an important role, being both in-between subsistence production and full commodity production, and a key means by which households retain some control over their livelihoods.

Figure 5.8   Petty commodity production is not only agricultural: bronze casting, Benin City, Nigeria.

In terms of the question 'Is there a sense in which people can be unemployed?', it may be difficult to find huge unemployment in the formal sense. But it is possible to conceive of a lack of 'quality' employment. People with expectations of wage work may lose it, fall back on petty commodity work or subsistence work, but still expect to go back eventually to 'better work'.

And the linked question: Is there a sense in which people can be fully employed, or fully engaged in work? The answer to that seems to follow quite naturally. People may not be employed in the formal sense, but may be relatively fully engaged in work. For example, because of low productivity and poor remuneration they may be obliged to work tremendously hard just to survive, engaged in petty commodity and subsistence production. Unsurprisingly, there is strong evidence that such people want better quality work and employment.

Moving from the micro to the macro, differing notions of development crucially involve different conceptions about what causes unemployment and underemployment and what to do about it.

5.3 Improving ways of making a living

What use are concepts of work and production? The purpose of this brief final section is to show that understanding of policy issues can be improved by use of these concepts.

Using the 'disguised unemployed' for development

One relatively early development policy idea was that there is a high level of 'disguised' unemployment (or **underemployment**) in the rural areas of countries in the South that could be drawn off and used for new development projects. The argument goes like this:

> Some (maybe even a significant proportion) of the population engaged in peasant agriculture is not strictly necessary for production to continue and reproduce itself. In other words, taking away a part of the labour force would not lower production output.

> **Underemployment:** Work that does not permit full use of someone's highest existing skills or capacities. This could mean, for example: working for shorter periods, less intensively than able or willing to work; working at a lower level of productivity than capable of doing; earning less than able or willing; or working in a production unit with abnormally low productivity.

Let us look more closely at this proposition. First, it is unlikely that any member of the family will not be working. I described earlier the high workloads of women. The existing data show women working much harder than men but they show men working hard also. Second, households are usually involved in petty commodity production and sometimes wage work so that income is shared in some way within the household. Intra-household distribution of income, uneven though it is, usually gives some rights to all household members while they are living in the household. But rights usually change when members leave the household. Third, it is likely that those in the peasant households have rights of ownership or control over land. Again, such rights may change for those who leave the household. In many of the poorest countries, people hand over control or access to land at the peril of famine and death. For these three reasons, and others, the idea of relatively free individuals able to take up employment elsewhere does not quite seem the way to describe the situation, though underemployment is certainly common.

The argument goes on to suggest that the 'disguised unemployed' or 'underemployed' can be transferred to more productive work. The implication is that such a transfer means rural to urban migration to provide the labour for economic development through industrialization.

Can you think of any problems with this argument? I introduced some problems above. Access to land can be the key to long-term survival, i.e. daily and biological reproduction of households. Thus we have seen above how households develop ways of linking employment in higher productivity units of production with continuing production on the land: for example, by some household members migrating for regular wage income at the same time as keeping a base on the land.

A second problem is that, in practice, opportunities for higher income wage labour have been easier to obtain in some countries than in others. Overall, it is important to emphasize that there has been significant growth in wage employment over time. But it has been unevenly spread.

The third issue is the actual level of spare time. You will remember the earlier descriptions of Shahanara's working day and lack of spare time, and of other working situations. The amount of 'spare time' is not great and often women are targeted as having more spare time than men. Many development projects have been criticized because they have targeted those who already work very hard. Put simply, they do not have much extra spare time; rather they need assistance in increasing their productivity of labour and thus their output, without further intensification of their work!

Overall then, our first look at policies to use the 'disguised unemployed' for development suggests the need for care.

Although our initial look at a concept for its usefulness has had only partial success, concepts can point to some useful openings for those interested in improving economic conditions. For example, underemployed people may not have spare time but may also work with very low productivity. Small interventions may improve productivity and conditions. An example might be the installation of a water pump close by that would lessen the time spent collecting water and thus free time for more productive activities, as happened in Shahanara's slum. Another example might be that people work hard but do not earn enough money. A development policy targeted at this problem might need to increase income-earning possibilities while avoiding loss of subsistence production and lowering time spent on domestic work.

Tackling social exclusion

The complexity of employment and poverty issues and the multi-dimensional causes of unemployment and poverty lie at the heart of a new concept. The concepts of **social exclusion** and inclusion were first developed in France but are now used widely in both industrially developed and developing contexts.

> **Social exclusion:** Defined by the European Foundation (1995, p.4) as: 'the process through which individuals or groups are wholly or partially excluded from full participation in the society in which they live.'

The power of these converse concepts is that they encourage policy-makers and development workers to address the full range of issues which inhibit people from taking employment or making adequate income. Such issues include human rights, legal and civic and democratic rights, education, health care provision and family and community support. It is the access which people have to basic rights and resources and the familial and community based relationships which impact on their ability to gain and maintain work and employment.

Table 5.6 shows the arenas which are encapsulated by the term 'social exclusion'.

Table 5.6 Arenas and elements of social exclusion

Key arenas	Elements
Rights	human
	legal/civic
	democratic
Resources	human and social capital
	labour markets
	product markets
	state provision
	common property resources
Relationships	family networks
	wider support networks
	voluntary organizations

Source: de Hann, A. & Maxwell, S. (1998) 'Poverty and social exclusion in North and South', *IDS Bulletin*, 29(1), p.3.

Inclusive social and economic development policies, which address all these issues rather than just pushing for macro-economic growth, are now widely advocated by development policy-makers. Kerala is often held up as an example of what can be achieved when a more holistic approach is taken.

Kerala's success is due to a number of factors including meaningful land reforms, promoting high literacy (especially among women) through free and universal primary education, and developing social movements through the establishment of a civil society to promote environmental conservation. Promoting people's rights, reducing inequalities and mobilizing workers and farmers also played a role (Randel & German, 1997, p.14).

Micro-finance to increase women's income

Micro-finance has become a key strategy for poverty alleviation and in particular as a tool to increase women's income. Micro-finance initiatives provide very small loans to people in order that they might set up as self-employed or start their own 'micro' businesses, usually defined as employing under ten people. Shahanara, you will remember, was able to take a loan from a micro-finance system through her non-governmental organization Proshika. Well-known schemes such as the Grameen Bank, which lends to small groups of mainly women in Bangladesh, and Banco Sol, which started in Bolivia, have replicated over much of the South and increasingly are being used as part of poverty alleviation strategies in the North. The idea is that by providing financial assistance directly to people they are able to organize themselves so that they can fit income generation into their lives. Micro-financeschemes often incorporate social development components such as training and childcare provision in order to provide more comprehensive assistance. In February 1997, the Micro-credit Summit in Washington brought together 2900 people from donor organizations, NGOs and grass roots organizations in 137 countries to:

"...launch a global movement to reach 100 million of the World's poorest families, especially the women of those families, with credit for self-employment and other financial and business services, by the year 2005."

(Results, 1997, p.3)

Women's work and development

The well-meaning policy mentioned earlier of targeting those who work hardest is especially important for policies addressed towards women. Consider this quotation from a policy document of a political party.

"[We] will strive to ensure that any new economic policy will have as an important policy objective the rapid successful integration of women into economic activity."

I chose this quotation because it is from a group which has made considerable efforts to integrate women and to increase their participation in politics. The quotation illustrates how persistent and easy it is to assume that women are not already integrated into economic activity.

From your reading of earlier parts of the chapter, what kinds of women's work may be hidden from policy-makers?

Childcare, production and preparation of food, possibly subsistence cultivation, may be 'invisible'. But there are other hidden elements that have been the key to failed development projects: the ignorance of the overall extent of women's work contribution – both paid and unpaid; the assumption that the household is male headed; not taking into account women's independent cultivation or other income-generating activities.

The fact that such policy statements can appear, even from groups cognizant of the dominant role of women in much economic activity, has serious implications for development projects. Women can be targeted for 'integration into economic activity', on the basis of massive misunderstanding of the extent to which their unpaid labour allows paid labour. There may be little 'free' labour time available.

Development interventions can affect existing social relations of production in various ways. One example is the provision of training courses to increase the skills of women. But such training courses can be set up without planning or provision to substitute for the women's unpaid labour. Courses can fail because women just cannot get free time. Other interventions have been designed to increase labour-intensive, low income-generating opportunities for women without thought for their already 'breaking point' working days.

Targeting women in development policy more sensitively could lead to increasing the priority given to unpaid over paid labour and would involve social as well as economic policy. Measures like those mentioned earlier (improving water provision under women's control or improved access to cheap fuel supplies for cooking) could dramatically free women's labour time in rural areas in many countries.

Finally, there is strong evidence that the structural adjustment policies pursued in the economic crisis from the 1980s have tended unequally to push women out of the development process and to increase the proportion of domestic, subsistence and low paid commodity production. Chapter 18 will deal with this in more depth.

Acknowledgement

We acknowledge Seife Ayele for his data collection work for this chapter.

Summary

1 Preconceptions of development include that it involves, for less developed areas, much unemployment and little employment. We found rather that work is characterized by its complexity and diversity and, importantly, by the relationship between paid and unpaid work. There are few, if any, situations where households are either all waged or where no members receive income.

2 Unemployment statistics, by themselves, do not give an accurate picture of those in work and those who need increased income to make a living.

3 Statistics do not adequately portray the large proportion of unpaid labour done by people, nor that much of this is done by women.

4 In economies in much of the South, there is a higher proportion of subsistence agricultural production, and also a higher proportion of petty commodity production.

5 Rather than people being unemployed, a major issue is that many work extremely hard but at levels of low productivity, receiving low financial recompense, and thus remaining in relative poverty. They require opportunities for better quality and better remunerated work.

6 Understanding work involves understanding the relationship between different forms of production:

- What is produced?
- How is it produced?
- For whom (division of labour)?
- What is the relationship between production and reproduction?

7 All over the world there has recently been an increase in the diversity of ways of making a living, with more part-time wage work, more self-employed and informal activities and more flexible work systems. These changes do not suggest a smooth process of development from subsistence to full-time wage labour.

8 Understanding of policy issues is improved by applying the concepts of commodity and subsistence production, reproduction, and waged and unwaged work, as well as an appreciation of how ways of making a living combine these types of work.

6

IS THE WORLD OVERPOPULATED?

TOM HEWITT AND INES SMYTH

"The unprecedented surge in population combined with rising individual consumption, is pushing our claims on the planet beyond its natural limits."

(Brown *et al.*, 1998, p.5)

"…increased population density can induce the necessary social and technical changes to bring about better living standards…"

(Tiffen, 1995, p.60)

There is clearly some disagreement over whether there is a population problem and what this problem is. Are there too many people in the world or is this an exaggeration?

Your immediate reactions may well be that there are too many people in the world: the greater the population, the less there is to go round; more people means less income and less food. In short, high population growth is a problem in itself and the cause of many other problems in the world. This is the traditional Malthusian view that population growth will sooner or later run up against the limits of the Earth's finite stock of resources. This has also long been the message from the major Western aid donors, at least up until the International Conference on Population and Development (ICPD) held in Cairo in 1994.

Alternatively, you may believe that population growth is not a problem at all. You may agree with Julian Simon (1992) or Mary Tiffen (in the above quotation) and think that population growth is a crucial impetus behind human progress.

These are two extreme views of the population issue. But you may realize there must be other, more complex, factors at play, and we need a wider set of questions.

Q Is the world overpopulated and, if so, in relation to what?

Q Is the majority of the world's population poor because there are too many people and not enough resources to go round or does the world's population continue to grow as a result of the poverty of the majority of people?

Q Is the population debate about more than population policies and birth control? Does the Programme of Action of ICPD offer new solutions based on a global consensus?

By the end of this chapter, you should be able to give reasoned responses to these questions. First, let's see what the problem is and examine its dimensions. You may find it helpful to have a look at the definitions of some demographic terms that will occur in the chapter.

Crude birth rate: The number of births per 1000 population in a given year. Not to be confused with growth rate.

Demographic transition (theory of) and **demographic trap:** See Box 6.1.

Fertility: The actual reproduction performance of an individual, a couple, a group, or a population.

Fertility rate: The number of live births per 1000 women aged 15–44 years in a given year.

Infant mortality rate: The number of deaths to infants under one year of age in a given year per 1000 live births in that year (see Chapter 4).

Population distribution: The patterns of settlement and dispersion of a population.

Population growth rate: The rate at which a population is increasing (or decreasing) in a given year due to natural increase and net migration, expressed as a percentage of the base population.

Replacement level: The level of fertility at which a group of women on average are having only enough daughters to replace themselves in the population.

Total fertility rate (TFR): The average number of children that would be born alive to a woman (or group of women) during her lifetime if she were to pass through her childbearing years conforming to the age-specific fertility rates of a given year. In the United States today a TFR of 2.12 is considered to be replacement level. (If there were no deaths before childbearing age and an equal number of male and female births, it would be 2.0.)

6.1 The size of the problem

What does Table 6.1 tell us about the size and distribution of the world's population?

First of all, note that the total world population in 1998 amounted to nearly 6 billion people, more than twice as many as 40 years earlier in 1950. You will also notice that in 1998 around 80% of the world's total population was to be found in 'low' income countries. This is hardly surprising since these countries comprise a large part of the world's land area. Yet the proportion of the population that is in low-income countries has been increasing over the years. Why do you think this is?

Table 6.1   Population size and growth rates by region (1950–2025)

(a) Population size by region (in millions of people)

Date	World	High-income countries	Low-income countries
1950	2515	832	1683
1970	3698	1049	2649
1998	5930	1182	4748
2025 projection	8039	1220	6819

(b) Average annual population growth (%)

Date	World	High-income countries	Low-income countries
1950–55	1.8	1.3	2.1
1970–75	2.0	0.9	2.4
1995–2000 projected	1.4	0.3	1.7

Source: UN (1989) *World Population Prospects 1988,* and UNFPA (1998) *The State of the World Population 1998.*

Look at Table 6.1(b). The population growth rate is much higher in low-income countries. You should also note that growth has *declined* in both high-income and low-income countries, although the decline has been less dramatic in the latter (see also Table 6.2 for selected countries). What the table does not tell us is that the lowest income countries continue to have an annual population growth rate of 2.6% on average, and in some parts, for example sub-Saharan Africa, this growth rate is higher still (UNFPA, 1998).

From the current level of 5.9 billion people, the world's population is projected to increase by 80 million per year to the year 2025. Most of this increase will be in developing countries (Figure 6.1). The United Nations Population Fund (UNFPA, 1989) projects that world population may stop growing at about 10 billion perhaps a century from now. We should stress, however, that projected population data which go further than the following decade should be treated with great caution.

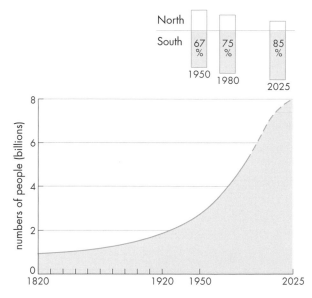

Figure 6.1 World population trends and North–South distribution.

Whatever the precise figures, the foreseeable future will produce many more people. But why does population grow and why do low-income countries have higher population growth rates?

Mortality and fertility

From a demographic point of view, two elements account for this: mortality and fertility. In most developing countries, while mortality rates have declined substantially, fertility rates are

declining more slowly and, in some parts of the world, very slowly. In developed countries, there is a much closer match between these two rates. When mortality rates are low, high fertility generates a 'population momentum', such that an increasing proportion of women in the total population is of childbearing age who will reproduce the next generation. This is why, even as growth rates in developing countries decline, they will still have greater shares of the world's population.

Improved health, as we have seen in Chapter 4, is a major factor in mortality decline in developing countries. Nevertheless, health and sanitary conditions are still far from satisfactory. Fatal disease is still prevalent in children and, for some of the countries under structural adjustment programmes, health indicators deteriorated during the 1980s (Commonwealth Secretariat, 1989; Watkins, 1995). This has a direct bearing on fertility. Why? Because the more the under-fives die from curable diseases or causes related to poverty and malnutrition, the more likely are parents to have more children to compensate for possible losses.

This is not the only explanation of high fertility. Farooq & DeGraff (1990) group many of the explanations of why fertility rates are high or low, into three types.

1 *Proximate variables*. This type of explanation recognizes that there is a series of social, cultural and economic factors which have an impact on fertility. However, between these and fertility outcomes there are a number of 'proximate variables' which affect fertility rates directly in a given social, cultural and economic context. These variables include:

- the proportion of people married;
- contraceptive use;
- the prevalence of abortion;
- post-birth infertility.

The explanatory power of such variables is not great. They provide a link between broader socioeconomic 'factors' and fertility, but questions remain about what are the underlying causes.

2   *Mechanisms of demographic transition.* In demographic transition theory (Box 6.1), no mechanisms are given precisely, but the following factors are suggested (individually or in combination) which all relate to a general process of industrialization and development, and which could all cause fertility to fall following an earlier reduction in mortality:

- urbanization, which increases the cost of raising children;

- a fall in the production value of children due, for example, to education, the introduction of labour laws, increased demand for skilled labour;

- increased education and age of marriage for women;

- the changing role of women and increased earning opportunities outside the household;

- intervening religious and cultural values;

Box 6.1   Demographic transition theory

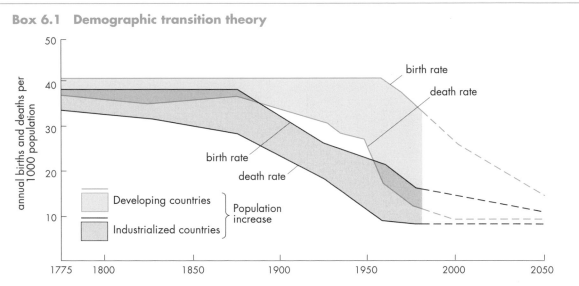

Trends in birth and death rates, actual and projected, 1775–2050 (World Bank, 1980).

This theory (much cited in books on population) is based on what was observed to occur in some of the industrialized countries. In the wake of the Industrial Revolution, death rates dropped dramatically, mainly as a result of improved sanitation and public health. Then, after a generation or so of higher population growth, the birth rate also began to fall.

In other words, there was a historical shift from a situation of high mortality and high fertility to one of low mortality and low fertility.

Today, in large parts of the world, as previously in Europe, death rates have been reduced. Demographic transition theory expects that after a period of transition (which according to World Bank estimates may be shorter than in industrialized countries), fertility levels and thus birth rates will also fall.

In developing countries, the experience is much more varied than that of the industrialized countries in the past. The theory would hold that with development and lowering mortality, fertility should follow suit and also reduce. But this has by no means always occurred. This has led some to a discussion of a 'demographic trap' where developing countries become stuck in the transition phase of low mortality/high fertility (King, 1990).

We should note that demographic transition is a model and like any other is open to question. That the model proposes that mortality and fertility rates will take a certain path does not mean that this will happen in practice. In fact the model is one based on a particular view of development – modernization theory (see also Chapters 1 and 13), which assumes an inevitable progression towards a 'modern' society, though at very different rates.

- a shift to greater individual control of fertility decisions;
- lower infant and child mortality;
- higher returns for education of children;
- more welfare and insurance schemes for the elderly;
- greater availability of contraception.

3 *Micro-level explanations.* Here there is strictly no single theory, but a range of analyses of specific situations. Their common denominator is that, one way or another, they are criticisms of grand theories, such as demographic transition. Among this category of explanation are the following:

- explanations based on the economic value of children, which is high in societies with low levels of social security for the elderly or where the value of children's labour is relatively high;
- the notion of intergenerational wealth flows: fertility is high where wealth flows from children to adults (as in different forms of child labour) and is low when it flows from adults to children (as in paying for school fees) (Caldwell, 1976).

Distribution

The third and often forgotten element of the population equation, after mortality and fertility, is the distribution of population. Density of population in the world is very uneven. Urban agglomerates are in stark contrast to rural regions in many countries. It is calculated that nearly half of the world's population was urban by 1995 (see Chapter 13, Box 13.3 and Chapter 20) and that this is projected to increase to nearly 60% in 2015, with the fastest urban growth rate occurring in the least developed countries (about 5% per year until 2015) (World Bank, 1998, p.175).

Population density varies greatly between and within continents. Africa, for example, is a continent where we find underpopulation and overpopulation side by side (Box 6.2).

The causes of unevenness in the distribution of population range from ecological endowments, colonial history and forms of production, to national and international migration and resettlements (or any combination of these).

From the perspective of development, migration is as important as size and growth of population. First, it is an integral component of the demographic equation: population change is a combination of natural increase (births minus deaths) and net migration (immigration minus emigration). Second, it has a complex, two-way relationship to development. The level and the nature of development in a given country or region determine migration patterns, while the latter in their turn impact on development. Finally, migration decisions have emotional and practical repercussions of great significance, affecting the quality of people's life in a way that is comparable to fertility- and mortality-related events.

People migrate in large numbers within and across international boundaries. The substantial migrations after the Second World War to Western Europe from many developing countries (frequently ex-colonies) are well known, as is the movement of Spanish-speaking labour from Central America to the southern states of the US, but there has been little consideration of the development impacts of other migrations. For example, it is estimated that in the early 1980s there were nearly seven million migrant workers in the oil-producing Middle Eastern countries from the Indian subcontinent and South-east Asia (Khan, 1990, p.88).

Other examples of substantial local and international population movements would include: the seventeenth-century slave trade, European migration to North and South America at the turn of the twentieth century, migration induced by war and famine such as from Indo-China and in sub-Saharan Africa, the urban evacuations imposed by Pol Pot in Cambodia, the Indonesian transmigration programme.

The movement of people forced from their place of origin by war, natural disaster and famine has increased dramatically. For example, in the period 1975–95 the number of refugees increased from something in the region of 2.5 million people to around 15 million people (Allen, 1998b; see also Chapter 8).

Box 6.2   Africa: overpopulation and underpopulation

Fertility

Sub-Saharan African countries are among those with the highest population growth rates, on average 2.7% per year compared with an average for all developing countries of 1.6% between 1990 and 1997 (World Bank, 1998, p.195). Fertility in Africa also remains high (see Table 6.2 for sub-Saharan Africa and selected countries).

There are regional variations in this but the overall pattern requires some explanation. Quite a large body of work (summarized by Dasgupta, 1993) has come up with the following:

• The 'household' is not a very meaningful organizing unit for fertility decisions in Africa: household budgets are often separate for men and women; polygyny is widespread; women become widows at an early age and remarriage is commonplace.

• Sexual division of labour: men are frequently absent (though not permanently!) and women control subsistence production. Children become an important resource. They are raised with diffuse responsibilities amongst kin rather than by parents directly or exclusively. This makes for diffused maintenance costs of children.

• Marriage for women tends to be early and universal with little reliance on contraceptive use.

• Most recently, the period of structural adjustment in sub-Saharan Africa (from the early 1980s) appears to have had an adverse effect on education and health access and expenditure (Watkins, 1995). Such indicators are significant in their longer term impacts on fertility rates, although the outcome will not be known for another generation.

Density

The average population density of sub-Saharan Africa is less than 25 people per square kilometre. The continent has millions of hectares of potential rain-fed cropland in the humid tropics, most of which is uncultivated and underpopulated.

Yet there are also areas of very high population density in the cities, along the coast, and in the highlands, where population pressure has contributed to environmental degradation. In Ethiopia, for example, the highest densities are in the drought-prone, environmentally vulnerable highlands, while there are thousands of acres of uncultivated arable land in the south and the east.

In West Africa the demand for labour is the crucial determinant of population densities and high fertility. There is a very low level of economic development and an undersupply of labour in many parts of the region. This can be traced back to the colonial era when the forced recruitment of labour, the forced growing of cash crops, taxation, and military reprisals by colonial troops compelled African peoples to produce as many children as possible to increase labour supply and reconstitute as much of their local economy as possible under colonial conditions. Added to this was the large-scale male migration to plantation zones and coastal cities for employment. It is estimated that 50% of the population will be urban by 2020. With husbands absent, women depend even more on children as a source of agricultural labour and security.

Today this same migration pattern continues. In Burkina Faso, for example, during certain times of the year when young men migrate to raise cash for taxes and consumer needs, there is not enough labour to clear bush for new farms or maintain wells, and food production suffers accordingly. A number of observers have in fact noted how low population densities serve as a brake on agricultural production in Africa.

(Sources: Hartmann, 1987, pp.17–18; Dasgupta, 1993; Dyson, 1996)

Table 6.2 Population indicators for selected countries and regions (1997 unless specified)

	GNP per capita (measured at PPP US$)	Under 5 mortality rate (per 1000)		Total fertility rate (births per woman)		Urban population (% of total)	Population total (millions)		Population average annual growth rate (%)	Maternal mortality ratio (per 100 000 live births)
		1980	1996	1980	1996		1980	1997	1990–97	1990–96
Bangladesh	1050	207	112	6.1	3.4	19	87	124	1.6	850
Brazil	6240	86	42	3.9	2.4	80	121	164	1.4	160
China	3570	60	39	2.5	1.9	32	981	1227	1.1	115
Ethiopia	510	213	177	6.6	7.0	16	38	60	2.3	1400
India	1650	173	85	5.0	3.1	27	687	961	1.8	437
Indonesia	3450	124	60	4.3	2.6	22	148	200	1.7	390
Kenya	1110	115	90	7.8	4.6	30	17	28	2.6	650
Mozambique	520	285	214	6.5	6.1	36	12	19	3.8	1500
South Korea	13500	18	11	2.6	1.7	83	38	46	1.0	30
Sri Lanka	2460	48	19	3.5	2.3	23	15	18	1.2	30
Thailand	6590	58	38	3.5	1.8	21	47	61	1.2	200
Uganda	1050	180	141	7.2	6.7	13	13	20	3.1	550
World regions (low and middle income countries only)										
East Asia and Pacific	3560	75	47	3.1	2.2	33	1359	1753	1.3	
Europe and Central Asia	4390	–	30	2.5	1.8	68	428	471	0.1	
Latin America and Caribbean	6660	82	41	4.1	2.8	74	358	494	1.7	
Middle East and North Africa	4580	141	63	6.1	4.0	58	175	283	2.5	
South Asia	1580	174	93	5.3	3.4	27	902	1289	1.9	
Sub-Saharan Africa	1470	193	147	6.6	5.6	32	379	614	2.7	
Low income countries	1400	175	113	5.6	4.1	28	1384	2048	2.1	
Middle income countries	4550	85	43	3.2	2.3	49	2217	2855	1.3	
Low and middle income countries	3230	133	80	4.1	3.0	40	3600	4903	1.6	
High income countries	22770	–	7	1.9	1.7	78	825	926	0.7	

Source: World Bank (1998) *World Development Report 1998–99*, Oxford University Press, New York.

6.2 Views on population

Thus in many countries of the world, mortality rates are declining while fertility rates remain generally high, though they are also declining in other countries. Given this, we now return to the original question: Is the world overpopulated? Already we can take a more considered approach because of what has been said about the patterns of distribution of populations around the world. So we must ask: In relation to *what* is the world overpopulated? Is it, as some believe, in relation to available resources such as food, or is the problem the distribution and, therefore, access to such resources? We know, for example, that food production has outstripped population growth in the last decades. Dyson (1996), in a comprehensive study on the matter, argues this to be the case in aggregate. The starkest regional exception is in parts of sub-Saharan Africa.

So is there a problem of overpopulation in the world? For some the question has to be asked not in absolute terms but in relation to distribution of, access to and use of resources.

> "...overpopulation is not a matter of too many people, but of unequal distribution of resources. The fundamental issue is not population control, but control over resources and the very circumstances of life itself."
>
> (Michaelson, 1981, p.3)

For others, 'overpopulation' is a problem in itself. In what follows, we present some of the most influential ideas concerning the world's population.

New Malthusian view
> "Let us act on the fact that less than five dollars invested in population control is worth a hundred dollars invested in economic growth."
>
> (President Lyndon Johnson, speech to the United Nations, 1965)

One of the most pervasive views in contemporary thinking on population is New (or Neo) Malthusianism, derived from the arguments of

---

Box 6.3 Malthus on population

Malthus (1766–1834) was an economist, most famous for his pessimistic *Essay on Population* (1798). In this he maintained that the human race tends to reproduce in geometrical progression (2, 4, 8...) while food supplies can only grow arithmetically (1, 2, 3...). Because of this law of Nature, humanity would breed up to the limits set by the supply of food, checked only by the inevitable consequences of its own growth: extreme poverty, famine, wars, pestilence, etc. Thus, as population grew, there would be a fall in average output of food per head, which would create growing misery and eventually could only be 'resolved' by famine or war. Malthus was renowned for his support of the landed gentry, which blinded him to the view that extreme misery was caused not so much by diminishing returns to labour as population grew but by the lack of political bargaining power of the peasantry vis-à-vis the landlords.

Malthus (Box 6.3). It shares Malthus' original view that population growth is a major cause of poverty but differs from Malthus in the belief that human intervention can put a check on population growth (through birth control). There are several variants of New Malthusian arguments, but the common feature of the more modern version is demographic determinism, i.e. that the weight of population itself is the cause of problems. This is the 'people versus resources' perspective (Lappé & Schurman, 1988) – epitomized by Paul Erlich's *The Population Bomb* published in 1968 – which states in no uncertain terms that there are (or will be) too many people for the available resources (Figure 6.2).

In the New Malthusian view it is argued that rapid population growth results in widespread poverty, economic stagnation, environmental destruction, rapid urbanization, unemployment, and political instability. During the years of the Cold War and the Vietnam War, in particular, the view prevailed that overpopulation, resulting in mass hunger, was a breeding ground for

Figure 6.2   Is population growth the cause of these conditions? Evicted squatters in Dhaka, Bangladesh.

revolutionary activity. Central to such views is that it is the poor who produce more children, because of their ignorance and lack of foresight.

The most recent variant of the New Malthusian argument comes from some of those concerned with the pace of environmental change in the world. Look, for example, at this statement from an editorial in the prestigious medical journal, *The Lancet:*

> "Human population has exploded five-fold in the past century and a half. For the first hundred years this explosion did not impose irreversible pressures on the biosphere. Over the past fifty, however, the inexorable growth of human population and increasingly numerous industrial off-shoots have come to threaten the health of the planet."
>
> (*The Lancet*, 1990, p.659)

The debate over environmental degradation is taken up in detail in Chapter 7. Suffice to say two things here. First, it is arguably those countries that are near or below population replacement level (as in Western Europe; see Table 6.2) which are the greatest consumers of non-renewable resources. Here, too, the worst environmental dangers are created, in the guise of global warming, acid rain, nuclear 'accidents' etc., and it is here that economic interests motivate the practices of deforestation and overexploitation of the soil and the sea, from which threats to the world's environment are generated.

Second, in certain parts of the world, land is overused as a result of the large numbers of people hungry for wood fuel, pasture or food crops. But again, this appears to be due to population distribution and an unequal access to resources rather than the sheer weight of humanity. In other words, there may be a link between population size and lack of resources in a given region but there is not always a direct relationship.

In the New Malthusian view, to set matters to rights, it is imperative that people, and especially the poor, should be persuaded (or forced, if this is necessary) to have fewer children. Improving the impoverished conditions in which they live is a secondary concern, reducing birth rates being the first. This can be achieved through family planning programmes, which have been promoted for over 40 years by international agencies as an efficient and cost-effective way to tackle the problems of development.

The New Malthusian orthodoxy sees the tendency to population growth as a constant factor in human history which needs no explanation in itself. When we ask *why* populations grow, the difficulties with the New Malthusian argument begin to appear. The *causes* of population growth may well be those aspects of socio-economic life which this argument puts forward as its *consequences*. Equally, we could ask why fertility decline has occurred in industrialized countries, and find answers in a complex set of socio-economic changes, not in population control policies.

Being able to understand the causes of high population growth (and of fertility decline, where it has occurred) would, logically, give us strong clues on how to reduce fertility rates more effectively in those countries or regions for which population pressure mounts by the decade.

The New Malthusian case, however, has not helped its credibility by its alarmist and pessimistic forecasts (the opposite, laissez-faire view is equally difficult to swallow). Overstating the case may have had the effect of alerting the world to try to do something about stemming high fertility rates, but the basis of the New Malthusian arguments is only partially true. Many of the New Malthusian assertions are measurable and have proved to be largely inaccurate or at least overstated (Dyson, 1996).

The most fundamental weakness, however, lies in the view that population growth itself is the cause of poverty (and ultimately human disaster). Questioning this assertion has given rise to alternative views and policy recommendations.

The social view

"Development is the best contraceptive."

(Bucharest slogan, 1974)

In 1974, at the Bucharest World Conference on Population set up by UNFPA, the New Malthusian argument was challenged by representatives from developing countries, on the basis that it diverted attention and money from the real causes of underdevelopment. Representatives from developing countries also reclaimed the right to define for themselves what they perceived their population problems to be and to resolve them, free of pressures from more powerful international agencies. Since 1974 a new wisdom has become accepted, incorporating some of the partial explanations of fertility rates mentioned above, that can, perhaps, be called a *social* view.

Central to this is the notion that rapid population growth is not the cause of social and economic problems, but rather a symptom. This also means that, rather than being poor because they have many children, people may have many children because they are poor. In fact, the economic value of children to the poor is one reason that fertility rates are high in some developing countries. We saw above that, when infant mortality rates are high, women tend to have more births to ensure that a sufficient number of children survive to adulthood. However, a 'sufficient number' is a variable quantity dependent on economic and security considerations such as the provision or not of pensions, and the level of savings. Poor women have children because children's labour is valuable in itself and also may release their mothers for work (Figure 6.3). In addition, in economies with little or no welfare provision, children provide parents with security in old age. Proponents of this view would point to remarkable declines in fertility in a few

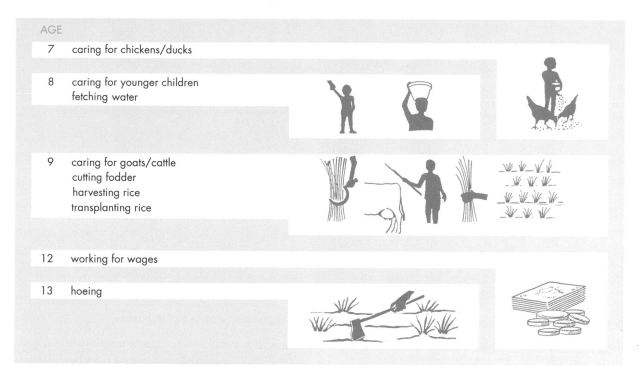

AGE	
7	caring for chickens/ducks
8	caring for younger children fetching water
9	caring for goats/cattle cutting fodder harvesting rice transplanting rice
12	working for wages
13	hoeing

Figure 6.3 Children's labour is valuable: (above) survey of child activities in Java, 1977, showing age from which different activities start; (left) boy tending water-buffalo, Indonesia.

countries with low per capita incomes (Sri Lanka, Thailand, Cuba, the Indian state of Kerala) and point out that in those cases there has been greater access to social resources such as health-care and education, particularly for women. It is lack of access to such resources rather than material poverty *per se* that tends to mean high fertility.

Can you imagine parents sitting at the kitchen table with a calculator, working out the future economic benefits of their children (Figure 6.4)? Of course, individuals do not take decisions only on the basis of economic calculations. Other, non-economic considerations are equally important. These include relations between women and men, social pressure, dominant norms concerning the family and the role of women, individual (men's and women's) desires and circumstances. Calculations over numbers of children are further influenced by the widespread phenomenon of son preference.

Figure 6.4   Why have children? Non-economic considerations are important.

Thus, it is argued that increasing living standards, lowering child mortality and improving the position of women via more equitable social and economic development will motivate people to have fewer children.

Family planning services, in this approach, are simply part of the necessary provision of health and other social services to the entire population, and a response to a genuine need for voluntary fertility reduction.

The counter to the New Malthusian view which emerged in Bucharest laid the ground for a much broader debate that went beyond population size and distribution in itself to a consideration of a multiplicity of reproductive rights and responsibilities.

Women at the centre

"... ethics, human rights and human development; women's empowerment; and reproductive and sexual health. These themes together present a new approach to population based on a solid ethical foundation and aimed at sustainable human development."

(Sen *et al.*, 1994b, p.3)

This angle on population is centred on the role of women. It is not entirely a separate approach, since the 'social view' has included a recognition of the importance of women in both development and demographic change. However, this view goes further in underlining the importance of the gender dimension of the population issue.

The close relationship between women's status and fertility is now accepted by demographers and policy-makers. More egalitarian gender relations in and outside the household are known to have a positive impact on fertility reduction. Women who have access to better education and employment opportunities tend to have less need to rely on their children for economic security and social recognition. Potentially, better educated women are more able to safeguard the health of their children, thus contributing to the reduction of infant mortality. They also have better access to contraceptive information.

This position has been adopted by international agencies. For example, the UNFPA chose women as their focus of the 1990s.

"In many societies, a young woman is still trapped within a web of traditional values which assign a very high value to child-bearing and almost none to anything else she can do. Her status depends on her success as a mother and on little else. Increasing a woman's capacity to decide her own future – her access to education, to land, to agricultural extension services, to credit, to employment – as an individual in her own right has a powerful effect not least on her fertility."

(UNFPA, 1990a, p.4)

Though this recognition of the centrality of women was inevitable because of the obvious role of women in bearing and rearing children, for some it has unsatisfactory connotations. There is a too narrow emphasis on statistical correlations between different aspects of women's life (e.g. education, employment) and fertility. Although these correlations are significant, they tend to hide the social mechanisms which are at the root of demographic behaviour. In addition:

1 High fertility may indeed be advantageous to some women (despite the possible health risks) as a route to higher status, economic security or access to financial and other resources.

2 Women are not always able to control their fertility and sexuality because of their lack of decisional and formal powers in their household, and in the community.

From the same sources comes the argument that consideration for women's reproductive and sexual behaviour should not be related exclusively and directly to fertility, but should be part of a concern for their social position, welfare and autonomy.

"The question of reproductive choice ultimately goes far beyond the bounds of family planning programmes, involving women's role in the family and in society at large. Control over reproduction is predicated on women having greater control over their economic and social lives and sharing power equally with men."

(Hartmann, 1987, p.34)

Many of those who are concerned with women's reproductive health argue that family planning services should be available not for population control but for birth control, and only as part of comprehensive health and welfare provisions (Box 6.4). One of the motivations behind this argument is the awareness of the past excesses of

---

> **Box 6.4   Population control versus birth control**
>
> The distinction between population control and birth control goes beyond semantics. *Birth control* refers to the right of individual couples or women to control childbearing (timing, spacing and total number of children) on the basis of individual choice. *Population control* refers to policies aimed at controlling the same for the population as a whole on the basis of demographic 'imperatives' such as the perceived need to cut the population growth rate (Rogow, 1986, p.74). The fundamental difference between these two approaches is in who is empowered to make decisions over fertility.

some family planning programmes which, in attempting to reduce fertility at all costs, have been notoriously negligent of human rights. Examples of this are the one child programme in China and the 'Emergency' in India. In sum, this view stresses women's right to control their own reproduction. One of the motivations behind this argument is the awareness of the excesses of population control, but it also gives a prescription for the way forward. While this position is championed mostly by women and health advocates (for example, Corrêa & Reichmann, 1994; Sen *et al.*, 1994a; Sen & Snow, 1994; Hartmann, 1995), it has also been adopted by international agencies.

6.3   A new consensus?

"...Cairo succeeded against dire predictions of doom and gloom in adopting a new global consensus on population embodied in the ICPD programme of action."

(Singh, 1998, p.161)

It may by now seem obvious that what is seen as a solution depends on what is perceived to be the problem. A government believing its territory to be relatively underpopulated may put forward policies aimed at increasing the birth rate. Conversely, many international agencies, and many developing country governments, still believe the problem is one of overpopulation, or at least of too high a rate of population growth, and their policies attempt to reduce the birth rate by reducing fertility rates. You should also realize that different views on causes and consequences will have different implications for deciding on how it is thought solutions can best be achieved. It is the views adopted by those agencies and governments which dictate what policy measures are actually implemented.

Over the last five decades, large and growing amounts of financial and human resources have been pumped into 'population control' in developing countries. In 1961, international population 'assistance' was US$6 million. In 1970 this had increased to US$125 million, by 1980 US$476 million, by 1990 US$972 million, and in 1995 it was US$2034 million (Singh, 1998, p.141). This comes mostly from USAID, The Population Council and UNFPA (UNFPA, 1990b).

In the 1950s and even more in the 1960s the activities of such international organizations and the countries funding them (donor countries) were clearly informed by the New Malthusian view. Massive support was given to direct population control initiatives as well as to contraceptive technology.

In later decades some positions appeared to change. The World Bank's *World Development Report 1984* (World Bank, 1984) was probably the most comprehensive and influential official document on population for the 1980s and early 1990s. So it is worth examining it more closely to see what official view prevailed at the time.

The Report states that 'Rapid population growth is a development problem' and that 'There are appropriate public policies to reduce fertility.' While there is welcome recognition that poverty can be a direct cause of high fertility (elements of the 'social view'), it also argues that poverty alleviation (improving income opportunities and social insurance, expanding education, employment and health opportunities for women, and so on) 'takes time to have an effect' on population. In other words, despite some acknowledgement of the importance of social factors, the official view is still largely the New Malthusian one which argues for direct population control measures (alongside development policies).

Indeed, most international population agencies and donors backed top-down programmes aimed at reducing fertility directly, rather than simply extending the availability of contraception and family planning services as one of a range of improvements to living standards (Figure 6.5).

Attempts at fertility reduction not only involved the imposition of direct means of population control: programmes used systems of incentives and disincentives aimed at increasing or decreasing fertility levels. For example, high fertility may be encouraged by increased child benefits, maternity grants, child care allowances and special family loans (as in many Eastern European countries). Disincentives include loss of tax exemption, low priority in access to education and housing for families that have more than a set number of children (as in China), or even penalties, such as delay in payments of salaries for civil servants (as in Indonesia).

Given the emphasis on population control, contraceptive methods were selected on the grounds of efficacy (for target reaching), costs, ease of delivery and duration, rather than to facilitate people's ability to determine the size of their families. Such methods included injectables (e.g. Depo Provera), implants and vaccines. It is perhaps unnecessary to point out that the most contraceptives are used by women who otherwise seem to have little control over any aspects of reproduction. Despite all these initiatives to control population, mostly in the direction of reducing it, not all people have had access to means of contraception. In many countries there is still a large 'unmet demand' for contraception from people who wish to control their fertility but do not have access to reliable means of doing so. For example, unmarried women often don't have access to contraception because of their marital status.

As mentioned earlier, ideas, emphases and priorities in population do change. An historical moment in the development of ideas about population and development has been the International Conference on Population and Development (ICPD), held in Cairo in 1994, and itself the culmination of three years of preparation. The reason for its importance is that a fundamental shift is perceived to have occurred

JANGAN RAGUKAN LAGI

KB SUDAH WAKTUNYA

Figure 6.5 All over the 'Third World' the message is the same.

there. The shift is to 'a new and broader reproductive rights approach that is fundamentally different from the prevailing family planning and demographic approach to population' (Bandarage, 1998, p.7). This is referred to as the 'new consensus'. The term is intended to reflect the coming together of two sets of positions. These are, on one hand, the position held by the organizations and individuals we have, broadly speaking, included under the 'New Malthusian view' and, on the other, those who can be broadly said to support the 'social view' and the 'women-centred view'. In fact, according to some, it was the pressure from women's and health advocates that has brought about this change (Smyth, 1996; Lassonde, 1997).

The ICPD's Programme of Action on Population and Development runs to 107 pages of recommendations covering three main areas of activity.

1 *Reproduction, women and the family.* Three significant steps, relative to thinking pre-Cairo, were accepted at the conference and feature prominently in the Programme of Action:

- the notion of 'reproductive health' replaced the term 'family planning';
- sexuality was recognized as a fundamental aspect of human existence;
- account was taken of women as people fully responsible for their own choices.

2 *The inter-relation between population dynamics and development.* Though less discussed and less pronounced than the items above, the conference adopted three programme aims – borrowed, it appears, from other UN conferences. Their significance lies in their explicit connection to population issues rather than being new ideas in themselves.

- to make the economic system sustainable;
- to stimulate economic growth in order to combat poverty;
- to recognize the right to development.

3 *Mortality, migration and the elderly*. Few commitments were made to these areas in Cairo, appearing in the Programme of Action more as issues than with 'actions' attached to them.

It is the view of some observers that the 'new consensus' has broken down long-standing differences of opinion (indeed enmities) and that outstanding issues in the population debate are 'essentially ethical rather than economic: What kind of world should we bequeath to future generations? How should resources be used and distributed? What are the limits of human rights – of the unborn and of individuals to determine what happens to themselves?' (Cassen & Bates, 1994, p.67).

However, while much is made of the 'new consensus' on the concepts of reproductive health and rights, and on the integration of concerns for population, environment and development, considerable scepticism exists. This is directed at two targets. One is the suggestion that the 'new consensus' emphasizes reproductive health and rights (especially of women) because they are instrumental to achieving population goals for their own sake (Smyth, 1996; Rosenberg, 1998). The other is that little exists in terms of mechanism and resources to ensure that meaningful changes to practices in family planning and related services actually take place. The 'new consensus' has still not put its money where its mouth is.

Summary

To summarize, let us reconsider briefly the questions posed at the beginning of the chapter.

1 Is the world overpopulated? If so, in relation to what? Overpopulation is relative: it depends on where you are talking about and on what you measure population against: food, the environment, wealth, employment, health and so on. One needs to look at the population of specific regions relative to specific factors.

2 What are the causes of population growth? Here the New Malthusians, who blame the world's ills on population growth itself, cannot help much. In fact, we have argued, they confuse consequences with causes. Continued high levels of fertility in many countries are real, but they will not be reduced without first identifying their causes. Other 'views' point to a variety of social factors largely related to poverty, and to lack of female autonomy, as partial explanations for high fertility. These views have been validated, at least in theory, by the 'new consensus' reached in Cairo.

3 Has the ICPD offered new solutions? As indicated in the last section, there has been a meeting of minds as a result of the Cairo Conference compared with the previous decades of entrenched opposing positions. The ICPD Programme of Action is, however, still just that, and the 'new consensus' has yet to be put to the test of time. The bulk of finance still goes towards population control. One may conclude that such programmes will continue to have a marginal impact on fertility until women, and men, have greater power of decision-making over the circumstances of their lives. To end on a more positive note, the new and more ample ways of thinking about population are at least now on the international agenda. Education and health provisions have entered the official vocabulary of international population agencies, as have women's empowerment and status.

7

ENVIRONMENTAL DEGRADATION AND SUSTAINABILITY

PHILIP WOODHOUSE

The second half of the twentieth century has witnessed a growing concern with the negative impact of human activity on the physical environment. By the 1990s concern with 'the global environment' had become one of the most potent factors shaping politics in industrialized countries, engendering a debate that concerns not only the environmental consequences of economic development through industrialization, but also environmental degradation in non-industrialized economies. As a result, the question of environmental change has become a key element in discussion and analysis of international development.

Q What factors determine the environmental outcome of development?

Q Are there forms of environmental degradation specific to particular patterns of economic development?

In addressing these questions, I shall first trace briefly the growth of an awareness of the 'global environment' and of a perception of the differential impact upon that environment of 'more developed' and 'less developed' economies. Secondly, I shall examine the ways that environmental problems are related to livelihoods. Finally I shall examine ideas of 'sustainable development' to see what implications they have for development policy.

7.1 The 'global environment'

A changing awareness: from 'conquest of nature' to 'managing the commons'

Transformation of the physical environment has been an integral part of the development of human society since its inception. The 'domestication' of plants and animals for agricultural production signified the modification through human intervention of the genetic composition, numbers and distribution of biological species. The construction of irrigation systems, and other systems of water control such as terracing of hillsides and dykes for flood control, constituted drastic transformations of natural ecosystems to improve conditions for human social existence. Even environments that seem natural have usually been modified by a degree of human intervention not apparent to the outsider. The pattern, common to semi-arid parts of west Africa, of scattered leguminous trees in land used for shifting cultivation and pasture, is beneficial to livestock and crops but is no more 'natural' than the traditional English landscape of hedgerows and fields.

Until comparatively recently human transformation of the environment was considered a necessary and creative activity: 'the conquest of nature'. Perception of a negative impact only began with the advent of industrial production and concerned the visible threats to health posed by 'the two great groups of nineteenth century urban killers – air pollution and water pollution, or respiratory and intestinal disease' (Hobsbawm, 1968, p.86).

The study of ecology in the post-war period, however, brought a perception of less visible dangers. Rachel Carson's book *Silent Spring*, published in the early 1960s, documented the way in which the insecticide DDT accumulated in successive stages of the food chain and reached toxic levels in the higher stages, thus killing large numbers of mammals and birds. The case of Minamata in the 1970s demonstrated a similar process in which a population of Japanese fishermen were the ultimate victims of an accumulation through the food chain of mercury entering rivers from local paper-processing mills.

This evidence of invisible but systemic damage, demonstrating interconnectedness of apparently separate processes and the cumulative damage caused by local activity, laid the basis for a questioning of the whole pattern of development through industrialization. A typical conclusion of such exercises is found in *The Limits to Growth*, published in the early 1970s: 'If the present growth trends in world population, industrialization, pollution, food production, and resource depletion continue unchanged, the limits to growth on this planet will be reached sometime within the next one hundred years. The most probable result will be a rather sudden and uncontrollable decline in both population and industrial capacity' (Meadows *et al.*, 1972).

In the 1980s, international concern was expressed through the setting up of the UN World Commission on Environment and Development (the Brundtland Commission). Its report stated:

"Over the course of this century, the relationship between the human world and the planet that sustains it has undergone a profound change. When the century began, neither human numbers nor technology had the power radically to alter planetary systems. As the century closes, not only do vastly increased human numbers and their activities have that power, but major, unintended changes are occurring in the atmosphere, in soils, in waters, among plants and animals, and in the relationships among all of these. The rate of change is outstripping the ability of scientific disciplines and our current capabilities to assess and advise. It is frustrating the attempts of political and economic institutions, which evolved in a different, more fragmented world, to adapt and cope. It deeply worries many people who are seeking ways to place those concerns on the political agendas."

(WCED, 1987)

Shortly after publication of the Brundtland Report, the 'deep worries' had indeed made their way onto the political agenda in the form of the Montreal Protocol to protect the ozone layer. This was the first international agreement on the various global effects of atmospheric pollution (Box 7.1).

Box 7.1 Managing the global commons: atmospheric pollution

Atmospheric pollution from coal burning has always been one of the more visible consequences of industrial development. As clean air legislation enforced measures to remove soot particles from flue emissions, the pollution effects of the invisible gases produced by burning coal and other fossil fuels became more apparent. In the late twentieth century vehicle exhausts overtook industrial plants as the main source of such gases in some urban areas. The principal gases produced are: carbon dioxide, carbon monoxide, sulphur dioxide, nitrogen oxides, and (in less efficient burning) hydrocarbons, such as methane. During the 1970s it was recognized that these pollutants, although comprising less than 0.1% of the atmosphere, were involved in chemical transformations in the atmosphere which created a number of hazards:

1 At a local level, in areas receiving large amounts of sunshine, ultraviolet radiation in sunlight causes nitrogen dioxide and hydrocar-

bons to react chemically, producing 'photochemical smog' close to ground level, where one of the reaction products, ozone, causes irritation to the eyes and respiratory system.

2   At a regional level, 'acid rain' results from the reaction of nitrogen oxides and sulphur dioxide with water droplets in clouds to form nitric and sulphuric acids respectively.

3   At a global scale, depletion of ozone in the upper atmosphere (stratosphere) is caused by chlorine released from compounds known as chlorofluorocarbons (CFCs). These compounds do not occur naturally, but have been manufactured since the 1930s for use as refrigerant gas, aerosol propellants, and cleaning fluids. Stratosphere ozone normally absorbs large amounts of ultraviolet radiation from the sun which would otherwise reach the earth's surface and damage biological organisms through its effect on genetic material.

4   Also at a global scale, infra-red absorbing gases (mainly carbon dioxide, methane, hydrofluorocarbons, perfluorocarbons, and sulphur hexafluoride) accumulate in the lower atmosphere (troposphere), trapping heat that otherwise would have radiated out into space and causing an increase in temperature at the earth's surface – the greenhouse effect.

The first attempts to establish binding international agreements to limit levels of atmospheric pollution were triggered by discovery of the ozone 'hole' over the Antarctic in 1985. Response was rapid. In 1987 the United Nations Environment Programme convened a meeting of 62 governments in Montreal to set out measures to halve the use of CFCs by the end of the century, a target which by 1990 had been changed to eliminate CFC manufacture completely by 2000. A key factor behind this more ambitious target was the discovery by ICI, in the UK, and DuPont, in the US, of new compounds that could be used instead of CFCs for the principal applications in refrigeration and aerosols. However, not only were these new compounds estimated to be about five times more expensive than the CFCs, but the production processes were protected by patent, unlike those for CFCs, on which patents had expired. The willingness of the UK to ratify the protocol was not shared by China or India, who argued that they had invested heavily in CFC technology and would ordinarily have expected to use CFCs in order to increase standards of living. By banning CFC use they were effectively having to accept lower living standards in order to clean up a mess created by richer nations. India finally signed the Montreal Protocol only on the understanding that international funding would be provided to assist India to acquire the new technology. Despite this international agreement, the effectiveness of the Montreal Protocol in safeguarding the ozone layer has yet to be confirmed. By 1998 NASA reported that, although CFCs in the stratosphere were no longer increasing, the ozone 'holes' above the Arctic and Antarctic continued to deteriorate – apparently an effect of a reduction in stratosphere temperatures because more heat was being trapped at the earth's surface by 'greenhouse' gases. 'It turns out that to repair the ozone layer we have to tackle the greenhouse effect too' (*New Scientist*, October 1998).

Action to reduce the greenhouse effect dates from 1988, when, at the height of a drought which destroyed much of the United States grain crop, NASA climatologist James Hansen told the US Senate's Energy and Natural Resources Committee 'the evidence is pretty strong that the greenhouse effect is here.' The same year the World Meteorological Office and the United Nations Environment Programme set up the Intergovernmental Panel on Climate Change (IPCC), which recommended in 1990 that total world emissions of carbon dioxide must be cut by 60% in order to stabilize the concentration of the gas in the atmosphere. At the 'Earth Summit' in Rio de Janeiro in 1992, 170 countries signed a framework document for a Convention on Climate Change, but commitment to specific targets for emission reduction has been slowed by sharp conflicts of interest, which came to a head at Kyoto in 1998. The US, responsible for 25% of global carbon dioxide emissions in 1990, insisted that recently industrialized countries, such as India, China, South Korea and Brazil, should commit themselves to emission reductions. While the US failed to have this included in the 'Kyoto Protocol' signed by 160 countries, it succeeded in inserting a number of provisions which allow it to achieve the same goal through bilateral negotiations. Thus, while the Kyoto Protocol commits industrialized countries to reducing their collective emissions of six greenhouse gases by an average of 5.2% by 2012, they may achieve this by action abroad, rather than at home, by means of:

1   'joint implementation', where an industrialized country builds or modernizes a power plant abroad and claims credit for reducing emissions;

2 'clean development mechanism', where an industrialized country introduces cleaner technology to a less industrialized country and claims credit for the emissions reduced;

3 'emissions trading', where emissions reductions achieved (or production foregone) in one country may be 'sold' to another country unwilling or unable to reduce emissions within its own territory.

By the time these proposals came to be discussed again, 10 months later, in Buenos Aires, it was clear that a number of industrial corporations were beginning to look for opportunities to act as 'carbon traders' by building wind, solar and other clean-energy projects in non-industrialized countries and reselling the 'carbon credits' so acquired in industrialized countries.

Environmental degradation in less industrialized countries

In the discussions of global environment by the Brundtland Commission and others, two specific concerns stand out in relation to environmental degradation in less industrialized countries.

Firstly, there is a fear that as these countries do industrialize there will be a large increase in pollution, particularly the atmospheric pollution which it has been claimed will cause catastrophic climatic change (Figure 7.1). This fear is derived from comparisons of consumption of resources, and particularly energy, in industrialized and non-industrialized countries. These show an average annual carbon dioxide emission of 5.4 tonnes per person in the United States,

Figure 7.1 Atmospheric pollution then and now: (top) contemporary painting of Manchester, 1830; (above) Shanghai 1980.

compared with only 0.3 tonnes per person in India.

The Brundtland Commission claimed that in order to supply everyone in the world with a level of consumption equal to that now enjoyed by those in industrialized countries, global energy consumption would need to increase fivefold, entailing a similar increase in the atmospheric pollution which results from energy generation through burning coal, oil or gas. Others have argued further that, whereas technological change has increased the efficiency of energy use in industrialized countries, large-scale industrialization using older (and more polluting) tech-

nology will cause a disproportionate increase in global pollution levels. Thus, of China's plans to industrialize by using its coal reserves to generate power (as Britain did in the nineteenth century), Greenpeace's Director of Science said 'It is an energy plan which spells death-by-climate for millions and disaster for all.'

There is evidence to support such fears. Where rapid industrialization has been attempted in the past – most notably in the Soviet Union and China – it has often employed 'dirty' technology on a vast scale with scant concern for environmental impact (Box 7.2). This experience continues to shape environmentalists' reactions to

---

Box 7.2   False economies on a grand scale: Soviet management of the Aral Sea Basin

In 1960 the Aral Sea, in Central Asia, covered 66 900 km^2 and was the world's fourth largest inland water reservoir. For centuries the Aral Sea Basin, which includes the Aral Sea and the area around its two tributaries (the Amu Darya and the Syr Darya), had been developed using irrigation and drainage systems to support agriculture around the ancient cities along the Silk Road. Irrigated land in the Basin in 1900 is estimated at 1 million ha. In the 1930s, the Soviet Union began expanding irrigated cotton production in the Basin by introducing large-scale irrigation systems. In the early 1950s, one of the Aral Sea's tributaries (the Amu Darya) was diverted into the Kara Kum desert of Turkmenistan to feed an accelerating expansion of irrigated cotton in the Aral Sea Basin to 4.5 million ha in 1960 and 7.5 million ha by 1992. Much of this expanded irrigation was inefficient (about 60% of water diverted from the Amu Darya is lost), and waterlogging resulted in widespread salinization of the soil. As a result, an increasing amount of water is needed simply to leach salt from the soil. The diversion of its tributary dramatically reduced the annual volume of water reaching the Aral Sea, from 45–55 km^3 in the early 1960s to 7 km^3 in the early 1980s. As a result, the current volume of the Aral Sea is a quarter of its 1960 level, and the Sea has shrunk into two lakes, with the larger and shallower lake in the south looking set to split again. Water quality in the Sea has also deteriorated. Salinity has increased to levels close to that of the oceans. Rudimentary sewage discharge from increasing populations

has resulted in frequent contamination with typhus, paratyphoid, and viral hepatitis. Profligate use of highly subsidized fertilizers and pesticides on cotton fields has resulted in heavy chemical contamination of water draining into the Sea. With fish stocks unable to survive in increasingly saline and contaminated waters, the fishing industry of the Aral Sea has been destroyed. In addition to deteriorating conditions for human health in the area, the shrinking of the Aral Sea has resulted in major ecological and local climate changes, some of which (such as the reduction in frost-free days) have negative implications for cotton cultivation.

With the break-up of the Soviet Union, the Aral Sea Basin has become subject to international management between the governments of upstream (and water-supplying) Kyrgystan and Tajikistan and downstream (and water-using) Uzbekistan and Turkmenistan. After the long period of unitary Soviet planning and management, the demands of co-ordination and co-operation over water use are unfamiliar. Further, the potential for conflict over water allocation is accentuated by the heavy reliance of all these governments on irrigated agriculture for employment, foreign exchange, and, increasingly, food. Improved efficiency in irrigation and drainage systems is urgently needed, but may be difficult to achieve because existing large-scale irrigation systems are likely to be even more problematic if moves to decollectivize them lead to fragmentation of water management.

(Spoor, 1998)

---

energy projects which could reduce greenhouse gas emissions, such as the Three Gorges Dam being constructed on the Yangtze river in China. The 690 km reservoir behind the dam will displace 1.2 million people but the dam's turbines will generate electricity that would have otherwise required burning 50 million tons of coal and the emission of 100 million tons of carbon dioxide annually (Xiong Lei, 1998).

Box 7.2 gives a different kind of example of a very large project aimed at accelerating development in a less industrialized part of the Soviet Union, and the enormous environmental problems caused. However, while criticism of such projects focuses on their scale, it is also clear that small-scale industry can be equally devastating, particularly when developed under a laissez-faire regulatory regime. To the example of coal mining in China (Box 7.3; Figure 7.2) can be added examples of major environmental hazards from mercury pollution of rivers caused by artisanal gold mining in Brazil, and chromium pollution in groundwater caused by small-scale tanneries in India. There is evidently no guarantee that small is always beautiful.

Yet the unfolding negotiations to agree action to reduce emissions of carbon dioxide show few industrialized countries willing to lead by example. The 'Kyoto Protocol' committing 160 signatory countries to quantitative emission

---

Box 7.3 Liberalization and enterprise in coal mining in Shenmu County, China

Shenmu County is at the centre of the coalfields in Shaanxi province, northern China. It is a semi-arid area (448 mm annual rainfall) and, in addition to drought, severe frost and hailstorms make farming hazardous. The loess (wind-blown deposits) soils are very prone to erosion and the area was subject to special conservation measures in the 1950s. Irrigated vegetables have for many years been grown along the banks of the Kuye river, a tributary of the Yellow river. Until the early 1980s coal mining was undertaken only by state-owned companies, and the commune system effectively imposed the prohibition on farmers engaging in mineral extraction. With the abolition of the commune system in the early 1980s came privatization of farming and an exodus of farm labour from agriculture. The Village and Town Enterprise schemes have assisted these erstwhile farmers to find alternative incomes in small-scale industry in rural areas. In Shenmu, this has led to a boom in small-scale coal mining.

Before 1980 only 8 state-owned mines existed in Shenmu County. After 1980, a further 225 mines were opened, of which 143 were still operational in 1994. The majority of these (128) were private or collective, and the remainder (15) were state owned. Output of coal grew from less than 4 million tonnes per year in 1985 to 19 million tonnes per year in 1994. However, most of this is produced from a few mines, since 113 small mines produced less than 30 000 tonnes per year between them. Nonetheless, lax regulation makes even very inefficient coal mining profitable. The priority given by the County authorities to maximizing economic growth means that the Environment Protection Bureau of the County's Department of Conservation is poorly resourced and 'acts as an ear for the deaf'. As a consequence, environmental regulations are routinely flouted, and statutory fines levied at token levels. The proliferation of small mining operations has had devastating consequences. Within Shenmu County, the 19 million tonnes of coal output, together with 36 coking plants consuming 150 000 tonnes of coal, generates 68 million tonnes of solid waste and 11 million tonnes of liquid waste each year. Of this, more than 60% is dumped in rivers, blocking channels and increasing risks of floods which in 1989 caused damage to infrastructure and land equivalent in value to the whole of the 1987 coal output (US$1.45 million). River pollution has resulted in the failure of irrigated crop production along the Kuye river since 1990, and growing health problems for people in the area, which has no water treatment plants. Air pollution by smoke and dust from coking plants, and from the 50 000 tonnes of coal estimated lost each year from accidental fires, has been measured as 59 times the statutory maximum allowed by air quality regulations. Within Shenmu County, coal mining is estimated to have resulted in the loss of 280 ha of arable land, further pollution damage to 1005 ha, and the death, on average, of one mineworker each month in 1994, mainly from mine roof collapse.

(From Wei Hu, 1998)

reduction targets was to become binding only after ratification by countries accounting for 55% of carbon emissions. Yet the US, accounting alone for 25% of global carbon emissions and therefore the key to ratification, refused to sign until the US Congress was satisfied that the Protocol provided scope for US emissions targets to be achieved through bilateral 'trade' with other countries (Box 7.1). Through this effective veto, business and consumer interests in the US sought to ensure that implementation of the Protocol would be responsive to their purchasing power, rather than the reverse. Thus, while in some parts of the European Union there appeared some commitment to political action to

reduce carbon emissions (for example, through taxation policy on production and consumption), in most of the industrialized world action seemed likely to be firmly anchored to the emergence of new business opportunities provided by cleaner technology, exemplified by heavy investments in the development of electric cars by Toyota and in solar power by Shell and BP. In the meantime, commentators on the 'discouraging fudges, missed deadlines, and disappointing targets' of international efforts to reduce greenhouse emissions looked in dismay at accumulating evidence of record temperatures and extreme, devastating, weather events (Figure 7.3). In the wake of a hurricane which left more than 11 000 dead

Figure 7.2   Coal mining in Shaanxi Province, northern China.

Figure 7.3   Is global warming causing more extreme weather as well as threatening a rise in average sea level? Devastation caused by Hurricane Mitch in Tegucigalpa, capital of Honduras, 1998.

in Central America in 1998, the *Guardian* newspaper (9 November 1998) observed: 'Dreadful though Hurricane Mitch's devastation has been, the threat from future disasters is of a much grimmer dimension: whole populations displaced as deltas – like the Nile, Mekong and Ganges – are submerged. Who will house, clothe, and feed the displaced?'

While the spread of industrialization typifies one set of environmental concerns, the lack of industrial development is often associated with another set of environmental pressures (Box 7.4). This view sees increasing rural population in non-industrial countries as the main cause for concern, not because they have high levels of consumption, but because their poverty is held

Box 7.4 A 'politics of scarcity'

In *The State of the World 1998* (Brown, 1998), Lester Brown asks: 'Can China, the world's fastest-growing economy during the 1990s, achieve US consumption levels? Can people everywhere expect to one day live like Americans?' (pp.3–4).

He then goes on to detail the challenges:

'As the economy grows, pressures on the Earth's natural systems and resources intensify. From 1950 to 1997, the use of lumber tripled, that of paper increased sixfold, the fish catch increased nearly fivefold, grain consumption nearly tripled, fossil fuel burning nearly quadrupled, and air and water pollutants multiplied severalfold. The unfortunate reality is that the economy continues to expand, but the ecosystem on which it depends does not, creating an increasingly stressed relationship.

'The vast rangelands that are used to support herds of cattle and flocks of sheep are not suitable for farming. Roughly double the area of world cropland, this land supports 1.32 billion cattle and 1.72 billion sheep and goats. With the growth of these herds and flocks tracking the growth in human populations, the growing demand for meat, milk, leather, and other livestock products has led to extensive overgrazing. As Africa's population has grown by leaps and bounds, so have its livestock numbers. Some of the most severe overstocking of rangelands comes in areas where people depend on cattle, sheep, and goats for their livelihoods, including much of Africa, the Middle East, Central Asia, the Indian subcontinent, and much of western and northern China...With rangelands now being pushed to their limits and beyond, future growth in the supply of beef and mutton can only come from feedlots, which in turn puts additional pressure on the world's cropland.

'As the consumption of grain and other agricultural products has tripled since mid-century, farmers have extended agriculture onto marginal lands, some of it in areas where rainfall is low and soils are vulnerable to wind erosion... In Africa, a continent where soils are shallow to begin with, soil losses can disproportionately shrink the grain harvest. Its rapid population growth and rapid soil erosion (perhaps the fastest of any continent) are on a collision course... Among the countries in Africa suffering heavy soil losses are Botswana, Lesotho, Madagascar, Nigeria, Rwanda, and Zimbabwe. Nigeria, Africa's most populous country, is suffering from extreme gully erosion...[N]ot one of these governments is addressing the soil erosion threat effectively. As a result, the next generation of farmers in Africa will try to feed not the 719 million people of today, but the 1.45 billion in the year 2025 – and with far less topsoil' (Brown, 1998, pp.8–9).

Brown then sets out a scenario in which agricultural productivity in the US has reached a plateau: 'The slower rise in world grainland productivity during the 1990s may mark the transition from a half-century dominated by food surpluses to a future that will be dominated by food scarcity...National security in this new era dictates that governments devise agricultural and population policies that enable them to avoid excessive dependence on imported food...At the root of these difficult problems is population growth...In the Middle East...the 1995 population of 215 million is projected to reach 443 million by 2030, forcing this water-limited region to import most of its grain...The projected growth in sub-Saharan Africa is even more staggering...With thin soils and a limited potential for irrigation, Africa seems destined to become a massive importer of grain – assuming that countries in the region can compete for what are likely to be scarce supplies' (Brown, 1998, pp.91–4).

to drive them to seek survival through means which degrade the resources on which they depend.

If you consider whether you have encountered similar ideas in earlier chapters, particularly those on population and food, you will probably identify the standpoint of the author as a 'New-Malthusian' one. Here let us note two particular problems with this view that you should be able to relate to criticisms in previous chapters.

First, aggregate statistics tell us very little about individuals' economic circumstances, which vary widely. In Chapter 3 we saw, for example, that, famines are not caused by a decline in total food availability (and in Chapter 6 we noted that world food production has consistently increased faster than world population for the past 30 years), but by a failure of 'entitlement' of individuals to that supply.

Second, the original Malthusian analysis rested on the assumption that the only way of increasing the production of food on a fixed land area was through the investment of more human labour, a process that Malthus considered ultimately self-defeating as an ever greater proportion of the total production would be needed to feed the labour force. As the economist Edward Barbier (1989, p.8) has observed: 'this constraint on growth in the Malthusian system would be broken through introducing the substitution of capital for labour in agriculture', i.e. by increasing the productivity of labour. Similarly, the modern idea of 'carrying capacity', implying a fixed relationship between a human population and its immediate environment, does not hold wherever technical or social change alters that relationship.

In addition to these aspects you have encountered earlier, the notion of a fixed 'carrying capacity' for human activity has been undermined by recent ecological studies which have pointed out that in many natural environments important features fluctuate so much that, on timescales relevant to humans, they should be considered not as tending to some single 'balance of nature' but of potentially shifting between different more or less stable states. In extreme cases, some ecosystems can be seen to

be in permanent 'disequilibrium'. Examples include mountainous areas subject to accelerated erosion and landslides, drylands subject to extreme fluctuations of rainfall from one year to the next, river floodplains, in which channels and sedimentation patterns alter from one flood to the next. This interpretation of nature has suggested that, to understand how human activity affects ecology, we need to be able to recognize the context of uncertainty which attaches to processes of environmental change.

We can see, therefore, that a variety of technical and social factors have a central role in determining the environmental impact of human populations. Thus, where environmental degradation is concerned, we should not be concerned with numbers or even densities of people, but rather with how they gain their livelihood. It is livelihoods which establish the relationship of human populations with their environment. If we wish to identify elements of environmental degradation characteristic of non-industrialized countries, we need therefore to consider the nature of economic activity in such countries and how it might have a different relationship to the environment from that in industrialized countries.

7.2 Livelihoods and environment in the global economy

Relating livelihoods to the environment

All human activity exploits the environment:

- through the use of natural resources as raw materials ('renewable' resources in the case of plants and animals, wind and water power; 'non-renewable' in the case of minerals for production and fossil fuels);

- through the use of the environment to accept waste products. The capacity of the environment to transform waste into harmless forms can be regarded as a 'renewable' environmental resource.

The intensity of exploitation of these resources determines the environmental consequences, in terms of the depletion of non-renewable resources and degradation of renewable resources.

An important distinction we need to make in economic activity is between primary commodity production and manufacturing. The former refers to agriculture, timber and other tree products, fisheries, mining, energy production; the latter includes food processing and relatively simple transformations to make paper, glass, or textiles, as well as extremely complex processes to make pharmaceuticals, or assemble machinery. The important point here is that complex manufacturing, which forms its products from a combination of different raw materials, offers more flexibility of resource use than primary commodity production. Whereas in primary commodity production the composition of the commodity (e.g. copper, or groundnuts) is fixed, and therefore so are the environmental resources used to make it, there is considerable scope to alter the composition of manufactured products: copper piping can be substituted by plastic or even steel; cooking oil can be made from a variety of different vegetable oils besides groundnut oil.

We should note here that the capacity to change the composition of manufactured output is critically dependent upon the availability of capital to invest in technological change, and cheap energy to allow transportation of raw materials from distant sources.

The importance of the distinction between primary commodities and manufacturing from an environmental standpoint is that an increase in output of primary commodities is more likely to be achievable only through increasing the intensity of exploitation of local resources, with attendant risks of degradation of those resources (exhaustion of mineral reserves, depletion of fish stocks, reduction in soil fertility etc.). By contrast, manufacturing output may be increased, if the capital and cheap energy supplies are available, by drawing on a multiplicity of more or less distant sources of raw materials. The local environmental impact from manufacturing is the waste energy and materials that cause pollution.

Table 7.1 has been assembled from UN statistics on world trade. It compares different regions in terms of their overall share in world exports, and also the percentage of their exports accounted for by manufactured goods and primary commodities, and, within the latter, by agricultural commodities.

The table shows clearly the way that primary production dominates the economic activity of sub-Saharan Africa, and to a lesser extent Latin America. The category 'East Asia' aggregates important manufacturing economies like Korea and Taiwan, in which manufactures form more than 90% of exports, and others like Malaysia and Indonesia, in which primary commodities make up over half of exports. Overall, however, as in China, East Asian exports rely even less on primary commodities than do those of the 'developed economies' of Europe, North America, and Japan. The first column of the table also shows the domination of world trade by manu-

Table 7.1 **Percentage share of total world export value, and percentage share of primary commodities and manufactures in merchandise exports for selected areas**

	Percentage share of total value of world exports	Percentage of exports accounted for by:		
		Manufactures	Food and agricultural raw materials	Other primary commodities
Developed economies	64	83	11	5
East Asia	15	84	8	7
China	3	86	10	4
Latin America	5	54	25	20
Sub-Saharan Africa	1	16	33	49

Source: *UN World Economic and Social Survey* (1998, p.141, table A16: Commodity Composition of World Trade: Exports 1985–1996), United Nations, Geneva.

facturing economies, and, conversely, the tiny proportion of total world export value accruing to economies dependent on primary commodity exports.

Implications of dependence on primary commodity production

This division of the world into countries producing manufactures and others producing primary commodities dates from the time of European expansion and colonialism (see Chapters 11 and 12).

During the latter half of the twentieth century prices of primary commodities have undergone a long-term decline relative to those of manufactures, with the exception of the period of economic boom following the Second World War (Figure 7.4). During the 1980s the fall in commodity prices became precipitate, reaching the lowest levels recorded in the twentieth century. Only in the mid-1990s did the fall in commodity prices appear to have slowed. The decline in commodity prices can be traced to four main changes in the pattern of demand, production, and trade in the industrialized countries.

1 Demand for primary commodity exports is closely linked to overall economic activity in industrialized countries, and this slowed down after the 1970s, relative to the boom of the postwar period.

2 The structure of consumption in industrialized economies has altered, with consumption of manufactured goods growing less quickly than consumption of services, which require little or no input of primary commodities.

3 Technological changes in manufacturing processes, involving greater efficiency in the use of materials, increased recycling of scrap materials, and increased substitution by synthetic materials, have reduced dependence on primary commodity inputs.

4 Agricultural protectionism has increased in industrialized countries. In Japan, the United States, and the EU countries, a willingness to pay high prices to local agricultural producers has stimulated overproduction of agricultural surpluses, which then need to be sold, often at much lower (i.e. subsidized) prices on the world market. This practice, which not only effectively closes markets for agricultural commodities in

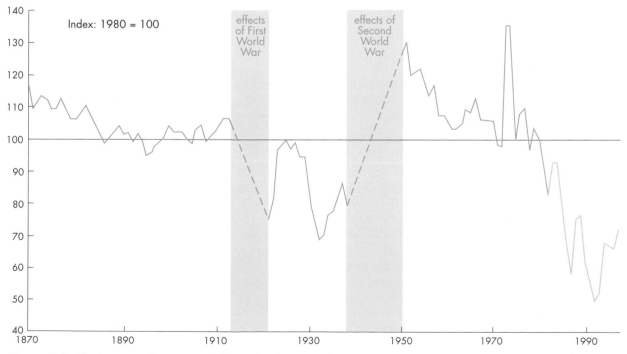

Figure 7.4   Real commodity prices deflated by the price of manufactures, 1870–1997. (Data to 1981 from ODI, 1988; data from 1982 from United Nations, 1998, table A19.)

industrialized countries to overseas exporters, but also generally lowers the world price for such commodities, was the object of trade liberalization measures negotiated during the Uruguay Round of GATT (General Agreement on Tariffs and Trade). However, the long timescale allowed for dismantling agricultural support programmes means its continuance beyond the millennium.

These trends have two main results. Firstly, the consumption of primary commodities is either declining or rising less than economic growth in general. Whereas environmentalists in the 1970s saw depletion of mineral reserves as an important limit to world economic growth, few were so preoccupied in the 1990s. Secondly, for countries whose export income depends on primary commodities, falling prices has meant reduced income. Each unit of output of primary commodities can be exchanged for a decreasing number of units of manufactured goods.

Governments of economies dependent on primary commodity production have responded to this situation by cutting imports, by borrowing, and by increasing the output of primary commodities and reducing the cost of such output. There is evidence, however, that these responses have not improved matters:

- Reduction of imports has reduced the capacity of manufacturing industry to maintain or replace equipment, thus further diminishing local manufacturing output.

- Borrowing was favoured in the 1970s as a means of 'recycling' the large surplus cash deposits of oil-exporting countries. In the 1980s, however, the drop in commodity prices and the increase in interest rates increased the debt liability of many primary commodity producing countries, while simultaneously reducing their capacity to repay. The burden of debt greatly increases the need for greater economic production, without producing any improvement in living standards or consumption in the indebted nation: in Brazil and Indonesia in 1988 the interest due on outstanding debt was equivalent to 42% and 40% of export earnings respectively.

- For governments of countries dependent upon exports of primary commodities, the need to 'service' their debts may present little option but to maximize output of these commodities, to try and recover lost revenues through greater volume of production. Indeed, this strategy was the one advocated by the World Bank in its prescriptions of 'structural adjustment' for indebted nations. However, increased production of the same commodity by different countries tends to depress prices further, and in some cases has precipitated a collapse in the market.

For example, in 1989 the Indonesian government was planning to double cocoa production within five years and take its share of the world market from 3% to 12% by the end of the century. At the same time, though, falling prices were wrecking the livelihoods of established West African growers, and causing an exodus of people from the countryside in Côte d'Ivoire and Ghana (Box 7.5; Figure 7.5). The main advantages of Indonesian producers were that their productivity was high, but also that the wages of rural labourers were extremely low. The decline in commodity prices therefore places a premium on low production costs, and the need to achieve these may require damage to the environment as well as to workers' standards of living.

Figure 7.5 An Ivorian farmer examines pods bulging with cocoa beans on a plantation near Gagnoa.

Box 7.5 Cocoa production in Ghana

Camp Number One is a cocoa-producing village in the Ashante region of Ghana. It has a population of 500 people, most of whom settled and planted their trees after the area was logged in the 1960s. Although cocoa farming provides most of their income, it also allows them to grow about 65% of their food by keeping chickens and intercropping yams, cassava, and bananas. From their cash income they buy cooking oil, sugar, salt, bread, dried fish, and sometimes meat.

In the late 1970s and early 1980s West African cocoa farmers were hit hard when world cocoa prices fell from almost US$4800 per ton to less than a third of that. Since the Ghanaian marketing organization, Cocobod, was paying farmers only 40% of the world price, the effect on farmers' income was disastrous. Many farmers left their cocoa farms and migrated to urban areas, while others switched to growing food crops, such as maize and cassava, whose prices were more stable. Ghanaian cocoa production fell drastically, from a third of the world total in 1972 to only 12% a decade later. Governments in Ghana and the Côte d'Ivoire, which relied on tax revenues from cocoa to fund public works, education and health, as well as to meet debt repayments, had little option but to accept intervention from the World Bank and the International Monetary Fund to 'rescue' the economy with a 'structural adjustment package' which resulted in higher prices for farmers but a 90% cut in Cocobod's staff and the loss of many subsidies and services for cocoa farming. Despite these measures, a continued fall in world cocoa prices through the late 1980s meant cash flow problems for marketing organizations and payment arrears and poverty for farmers. By the mid-1990s cocoa prices were on the increase. Cocobod paid farmers 50% of the international price and committed itself to raising this to 65%. However, removal of subsidies and devaluation of the Ghanaian cedi pushed agrochemical inputs beyond the reach of most cocoa farmers: a two-year increase of 107% in cocoa prices was outstripped by increases of 657% for insecticides, 250% for fungicides, and 400% for spraying equipment.

Today, few young people see a future in village life farming cocoa. Many of Ghana's 500 000–600 000 cocoa farmers are in their sixties and seventies. Increasingly, cocoa farm owners are absentee city-dwellers who leave the production of the crop to a million or so 'caretakers' who receive 30–50% of the income, depending on the level of their input to the farm. The future contribution of cocoa to livelihoods in Ghana depends critically on the way cocoa consumption develops. Downward pressure on prices will continue because major chocolate producers are reducing the cocoa content of their products and replacing it with cheaper fat substitutes. Ghanaian cocoa production on smallholdings averaging 2 acres faces stiff competition from lower-cost producers on large plantations in Brazil and Indonesia. Attempts to create more jobs from cocoa in Ghana, by establishing a chocolate industry in Tema and Takoradi, have been hindered by high tariff walls in export markets (34% in the EU), by the small domestic market, and by competition in the West African region from multinationals like Nestlé and Cadbury. On the positive side, Ghanaian cocoa is valued for its quality and commands a premium price. This has been exploited by a Ghanaian farmers' organization Kuapa Kokoo which established a cocoa-purchasing company in 1993 with the aim of selling to fair-trade organizations in Europe. With 30 000 members organized in 160 local societies, in 1997 the company was able to pay members 500 cedis per bag more than Cocobod, contributed 300 cedis per bag to the local societies, and make a profit of 700 cedis per bag. The organization has successfully reduced marketing costs by giving farmers a larger role in local purchasing, and has achieved higher margins by selling all but 11% of its cocoa to fair trade organizations which offer a premium of 10–12% on the world price. Kuapa Kokoo is seeking to further bolster the premium for its cocoa by assisting farmers to qualify as organic producers by adopting integrated pest management methods. It remains to be seen, however, whether enough European consumers are ready to pay higher prices for higher quality for this strategy to secure the livelihoods of Ghanaian cocoa farmers.

(Adapted from Swift, 1998, pp.7–30)

A similar process occurred in tin mining in the 1980s. In 1985 the price of tin collapsed as a result of the failure of the International Tin Council to maintain market stabilization operations on the London Metal Exchange. In the following three-year period tin production remained static or fell in all the principal producing countries except China and Brazil. The International Monetary Fund (IMF) observed:

> "World mine production of tin is estimated to have risen in 1988 by 11%. A large part of the increase occurred in Brazil where mine output was raised by over 50% to 44 thousand tons. As a consequence, Brazil accounted for over 20% of world mine production in 1988 compared with less than 4% in 1982 and is now the world's largest producer. The increase in 1988 came largely from the Amazon State of Rondônia where production from a new low-cost mine began in September 1987."
>
> (IMF, *Primary Commodities. Market Developments and Outlook*, July 1989)

In 1989, British Petroleum, which owned 49.5% of the open-cast tin mine in Rondônia, was defending itself against newspaper reports of devastation of thousands of hectares of rainforest by its mining operation:

> "The company admitted that re-afforestation had not been attempted, because the land that had been used for extraction of prime-grade tin ore, and was now lying spoilt, might be brought back into use for lesser grades if the price of tin rose. The mine management did have a plan for eventual re-afforestation, the company said, but BP's stake was in any case about to be sold to another large British company, RTZ. There were no environmental restrictions on the sale, a BP spokesman said."
>
> (*The Times*, 19 June 1989)

The pursuit of increased output of primary commodities may intensify the exploitation of environmental resources to the point where degradation of livelihoods may be catastrophic. It has been argued that the Sahelian famine of the 1970s (Box 7.6) was an outcome of this kind, the result of reckless extension of groundnut cultivation into marginal rainfall areas.

At the level of individual livelihoods, what is the response to low commodity prices? In Box 7.5 we saw two general effects of a crash in agricultural prices: a migrant labour force, on the one hand, and on the other, a residual, part-time, under-resourced agriculture. For those left on the land, lack of resources confronts the immediate need for subsistence and reproduction. A more intense exploitation of local resources (land, trees, pasture) may present the only alternative, despite the environmental degradation which results. Here we have an agent of environmental destruction we can perhaps identify from the extract in Box 7.4.

In this section I have argued that the specific form that environmental degradation takes in different parts of the world has its roots in the structure of the world economy. It is not that environmental degradation in less industrialized economies is worse than that in developed countries, but that it appears to many that it is less amenable to intervention because it is the result of economic desperation rather than profligate consumption.

7.3 Sustainable development

Whose development, whose environment?

When we considered the 'New Malthusian' diagnosis of the causes of environmental degradation (Box 7.4), we observed that reliance on aggregate statistics is one reason why such an approach fails to identify why environmental change happens. By looking at environmental problems such as deforestation in specific cases, we can quickly see the extent to which 'New Malthusian' views misrepresent the agencies at work in deforestation. Box 7.7 gives an account of deforestation in Malaysia constructed from press reports in 1989–98 (also see Figure 7.6), and it is worth taking a little time to note all the different groups and interests involved.

Box 7.6 Groundnut cultivation and environmental degradation in Niger

In the postwar period European consumption of vegetable oils far outstripped local production and so US exports of soya beans to Europe were vigorously promoted. The trade quickly incorporated sales of seedcake (residue after extracting the oil) for incorporation into animal feed, and US soya bean processors established milling plants in Europe to supply the animal feed and vegetable oil markets. As a result, US exports of soya increased from 47 000 tons of soya seedcake in 1949 to 5 million tons of seedcake and 13 million tons of soya beans in the early 1970s. The near total dependency of the rapidly expanding intensive livestock (pigs and poultry) industry in Europe on American soya bean imports caused alarm to the French authorities who attempted to secure alternative sources of oilseedcake by stimulating the production of groundnut in its Sahelian colonial territories. In some of these, such as Senegal, groundnut production had been established at the turn of the century and the efforts to increase production emphasized the provision of credit and subsidized supply of seed and other inputs. In Niger, the area of groundnut cultivation increased rapidly, from 142 thousand hectares in 1954 to over 300 thousand hectares in 1957.

Intensive promotion of research by the colonial government resulted in the development of varieties with shorter growing seasons and, assisted by a number of seasons of favourable rainfall, the years following formal independence of Niger from France in 1961 saw a further expansion of groundnut cultivation, which covered 432 000 ha in 1968. Research by Richard Franke and Barbara Chasin (1981) indicates that the expansion of groundnut cultivation in Niger profoundly changed patterns of land use. Land was brought into cultivation that would have remained fallow, thus reducing recuperation of soil fertility and eliminating vegetation that would normally serve for grazing: cultivation was also extended into marginal rainfall areas traditionally used by pastoralists for grazing livestock according to a 'transhumant' management pattern (moving seasonally from one area to another to take advantage of seasonal vegetation growth). The overall effect was seriously to reduce the pasture available for pastoralists' herds and to generate conflict between pastoralists and cultivators for control of land.

The onset of drought in 1968 found pastoralists very vulnerable to shortage of pasture, therefore, and by the end of the drought, in 1974, FAO estimates suggested some 39% of the total cattle in Niger had died through lack of water or lack of pasture. The loss of their animals left many pastoralists entirely destitute, and the ensuing famine conditions established an imagery of African agriculture that was to be reinforced throughout the following decade, providing many environmentalists with the evidence of the eco-catastrophe that they had been predicting.

Of the struggle by the French government to resist dependency on American soya bean imports, Franke and Chasin have observed: 'It was ultimately a losing battle: by 1971, France imported 1.3 million tons of soya, of which 773 544 tons came from the US as opposed to only 318 332 tons of groundnuts. Nonetheless, this losing battle was fought not only on the fields of France, but also in Niger.'

The balance of the oilseed war changed by the 1980s: the US monopoly of soya bean exports was effectively broken by the rapid increase in production of soya beans in Brazil and Argentina, who between them accounted for nearly of a third of world production in 1989. European dependency on oilseed imports was reduced by increasing production of rapeseed and sunflower seed within Europe supported by the Common Agricultural Policy. By 1988 Niger's dependency had also undergone a change, although one promising dubious long-term security: 76% of the country's export income was derived from the extraction of uranium ore.

Figure 7.6   (top) Logs awaiting shipment from Limbang in the north of Sarawak; (above) Penan spokesman Unga Paranb and Mutang Urud of the Kelabit people at an international meeting in London.

Box 7.7   'Developing' the rainforest in Sarawak

Sarawak, in north-west Borneo, is one of the states of the Malaysian Federation. It has been for some time the largest source of unprocessed (log) tropical timber in the world. During the 1980s the annual output of logs doubled, reaching about 15 million cubic metres, worth about £2.5 billion, in 1990. The rapid increase in Sarawak's output accompanied reductions in supply from other important sources of timber in South-east Asia: log exports from Indonesia were banned in 1985 and all logging in Thailand was banned in 1988.

Two-thirds of Sarawak's log exports go to Japan, and Japanese companies Mitsubishi, Marubeni, and C.Itoh are active in logging operations, either directly or as owners or partners of local logging companies. Logging companies gain access to the Sarawak forests by obtaining 'concessions', of 10–20 years' duration, from Malaysian concession owners. In

1987, the State Chief Minister, Abdul Taib Mahmud, accused his predecessor of corruption in the distribution of concessions. It subsequently emerged that many state politicians had acquired concessions and other interests in logging. Two of the most prominent were the State Chief Minister himself, who was also Minister for Forestry, and James Wong, Minister for the Environment, whose logging company, Limbang Trading, had a logging concession of 300 000 ha.

Most of the concessions are for 'selective logging', in which a maximum of 10 mature trees per hectare are supposed to be cut, allowing the remaining trees to regenerate the forest cover sufficiently to allow a similar cutting after 30 years. Critics say that the selective logging process is poorly policed and that in practice the impact of logging roads and damage to other trees during felling and log removal results in a loss of 40% of the tree cover.

In 1990, a report commissioned by the timber traders' association, the International Tropical Timber Organization (ITTO) concluded that logging in Sarawak was not sustainable and, unless annual output was cut to less than 9 million cubic metres, the primary forests in the state would be 'logged out' within 11 years. In practice logging continued at about double this rate for the next five years and timber exports became Malaysia's 'green gold': the second largest source of export earnings, after oil. The impact of the logging process was felt particularly by the 200 000 native inhabitants of the forest, whose livelihood is based on small-scale agriculture (2 ha cleared each year by each family, estimated to account for a total of 72 000 ha of cultivation per year), hunting, fishing, harvest of nuts, resins, and making rattan products. Encroachment of logging activities on forest people's land frightened away wildlife, caused soil erosion which increased sediment loads in rivers, with negative consequences for fishing and drinking water supply, and damaged large numbers of nut- and resin-producing trees.

In 1988, one group of rainforest people, the Penan, started blockading the logging roads where they entered their part of the forest, and disrupted logging operations. Through Harrison Ngau, a member of Malaysian Friends of the Earth, and one of the protest organizers, the conflict received publicity in London and New York. In 1989 the World Rainforest Movement petitioned the UN General Assembly to defend the land rights of forest peoples against their governments.

Justifying his government's rejection of the Penan's claims, the Malaysian Prime Minister was quoted in 1989 as saying that the Penans were 'unfortunate people exploited by crusading environmentalists who wanted the tribe kept as ill-fed and disease-ridden museum pieces.' Throughout the 1990s resistance to logging in Sarawak was mounted through international campaigns to boycott Malaysian tropical timber exports, and through continued blockades mounted by Penans on logging roads. The Malaysian authorities responded uncompromisingly. By 1995 some 700 people had been arrested, detained and fined, and in 1993 forest legislation was altered to allow easier prosecution for disrupting logging in Sarawak. However, High Court judges repeatedly upheld Penan refusal to pay fines, and released them, often

on grounds of local police and magistrates' failure to observe legal procedure. In 1990, Jewin Lehnen, chairman of the Sarawak Penan Association, had said: 'It's simply wrong to say we don't want development. But by development we don't mean timber companies invading our land. We want the right to live here, and use our land, without disturbance. Then we want development in terms of schooling for our children and clinics to treat illnesses. But all these things we can get only when the logging stops and our rights are recognized.' By 1996 he had been reduced to despair. Of 9500 Penan, all but a few hundred had been relocated to government settlements, and environmentalists conceded defeat: 'It's pretty much over in Sarawak. The bulldozers are on ships steaming toward PNG and other fresh rainforests.'

One outcome of the logging of Sarawak has been to establish Malaysian logging companies as a major force internationally. In 1997, the largest, Rimbuuan Hijau, controlled 60% of government concession areas in neighbouring Papua New Guinea. In the same year, Malaysian Samling in consortium with a Korean partner obtained a concession of nearly 1.6 million hectares in Surinam, and WTK purchased a quarter of a million ha in the Brazilian Amazon. In Sarawak, the Asian recession in 1998 caused a slowdown in logging rates, but half the land remains zoned for logging, 8% is to be permanently protected, and the rest is to be deforested, mainly for plantations of oil palm and other trees to feed a major expansion of Malaysia's paper industry, with six integrated pulp and paper mills planned for Sarawak by the year 2000. In 1996 the government announced tax concessions to encourage plantation investment, and modifications to the land code 'to streamline the identification and acquisition processes of Native Customary Rights Land and protect the interests of investors in the tree plantation sector.' In 1997, newspapers reported the release of 42 Iban – neighbours of the Penan – who had been arrested during protests against the establishment of an oil palm plantation on their land. The High Court's decision alleged procedural irregularities in the issue of warrants and summons. In 1998, for the second year running, a state of emergency was declared in Sarawak due to widespread forest fires following 'freak' droughts.

As in most cases, a complexity of conflicting interests implies conflict over what kind of development is desirable. You should have noted the following: the environmentalists of the industrialized countries wishing to prevent destruction of the rainforest; the members of ruling groups in Malaysia wishing to generate wealth through the sale of timber concessions; multinational, and latterly Malaysian, logging companies wishing to cut and sell tropical hardwood; international timber and paper companies seeking cheaper raw materials and opportunities for regional expansion; the traditional inhabitants of the forest, such as the Penan and Iban, who see their livelihoods as hunters or shifting cultivators being destroyed by the incursions of the logging and plantation companies into the forest.

For another example, consider this description of the Brazilian government's goals in Amazonia:

"The roots of the environmental pillage in the Amazon can be traced back to the strategy for regional development elaborated by the Brazilian military whose influences in national and Amazonian policy expanded steadily from the first days of President Getulio Vargas's schemes of the late 1930s to develop the northern half of the country…The generals who drove out President Joao Goulart – with active US connivance – took power on April 1, 1964, with a long-nourished geostrategic vision. It was tersely expressed by their chief theorist, General Golbery do Couto e Silva… Brazil's manifest destiny, Golbery wrote, would be to occupy 'the vast hinterlands waiting and hoping to be roused to life'. Such a project would provide a disgruntled population with a sense of purpose and achieve the all-important settlement of empty lands and unguarded frontiers. The march to the west would integrate the Amazon into a new economic sphere. The central ambition, Golbery said, was 'to inundate the Amazon forest with civilization'."

(S. Hecht and A. Cockburn, *The Guardian*, 25 November 1989)

On this interpretation, then, rainforest destruction has little to do with population growth, and much to do with a particular vision of national development and 'civilization' – arguably the same vision that operated among European immigrants to North America who also 'won the West' at considerable ecological expense. The agencies that benefit from this form of development are those with commercial interests in mining, timber, and construction (particularly of transport infrastructure), and those favourably placed to take advantage of changing rights to land tenure. Those whose livelihoods are threatened by this form of development are existing users of the land and other natural resources, and those whose influence over land tenure is weak (Figure 7.7).

Views of sustainable development

For the Brundtland Commission, the basic issue was whether or not the activities such as logging just described are sustainable in the medium to long term. The Commission's definition of **sustainable development** has since been widely quoted.

> **Sustainable development:** Development that meets the needs of the present without compromising the ability of future generations to meet their own needs.

Interpretations of 'sustainable development' diverge greatly, however, and in the following paragraphs I outline three: a neoliberal view, a people-centred development view, and an interventionist view emphasizing the need for international co-operation, which I call a 'global environmental management view'.

Neoliberal view

The environment is natural 'capital'. The services derived from air, water, soil, biological diversity, and recreation (the countryside etc.) depend on maintaining those environmental 'assets' intact, or renewing them. If this is not done, those services will sooner or later decline. This evidently parallels the distinction between income and capital, whereby 'income' is the

Figure 7.7 Conflicting interests in the development of the Amazon: (top) 'Indian' women gathering forest products; (middle) construction of the trans-Amazonian highway; (above) the funeral of the rubber tapper union organizer 'Chico' Mendes, assassinated by gunmen in 1989.

amount that can be consumed in a given period without being any worse off at the end of it. In these terms, if a forest can be used for various purposes without reducing its long-term value in those uses, this can be regarded as 'sustain-

able development'. Similarly, discharges of waste are considered 'sustainable' if they are within the capacity of natural systems to transform them into harmless forms.

If values can be assigned to natural 'capital', then sustainable development can be secured by classical economics criteria, valuing the income from a particular course of development against any depletion of environmental capital. While considerable interest has been generated among economists over the possibility of incorporating environmental valuations in accounting procedures, there appear to be considerable unresolved difficulties in providing valuations of natural 'capital', particularly since these need to take account of future values of resources to future generations with unknowable lifestyles (livelihoods and consumption patterns). The concept of pricing present-day consumption of environmental 'services', such as waste discharge, has found easier application in development policy, however. It is widely accepted, for example, in the form of the 'polluter pays' principle incorporated into pollution control legislation. It also underpins proposals for reducing 'greenhouse gas' emissions under the Kyoto Protocol (Box 7.1).

These ideas have been received with suspicion by governments of less industrialized countries, some of whom regard such proposals as a means of transforming their (unpolluted) atmosphere into yet another primary commodity to be exported to industrialized countries. Moreover, in the absence of cheap, non-polluting, energy sources, selling carbon dioxide emission rights may be tantamount to selling options to industrial development. A similar mechanism, known as 'debt-equity swaps', has enabled concerned agencies in the industrialized world to 'buy' part of the debt owed by countries with 'threatened' ecological resources, in return for the right to determine the conservation of those resources, usually through the establishment of reserves. Advocated by international agencies like the World Wide Fund for Nature, such deals have also been denounced as (for example) 'neo-colonialism in its most stupid splendour' (Hayter, 1989).

People-centred development view

An alternative definition of 'sustainable development' may be identified in the declarations of environmental movements in some developing countries. The Inter-Regional Consultation on People's Participation in Environmentally Sustainable Development, held in Manila in 1989, stated:

> "The concept of sustainability is best understood in terms of the sustainability or non-sustainability of a community. Authentic development enhances the sustainability of the community. It must be understood as a process of economic, political and social change that need not necessarily involve growth. Sustainable human communities can be achieved only through a people-centred development."

A similar view of sustainable development can be found among writers who emphasize the need for priority in development to be given to securing 'sustainable livelihoods' for the poorest groups within communities (e.g. Chambers, 1988).

In this interpretation, sustainable development concerns local trade for local needs, and is often profoundly opposed to urban and industrial development, and the national government with which these are associated. Of the environmentalist peasant movements in India, Ramchandra Guha (1989) wrote: 'At one level they are defensive, seeking to escape the tentacles of the commercial economy and the centralizing state; at yet another level they are assertive, actively challenging the ruling class vision of a homogenizing, urban-industrial culture.' He traces the environmentalism of these movements as originating in resistance to the creation by the British colonial government of reserves for 'rationalized timber production'. The exclusion of the peasants from the reserves deprived them of their traditional use of the forest for pasture, fuel, herbs and medicines. Re-assertion of such 'sustainable' use of the forest is more than an environmentalist statement, therefore: it is also a reclamation of economic control of forest resources. Through the 1990s the influence of 'alternative' or 'people-centred development'

ideas is evident in widespread advocacy of environmental management which is 'local', 'participatory', or 'community-based'. A major question mark over such an approach is the degree to which such 'sustainable' exploitation of forest products can survive integration into the world economy. Antonio Macedo, Co-ordinator of the National Council of Rubber Tappers in Brazil, following his murdered predecessor Chico Mendes, emphasized the use of local rubber extraction for local manufacturing to supply local markets, rather than international traders. However, entrepreneurs – whether individuals or multinational corporations – are active in exploring marketing opportunities for exotic rainforest products from cosmetics to ice cream. Observers are sceptical of the ability of forest dwellers to retain control of any trade with world markets:

> "Once botanists have taken their samples and repotted them or tucked away the seeds in gene banks, the forests are often no longer needed. Either, like rubber or cocoa, production is transferred to plantations, or the required chemical is synthesized in Western laboratories. Certainly neither Third World governments nor forest people receive any reward from the subsequent exploitation."
>
> (F. Pearce, *New Scientist*, 7 July 1990)

These fears were borne out by the experience of the Amazonian 'extractive reserves', which the governments of Brazil and Bolivia leased to groups such as the rubber tappers and brazil nut gatherers. According to one evaluation 'there are considerable doubts about economic viability. There is high dependence on outside support, and low product prices and marketing diseconomies of scale have forced extractivists into less benign forms of land use, such as cattle ranching' (Richards, 1997).

The global environmental management view

The Brundtland Commission envisaged international co-operation to achieve environmental management at a 'global' level, through international environmental treaties enforced by international agencies. These ideas received their formal adoption by the United Nations, at the 'Earth Summit' in Rio in 1992, in the form of Agenda 21, the opening paragraph of which asserts:

> "We are confronted with a perpetuation of disparities between and within nations, a worsening of poverty, hunger, ill health and illiteracy, and the continuing deterioration of the ecosystems on which we depend for our well-being. However, integration of environment and development concerns and greater attention to them will lead to the fulfillment of basic needs, improved living standards for all, better protected and managed ecosystems and a safer, more prosperous future. No nation can achieve this on its own; but together we can – in a global partnership for sustainable development."

The practicalities of implementing Agenda 21, and the international environmental conventions (on Biodiversity, Climate Change, and Desertification) linked to it, are unsurprisingly marked by the conflicting interests of governments and peoples in industrial and non-industrial economies (Figure 7.8). One commentator at Rio observed: '...this was not a conference about the environment at all, it concerned the world's economy and how the environment affects it...(T)his was the first meeting of world leaders since the end of the Cold War. The old East/West agenda is dead, attention is now focused on North and South' (Sandbrook, 1992, p.16).

We have seen (Box 7.1) how the industrial countries' enthusiasm for international treaties to curb atmospheric pollution, the Montreal Protocol and, later, the Kyoto Protocol, were largely dependent on governments' perception of their own industrial capacity to exploit any proposed international regulations. Thus, in 1998, once it had been agreed in January (in Kyoto) that emissions reduction would be achieved through trading mechanisms, such as the earning of saleable 'credits' from construction of 'clean' (e.g. wind, hydro, or solar powered) power-generating plants in less industrial countries,

Figure 7.8   Conflicting interests at the international level.

the resistance earlier mounted by the industrial lobby could be seen swiftly melting away. By November (in Buenos Aires), agreement was reached on proposals to start trade in carbon credits in the year 2000.

In addition to the conflicting economic interests which confront a 'global' environmental management, in much of Agenda 21 and its associated Conventions there is an evident ideological tension between a neoliberal emphasis on market allocative mechanisms and an alternative emphasis on local, participatory, and communitarian processes of environmental management. In this sense, the 'Global Management' view of Agenda 21 can be seen as a field of negotiation between proponents of globalizing market forces and those who see in the local and 'participatory' some protection from the greater inequality and poverty that market forces may produce. Some have argued that these inherent contradictions mean that 'Global Management' is doomed to founder on conflicting interests: 'it is impossible to arrive at the optimum mix of resource uses without preconceived, value-based criteria. Once you agree about the kind of society you want, then agreement about environmental goals may not be difficult, but a consensus does not exist' (Redclift, 1987). Others suggest that conflicting environmental views or 'discourses' are precisely the expression of different value-based criteria for the future of society and its relationship with nature: 'Each society carries what we refer to as an "environmental imaginary", a way of imagining nature, including visions of those forms of social and individual practice which are ethically proper and morally right with regard to nature' (Watts & Peet, 1996, p.263). From this standpoint, the struggle over the environmental implications of 'sustainable development' is a struggle to legitimate particular models of social and economic development. We have seen in this chapter how debates about 'sustainability' are often also about who may legitimately access, use and manage natural resources. This suggests that our interpretation of 'sustainability' may therefore have as much relevance to future social and economic relations between people as to relations between human society and nature.

Summary

Concern about environmental degradation generally has two aspects: worries about the problems of pollution which are likely to be made worse by wider industrialization, and concerns about overexploitation of environmental resources. I have argued that to understand environmental degradation, we need to consider people's livelihoods, for these establish the relationship between economic activity and environment. Characteristically 'non-industrial' forms of environmental degradation are generated by livelihoods based on primary commodity production, such as those of wage labourers in mining, forestry, agriculture, or 'petty commodity' producers (sometimes degraded to 'subsistence' producers). I have introduced three views of the environment and its role in development: neoliberal, 'people-centred', and 'global environmental management'. I have emphasized that all such views must be interpreted in relation to the interests of those concerned and the manner in which they participate in the global economy and the development process.

8

A WORLD AT WAR

TIM ALLEN

Figure 8.1   War games in the divided city of Mostar (Bosnia & Herzegovina), 1994.

For many people concerned about development issues, the most disturbing aspect of the 1990s was the apparent spread of war, particularly civil war. The tragedy of the decade seems to be best illustrated by images of distraught and destitute people fleeing for their lives. In the middle of the decade, at the time of the World Summit for Social Development, held in Copenhagen, and the 'golden anniversary' of the founding of the United Nations system, the seriousness of the situation was highlighted in several major reports published by international agencies. The title 'A World at War' is in fact taken from a chapter of one of these reports, *The Oxfam Poverty Report* (Watkins, 1995). In this report it is

pointed out that the UN system was essentially a product of the blood-letting which had made the first half of the century so violent. The founders of the UN saw conflict prevention as the ultimate criterion against which the post Second World War order would be judged. Thus, the first Article of the UN Charter committed governments to:

"maintain international peace and security, and to that end to take effective collective measures for the prevention and removal of threats to the peace, and for the suppression of acts of aggression or other breaches of the peace."

However, according to the Oxfam report,

> "Fifty years after the Charter was adopted, the world's citizens are in greater need of a collective security system than ever. Throughout the world, the level of human rights violations resulting from current conflicts and rising violence is unprecedented. The costs are to be measured in deaths, broken lives, the destruction of livelihoods, loss of homes and increased vulnerability. Yet as the human suffering mounts, the international community's response to conflict appears ever more inadequate."
>
> (Watkins, 1995, p.42)

Similar sentiments could be found in the report from the Office of the United Nations High Commissioner for Refugees (UNHCR), *The State of the World's Refugees*. At the beginning of 1995, the total number of official refugees and 'other persons of concern' to UNHCR was more than 27 million. For one staff member quoted, 'We are living a scenario…that not even the most pessimistic among us could have predicted' (UNHCR, 1995, p.97).

Meanwhile, the *Human Development Report* of the previous year from the United Nations Development Programme (UNDP) claimed that there were 52 major conflicts in 42 countries and another 37 countries affected by political violence. Of these 79 countries, 65 were in the developing world. It also noted that about half of the world's states had recently experienced 'interethnic strife'. A new approach was called for in international affairs, one premised on a 'profound transition – from nuclear security to human security' (UNDP, 1994, pp.22,32,47).

More recently, Oxfam's director for emergencies has claimed that the highest crude mortality rates ever recorded by his organization were found in the war zone of central Africa in 1997, and UNHCR officials privately admit that they have 'lost' more people who were formally under their protection between 1994 and 1998 than the cumulative 'loss' for all preceding years (Stockton, 1998). This latter point was confirmed to me in an interview with the UN High Commissioner for Refugees herself in 1999. She talked of her disappointment at the lack of 'humanitarian compassion' in rich countries, particularly for events outside Europe, and of her 'despairing feeling' when the rebellion in Zaïre expanded in 1996, and her organization 'lost track of a million people' (Sadako Ogata, interviewed in Geneva, February 1999).

Yet, in stark contrast to all these statements, other commentators suggest that things are actually improving. Peter Wallensteen and Margareta Sollenberg of the Department of Peace and Conflict Research at Uppsala University have argued that there is a 'clear pattern of a global reduction in armed conflict' which 'does not correspond to the common understanding of the world as becoming more insecure after the end of the Cold War' (Wallensteen & Sollenberg, 1998, p.623). The eminent British military historian, John Keegan, has gone further, asserting in the first of his 1998 BBC Reith Lectures on the subject of 'War and Our World' that:

> "…the worst of war is now behind us and…mankind, with vigilance and resolution, will henceforth be able to conduct the affairs of the world in a way that allows war a diminishing part."
>
> (Keegan, 1998, p.1)

Three questions follow from the above:

Q What is the scale of contemporary war?

Q Are there special characteristics of contemporary wars, which make them particularly awful?

Q What are the prospects for 'human security' in war-torn areas?

The three subsections of this chapter address each of these questions in turn.

8.1 The scale of contemporary war

A basic problem with trying to make an assessment of the scale of contemporary war is that it is not clear what it is that we are discussing. A standard dictionary definition of war is: 'strife, usually between nations, conducted by force, involving open hostility and suspension of ordinary international law' (*The Concise Oxford*

Dictionary). But if this is what war is, then most of the recent events which are commonly described as wars are exceptions, in that they are not fought between recognized nation states, and their connection with 'ordinary international law' is tenuous.

Ostensibly recognizing the problem, John Keegan made the following observations towards the end of his fifth and final Reith lecture:

> "War is a protean activity, by which I mean that it changes form, often unpredictably. It is for this reason that I have avoided attempting to define the nature of war throughout these lectures. Like disease, it exhibits the capacity to mutate, and mutates fastest in the face of efforts to control or eliminate it. War is collective killing for some collective purpose; that is as far as I would go in attempting to describe it."
>
> (Keegan, 1998, p.72)

But this does not correspond well with his own usage. It should include kinds of criminal activity which are not usually thought to be manifestations of war, as well as various forms of human rights abuses, including genocide. It should also include violent feuding and other innumerable small-scale and locally contained conflicts of the kind sometimes studied by anthropologists. In one of his lectures, Keegan mentions in passing things like the military practices of the Yanomamo tribesmen of Brazil. But the vast majority of his examples are drawn from big wars fought between states or for the control of states, and most of them took place in Europe or North America. This is one of the reasons for his optimism, because the number of these sorts of conflicts have clearly been declining, and the populations of north America and western Europe have mostly enjoyed a period of continuous peace since 1945. When Keegan talks of 'War and Our World' he really does mean *'our'*.

In practice, it seems that 'war' is used in various ways as a means of indicating the occurrence of a kind of violence in which collective public killing can be expected to occur. It is often employed as a means of conferring status on a conflict, suggesting that a particular situation should be taken seriously and not just treated as criminal activity or dismissed as petty squabbling. The conferring of such status can be a point of controversy, especially in situations occurring within a state, and use of the label sometimes reveals as much about the user as it does about those who are fighting. It may be a way of highlighting the scale of killing in a particular place by an affected group (e.g. northern Uganda in the 1990s), or it may be used to suggest that killing can be partly or even entirely condoned (e.g. by the US and its allies during the 1991 war with Iraq).

More broadly, there seems to have been an increasing acceptance of the term 'war' at international fora and in the international media for localized conflicts which formerly would have been ignored. In other words there has been a shift in usage of the term. This raises the question: is the violence which is commonly called war really becoming more serious or is it just that some commentators are allocating the status of war to conflicts more readily? The obvious response is to try to avoid the ambiguities of the term by deciding upon a specific set of measurable indicators.

Probably the most established approach is that employed by the Stockholm International Peace Research Institute (SIPRI). This is commonly used as a source for the number of wars (e.g. Thomas, 1994; Carnegie Commission, 1997), even though it actually avoids the term 'war' itself in its annual *Yearbook*, preferring to use the less overtly problematic expression 'major armed conflicts'.

SIPRI defines 'major armed conflicts' as:

> "prolonged combat between the military forces of two or more governments, or of one government and at least one organized armed group, involving the use of weapons and incurring the battle-related deaths of at least 1000 people during the entire conflict and in which the incompatibility concerns government and/or territory."

According to SIPRI there were 36 such conflicts in 1986 (the first year that this indicator was used in the *Yearbook*), 37 in 1990, 31 in 1994 and 25 in 1997.

Other organizations and analysts adopt a somewhat similar method, but take different casualty rates, and end up with very different results. Wallensteen and Sollenberg (1998), for example, classify three kinds of armed conflict:

minor armed conflict, where the number of battle-related deaths during the course of the conflict is below 1000,

intermediate armed conflict, with more than 1000 battle-related deaths recorded during the course of the conflict, but fewer than 1000 in any given year,

war, with more than 1000 battle-related deaths during any given year.

Findings from this study are presented in Table 8.1. As can be seen, the number of wars defined in this way seems to have dropped dramatically from 18 in 1989 to just 7 in 1997.

Such assessments exclude many situations sometimes described as war in newspaper articles or by anthropologists working among small population groups. SIPRI and Wallensteen and Sollenberg aim only to indicate the prevalence of larger scale conflicts. However, even if this limitation is accepted, there are important flaws in their approach which need to be recognized.

It is usually impossible to know if combat-related casualty rates are accurate. They are often no more than a guess, and they are commonly linked to a political agenda. Estimates of those who have died in Bosnia & Herzegovina in 1992–95 vary from 400 000 in one UN source, to the most commonly quoted figure of 200 000 (which seems to

have originated with the Bosnian Information Ministry in June 1993), to as little as 20 000 in *The World Disasters Report*, published by ICRC (the International Committee of the Red Cross). Obviously even the low figure for casualties is enough for Bosnia & Herzegovina to appear in both the SIPRI and Wallensteen and Sollenberg surveys. But the variation in assessments is striking, and is equally apparent in smaller scale conflicts, many of which should also perhaps have been included.

In parts of the world there is organized armed combat that frequently results in the deaths of many more people than in the past. An increasing ease of access to sophisticated light weapons (such as automatic assault rifles) means that fighting which in the past would lead only to a few casualties, now can escalate very quickly (an issue which will be explored in Box 8.1). Anthropologist David Turton has described one such incident which occurred in Omo Valley of south-west Ethiopia on 21 February 1987, when a Nyangatom war party crossed the Omo and attacked a group of Mursi – mostly women and children (Turton, 1994). The Nyangatom had obtained Kalashnikov rifles in return for cattle from warring factions in Sudan. Several hundred Mursi were killed, perhaps as much as a third of the whole Mursi population. Subsequently, there have been further attacks, and the Mursi have also managed to obtain Kalashnikovs with which to launch a counter-offensive. No one really knows how many have been killed in the area, but there is no doubt that more than a thousand casualties have occurred. Possibly there have been more than a

Table 8.1 Armed conflicts, 1978–1997

Level of conflict	1989	1990	1991	1992	1993	1994	1995	1996	1997
Minor	15	16	18	23	15	16	12	17	12
Intermediate	14	14	13	12	17	19	17	13	14
War	18	19	20	20	14	7	6	6	7
All conflicts	47	49	51	55	46	42	35	36	33
All locations	37	39	38	41	33	32	30	29	26

Source: Wallensteen, P. & Sollenberg, M. (1998) 'Armed conflict and regional conflict complexes, 1989–97', *Journal of Peace Research*, 35(5), pp.621–34.

thousand in a single year if all the groups in the Omo Valley region are included, so a case could be made for the area to be listed as a war zone by Wallensteen and Sollenberg. Arguably it is reasonable to exclude it from the SIPRI survey, because government forces have not been directly involved, but elsewhere in Ethiopia, and in other countries, this is not the case.

Moreover, even if it was possible to use data on combat-related deaths with confidence, it may be a misleading indicator. It is a matter of opinion, for example, how many of those who died in Bosnia were casualties of this kind. Many seem to have been unarmed people who were rounded up and murdered. In many modern wars, being a combatant can be relatively safe. According to some sources, at the beginning to the twentieth century, 90% of all war casualties were military, whereas today about 90% are civilian (UNDP, 1994, p.47). This too can be no more than a good guess, and it also begs the question what is a civilian in a civil war? Nevertheless, it is the case that many insurgents and government forces seem to spend most of their time avoiding each other. The immediate military objective of warring factions may not be to defeat the other side in combat, but to exhort a livelihood from or traumatize a population as a whole.

One response to the difficulties of using casualty rates is that adopted by the Study Group on the Causes of War at Hamburg University. This group sets them aside as a defining characteristic. Their key indicator is that regular armed forces of a government must be engaged at least on one side. This is perhaps an even more narrow way of categorizing war, but it is much more easy to verify and it can be easily used to give a longer term perspective. The group has recently published findings for the period 1945 to 1993 (Gantzel, 1997). Figure 8.2 shows the annual frequency of wars, defined in this way, between 1945 and 1992.

According to this source (Gantzel, 1997), there have been 184 wars between 1945 and 1993. The annual frequency of outbreak oscillates in an irregular way, which does not differ from earlier periods. However, since the end of the 1950s, the number of wars on-going from year to year has increased. This means that more wars have begun than have ended, and that new wars last longer. From 5 wars in 1945, the trend resulted in a peak of 51 on-going wars at the end of 1992. In 1993 the number declined to 42, but this still indicates that nearly a quarter of all wars which have broken out since the end of the Second World War were being waged in that year. This is a very different, and more worrying, interpretation from that suggested in the surveys linked to battle-related deaths.

Whatever the limitations of the way that the Hamburg study classifies war, it does demonstrate something very significant: that the military forces of more and more states have become involved in serious armed conflicts within the territories which they are supposed to govern. Many of the affected states are former colonies which became independent in the two decades after the Second World War. It seems that their

Figure 8.2   Annual frequency of wars, 1945–92, according to Gantzel (1997).

political integrity and legitimacy has increasingly been challenged. The data also suggest that the challenge has been growing in significance fairly consistently since the late 1950s. In other words, the end of the Cold War is not in itself an adequate explanation, but may be seen as part of a longer term process, whereby artificially formed and fragile states increasingly face violent dissent from within.

It is also important to note that all three studies reviewed here are in agreement on two things: most wars are not being openly fought between states, and not being directly waged by rich states. The first point is illustrated in Figure 8.3, taken from the Hamburg University study. Of the wars counted in the study since 1945, 22.8% have been waged between states, 11.2% have been intra-state wars with an international involvement (i.e. situations in which a state directly intervenes in a foreign civil war), and 66% have been 'internal' or civil war (i.e. wars in which the combatants themselves are mostly citizens of the same internationally recognized state – although, of course, they may be receiving a great deal of external support).

The second point is clear from a glance at Figure 8.4, which is mainly based on SIPRI data in Table 8.1. Most of the major armed conflicts surveyed in the 1990s took place in Africa and Asia. Meanwhile, the Hamburg University study found that 93% of all situations categorized as wars since 1945 have taken place in developing countries. Figure 8.4 shows that the main troublespots of the 1990s have mostly been located on a north–south axis running from eastern Europe and western Asia to South Africa. Relatively few wars are indicated in eastern Asia or South America. In previous decades these regions were severely affected, largely due to the effects of Cold War politics. This suggests a shift in the concentration of major war towards some of the world's most impoverished places. Many of the affected countries are now often referred to as being in a state of 'complex emergency', characterized by protracted crisis and the collapse of state structures.

The usual location of contemporary large-scale warfare helps explain why those most vocifer-

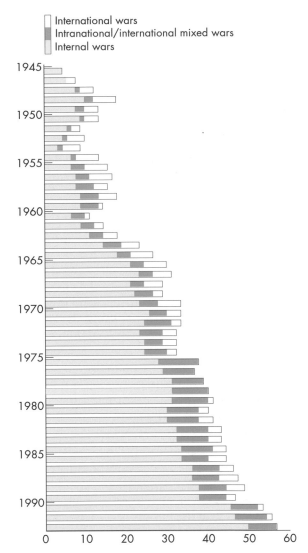

Figure 8.3   Annual frequency of types of war under way, 1945–92, according to Gantzel (1997).

ous in asserting the seriousness of the situation tend to be individuals and organizations representing the interests of people from developing countries. Often they will present their own statistics making their own estimates of the number of wars (like the UNDP figures mentioned at the start of this chapter). In addition they commonly refer to other kinds of indicators, focusing more on the social effects of the fighting.

For example, it was noted in Chapter 3 how in parts of central Africa during 1994 and again in 1997 staggering crude mortality rates (CMRs) were recorded of around 60 deaths per 10 000

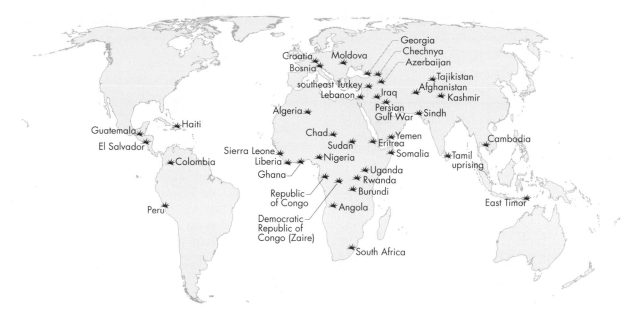

Figure 8.4   Major conflicts of the 1990s.

persons per day (Stockton, 1998, pp.352–3), compared with a 'normal' CMR of less than 0.5. These data highlight that something dreadful must have been occurring in the places in which they were collected. However, this sort of information cannot be readily used for comparative purposes. CMRs based on local level surveys are usually hard to come by, and where they are available it is often not clear what sampling methods have been used. In practice it is virtually impossible to gather this kind of data unless a population is relatively static (i.e. not actually in the process of fleeing) and the security situation is such that researchers are not going to be killed.

Another approach is to assess levels of forced displacement (Figure 8.5). It can be argued this is a relatively good indicator of the intensity of social upheaval, and longitudinal data is readily available on refugees in annual surveys.

Figure 8.5   Refugees from Rwanda at Benaco camp, Tanzania, 1994.

The first chapter of a 1997 Médécins Sans Frontières (MSF) Report, entitled *World in Crisis*, begins with the observation that:

> "Civilians have always been under threat in war. But the methods of modern warfare seem sometimes to threaten more of them more of the time. In recent years wars have seemed characterised by endless streams of wretched refugees, fleeing violence or mayhem or starvation…"
>
> (MSF, 1997, p.1)

A later chapter refers to 'a world in a state of upheaval', and notes that the 'multiplication of conflicts and violent situations has swollen the ranks of refugees and displaced populations to over 50 million people' (Jean, 1997, p.42). A similar figure is given in the 1996 edition of *The Blue Helmets*, the United Nations official report on peace-keeping (UN, 1996, p.4). *The Oxfam Poverty Report* suggested in 1995 that, unless something was done, there might be 100 million refugees by the year 2000 (Watkins, 1995, p.43).

But once again, we need to be cautious about such estimates. There are four main reasons why refugee figures may be inaccurate:

1 The numbers may have been exaggerated in order to secure international aid.

2 It can be impossible to register refugees accurately when they are dispersed in a host population.

3 It may not be known when refugees have returned to their place of origin.

4 If refugees do not return to their country of origin but are absorbed into a host population, it may be unclear when they should stop being included in refugee statistics.

In addition, it needs to be remembered that official data on refugee flows have not always been collated on the same basis, and some very large displaced groups were never formally registered as being refugees. For example, perhaps two million Vietnamese were displaced between North and South Vietnam in 1954, and an estimated 10 million people crossed into India during the Bangladesh war of independence in 1971. Such groups have been largely overlooked, and as a consequence graphs indicating rising refu-

gee numbers over time may seriously underestimate the scale of the problem in the past.

Moreover, in civil wars, most of those who flee the fighting may not actually cross an international border. This may be because the border is too far away or too dangerous to reach, or because a neighbouring country offers no advantages in terms of security, or because a border has been closed. Internally displaced people are not technically refugees, and there is no established system for effectively categorizing, surveying or protecting them (although various *ad hoc* measures have been introduced to extend UNHCR's mandate in specific cases). It is therefore hardly surprising that figures quoted sometimes vary widely. The World Refugee Survey, for example, claims that in 1996 there were one million internally displaced people in Liberia alone – more than three times the corresponding UNHCR figure.

A recent attempt has been made by the Norwegian Refugee Council to collate the best available information on refugees and internally displaced people (Norwegian Refugee Council, 1998). Some of the findings are presented in Figure 8.6. Drawing on usually conservative estimates from UNHCR and the US Committee for Refugees, this survey suggests that official refugee numbers rose from under 3 million in the early 1970s to over 10 million in the early 1980s to around 17 million in the early 1990s. They subsequently declined to around 10 million in 1996. However, the decline is somewhat misleading, because from 1993 UNHCR became responsible for 'safe havens' – areas within war-torn countries in which people were supposedly protected, and from which they were effectively prevented from fleeing across international borders. Figures for internally displaced people from the mid 1990s include around 10 million people in these safe havens (classified as 'other people of concern to UNHCR' in *The State of the World's Refugees*; UNHCR, 1995). Norwegian Refugee Council assessments of the overall number of internally displaced people suggest a rapid rise from the early 1980s, from under 10 million, to around 25 million in 1994, then a decline to about 18 million in 1996.

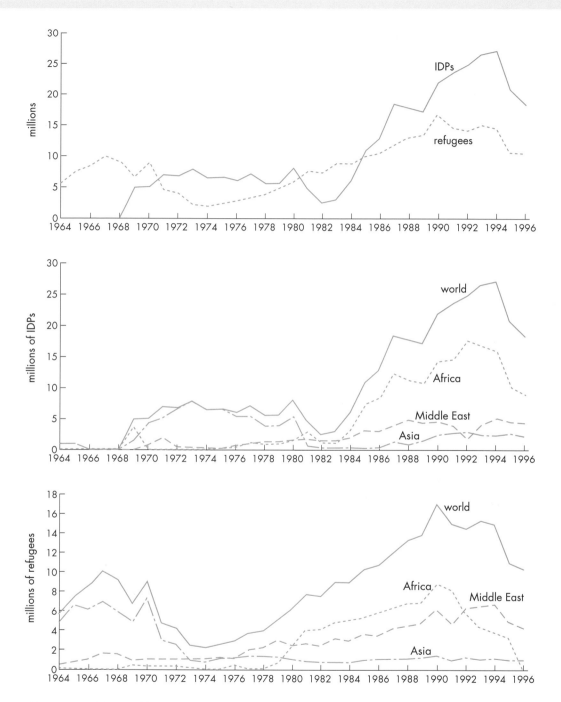

Figure 8.6 Internally displaced persons (IDPs) and refugees: (top) world totals; (middle) IDPs by world region; (above) refugees by world region. All figures are estimates.

Figure 8.7   Mass return from Tanzania across Rusumo Bridge into Rwanda, 1996.

The decline in estimates of the number of both refugees and internally displaced people since the early to mid 1990s seems to coincide with a decline in the number of on-going major wars suggested in the surveys discussed above. But it may just reflect a growing unwillingness for many governments to recognize and take responsibility for displaced populations. This has been evidenced by the concerted attempts of rich countries to restrict the arrival of asylum seekers on their territory as well as attempts to prevent populations from moving out of war zones (something which was, for example, an explicit strategy of Western European countries in former Yugoslavia). There have also been an increasing number of violations of the established principle of voluntary return. In 1996, for example, 1.2 million formally registered refugees were expelled from Tanzania (Figure 8.7) and Zaïre, and 18 other states also expelled refugees in that year (ODI, 1998, p.2).

So what conclusions can we derive from the foregoing discussion? While it is not possible to be exact about the scale of contemporary warfare, there does not seem to have been a massive increase since 1990. Or rather, the prevalence of wars involving formal armed forces continued to rise in the early 1990s at about the same rate

as previously, and may have declined slightly since the middle of the decade. It is also apparent that most of these wars are not being fought between states, and that they mostly occur in parts of the world which are relatively poor and which are least equipped to recover quickly. Finally, there is evidence that the adverse social effects of wars have become more extreme, including very high CMRs in some locations, and a rise in the number of forcibly displaced people between the early 1980s and mid 1990s.

8.2   Characteristics of contemporary war

A reason often given for why many contemporary wars seem to be so awful is that they are civil conflicts characterized by what the 1994 *Human Development Report* calls 'interethnic strife' (UNDP, 1994). Many commentators have suggested that the end of the Cold War has lifted the lid on a social pressure-cooker, and scores of ethnic groups are ferociously competing for power and influence. In this view, what we have witnessed in Bosnia, Liberia, Rwanda and elsewhere is the expression of long-repressed primordial identities.

John Keegan, for example, argues that the:

> "withdrawal of superordinate authority has cast the populations back into a condition that…is certainly a regression from civilized order. The practices of territorial displacement, massacre, deliberate desecration of cultural symbols and systematic mistreatment of women, all evidently rife in recent non-state warfare… undeniably resemble those of the surviving Stone Age peoples of the world's remote regions – at their most savage."

(Keegan, 1998, pp.67–8)

Leaving aside Keegan's insult to Stone Age peoples (whoever they might be), the kind of interpretation he makes seems to me to be fundamentally incorrect. In this section I comment on some characteristics of contemporary wars, and suggest that they are not throw-backs to an uncivilized past, but are the products of modern political economy.

To begin with, the shocking brutality of recent civil wars does not reveal a sudden change of behaviour. Many civil wars in the past have been characterized by appalling atrocities perpetrated on non-combatants: those which took place between the American states in the 1860s and in Spain in the 1930s being good examples. Between the 1950s and 1980s, the people of Korea, Algeria, Nigeria, Vietnam, Bangladesh, Afghanistan and several other countries were similarly torn apart by ferocious conflicts, all marked by the savage practices which Keegan finds in the wars of the 1990s. It is also significant that when the armies of supposedly civilized states have been drawn into such conflagrations, they too have sometimes ended up performing atrocious acts. French forces in Algeria and US forces in Vietnam, for example, vigorously adopted strategies aimed at deliberately terrorizing whole populations. While not wanting to underestimate the horrors of wars that have been fought openly between states, there seems to be a number of reasons why civil wars are prone to extreme forms of social trauma.

First, in civil wars it is the civilians who tend to be the object of the fighting and who bear most

Figure 8.8   The human cost of war in Bosnia &Herzegovina. Sarajevo, 1994: a boy covers his face with his hands and prays at the grave of his older brother, killed fighting at the front.

of the consequences (Figure 8.8). In some instances they also do most of the slaughtering. This is why relatively few soldiers, guerrillas or warriors are killed. Effective military strategy depends less on victory in particular battles than on either changing the attitudes and allegiances of a part of the population, or removing it altogether. The material resources and social networks which made former activities of daily life possible are destroyed. People are given no option other than to find alternative modes of livelihood, sometimes necessitating an antagonistic relationship with old friends who are now defined as outsiders. Customs of trust, moral probity and duty are made inadequate to ensure social accountability, except perhaps within a 'purified' locality or an extended family. Long-standing arrangements of exchange between groups are often forcibly broken down.

Second, the protagonists in civil wars know each other, and if constraints on violence are abandoned, they can find ways of hurting each other in special ways that make it impossible for people to return to former ways of life. Places of religious importance are likely to be targeted, venerated or knowledgeable individuals killed, and rape practised systematically. Atrocities may be finely tuned; for example, being forced to undress in public, leaving the dead to rot in the open, cannibalism, slavery, the mutilation of particular parts of the body, being made to eat faeces, the deflowering of virgins, sexual violation of the anus, and torturing victims with everyday objects (like telephone handsets) so that they will always be reminded of what has happened to them.

Third, civil wars are usually linked to alternative conceptions of social cohesion. War (and the threat of war) has played, and continues to play, an important role in the formation and regulation of human societies in that it promotes internal cohesion in relation to an enemy, and also tends to justify modes of social control, hierarchy and conformity. But whereas wars between states have normally helped to reinforce an existing social category such as 'France' or 'Argentina', in civil war the promotion of social integration will often directly challenge former notions of where the boundaries of collective identity should be located. As a result, established institutions regulating cultural specificity, social order and moral behaviour are likely to be directly threatened.

Fourth, there is less regulation on levels of violence in civil wars. There are long-established codes of conduct which are supposed to govern military action in wars between states, and, since the first Geneva Convention of 1864, there has been a degree of formal monitoring. Such mechanisms have been fruitfully developed, especially since the Second World War. The UN Charter, the Geneva Convention of 1949 and the Additional Protocols of 1977, the 1948 Convention on the Prevention and Punishment of the Crime of Genocide, the 1951 Convention on the Rights of Refugees, and a host of other agreements between governments have elaborated various sets of norms and rules. Violations have often occurred, but it would fair to claim that some headway has been made in limiting both the number and the effects of wars between states. However, most of these conventions and protocols do not apply to wars occurring within states. Especially in the late 1980s and early 1990s, attempts have been made to broaden their reach so that they could be applied to civil wars, but this has proved very difficult.

Thus it is not altogether surprising that the civil wars of today, like those of the past, are marked by extreme forms of violence against whole populations. But it still needs to be explained why there are so many, and why perpetrating mass violence seems to have become relatively easy. The reasons can be found in the following: processes of economic exclusion, erosion of state institutions, vigorous encouragement of ethnic essentialism, the role of news media, the changing nature of the arms trade, and the evolution of new modes of fighting. The following subsections reflect on each of these in turn.

Economic exclusion

Several recent studies have convincingly demonstrated that civil wars can have a highly negative effect on economic growth and welfare indicators (e.g. Cranna, 1994; Stewart et al., 1997). But it would be an error only to see war as the cause of impoverishment. It is also the case that economic deprivation is a cause of war. Obviously social stratification linked to highly inequitable distributions of income is not something new, and has often been a cause of violent conflict in the past. In recent years, however, the exclusion of populations from the benefits of economic growth has taken on a more overtly structured and regional dimension.

Economic power has become concentrated in three blocs, North America (and parts of Latin America), Western Europe and Eastern Asia. These blocs have become increasingly integrated with one another and have undergone a remarkable technological revolution. What has been termed the 'new world trade order' has helped maintain the expansion in international trade, and, since the early 1980s, international trade has grown half as much again as the growth of national products. However, while countries within the trading blocs continue to profess liberal economic policies, and vigorously promote open markets when it comes to their own exports, there has been a marked tendency to limit imports from non-bloc regions by increasing protectionist barriers. Therefore, countries (or areas within countries) which have been excluded from the major trading blocs have become relatively poorer. In parts of Eurasia and much of Africa the effects have been especially severe.

The decline of state institutions

The decline of state institutions as they are conventionally understood appears to be a global trend, although it is much more pronounced in some countries than in others. It has also been occurring for some time. As noted above, a growing number of governments have been deploying their armed forces against their own populations since the end of the 1950s. In recent decades, open market economic strategies, multinational companies, the large-scale migration of populations, and the far-reaching effects of new media technology have all helped undermine the notion of national sovereignty. So have international aid agencies (a point taken up below). In some places, the lifting of Cold War constraints has combined with these factors in encouraging demands for greater autonomy for populations within states, and the restricting of central government controls. These points are discussed elsewhere in this book (e.g. Chapter 9), and need not detain us here, other than to note that most African states were always more fragile than those in Soviet-dominated Europe, and, with a few exceptions, had already become very weak well before the turn of the 1990s.

Ethnic essentialism

One effect of the weakening of the institutions of statehood has been to highlight the superficiality of formally ('internationally') recognized national collective identities. With the collapse of services and the inability of the central government to maintain the rule of law, the tendency is for people to emphasize other notions of ethnicity. Again this is an issue discussed elsewhere in the book (Chapter 23), so only a few observations are made here.

It is very important to recognize that ethnic distinctions do not always relate to long-standing social divisions. It is, for example, bad history to suggest that the ending of the Cold War has

lifted the lid on a pressure cooker of ancient ethnic divisions in eastern Europe. Current politicized ethnic categories are largely the product of policies implemented under Communist rule, media coverage, and the machinations of leaders seeking a power base. However, when ethnicity is asserted to be a primary reason for conflict by many of the protagonists themselves, perceived ethnic differences are likely to be essentialized (i.e. qualities associated with an ethnicity are articulated as if they are primordial or natural).

Once the ideologies of internal wars become closely bound up with such localized notions of ethnic essentialism, it is exceedingly difficult to contain the spread of violence. Whatever an individual's own views, participation in the struggle or migration are likely to be the only options. Whereas enemies during the Cold War era often used to label each other as politically misguided 'imperialists' or 'communists', partly in order to obtain Soviet or Western support, now they can vigorously promote views of each other as inherently inferior or evil. National and international constraints on such assertions have been eroded. Combatants have always found ways of emphasizing the brutality of their opponents, and ethnic genocide is nothing new. It is also the case that no war can only be explained with reference to identities. To suggest that people kill each other in Rwanda because Hutu are Hutu and Tutsi are Tutsi is no more insightful than to suggest that the Iran/Iraq war was fought because the Iranians were Iranian and the Iraqis were Iraqi. Nevertheless, in many more war zones than in the past, the protagonists themselves openly place greater emphasis on apparently immutable ethnic characteristics as a justification for slaughter – something which can make conciliation all but impossible.

The media

Another aspect of overtly ethnicized wars is that they are likely to spread into more stable areas. Refugees provide information about atrocities, engendering sympathy, anger and fear among groups culturally related to those caught up in the fighting. Nowadays this tendency is exacerbated by widespread vicarious participation in violent events through the media. Even those who have not witnessed the killing themselves, nor talked to those who have, will be kept informed by newspapers, radio and television – media of communication which are commonly used for sensationalism or propaganda.

This is not a recent development, but the scale of audiences and the immediacy of coverage are new. Even in isolated areas, people watch television or listen to the radio and expect to find out about things that have happened on that day. In many countries, CNN-style reporting has become enormously influential, and sometimes one particular story can radically alter responses to a complex situation. For example, when Bosnian Serbs fired a single mortar shell into a Sarajevo bread queue, in local terms it was not an especially shocking atrocity. It was the fact that it was captured on film that made the difference, and prompted a threat of military action by NATO. The media now sometimes directly influence the agenda of confrontations, the pace of escalation and the response of the international community. On occasion this may be something positive, but as Cornelio Sammarunga, the head of the International Committee of the Red Cross, has observed, 'television is driven by images, which is an inappropriate way for others to make policy.'

The superficiality of much international reporting is such that it can also have an important influence on the fighting itself. This is particularly so where coverage makes no effort to look beyond the public ideologies of combatants or highlights what appear to be exotic aspects of a conflict. In former Yugoslavia, for example, the national media played a part in encouraging the emergence of populist nationalisms, and in the creation of mass panics which reinforced closed definitions of community. Little was done to reverse this trend in international coverage as warfare spread. The ethnicity of 'Serbs', 'Croats' and 'Muslims' was reported as if these were immutable, obvious, and a natural focus for group division. Although some newspapers and reporters tried to dig deeper into events, the main thrust of international coverage was not to provide an alternative, more objective commentary on the fighting, but to confirm as 'facts' the constructed populist nationalisms of local politicians and war-leaders.

The arms trade

The international arms trade has changed significantly since the mid 1980s, with increased availability of modern military equipment strongly affecting the way in which civil wars break out and escalate (Figure 8.9). This is discussed in detail in Box 8.1.

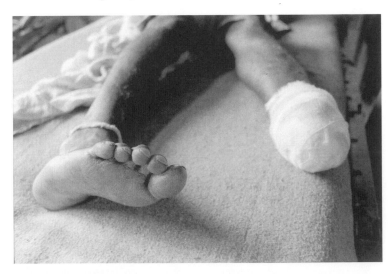

Figure 8.9   A land-mine victim: one of the 'lucky' twenty per cent who survive, Angola.

Box 8.1 The changing arms trade

It is well known that industrialized countries compete with each other to secure lucrative export contracts for military hardware and know-how. This continues to be the case. Between them, the five Permanent Members of the UN Security Council – the US, Russia, China, France, and Britain – account for over four-fifths of weapons officially exported to developing countries. But competition has become more intense for the major arms suppliers. Several newly industrializing countries have sought to expand their share of the market, notably Egypt, North Korea, South Korea, Brazil, India, Israel, South Africa, Taiwan, and Argentina. In the mid 1990s there were over 250 officially registered arms manufacturers based in some 70 countries. At the same time, the end of the Cold War has led to a decline in demand for newly manufactured products, because the former superpowers are no longer willing to prop up client regimes by financing their 'defence' budgets. Between 1987 and 1993 there was a 15% decline in non-covert worldwide military spending and a 25% reduction in official arms exports.

Moreover, the nature of most armed conflict in the world at present is such that heavy equipment and even military training, let alone 'smart' weapons, are becoming less important. They appear to have been significant in the Gulf War of 1991, but that was an exception. Nowadays, the vast majority of wars are not being fought with tanks, heavy artillery and aeroplanes, but by infantry, guerrillas and civilian militia using small arms. In some situations, a great deal of the killing may be done with knives and clubs. But this does not mean that warfare has become 're-primitivized'.

A major catalyst in the outbreak and escalation of contemporary warfare has been the increased access to highly effective military equipment, notably land mines, grenades, mortars and low calibre, automatic and semi-automatic guns. This equipment is obviously more expensive than knives and clubs and some of it would be regarded as outdated by NATO armies. Nevertheless, in large parts of the world it has transformed the experience of war. Indeed, far from being 're-primitivized', armed conflict has been disturbingly modernized. This was the case even in what has become a paradigm for new genocides: the events in Rwanda during 1994. It is true that thousands of people were slaughtered by hand,

but thousands were also killed with bullets and grenades. The Rwandan Presidential Guard, the army, the police and the *interhamwe* militia were all well-armed, and where they did not actually do the killing, they created the conditions in which it occurred. Sophisticated weapons have become widely available in central Africa and elsewhere for five main reasons.

First, arms continue to be openly supplied. For example, arms had been supplied to the Rwandan government by Belgium up until the war broke out with the Rwanda Patriotic Front (RPF), and France, Egypt, South Africa and some Eastern European countries continued to provide weapons subsequently. In 1991, almost $6 million-worth of mostly small arms were supplied to the Rwandan government by Egypt (made possible by credit extended by the French bank Crédit Lyonnais). The shipment included 450 Kalashnikov assault rifles with more than three million rounds of ammunition, fifty mortars with 16 000 mortar shells, 2000 rocket-propelled grenades, 2000 anti-personnel land mines, and six long-range artillery guns with 3000 shells. This is not so different from the way that weapons were provided to several war zones during the Cold War, but distribution is no longer the preserve of a few major powers and it is much less concentrated. Although political alliances can still be significant, as they certainly were between the French and Rwandan governments during the early 1990s, supply follows demand more obviously than it used to. It is, in fact, a buyers' market, and there has been a rise in the sales of cheaper products and services, and a growing market in discounted goods. In addition to the increased competition between manufacturers, there are large stockpiles of weapons, mostly light arms, which are no longer needed due to reductions in the size of standing armies, particularly in Europe. Obviously, countries wishing to sell military equipment have an economic incentive to encourage war, whatever their political commitment to global peace.

Second, availability of small arms has spread within and around war zones in which combatants were supplied by the major powers in the 1980s. For example, huge quantities of weapons were pumped into Afghanistan by the Soviet Union, the US and several other countries, including China, Saudi Arabia, Egypt and Iran. At its height, US military support to the *mujaheddin*

in economic activities such as cattle raiding or smuggling. Others have successfully managed to maintain themselves and their followers by 'taxing' international relief organizations operating in zones under their control. A few have received support from the Sudan government itself, and have switched sides, acting as mercenary militia, usually linked to particular ethnic factions engaged in localized disputes (such as confrontations between groups of pastoralists over grazing rights).

Another characteristic of many war zones is the adoption of new military tactics which have been found to be particularly effective at traumatizing populations. People using land mines and small calibre weapons do not have to be highly trained, and numerous combatants in contemporary wars are very young (Figure 8.10). An automatic assault rifle, such as an AK-47, can be stripped and reassembled by a child of 10; a semi-automatic hand-gun, such as the Cobray M11/9, weighs no more than a new-born baby; and half a dozen anti-personnel land mines can be carried around in a rucksack. In Mozambique, Uganda, Angola, Liberia and several other countries, guerrillas have forced children to kill or maim members of their own families. The children are subsequently branded or indelibly marked, and then incorporated into the guerrilla army, knowing that they can never go home because their relatives will exact revenge for what they have been forced to do. It has been found that children are often more ready to perpetrate atrocities, because they have less sense of the implications of their actions than adults. They are also more likely to follow orders, require little remuneration, and can have a profoundly disturbing effect on the groups they attack in that established codes of conduct are so dramatically inverted.

Finally, it is important to recognize that contemporary internal warfare has beneficiaries as well as victims. Not surprisingly, with the localization of conflicts in many parts of the world, many beneficiaries are local people. They include young men whose livelihoods become bound up with the on-going violence, and 'war lords' whose power depends largely on there being no authority able to impose the rule of law. In some places, such as in parts Afghanistan and Sudan, civil wars have been waged for so long that they have become the norm. Much of the population has had no experience of peace. This raises enormous difficulties for humanitarian intervention, not least because operating in a war zone tends to require negotiation and logistical agreements with those who are gaining most from the current situation, and may have least interest in a resolution.

Figure 8.10   Child soldiers: (left) Albania; (right) Angola.

8.3   Prospects for 'human security'

At the start of this chapter it was mentioned that the *Human Development Report* of 1994 called for a new approach to international affairs, premised on 'human security'. In retrospect, that year can indeed be seen as a turning point, but the change has been in the opposite direction.

This is clearly indicated in Figure 8.11. In 1994, the amount of bilateral ODA (i.e. Official Development Assistance allocated directly by a donor country) specifically allocated to aid in emergency situations reached its highest level both in absolute terms and as a percentage. There has subsequently been a rapid decline. After remaining at a roughly constant level during the 1980s and early 1990s, total ODA has decreased from around US$59 000 million in 1994 to US$48 000 million in 1998. Bilateral emergency assistance has fallen at an even faster rate from US$3400 million to about US$2000 million, and this decline is also apparent in multilateral emergency aid flows (e.g. through the European Union and UN agencies), in private donations and in UN peace-keeping operations. Far from there being an increased commitment to human security, it is apparent that there has been a general withdrawal of concern.

The reasons are not hard to find. They relate to a series of much publicized failures, perhaps most notably in Somalia. The following subsections briefly trace the rise and fall in expectations that 'human security' might be a possibility.

The mid 1980s to 1993

Although Article One of the UN Charter committed governments to 'maintain international peace and security', the Charter also recognized national sovereignty, and interventions which infringed upon 'the territorial integrity or political independence' of a member state could be interpreted as a violation of Article Two. The UN Security Council's authorization of member states to undertake enforcement action in Korea between 1950 and 1953 had set an im-

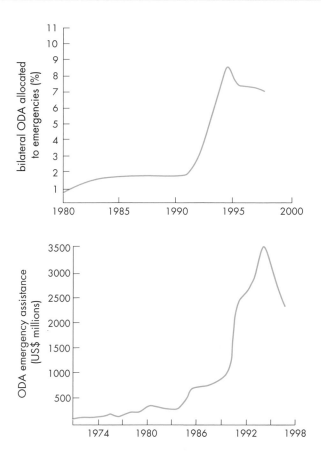

Figure 8.11   (top) Percentage of bilateral ODA (Official Development Assistance) allocated to emergencies, excluding multilateral ODA (unless specifically earmarked by bilateral donors) and food aid. (above) Total ODA emergency assistance (excluding food aid, etc.). Note: Non-earmarked multilateral ODA and food aid allocated to emergencies are omitted because data are not given in ODA reports.

portant precedent for a highly interventionist approach in war zones. However, rivalries between the major powers during the Cold War and the consequent frequent recourse to the veto within the Security Council meant that most subsequent involvements of the UN in situations of on-going armed conflict were very limited. It became established that the UN's role was largely one of peace-keeping, which essentially meant monitoring cease-fire arrangements. The seeds of change were sown in Africa, with precedents initially being set by international non-governmental organizations (NGOs).

Since the time of the civil war in Nigeria in the late 1960s, international NGOs had gained considerable experience of providing relief aid to traumatized populations, even when governmental approval was not forthcoming. From the early 1980s, a combination of factors resulted in an increasing amount of ODA being channelled towards these organizations, either through the UN specialist agencies, such as UNHCR (the Office of the United Nations High Commissioner for Refugees), or through direct official aid allocations. In addition to the continuing restrictions on the activities of UN agencies, these factors included the cutting back of African state sectors as part of structural adjustment programmes, a growing reluctance of aid donors to channel funds through African state institutions on the grounds that they were corrupt or unaccountable, and demands from electorates in rich countries for an adequate response to heart-rending media reports about the human costs of wars and droughts. A consequence was that, in effect, many international NGOs became contracted to the major donors.

Scores of agencies started running top-down operations, aiming at rapid provision of relief, and making a virtue out of their emergency focused short-termism, competing for lucrative aid contracts wherever they were on offer. Indeed, many new NGOs were established specifically for this purpose. The fact that relatively large sums of money and other resources tended to become available for specific locations and for short periods, meant that even some of the best international NGOs were drawn into situations where scores of agencies fell over each other, occasionally going so far as to deliberately undermine what were perceived as being rival projects. Counter-productive conflicts between international NGOs were well documented for most of the main African emergencies in the 1980s, including those in the Sahel, Uganda, Sudan, Ethiopia, Somalia, Zimbabwe and Mozambique.

A further problem was that their interventions were not intended to be sustainable. In attempting to assist those in acute need they persistently bypassed or co-opted the structures by

means of which African states had (however inadequately) attempted to provide welfare services, and in many cases they also undermined important local networks of exchange and accountability. 'Aid dependency' was often created by the very organizations which complained about it. In some places, such as southern Sudan and Mozambique, international NGOs, in effect, took over civil administration, and government officers become informal (and occasionally formal) employees of expatriate-run programmes. In Mozambique a virtual invasion of international NGOs from 1984 onwards helped undermine the policies and achievements of the Frelimo administration. Perhaps several of the relief schemes that the aid agencies implemented succeeded in their immediate objectives. Nevertheless, according to World Bank tables, by 1990, Mozambique had become the world's poorest, hungriest, most indebted and most aid-dependent country (Hanlon, 1991).

There was also some evidence that the willingness of international NGOs to work in war-affected areas helped institutionalize armed conflict, and supported local war economies. Populations fighting civil wars were supplied with food and other necessities, while war-prone regimes and their local allies obtained resources from aid programmes by a range of means, from straightforward robbery to the imposition of inflated exchange rates for foreign currency transactions. In such circumstances, humanitarian neutrality was inevitably seen to be compromised. NGOs themselves effectively took sides, and directly or indirectly supported anti-insurgency operations or guerrilla resistance.

Nevertheless, as the constraints on the UN system began to be lifted with the easing of Cold War tensions, these issues were overlooked. From 1986 the UN began using threats of sanctions and other pressures to help negotiate access with warring factions in order to provide humanitarian assistance. Initially an effect was that UNHCR and other UN specialist agencies became operational in the field (something which had rarely happened before), but it rapidly became apparent that they were too bureaucratic and top heavy. Instead, the somewhat *ad hoc* arrangements between NGOs and the UN started to be systematized. In several cases this new UN/NGO collaboration involved establishing formally recognized corridors of relative peace, from which food, water and relief items might be distributed and a kind of welfare safety net maintained. An early example of these arrangements was Operation Rainbow in south Sudan, set up in 1986. Two years later, General Assembly Resolution 43/131 of 8 December 1988 legitimized the crossing of national boundaries in order to reach the victims of emergencies; in subsequent years, quite large-scale, UN coordinated, safety net programmes were run in several African countries, including Sudan, Ethiopia and Angola.

The enthusiasm for these programmes has to be set in the context of post-Cold War euphoria in industrial countries. For a few years there was a genuine expectation in influential circles that armed conflicts would become increasingly rare. However, the co-ordinating role assumed by the UN failed to result in more cohesive or longer term approaches to humanitarian assistance. There were numerous instances of aid being hindered by fierce antagonisms within UN specialist agencies, between them, and with NGO partners. This was partly because the UN as a whole was prone to the same kind of funding and media pressures that have affected international NGOs. It had to be seen as acting in a decisive manner in exceedingly complex situations, and has needed to achieve results rapidly in order to secure resources from member nations to intervene somewhere else. As it became apparent that negotiated 'corridors of tranquillity' were not going to serve these purposes adequately, a more dramatic response was probably inevitable. In the early 1990s, the logical next step was taken, and humanitarian assistance became associated with armed action.

The presence of large numbers of UN-affiliated troops in the region in the aftermath of the 1991 Gulf War provided an obvious solution, and the principle of using military personnel to protect a UN relief operation was established. Security Council Resolution 688 insisted that 'Iraq allow immediate access to international humanitarian organizations to all those in need of assistance in all parts of Iraq'. Little was done for the Shiites in the south of the country, but in Kurdistan the idea of 'corridors of tranquillity' was superseded by the concept of 'safe haven'. The decision to use military means in order to protect the Kurds within Iraq was clearly a violation of Iraqi national sovereignty, and indicated that the integrity of recognized states would no longer always be a premise of international affairs. This point was reiterated in 1992 when the Secretary General's report *An Agenda for Peace* was adopted by the General Assembly, with its statement that 'the time of absolute and exclusive sovereignty has passed'.

However, there were also other factors at work in the setting up of the safe haven in Iraq. Most obviously, it reflected concerns within influential countries about influxes of refugees (a fact which helps explain why efforts were largely focused on northern Iraq). Indeed, it is hard to avoid the conclusion that an overriding criterion shaping recent international approaches to displacement in war zones has not really been protection at all, but only a determination to prevent people from becoming refugees. That protection was not really the priority was made shockingly clear in Kurdistan. Between October 1991 and January 1992, for example, some 300 000 Kurds were forced to flee their homes within the safe haven due to continued attacks by Iraqi government forces. In October 1992, when there were around 100 000 Iraqi troops located in the vicinity, there were only 30 UN guards deployed in the whole of northern Iraq (Keen, 1994, pp.170–1). By that time, however, international media attention had moved elsewhere.

In 1992–93, what might be called armed humanitarianism was attempted on a much larger scale in Cambodia, and was also attempted in situations of on-going war in Croatia (1992), Bosnia (1992 onwards) and Somalia (1992–93). This was the high-water mark of post-Cold War international interventionism. But, with the partial exception of Cambodia, all these operations proved to be very costly, in terms both of the funding required for implementation, and of the political credibility of the UN and the major powers. Bosnia and Somalia (see Box 8.2) were perhaps the most humiliating failures, and occurred in the full light of international media coverage (Figure 8.12). Here the manifest incapacity to prevent or stop the fighting was combined with all the problems that had arisen with the 'negotiated access' schemes of the 1980s. In spite of the setting up of a special UN agency to promote co-ordination between agencies, this proved to be extremely difficult. Conflicts remained common, and so did support for unsustainable and often inappropriate programmes, and the fuelling of local war economies. By the end of 1993, there was a major crisis of confidence.

Figure 8.12 The UN High Commissioner for Refugees, Mrs Sadako Ogata, arriving at Bardera during a mission to Somalia in April 1996.

1994 to the present

Following the débâcle in Somalia, there was a marked shift in the international approach to civil wars. Initially this was not reflected in a decline in emergency aid flows (indeed, 1994 proved to be a record year), but there was a new reluctance to deploy military forces.

In 1994, the world witnessed an extraordinarily efficient genocide. About 800 000 people were killed in Rwanda in a couple of months. In April there was also the largest single exodus of official refugees as an estimated 200 000 people fled into Tanzania. Then in August, an even larger movement occurred as around 850 000 fled into Zaïre. This group rapidly set yet another grisly record. In the huge refugee camp at Goma, a dysentery and cholera epidemic claimed about 60 people per 10 000 per day. Perhaps 50 000 people died in a week (Stockton, 1998, p.352).

The international response to these disasters was a strange mixture of action and inaction. There was no military intervention to prevent the killing, even though events in Rwanda were covered under the terms of the 1948 Convention for the Prevention and Punishment of the Crime of Genocide. The UN Secretary General openly used the word genocide to describe what was occurring, but implementation of the Convention required Security Council approval, and this was not forthcoming. In fact, as news of the killing spread during April, the Security Council took the decision not to reinforce the small UN peace-keeping force in the country. Sir David Hannay, Britain's representative on the Council argued that it would only mean 'a repetition of Somalia with its well-known and dire consequences' (*The Guardian*, 7 December, 1998). On 21 April, the Council voted to withdraw the force altogether. A week later, the New Zealand representative, who was also acting as Council president, attempted to have the genocide officially recognized so that the 1948 Convention could be applied. But this was resisted vigorously, with Sir David Hannay maintaining that, having already withdrawn the peace-keeping force, the Council would become a 'laughing stock' (ibid.).

Box 8.2   The humanitarian intervention in Somalia 1992–93

The circumstances behind the military intervention in Somalia in December 1992 are not entirely clear. Nevertheless, they seem to demonstrate the close relationship between the UN-endorsed armed interventions of the early 1990s and the activities of interventionist NGOs in the 1980s. Indeed, it appears that a group of international NGOs were instrumental in creating the conditions for the intervention to occur. The most prominent of these NGOs was the US-based CARE-International (De Waal, 1994, pp.152–4). In October 1992, the president of CARE advocated sending a force of 15 000 to Somalia to ensure that fighting in the civil war would not interfere with distribution of essential famine relief. Two million Somalis were said to be facing imminent death by starvation. The food situation in Somalia had in fact already much improved. However, there had been intense media interest in Somalia for several months, and President Bush was keen to leave office on a high moral note. As a result, on 3 December 1992, the Security Council unanimously adopted Resolution 794 'welcoming the offer by a Member State to help create a secure environment for the delivery of humanitarian aid in Somalia and authorizing... the use of "all necessary means" to do so' (UN, 1996, p.294).

As is well known, Operation Restore Hope was a farcical but tragic débâcle. According to Africa Rights, by August 1992 Somalia had already become a kind of 'media–NGO circus' in response to the famine (African Rights, 1994, p.18), but as media coverage intensified following the arrival of US troops, scores of new NGOs quickly became involved in relief work. Many aid agencies clearly hoped to obtain a high profile in their home countries, and concentrated on dramatic assistance schemes involving food distribution, even though the food supply situation was no longer a serious problem. Thousands more Somalis died due to diseases rather than famine, but public health programmes were not made a priority, and even mass inoculation of children against measles was not attempted. NGOs tried to outdo each other in giving out food relief, and some went to ludicrous lengths to 'steal' customers from each other. Incentives were offered to people so that they would attend a particular agency's feeding centre rather than go to those run by others. There were cases of T-shirts being distributed so that agencies could publicize their activities when the international media arrived to film their projects (UNRISD, 1993).

Meanwhile the UN-authorized armed forces were drawn into open conflict with one of the main Somali armed factions, that of Mohamed Farah Aidid. There are various views as to how this came about, but an important factor seems to have been the way in which the US-dominated UN force was influenced by the interventionist NGO agenda (African Rights, 1994, pp.19–20). During the crucial first five weeks of the operation, no attempt was made to disarm the Somali militia. Instead, the US ambassador entered into agreements with the leaders of the main warring groups in order to ensure that relief food supplies could be distributed. In other words, Restore Hope was initially a kind of armed, negotiated access operation. The fighting could continue, provided humanitarian aid agencies were able to do their work, and the position of the war lords was in fact enhanced by the UN's recognition of their status.

By March 1993, the limitations in the policy had become abundantly clear. Among other embarrassing events, in February Mohammed Said Hersi's forces had been able to take Kismaayo, while US and Belgian soldiers merely watched. The Security Council's response was to shift from negotiated access to an approach similar to that adopted in Iraq and Cambodia. Areas under UN control were to become a kind of 'safe haven' in which peace would be imposed. Thus, Resolution 814 of 26 March 1993 authorized a new UN force to take over in Somalia, and insisted that 'all Somali parties...desist from all breaches of international law', and reaffirmed 'that all those responsible for such acts [would] be held individually accountable.' In making these assertions the UN crucially over-reached its capacities, and revealed an extraordinary lack of understanding of the situation on the ground. To those militia which had suffered reverses since the UN soldiers arrival, the new strategy was viewed as confirmation of UN bias in favour of their enemies. It lead inexorably to the events of 5 June 1993, when 23 soldiers of the UN forces were ambushed and killed.

Operation Restore Hope was the high-water mark of naive enthusiasm for relief-oriented, humanitarian intervention. It also marked its nemesis. Response to the failure has not so much been a careful assessment of what went wrong, as confirmation that disengagement and containment of internal war is the only viable approach. The commission of enquiry established by the Security Council in November 1993 concluded that the UN should abandon 'peace enforcement'. In the US, Presidential Decision Directive 25 of April 1994 placed restrictions on the deployment of American forces, and on UN operations in general – 'restrictions that have more to do with avoiding military casualties and embarrassing media coverage than with solving the problems in the countries concerned' (African Rights, 1994, p.20).

This abrogation of responsibility was perhaps one reason for the fairly generous response to the humanitarian crises which followed. About a hundred aid agencies, mostly NGOs, were funded to provide relief to the refugees in Goma. However, the quality of this aid was mixed. As Nicholas Stockton, Oxfam's Emergencies Director, put it:

"The place was awash with the modern symbols of international aid: T-shirts, car stickers and flags. Humanitarian 'heralds' were there, the NGO press officers, doggedly pursuing journalists, brandishing their new angles on the story, often relating to their own agency's courage, skill and impact. All clamoured for television coverage and made claims about what could be achieved, some of which were indeed outrageous."

(Stockton, 1998, p.358)

Unlike many other agencies, Oxfam received praise for its work in Goma from the major review of the humanitarian response to the crisis (JEEAR, 1996), in particular for managing to provide adequate water to the settlement. However, criticism was scathing of other organizations. Perhaps most damning of all, in spite of the presence of numerous NGOs specializing in emergency health care, it seems that the cholera epidemic more or less ran a natural course – in other words, the same number of people died as would have been expected had there been no intervention at all. Many commentators, including influential journalists, argued that the mess in Goma revealed that the relief system was out of control, 'having become a self-perpetuating expatriate industry unscrupulously exploiting other people's misery', and characterized by 'gross naivety and amateurism' (Stockton, 1998, p.358).

Moreover, the refugees that were the target of the relief effort had fled the new RPF government in Rwanda, and within the camps were the very people who had organized the genocide. Calls from some sources for military deployment to separate the refugees from the extremist *interhamwe* militia were not heeded. The 1995 *Oxfam Poverty Report* made the following observations:

"Having condemned the genocide and demanded that its perpetrators be brought to justice, Oxfam and other agencies have found themselves in the invidious position of delivering aid through structures controlled by the very people responsible for the crimes committed in Rwanda. Hutu militia leaders control the camps and are using them as a base from which to plan armed incursions into Rwanda, and are forcibly preventing refugees from returning home. It is difficult to imagine a graver abuse of international assistance."

(Watkins, 1995, p.52)

In the event, this was the last big humanitarian intervention of the mid 1990s. During the following year, the fall of the UN 'safe haven' of Srebrenica to Bosnian Serb forces confirmed that, even in Europe, expectations about a New International Order were misplaced. It had now become widely accepted that, as an MSF report put it, relief operations can 'reinforce the war parties and extend the war' (MSF, 1997, p.2). Humanitarian operations have continued but, with the partial exception of Kosovo, they have been on a much smaller scale. Central Africa has been more or less abandoned. Hundreds of thousands of people who were formally under UNHCR protection were left to their fate. In May 1997, MSF and Oxfam both found crude mortality rates (CMRs) in eastern Zaïre that were as high as those in Goma in 1994. According to Stockton, for a few days Oxfam's staff estimated that the CMR reached 300 deaths per 10 000 per day, 'a public health disaster that Oxfam has not encountered elsewhere' (Stockton, 1998, p.353). But there was little media coverage and no appeal for funds.

The current mood seems to be one of resignation. In the immediate future it is unlikely that there will be attempts at UN-endorsed, armed intervention to enforce peace and provide humanitarian aid (let alone to stop genocide), except in places where the interests of the US and/or its more affluent allies are seen as being affected. It is surely significant in this respect that the 'humanitarian' bombing of Yugoslavia by NATO forces in 1999 occurred without the specific sanction of a UN Security Council resolution. There has been a return to the approach of the 1980s, with official funding being channelled through contracted NGOs. But there is now much less optimism about what might be achieved and, it would seem, less pressure in rich countries for governments to provide aid. Stockton and others have argued that the experiences of delivering humanitarian aid in war zones during the 1990s, and the criticisms that have been made of many operations, has had the effect of greatly improving aid agency capacity. Certainly there have been important steps taken to regulate activities according to agreed codes of practice, and to monitor results more closely. Stockton also points out that the withdrawal of emergency aid from Central Africa contributed to the horrors of 1997, as warring factions perpetrated atrocities with impunity. As noted at the end of Chapter 3 he has called for a renewal of humanitarian commitment. However, it would seem that few are listening. Far from there being widespread belief in the possibility of achieving global peace, there is now a disturbing acceptance that large parts of the world are going to be very violent for a long time.

Summary

Assessments of the scale of contemporary wars vary widely. This is partly because there are ambiguities in the concept of war itself, and partly because of difficulties in establishing objective indicators and reliable statistics.

However, certain observations can be made with some confidence. First, the overall number of large-scale armed conflicts has not risen dramatically during the 1990s as is sometimes supposed, but has been rising steadily since the late 1950s. Second, the vast majority of these conflicts are civil wars. Third, most of them occur in economically poor countries. Fourth, the social devastation caused by war has been increasing during the past two decades. Indicators of this include extremely high crude mortality rates (CMRs) and huge numbers of forcibly displaced people.

The reasons for the prevalence of civil war and for their devastating impact are complex. They cannot simply be explained by the end of the Cold War, and it is highly misleading to interpret them as the product of resurgent ancient ethnic identities. The changing nature of international alliances and the promotion of ethnic essentialism by political leaders have certainly been significant. But so have other factors, such as economic marginalization, the long-term erosion of state institutions, superficial media coverage, the arms trade, and the development of a range of new military strategies.

The possibilities of providing for human security do not seem to have been enhanced during the 1990s. On the contrary, the experiments with militarized humanitarianism between 1991 and 1993 resulted in embarrassing failures, and a crisis of confidence. This was manifested in the refusal to act to stop the genocide in Rwanda in 1994. The effectiveness of humanitarian aid has also been questioned, and funding has sharply declined. At the turn of the century, the prospects for many war-torn populations, particularly in Africa, are very bleak.

9

AGENCIES OF DEVELOPMENT

ALAN THOMAS AND TIM ALLEN

The previous chapters in this section have considered the world as a world of problems. Each chapter has dealt with an aspect of poverty (hunger and famine, ill health and disease, unemployment, and so on), or with problems which together with poverty make up what has been called the 'global threefold human crisis' (Chapter 1). From another point of view, each chapter has dealt with evidence of the 'disordered faults of progress' which according to Cowen and Shenton (1996) are to be ameliorated by intentional development in order to avoid chaos (Chapter 2). This suggests that things should be looked at from the other side. If indeed they are building up to a global 'crisis', then in addition to looking at the causes and qualities of the problems themselves, we might focus on efforts to 'ameliorate' them.

Thus we give more emphasis here to issues of **agency** rather than **structure**. These are terms worth considering in their own right.

You may recall from Chapter 2 that Cowen and Shenton identified the 'problem of development' as one of 'trusteeship' – *who* will take on the task of acting on behalf of others to promote improvements? to 'develop' them? The very notion of intentional development requires development agencies to be taking on trusteeship roles in this way. This leads to the question of evaluating development agencies in terms of their legitimacy and their capacity (political and technical). In other words, do they have the *right*

Structure: The pattern or framework of relationships between social institutions, such as markets, families, classes, and political factions. It includes rules of behaviour associated, for example, with moral norms and hierarchies.

Agency: The actions of individuals or groups, and their capacities to influence events.

In practice, social analysts combine both concepts, although some tend to favour one over the other.

to implement development on behalf of others, and do they have the *power* to do so?

As was also noted in Chapter 2, for much of the 200 years since the 'invention' of intentional development there has been an assumption that it is the state (colonial, metropolitan or postcolonial) which is the agency best able to take on this trusteeship role. Indeed, for long periods development was virtually synonymous with the development activity of the state. In practice the state had a virtual monopoly of development activity within its boundaries. However, the lack of alternatives did not mean the state was always a positive force for development. Moreover, in the last years of the twentieth century various trends have weakened the state's claim to this monopoly, while other agencies of development have been gaining a higher profile, notably inter-governmental organizations such as the United Nations and its affiliated agencies (the World Bank, IMF and others) on the one hand, and non-governmental organizations (international, national and local) on the other. Add to this the now frequently asked question of whether there is not another way altogether of answering Cowen and Shenton's problem of development without resorting to the notion of trusteeship: for example, might not people be their own development agents? We see that there is plenty to discuss in a chapter on agencies of development. Here we ask:

Q What are the characteristics of states and what roles can they play with respect to development? What are the forces weakening the claim of states to a monopoly on development activity?

Q What are the possibilities and limitations of inter-governmental (multilateral and bilateral) and non-governmental organizations as development agencies?

The two main parts of this chapter address each of these questions in turn. It should be stressed, however, that only certain aspects can be dealt with here. Concerning the state, you should also look especially at Chapter 12 on colonial states, Chapter 13 on state-led development strategies, Chapter 14 on socialist states, Chapter 17 on democratization and 'good governance', Chapter 23 on nationalism, and Chapter 24 on arguments about states requiring autonomous 'national' industries.

9.1 The state as a development agency

In an extreme or pure form of capitalism, there would be only a minimal role for states or any form of collective or public action. In practice, in contemporary or 'advanced' capitalism, states have an important role to play. Development in particular has to be seen not only within the economic context of global capitalism, but also in the political context of a world of formally constituted states. These states differ hugely, but also share certain key features.

Key features of states

1 Each state claims the right to regulate affairs within the boundaries of its own territory and aims to provide security from foreign intervention for people within its boundaries by conducting relations with other states. Such interstate relations can be peaceful (e.g. diplomacy) or warlike. The military capability that states acquire can also help to make them exceptionally powerful and dangerous within their own territories.

2 The state's claim to 'a monopoly over the use of force' within its boundaries goes with its being 'distinguished from the myriad of other organizations in seeking predominance over them and in aiming to institute binding rules over the activities of other organizations within its boundaries' (Azarya, 1988, p.10). Notice here the note of conditionality regarding the state's power – the state *seeks* predominance and *aims to institute* binding rules. The state's predominance and maintenance of binding rules might be strong and effective, but equally it might be weak and reflexive – so weak indeed that the state's power is really of no consequence beyond the walls of the political leader's compound.

3 The state also provides 'identity and cohesion' (Jordan, 1985, p.1). In order to enjoy the enormous advantage of having their rule accepted by the people (or at least some of the people) as legitimate, states continually promote a sense of national identity and common citizenship, and seek to define away, or suppress, competing ideologies subversive of their rule. This process of legitimation involves the reproduction of a common culture, a 'national interest', through the use of the mass media, the educational curriculum, religious organizations, and other interest groups and associations. The working of political institutions, the 'majesty of the law', and the pomp and circumstance that attend state ceremonies can also contribute to the process of legitimation so central to the reproduction through time of any state form.

4   The state is not coterminous with society; it is one of many organizations or spheres of activity *within* society. It is therefore both an agent and a structure. It acts as an agent within a broader social structure (and international arena) and is always influenced to some extent by this structure. At the same time, the state also provides a structure of binding rules (more or less) that influence or control to some extent the actions of other agents within society.

5   The state sustains relationships with other agents within society; it 'coexists and interacts with' families, economic enterprises, religious organizations, and so on (Azarya, 1988, p.10) and presides over 'different spheres of the community' (Jordan, 1985, p.1). Perhaps the most crucial of these relationships is the one between the state and the economy: broadly speaking, states participate directly in the processes of productive capital formation, they provide infrastructure, and they affect private sector resource allocation through monetary and fiscal policies.

6   Although a state can be considered as a single cohesive entity or organization distinct from others in society, it is at the same time a set of organizations or an ensemble of political institutions – coercive, administrative, legal – which may not always act as one or in concert. The state in India in 1990, for example, had assemblies of political institutions at the centre and in each of 20 state governments, one of which in West Bengal was controlled by the Communist Party of India (Marxist) which was pursuing policies different from those in the other 19 states and at the centre. Even within West Bengal 'the state' behaved differently in different districts, development blocks and villages.

7   States require bureaucracies. These are a type of organization usually thought of as ideally characterized by *hierarchy*, *continuity*, *impersonality* and *expertise*. They are also supposed to be distinct from the governing bodies which employ them, although clearly this is not always the case (a point taken up below). Not all bureaucracies within a state are part of the formal state structure. But state bureaucracy helps provide a framework of predictable social action, within which other bureaucracies can operate (Figure 9.1).

Figure 9.1   Bureaucracy at work. Officials of a co-operative credit agency in India getting the thumb impression of a peasant on documents before giving him a loan for agricultural operations.

8   The term 'state' is often associated very closely with the term 'government'; indeed, the two are commonly treated as synonymous, and a 'strong state' is often taken to mean a powerful government. However, this can be misleading in that the state is a broader category, which includes, for example, the civil service and the legal system (Figure 9.2). A distinction between the concept of government and the concept of the state has become clearer with the demise of all-encompassing, state-controlled, economic planning on the one hand, and the questioning of market-driven strategies on the other. There is now much greater emphasis on institution building. Thus, a United Nations Development Programme report on *The Shrinking State*, published in 1997, explains that:

> "The state is the network of government, quasi-government and non-government institutions that co-ordinate, regulate and monitor economic and social activities in society. A weak or 'small' state is one in which the institutions and regulations are undeveloped, so that relations between individual, communities and groups are erratic and subject to uncertainty and insecurity. A strong state does not necessarily require or equate with a 'large' government."
>
> (UNDP, 1997a, p.6)

The role of the state in development

From these features we can see that the state must always play a major role in development, though this can be in at least three different ways.

First, the state itself can be a *primary agent* for development initiatives in society. Political decisions can be taken regarding development as contained in national and local plans; development departments can be established employing trained personnel with development expertise; funds and other resources can be obtained and allocated; bureaucratic rules and regulations can be laid down regarding how the development programme is to be implemented; and so on.

Second, the state can provide an *enabling structure* for development by other agencies. That is, development can be taking place primarily through the activities of economic and other organizations outside the state. This is what occurs in the case of capitalist development, when the state provides essential infrastructural support, including the maintenance of order in society, establishing a set of economic policies favourable to capitalist accumulation, changing the domestic economy in response to the changing demands of global capital, controlling the labour force, providing necessary transport and communications, and so on. Actually, a strict

Figure 9.2   Political parties may be viewed as part of the state, but they are not synonymous with the state, although some have claimed to be so. Above are those present at the foundation of the All-India Muslim League at Dhaka, 1906. The League was eventually, as a political party, to lead the movement for an independent Pakistan.

separation between the state providing infrastructure and capitalist enterprises spearheading development is not easy to make in many countries where there is a long tradition of state involvement in the economy. For example, state guidance of capitalist development was central to the exceptional growth of the newly industrializing countries of South Korea, Taiwan and Singapore.

Third, the state can be a *structural obstacle* to development, resulting in development efforts through collective struggle against the state. Workers and peasants may perceive the state and its allies as maintaining forms of exploitation and oppression that block any genuine development from which they might benefit. Development for them can only begin with collective struggles which 'can combine elements of *defence* against further exploitation and oppression; of *resistance* to the power of capitalists and landlords, and the legal, political and ideological forces that support them; and of *transformation* when such struggles develop ideologies and forms of organization and solidarity that challenge existing structures of exploitation and oppression and point the way beyond them to alternative forms of society' (Johnson & Bernstein, 1982, pp.266–7). In such cases, the state is neither the main agent of development nor does it provide infrastructural support for development by others; it is central to the problem of development because it does not allow development to occur.

These three cases should not be seen as mutually exclusive. The state has been viewed both as the most important form of political organization which can act as an agency of development (or, for that matter, block to development), and as the main political context in which development agencies operate.

The state and the politics of development

Politics here refers to processes of ordering and influencing society at different levels, including the means by which some people or groups attain positions from which they can effectively promote their own interests and values. These levels range from the very local, such as in a village or even a single family, to international relations between states. Thus development fits into wider political processes which involve the following aspects.

Interests and influence

Any deliberate action to bring about change in society in a desired direction always involves choice. To choose one development programme means not choosing another, and that choice is political because it benefits some people more than others. Plans and strategies also relate to interests and values. They express certain values in the sense that they rest on certain preferences and moral assumptions about what is good or desirable. For example, a preference for competition as broadly the right approach to development efforts usually rests ultimately on some moral conception about the value of individual freedom. A development strategy which gives strong emphasis to collaboration usually is grounded in a more egalitarian moral premise. Interests, on the other hand, are about material benefits. Any development choice or action is going to benefit certain interests more than others.

Usually, dominant interests and values in any development initiative reinforce each other. For example, development schemes which spring from those who value competition usually best serve the interests of those who are already dominant, with the result that there is little immediate change in the existing structure of rewards and benefits. This is frequently what happens with top-down initiatives by bureaucratic and political agents within the state. As Goldsworthy (1988, p.511) suggests, decisions and actions by such agents will commonly reflect either bureaucratic self-interest or the interests of friends, clients and class allies, or will at least 'objectively serve' those interests, resulting predictably in 'a pattern of development that both reflects and consolidates existing disparities'. But that may be too static a view. Over time, patterns of development can also change as the relative power of clients and classes changes.

Thus, politics always involves certain material interests and valued preferences. Those doing the ordering or influencing usually have a political project or purpose of some kind, which may or may not be shared by those being ordered or influenced. The project may be rather narrow – to enrich the leader and/or a dominant class. It may be more broad – to enrich and fulfil the lives of all the people through increased empowerment, the abolition of poverty, and the creation and optimal distribution of wealth. Political content produces conflict. It also inspires and mobilizes people in collective political effort.

This is why politics (or more precisely, political agency) at the level of the state has been likened to steering a ship at sea ('the ship of state') – and has several similar requirements, like trying to stay in control, charting a specific course and trying to achieve a particular objective (reach a destination). Another, and perhaps better, analogy has been around in Asia for a long time: that of trying to ride a tiger in a particular direction, the tiger being the more or less obedient masses who must be coaxed along and who may, if goaded too hard, turn on the ruler and make big trouble.

Political agents and institutions

Politics is about people getting into sets of positions and their supporters pursuing their interests and purposes. People in such sets of positions may be called political agents. They make up political institutions that endure over time such as legislatures, courts, chief executives, councils, commissions, military junta, the police, the armed forces, civilian bureaucracies and political parties. Combinations of political institutions make up the state apparatus. Also part of politics are the processes by which some people get into these sets of positions; such processes include elections, appointment, inheritance, military coup, revolution. Here we consider how development relates to two important examples of political institutions: political parties and civilian bureaucracies.

There are different types of parties and party systems, from (for example) those where only one party exists, to those where parties are ephem-eral or non-existent, to multi-party regimes where there are decentralized patronage-based parties seeking votes. A conventional view of parties sees them as agencies representing certain views or interests in society and, when a party's leaders are in power, having a controlling or influencing say over government policy, including development policy. Political parties would thus provide a major political input into the development process.

This conventional conception of parties is not wrong, but it can be misleading if it is assumed to hold universally and if too much emphasis is put on it. In much of the South, pol-itical parties are more important as political outputs, as instruments of government. They frequently are created and used by political leaders to help legitimize their regimes, as well as to provide a structure in society through which, generally via the distribution of patronage, a coalition of powerful political interests sufficient to sustain the government can be secured (Randall, 1988, p.184). Parties can be used by governments to knit together alliances between certain groups in society at different levels, through which development efforts can be channelled.

One also has to be wary of conventional definitions when it comes to bureaucracies. Few if any bureaucracies in the South or elsewhere would fit closely the ideal type represented by a standard definition of bureaucracy (see above). Hierarchy? Formal organization charts frequently hide the reality of pyramids of informal, patron–client groupings. Continuity? Bureaucratic tenure for officials can be short or uncertain as determined by the rapidly shifting fortunes of ministers, generals or other political leaders. Impersonality? Bureaucratic decisions are frequently determined by particularistic loyalties rather than by impersonal application of general rules. Expertise? Training programmes are frequently inadequate or non-existent and selection can be influenced more by political loyalty than by the qualifications of the candidates. Indeed, some bureaucracies appear to depart so far from the model that it might seem misleading even to refer to them as bureaucracies.

But that goes too far. Most countries do have organizations accountable to political leaderships, with noticeable elements of hierarchy, continuity, impersonality and expertise which distinguish them from other types of political institutions. Development takes place in a political context in which such bureaucracies play a considerable role in several ways.

First, bureaucratic officials make an input into the making of development choices, by providing necessary information, suggesting likely political outcomes of different policy options, even framing the options. There are also a host of bureaucratic decisions to do with finance, budgeting, scheduling, methods of recruiting and training necessary personnel, and so on, as well as the detailed allocations of resources at a local level.

Secondly, the implementation of any development effort involves power and control. The way bureaucracies are organized helps higher civil officials and political leaders to ensure that people working lower down in government departments are behaving appropriately. Also, people on the receiving end of development programmes normally must enter into a power relation with bureaucratic officials whenever government funds are involved. For example, conditions to be met before grants and loans can be released are enforced by local bureaucrats.

Thirdly, the results of development will be affected by informal political and social structures and alliances in society at different levels. Bureaucracies, like political parties, can help to knit together such alliances. Even when there is a comparatively rich assortment of local structures and alliances, bureaucratic and party institutions may together dispense development funds to local élites and others, thereby helping to sustain the alliances of those who benefit from development.

Finally, and most importantly of all, politics concerns power relations in society, both authoritative power (perceived by those subject to it as legitimate) and coercion or 'naked power'. Within states the maintenance of order in society depends on the power of that state's institutions.

This includes the efficiency of the state bureaucracy. But of course it also involves other things too, most crucially the cohesion, loyalty and discipline of the armed forces.

> "From one point of view, the state is society's way of controlling itself, and of making sure that others do not control it. From another, it is a sort of protection racket which claims a monopoly over the use of force."
>
> (Jordan, 1985, p.1)

The developmental state

The fact that the state is supposed to have a capacity to exercise legitimate coercion and at the same time is supposed to represent the will and desires of the 'nation', helps explain why state-induced development gained such a currency, and retained it for so long. There was continuity in the idea of the state as agency of development from the activities of both colonial administrations and metropolitan states in the nineteenth and early twentieth centuries through to post-colonial states after independence in the later twentieth century. As explained in Chapter 13, the idea remained dominant in development thinking throughout the 1960s and most of the 1970s, and only began to be questioned seriously from the early 1980s, with the shift towards neoliberal strategies.

In the course of the 1980s, the obvious failures of many state-led schemes was emphasized (perhaps exaggerated). However, as several scholars pointed out, this ignored several very striking success stories, notably in Asia. For some, these seemed to indicate the possibility of a 'developmental state', i.e. a state which reaped the benefits of state-led development, and avoided the problems.

The idea of the developmental state derives from the work of Chambers Johnson on Japan, Gordon White on South Korea and Taiwan and Robert Wade also on Taiwan. These authors suggested a number of features of these states which might explain why they were able to undertake intentional development whereas most states around the world attempted to do so and failed. These features include:

- a leadership ruthlessly committed to national economic development (and not to partial interests or its own enrichment)

- a developmental élite commanding a strong bureaucracy

- a bureaucracy relatively insulated from powerful interest groups

- the availability of possibilities for strategic intervention to govern the market.

Leftwich (1994) took on the idea of the developmental state and applied it to explain why a group of eight countries (seven in East and South-east Asia, plus Botswana) had performed outstandingly in terms of economic growth compared with others in Asia and Africa over a twenty-five year period from the mid 1960s. Leftwich suggested that both autocratic and democratic states could be developmental, since what was required was a question of political capacity which could be achieved under more than one political system. In the case of Botswana, his views concur with other commentators such as Charlton (1991) who characterized that country's governance as 'paternalistic developmentalism'. Leftwich also suggests another condition for a developmental state to succeed:

- a relatively weak civil society.

Others such as Peter Evans (1995) have pointed out the importance of embeddedness as well as autonomy. This implies that while, for effective development to occur, the political and administrative élites have to able to act relatively independently and forcefully on behalf of the nation as a whole (and hence need to be autonomous from any one interest group), they also need to enjoy the trust and co-operation of the whole of society (and hence to be embedded within it, not isolated and out of touch). Thus the idea of the developmental state is broadened to include notions such as that of social capital (Chapter 2) and relates strongly to contemporary debates about democratization and 'good governance' (Chapter 17).

Before moving on, we should note that the idea of 'developmental state' sees development in terms of achieving economic growth, generally through state promotion of industrialization. As you will recall from Chapters 1 and 2, this is only one of the several competing views of what is meant by development. There are other examples of states which have succeeded to greater or lesser extents in promoting human development, in some cases at the same time as failing in economic terms. Two notable cases, which stood out as exceptions in Chapter 4 in terms of their success in promoting the health of their populations despite relatively low material standards, are Sri Lanka and Cuba.

The decline of the state as a development agency

The authoritarian, developmental state model has been growing in influence. In part this is a reflection of the growing global significance of Asian states, especially Japan and China. Nevertheless, the general trend seems to be in a different direction. In 1992, the Secretary-General of the UN made the following revealing statement in a major report: 'The time of absolute and exclusive sovereignty...has passed; its theory was never matched by reality...' (Boutros-Ghali, 1992). This reflected a widespread recognition that state institutions were becoming more constrained.

In the early 1980s, the neoliberals had reacted to what they perceived to be the excessive controls exercised by states. They essentially viewed the power of states as blocking development. But nowadays, even the World Bank has become concerned that many states have too little authority. This is why the *World Development Report* of 1997 argued that it is essential both to 'reinvigorate state institutions', and to introduce 'skilful regulation' in order to 'make markets work more efficiently' as well as to 'influence market outcomes to achieve public purposes' (World Bank, 1997b, pp.7, 64–5). States are under pressure both from above and below: from 'globalization' (Chapter 16) and from 'localization'. These are two of the four 'key trends' which, according to the World Bank (1999b), will 'dominate the early 21st century' (the others being urbanization and environmental change):

"Globalization has reinforced the influence of market forces while attenuating the constraint of geography through advances in communication and transportation. Steeply declining telecommunications costs are tightening financial integration, opening up the possibilities for new kinds of international trade, and promoting the diffusion of ideas. Globalization has greatly increased the importance of MNCs, NGOs, regional trading blocs, of policy coordination between countries and the need for mechanisms, national as well as local, to enforce credible rules…

Side by side with globalization, we are also witnessing a shift in the focus of political activity to the subnational level, a process known as localization. It has many causes. Powerful forces have been released by the end of the Cold War, the conspicuous failure of the centralized economic model, the international circulation of ideas among a growing and politically more sensitized urban population, and a belief that many governments are failing to realize broad-based development. All these are diminishing the authority of the centralized state, have sharpened local identities and are arousing a popular demand for greater participation in public decision-making. In some regions, this is leading to the redefinition of borders and outright secession: 21 new countries were created since 1990. In other countries, where political accommodation has proved possible, the spread of localization is evident in the increasing share of subnational governments in total government spending."

(World Bank, 1999b, http://www.worldbank.org/wdr/2000/overview.htm)

The World Bank's overall assessment of the state of the world as we enter the twenty-first century is relatively up-beat. Some commentators are much less sanguine. Instead of a 'new world order', they paint a picture of increasing anarchy as particular groups pursue their interests both inside and across national borders in defiance of state controls (Chapter 23). Yet although the pace of disintegration seems to some as having accelerated since the end of the Cold War, it would be a mistake to limit the discussion to recent events.

The nation-state is quite a recent creation and its world-wide dissemination was shaped by European colonialism and anti-colonial independence movements. Just at the time when the nation-state became the almost universal mode of governance the cracks within its edifice began to appear. Since the end of the 1950s the rifts between the state and people were revealed as an increasing number of governments began to use force against those whom they claimed to represent. With the benefit of hindsight we can see that two disastrous world wars between European nation-states and the onset of the Cold War encouraged Western political élites to move towards economic and political union. Since the late 1940s substantial areas of nation-state sovereignty have been gradually abandoned in the creation of a supra-national European Community/Union. This has been matched by greater demands for recognition of sub-state units and the rights of particular 'nationalities' (such as Catalunya, Scotland and North Italy). Tensions have arisen but, so far, most Western European 'nationality' and regional autonomy movements have entered into negotiations with central governments without recourse to violence, and some have secured major concessions (obvious exceptions are the IRA in the UK, and ETA and Enbata in Spain and France).

The governments of less affluent states, however, have in general had much less room to manoeuvre. Some have become (or have managed to remain) affiliated to more powerful neighbouring supra-national regions. States in North Africa, for example, have a special relationship with the European Union, and are still considered strategically important enough for Western countries to help preserve 'friendly' administrations in Algeria and Egypt. A few governments of less developed countries have been able to use this kind of patronage to maintain or reinforce their authority within their territories in the face of ever growing demands for change (e.g. Turkey), but they often have to resort to human rights abuses to do so. Elsewhere, the governments of several newly industrialized states (particularly in eastern Asia) have been strong enough to act in a similar way (examples are Burma/Myanmar, China and Indonesia). But it is hard to see how policies of centralized oppression can be maintained in the long run.

Pressures on the integrity of states have become particularly intense along the Africa/Eurasia axis discussed in Chapter 8. Here, the institutional structures of internationally recognized states have been revealed to be very weak. In many instances the formal arrangements of statehood had been externally introduced or imposed, often joining together culturally diverse populations. Several Eurasian states were 'multi-national', and most African states were 'multi-tribal'. Often mutually antagonistic populations found themselves thrown together as a single unit and, in retrospect, many states were obviously artificial creations which were unlikely to turn into Western European-style nation-states. The wonder is that they appeared to hold together as relatively cohesive entities for so long.

The concentration of power in the Eurasian centrally planned states has made the end of the Cold War particularly dramatic. Numerous repressive, externally supported or unpopular regimes have fallen, but a transition to more democratic or accountable government has often not been possible. Some governments have been unable to maintain the rule of law (or even a dominance in the use of force) within their territories. The collapse of one communist government after another has contributed to a power vacuum. Scores of groups have fiercely competed for a voice at a time of rapid social changes, and several states have disintegrated into smaller polities.

In parts of Africa a somewhat similar scenario has unfolded. In the mid 1980s, Soviet aid to Africa was concentrated on the MPLA in Angola and Mengistu's regime in Ethiopia. The parallels between developments in these two states and some of those in parts of Eurasia formerly dominated by the USSR are obvious. Following the end of the Cold War, externally supported, centralized state systems have proved to be unsustainable when assistance was withdrawn. However, in certain respects developments in Angola and Ethiopia have been relatively unusual in the African context, and the influence of events in Eastern Europe has been more limited than is sometimes suggested. By the early 1980s the possibility of more communist governments coming to power had become remote in most of the continent. The USSR was overextended, and much of Africa was left largely to the West's 'sphere of influence'. The eroding of central government authority and the weakening of state institutions have continued in the 1990s, partly as a consequence of what has happened in Eurasia. But in much of the continent, the continued provision of diplomatic, humanitarian and financial aid disguised the fact that the majority of states had already suffered a serious loss of sovereignty and capacity, and were facing intense political pressure from within during the 1980s.

It is well known that most African states were the creations of European colonialism, and several were always very fragile indeed. Chad, for example, only came into existence as a discrete territory in 1960, has been almost continuously affected by civil war since 1965, and on occasion has had no internationally recognized government. There is little doubt that some African states would have broken up long ago if the Organization for African Unity and other international bodies had not been so committed to maintaining the often arbitrary boundaries inherited at independence, and generally discouraging secession movements.

Of course, not all the post-colonial states of Africa were as weak as Chad. In some countries a sense of national identity had been forged out of armed struggle against European imperialism (e.g. Algeria, Mozambique, Guinea Bissau, Zimbabwe), or was promoted with a degree of success by governments after independence (e.g. Tanzania). Also, in most African countries there were improvements in social welfare following independence which were linked to public services run by the state.

However, in the course of the 1970s and 1980s, these achievements were slowed or reversed. Even some of Africa's apparently most successful administrations faced enormous difficulties. Specific factors weakening states varied from one country to another, partly depending on natural resources and relations with former colonial rulers and the superpowers, but they usually included the effects of oil price rises, mounting foreign debt, structural adjustment programmes, some of the activities of international aid agencies, severe droughts, shifting terms of trade in primary products, externally supported destabilization campaigns, and increasing internal resistance to central government authority.

9.2 Other development agencies

The apparent erosion of state capacities has highlighted the issue of what other kinds of actors might try to respond to aspirations of social well-being. In this section we discuss two categories of such actors: official development agencies and non-governmental organizations.

Official development agencies

The first part of this chapter has indicated that, in a sense, all formally constituted states are 'official development agencies'. But here we use the expression to refer to 'bilateral' organizations representing those relatively affluent states which provide resources for development in other, poorer countries. We also use it for intergovernmental or 'multilateral' organizations, which promote or implement development programmes.

These bilateral and multilateral organizations allocate or spend resources known as **ODA**

(**official development assistance**). However, we also include reference to some official organizations which do not deploy ODA, but are nevertheless involved in development work. These obtain funds by other means. The landscape of these various agencies may conveniently be mapped out under three subheadings: the UN system, the World Bank and IMF, and official aid programmes.

> **ODA (official development assistance):** A term used by the Development Assistance Committee (DAC) of the Organization for Economic Co-operation and Development (OECD). It refers to grants and soft loans (with a grant element of at least 25%) which are provided by OECD members, with the 'promotion of the economic development and welfare of developing countries' as the 'main objective' (OECD, 1985, p.171).

The UN system

The United Nations has been involved in the promotion of development since its inception in 1945. The preamble to the Charter calls for an 'international mechanism for the promotion of the economic and social advancement of all people', and Article 55 states that the UN shall promote 'higher standards of living, full employment, and conditions of economic and social progress and development.'

However, until the 1960s, the role of the organization was limited to improving methods of assessment, and providing advice to the governments of member states. In general it recommended a somewhat expanded role for government in the promotion of development, going beyond the simple provision of physical infrastructure, social services and administration. This approach reflected assumptions about a relatively benign global environment, marked by rapid economic growth following the Second World War. Also, the dominance of the major powers within all the UN's principal organs meant that there was initially little recognition of a need to address structural arrangements underpinning international economic relations.

Things changed during the UN First Development Decade, declared in 1962. For some years, Raul Prebisch and his colleagues at the UN's Economic Committee for Latin America had been at the forefront of highlighting inequitable, 'centre-periphery' relations existing between the North and the South. As the number of former colonies achieved independence and took their seat in the General Assembly, pressures began to be brought to bear for this to be more fully recognized. In 1964, the first UN Conference on Trade and Development (UNCTAD) was held, with Prebisch as its Secretary-General. From this point, the UN system, or at least important parts of it, has tended to take a more radical and pro-South line on development issues than many Northern governments. This is reflected, for example, in the annual Human Development Report, which played an important role in critiquing the effects of neoliberalism during the early 1990s, and drawing attention to issues of poverty and deprivation. It also helps explain why the US and several other governments have been so unwilling to pay their assessed contributions to the organization's regular budget on time or in full. Another consequence has been the growth of a host of specialized agencies and programmes which are engaged in development activities, but are not funded through the core UN budget. These are mostly dependent on ODA, and therefore have to take care not to be too critical of the main aid donors.

The regular budget of the UN is derived from assessed contributions (which do not include ODA). These are based on a variety of factors, of which the most important are GNP and per capita income. The US is expected to contribute 25% of the budget, Japan almost 18%, Germany almost 10%, the United Kingdom just over 5%, and China just under 1%. However, in 1998, accumulated unpaid contributions from a total of 85 member states totalled $990 million. Peace-keeping operations are funded separately, with contributions being made as the need arises, and

being based on a modified version of the same scale. The cost of peace-keeping peaked at $2.8 billion in 1995. It then declined to around $1 billion per year, but rose again in the wake of the situation in Kosovo at the end of the decade.

Figure 9.3 shows the structure of the UN system. It can be seen that there are six principal organs:

The Trusteeship Council was established to supervise the administration of territories that were placed under the UN trusteeship system, such as Tanganyika (which later became Tanzania). All Trust Territories have now attained self-government or independence, and the Council now meets only as occasion might require. There has been some talk about it being reactivated to take responsibility for new territories placed under UN protection, notably Kosovo.

The International Court of Justice is the main judicial body of the UN. It settles legal disputes between states (such as the border dispute between Libya and Chad), and gives advisory opinions.

The Secretariat is an international civil service, employing some 8600 people from the UN's regular budget, and carries out the diverse day to day work of the organization. It includes the Department of Peacekeeping Operations and also the Office for the Co-ordination of Humanitarian Relief, both of which were established in the 1990s, as part of the huge expansion in international interventions in situations of ongoing war (see Chapter 8).

The General Assembly is where the main deliberations of the UN are supposed to take place. It is made up of all the member states, with each having one vote. This means that representatives of the South are in the majority, and that resolutions sometimes run counter to the views of the US and its allies. However, General Assembly resolutions are not binding on the UN's members, but are only recommendations. This has meant that much of what occurs in the General Assembly can be largely ignored by the major powers.

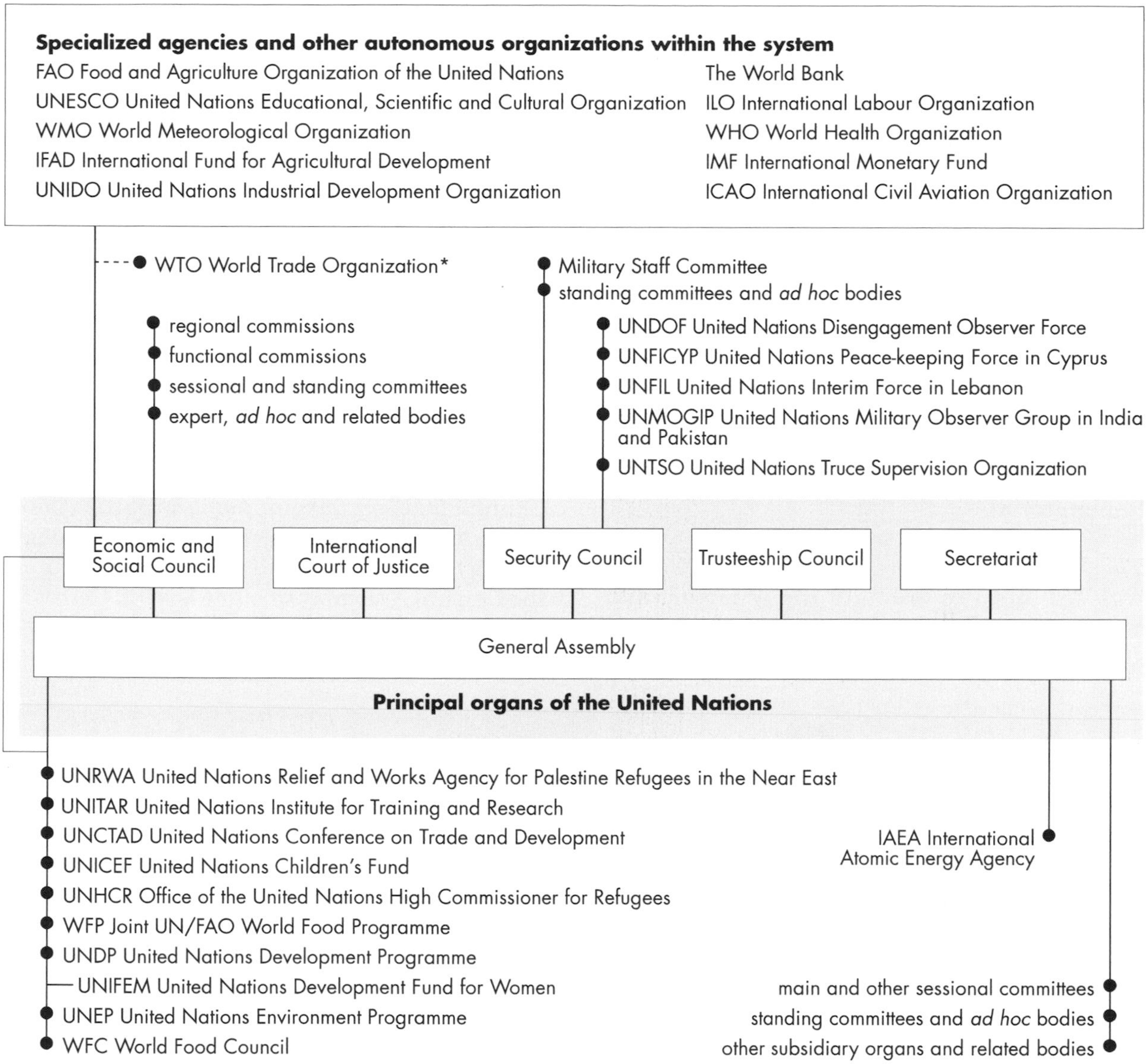

Specialized agencies and other autonomous organizations within the system

FAO Food and Agriculture Organization of the United Nations

UNESCO United Nations Educational, Scientific and Cultural Organization

WMO World Meteorological Organization

IFAD International Fund for Agricultural Development

UNIDO United Nations Industrial Development Organization

The World Bank

ILO International Labour Organization

WHO World Health Organization

IMF International Monetary Fund

ICAO International Civil Aviation Organization

- WTO World Trade Organization*
- regional commissions
- functional commissions
- sessional and standing committees
- expert, *ad hoc* and related bodies

- Military Staff Committee
- standing committees and *ad hoc* bodies
- UNDOF United Nations Disengagement Observer Force
- UNFICYP United Nations Peace-keeping Force in Cyprus
- UNFIL United Nations Interim Force in Lebanon
- UNMOGIP United Nations Military Observer Group in India and Pakistan
- UNTSO United Nations Truce Supervision Organization

Economic and Social Council	International Court of Justice	Security Council	Trusteeship Council	Secretariat

General Assembly

Principal organs of the United Nations

- UNRWA United Nations Relief and Works Agency for Palestine Refugees in the Near East
- UNITAR United Nations Institute for Training and Research
- UNCTAD United Nations Conference on Trade and Development
- UNICEF United Nations Children's Fund
- UNHCR Office of the United Nations High Commissioner for Refugees
- WFP Joint UN/FAO World Food Programme
- UNDP United Nations Development Programme
- UNIFEM United Nations Development Fund for Women
- UNEP United Nations Environment Programme
- WFC World Food Council

IAEA International Atomic Energy Agency

main and other sessional committees
standing committees and *ad hoc* bodies
other subsidiary organs and related bodies

- **Other United Nations programmes and organs whose governing bodies report directly to the principal organs (representative list only).**

* **The WTO is not formally part of the UN system but has co-operating arrangements and practices with it. It is the successor to the General Agreement on Tariffs and Trade (GATT), which, like the World Bank and the IMF, emerged from the Bretton Woods conference of 1944 (see Chapter 13).**

Figure 9.3 The structure of the United Nations system.

The Security Council has primary responsibility for the maintenance of international peace and security. It has 15 members, of which 5 are permanent – China, France, the Russian Federation, the United Kingdom and the United States. Permanent members have a veto, which means that if any one of them votes against a proposal it cannot be passed. Thus, the Council is dominated by the victorious allies of the Second World War. This is particularly significant because the Security Council alone has the power to take decisions which member states are obliged under the Charter to carry out. During the Cold War, the Council was hamstrung, but in the 1990s it became much more active, in many ways setting the agenda for international humanitarianism.

The Economic and Social Council (ECOSOC) was set up to co-ordinate the economic and social work of the UN and the specialized agencies, programmes, and autonomous organiz-ations within the system. The Council has 54 members, who serve three-year terms. Voting is by simple majority, with each member having one vote. It usually holds one five-week long session each year, at which high-level meetings take place between various government ministers and other senior officials. The year-round work of the Council is carried out in subsidiary bodies, such as the Economic Commission for Latin America. However, in practice, many of the agencies nominally under the Council are able to operate quite independently and, as indicated above, are often more affected by the priorities of their main funders. The president of the World Bank and the managing director of the IMF are amongst those who report to the Council. Other development organizations which are supposed to be co-ordinated through ECOSOC (and in some cases also directly from the General Assembly) include UNDP, UNHCR, UNICEF, WFP, FAO and WHO (see Box 9.1 and Figure 9.4).

Figure 9.4   UNHCR at work, mid-1990s. Children displaced by the civil war in Sri Lanka at the UNHCR reception centre in Trincomalee, before returning home.

Box 9.1 Some UN programmes and specialized agencies

UNDP (United Nations Development Programme) was established in 1965. Managed by an executive board representing both Northern and Southern countries, it provides grants for 'sustainable human development'. Most of its resources go to the world's poorest countries, and most of its staff is based in these countries. Its budget is derived primarily from voluntary contributions made by UN member states (most of it being ODA). In the late 1990s, its annual budget was around $2.16 billion. During the 1990s the organization has been under considerable financial pressure due to a combination of declining aid flows and a concentration of resources on humanitarian relief, rather than longer-term development. UNDP publishes the annual *Human Development Report*, which offers a very important alternative (but still official) perspective to that of the annual *World Development Report* of the World Bank.

UNHCR (Office of the United Nations' High Commissioner for Refugees) was established as a UN organ by the General Assembly in 1951. Its mandate is to provide protection and assistance to refugees, but this has been extended on an *ad hoc* basis to include some groups of returned refugees, and internally displaced people. The organization has expanded with the rise in the number of displaced persons. Its budget for 1997 was $1.22 billion, most of which came from ODA. The High Commissioner is supposed to follow policy directives given to him or her by the General Assembly and ECOSOC. However, during the 1990s, the current High Commissioner worked closely and controversially with the Security Council. For some commentators, this weakened the agency's independence, and thereby its capacity to protect refugees in an even-handed manner.

UNICEF (United Nations Children's Fund), was founded in 1946 as a programme to meet the emergency needs of children. It expanded rapidly during the 1980s, attracting considerable funds with its high profile 'selective primary health care' programme in impoverished countries. In the 1990s, it shifted focus, working within the framework of the Convention of the Rights of the Child, adopted by the General Assembly in 1989. Towards the end of the 1990s, its total annual income was $900 million, of which 70% was derived mainly from ODA. The remainder came from non-governmental contributions. UNICEF is unique among UN agencies in also having 'non-governmental' status through its national committees. In some countries these have been successful at raising money through the sale of Christmas cards.

WFP (World Food Programme) was established in 1963, and is governed by a committee, half of which is made up of staff members, and half of which is appointed by ECOSOC. It specializes in providing food aid to populations caught up in 'natural' and 'man-made' disasters, and wars. Most of its resources, 70%, are used for emergency relief. Much of the food which it distributes is pledged in kind by donor countries. This has served the purpose of disposing of surplus production in North America and Western Europe in such a way as to maintain food prices. It has also sometimes had the effect of undermining local markets in regions where the food is distributed, with adverse effects on farmers' livelihoods. But in recent years efforts have been made to avoid this problem. WFP also purchases food with mainly ODA finance. In the late 1990s, it was spending about $300 million per year.

FAO (Food and Agriculture Organization) is a UN specialized agency, founded in 1945. It aims at promoting rural development by improving agricultural production and increasing food security. It provides support to states preparing for emergency food crises, sometimes provides food relief (in conjunction with WFP), and is often involved in efforts to re-establish production following floods, livestock disease outbreaks and other disasters. An important development for the organization in 1994 was that it became the custodian of the important germplasm collection of CGIAR (the Consultative Group on International Agricultural Research). This followed an attempt by the World Bank to take control of CGIAR, and a vigorous campaign mounted by concerned non-governmental organizations, who maintained that the germplasm collection should be managed by an intergovernmental organization governed by the one-country-one-vote system. FAO is governed by a Conference of Member Nations, which meets every two years and approves the budget. The regular programme is financed by member states, who contribute according to levels set by the Conference. This forms part of the approved regular budget of the UN system as a whole. In 1998–99 it was $650 million. FAO's field programmes are partly funded from this source, but also from trust funds and from funds provided by UNDP (mainly from ODA sources). Joint financing of projects with other agencies and with governments is also common.

WHO (World Health Organization) is also a UN specialized agency. It was established in 1948 to give worldwide guidance in the field of health. It co-operates with governments in planning and management and evaluation of national health programmes, and promotes the development and transfer of appropriate health technology, information and standards. The governing body of the WHO is the World Health Assembly, which is composed of all member states, and meets every year. It was set up to be the UN's premier institution working on health, and nominally this is still the case. It

plays a key role, for example, in monitoring disease control research. However, especially since the 1980s it has found itself in competition with other parts of the system. UNICEF, which is much more directly influenced by the major aid donors, has attracted considerable funds for its public health activities, and the World Bank too has become increasingly interested in the health sector. The regular budget of the WHO, which is derived from the assessed contributions of member states in the same way as the regular budget of FAO, is only $842 million. As was noted by the Director General in the 1998–1999 proposed budget, this is about the same as for a medium-sized teaching hospital in any industrialized country. It is also somewhat less than the organization raises from voluntary contributions (around $950 million), including ODA, much of which is 'earmarked' for specific projects, with by far the largest portion being spent on WHO's integrated disease control programme.

The World Bank and IMF

The main part of the World Bank, known as the International Bank for Reconstruction and Development (IBRD), and the International Monetary Fund (IMF) were both products of the Bretton Woods Conference of 1944 (see Chapter 13). They were set up essentially to regulate the global economy under the sponsorship and direction of the US, initially with the acute needs of war damaged Europe in mind. The IBRD would guarantee European borrowing in US financial markets, and the IMF would smooth the flow of repayments (Raffer & Singer, 1996, p.46). Subsequently they have both turned their attention to the South. In the case of the IBRD this occurred quite quickly, because Marshall Plan grant aid to Europe, and US loans to the UK, bypassed and sidelined it.

In theory both the World Bank (which, in addition to the IBRD, includes the International Development Association, the International Finance Corporation, and the Multilateral Investment Guarantee Agency) and the IMF are included in the UN system. Like the FAO, the WHO and the International Labour Organiz-

ation (ILO), they are specialized agencies which report to ECOSOC. However, in reality they form a separate system from that of the rest of the UN.

Other UN affiliated agencies are nominally managed on a 'country-a-vote' basis, even if there tends to be pressures placed on them by those affluent states which are their main funders. With respect to the World Bank and the IMF, the dominance of the North is much more transparent. Both are run on a 'dollar-a-vote' basis. This means that voting power fluctuates, and is weighted according to financial contribution. Thus, within the IBRD, the US vote counts for around 17%, and the UK vote counts for around 5%, whereas that of India and China both count for about 3%. The voting weight of the North as a whole is well over 60%, while that of the South (excluding the affluent east Asian countries, such as South Korea) counts for around 30%.

This arrangement has placed the Bank and the Fund under the direct control of the rich industrial countries – underlined by the fact that the president of the Bank is always a US citizen and the managing director of the Fund is always a western European. Northern governments have also made it clear that any change in this situation will be resisted. During the 1970s, some oil-producing states from the South tried to increase their voting power in exchange for larger financial contributions, but were blocked from doing so. More recently, in the mid 1990s there was an adamant refusal to accept closer coordination under a proposed ECOSOC executive committee.

One effect of the Bank's and the Fund's lack of accountability to the rest of the UN system has been that they have been much more significant in providing development assistance than had originally been anticipated, because the governments of rich countries could more easily ensure that their contributions were used for policies which they supported. This is most obviously the case with respect to the World Bank.

The IBRD was not set up as an aid agency, and is not supported by ODA. It was established to promote the international flow of capital for what were deemed to be productive purposes. Although voting power relates to the amounts paid to the organization by each member, 90% of its lending is funded by borrowing. The IBRD is able to raise money from finance markets at a much lower rate of interest than many governments, because it is effectively guaranteed by its rich shareholders, notably the US. It can then pass on this favourable rate to all its members. Thus the government of Uganda, for example, can borrow at a very favourable rate of interest from the IBRD compared with the interest it would have to pay if it borrowed directly from a commercial Bank. Since it was established, the IBRD has only received $11 billion in capital paid in by its members, but has leveraged more than $280 billion in loans.

In 1997, the IBRD's commitments amounted to $14.5 billion, of which $7.4 billion were loans approved to the poorest countries (defined as those with a per capita GNP of $785 or less). This is not a huge amount, far less than total ODA, let alone private capital flows. However, the IBRD's influence should not be underestimated. Together with the IMF it audits the economies of countries, and without its approval it is very difficult to obtain finance from other sources. Moreover, from 1960 the IBRD became responsible for the administration of an ODA-supported, soft-finance facility known as the International Development Association (IDA), and has become a leading think-tank on Southern issues.

During the period 1948 to 1953, the US spent 2–3% of its GNP on Marshall Plan aid to reconstruct Western European economies and contain communism. It was generally regarded to have been a resounding success, and it has been seen as a model which might potentially have similar effects in the South. Yet, in spite of Truman's enthusiasm for the fight against 'underdevelopment', expressed in his 1949 inaugural address, similar funds were not made available for the rest of the world. A UN fund was set up to administer large-scale soft aid, but was never adequately resourced. However, in 1960 the political climate in the US changed, largely in response to concerns generated by Castro's coup in Cuba. Congress was prepared to make more funds available for development in the South, although on nothing like the scale that had been allocated for Europe. But by this time many former colonies had become independent, and the major powers did not have control of the General Assembly or ECOSOC. It was therefore decided to ignore the UN fund, and to set up the IDA, which was placed under the control of the IBRD.

The IDA loans, known as 'credits', are made available for a period of 35–40 years, only to the poorest countries. No interest is charged, except for a small fee to cover administrative costs, and repayment does not begin until after a 10-year grace period. 'Credits' are financed from IBRD profits, and from replenishments to IDA funds made by member states every three years, most of which is classified as ODA. In 1997, IDA disbursements reached a record figure of just under $6 billion.

Taking control of the IDA, however, did not immediately lead to a huge expansion of the World Bank's power in the South. Until the late 1960s, the Bank was constrained by a policy of project lending. This meant that it could only lend for specific schemes, such as a dam. In each case an argument had to be made that the project was needed. Technical feasibility studies had to be made, and the costs and benefits assessed. It was a very time-consuming business, and could only ever have a limited impact.

Understandably, the policy irritated Robert McNamara when he became the Bank's president in 1968. He had been used to handling much larger budgets when he had been US Secretary of Defence. It had also proved difficult to find very successful projects. By any criteria, many had failed. It was pointed out by analysts at the time that this was at least in part because a project could not be separated from the economic and political context in which it was located. In response, McNamara led the Bank away from exclusively project-oriented lending during the 1970s, towards programme lending. Larger sums of money were loaned, with the intention of encouraging fundamental transformations in recipient countries. Inevitably, the approach went hand in hand with much tighter conditionality on the loans, because ultimately the objective was to alleviate poverty by changing social structures and, less explicitly, to combat more effectively the spread of communism.

Following McNamara's departure from the Bank, and the shift towards a neoliberal ideology in the US, the Bank moved away from direct poverty alleviation towards an emphasis on free-market strategies. At the same time, the oil price rises and the debt crisis had greatly increased its importance, particularly for the poorest countries. The Bank moved much closer to the IMF, and the two organizations used the programme-lending approach to promote structural adjustment vigorously throughout the 1980s. More recently, the Bank has shifted again. Since 1990, poverty has been put back on the agenda, and there has been a growing emphasis on institution building. The Bank now makes recommendations in just about every area of development, from the health sector to information technology. Again this reflects a shift in emphasis in the US, but it is also a response to

the growing influence of Japan within IBRD (Japan has wanted to give more emphasis to the role of government), and to the rise in private capital flows to developing countries (which are now four to five times annual World Bank lending). At the turn of the millennium, the Bank is keen to reinvent itself as the world's major repository of knowledge on poverty and how to eradicate it (hence the interest in CGIAR's germplasm collection mentioned in Box 9.1).

While the World Bank has always had a development assistance orientation, this has been less clear with respect to the IMF. Initially the Fund was not much involved in the South at all, but mainly functioned as a means of keeping the currencies of member states at par value to gold and the US dollar. It provided short-term finance to members in order to resolve balance of payments problems. Unlike the Bank, the Fund has never been expected to raise funds by borrowing on financial markets, but, as its name suggests, it is a fund. Each member pays in a certain amount depending on the size of its economy, and can borrow from the Fund on a short-term basis, under strict conditions to ensure repayment within a short period. At present the Fund's financial resources total almost $200 billion.

Until the 1970s, special measures for aiding Southern countries with longer-term problems were very limited. In the course of the decade, however, the character of the Fund changed. The system of fixed exchange rates collapsed in 1973, and was replaced by all the major industrial countries with floating exchange rates. Also, private banks took centre stage in the expansion of international credit. The IMF shifted attention to the South, and as the debt crisis worsened in the early 1980s, moved to a lead role in deliberations over rescheduling. In effect the IMF became a means by which Northern governments tried to prevent defaulting. In the course of the 1980s, the Fund worked closely with the World Bank in promoting structural adjustment measures, which were at least partly motivated by a perceived need to ensure continued repayment of outstanding debts.

In the 1990s, the Fund was less prone than the Bank to shift ground. It collaborated in the administration of the so-called Enhanced Structural Adjustment Facility, which has a grant element of over 25%, and is supposed to ensure that poverty is not exacerbated. However, far from trying to reinvent itself, the Fund has remained a much smaller organization than the Bank, specializing in providing members with a particular short-term facility, and providing technical and economic advice. It is hard to obtain private investment or finance without its seal of approval, and it continues to encourage neoliberal, free-market policies. This had led to some tensions with the Bank. The Fund has, for example, been much less willing than the Bank to consider the possibility of extensive debt cancellation for selected impoverished countries.

Official aid programmes

UN agencies and the IDA of the World Bank are multilateral organizations which receive donations (official development assistance, ODA) from the 20 countries which make up the Development Assistance Committee (DAC) of the OECD. These aid donors also provide ODA for other multilateral operations, such as the European Union's aid programme. They also run their own bilateral ODA schemes. In theory, multilateral aid is less prone to donor influence than bilateral aid, although (as we have seen) this is not necessarily the case in practice.

Donors give very different amounts. According to data presented in *The Reality of Aid 1998/*

1999: an independent review of poverty reduction and development assistance (German & Randel, 1998), in 1997 Japan's ODA was $9.4 billion, France's was $6.3 billion, the US's was $6.2 billion, Germany's was $6 billion and the UK's was $3.4 billion, while Portugal's was $251 million, Ireland's was $187 million, New Zealand's was $145 million and Luxembourg's was $87 million. However, if ODA is expressed as a percentage of GNP, then Denmark gives the most (0.97%) followed by Norway, the Netherlands and Sweden. These are the only states which have met or exceeded the agreed UN target of 0.7%. At the other end of the scale are Japan, which gives just 0.22%, Italy which gives 0.11% and the US which gives 0.08%. The UK gives 0.26%. Total ODA in 1997 was $47 580 million, which was 0.22% of the total GNP of all 20 DAC donors. Figure 9.5 provides a range of information about ODA in 1997. It can be seen that, in terms of GNP, it was at the lowest level that year since the 1960s. During this period, US ODA has plummeted from 0.56% of GNP in 1965. But even this seems very low when it is compared with the 2–3% allocated for Marshall Plan aid for Europe.

Bilateral aid is deployed in a variety of ways. Some countries, including the UK, have used bilateral ODA to indirectly subsidize their own arms industries or, like the US, have used ODA to fund military debt cancellations. Others concentrate their donations on particular problems

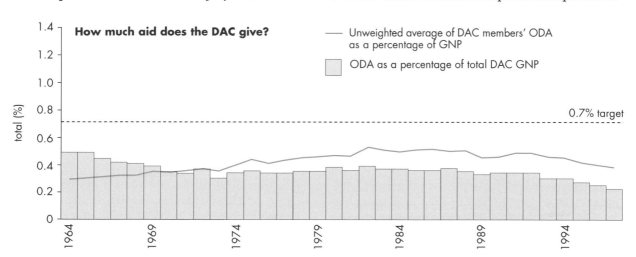

Figure 9.5 Official development assistance in 1997.

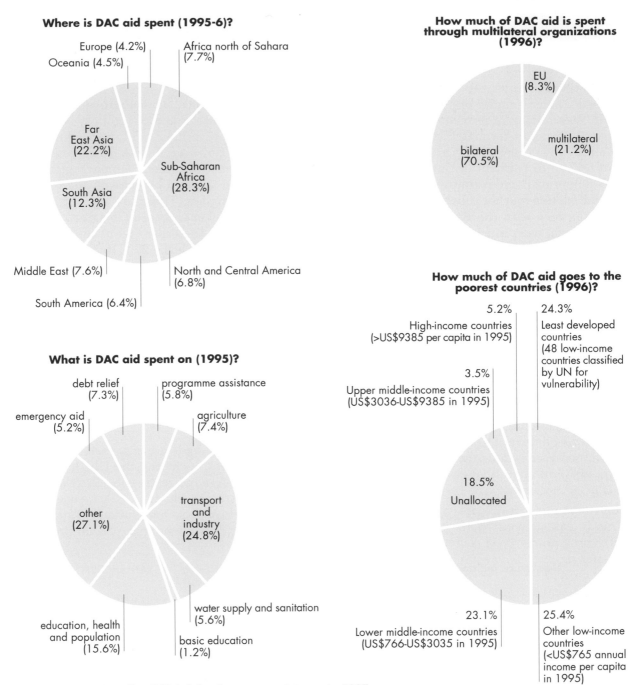

Where is DAC aid spent (1995-6)?

Europe (4.2%)
Oceania (4.5%)
Africa north of Sahara (7.7%)
Far East Asia (22.2%)
Sub-Saharan Africa (28.3%)
South Asia (12.3%)
Middle East (7.6%)
North and Central America (6.8%)
South America (6.4%)

How much of DAC aid is spent through multilateral organizations (1996)?

EU (8.3%)
bilateral (70.5%)
multilateral (21.2%)

What is DAC aid spent on (1995)?

debt relief (7.3%)
programme assistance (5.8%)
emergency aid (5.2%)
agriculture (7.4%)
other (27.1%)
transport and industry (24.8%)
education, health and population (15.6%)
water supply and sanitation (5.6%)
basic education (1.2%)

How much of DAC aid goes to the poorest countries (1996)?

5.2%
High-income countries (>US$9385 per capita in 1995)
24.3%
Least developed countries (48 low-income countries classified by UN for vulnerability)
3.5%
Upper middle-income countries (US$3036-US$9385 in 1995)
18.5%
Unallocated
23.1%
Lower middle-income countries (US$766-US$3035 in 1995)
25.4%
Other low-income countries (<US$765 annual income per capita in 1995)

Figure 9.5 (continued)   Official development assistance in 1997.

or issues. Portugal, for example, allocates 57.9% of its ODA to general debt relief, and Japan allocates 46.2% of its ODA to supporting the infrastructure of transport and industry. Certain donors continue openly to use ODA to subsidize governments which they perceive to be strat-

egically important – between a quarter and a third of US ODA has traditionally gone to Israel and Egypt. Several countries require a percentage of their bilateral aid to be spent on their own goods and services. For example, 38.7% of Danish bilateral ODA, 25.1% of French bilateral ODA, 13.8% of UK bilateral ODA, 6.1% of Swedish ODA, and 0.2% of Japanese ODA must be used in this way. There is also considerable divergence in the amounts allocated to the 48 least developed countries (as classified by the UN): 96.3% of Portuguese ODA, 51.4% of Norwegian ODA, 46.9% of Danish ODA, 40.8% of UK ODA, 20.6% of German ODA, 18.2% of US ODA, 15% of Japanese ODA, and 13.7% of Austrian ODA. Allocations for emergency relief vary from 22.5% of Norway's ODA, to 14.2% of the UK's ODA, to 0.2% of Japan's ODA.

Thus the total amount of ODA allocated by all the major donors is very low, and it is also clear that only a relatively small amount of it is used directly to alleviate poverty. It is even questionable that most of ODA has 'the economic development and welfare of developing countries as its main objective' (a characteristic which is supposed to be part of the OECD's definition). Although there appear to be altruistic motives behind the allocation of some ODA, reflecting the concerns and demands of electorates in Northern countries, much of it is manifestly deployed to promote the political and economic interests and concerns of the donors. This has been underlined during the 1980s and 1990s by the increased emphasis on aid **conditionality**. It is no longer just the World Bank and the IMF that require recipients of their assistance to adhere to certain policies. This is now a requirement of many bilateral ODA programmes. Aid is viewed as a means of promoting what donors perceive to be 'good governance' and 'sound' economic practices. Such strategies might have beneficial consequences where governments are especially corrupt and undemocratic, but they are not applied consistently. Little pressure is placed on China or Indonesia, for example, while the Kenyan government has been forced to accept a rather half-baked form of multi-party democracy.

These factors have prompted many analysts and politicians to become very critical of aid. It has been argued that no amount of conditionality can disguise the fact that ODA has subsidized oppressive and inefficient regimes. Some maintain that official aid should really be understood as a form of government-to-govern-

Conditionality: Giving loans or grants subject to specific conditions, such as the World Bank's frequent insistence from the early 1980s, on neoliberal economic policies through structural adjustment programmes, or more recent insistence on moves towards multi-party liberal democracy or 'good governance'.

ment subsidy, and that it will always have the effect of encouraging poor administration. It allows politicians in the South to line their own pockets or invest in military expansion, while appearing to offer welfare services to their people. In addition, there appears to be no evidence that aid is beneficial for growth, or that it has any overall and sustainable effect on deprivation.

These criticisms have to be taken seriously, and are at least one reason for the decline in ODA flows. However, just as it is hard to show that aid has beneficial results, it is difficult to prove that it has negative ones. It may fund some corruption in some places, but it has also been used to provide services to at least some poor people. Food aid, for example, may create all sorts of problems, from undermining local markets to feeding warring factions, but it cannot be denied that it has occasionally saved lives. In any case, the amount of ODA that has been available since the 1960s has never been high enough to have a really significant impact. It can only be a partial measure, and therefore has to be looked at in particular contexts. Danish aid to Uganda, for example, is not the reason why the Ugandan economy has been growing quite quickly since the 1980s, but Danish support for road construction has meant that some farmers and fishermen in some parts of the country have been able to transport more of their produce to markets. Moreover, in the post Cold War era there have been certain potentially positive developments. The initial reason for providing ODA in the 1950s and 1960s is no longer an issue. Indeed, a considerable portion of ODA is now being spent in former communist countries, and even some countries which are still communist, such as Vietnam. This has meant that the purpose of giving ODA and the way in which it is deployed is more open to scrutiny. One response has been an increased interest in supporting environmental projects. Another has been increased funding for non-governmental organizations, which are generally thought to have a much greater capacity to reach down to the local, grassroots level. Many bilateral and multilateral aid programmes now seek to assert their political neutrality and altruism by, in effect, contracting NGOs to spend resources on their behalf. In the mid 1990s, for example, the US amazed observers by asserting that it intended to channel half its aid through NGOs (Todaro, 1997, p.558), although exactly what this means in practice is still not entirely clear.

Non-governmental organizations

Having surveyed official development agencies, we now turn our attention to NGOs. However, the distinction may be much less clear than it first appears. Many organizations calling themselves NGOs are in fact largely funded by governments, or from official state resources. Norwegian Church Aid is largely financed by the Norwegian state, and some Japanese NGOs have been set up by government ministries. In Zimbabwe, the President's Fund has, as the name suggests, close links with the ruling party. Moreover, even those NGOs which try to distance themselves from governments, and receive most of their support from private contributions, may also obtain some funds from ODA, and may end up operating under an aid umbrella in which policy is largely determined by multilaterals (in a war zone, for example, where UNHCR is the lead humanitarian agency). In general the term NGO is restricted to non-profit-making organizations. But this too can be an ambiguous concept. On the one hand, many other organizations, such as UN agencies, are non-profit making, and on the other hand, NGOs have to survive as bureaucracies, something which requires considerably more finance than that which is spent on their supposed beneficiaries.

In general, the question of what is meant by an NGO is dealt with differently in different sectors. Development NGOs are often viewed as a category which is distinct from NGOs involved in environmental protection and human rights. The latter are primarily membership organizations based in the North which promote and lobby for environmental and human rights interests within their own countries and internationally. On the other hand, development NGOs mostly began as charitable relief or missionary welfare organizations, often running very localized projects, and are often evaluated against goals such as their direct impact on rural poverty. It is relatively recently that such NGOs have broadened their activities to include attempts at policy influence or advocacy at both international and national levels.

Korten (1990) has suggested that NGOs which began as charitable relief or missionary welfare organizations have typically moved on to the promotion of small-scale self-reliance and then to a 'third generation strategy' of 'sustainable systems development' involving 'facilitating development by other organizations, both public and private' (1987, p.149). However, as Edwards and Hulme (1992, p.13) have pointed out, despite many small-scale successes the impact of development NGOs is 'highly localized, and often transitory'. This has prompted efforts at 'scaling up', in order to make a real difference. These include 'additive' strategies where the size of programmes is increased, 'multiplicative' strategies involving 'deliberate influence, networking, policy and legal reform' and 'diffusive' strategies spreading ideas informally and spontaneously (ibid., p.15).

Thus the role of development NGOs has broadened to include advocacy as well as the provision of relief and welfare services. At the same time NGOs originally set up for advocacy, say on the environment or human rights, often end up providing services aimed at development in a way that complements their promotional and lobbying work. For example, in Zimbabwe the World Wide Fund for Nature (WWF) actively supports the 'CAMPFIRE' programme for the sustainable utilization of natural resources (particularly wildlife) at community level; in Nigeria the Royal Society for the Protection of Birds (RSPB) has been involved in community development alongside its bird protection activities.

Types of NGO

It is perhaps most important to distinguish *mutual benefit* organizations, based on membership, from *public benefit* organizations, including charities and other NGOs set up to supply services to others as well as campaigning or research organizations which do not necessarily have a defined client group. It is also useful to recognize differences in scope and scale; NGOs working variously at local, national and international levels should not be expected to work in similar ways. Starting from these principles, and excluding political parties, religious congregations, and trade unions, we might distinguish the following main types of NGOs which aim, in one way or another, to promote development.

At the international level, we can differentiate between campaigning and charitable or service-providing NGOs. Both of these are generally based in the North. International campaigning NGOs are epitomized by Greenpeace. Such NGOs will only become involved in development policy issues from a distance. There are also a few Southern-based international campaigning NGOs, some of which have several country branches. ENDA-Tiers-Monde is a notable example, set up following the 1972 UN Stockholm Conference on the World Environment. ENDA stands for 'Environment and Development Activities'.

Northern-based, service-providing NGOs include organizations like Save the Children, Oxfam, Christian Aid, World Vision, and so on. These generally have branches in the Southern countries in which they work. Often they will run their own projects, sometimes setting up their own bureaucracies, effectively bypassing those of the state (or in certain war zones, those of rebel groups). In other circumstances they will fund and monitor local service-providing NGOs or membership organizations (see below). Some agencies, such as Christian Aid, operate only in this way. Several of these agencies have been established recently, partly as a consequence of the increasing availability of ODA funds to contracted NGOs. Others, such as Oxfam, have a relatively long history (Oxfam was founded during the Second World War). They also vary enormously in professionalism and size. Oxfam (Figure 9.6) is one of the most highly respected, and one of the largest (it has an annual income exceeding £100 million).

Moving to the national level, there are many NGOs which are public interest research or campaigning organizations. Some of these are

Figure 9.6   Refugees from Rwanda at Katele Camp, Zaïre, 1994, helping to install a water tank provided by the British aid agency, Oxfam.

Western-style human rights or conservationist NGOs, but they are usually relatively few in number, and often have very limited local support. More often they represent the concerns of particular groups, such as landless labourers or farmers requiring agricultural services. Some may reflect the aspirations and social demands of specific professions, such as public health workers.

Another type are indigenous, national (and provincial) service-providing NGOs – mostly concerned with welfare and rural development. They are like the previous type (and differ from the next) in being clearly for public rather than mutual benefit. Some aim at particular constituencies or interests, such as women or the rural poor, and some of them may adopt a participatory style and attempt to build up local membership. Many of the international NGOs have moved from direct running of projects to working through partnerships with NGOs of this type and the next. Thus there is a tendency for some of these NGOs to be rather artificial products of the need for international NGOs to have local partners. Nevertheless, they are essentially based on trust, charity and private initiative aimed at social and development goals.

Lastly, there are membership organizations which exist to further their members' interests. The term 'grassroots organization' is often used to refer to local organizations of this type. Local member-benefit NGOs may also combine into regional or national federations or there may be national associations or unions. In principle there is a clear distinction between this type of NGO and those of the public-benefit type, even if the latter are set up with a fully participative style of working. In practice the differences may not be so clear cut. A public-benefit NGO may be set up from the top with the intention of attracting local members to whom the staff should be accountable. Alternatively, a member-benefit NGO may originally be based on some local campaign. It is quite common in cases where local political activity through other channels is suppressed for NGOs to be set up in order to allow the political demands of a particular community or ethnic group to be expressed. In Nigeria the Movement for the Survival of the Ogoni People (MOSOP) did this via an environmental campaign. In the end, however they are started, NGOs may well work both for member benefit and for general public benefit.

The potential for variety amongst NGOs is enormous. For example, we might construct an additional type of NGO with membership consisting of other NGOs, to include the various representative bodies which exist in most countries as well as internationally. However, the main types and how they have arisen is as described. It should be noted that different types have different histories and concerns. Not surprisingly, we are likely to find that NGOs of different types act as development agents in very different ways.

The growth of the NGO sector

There is a widespread recognition that the NGO sector has expanded hugely. At the international level, the number has risen from just over 1000 in the late 1950s to 29 000 in the early 1990s (see Figure 16.4 in Chapter 16). The number of NGOs with consultative status with the United Nations Economic and Social Council (ECOSOC) has increased steadily from about 200 in 1950 to almost 1000 in the early 1990s and 1500 by 1995. Since the late 1980s, over 4000 development NGOs based in OECD countries have been spending about US$6 billion annually for relief and development work from privately raised resources. In addition, as mentioned above, during the 1990s they were commonly contracted to implement projects by bilateral and multilateral organizations. The amounts deployed in this way vary from year to year, largely in accordance with the incidence of emergencies, and are sometimes difficult to assess because they may be transferred rapidly and on an *ad hoc* basis to a wide variety of types of NGOs, including some national (i.e. Southern) NGOs. Nevertheless, for some years in the mid 1990s they were certainly in excess of $5 billion, and were perhaps as high as $9 billion. This caused a sudden proliferation of NGOs, many of them being set up specifically to compete for ODA funds (and, as noted in Chapter 8, also a worrying decline in the quality of activities in some places).

Partly because of the problem of definition, and often the lack of formal registration, the overall number of national or grassroots NGOs cannot be adequately assessed. Some sources suggest that there are now over 200 000 grassroots organizations which may be termed NGOs in Asia, Africa and Latin America. This can be no more than a guess, but it does seem to be incontrovertible that NGO activity is on the increase virtually everywhere, and has increased more rapidly during the 1990s. In Nepal, for example, the number of NGOs registered with the government rose from 220 in 1990 to 1210 in 1993 (Edwards & Hulme, 1995, p.3). One commentator has gone so far as to assert that:

> "a veritable associational revolution now seems underway at the global level that may constitute as significant a social and political development of the latter twentieth century as the rise of the nation state was of the nineteenth century."
>
> (Lester Salamon, quoted in Edwards & Hulme, 1995, p.3)

However, the discussion in previous sections of this chapter will have made it apparent that this increase is not likely to be the result of a sudden expansion of interest in charity work, or of an outbreak of solidarity with the poor. It may be largely connected with the decline of the state as an institution, and the emergence of various kinds of agencies which have taken over some of its former roles, or which can now resist state dominance more openly.

With respect to international, service-providing NGOs, this has been clear. The growth of their activities since the 1980s has in fact largely been a consequence of the way in which ODA has been allocated. Many bilateral and multilateral agencies have been less willing to transfer resources to Southern governments, both because they are viewed as inefficient and possibly oppressive, and because of the neoliberal view that states should be cut back as much as possible. In the 1990s, the extreme neoliberalism of the 1980s may have eased, but there was also less need to prop up 'friendly' regimes. In the 'New Policy Agenda', which combines market economics and liberal democratic politics, NGOs are simul-

taneously 'viewed as market-based actors' and 'placed ... in a central position as components of 'civil society'" (Edwards & Hulme, 1995, p.849). Thus the increase in provision of services by NGOs is seen as part and parcel of the privatization of state services, despite NGOs' non-profit basis. This is often described as 'gap-filling' (e.g. Vivian, 1994), and occurs where states, especially in the South, do not have the capacity to maintain universal services or are obliged to reduce them as part of a structural adjustment or donor-promoted 'reform' package.

NGOs have also served the purpose of allowing official aid agencies to claim that at least some of their activities benefit the poor. Transferring ODA to NGOs has become a means of asserting good intentions, because NGOs are viewed as apolitical, socially accountable, and integrated into the communities which they serve. But this, of course, is something of a fiction. Indeed it raises a crucial problem, which NGOs themselves have found difficult to resolve. Except where an NGO is in fact a mutual benefit group, the issue arises of what right do those who run the NGO projects have to decide what is best for people. The dilemma is especially acute for the international NGOs. Their survival as organizations depends on private donations and ODA, not on the successful provision of services to those they want to help. In other words, NGOs are in practice more accountable to their donors than they are to their beneficiaries (however much they would like the situation to be otherwise). This inevitably affects what they end up actually doing on the ground, and shapes the way they present their interventions to the public and international meetings.

Finally, we need to keep in mind the most acute limitation in the NGO sector. In spite of the enormous amount of hype that is generated by some development NGOs and their supporters about 'making a difference' and 'empowering' the poor, and the fact that NGOs can obviously achieve a great deal in certain situations, they are never going to change the world. There just is not enough money involved. At less than $50 billion, total global ODA is little more than a pittance. The fact that NGOs receive some 10% of

Figure 9.7 Challenging structures through social agency: two examples of the growing number of social movements which are broader than single NGOs. (top) Brazilian landless movement, Movimento sem Terra: members shout 'Reforma agraria: uma lutta de todos' ('Agrarian reform: everyone's struggle') at the first assembly held on land occupied by people from favelas and the streets of São Paulo and smaller cities. (above) Up to 50 Indian farmers, in Britain as part of the intercontinental caravan highlighting the unfairness of free trade and world debt, protest outside the Nuffield Council on Bioethics, May 1999, at its recent report suggesting genetically modified food could help stop the poor going hungry.

it is probably a step in the right direction (it is certainly better than using ODA to subsidize arms deals), but even when this is combined with private aid donations, we are still only talking about $10 billion to $15 billion per annum.

9.3 Conclusion

In this chapter we have reviewed different kinds of agencies of development. We ended by making reference to accountability – or, as we put it at the beginning of the chapter, the issue of trusteeship. What right have NGOs to speak for the impoverished? The same question might be asked of all the other agencies we have mentioned, from the World Bank to the governments of states. By and large they must be assessed to be less accountable to the poor than many NGOs, who at least encounter them on a regular basis. This may not necessarily mean that they implement harmful policies, but it does indicate a certain lack of legitimacy. We fall back on altruism. Philanthropy may help, even if those in positions of power and influence are not compelled to act in ways that benefit those in most need. But it cannot be enough. In the end poverty reduction requires accountability or, to put it another way, the institutionalization of altruism. This in turn requires another kind of agency. Not an organization which promotes what it views as development for those in need, although such organizations have a role to play, but agency in the general social sense. Individuals and groups must have expectations and make demands in order for structures to be challenged (Figure 9.7). Services provided out of goodwill have to become a right. To the extent that it is not just more empty rhetoric, the current emphasis on building democratic institutions and embracing human-rights approaches to policy-making, reflects a recognition of this (although it also implies a very different set of strategies from those exemplified by the authoritarian Asian 'developmental states'). But with the best will in the world, the current scope for using development assistance to transform livelihoods on a large scale is very small. It seems more likely that things will really change only when the affluent have no choice.

Acknowledgement

We wish to acknowledge our debt to David Potter, whose ideas are drawn on heavily in this chapter. Large parts of Section 9.1 are based on his work from the previous edition of this book (Allen & Thomas, 1992, ch.6).

Summary

The basic agency of development, in the sense of an institutional source of action to promote well-being, is usually perceived to be the state. The state can be the primary agent for development initiatives and it can provide an enabling structure for development by other agencies. It can also be a structural obstacle to development.

In the past it was assumed that the state would take the lead in directing planned development. Since the late 1970s, this has been questioned. However, there has been an important discussion about the possibility of a special kind of 'developmental state'. This is a model associated with some Asian states, with authoritarian governments and apparently independent bureaucracies.

Elsewhere in the world, and arguably even in these Asian countries, institutions of state have been under considerable strain for some time. Neoliberal policies involved cutbacks in state sectors and state capacity. Also, the end of the Cold War has undermined support for some regimes. More generally, processes of globalization and localization have challenged conceptions of state sovereignty.

Other development agencies include official international organizations, like the UN agencies, and NGOs. Many of these organizations receive resources known as Official Development Assistance (ODA), provided by those states which are the main aid donors. Others, notably the NGOs, also receive private donations.

The UN was set up partly to promote development, but it has been hindered by a lack of commitment from many Northern governments. This has partly been due to the arrangements for voting in the General Assembly and ECOSOC, which means that the major powers do not have control. Several UN programmes and specialized agencies working on development issues are mainly funded by ODA, rather than from the UN regular budget. This places them under certain constraints, directly and indirectly imposed by the major aid donors.

The World Bank and the IMF are technically part of the UN system, but in practice operate separately. Northern governments have been much more willing to support them, because voting power within both organizations is weighted according to financial contribution. Both the Bank and the Fund have been used to further the interests of the major powers, although the Bank has had some interest in measures to alleviate poverty, particularly in the 1970s and again in the 1990s (this is partly because the Bank includes the ODA-financed, soft loan facility known as the IDA).

ODA is given by 20 countries which make up the Development Assistance Committee of the OECD. It is given in a variety of ways and for a variety of purposes. Some of it is spent on a bilateral basis, and some of it is paid to multilateral development organization, like the UN agencies, the IDA and the EU. Much of it is openly used to further the interests of the donor country, and only a relatively small portion has been deployed with the specific purpose of directly alleviating poverty. Total ODA available for developing countries has never approached the agreed UN target of 0.7%, and has been declining since the 1960s. It is now a mere 0.22%.

During the 1980s and 1990s, an increasing amount of ODA was being deployed through NGOs. In some years this has been more than 10% of total ODA. NGOs also raise their own funds from private donations. They differ significantly in size, approach and policy orientation. By no means all NGOs promoting development are service-providing agencies. Some, for example are mutual interest groups. There is no doubt that some NGOs have achieved remarkable things in particular situations, and with increased funding and the decline in the strength of formal state institutions, they have become much more important than hitherto. However, the NGO sector is not adequately funded to transform livelihoods on a huge scale, and most NGOs lack a capacity to be truly accountable to those they seek to assist. Overall poverty reduction requires the institutionalization of altruism and for services to be provided as a right rather than from goodwill.

THE GREAT TRANSFORMATION?

itself or for those regions which it dominated. Now that the transformation to global industrial capitalism has taken place, the world can be regarded as a single market society, but it is by no means uniform. One reason for this lies in the diversity of the pre-capitalist societies, elements of which have survived.

Q What impression can we gain of that pre-capitalist world which was undermined by European colonialism?

Q What can we learn about the pre-capitalist world which will help us to understand the diversity of today's world now that it is transformed to global industrial capitalism?

10.1   A two-sided equation

The 'great transformation' to industrial capitalism and a global market society began in the second half of the eighteenth century. However, the conditions for this transformation had been building up for a long time, both within Europe and in its colonial relations with other parts of the world. When we remember that the first European trading stations were established on the west coast of Africa in the fifteenth century, and that the European metropolitan powers were still squabbling about the boundaries of their colonial empires more than four centuries later, it becomes clear that in considering world development today we are analysing but one moment in a long historical process. The 'great transformation' was the latest, though arguably the most thoroughgoing, of several transformations undergone by European capitalism during this period (see Chapter 11), and the regions which Europe brought under its domination were diverse in character.

In the period of European mercantilism (the accumulation of capital via trade) Spain, Portugal, England, Holland and France vied with each other to dominate the trade to and from particular areas – a trade in precious metals, luxury goods and slaves. In more fully fledged phases of European capitalist development (when the accumulation of capital began to derive from the

harnessing of working-class labour power to new techniques of production), a whole variety of demands were made of less economically developed regions of the world: to supply the essential raw materials without which Europe's (or more particularly, in the first instance, Britain's) industry could not operate; to buy the finished goods which were the products of its manufacturing sector; to become investment areas for the wealth accumulated through European industrial expansion, so that more wealth could be created to feed back into that same process; to absorb Europe's surplus population; and so on. Different areas might play different roles, and the significance of their contribution to metropolitan expansion might change over time.

European demands, then, were one side of the equation, but the other side depended on what the colonized regions had to offer in the first place, and how their inhabitants could be persuaded to part with what was theirs; in other words, it depended on their level of material development and forms of social organization. It is often assumed that these dominated regions were by definition 'less advanced' than Europe, and hence that the latter had some acceptable rationale for intervention. Such rationales certainly existed as part of the ideology that justified imperial expansion. But in many cases it is open to question as to whether this was the real state of affairs.

When François Bernier visited the Mogul empire of India in the seventeenth century he was impressed by the sophistication and skill of its craftsmen, by the range of its products, and by the way in which manufacture was organized and controlled by the state (Bernier, trans. 1916). At that period Europe could not compete with India in the production of fine muslins and silks; indeed, it was the import of such luxury goods into Europe that was the mainstay of the British East India Company.

This high level of material culture and social organization had in fact to be *destroyed*, so that European capitalism might arise and transform the world. At the end of this process (it took some two centuries to complete) the East India Company was to boast in 1840 that, 'encouraged and assisted by our [own] great manufacturing ingenuity and skill, [we have] succeeded in converting India from a manufacturing country into a country exporting raw produce' – in particular cotton, to supply the burgeoning mills of Manchester (quoted in Davey, 1975, p.46).

It is worth comparing the respect with which European commentators regarded India in the seventeenth century with the lofty attitudes of travellers in Africa in a later phase of imperialist expansion. Thus, for instance, when John Hanning Speke visited the East African kingdom of Buganda in the mid-nineteenth century he was astonished at the scale of the king's palace, consisting of 'gigantic grass huts, thatched as neatly as so many heads dressed by a London barber' (quoted in Perham & Simmons, 1948, p.157); Sir Henry Morton Stanley commented on the King's navy of near 20 000 men in canoes; and Lord Lugard praised the 'superior' skill of Baganda craft production of barkcloth, soap and pottery.

By now, however, such technical virtuosity was no longer comparable to that of contemporary capitalist Europe. As no demand was anticipated in Europe for Baganda barkcloth or pottery, the British paused briefly to admire and then proceeded to undermine this indigenous economic development. Within a decade or so after colonial rule had created the state of Uganda (1894), the traditional craft industries had almost disappeared, internal demand was being satisfied by imports from Britain, and the Baganda peasants were set to producing cotton and coffee for export to Europe.

In these two examples we have seen that the societies brought under European domination were not always markedly inferior in economic development to contemporary Europe (though it is clear that on the whole they were), and that as capitalist transformation revolutionized European production, this relative economic inferiority became increasingly marked. It is also clear that if we compare Mogul India with Buganda, at the point when they came under European domination, we find that they were quite different from each other. If this is true of levels of *material* development it is even more the case when we consider other aspects of cultural and social organization.

There were peoples whose mode of life was a constant struggle for survival against nature, and there were others whose grand cities, manufactures and fine arts excited the admiration of European society. There were societies in which everyone was a farmer, others in which the farmer supported a nobility and a merchant class. There were peoples with written languages and a literature of their own, whereas others had only the spoken word. There were societies whose gods existed for them alone and others who recognized that the same world religion united them with other peoples in diverse areas of the globe.

These societies certainly had no original cultural uniformity. If their descendants have anything in common today, it is as the result of a long historical process of subordination to the expansion of European capitalism in its various forms, or because, by and large, they did not experience the social and economic upheavals of industrialization, but remained agrarian societies, producing raw materials for industry elsewhere.

But we cannot hope to understand the world under global capitalism today if we see it simply as a one-sided product of European capitalist expansion. The manner in which this expansion took place varied considerably, depending on the pre-existing and co-existing forms of social organization of the dominated peoples and the differences between the colonial powers.

10.2 Subsistence producers

The world in which Europe discovered itself included pre-capitalist states and empires as well as communities of people living on the margins of subsistence. Many of the pre-capitalist states had swallowed up pre-existing communities of independent producers, while in other areas such communities still maintained a viable existence. It is vital that we look at both of these phenomena.

This pre-capitalist world is not easily recoverable. Its own voice has been muffled by centuries of domination, especially in areas where the spoken language had no written form. Our understanding is often dependent on the perceptions of European colonizers, missionaries and scholars who belonged only to their own, European, culture. Or it may be based on twentieth-century studies of those groups of hunters and gatherers, pastoral nomads or shifting cultivators that have survived – and none has survived in original form. Pre-capitalist states and empires have long succumbed to superior European force, and what we know of them comes from historical accounts, often written by the victors and flawed by their intrusive arrogance.

We look first at what are often termed 'subsistence' producers. Such groups seem to have generally formed the base on which states were built and, even though they were rarely independent, in some places small communities producing mainly for subsistence succeeded in maintaining their integrity right through to colonial times and beyond. Communities previously unknown to Europeans were being discovered as late as the 1930s in New Guinea (Connolly & Anderson, 1988). A closer view of how such a way of living might have been organized is important for three reasons:

1   A global historical process can be discerned, whereby self-sufficient communities producing little more than their own subsistence were overwhelmed in the expansion of centrally organized states (pre-capitalist as well as capitalist) founded on the appropriation of surplus.

2   When such communities were swallowed up by more powerful states, they resisted in a variety of ways which the superior power had to accommodate. They might retreat into relatively inaccessible areas or refuse to yield up tribute.

3   People in many parts of the world today live and work in ways which owe much to their grounding in such small rural communities.

One group which survived Spanish intervention in Latin America, and some of whose descendants still lived in the 1950s as hunter–gatherer–cultivators in the Brazilian Amazon, were the Mundurucu 'Indians' (Murphy & Murphy, 1974). Although an account of the Mundurucu at that point can only be suggestive as far as earlier times and places are concerned, the study by the Murphys is a first-hand account.

The Mundurucu

In the 1950s, the Mundurucu were divided between those who lived a relatively independent existence in the savannah contiguous with the Amazon forest (Figure 10.2), and those who had given up this life to become little more than outworkers, collectors of wild rubber for the handful of traders established on a tributary of

Figure 10.2   Some 'Indians' of the Brazilian Amazon have tried to maintain older ways of life in the face of the forest's destruction: a man carving a bird for a fertility festival.

the Amazon river. It is the former category, reduced in the 1950s to a mere 350 people living in a series of tiny villages, that we shall consider.

Kinship and the sexual division of labour

In capitalist society, we are accustomed to think of family affairs as belonging to the realm of private life, and private life, while often of central importance to individuals, as peripheral to public affairs. Amongst the Mundurucu things were different. There was no sharp dichotomy between the public and private: family relations were also work relations and exchange relations, and they determined the form and pattern which learning took. Kinship – the network of relationships stemming from 'blood' and from marriage – was central in Mundurucu social life. It was 'the anvil on which social relationships are forged and the language in which they are conducted' (Murphy & Murphy, 1974, p.68).

The central social relations in any society are those which organize production and reproduction. The Mundurucu lived by a combination of exploiting what nature provided in the immediate neighbourhood and of actively intervening in natural processes through cultivation. The major item in their diet was manioc, made into flour, which they cultivated on patches cleared in the forest and fertilized by burning the undergrowth ('slash and burn' cultivation). A variety of fruits and vegetables was also grown, and their diet was supplemented by hunting, fishing and the gathering of wild foodstuffs.

It was kinship which structured the organization of work in these Amazonian villages, but whereas women tended to work with immediate family relatives (a mother and her daughters, her sisters and her sisters' daughters), men were forced to co-operate with more distant kin. We shall see presently why this was so.

The sexual division of labour was very marked in this society. Women did the major and most tedious work of cultivation: planting, weeding and harvesting. It was they who shouldered the time-consuming task of processing the manioc flour; they also gathered wild nuts and fruits, did a little net fishing, and took on the major

share of household labour – cooking and the care of small infants. Men were the hunters, they caught most of the fish and did the heavy work of clearing the ground and firing undergrowth in preparation for cultivation. Nevertheless, it was on women's work that the major subsistence depended, and it was they who controlled food distribution, even where that food was produced by the men.

> "The distribution of [manioc flour]...is handled completely by the women. It is a women's product, and women control its disposition. But even the distribution of game eventually falls under female control. The man brings his kill to his wife, or his closest female relative if he is unmarried, and she and her housemates butcher it. They send pieces to other houses, but they determine who gets which parts. And if the take has been small, the food may be shared with only one household – the choice is the woman's and she generally opts for the one housing her closest relatives."
>
> (Murphy & Murphy, 1974, p.131)

This sexual division of labour was reflected in living arrangements. The houses of a village contained clusters of closely related women and their children, 20 or more per house; the men lived and ate in a separate men's house, visiting their wives discreetly at night. The women of different households in the village were generally related to each other, so that the co-operation of women beyond the household could also be validated in terms of kinship. And indeed, many of the tasks women performed (in particular the production of manioc flour) required a wider grouping than that of the household. Men's tasks were also communally organized, even though most of the men living in the men's house were not closely related. These patterns of work and residence resulted from the fact that the preferred pattern of work and residence after marriage was matrilocal: men moved to live in their wife's villages and women stayed with their mothers. 'How would a girl manage without her mother to help her?'

asked the Mundurucu, thus explaining marital residence patterns in terms of the organization of household labour (Murphy & Murphy, 1974, p.122).

In terms of village co-operation, then, Mundurucu men related to each other effectively through their wives, and this is illustrated neatly by the distribution of the kill. But the people also related to each other in terms of patrilineal descent, which meant that children belonged to their father's line. The Mundurucu were divided into two categories or 'moieties', the 'White' and the 'Red', and each moiety was subdivided into clans. Both clan and moiety were groups claiming a common ancestry, although this could not be precisely traced. These kinship divisions structured marriage choices, for a White had to marry a Red; this meant that whereas it was unusual to find a father and son, or two brothers, sharing the same men's house, men could relate to each other by more distant associations of clan or moiety, and could discover such links wherever they might go in search of a wife. Ultimately all Mundurucu believed themselves to be related.

Political organization

Although citizenship of a modern nation state may be spoken of in the idiom of kinship ('the mother/fatherland'), we do not generally believe ourselves to have a single ancestry as did the Mundurucu. We are more likely to define ourselves as members of a single political unit, within which ethnic diversity is the norm. It is clear that our kind of society depends for its maintenance on centrally organized political institutions and a bureaucratic structure, backed up by the law and ultimately by control of means of coercion. The Mundurucu had none of this, and indeed in no real sense did all the Mundurucu villages constitute one political unit: each village organized its own affairs. Political effectiveness, as opposed to vaguer feelings of cultural identity, was restricted to the organization of relationships essential to production.

Each Mundurucu village had a chief, but he had no authority, only influence.

"He does not make decisions on his own, nor does he give orders to others. Instead, decisions affecting the entire community (hunting, raiding, trading) are made in the course of conversations in the men's house with most of the adult males present, and the older and more prestigious men exercising the most weight. The chief acts as the manipulator of the consensus, guiding the discussion and seizing upon the moment when compromise is possible."

(Murphy & Murphy, 1974, p.79)

The chief's influence was enhanced by a subtle twist of the normal rules of marriage. When the chief married, his wife had to come and live in his village rather than he removing to hers; similarly his sons stayed with their father after marriage, and in addition he attracted sons-in-law for his daughters. This already gave him a core of probable supporters, but he remained a 'first amongst equals': he had to earn respect, rather than automatically commanding it.

Real power requires control over vital aspects of people's lives. The Lord of the Manor in feudal Europe had power over his serfs because he held the land on which they depended in order to live, and he used his power to make the serfs labour for him as well as for themselves. Among peoples like the Mundurucu no one controlled resources on which others depended. All had free access to what nature could provide, but they depended on each other to exploit their natural environment more effectively. People did not co-operate here as a consequence of coercion by higher authorities; they co-operated partly because it was in their interests to do so as a contribution to the general well-being, partly because of sanctions from others if they did not. Such sanctions were not in the form of prison sentences, whippings or fines, but expressed in public scorn, derision and ostracism, or the fear that the co-operation of others might be withdrawn in retribution.

The supernatural

Each Mundurucu men's house contained a set of sacred instruments, the *Karökö*, which were believed to be the repositories of the ancestral spirits of the patrilineal clans. The *Karökö* were long horns, hidden away in an inner room so that women might not see them, although they often heard them being played. When men hunted, a portion of the meat always had to be laid before each instrument: 'the ancestral spirits are pleased by the playing of the *Karökö*, just as they are by the presentation to them of meat after a successful hunt' (Murphy & Murphy, 1974, p.93).

The beliefs and rites surrounding the *Karökö* served to reinforce certain basic features of Mundurucu society: patrilineal descent and male forms of co-operation. Restatements of the interrelatedness of all Mundurucu seemed to be more important for men than for women – presumably because women's daily activities were carried on with other closely related women, with whom patterns of co-operation had become familiar since childhood, whereas men had to co-operate with others to whom they were not close kin.

The *Karökö* also carried other symbolic references, however: they selectively emphasized one aspect of the Mundurucu mode of livelihood – hunting. The Murphys point out that although women's labour accounted for the bulk of the Mundurucu diet, meat was valued above vegetables and 'it is the skilful hunter who is honoured, not the industrious tiller of the soil' (ibid., p.62). One of the major Mundurucu myths may give you pause for thought. It recounts how it was *women* who found the sacred *Karökö* and how they forced men to do 'women's work' and to submit to women's sexual desires. 'The men could not refuse, just as the women today cannot refuse the desires of the men' (ibid., p.89). But women were unable to maintain their hold over the sacred instruments because they could not present them with offerings of meat; women did not hunt and therefore they lost their ascendancy in society.

'Science'
When Mundurucu women engaged in the complex process of producing manioc flour so that the prussic acid which it contains was elimi-

nated, could one understand them to be applying science to survival? Similarly, what of the Mundurucu practice of fishing by introducing a poison into the streams – enough to kill the fish but not to poison those who ate them? The differences between these practices and the image we commonly have of science is that the principles and logic behind such effective action could not be stated abstractly by the Mundurucu – they knew only that it worked, and that they had 'always' done it so.

Another craft which is often a repository of practical wisdom is that of healing. The Mundurucu knew of, and used, drugs such as ginger root and quinine bark which are used in modern medicine. Efforts are now being made in many parts of the world to record the knowledge of 'traditional doctors', as it is now recognized that in many cases their expertise has a sound basis and can be incorporated into primary health care programmes.

Some general comments
Encountering peoples like the Mundurucu, the Sioux Indians of North America, the !Kung of the Kalahari, the Maori of New Zealand, or the Masai of eastern Africa, Europe confronted societies unlike its own. Although culturally different from each other, such peoples shared certain characteristics of socio-economic organization.

1 These societies were not organized to produce a surplus above comfortable subsistence requirements. Given favourable conditions, 'subsistence' might allow for the occasional feast, or for the expenditure of energy on non-utilitarian activities such as house decoration, rituals or celebrations. Certainly it allowed for periods of rest between bouts of work – there was no pressure to *maximize* productive activity above what could be consumed in everyday life.

2 Such societies were relatively egalitarian, since no surplus-appropriating class had arisen. However, this egalitarianism did not always include women. Although women were almost always the major producers of daily food, they were often excluded from political life and it was men's activities that were more publicly valued. Some feminists have seen this as evidence of the universality of male domination in human society: what do you think?

3　Everywhere kinship provided the framework for society as a whole, and in particular it validated the forms of co-operation which ensured people's livelihoods. There were many variations upon this theme: some peoples emphasizing descent through the father, others organized into networks of co-operation through the female line, others drawing equally on both. These systems of kinship were linked to rules of marriage, residence and patterns of inheritance.

4　Since co-operation was essential in producing the basic subsistence, various devices existed to enhance the unity of the co-operating group (myth and ritual, political leadership, etc.) and to punish those who failed to conform (ridicule, sickness caused by ancestral ghosts, etc.). These were not communities held together by political coercion. Their lack of authoritarian structures made them pathetically vulnerable to the more technologically advanced and predatory state-organized societies.

10.3　Pre-capitalist states

The kingdom of the Bakongo

In 1483 the Portuguese discovered the estuary of the River Congo, and some time later, 150 miles inland, the capital of the kingdom of the Bakongo people, in what is now Angola. The king of the Bakongo maintained an 'empire' which was estimated to number two and a half million people and covered an area at least as big as England. The Portuguese received gifts of carved ivory and cloth made from palm raffia, and on their return highly embroidered accounts of the grandeur of the Bakongo king's court were published.

At the base of this empire were communities of subsistence agriculturists probably like those I have described above. In this case they cultivated millet and sorghum by slash-and-burn techniques, and supplemented their diet by gathering wild fruits and by hunting.

The king was able to maintain a hold over this territory by a system of provincial chiefs, who rendered tribute to the capital in the form of raffia cloth and other commodities. The founders of the kingdom were said to have been smiths who could work both iron and copper and who thereby became skilled as hunters and warriors. The Bakongo, therefore, could produce weapons, and knives and hoes for cultivation, in addition to cloth and pottery. It would appear that such items were bought and sold within the country. Exchange was facilitated by the existence of a currency in the form of cowrie shells, which came from the island of Luanda, controlled by the king. This empire was extended by conquest, although the loyalty of its outlying provinces could not be guaranteed; indeed, several had asserted their autonomy by the time the Portuguese appeared on the scene. In extending the kingdom, the Bakongo took captives; it is said these became slaves of a kind, though we do not know what labour they did.

The Portuguese were able to gain a foothold here, as in so many other instances of imperial expansion, by exploiting internal dissension, in this case over succession to the throne. When a pro-European candidate emerged, they worked out a mutually advantageous agreement. It required the Bakongo to capture slaves from their neighbours to be shipped off by the Portuguese to the sugar estates of São Tomé off the West African coast, and, later and more importantly, to Brazil. By the 1520s around 5000 slaves a year were leaving the port of Mpinda. In return, the Bakongo received beads, cloth, tobacco, metal goods, and new crops such as cassava and groundnuts; but also the services of artisans (masons and blacksmiths) and the concern of missionaries for their spiritual well-being. The Bakongo king had been converted to Christianity as early as 1491.

Imperial expansion and pre-capitalist states

In many ways the colonists, merchants and missionaries found it easier and more profitable to deal with societies that had already developed centralized political institutions (Figure 10.3).

Engraved for MILLAR's New Complete & Universal SYSTEM of GEOGRAPHY.

The KING of CONGO

surrounded by his Attendants, giving Audience.

Figure 10.3   King Alvaro II of Congo receiving Dutch ambassadors (from an eighteenth-century text).

To begin with, the very existence of such states spelled the presence of a surplus to be exploited, and sometimes of great riches to be plundered. Secondly, where territorial acquisition was the goal, a ready-made structure of administration and a people used to political control were tempting prizes.

Some pre-capitalist states were more vulnerable than others to European intervention. The rise of European mercantile power coincided with the decline of an earlier Islamic mercantile expansion, but the declining Islamic empires of the Middle East, North Africa and India were still equal to Europe in technical and maritime skills as well as in military capacity (see Section 10.4). It was a different matter in the rest of Africa, or in the Americas, where resistance to conquest pitted spears, clubs and knives, even bows and arrows, against guns and cannonry. An example of the ease with which Europeans exerted domination over native kingdoms is shown by the conquest of Peru.

The Incas of Peru

The Inca peoples had created a highly organized social and political system by the time the Spanish *conquistadores* arrived in the early sixteenth century. At its foundation were small communities of cultivators, apparently co-residing patrilineages or patriclans, each with its senior elder. Over the considerable region that now includes Peru, part of Ecuador and part of Chile, such communities were welded together by a remarkable state apparatus which allowed the common people a subsistence living but was also able to support a superstructure of people withdrawn from directly productive labour. At the apex of the state was the Inca king and his queen, who was always his own sister. Believed to be descendants of the sun and moon (Inca religion was focused on great sun festivals) they had always practised sibling marriage in order, as they said, to preserve the purity of the royal blood line.

The Incas could work gold and silver and other precious metals; they had philosophers and poets, a developed knowledge of medicinal herbs, purgatives and blood letting, and a complex mathematical and architectural ability. Their language was, however, unwritten and the technology applied to agricultural production extremely simple. Cultivation was carried out by hand-plough, and commerce occurred only in the form of barter, as there was no currency.

This sounds like a bundle of cultural contradictions: how could such a state operate? The major factor seems to have been the centrally organized and to some extent coercive state apparatus, which played an active role in the organization of labour and the creation of an infrastructure for productive activity. State artisans were employed to construct and maintain irrigation works, and to carry out the terracing of slopes so that productivity could be increased (Figure 10.4). At harvest time each community had to pay its tribute to the king, and since the Incas had a good knowledge of storage procedures, these levies of grain and agricultural produce could be used to feed the nobility, the intelligentsia, the administrative functionaries and the artisans. Not only did the ordinary people have to provide tribute in the form of food: they also had to produce clothing, shoes and weaponry for the Inca army, which was composed of enlisted men. The army was engaged mainly in extending the Inca empire, and to each new area the Incas extended their state-organized techniques of production.

A system of courts ensured that Inca law was obeyed and miscreants punished. Control was also exerted over the populace by a system of accounting, remembered here in the early seventeenth century by Garcilaso de la Vega, the half-Inca son of a Spanish *conquistador*:

"Accounts…were kept by means of the knots tied in a number of cords of different thicknesses and colours…[O]ccasionally other, thinner cords of the same colour could be seen among one of these series,

as though they represented an exception to the rule; thus for instance, among the figures that concerned the men of such and such an age, all of whom were considered to be married, the thinner cords indicated the number of widowers of the same age, for the year in question; as I explained before, population figures, together with those of all the other resources of the empire, were brought up to date every year."

(quoted in Gheerbrant, 1961, p.198)

The Spanish destroyed this ancient empire with a minimal show of force, by trading on Inca beliefs (a former king was said to have foretold the coming of bearded men, 'superior in every way', who would conquer the empire), and by exploiting rivalry between two heirs to the throne.

Elsewhere in Latin America, the Aztec civilization of Mexico had been subdued some few years earlier, though after rather more resistance. These highly organized and stratified societies, rich in skills and treasure but pathetically vulnerable, were annihilated almost without trace under Spanish rule. Other colonial powers (e.g. Britain in India and Africa) exploited the

Figure 10.4   The terrace, housing and stone construction of the Inca ruins at Machu Picchu.

existence of such societies by preserving the structures of authority, but subjugating them to new ends (see Chapter 12).

Some general characteristics of pre-capitalist states

Pre-capitalist states often seem to have arisen as a result of the extension of control by one people over another, rather than as an outcome of internal differentiation within communities of subsistence producers.

In the pre-colonial kingdom of Rwanda, for example, a complex stratification system had emerged, apparently from successive waves of immigration. At its apex were the pastoral Tutsi, who ruled over agriculturalists calling themselves Hutu, while at its base were the Twa, pygmy hunters and gatherers. The occupational and ethnic differences between the strata in this society led Maquet, a Belgian anthropologist, to liken it to the caste system of India.

In contrast with the relative egalitarianism of subsistence communities, these were states based on the 'premise of inequality' (to use Maquet's term). The labour of the many supported an élite who were no longer engaged in productive work. In many cases people continued to produce by the same methods as they had always done, but in addition to feeding their own families they now had to labour longer and harder to produce a surplus as tribute to their overlords.

Such communities could remain relatively unaffected in other ways by the overriding state apparatus. They might continue to define their community and its forms of co-operation in kinship terms, but this was rarely the bonding force for society as a whole. The relatively egalitarian notion of 'we of one blood' was out of place in a divided and unequal society. Bonds of a more overtly political nature had to be forged, and the genealogical tree was replaced by the administrative hierarchy.

Local beliefs regarding the supernatural might also persist: the fear of witchcraft or of witchcraft accusations was a potent force for social control in local communities. The Azande com-

moners in east-central Africa consulted 'oracles' to discover the witch responsible for a person's sickness or death. This was done mainly by administering a poison to fowls, some of which died while others survived. In this small-scale kingdom, however, there was a hierarchy of oracles; courts administered justice according to their verdicts, with the king's oracle as the final arbiter. Sometimes, however, we find a ruling group so effectively organized that all are drawn into the practices of a state religion – as with the cult of the sun promoted by the Inca kings.

Where the state was simply parasitic on the labour of simple farmers, hunters and cattle herders who continued to control the means to, and conditions of, their own production, it was always vulnerable. Where power was maintained simply by coercion and there was no reciprocal dependence of the populace on the state, secessions were a frequent occurrence. Occasionally, however, as among the Incas, there was *state intervention* to promote and improve production. State works such as irrigation projects have long been recognized not only as a means of raising productivity so that a surplus can be produced, but also as the basis of effective, strongly centralized and bureaucratized states (Wittfogel, 1957).

In many of these early states most production was still for consumption, even if the levels of consumption were progressively greater as one moved up the social hierarchy. Foodstuffs particularly, but even weapons, clothing, ornaments or pottery had not necessarily become commodities for sale: the payment of tribute is not yet commerce. For the Baganda of East Africa, the aim of taxation:

> "…was not the accumulation of wealth, for commerce seems to have been relatively undeveloped. Rather [it was]…to provide the Kabaka [King] with surpluses with which he could reward his favourites. The circulation must have been quite rapid for the buildings shown on [a] chart of the palace as constituting the treasury…would hold only a small part."
>
> (Fallers, 1964, p.109)

Thus, surpluses were usually redistributed in such a way as to retain the political loyalties of powerful allies or subordinates, whereas in subsistence communities, although inequalities existed, resources were more likely to be distributed evenly among producers.

Not all the pre-capitalist states which were brought under the sway of European capital expansion were of this *pre-mercantile* character. In West Africa, ancient inland kingdoms such as Songhai or Mali flourished through their hold over trade routes spanning the Sahara (see Section 10.4). The Portuguese early traded with such kingdoms, though at one remove – through middlemen at the coast. In India, European commerce confronted an even more economically and militarily powerful society: the Mogul empire, contemporaneous with early Spanish and Portuguese exploration overseas.

The Mogul empire (1526–1761)

Long before the Moguls (sometimes spelled Mughals) established their sixteenth-century empire, a surplus-producing economy existed in north-west India – the ancient civilization of Harappa. City ruins and archaeological remains show that already, 4500 years ago, Harappan agriculture was sufficiently productive to support a sizeable city population engaged in non-agricultural production. Among the relics are depictions of agricultural technologies still widely used in India – wooden-wheeled bullock carts and bullock-drawn ploughs, for example. Other remains show that production here was not simply for use: *production for exchange* had become important. Amulets and beads from the Indus Valley have been found in Mesopotamian cities and, conversely, luxury products of Sumeria and Mesopotamia found their way to Harappa. Clearly a *merchant* class had emerged, whose transactions served the demands of a leisured élite as well as allowing for their own enrichment. These features, of surplus production and of production for exchange, were further developed by the Moguls.

Over the centuries the Indian subcontinent has been subject to many waves of invaders and settlers from the north. The Mogul era began as one such invasion by Muslim northerners who, in the course of their 200-year rule, welded together the pre-existing petty kingdoms of north and central India into an administratively united country, making a qualitative break with the past and a significant step towards the modern nation state.

At the base of this empire was the village community, a more or less self-sufficient unit of peasant producers and artisans. Local chiefs or *zamindars* took a share of the products of the peasantry; more significantly, villagers also had to pay taxes to the central government. On this basis was erected an economic system characterized by a complex division of labour, with a good proportion of the population producing the necessities of life but specializing in various branches of manufacture. It was a system marked by cruel discrepancies in the conditions of life: at one extreme were the hard-pressed and illiterate peasantry, while at the other there was the Emperor with his peacock throne of precious stones, gold and pearls (Figure 10.5). There was also a flowering of the arts: literature, painting, philosophy, theology and music.

How did the Mogul empire extend to dominate almost the whole of northern and central India? A facilitating factor here was that Mogul India had a monetized economy. Habib (1969) tells us that, by the early seventeenth century, taxes on the peasantry accounted for approximately half the value of their production, and were predominantly in the form of cash rather than kind. Members of a village sold their produce in nearby markets in order to pay their taxes, or the produce was collected by the authorities for sale and the proceeds forwarded to the imperial coffers. Artisans within the village community were remunerated in kind by peasant cultivators, but in the urban areas they produced for cash.

The monetization of the economy eased the technical problems of storing and redistributing agricultural surplus. It also allowed for the rise of a class of merchants and money-lenders dedicated to the accumulation of money capital. In the city of Swat alone, Europeans found immensely rich merchants possessing between them 50 ships, some as much as 800 tons,

Figure 10.5   The Taj Mahal, a mausoleum built by the Mogul Emperor for his wife, as depicted by Thomas Longcraft, 1786.

trading with overseas countries (Persia, central Asia and Arabia). In addition, this cash economy greatly facilitated the division of labour, by allowing for an impersonal medium in which relations of exchange between strangers could take place (Figure 10.6).

More than the cash nexus was required to integrate such a vast empire, however. There was no unifying religion in Mogul India for (as we shall see in Section 10.4) the ruling élite were Muslims while the mass of the people remained Hindus. Nor could the bonds of kinship provide a framework here. Even at the village level ordinary people were divided into *castes* – hereditary ranked categories, the members of which did not intermarry, and whose relations were governed by a host of ritual regulations.

Caste is an institution whose origins are lost in antiquity, though it is probably the outcome of successive waves of invaders into India, each one exerting dominance over its predecessors. Its form was well established by the Mogul period. As a system, caste affected all aspects of life, from kinship to ritual, from consumption to production. Caste can be seen as a form taken

by the *division of labour*, since each caste group was associated with a customary occupation: cultivating, weaving, soldiering, etc. More fundamentally still, the system was based 'on the exchange of labour and services for food between castes who had land and those who had little or none' (Moore, 1967, pp.333–4). It is clear that caste has always been concerned with access to the means of production.

The Mogul ruling class found that its interests could easily be accommodated by such a system. In each area the land was controlled by a dominant caste, always high in the caste hierarchy. Caste ideology provided a religious validation for economic inequality, presenting it as part of the sacred order and thereby unalterable. By means of their control over the local chiefs or *zamindars*, the Mogul rulers were able to capitalize on caste, both as a system within which a surplus was extracted from the direct producers and as an ideological reinforcement of the social order. A divided society was thus effectively subjugated.

The integrity of the Mogul empire also owed a good deal to its political structure. A large and powerful ruling class emerged, whose varied economic interests complemented each other and

*Figure 10.6   Workmen building the royal city of Fatehpur Sikri
(an illustration from an Akbar Nama manuscript, c.1590).*

provided a joint interest in perpetuating the *status quo*. This dominant and largely urbanized category was composed of the nobility, the bureaucracy, merchants, and an intelligentsia dependent on patronage. Although members of the nobility were rewarded for their loyalty by the rights to taxes from particular blocks of land, they were never allowed to put down local roots.

The rights to a share in revenue were assigned at the pleasure of the ruler and frequently ceased at the death of the assignee, when his wealth reverted to the Mogul treasury – a practice which encouraged the consumption rather than the accumulation of wealth. If the nobility were thus held in check, tendencies to fragmentation in the empire were also inhibited by the existence of a vast standing army, said to number over 200 000 in 1647, and employing matchlocks and cannon.

Although as a political entity the Mogul empire was highly successful, in terms of economic development it had severe limitations. High levels of aristocratic consumption left little surplus available to transform methods of production, and the peasantry had no incentive whatsoever to increase their level of production. The more the peasant produced, the more went in taxes to the imperial treasury.

In the end it was these harsh exactions which led to the decline of the empire. Increasing pressure on the peasantry sparked off revolts, helped on by minor chiefs in the countryside. New and smaller states, such as Maratha, were established as the Mogul empire fragmented (Bayly, 1983). At the same time inroads were being made from without, as a consequence of the rise of European mercantilism. English, French and Dutch merchants competed to gain footholds on the margins of the empire, aiding and abetting as they did so various ambitious and disaffected elements within.

It has been suggested that, given time and left to itself, Mogul India could have developed a capitalist economy. Habib discusses this possibility, and Basil Davidson (1978, ch.5) has asked the same question of certain of the African mercantile states. Other writers dispute this suggestion. Can you see any reasons why such a development might have been inhibited?

10.4 Cultural movements: commerce, politics and the rise of Islam

Pre-capitalist societies did not exist in isolation one from another. Patterns of interaction had always existed, even apart from outright conquest: barter, commerce, raiding, safe passage, intermarriage, tribute and so on. The expansion of Islam flowed along existing routes of this kind, as well as ideologically reinforcing the creation of new ones.

It is important to consider the rise of Islam for two reasons. First, because it is not only a religious system but was also the codified practice of new and expanding empires and mercantilist ventures. It carried with it not only literacy but also a set of rules governing the whole of social life. Its extended influence testifies to the vitality of merchant classes and circuits of exchange linking many parts of the pre-capitalist world.

Secondly, Islam had a powerful effect on European cultures, extending back to the mid seventh century. Although Islamic influence had largely been excised from Europe by medieval times, it continued to be a potent and unifying force in many of the regions later to come under the political and economic domination of Europe. From West Africa to Indonesia in colonial times, Islam offered an alternative to that other world religion, Christianity, introduced largely by European settlement.

World commerce and the origins of Islam

Samir Amin (1976), in his account of the precolonial Arab world, notes that Islam was associated with the rise of 'rich and specifically urban civilizations'. He then asks an important question: From where did the wealth come, on which these civilizations were built? Answering his own question, Amin contends that the Arab world was:

"a turntable between the main areas of civilization of the Old World. This semi-arid zone separates three areas whose civilizations were essentially agrarian: Europe…Africa, [and] Tropical Asia. The Arab zone fulfilled commercial functions, bringing together agrarian worlds which otherwise had little contact with each other… the crucial surplus which was the life blood of its great cities at their height did not come mainly from the exploitation of its [own] rural world."

(Amin, 1976, p.12)

The logical conclusion to such reasoning is that the surplus which created the Arab world came ultimately 'from the peasantries of other countries'.

This is a thought-provoking idea for, if we accept the argument, it distinguishes the major Islamic empires from those surplus-producing societies that we have considered so far which flourished on a peasant base (peasants being defined in this case as subsistence producers forced into producing a surplus for the state). Of course, once Islam spread beyond this Arabian epicentre it was no longer simply a 'trading formation'. We have seen this in the case of the Islamic Mogul empire which, while it was strongly mercantile in character, depended vitally on exactions from the peasantry.

Let us consider the extent and character of the commercial nexus within which Islam arose, looking first at the role of Mecca, the birthplace of the Prophet Muhammad. The Arabian peninsular is very largely desert, still occupied by semi-nomadic Bedouin whose livelihood depends mainly on their camels, sheep and goats. Scattered throughout the desert there are some small and large towns, generally situated at oases, whose inhabitants are settled townspeople. Mecca was one of the most important urban centres in Arabia during Muhammad's life (c.572–632). Its importance was due to its situation as a link in a network of trading routes connecting the Byzantine empire and Persia with southern Arabia, India and Africa.

As Shaban notes: 'It is impossible to think of Mecca in terms other than trade; its only *raison d'être* was trade' (Shaban, 1971, p.3). Muhammad himself was a member of the dominant Quraish tribe, which operated in this region as a trading community, and whose merchants collectively and regularly despatched great caravans (the guiding and safe passage of which depended on the Bedouin) to north and south. Muhammad himself was probably a merchant at one time, before he began to preach a form of monotheism which was at first unacceptable to his fellow Quraishi in Mecca. He found a base in another oasis town 200 miles to the south (later to be called Medina). Since there was no overall authority in this area, and since the profits of trade had always been subject to rivalry between the merchants of different towns and their Bedouin allies, Muhammad and his follow-

ers were merely exploiting pre-existing conflicts in making this move. From Medina he later mounted a successful attack on Mecca, after undermining its trade position.

The expansion of Islam

This first success was the forerunner of an amazing expansion of Islam after Muhammad's death in 632: by the end of the following decade his successors had conquered Syria, Egypt and Iraq. The initial impetus for this expansion was in response to the disruption of trade (and hence prosperity) in the region caused by Muhammad's activities and the wars which followed his death. In the process, energies were unleashed which led, as Shaban puts it, to the Arabs 'unintentionally acquiring an empire' (Shaban, 1971, p.14).

At first the military engagements against the crumbling Persian empire were merely for booty. The Byzantine empire, then in control of the area around the important merchant towns of Damascus and Jerusalem, was more vigorous, and greater organization was required to make inroads upon it. These initial conquests were made not as the result of a centrally organized plan of action but as the outcome of decisions made by field commanders, faced with the necessity of feeding their troops and eager to advance the cause of Islam. The Arab tribal armies which had conquered this empire also settled and governed it – partly by taking advantage of existing systems of revenue collection and partly by taxing trade. Each area had its governor, at first either an army commander or his appointee. The Arabs did not, in the initial stages, integrate with the populations they had subdued: they remained segregated in garrison towns, each entitled to a share of the revenues. Not surprisingly, such towns gradually became rich and expanding urban centres, the locus of trading operations and production by artisans.

As the empire extended it became less and less possible to exert control over its far-flung provinces. At first a fixed percentage of the booty taken was sent back to Medina, and attempts were made to impose Medina appointees as governors of the provinces; but, given the communications of the period, it is not surprising that success was limited. Twice the capital of the empire was moved (from Medina to Damascus and later to Baghdad) in an unsuccessful attempt to exert centralized control. This was an empire held together by bonds of trade and religion more than by administrative control.

By the early Middle Ages Muslim influence extended from Spain in the west to Indonesia in the east; control of Spain lasted until the end of the thirteenth century, and in Granada it persisted a further 200 years. Such an empire was inevitably prone to fragmentation. When Mongols captured Baghdad in 1258 they destroyed the Caliphate (central leadership), and thereafter the empire became merely a collection of autonomous states. It did not, however, lose its impetus: these same Mongols became Muslims and went on to found the Mogul empire in 1526.

In the fourteenth century the traveller Ibn Batuta set off from his home in Tangier to make the pilgrimage to Mecca, and from there he was able to travel for a further 25 years in Muslim lands before returning home. He crossed Persia, Asia Minor and the Crimea to Constantinople, then went overland to India (parts of which were under Muslim rule) and on to China. On his return he visited Sumatra, Arabia, and East and West Africa.

Though China was not part of the Islamic empire, Ibn Batuta found that 'in every Chinese city there is a quarter for Muslims, in which they live by themselves, and in which they have mosques' (McNeill & Waldman, 1973, p.293). Here Ibn Batuta met again a Muslim religious doctor, originally from Ceuta in North Africa, whose family he knew well and whom he had assisted earlier in India. This incident illustrates that Muslims from one part of the empire could feel equally at home in others, and that the pursuit of wealth by trade scattered rich families throughout its length and breadth. It also illustrates the intimate links which existed in Islamic countries between trade and religious learning: Ibn Batuta himself combined the two vocations quite profitably.

Islam: religion and society

What kind of religion, then, was Islam, and how did it come to play such a powerful ideological role in mercantile expansion and empire-building? One respect in which it made a break with the past was in its emphasis on *community* rather than kinship – the moral community made up of believers, not simply those who happened to co-reside. Prior to Muhammad's teaching, each Arab clan had its totemic deity, but Muhammad had the totemic 'idols' destroyed and demanded allegiance to a single God – Allah.

Islam did not repudiate Judaism and Christianity, except in certain important details, but claimed to build on them. Muhammad saw himself as the last in a long line of prophets which had begun with Abraham and which included Jesus Christ. Muhammad did not himself claim divine birth, which is why it is incorrect to refer to Muslims as 'Muhammadans'.

Allah is believed to be stern in his punishment of wrong-doers, but also compassionate and merciful towards the weak: Muslims are enjoined to help those who cannot help themselves, in particular the poor, orphans and widows. While fiercely egalitarian in some respects (at least as regards men), it does not disallow the accumulation of riches by trade. The merchant's occupation is an honourable one, though he must not profit by dishonesty, cheating or usury, and he must always do his duty towards the poor. As with certain versions of puritanical Christianity, abstemious accumulation is commended, together with a life of self-discipline (e.g. abstention from alcohol, fasting during Ramadhan). Political rulers are to be simply the first among equals in this moral community, and to rule by consultation, not fiat. Islamic legal codes cover the whole of social life.

Many attempts have been made to interpret Islam sociologically. There are those who have seen in it a reflection only of the harsh realities of desert life, of 'tent and tribe'. Others have fastened on it as a political manifesto rather than religious inspiration, and there are those to whom its essential significance is its tolerance of other religions. Elements of all these positions are present in Islam, but perhaps the essential point is that in its stern simplicity Islam equipped its believers with guidelines to which they could fully subscribe while at the same time interpreting them in relation to their own particular environment. The surface appearances of unity were always there, in the forms of worship and the social codes relating to vital human relationships. In addition there was the language of the Holy Book, Arabic: 'mastering the Arabic language to grasp the Qur'an's [Koran's] meaning, and learning it by heart became the necessary first step into the nascent civilization of Islam' (McNeill & Waldman, 1973, p.29). Arabic became the language not only of religion, of trade and of administration, but also of education and culture.

What I want to consider next is the impact that Islam had on the kinds of society we have been considering so far. I shall look first at some of the ancient African kingdoms of the southern Sahara; then return again to the Mogul empire.

The impact of Islam on ancient African kingdoms

Kingdoms such as Mali, ancient Ghana, Songhai and Kanem were in existence *before* the spread of Islamic influence and Arab empire in North Africa. We owe our first written account of ancient Ghana (situated roughly in the west of modern Mali) to an eighth-century Muslim traveller, Al Bakri of Cordoba (Spain), who made it clear that this was a pre-Islamic kingdom: 'the religion of the people of Ghana is paganism and the worship of idols.' He described how its kings were buried in huge mounds, accompanied by human sacrifices and 'offerings of intoxicating drinks' (quoted in Oliver & Fage, 1962, p.46). Regarding the ancient kingdom of Kanem (in the east of what is now Niger), a tenth-century Muslim traveller, Al Muhallabi, wrote: 'their King...they respect and worship to the neglect of Allah the most High... they believe that it is [their kings] who bring life and death and sickness and health' (ibid., p.47).

The prosperity of such kingdoms lay in their control of the trans-Saharan trade routes. Such routes had perhaps always existed, but they were given impetus by the extension of the power of Rome to North Africa (third century), to be followed by the Byzantine and Islamic empires. This trade came to consist of items such as gold, salt, copper and to a lesser extent slaves, ivory, ostrich feathers and hides (ibid., p.64). Al Bakri notes that the Ghanaian king levied tolls on this trade, and it would appear that certain mercantile devices such as credit were already being used by traders along the route. Following the establishment and extension of Muslim power in the north, an attempt was made to subdue such kingdoms, but this turned out to be not so easy as had been supposed – Ghanaian defences were well organized and it took 14 years before resistance could be overcome. The capital (Kumbi Saleh) was finally captured and sacked in 1076.

But it turned out to be an empty victory, since trade had already been disrupted as a result of the political upheavals in the north. The agricultural base of the Ghanaian kingdom was undermined by the process of conquest, and its constituent communities reverted to their previous mode of subsistence production, while the merchants moved further east, to Mali and Kanem. The kings of these states were converts to Islam; the best-known king of Mali, Mansa Musa, made the pilgrimage to Mecca in the fourteenth century.

There were at least two advantages which conversion to Islam gave these kingdoms. The first was in the field of trade: once they were Muslims, the ruling class and its merchants were treated as allies rather than infidels (Islam had its own ideology of cultural inferiority), and the good will of Muslim states to the north was clearly vital for the prosperity of trade. In turn the itinerant merchants helped to spread Islam to the south.

The second advantage, here as everywhere, was that Islam acted as a symbolic unifying force, its significance extending over and above the divisive loyalties of kinship and locality. To some extent the state religions of Ghana and Kanem had already provided such an ideology of nationhood, but its force had become progressively weaker as the kingdoms extended their control. Islam, by contrast, offered a developed and uniform system of formal education which, once instituted, could ensure the reproduction not only of religious adherence but also of a formally educated élite.

This process was strongly entrenched in Islam, so that the act of conversion, in theory at least, entailed an obligation on the part of the converter to instruct the convertee in religious knowledge. As we have seen, the repository of knowledge in Islam was in the Qur'an, a *written* document, so a basic literacy was demanded of all true converts.

The net effect of these processes was the production, in these ancient African kingdoms, of a ruling class of educated and literate merchants and officials whose 'interests were closely tied to the maintenance of the imperial administration and peace' (Oliver & Fage, 1962, p.88). Moreover, the ideological form taken by this process of class reproduction now linked Africa with the rest of the Islamic world. By the six-

teenth century the Songhai empire could boast a university, situated at Timbuktu, where theology, Muslim law, rhetoric, grammar and literature were taught by lecturers from Cairo and Fez as well as local scholars.

By the seventeenth century these empires were falling into decay. Attempts by Morocco to dominate the trade routes more effectively led to the downfall of the Songhai empire; when attacked, it fragmented into petty kingdoms, and the trans-Saharan trade collapsed. It picked up again from new centres in the smaller Hausa states of what is today northern Nigeria (Figure 10.7), but by the time this adjustment was being made, European traders had already begun to turn their attention to the West African coastline as a source of gold, ivory and slaves. The focus of trade shifted from north to south and the new religion of prosperity became Christianity.

The Mogul empire: Islam and Hinduism

Islamic influence in India dates back to the thirteenth century, though at first it was restricted to the north-western corner of the country. As we have seen, the Mogul empire was founded

Figure 10.7 Artist's impression of the city of Kano, capital of a Hausa state in northern Nigeria, 1877.

in 1526 by invaders from the north, Turko-Mongols and Afghans, and survived until the eve of European penetration. In India, Islam faced a religion so deeply embedded into national life that it is difficult to define without describing Indian social structure. What was the impact of Islam on Hinduism, and vice versa? Before we can answer this question we need to look at the character of Hinduism itself.

Unlike Islam, Hinduism is polytheistic – a religion of many gods. In some of its versions there is an emphasis on a single personal God, while in others the conceptions of 'God' are so abstract as to be completely impersonal. There is no central theology in Hindu belief, nor any centrally organized priesthood. It was not founded at any precise period nor by any particular prophet; rather it unfolds as a set of diverse traditions which allows the individual believer a great deal of latitude.

One of its central ideas is *dharma* – the sacred order of things – and one aspect of that sacred order is the caste system. In Section 10.3 we looked at caste as a form of division of labour, and this is indeed one of its central features. However, it is not simply an economic phenomenon, but involves a structuring of the whole of social life. Not surprisingly, then, the caste divisions are given religious validation by Hindus.

The basic idea comes from the Vedic scriptures where four categories in society are said to spring from different aspects of the Cosmic Being. The concept of *varna* (colours) is associated with these different categories: white for the Brahman (religious functionaries), red for the Kshatriya (warriors), yellow for the Vaishiya (cultivators and herdsmen), black for the Sudra ('one occupation only the Lord prescribed to the Sudra, to serve meekly the other three castes') (Manu I, 91, quoted in Burridge, 1969, p.89). Outside the *varna* altogether were the Untouchables.

Although social divisions in real life (the local caste grouping or *jati*) corresponded only roughly to this sacred model, caste was a clear determinant of life chances. One was born into and died within a particular caste group, and one's marriage choices were restricted within it. A host of ritual injunctions, many concerned with matters such as food preparation and bodily contact, regulated the relationships between members of different castes. It will now be clear that Hinduism is not so much a religion as a way of life. People do not become Hindus: they are born Hindus, and proselytization is rarely practised; indeed it is frowned upon by the orthodox.

After several centuries of Islamic influence the caste system remained intact, even though Islam promoted an overtly egalitarian message; indeed, India's Muslims were absorbed *within* the caste system. How did this happen?

In the era of Muslim expansion there was forcible conversion of Hindus in some areas. Later, however, there were two categories who most commonly became Muslims. On the one hand there were individuals in the highest ranks of Indian society who found it politically expedient to espouse Islam, the religion of the ruling power. Most conversions, however, took place at much lower social levels: for the socially disadvantaged in Indian society the attractions of conversion were clear enough. At this social level, however, conversion was rarely an individual matter; more commonly, a whole *jati* would convert *en masse*. Apart from their new ritual practices, the mode of life of such categories did not change, so in certain areas Muslims have a monopoly of particular occupations: weavers, butchers and tailors are common examples.

Most significantly, the wealthiest groups in Indian society – landowners and merchants – remained loyal to Hinduism. India's external trade during this period was in the hands of Arabs and Persians, but Hindus monopolized trade within the country. The Muslim rulers were careful in their treatment of such powerful social groups. Indeed, since they did not transform the economy of India but merely centralized its political organization, they depended on these groups to organize the production of an economic surplus.

Two processes were set in motion by the interaction of Islam with Hinduism. On the one hand the Muslims took on many traits that were Hindu in origin, while on the other there were philosophical initiatives from Hindus to come to terms with Islamic concepts.

Writers have described the first process as the Indianization of Islam. Akbar, one of the most famous of the Mogul emperors, was accused by a Muslim faction of favouring Hindus, even of having Hindu sympathies. The Mogul rulers were not only tolerant of Hindu sages, they also adopted much in the way of Indian culture – food, dress, art and architecture. The *lingua franca* of the empire, Urdu, evolved out of a combination of Hindi syntax with Persian–Arabic vocabulary. The majority of Muslims were not foreigners but ex-Hindus, and they naturally reinterpreted Islam in ways that seemed appropriate to their situation.

Although most Hindus ignored the message of Islam, there were others who attempted a synthesis between Hinduism and the new religion. One such attempt resulted in the religion of the Sikhs, where the emphasis is on the oneness of God, the equation of Hindu and Muslim concepts of God, and on the promotion of a society that does not differentiate between castes.

We can make some general observations arising from our consideration of Islam in Mogul India. The first is that world religions must adapt to the particular environments into which they are transplanted – Islam in Mogul India was not the same as Islam in Mali. But Islam has a core of universalistic tenets of faith held to be applicable everywhere; Hinduism, on the other hand, is embedded in particular cultural forms that are not easily transplanted. Ask yourself: is Hinduism like this because the Hindus never created an empire, or did they refrain from creating an empire because their religious faith, being inwardly and specifically focused, contains no impetus for such action?

Summary of Section 10.4

Throughout this account of Islam I have emphasized a certain 'fit' between ideology and economic practices – in particular, in this case, between Islam and international trade. It would be imprecise to see this 'fit' as deriving from Islam's religious message; it had more to do with the common language and code of social practice that Islam carried with it, and which undoubtedly facilitated economic transactions between people in far-flung corners of the globe.

It is clear that many other ideologies have promoted commerce, for international trade preceded the rise of Islam and persisted, indeed expanded, after the decline of its empire. Islam is but one 'appropriate' ideology among others. It is significant to us here, first because of its non-European origins, and secondly because of its success. The extent of that success is often unknown to those of us brought up on the glorious history of Western empires and European 'civilization'.

Pre-capitalist empires, as we have seen, were marked by their relative fragility. The common code of Islam, and the mercantile prosperity which it brought in its train, were factors making for a remarkable degree of cohesion, given the lack of any transformation in the organization of peasant production on which mercantile accumulation ultimately rested. When the empire dissolved into its constituent parts, Islamic culture persisted, providing a focus for resistance and identity in the face of European domination.

Summary and conclusion

I have emphasized above the diversity of the elements which became part of the global capitalist system centred on Europe. The commercial and territorial expansion of Europe incorporated peoples whose modes of life and work were, at one extreme, similar in form to those of contemporary Europe, at the other completely different.

I have argued that in terms of material development in the seventeenth century, Mogul India was equal if not superior to contemporary Europe. If we consider its social organization we find a class-divided society held together by a strongly centralized state. At its base were the peasants, whose labour had to support not only themselves but also a hierarchy of officials, a military establishment and the nobility. A monetary economy and the existence of a wealthy merchant class distinguished Mogul India from, say, Inca Peru. In Mogul India we have a society comparable in many ways to the societies of feudal Europe. There are no exact parallels, however, for social phenomena such as the caste system or Hinduism.

Other societies which Europe confronted were quite unlike its own, smaller in scale, and more egalitarian. Communities such as these were beginning to be incorporated into more powerful and hierarchically organized states long before the arrival of European merchants and colonists. Subsistence producers were forced to sustain others more powerful than themselves. This did not necessarily mean that they began to produce in different *ways* – simply that they had to produce *more*; technology and forms of co-operation often remained unchanged. What was lost was the *control* of the producers over the intensity of their work and over the fruits of their labour. Adoption of the rulers' language and customs (what we might call 'cultural incorporation') was sometimes total, but often the conquered peoples maintained a degree of cultural identity – as the Hindus retained their distinctiveness from their Muslim rulers in Mogul India.

In many respects, the empires which Europe created in Africa, Asia and Latin America were merely the last (to date) in a long line of imperial ventures. There were few areas in the world which had not previously been subject to overlordship by external forces, sometimes to the suzerainty of successive powers. We still need to ask why (for example) the Islamic empire fragmented and lost its impetus, while European imperialism transformed the world economy. There were, in fact, two vital differences between the new empires and the old.

1   Whereas in previous empires merchants had merely served the demands of wealthy minorities for luxury goods (and in the process accumulated hoards of wealth themselves), now these stocks of wealth began to go *directly into the transformation of productive processes in Europe* (the Industrial Revolution) rather than into consumption. This transformation did not occur everywhere – the empires of Spain and Portugal (like that of the Arabs before them) were largely of the ancient kind, and their decline when mercantilism had been exhausted is evident.

2   Territorial acquisitions in the old empires were generally a means to ensure the appropriation of a surplus, *whose manner of production was usually of little concern to the colonizers*, whether it was in the form of agricultural or artisan products or slaves. (This generalization is not of course applicable to areas which were settled by large numbers of Europeans – in particular North and South America, where indigenous peoples were either wiped out or their cultures largely destroyed). In the new phase of empire the growth of capitalism in Europe led to the need for a closer control over the type and extent of production in areas under imperial domination. The sixteenth and seventeenth century trade in silk and spices, plus the plunder of the treasures of other nations, began to give way to the more direct organization of the production of specific items, vital as raw materials or as intermediate inputs to European industry.

European imperialism was thus the harbinger of a new world economic order. The harnessing of the labour of many millions to the creation and recreation of *industrial capital* in Europe led to the development of capitalist societies in the West, but it transformed a large part of the rest of the world into a backwater, supplying raw materials for European industry and consuming European manufactured goods. It played a major part in creating economic dependency in many parts of the world, whose capacity to develop autonomously was – at least for a period – stifled.

11

COLONIALISM, CAPITALISM, DEVELOPMENT

HENRY BERNSTEIN

This chapter explores some of the connections between the three terms of its title. They are such encompassing terms that discussion of them in a single chapter is unavoidably schematic in (at least) two senses. One is that it is schematic conceptually: we cannot explore all the different meanings and interpretations of colonialism, capitalism and development, and of the connections between them. The other is that the discussion is schematic historically: it compresses a great deal of time and variation, to which different understandings and interpretations of colonialism, capitalism and development are applied and debated.

The method of the chapter then, to adapt the words of Gilsenan (1982, p.51), is to investigate some general themes rather than the complex variations that specific histories weave of them. The point, as Gilsenan demonstrates so well in his account of the diverse social histories of Islam, is that it is difficult to make sense of complex variations without a grasp of the general themes (processes, dynamics) that underlie them.

The central theme here concerns the implications for the rest of the world of the 'great transformation' in western (and especially north-western) Europe. As for Karl Polanyi (1957), who coined the term, that great transformation is understood as the rise of industrial capitalism from, roughly, the late eighteenth century. The emergence of industrial capitalism at that time, in what was hitherto a quite peripheral part of the world, had its own history, of course, including European

overseas expansion from the late fifteenth century. For simplicity of exposition, the period from the late fifteenth to eighteenth centuries is designated as the transition to capitalism in Europe, and thereafter the period of industrial capitalism – its emergence, spread and dominance. Both periods have distinctive features and effects in shaping the regional patterns of development of the 'globalized' world we inhabit today as well as the contradictory processes of integration and marginalization between and within the societies it incorporates.

Q What are colonialism and capitalism, and the connections between them, conceptual and historical?

Q How did (north)western Europe come to dominate so much of the world by the end of the nineteenth century?

Q What are the implications of colonial economy and society for development?

11.1 Colonialism and capitalism

The initial task is to define the first two of our three key terms, to give them a content that can be applied consistently in what follows. Even this conceptual task requires reference to an historical framework, as will become evident. The discussion of colonialism and capitalism then provides a basis for exploring our third question, and its issues of development, later in the chapter.

The terms 'colonization' and 'colonialism' derive from the (ancient) Greek word for, and idea of, the permanent settlement of a new territory by a group of people who have moved there from their original home: a colony. **Colonization** is used to refer to this process, while **colonialism** refers to political control or rule of the people of a given territory by a foreign state. It is thus possible for colonization to occur without colonialism. However, in the period of the formation of the modern world with which this chapter is concerned, 'colonization' is also often used to refer to the process of establishing the colonial rule of a state over the inhabitants of other territories, whether or not this is accompanied by significant movements of population from the country of the colonizing state to its colonial territory. When this does occur, it can be distinguished by the term 'settler colonies'.

> **Colonization:** (a) The settlement of new territory by a group of people; (b) the imposition of colonial rule by a foreign state (colonialism).
>
> **Colonialism:** The political control of peoples and territories by foreign states, whether accompanied by significant permanent settlement ('settler colonies') or not.

These various distinctions can be illustrated in the periods we are concerned with. For example in the Americas settler colonies were established by Portuguese, Spanish, French, English and other Europeans in the centuries following Columbus's fateful voyage of 1492, while a permanent settler presence was (demographically) insignificant in the European colonies of Asia. Africa presents examples of both settler colonies – the French in Algeria, Portuguese in Angola and Mozambique, British in Kenya and Rhodesia (now Zimbabwe), Dutch and then British in South Africa – and other colonies where the European presence was mostly limited to the agents of political rule (civil and military officials) and economic activity (merchants, plantation managers, mining engineers), who returned 'home' on retirement.

The distinction in terminology and its uses also implies that a key difference in patterns of colonization is whether territories thereby settled and/or brought under colonial rule are already inhabited by other (indigenous) peoples – and what are the consequences for them of colonization and colonialism. Typically, the territories colonized by European overseas expansion were already inhabited by people of different cultures and, moreover, 'people of colour' (or various colours). European colonialism, then, was almost invariably accompanied by ideologies of racial superiority – of various kinds, intensities, and mutations – that are among its most enduring and intractable effects, whether indigenous peoples were exterminated (the Caribbean, Tasmania), dispossessed and marginalized (the native Americans of North America, native Australians), or their labour pressed into the service of colonial exploitation (see Figure 11.3 below).

We address next the definition (or understanding) of **capitalism** used in this chapter, and throughout this book more generally. Many, perhaps most, people would agree with a definition of capitalism as a system of production of goods and services for market exchange (rather than consumption by their producers) in order to make a profit. More contentiously, this economic system is also understood here – in the theoretical tradition of classical political economy (by which Polanyi was strongly influenced) – as based in a distinctive type of social relation between capital and labour, which generates the two principal social classes of capitalism: the capitalist class or bourgeoisie (owners of the means of production) and the working class or proletariat (owners solely of their own labour power, or ability to work).

> **Capitalism:** (a) Production of goods and services for market exchange (commodities), to make profits; (b) founded on a definitive social (class) relation between owners of capital and owners of labour power; (c) to which other social relations and divisions are linked, e.g. those of gender, urban/rural differences, nationality.

This social – or social class – relation is the definitive, hence most fundamental, feature of capitalism for classical political economy, which is not the same thing as an adequate description of the world as we experience it. Even at a theoretical level, it requires elaboration in terms of other axes of social differentiation that manifest the ramified social divisions of labour of capitalist society: for example, in the relations and divisions of gender, of town and countryside, and indeed of nationality and the political conditions of economic activity – forms of the state in capitalism, and the (international) relations of states.

For the tradition of classical political economy, therefore, capitalism is not just an economic system, narrowly defined, for example, in notions of 'the market', as consisting of atomized individuals engaged in the rational pursuit of their self-interest, and relating to each other only as producers and consumers, sellers and buyers, of commodities. Rather, capitalism is understood as a system of social relations, with particular political forms, and also cultural and ideological processes, that are necessary to, and intimately linked with, its distinctive economic dynamism. We can 'unpack' this rather more encompassing view of capitalism, by illustrating it in relation to the historical emergence and development of capitalist society.

We saw in Chapter 10 that the production of commodities (i.e. goods for exchange), the existence of markets for them, and the use of money as a medium of exchange, are not exclusive to capitalism. Pre-capitalist societies generally produced a surplus and often had well-developed markets and trade networks, considerable specialization in the social division of labour, and classes of rich merchants and money-lenders – all, however, without having undergone a transition to capitalism as a distinctive mode of *production*. The word 'production' is stressed here because capitalism is distinguished by the emergence and central importance of *productive capital* – capital invested in production. Productive capital invests in means of production (land, tools, machines, etc.) and labour power,

which it then organizes in a production process, making new commodities and creating new value as the necessary step towards realizing a profit. By contrast, *mercantile* capital is invested in the circulation of commodities (by wholesalers, chain stores) and *finance* capital in the provision of finance and credit (by banks). Of course, mercantile and financial capital play an important role in a capitalist society in which commodity production is generalized, but it is the activities and needs of *productive* capital that give that society its special characteristics.

Only productive capital presupposes that labour power and the means of production are available as commodities. As most pre-capitalist societies were predominantly agrarian (hence the common synonym 'pre-industrial'), a crucial step in the transition to capitalism was that land should become a commodity, to be freely sold or rented without restriction by customary laws, the rights of monarchs, feudal lords, peasant communities, or whatever. In England such restrictions on the commercialization of land, imposed by the class relations of feudalism (one type of pre-capitalist society), were undermined far earlier than anywhere else in Europe. Historians have stressed the importance of the capitalist 'agricultural revolution' in England that preceded, and undoubtedly contributed to, the more celebrated industrial revolution.

Productive capital invested in means of production can do nothing, however, without labour power to use those means. Just as land and other means of production had become commodities, there had to come into existence a class of people possessing no other commodity than their labour power. The related emergence of productive capital and a working class – basic conditions of capitalist production – are part of the process called *primitive accumulation* that resulted from particular processes of change and disintegration in pre-capitalist societies. This meaning of 'accumulation' is broader than the usual notion of amassing wealth or capital, since it includes the historical formation of a class of people whose labour power is necessary to the production of wealth and capital.

The process of transition to capitalism in north-western Europe took place over a long historical period, mainly the sixteenth to the nineteenth centuries, when the industrial revolutions took off. This period of transition was one of continuous (albeit uneven) expansion of commodity production and exchange, facilitated by a range of social, political and cultural changes.

The process of primitive accumulation was helped by the 'expansion of Europe' in the same period, as a result of which vast amounts of wealth flowed into Europe from the plunder, conquest and colonization of many of the pre-capitalist societies of Latin America, Asia and Africa. In itself, this flow of wealth was not different in character from the riches amassed through other great imperial ventures in history, such as those of the Ottomans, the Moguls and the Manchus. It would not have led to capitalism if it had not been able to feed into changes already taking place in Europe. For example, much of the treasure extracted from their colonies by Spain and Portugal went to buy commodities from north-western Europe, where the transition to capitalist production in manufacturing as well as agriculture was taking place. The relatively slow transformation of feudal relations in Iberian society resulted in the declining wealth and power of Spain and Portugal compared with those countries that were pioneering capitalism.

The development of capitalism had a global dimension from the beginning, therefore, which was experienced by the pre-capitalist societies of Latin America, Asia and Africa through their incorporation in an emerging world market and an international division of labour, typically initiated during a period of European colonial rule. In this sense, capitalism came to these societies from the 'outside' rather than resulting from their internal dynamics.

One is struck by the long period (about three centuries) between the beginning of the breakdown of feudal society and the onset of the industrial revolution, which provided the emerging capitalist society of Britain with its distinctive type of production process – large-scale machine production. Once capitalist industrial production was firmly established and had begun to develop elsewhere in Europe, in the USA and in Japan, the striking feature by contrast was the 'acceleration' of history, caused by the tendency of capitalism constantly to revolutionize technology and methods of production and to accumulate capital on an ever larger scale.

This framework suggests key themes in the relationship between capitalism and colonialism, and also significant variations in the colonial experience. Such variations arose from:

1   different stages in the emergence of capitalism, and its uneven development between colonizing powers and within the areas they colonized;

2   different types of colonial state and the interests they represented;

3   the diversity of the pre-colonial societies on which European domination was imposed.

With respect to the first point, for example, Spain and Portugal colonized Latin America while they were still feudal societies, and did so at an early stage of the transition to capitalism in north-western Europe. At that time, the demands of the emerging international market focused on precious metals (gold and silver) and on tropical products for 'luxury' consumption by the wealthy classes of Europe (e.g. sugar, coffee, spices, precious woods and fabrics). But by the time Britain, France and Germany were competing for colonies in Africa in the last quarter of the nineteenth century, they were already industrialized or rapidly industrializing capitalist countries. The international market had changed with the industrial revolution to produce an enormous demand for raw materials for manufacturing (minerals and agricultural products like cotton, jute, rubber and sisal) and for mass consumption by new and large urban populations (e.g. tea, sugar, vegetable oils). It should also be remembered that periods of colonial rule in different regions cut across those stages in the development of capitalism. For example, most of Latin America consisted of independent states, created from struggles against the Spanish and Portuguese crowns, before most of sub-Saharan Africa was incorporated into the colonial empires of European powers.

This connects with the second and third points, which entail consideration of the duration of colonial rule as well as when it was initially imposed. Most of Latin America, for example, experienced at least three centuries of colonialism, while in parts of Africa the period of colonial rule lasted less than the lifetime of some individuals. Again, for Latin America and the Caribbean colonialism was a brutal first introduction to the emerging world economy of the sixteenth century, and existing ways of life were shattered. In some parts of West Africa, on the other hand, the development of an agrarian commodity economy involved in international trade – 'the major revolution in the lives of the peasants' (Crowder, 1968, p.7) – had begun long before the beginning of the colonial era in the late nineteenth century, although it was certainly restructured and intensified under colonialism.

11.2 Stages of colonialism and capitalism

Periodizing the 'stages' of European colonization and the development of capitalism enables us to trace some key connections between them, albeit still in a schematic fashion. This further specification and illustration of our general theme is not the same as, nor a substitute for, the detailed histories of particular countries (including their formation, and incorporation in the international economy and state system), of which many illuminating accounts have been written using this kind of framework. This section elaborates the elements of a periodization which is also summarized in Figure 11.1.

The crisis of feudalism and the first stage of expansion (sixteenth century)

It can be suggested that the motivations, forms and cumulative intensity of the expansion of Europe in the sixteenth century were closely linked to the crisis of feudalism there (Barratt Brown, 1963). One aspect of crisis in the old order was a transition from one kind of commodity economy, controlled and constrained by the power of landowning aristocracies, to another that was being initiated by increasingly independent groups of merchants based in the towns. They encouraged the development of urban production (crafts, simple manufacturing) and exploited the weakening control of feudal lords over the agrarian economy and its peasant producers.

Late feudalism was marked by dynastic wars for sovereignty within and between existing political territories, and the emergence from them of new states confronting the effects of the massive costs of continuous military expeditions, the disruption of the agrarian economy, and a series of peasant uprisings. The need of these states for further sources of revenue stimulated the search for, and seizure of, the wealth of other societies.

The agents of this first wave of expansion were explorers, mercenaries and merchant adventurers. From their forts and trading posts, these gangster entrepreneurs collected from local societies the luxury goods valued by the wealthy classes of Europe, whether by plunder, trickery, or establishing commercial monopolies.

In the sixteenth century, systematic colonial rule was imposed only in the Caribbean and Latin America where the aftermath as well as the immediate methods of conquest had devastating effects. The quest for treasure that had first spurred exploration of a western route to the Indies led to the opening of the great silver mines of Mexico and Peru. It is estimated that the 'silver mountain' of Potosi absorbed the forced labour of about 15% of the male population of Peru in the second half of the century. From 1503 to 1660, shipments from Spanish America to sCastile tripled the amount of silver in Europe.

At the same time, although American silver sustained the feudal regime of Spain, it did so at the expense of that regime over the longer term. The domestic economies and overseas trade of Spain and Portugal were to face increasing

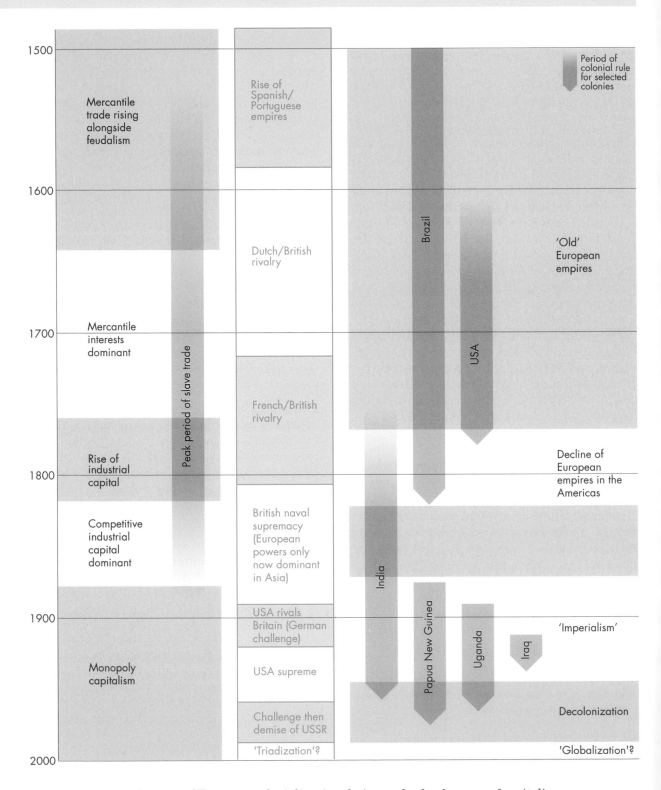

Figure 11.1   Periodization of European colonialism in relation to the development of capitalism.

competition from England and Holland in particular – small countries on the periphery of Europe that were moving much more rapidly
towards capitalism.

Merchants, slaves and plantations (seventeenth and eighteenth centuries)

In the course of the seventeenth century, a different kind of European expansion was added
to the Spanish pursuit of treasure by plunder
and mining in the west, and to merchant–
adventurer trade in luxury items from the east.
Alongside these 'feudal' types of colonization
and commerce, and ultimately displacing them,
new forms of settlement and trade, exemplified
by British interests in North America and British and Dutch activity in the Caribbean, linked
more directly with the development of manufacturing and the transition to capitalism in
Europe.

An example of this new type of colonization was
the Virginia colony in British North America,
where a plantation economy based on slave and
indentured labour was established. Tobacco and
cotton exports from Virginia became far more
important to the British economy, and especially
its emerging class of manufacturers, than the
luxury spices and silks of the Asian trade, and
the American colonies later became the main
export market for the products of England's new
manufacturing enterprises (Barratt Brown,
1963, p.37).

In short, British colonization of North America
and the Caribbean initiated a new kind of international trade linking the systematic large-
scale production of raw materials for
manufacturing in Europe, the development of
markets for European goods in the colonies, and
also, for several centuries, the procurement from
Africa of slave labour for plantation production
(Figure 11.2).

The first recorded slaves arrived in the New
World from West Africa in 1518. Until the mid-
seventeenth century their principal destination
was the sugar plantations of coastal Brazil. The
Dutch then played a leading role in the spread
of slave production to the mainland coasts and

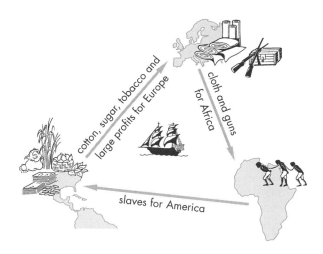

Figure 11.2   The triangular trade.

islands of the Caribbean, to meet the demand
by merchants and sugar refiners in Holland,
while the British developed the slave plantation
system of what is now the southern USA.

Despite these important moments in the process of colonization, and its connections with the
transition to capitalism, the latter half of the
seventeenth century experienced a relative decline in international trade and the fortunes of
European merchant companies. This was connected with turbulent events in Europe, including dynastic wars and, significantly, a new type
of mercantilist trade war conducted principally
at sea by armed fleets. The eighteenth century
saw a revival and further intensification of European expansion, both reflecting and contributing to the resumed pace of the transition to
capitalism. This was manifested in the growth
of the Atlantic slave trade to meet the increased
demand for tropical commodities. It was estimated by Curtin (1969) that between 1701 and
1810, 6 million slaves left Africa, of whom 2.7
million were destined for the British and French
Caribbean, 1.9 million for Brazil, and the rest
for the Dutch Caribbean, Spanish America, British North America and the USA.

It was merchants who financed and organized
the slave trade and the shipment of tropical commodities and European goods, to their own benefit and that of the emerging industrialists of

north-western Europe (Figure 11.3). During this period, adventurers and merchants also extended their exploration, pillage and pursuit of commercial advantage along the coasts of Africa and within Asia. These activities continued and developed the forms of European expansion that had begun in the sixteenth century, and were marked by armed conflict between Europeans (as well as between them and the people of the areas on which they sought to impose their domination) – for example, between the Portuguese and the Dutch in the Spice Islands (now Indonesia, Malaysia, and the Philippines), and between the French and the British in India where the power of the Mogul emperors was in decline.

The Dutch wrested control of the Spice Islands from the Portuguese after a long struggle. The Dutch East Indies Company profited consider-

Figure 11.3   Carved ivory tusk depicting an African view of mercantilism as a hierarchy: slaves at the bottom, African producers in the centre and a European merchant at the top.

ably from remittances, dividends and exporting spices between 1650 and 1780, and then from the establishment of systematic plantation production in Java. In India, Clive's bloody victory in Bengal in 1757 put paid to French hopes and hastened the downfall of the Mogul order.

While France also lost Canada to Britain at the end of the Seven Years' War in 1763, and twenty years later Britain in turn lost its original North American colonies, both countries were able to increase their importance as colonial powers in Asia and Africa in the course of the nineteenth century, as industrial capital rose to dominance in their economies.

This extremely schematic outline has suggested that, in the course of the seventeenth and eighteenth centuries, the expansion of Europe intensified in ways connected with its accelerated transition to capitalism and the international division of labour that was emerging from it. At the same time, most colonization in this period was undertaken by merchant companies rather than by European states themselves (however much these states assisted their merchants through political, diplomatic, and military – above all naval – measures).

Colonialism in the era of industrial capitalism and imperialism (nineteenth and twentieth centuries)

The consolidation of more systematic colonial rule including state formation (see Chapter 12) during the nineteenth century, as well as the last great wave of colonial expansion towards the end of the century, involved a more direct role for European states in an international context structured by the effects of industrial revolution. Again, it is highly suggestive that the original 'feudal' colonialisms of Spain and Portugal were losing their American possessions at a time when capitalist colonialism was about to embark on its most significant period of domination, from the mid-nineteenth to the mid-twentieth centuries.

The types and volumes of raw materials needed by a rapidly industrializing Europe, new market outlets for its factory-produced commodities, the character of overseas investment, new types of shipping and of communications more generally (railways, telegraph), together with their strategic implications, all made the capitalist colonialism of the nineteenth and twentieth centuries very different from its sixteenth-century antecedent in Latin America.

In India, the rule of the East India Company was replaced by that of the British state after the 'mutiny' (uprising) of 1857–58. In subsequent decades, colonial rule was also imposed and/or consolidated by the British in Burma, Sarawak and the Malay States, and by the French in Indo-China. The most rapid and dramatic wave of European expansion in this period, however, was 'the scramble for Africa'. In 1876, European powers ruled about 10% of Africa. By 1900, they had extended their domination to 90% of the continent, which was thus the last great 'frontier' of colonial capitalism. Africa was carved up principally between Britain and France, with substantial areas also seized by Belgium, Germany and Portugal.

The causes of the partition of Africa in the late nineteenth century are fiercely debated by historians. Colonialism was a controversial issue among leading European capitalists and politicians of the time, not least in Britain where some preferred the 'imperialism of free trade' to that of direct political rule, with what they considered its unnecessary costs. Even the advocates of such international free trade, however, had to recognize the strategic nature of their trade routes (and the sources of their raw materials) and, hence, the need to guard them. This meant, at the least, an effective network of naval bases, and often the political and military capacity to guarantee communications and the flow of commodities across great land masses (Figure 11.4).

The scramble for Africa occurred during the great depression of late nineteenth century Europe (1873–96), which was the first major manifestation of the cycles (boom followed by slump and crisis) of the new world economy of industrial capitalism. A connection between these two processes was suggested by Lenin in his pamphlet *Imperialism: the highest stage of capitalism*, written in 1916 with two immediate and related objectives: explaining the causes of the First World War, and winning the workers of Europe away from mutual slaughter in the interests of 'their' ruling classes (Lenin, trans. 1939).

For Lenin, the great depression of the late nineteenth century marked a critical turning point in capitalism, from an earlier 'competitive' stage to what he termed **monopoly capitalism**. This does not mean that competition ceased to exist, but rather that it took more extreme and dangerous forms (leading, in 1914, to war).

DIGNITY AND IMPUDENCE.

Figure 11.4   Rivalry between European nations was exemplified by Britain's occupation of Egypt despite French claims.

Imperialism: Whereas *colonialism* means direct rule of a people by a foreign state, *imperialism* refers to a general system of domination by a state (or states) of other states, regions or the whole world. Thus political subjugation through colonialism is only one form this domination might take; imperialism also encompasses different kinds of indirect control.

Monopoly capitalism: A stage in the development of capitalism dominated by giant corporations, each of which controls a relatively high proportion of the local or world markets for its products. This means that instead of simple price competition between small independent producers, there is greater importance for finance and investment. Competition between large corporations each with monopoly control in different areas takes the form of competition for finance, for sources of raw materials and for profitable investment opportunities.

Lenin also argued that the expansion of colonialism in this period was due to the need to find new outlets for the export of capital for two reasons. The first reason was competition for overseas sources of raw materials and markets for European manufactured goods (both in ever-increasing volumes). The second was the search for investment opportunities that would be more profitable than those available in Europe itself.

Britain at this time provided the best example of Lenin's thesis of capital export. British capital exports accelerated rapidly in the later nineteenth century and early twentieth century, and from the 1880s about 40% of British overseas investment was directed to railways, plantations, factories, government stocks and finance in the empire.

It was Germany, on the other hand, that best exemplified the concentration of capital in the form of giant industrial corporations closely linked with banks. Lenin termed this particular combination of industry and banking 'finance capital', which he saw as the distinctive and dominant form of capital in the period of imperialism or monopoly capitalism.

Lenin's account has been criticized on various grounds, analytical, empirical and, of course, ideological. For example, his analysis may be considered 'exaggerated' in that two of the principal characteristics of imperialism he identified (capital export and the formation of modern finance capital) were respectively exhibited by two countries with quite different paths of capitalist development (Britain and Germany) rather than being combined.

However, Lenin's approach still attracts interest, at least for some of the issues it posed, if not necessarily his arguments about them. One reason is that the trends in the internationalization of capitalist production and finance which preoccupied Lenin have become much more powerful and evident since then, notably in the operation of transnational corporations and banks, as contemporary concerns with 'globalization' suggest (see Chapter 16).

A second reason is that Lenin's analysis highlighted a striking feature of capitalism in its 'imperialist' phase, namely the (growing?) gap between the continuously increasing internationalization of capitalist production, finance and markets, and the persisting political organization of capitalist societies through national states. This also resonates with a leading theme of current debates about 'globalization', namely the view that economic globalization inevitably diminishes the functions and capacities of the state and requires more effective institutions of supranational governance – and whether this thesis and prospect is embraced as a welcome opportunity or deplored as inimical to democracy.

While Lenin sought to connect the great depression of late nineteenth-century Europe, the emergence of imperialism, and the last great wave of capitalist colonization in Africa, a third reason for the continuing interest of his analysis is its insistence that imperialism, as 'the highest stage of capitalism', does not necessarily depend on colonies (Figure 11.5). In the world of 1916, Lenin illustrated this in relation to Argentina as a

Figure 11.5   *European domination without direct political control. China remained independent throughout the period of European colonialism, but, in the late nineteenth century at least, European powers were able to suppress anti-Western movements. (left) A French magazine reports massacres of Christians and missionaries in China in 1891; (below) Punch's view of Western action in China against the 'Boxer' movement of 1900.*

THE AVENGER!

'semi-colony' of British finance capital, and in relation to Portugal as a kind of client state of Britain which was at the same time a (minor league) colonial power in Africa and Asia (having lost Brazil, until its independence the jewel in Portugal's colonial crown).

As this indicates, imperialism in the sense of the distinctive form of modern capitalism has a different and more precise meaning from imperialism in the colloquial usage of 'empire'. The latter tends to include the British Empire, for example, as simply one of a line of great empires in history. Lenin suggested that British imperialism could survive the end of its formal empire and decolonization (on the analogy of Argentina and Portugal). In this respect, too, it is worth noticing that the First World War, caused by the rivalry of industrial capitalist powers, also resulted in the final demise (after long decline) of the remaining pre-capitalist empires of Eurasia: those of the Hapsburgs (Austro-Hungary), the Romanovs (Russia), and the Ottomans (Turkey and its possessions).

In fact, the inter-war years saw an increase in the number of British (and French) overseas dependencies. The vehicle of a League of Nations 'mandate' was used to allow what were effectively new areas of colonial rule in the Middle East,

where various parts of the old Ottoman empire were divided between Britain and France. Although Iraq, for example, was ruled by Britain for only 16 years, during that period that rule was enforced as strongly as anywhere in the British Empire, and new weapons technology in the form of air raids and mustard gas was used in policing parts of the rural population in order to enforce payment of taxes.

The Middle East also gave rise to new examples of imperialism continuing beyond a period of direct political control. New boundaries were drawn and states granted independence at different times in such a way that what was becoming a vital natural resource, namely oil, was divided geographically between several countries so that the capitalist states of Europe and the USA were able to control supplies through the various giant oil corporations.

League of Nations mandates granted Germany's West and East African colonies to France and Britain (plus what is now Namibia to South Africa, and Papua New Guinea to Australia). Apart from Namibia, which remained occupied until 1990, these were treated like other colonies. Japan also consolidated the area of its overseas control in this period, and the Soviet Union was established as a non-capitalist rival to the imperialist powers.

Imperialism without colonies?

In the decades following the Second World War, the European colonial empires were dismantled. Decolonization occurred relatively quickly in the Caribbean, Asia and Africa, compared with the period during which European domination had been established over these areas. The end of empire was primarily the result of anti-imperialist struggles pursued by the peoples of the colonies, but post-war decolonization was also supported by both the USSR and the USA, though for different reasons.

The USA was the dominant international capitalist power after 1945, hence the dominant imperialist power in Lenin's sense (and leaving aside the question of whether 'globalization' in the late twentieth century marks a shift from American economic dominance to a 'triadization' of the world economy based on three dominant countries/regional blocs, namely the USA/North America, Germany/the EU, Japan/East Asia). It had little in the way of formal colonies; the Philippines which had been taken over by the USA from Spain in 1898 (having been Spain's principal Asian colony for nearly four centuries) became politically independent in 1946. The expansion through which the economic power of US capitalism emerged had taken place mostly through its own internal 'frontier', at the expense of indigenous Americans and of Mexico to the south. Before the First World War, however, US

capitalism had actively expressed its imperialist character in the countries of Central America and the Caribbean (as well as in the Philippines). Following the decolonization of Asia and Africa, its economic, political and military activity extended to other areas and intensified, confirming the role of the USA as the leading power in an international capitalist economy now largely without colonies.

This section has gone a considerable way – by means of the particular theoretical framework adopted, and conscious of the strains of historical compression – to answering the second question posed at the beginning of this chapter. It has done so mostly by focusing on the broad historical contours and issues of European colonization: its impulses, stages and (changing) dynamics, and how these were shaped by profound economic, social and political changes in the countries of the colonial powers and by conflicts between them. How colonialism – in its 'feudal', mercantilist and (industrial) capitalist manifestations – impacted on the lives of hundreds of millions of people subjected to it, is the general theme we turn to next.

11.3 The making of colonial economies: the labour question

Whether the initial reason for the colonization of a territory was strategic or economic, few metropolitan governments were prepared to bear the financial cost of colonial administration for long. It was therefore necessary to organize the productive capacity of colonial territories, so as to generate sufficient income to sustain the administrative and military presence that maintained European control. This was seen as a minimal requirement, though it was one that some colonial territories were barely able to satisfy. In addition, colonies were expected to contribute to the economies of their metropolitan rulers.

Colonies therefore had to be integrated in an international economy, initially formed by the expansion of Europe in its period of transition from feudalism to capitalism, and subsequently shaped and reshaped by the dynamics of capitalist development on a global scale. The making of colonial economies within the international division of labour occurred through the production of commodities for export, above all from extractive industries and tropical agriculture. The production of these commodities took different forms. Mining and larger scale agriculture (whether organized by plantation companies or by individual colonial settlers granted large areas of land for this purpose) required some initial capital and a sufficiently large (and cheap) labour force. Alternatively, peasants were 'encouraged' to grow particular crops for sale and export, by various means ranging from direct coercion to more indirect pressures, including the need for a money income to pay taxes and to purchase the new kinds of goods and services introduced with colonialism.

The kinds of commodities produced in the colonies, and how they were produced, varied in time and place according to the interests represented in different colonialisms. Large-scale trade dominated by metropolitan companies and colonial entrepreneurs was a consistent interest throughout the history of colonialism, although the composition and scale of that trade changed as industrial capitalism developed. In the sixteenth and seventeenth centuries, the mining of gold and silver in Spanish America and their transport to Europe provided the profits of colonial entrepreneurs, shipping and mercantile interests, and also met the needs of the Spanish Crown for revenue to finance its dynastic ventures in Europe. But as the growth of industrial capitalism in Western Europe and the USA accelerated during the nineteenth century, it required a more diverse range of products for processing and manufacturing, and in ever larger quantities: minerals like copper, and industrial crops like cotton, rubber, sisal and jute. The rapid urbanization that accompanied industrialization in the Western countries also resulted in a new market demand for tropical products that became items of mass consumption (sugar, tea, coffee, palm oils) and their production in the colonies was consequently expanded.

Changes in the international economy also led to changes in forms of colonial exploitation. For example, the massive development of the mining industry in South Africa in the late nineteenth century was a very different matter from the earlier Spanish adventurers' colonization of Latin America in search of 'treasure'. In the late nineteenth century, gold was needed to support the Gold Standard, on which the stability of vastly expanding international trade and international monetary transactions was held to rest. Diamonds were needed for new industrial processes, as well as continuing to be an item of luxury consumption.

The variation and complexity of the economies created by European colonialism was thus a result partly of different stages in the formation of a capitalist world economy, and also of different forms of colonial incorporation and exploitation of different types of pre-colonial economies and societies. The making of colonial economies required the 'breaking' of pre-existing types of economy and their social relations. In different cases, the rupture could be more or less abrupt, more or less brutal, and effected by more or less direct means.

In examining and illustrating the general theme of the impact of colonialism on the lives of its subjects, we focus principally on questions of labour and different types of *labour regime*. This is because the formation of export economies under colonialism required reorganization of the economic activities of their 'native' populations. The term 'labour regime' refers to different methods of mobilizing labour and organizing it in production. The essential mechanisms of four broad types of labour regime are described, namely forced labour, semi-proletarianization, petty commodity production and proletarianization. Connections between those labour regimes and the development of capitalism are then suggested.

Forced labour

Of the regimes of **forced labour**, slavery in the Caribbean and the Americas is probably the most widely known because of its scale, its duration over more than three centuries, and the intense violence of the slave trade and of the conditions of plantation production.

Forced labour: The mobilization and organization of workers based on extra-economic coercion. Workers do not enter the arrangement by their own volition or by selling their labour power in the market. Examples of forced labour are *slavery*, *tribute labour* (labour services or payments in kind) and *indentured labour*. In some circumstances, forced labourers may own or have access to their own means of production, from whose produce they may make forced payments in kind as well as, or instead of, providing labour service.

There were two main historical factors that contributed to the development of the slave trade.

1 The demand for certain products (sugar, cotton, tobacco) increased with the expansion of production, trade and incomes in Europe, which was associated with the development of capitalism, itself stimulated by the in-flows of precious metals and treasure acquired from colonial conquest in Spanish America, and subsequently from the plundering of large areas of Asia.

2 The indigenous people of the colonized areas of the New World were too few to provide sufficient labour to produce these commodities, or were resistant to enslavement, or were destroyed by European arms and diseases, or some combination of these factors.

Significantly, the slave trade and plantation production reached a peak in the eighteenth century, as north-western Europe was completing its long transition to industrial capitalism. Slavery was profitable as long as a plentiful and cheap supply of slaves could be assured. This might be met by the reproduction of the existing slave population, although reliance on this placed limits on the intensity with which slaves could be exploited: the slave population could not be replaced at the desired rate if they were literally worked to death after a few years or less (Figure 11.6). Alternatively, plantation owners had to rely on continuing shipments of slaves from Africa at prices that suited them. This strategy was undermined by the abolition of the slave trade by Britain in 1807.

Two other factors in the eventual decline of slavery are worth noting. The first is that in the course of the nineteenth century, new and superior technologies made available by the industrial revolutions of Europe and the USA were increasing the productivity of labour in agriculture as well as in manufacturing, thereby rendering slave production less competitive. The nature of slave production on plantations, including brutal forms of control and slaves' resistance to them, meant that it was very difficult to operate new and more sophisticated techniques of production with coerced and antagonistic workers. Secondly, the social and political costs of maintaining control over slave

Figure 11.6   Slaves on a treadwheel in Jamaica.

populations grew as they themselves increased in number, both absolutely and as a proportion of the population in plantation colonies. There were numerous strike waves and slave revolts in the sugar regions of Central America and the Caribbean throughout the eighteenth and early nineteenth centuries, and the ratio of slaves to others was ten to one in Jamaica by the time of the abolition of slavery in the British Empire in 1833.

The major effects of slavery over this long period illustrate the spatial dimensions of the processes contributing to the formation of a capitalist world economy.

1 In West Africa, slave trading brought about massive social disruption and depopulation. The raiding and warfare necessary for the provision of slaves was mostly carried out by indigenous groups (who consequently increased their own wealth and power by, for example, acquiring European firearms), in collaboration with European traders on the coast.

2 In those societies it created (in the Caribbean, Brazil, the southern USA), the experience of slavery had profound consequences for social differentiation and cultural patterns that are still felt today.

3 For Europe, where the often vast profits of slave traders and shippers and plantation owners were directed, slavery contributed to the accumulation of wealth and facilitated the transition to industrial capitalism.

Having said that, the long history of New World slavery provides an exemplary warning against an overly schematic division of historical periods (or 'stages'). After slavery was abolished in the French and British Caribbean, and in the newly independent republics of Latin America, plantation production by slaves underwent a further wave of expansion in the southern USA, Brazil and Cuba (where slavery was not abolished until 1865, 1888, and 1889, respectively).

The historian Charles Post gives a subtle summary of the contribution of slavery to the development of capitalism in the USA, and of the historical conditions in which it then became an obstacle to (industrial) capitalism (Box 11.1). Post makes two further observations of interest. First, the Civil War of 1861–65 (despite its subsequent mythology) was not a war to end slavery but to prevent its expansion into the south-west of the USA, as an obstacle to capitalist development (Post, 1982, p.37). Second, the abolition of slavery in 1865 was a *contingent*

Box 11.1   Slavery and the development of capitalism in the USA

It is clear that slave production of cotton was a profitable investment prior to 1860... the source of the cotton plantations' profitability was neither the high productivity of slave labour, nor economies of scale achieved under the plantation regime, but the demand for raw cotton by industrialist capitalists in England, and the complete domination of the world market for raw cotton by the plantations of the American South...Northeastern merchants, who facilitated the trade of cotton with the capitalist world market, accumulated mercantile wealth from the circulation of cotton. Cotton, as the major export of the ante-bellum US, also created a favourable balance of trade and sound international credit for American merchants and bankers. The expansion of commercial slavery provided the basis for both the geographic expansion of merchant capitalist operations (land speculation) and the importation of money from Europe for merchant-sponsored transportation projects in the 1830s... the commodity producing character of plantation slavery was a catalyst to capitalist development as long as merchant capital was the major agency for the expansion of commodity production and the deepening of the social divisions of labour. As merchant capital created the conditions for its [own] subordination to industrial capital, by generalizing commodity relations in the Northern US, slavery's non-capitalist relations of production became an obstacle to the dominance and expanded reproduction of capitalist production in the US social formation.

(Post, 1982, pp.31–2, 37, 38)

outcome of civil war: 'a measure forced upon the industrial bourgeoisie by military exigencies and the struggle of the slaves' (Post, 1982, p.49). The more general point he derives is that however potent the underlying 'economic logic' of abolition in the USA, that logic was only – and necessarily – realized through 'political class struggle' between northern industrialists and southern slaveowners, and their allies (the complex politics of abolition in the colonial Caribbean and independent Latin America is also central to the authoritative account by Blackburn, 1988).

More or less contemporaneous with the long history of slavery was a variety of other forced labour regimes in the Spanish colonies of the Caribbean and Central and South America. Originally adapted from the feudal institutions and practices of Spain, these allowed the Spanish settlers to establish themselves as a colonial aristocracy, in relation to the subjugated indigenous populations on one hand, and to the Spanish Crown on the other.

In the first half of the sixteenth century, individual colonists, churches and agents of the Spanish Crown were given rights to exact tribute from the labour of indigenous 'Indian' communities, which they could extract as *labour service* (for agricultural production, porterage, construction, personal services, etc.) and/or *tribute in kind* (agricultural and craft products). This was the *encomienda* system. Technically it did not bestow rights to Indian land, although individual grants of land could be made by the Crown independently of the *encomienda*.

With the massive decline of the indigenous population (in Mexico, for example, from about 11 million in 1519 to 6.5 million in 1540 and 4.5 million in 1565), as the direct and indirect result of conquest and early colonization, and with the arrival of new colonists demanding their grants of Indian labour, there were conflicts over access to a diminishing labour supply. These were intensified by the discovery of massive silver deposits in Mexico and Peru in the mid sixteenth century. The Crown introduced new mechanisms of forced labour service (known in Mexico as *repartimiento* or *cuatequil* and in Peru as *mita*), through which colonists had to apply to the state for 'Indian' tribute labour (Box 11.2).

Box 11.2 Women and forced labour in Peru

From the beginning of the Spanish Conquest, women were brutally exploited by colonial administrators and *encomenderos* (recipients of royal *encomienda* grants) who needed women's labour to produce goods (particularly cloth) destined for the colonial and European markets. The first forms of industrial labour draft emerged…when the *encomenderos* established a tribute in cloth. Many *encomenderos* introduced the practice of locking women in rooms and forcing them to weave and spin; these women were so exploited that in 1549 a royal decree was published prohibiting the continuation of the practice… this decree, like many others issued to alleviate the burden of the peasantry, was effectively ignored.

One hundred and fifty years later, the judge responsible for indigenous affairs in Cuzco was imprisoned because he had a private jail in his house where he forced Indian women to weave…Colonial magistrates (*corregidores*), who primarily saw their stay in the colonies as a way to make a fast buck, forced women to weave clothing for them for less than half the free market rate… Spanish tribute demands and taxes were so high that women saw themselves by necessity having to weave…in their homes in exchange for grossly depressed wages, while their husbands and male kin were away working in the *mita* service…In addition, the wages paid to a *mitayo* (a man performing *mita* service) in the mines were equivalent to approximately one-sixth of the money needed to cover his subsistence requirements. Since *mitayos* often were accompanied by their wives and children…one way in which the difference may have been made up was for the labourer's wife and children to work also…but at wages which were certainly lower than the already depressed wages of their husbands.

(Silverblatt, 1988, pp.167–8)

Figure 11.7   Mining at Potosi, the Peruvian 'silver mountain'.

In this sense, the allocation of labour was centralized and bureaucratized as an action of the colonial state against colonial settlers (who accumulated large numbers of Indians through *encomienda* and passed them on to their heirs). At the same time, the aim of the new systems of tribute labour was to rationalize the supply of labour from wider areas for the concentrated demand brought about by the new mining boom. This resulted in long journeys undertaken by large convoys of Indians to work out their labour service at distant mines – from which many of them never returned (Figure 11.7).

The real practices of forced labour regimes in Spanish America differed considerably from the legal theory, and both changed over the centuries with changes in patterns of economic activity and with social and political struggles between settlers and 'Indians' and settlers and the Crown. Without going into the intricacies, it should be noted that when the new republics were established in the first half of the nineteenth century following wars of independence against Spain, their constitutions granted Indians equal citizenship and abolished forced labour. However, during the course of the eighteenth century many of the formal mechanisms of labour coercion had already given way to other labour regimes based on debt bondage (see below), to secure labour for the estates of what had become, in effect, a *landed* aristocracy.

"In the process of debt bondage, the employers gave an advance on wages, or paid their labourers' tribute debts, after which the debtor was obliged to work for the man who had loaned him money until such time as he was able to settle the debt. However, since the debt slaves always received very low wages, and since the employers provided them with essential commodities and possibly also tools at a very high price, the workers became more and more involved in debt the longer they worked – so that the system really in effect boiled down to lifelong compulsory labour."

(Kloosterboer, 1960)

Forced labour regimes were also features of other colonies at other times, particularly during the early stages of colonization. Throughout sub-Saharan Africa in the late nineteenth century, and in a number of Asian colonies, tribute labour was directed to the construction of railways and roads and to work on European plantations. The control over labour and the conditions experienced by workers were little different from those of slavery.

Another distinctive type of forced labour regime was that of *indenture*. Indentured labour is a practice whereby people contract themselves to work for an agreed number of years for a particular employer. This was an important device in the early settlement of British colonies in the Caribbean and the southern USA, those who were indentured as workers and servants coming from the poorest sections of the British population. Probably some of the small settlers in the Caribbean, who were displaced by the spread of sugar plantations in the seventeenth and eighteenth centuries, had first gone there as indentured workers and had become small farmers when the period of their indenture was worked out.

In the nineteenth and early twentieth centuries, indentured labour occurred on a far larger scale, drawing particularly on those masses of people in India and China whose poverty and destitution resulted from European domination (even though China was not formally colonized). Most of them were peasants driven from the land by crippling debt or hunger produced by intensified commercialization and exploitation, and craft workers like spinners and weavers, whose livelihoods were destroyed by competition from the cheap textiles of Britain's new factories.

Indian and Chinese indentured workers went to the plantations of the Caribbean, Mauritius in the Indian Ocean and Fiji in the South Pacific; to the rubber plantations of Malaya; to British East Africa, where the economically strategic railway from the port of Mombasa to Lake Victoria was built by Indian indentured workers in the first decade of the twentieth century; and to South Africa, as workers in agriculture and mining.

In principle, indenture was a contract freely entered into by workers for a limited period, and in this sense it differed from slavery, where the body and person of the slave was exchanged and used as a commodity. However, given the circumstances of destitution that drove people into indenture, the tricks and coercion often employed by licensed labour recruiters to get them to sign the indenture contract, and the power of the plantation owners and other employers (backed up by the colonial state) in the countries where they went to work, the experiences of indentured workers were often similar to those of the slaves of earlier generations (whom they replaced in the Caribbean). This has been amply documented by Hugh Tinker (1974) who termed indenture 'a new system of slavery'.

Semi-proletarianization

Indentured workers who completed their contracts often stayed in the colonies they had been shipped to, some of them subsequently becoming semi- or fully proletarianized. Full proletarianization refers to a generalized process of wage labour employment. When Karl Marx analysed capitalism, he called wage labour 'free' because workers own no means of production and are 'free' to sell their labour power as a commodity in the market without any form of coercion beyond the economic necessity of earning a living.

The meaning of **semi-proletarianization** is often elusive, but two somewhat different uses of it can be suggested. The first refers to conditions where producers are unable to pay back debts and are required to carry out labour services or make payments in kind to creditors (usually landlords). This is called *debt bondage*. This kind of situation was (and still is) found among the poorest strata of peasants and rural semi-proletarians, caught in a permanent cycle of debt to their landlords and others with a claim on their labour. It was indicated above that in the eighteenth century, with the consolidation of the colonial aristocracy of Spanish America as a landed class, many of the former forced labour regimes gave way to debt bondage as a means through which landowners secured a 'captive' (and resident) labour force for their estates.

> **Semi-proletarianization:** A process where people who have inadequate access to means of production, or have been dispossessed of them, have to provide labour for others. One mechanism of semi-proletarianization is *debt bondage* in which producers provide labour because they have fallen in debt with their creditors over land rents, cash loans or other resources. Another type of semi-proletarianization occurs through *periodic labour migration*. Historically, semi-proletarianization has involved a dimension of extra-economic coercion as well as economic compulsion. Current forms of semi-proletarianization may mirror characteristics of colonial forms but are generally regarded as being based on economic compulsion. Additionally, contemporary semi-proletarianization often combines production using own means of production with wage labour for local farms and industrial enterprises.

Significantly, the introduction of new and profitable commercial crops into particular areas was often accompanied by new types of debt bondage, or the intensification of existing ones. The term 'semi-proletarianization' seems appro-priate here to the extent that debt bondage is a way of securing labour for commodity production within capitalism, but labour that is clearly not 'free' in the full sense suggested by Marx. In most Latin American countries, legislation to abolish debt bondage was passed between 1915 and 1920, but debt bondage as one type of labour regime established within capitalism (and not only colonial capitalism) remains widespread today.

Those who have to supply their labour because of debt bondage may also have some land of their own or other resources which contribute part of their livelihood through subsistence or small-scale commodity production. This is the major characteristic of the second form of semi-proletarianization in which *periodic labour migration* is combined with other economic activity (and especially subsistence agriculture) to provide a means of livelihood and household reproduction. Cyclical or periodic labour migration regimes were a major feature of many colonial economies, notably in sub-Saharan Africa where semi-proletarianized migrants supplied much of the labour for mining and commercial agriculture – both large-scale (particularly in southern Africa) and small-scale (particularly in West Africa) – and continue to do so. Like debt bondage, then, the regime of semi-proletarianized migrant labour is reproduced, or even recreated, more generally within capitalism beyond the specifically colonial origins it had in many cases.

Petty commodity production

Petty commodity production is widespread today within an international division of labour (see Chapter 5). Under colonialism its conditions were typically established by the need for a money income to pay taxes, and subsequently also to purchase new means of production and consumption that the extension of the capitalist market made available (and often necessary). In some cases, colonial states ordered particular cash crops to be grown and attempted to regulate their methods of cultivation; in other cases, peasants seized or created opportunities to pioneer new cash crops and ways of farming.

Petty commodity production: The production of commodities for sale based on economic necessity and using own means of production and household labour. Petty commodity production is therefore small scale but is based on a high level of integration in product markets, frequently leading to integration in credit and input markets. The use of family or household labour is an important characteristic, although temporary or seasonal wage labour may also be employed.

Here is an example from late nineteenth century Guinea:

"A considerable poll tax was imposed on a population which had little or no contact with a cash economy and thus quite literally had no money to pay with. So Africans were forced to gather rubber to sell at derisory prices to the companies in order to get the money with which to pay the tax. Indeed, in the early days the tax was itself payable in rubber. The Fonta and Savannah areas were systematically defoliated of rubber plants as every year the African peasants moved out in ever wider circles from their villages to gather rubber. Thus the Administrator's fiscal policy was aimed at coercing Africans into the cash economy for the greater profit of the trading companies, and coincidentally to help balance the Administration's budgetary books."

(Johnson, 1972, p.235)

Generally, rural populations preferred to meet the new needs for cash imposed on them through petty commodity production, in which they could exercise some control over the uses of their labour, rather than periodic wage labour for others in the harsh conditions of plantations, settler estates and mines. There is a parallel here with *encomienda*, in which the payment of tribute in kind was experienced as relatively less oppressive than labour service.

In some colonial economies the preference of rural people to undertake petty commodity production, and their success in doing so, confronted capitalists requiring large numbers of workers at low rates of pay. The historian Colin Bundy (1979), in a famous thesis, argued that in the latter part of the nineteenth century a thriving African commercial agriculture developed in the Eastern Cape and other parts of South Africa. With the discovery of diamonds at Kimberley, and subsequently gold on the Rand, the rapid growth of mining (and the stimulus to settler agriculture that it generated) required a plentiful and continuous supply of cheap labour (in 1889 the gold mines employed some 17 000 African workers and 11 000 whites; by 1909 those numbers had grown to 200 000 and 23 000 respectively). Following the Anglo-Boer war of 1899-1902, the subsequent 'historic compromise' between British imperial and mining interests and Afrikaner landowners, and the establishment of the Union of South Africa in 1910 – outcomes of 'political class struggle' analogous to Post's (1982) account of the American Civil War – the state moved to restrict African access to land and incomes from farming as part of the 'economic logic' of ensuring a plentiful supply of cheap labour to the mines and settler agriculture, thereby engineering 'the fall of the South African peasantry' as Bundy (1979) put it.

This example can be repeated for many other areas where the interests of powerful types of capital demanded a plentiful and 'cheap' supply of labour rather than commodities produced by peasants. In colonial eastern, central and southern Africa the solution to the problem of competition over labour between (European) capitalist and (African) peasant production was to undermine the ability of the latter to generate an adequate income through growing cash crops. This was done by restricting African farming and rural residence to limited and usually agriculturally marginal areas (the 'Native Reserve' system), and discriminating against peasant commodity production in terms of prices, transport charges, access to credit, etc. These various measures, directly imposed or facilitated by colonial states, thus institutionalized some of the conditions of semi-proletarianization.

Proletarianization

Full **proletarianization** in colonial economies occurred when impoverished peasants and craft producers (including previously indentured workers) either lost access to land and other means of production, or were driven by debt or hunger to try to secure a living through selling their labour power. From the side of capital, there was sometimes a demand for a more stable and skilled workforce than the labour regime of semi-proletarianization could provide. This applied to some jobs in mining, in manufacturing (although this was very limited in most colonial economies), and in such branches as railways, ports and road transport, which played a strategic role in the circulation of commodities and in the administration of the colonial state.

> **Proletarianization:** The process (and result) of generalized employment of wage labour in commodity production. Proletarian labour is formed when producers are separated from their means of production, and have to sell their labour power to capitalists (owners of capital). The notion of 'generalized commodity production' (often used to describe capitalism) therefore suggests not only the generalized production of goods for sale but the employment of commoditized labour (i.e. wage labour) to do so. Proletarianization is based on economic compulsion.

While the emergence of a stable working class in colonial economies was usually limited relative to the numbers of those proletarianized, that working class was able to develop trade unions and other forms of political action (both legal and illegal) which often played an important role in the movements for independence from colonial rule.

Colonial labour regimes and capitalism

The different types of colonial labour regimes discussed here are summarized in Table 11.1. The table does not represent a rigorous classification of mutually exclusive categories, which

in any case could be misleading. In particular, if we view the global history of capitalism, we see that it has absorbed, created and combined many diverse social forms in the course of its uneven and contradictory development. For example, capitalism is usually characterized by the employment of wage labour (or full proletarianization) but other labour regimes can and do co-exist under capitalism.

Directly coercive labour regimes were characteristic of the period of primary or 'primitive' accumulation on a world scale, during the sixteenth to eighteenth centuries when Europe was undergoing its long transition from feudal to capitalist society. This does not mean that directly coerced labour then disappeared all at once. Various forms of tribute labour were imposed on the people of the new colonies of Africa and Asia in the late nineteenth and early twentieth centuries (and, in the case of Portugal's African colonies, continued until the 1960s).

Nevertheless, from the turn of the nineteenth century, there were important changes that led to the establishment of forms of production in colonial economies based on semi-proletarian and proletarian labour (capitalist production) and household labour (petty commodity production). Whereas the initial creation of these types of labour within capitalism (as distinct from, for example, pre-capitalist and pre-colonial peasant production) often required direct and indirect forms of extra-economic coercion, the latter were replaced sooner or later by economic compulsion. That is, people came to depend on commodities for consumption (and in the case of petty commodity production, for means of production too) and therefore needed cash incomes to buy these commodities. Semi-proletarian, proletarian and household labour were all reproduced within capitalism as a result of economic compulsion, and consequently persisted after the demise of colonialism.

This is the reason why these three types of labour are shown in Table 11.1 as not requiring extra-economic coercion as a condition of their reproduction. At the same time, one should not regard the 'freedom' of labour under capitalism too literally. Marx's reference to such 'freedom' was ironic: it consists precisely in economic compulsion rather than other types of compulsion. Nevertheless, capitalists also use political, ideological and legal means of coercion to structure, or to augment, economic compulsion in ways that will deliver the kinds of labour they want on the terms they want (levels of pay, conditions of control and discipline, etc). This is evident in labour regimes using debt bondage to try to secure a captive and compliant work force, but it also applies to class struggles more generally, including those circumstances in which labour power is 'freely' exchanged through the market.

A similar point applies to the separation of the producers from the means of production as a condition of 'free' wage labour. Semi-proletarian labour is generated within capitalism no less than full proletarian labour. But conditions which produce semi-proletarian labour are usually regarded as 'transitional'; i.e. they are considered to be only part way towards proletarianization in its full sense. In practice, semi-proletarian labour is not necessarily transitory or short-lived, and, along with fully proletarianized labour and petty commodity production, is a general feature of most economies of Africa, Asia and Latin America today.

Table 11.1 Colonial labour regimes

Labour regime	Separation of producers from means of production	Extra-economic coercion	'Free' wage labour	Examples
1 Forced labour				
Slavery	Complete	Yes	No	Caribbean, Brazil, southern USA, 16th–19th centuries
Tribute, tax in kind	No	Yes	No	Spanish America, 16th–17th centuries; Africa, 19th to early 20th centuries
Labour service	Partial	Yes	No	Spanish America, 16th–18th centuries; Africa, Asia, 19th to early 20th centuries
Indenture	Complete	Partial	'Transitional'	Caribbean, East Africa, Malyasia, Mauritius, Fiji, 19th–20th centuries
2 Semi-proletarian labour				
Debt bondage	Partial or complete	No	'Transitional'	Spanish America, 18th–20th centuries; Asia 19th–20th centuries
Periodic labour migration	Partial	No	'Transitional'	Africa and more generally, 20th century
3 Petty commodity production	No	No	No	India and Africa, 19th century; more generally, 20th century
4 Proletarianization	Complete	No	Yes	Some sectors of colonial economies: 18th century (Latin America), 19th century (India), 20th century (Africa)

11.4 The experience of colonialism

Closely associated with issues of labour and labour regimes in the political economy of colonialism were issues of land. Given that most people in pre-colonial societies gained their living from the land, changes in ownership of, access to, and uses of land had profound effects.

Throughout Latin America, in much of eastern, central and southern Africa, and in regions of South and South-east Asia where plantation economies were established, land was expropriated by settlers and colonial companies, whether by formal decree or outright land-grabbing, and its indigenous inhabitants restricted to agriculturally marginal (and, sooner or later, overcrowded) areas of the countryside (Figure 11.8). Even in colonial economies of a more 'peasant' type – in West Africa, most of South Asia, much of South-east Asia – the development of export crop production led to the commoditization of land and associated struggles over its control and uses, whether land was constituted as private property under colonial legal codes or not (see Bernstein *et al.*, 1992, chapters 2 to 4).

Like labour then, land was also a key (and closely connected) aspect of the general theme of the making of colonial economies, and its 'breaking' of pre-colonial modes of production and livelihood, hence of ways of life. For labour and land were not simply 'economic' resources, or discrete 'factors of production' exchanged as commodities in discrete 'factor markets', as they appear in capitalism. Rather, command over labour and land, and their uses, were deeply 'embedded', in Karl Polanyi's term, in (different) sets of social relations, institutions, beliefs and values: in short, in entire ways of life rooted in material and symbolic cultures.

Attempts to reproduce, preserve or adapt those ways of life in the face of colonial imposition were expressed in a spectrum of resistance to colonial rule ranging from rebellion to evasion, through collective and individual action, on a larger and smaller scale. And this explains the remarkable continuity of the 'labour problem' as a preoccupation of colonial authorities, despite all the complex variation of time and space encompassed by the history of European colonialism, as the following examples show.

A Spanish decree on *encomienda* in 1513 stipulated that 'Indians…were to work nine months a year for the Spaniards (i.e. without pay), and were to be compelled to work on their own lands or for the Spaniards for wages in the remaining three months'. The stated intention was *'to prevent them spending their time in indolence and to teach them to live as Christians'* (Kloosterboer, 1960, emphasis added). More than 400 years

Figure 11.8

later, the 1922 Annual Report of the Governor-General of the Belgian Congo stated that 'under no circumstances whatsoever should it be permitted to occur that a peasant, who has paid his taxes and other legally required obligations, should be left with nothing to do. The moral authority of the administrator, persuasion, encouragement and other measures should be adopted *to make the native work*' (Nzula *et al.*, 1979, emphasis added).

These examples also illustrate how colonial authorities sought to justify their objectives, and the means by which they pursued them, on *moral* as well as practical grounds (as, indeed, most states try to do most of the time). We shall come back to this in the next section, but first we amplify briefly other aspects of social and cultural change under colonialism generated by its central purpose of economic exploitation.

Social and cultural change

First, as just noted, the colonial experience involved resistance and adaptation (sometimes combined) by colonial peoples to the changes imposed on them. Two major instances in the sphere of cultural change concern the introduction of Western education and of the Christian religion (sometimes closely connected, as in most of Africa). Both illustrate contradictions of colonial rule, and the impossibility of ensuring its effective legitimacy over the colonized. Western education was introduced to train people for the lower ranks of the colonial civil service (as clerks, medical assistants, teachers) but some who acquired literacy in Western languages were able to continue their education beyond the limits set by their colonial (often missionary) teachers. They were able to articulate their resistance to foreign domination through turning Western principles of democracy and justice (and sometimes the vocabulary of socialism) against their colonial masters.

Similarly, while Christianity was a central element of Western imperialism's ideology of its 'civilizing mission', and missionaries often functioned as informal agents of the colonial state, the meaning of Christianity could be assimilated and interpreted in different ways. It could facilitate the acceptance of colonial rule by preaching the virtues of hard work, sobriety and due deference to authority, both spiritual and temporal. On the other hand, its message of universal brotherhood and equality in the sight of God could be used to criticize the inherent racial oppression and inequality of colonial society.

Second, responses to colonial incorporation included initiatives and innovations by those who were colonized (often using their ability to draw on aspects of their culture and social organization of which colonial authorities were ignorant, or which they misunderstood). Within the (varying) constraints set by different forms of economic domination, some of the colonized became entrepreneurs and were able to accumulate through trade, land grabbing and renting, agriculture and transport. In the sphere of religion, many 'native' churches in Africa developed in opposition to the European monopoly of Christianity (as also happened among the black populations of the Caribbean and the USA, themselves descended from African slaves). Whether overtly resistant to colonial rule in their teachings or not, these independent churches were necessarily subversive of the ideology that tried to justify European domination.

Third, colonial society was marked above all by the ethnic divisions of labour, of legal status, political influence and social standing, between colonizers and colonized, justified by ideologies of European racial superiority. This was a potent factor contributing to the unity of anti-colonial movements, overriding (at least temporarily) many of the differences emerging among the colonized people themselves. However, such unity could be fragile and subject to intense strains following independence from colonial rule (decolonization).

The final point is that the fundamental racial differentiation of colonial society could obscure the developing social differentiation among the colonized, often abetted, whether intentionally or unintentionally, by the policies and practices of colonial states. These included strategies of 'divide and rule' (contributing to the potentially explosive combination of extreme regional economic and social inequality with distinct cultural identities, including language and religion), incorporating and reconstituting ruling groups from pre-colonial society within the hierarchy of the colonial order (giving offices to chiefs and princes and educating them, granting land and tax offices), and conducting other experiments in 'planned' class formation. For example, the Tanganyika Agricultural Corporation was set up by the colonial government in 1953 to promote 'a healthy, prosperous yeoman farmer class, firmly established on the land, appreciative of its fruits, jealous of its inherent wealth, and dedicated to maintaining the family unit on it' (quoted in Cliffe & Cunningham, 1973, p.134). This was partly a response to events in Kenya (Mau Mau), and partly an attempt to create social groups which, it was hoped, would underwrite social stability and friendliness towards the former colonial power (and the West more generally) following the inevitable moment of political independence.

11.5 And the origins of development?

The overview of social and cultural change under colonialism, brief (and schematic) as it is, contains some significant, more specific, historical markers. For example, the ability of an emergent indigenous intelligentsia (and working class) to articulate its opposition to colonial rule (and exploitation) in terms of universal principles of democracy and justice, and subsequently socialism, was related to the historical moments in which discourses about such principles and rights emerged – and were fought over – in Europe. The discourse of republican liberty generalized by the experience of France in 'the age of revolution' (Hobsbawm, 1962) loomed large in the struggle for independence of Spain's colonies in the Americas. Likewise, the discourses of democracy and nationalism that developed in Europe (and the USA) in the nineteenth and twentieth centuries were taken up by Asian and African anti-colonialism, while that of socialism exerted its appeal with particular force after the Bolshevik revolution of 1917 and formation of

the Third (Communist) International, with its support for anti-colonial and anti-imperialist movements.

Another historical marker is that the moment of independence from colonial rule in Asia and Africa only appeared 'inevitable' in the reshaping of the international political system after the Second World War when, as noted earlier, the strategies of the new definitive 'superpowers' (the USA and USSR) included the dismantling of Europe's colonial empires, above all that of Britain. Finally, as the example of the Tanganyika Agricultural Corporation in the 1950s suggests, the idea of development was established by the late colonial period – and, moreover, the idea of development as a process in which state funding, agencies and initiatives had a central role to play.

Ideas and practices of development – and their various complexities and contestations – are the central theme of this book. Here we can only sketch some of the contexts and contours of their historical career, in relation to the third and final question of this chapter, concerning the implications of colonial economy and society for development.

Systematic colonization, under the aegis of the state from the beginnings of Spanish rule in sixteenth-century Latin America to the colonialisms of Asia and Africa in the epoch of industrial capitalism, sought to theorize and justify the domination of colonial rule. These theories and justifications typically presented colonialism as in the interests, both practical and moral, of both colonizers and colonized. The earliest formulations of such ideology (and that persisted, with variations, throughout the long period of colonialism) centred on the mission of spreading Christian civilization. As the extract quoted earlier from a Spanish decree on *encomienda* shows, getting colonial subjects 'to live as Christians' entailed an opportune combination of elevating their belief through conversion and their practical morality through hard work.

The mercantilist phase of colonialism allowed the civilizing quality of 'commerce' (commodity production and exchange) to be coupled with that of Christianity. The rise of industrial capitalism, the new colonialisms it generated (as in Africa and Indochina) and the older colonialisms it reshaped (of the British in India, the Dutch in Indonesia), generated additional – and more recognizably modern – justifications of colonial rule in the form of ideologies of *progress* (Box 11.3). Ideas of progress, with their own combination of elements of material advance and moral quality, could be proposed in secular, hence more universal, versions: from Christian civilization to industrial civilization, and the latter from 'westernization' to visions of 'modernization' and 'development' finally liberated from any explicit ethnocentric (as well as religious) associations.

Doctrines of development

Chapter 1 introduced the original and provocative study of the historical origins and career of 'doctrines of development' by Cowen and Shenton (1996). They suggest (p.12) that 'the modern idea of development was created in the crucible of the first half-century of Western European transition to industrial capitalism' (by which Cowen and Shenton mean the first half of the nineteenth century):

1   Prior to the crucial half-century of 'the great transformation', earlier liberal views of progress – formulated by enlightenment philosophers and social theorists – saw progress as an immanent or 'natural' process.

2   In the period of profound change of the transition to industrial capitalism, its key contradictions – generated by its social class relations and manifested in patterns of inequality, poverty and unemployment, and their implications for social order (fear of revolution) – stimulated the invention of the idea of development as a process requiring intention and design.

3   The content and purpose of 'development' is thus to reconcile progress and order, to contain and manage the potential social disorder of the dynamics of immanent (or unchecked) capitalist development.

4   Doctrines of development combine this need for order with the agency of its intention and design by an appropriate 'trustee' of society's progress with stability: '(development) became the means whereby an epoch of the present was to be transformed into another through the active purpose of those...*entrusted* with the future of society' (Cowen & Shenton, 1996, p.25).

5   Typically, such trusteeship has been vested in, or claimed by, the state.

This is only a partial summary of some key ideas of a large, complex, and (it has to be said) often very difficult book, but a summary that throws light on our question about colonialism and development. Cowen and Shenton propose the challenging thesis that doctrines of development, as they theorize the concept, address not only the prospects of change in poorer (colonial and former colonial) countries, and are not only relevant to the conjuncture of late colonialism and decolonization with which they are convention-

---

Box 11.3 'Progress' and forced labour in the 1920s: Railway construction in the Belgian Congo

'I work on track repairs with a group of fellow villagers. Men work on one side of the track, women on the other. When a woman can't be sold or gets too old, she is made to do more work than a man. In scorching sunshine they carry large stones on their heads, level the ground and drag blocks of marble along, all to the sound of continual sad moaning. There is also a black overseer. The monotonous beating of a drum gives rhythm to the work, but when the music stops, the negro overseer brings down his whip on the shoulders of 50 or 100 male and female workers, passive, weakened and hungry. This is how we build the road to civilization. That's how progress goes. The engine's whistle blows where there was once the silence of the impenetrable forest. But the train runs on the bones of the thousands who died without even knowing what was this progress, in whose name they were made to work.'

(Congolese worker's letter to the International Trade Union Committee of Negro Workers, quoted in Nzula *et al.*, 1979 edition, p.85)

ally identified, but also have deeper historical roots in the epoch of industrial capitalism. In the second part of their wide-ranging book, they explore and illustrate this thesis in relation to the settler colonies (later 'white' Dominions) of Australia and Canada in the mid-nineteenth century, late nineteenth- and early twentieth-century Britain, and colonial and independent Kenya in the second half of the twentieth century.

The strategic conclusion they derive is that while European colonialism incorporated the territories of so much of the world in an (evolving) international capitalist system, and harnessed their resources – above all the labour of their inhabitants – to its purposes, it did so through doctrines of development and practices of trusteeship that inhibited the fuller development of capitalism. The principal reason is that while development was invented in Western Europe to control and manage the social *effects* (contradictions) of 'the great transformation' that had occurred there, in the colonies it was applied *pre-emptively*, as it were: to engineer progress within a framework of order, intention and design to anticipate and contain the social and, above all, class contradictions of capitalist development experienced in Europe.

It was this aspiration, argue Cowen and Shenton (1991a,b), that explains the apparent paradox of the colonial promotion of peasant export crop production for imperial and world markets on the basis of 'traditional' or 'customary' land tenure and forms of labour organization (household and 'co-operative'), rather than the formation of indigenous classes of agrarian capital and labour, which colonial states in Africa tried to inhibit. Similarly, such concerns and notions informed the colonial anthropology of native custom, 'community' and 'tribe' as anchors of social stability, and the constitution of local government (indirect rule) on the basis of an ethnicity opportunely deemed both 'natural' to Africans and cost-effective to the colonial state (Mamdani, 1996, and Chapter 12 following).

The corpus of Cowen and Shenton's (continuing) intellectual project is an original and comprehensive account of the historical origins and career of ideas of development, applied in case studies of economic and social change, and (related) political, ideological and policy processes in a range of contexts (which exemplify the complex variations on their general themes). It also provides an analytical reference point to which other aspects, and accounts, of the relationship between (capitalist) colonialism and development can be linked, in all its ambiguities and tensions.

The ambiguous relationship of colonialism and development

Modern colonial doctrine – as elaborated and applied in the century or so of colonial expansion and restructuring in the age of industrial capitalism – increasingly featured notions of development as a rationale of colonial rule and its responsibilities. Developmental notions ranged from the creation of law and order within a modern administrative framework, to the building of infrastructure and communications to facilitate both the exercise of law and order and the growth of markets and trade, the introduction of Western education and medicine, and the gradual formation of new tastes and disciplines, new capacities and values (Figure 11.9).

As with so much fundamental change elsewhere in the twentieth century, the decades of the 1930s to 1950s – marked by the great Depression, the Second World War, and its aftermath – were the crucible of a more explicit and comprehensive application of 'doctrines of development' in the colonies of Asia and Africa. Britain's first Colonial Development and Welfare Act of 1939 could not be implemented because of the war, but a similarly titled Act of 1945 was the legislative framework of colonial state 'developmentalism' in the next 15–20 years prior to independence. The Tanganyika Agricultural Corporation, referred to above, is a typical example of a colonial development intervention of this period: premised on state initiative and management to engineer a more productive agriculture with explicit welfare objectives, through the social creation of an (idealized) 'yeoman farmer class'. The example of the TAC also exemplifies the 'trusteeship' of the colonial state in gradually 'elevating' (a term dear to French

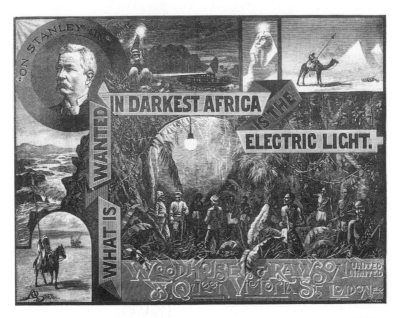

Figure 11.9   Lighting up Africa: an advertisement from the 1890s.

colonial discourse) colonial peoples to a level of civilization – material and productive, moral and civic – at which they would (eventually) be equipped to govern themselves.

From the 1930s, and accelerating after 1945, late colonialism in sub-Saharan Africa was thus marked by a more intensive and comprehensive series of interventions to promote development, manifested in a range of 'model' agricultural schemes, together with land use planning and environmental conservation; infrastructural development; urban planning and housing; labour relations and social services; education and health; local government reorganization and limited elements of 'self-rule'. All this occurred within the framework of state tutelage or trusteeship, intellectually shaped by Fabian ideas of social engineering (Cowen & Shenton, 1991a) and by contemporary experiments with Keynesian policies in the metropolitan centres of the colonial powers.

At the end of colonial rule, then, colonial doctrine could say to its former subjects: 'we have given you foundations of development' – new crops and ways of growing them; a thriving international trade; ports, railways and roads; schools, clinics and hospitals; the apparatuses

and procedures of modern state administration – 'and so now it is up to you'.

Of course, there are other, less sanguine assessments of the relationship of colonialism and development, of the 'balance sheet' of achievements and failures, problems and prospects, of development, at the end of colonial rule. As we saw, Cowen and Shenton's perspective suggests that how colonial states attempted to engineer economic and social change – through the commitment to balance progress and order – significantly inhibited the fuller development of the social conditions of capitalist production (class formation) among the colonized.

There are other arguments, too, about how the contradictions of the colonial project of social enginreering limited the realization of the claims of colonial doctrine, as summarized above. Recent historical research on colonialism in the modern (industrial capitalist) epoch, and especially the late colonialism of the twentieth century, has emphasized how ostensibly 'rational' (or rationalistic) and 'scientific' (or scientistic) doctrines and designs of development that permeated colonial policies and practices – of agricultural growth, conservation or health care – were often intrinsically flawed and/or inappropriate to the conditions of the colonies, both environmental and social (e.g. Little, 1992; Peters, 1994, on pastoralism in northern Kenya and Botswana respectively; Moore & Vaughan, 1994, on agriculture, conservation and nutrition in northern Zambia; Chandavarkar, 1998, ch.7, on state responses to outbreaks of plague in colonial Bombay). Such doctrines and designs, and the specific policies and practices they generated – however misconceived or inappropriate – could be imposed on colonial subjects with all the confidence of modernity and arrogance of trusteeship, even though their consequences might prove to be negative or simply ineffectual.

Beyond the kind of research cited and its findings on late colonial developmentalism, a contemporary, and more fundamental, issue was how colonial subjects themselves perceived the changes they experienced under colonial rule, and especially (for present purposes) the leadership and intelligentsia of the nationalist parties and movements which formed the governments of the independent states of Asia and Africa. Once again this is a general theme about which it is difficult to generalize empirically. However, it is possible to 'unpack' two aspects of it.

One is straightfoward: the nationalist demand for independence was political and ideological, i.e. freedom from the oppression of rule by another state. The other proved more ambiguous in practice. This started from the belief that foreign rule entailed economic exploitation and obstacles to development, that colonies were established and ruled for the benefit of the colonial powers and not that of their subjects. This could encompass views that:

1 patterns of economic change under colonialism were 'distorted' towards the export production of raw materials needed by the markets and industries of the colonial powers;

2 the development of manufacturing industry, above all in capital goods and engineering – the definitive sector of modern economic progress – was blocked or otherwise inhibited by colonial states, whether through design or neglect;

3 the profits, hence accumulation, from the activities of colonial production and trade accrued to the economies of the colonial powers rather than being invested to promote the economic development of the colonial territories.

In sum, this position was not a rejection of ideas of development, nor of development doctrines that constructed them in particular ways, but a statement of the belief that political independence is a necessary condition of more rapid and comprehensive – and indeed of more properly 'national' – development: to overcome the colonial legacy of 'poverty, ignorance and disease' (a standard expression of the time), and to yield the fruits of prosperity and well-being. Achieving the progress of 'national development' was also widely seen, together with the connected ambition of 'nation building', as primarily the role of the now national state established at independence.

The element of ambiguity – and irony – in the project of post-colonial developmentalism, then, was that it inherited, adapted, reproduced, and in some instances reinforced, many of the specific ideas and methods of colonial doctrines of development and their constructions of modernity: what it means to be modern, and how to get there.

11.6 Conclusion

In 1961, Julius Nyerere expressed the hopes of the moment of independence: 'This day has dawned because the people of Tanganyika have worked together in unity...[F]rom now on we are fighting not man but nature.' In quoting these words at the end of his authoritative history of colonial Tanganyika, Iliffe (1979) commented 'but it was more complicated than that.'

It proved to be more complicated precisely because the end of colonialism was not the end of capitalism. The former colonies of Asia and Africa still had to confront the unequal structures of the international division of labour and capitalist world market in their efforts to achieve economic development. In addition, the contradictory social relations and divisions of capitalism were now as much part of their societies as of those societies in which capitalism had its origins; and many of the assumptions, methods, institutions and practices of colonial doctrines of development, with all their intrinsic tensions, were assimilated in the designs for development of the newly independent states.

Summary

1   The three main phases of European colonialism were connected with the development of capitalism in Europe: the crisis of feudalism; mercantilist expansion during the transition to capitalism and its 'primitive accumulation'; more systematic colonization through both expansion and the restructuring of colonial economies with the emergence and dominance of industrial capitalism.

2   The peak period of European colonialism from the mid-nineteenth to mid-twentieth centuries, in the era of industrial capitalism, involved more systematic and comprehensive exploitation of the colonies as sources of raw materials for industries in Europe, and as outlets for investment and markets for manufactured goods.

3   The making of colonial economies – through the organization of commodity production and trade by colonial states, settlers and companies – entailed the 'breaking' of existing patterns of production and social existence, of whole ways of life.

4   This process was encapsulated in the formation and functioning of colonial labour regimes, which underwent a broad, if uneven, sequence of change from direct coercion during the period of 'primitive accumulation' (slavery, tribute labour, indentured labour) to semi-proletarian, proletarian and household labour (petty commodity production) by the late nineteenth century.

5   Other aspects of social and cultural change under colonialism also contributed to new forms of social differentiation among the colonized, and exposed the contradictions of colonial rule, not least in challenging its legitimacy.

6   Colonial doctrine justified European colonization in terms of its 'civilizing mission', typically connected with ideas of racial superiority: from conversion to Christianity, to the civilizing effects of trade and, in the era of industrial capitalism, notions of progress universalized as 'modernization' and 'development'.

7   The European colonial empires were dismantled in the decades following the Second World War: anti-colonial movements became stronger, and international capitalism led by the USA no longer required the direct political rule of Asia and Africa (an 'imperialism without colonies'), while the proclamation of strategies of 'national development' by the newly independent states assimilated many of the tensions and ambiguities of the 'doctrines of development' of the era of (industrial) capitalist colonialism.

12

THE POWER OF COLONIAL STATES

DAVID POTTER

One of the things that has conventionally distinguished developing countries in the Americas, Asia, Africa and the Middle East from the rest of the world is that nearly all such countries experienced some form of European colonial rule. Some of the reasons for the Europeans going to these parts of the world have already been mentioned in Chapter 11. They include the economics of the expansion of Europe, the development of capitalism, and the creation of a world market and international division of labour. Wherever and whenever the colonialists established themselves, they were gradually drawn to control the area they had conquered or in which they had their investments. Eventually these political interventions resulted in the formation of what came to be called colonial states.

Colonial states gradually ripped apart pre-existing economic and social relations and created colonial economies, including various labour regimes as discussed in Chapter 11. These and other actions of such states were more or less resisted by those on whom their rule was imposed. The result was that colonial rule was never easily created and maintained. In the end, the problem of rule became insuperable and the European colonialists withdrew or were driven out.

The 'problem of rule' from the European point of view had two related aspects. One was that lines of communication between Europe and far-flung colonies, and between the seat of government in a colonial city and the rural countryside, were extremely slow and uncertain during nearly the entire period of colonial rule. Colonial powers in Europe therefore had to rely on officials in the colony whom they could trust to rule on their behalf. For the most part such trusted officials were recruited in the European country and sent out to the colony. But, and this is the other aspect, only a minuscule number of such officials relative to the indigenous population could be sent. For example, in 1906 shortly after the British took control of northern Nigeria the ratio of European civil officers to the indigenous population was 1 to 45 000; in terms of area it was 1 to 2900 square miles (Okonjo, 1974, cited in Mamdani, 1996, p.73). In 1939 the ratio of European officials to Africans in both the Belgian Congo and in French West Africa was about 1 to 4000 (Delavignette, 1950 cited in Mamdani, 1996, p.73). In India, Mahatma Ghandi used to put the same issue this way: 'We in India may in a moment realize that one hundred thousand Englishmen [his estimate of their number in India] need not frighten three hundred million human beings' (Gandhi, 1920, cited in Low, 1974, p.8).

Such ratios frame the key political question about the power of colonial states, the question with which this chapter is primarily concerned:

Q How was it possible for so few Europeans to hold down so many colonial peoples?

I shall argue that the beginnings of a useful answer to this question can be found through an understanding of seven political features that all colonial states shared: (1) an international political dimension, (2) bureaucratic élitism and authoritarianism, (3) use of 'traditional' or 'customary' authority figures in colonial society, (4) use of force, (5) technological advantage, (6) statism, (7) hegemonic ideology.

Towards the end of the chapter I also briefly address two other questions:

Q Why did colonial rule end when it did?

Q What were the legacies of colonial rule for post-colonial states and state-led development?

The subject matter of this chapter is, of course, enormous. To make it a little less unmanageable, I have focused the discussion on India and sub-Saharan Africa.

12.1 Seven features of colonial rule

I want now to draw attention to the seven political features of colonial rule that help to explain the power of colonial states.

International political dimension

First, all colonial rules in Africa and India involved *political direction and control* of a subject society ultimately *by a foreign power*, be it a Board of Directors (like the East India Company prior to 1858) or a government organization of the metropolitan power in Europe (like the British or French cabinet). This international dimension has been frequently forgotten by students of colonial rule who have tended to be preoccupied with how rule was maintained locally. Such foreign direction and control had important consequences. For example, economic policy in India in the latter part of the nineteenth century was shaped by directives from London which included restrictions placed by London on purchase in India of locally manufactured goods and refusal to allow protective tariffs in India to assist the growth of Indian industry. As an Indian historian has pointed out, 'other nations were able to develop their industries under the umbrella of protective tariffs, but the Secretary of State for India in London stubbornly maintained a policy of *laissez-faire,* prepared neither to impose protective tariffs nor actively to encourage domestic industries in other ways in India' (Rungta, 1970, p.69). Such a policy, however, was advantageous to capitalist interests and industrialization in Britain. More broadly, the economic surplus being generated in the Indian countryside was not directed toward industrial growth in India because of government policies determined in London.

Foreign rule also had the consequence of there being little resource to assist agricultural development. In the 1870s, departments of agriculture were set up in the provinces of British India, but they were always desperately short of money. Nearly all the land revenue was consumed by the high costs of maintaining the Government of India and the imperial system. The land revenue helped to meet the costs of the civil service, the army, the police, the Afghan wars, the magnificent public buildings, the pomp that attended the Viceroy and his staff, and so on. In addition to the actual costs of the government in India, there were various other expenses in Britain and elsewhere that were met from the Indian revenues. For example (Whitcombe, 1972), every government item in London that remotely related to India, from the cost of training Indian regiments in preparation for duty in India to the fees of the charwomen in the India Office at Whitehall, were charged to the Indian account. Indian peasants – as the original source of the government's land revenue – paid, among other things, for a lunatic asylum in Ealing, gifts to members of the Zanzibar mission, the consular and diplomatic establishments of Great Britain in China and Persia, part of the permanent expenses of the Mediterranean fleet and the entire cost of the telegraph line from England to India. When the Sultan of Turkey made a state visit to London in 1868, his official ball was held at the India Office and the bill charged to India. Little was left after all this for state support for agricultural improvement in Indian provinces.

In colonial Africa (Figure 12.1a), the subordination of colonies there to trends in the capitalist economies and interests in Europe and North America is well illustrated by the history of Africa in the early 1930s following the Wall Street crash of 1929. The depression slashed demand for African staples. World prices for East African sisal, coffee, maize and hides fell by 70% between 1929 and 1932; the price of cotton fell by 60%; raw cocoa from West Africa which sold at Liverpool for nearly 38 shillings per hundred-weight in 1930 dropped to 23 shillings in 1939; palm oil from the Belgian Congo fell to less than one-fifth of its value between 1929 and 1934 and the money paid for rubber production there plunged by 90% between 1929 and 1932 (Wilson, 1994, p.32). Falling prices shrank customs receipts for colonial states. In the Gold Coast and Sierra Leone, for example, revenue fell by about one-third. Metropolitan governments in Europe, responding to the advice of orthodox economists, instructed their colonial states in Africa to cut

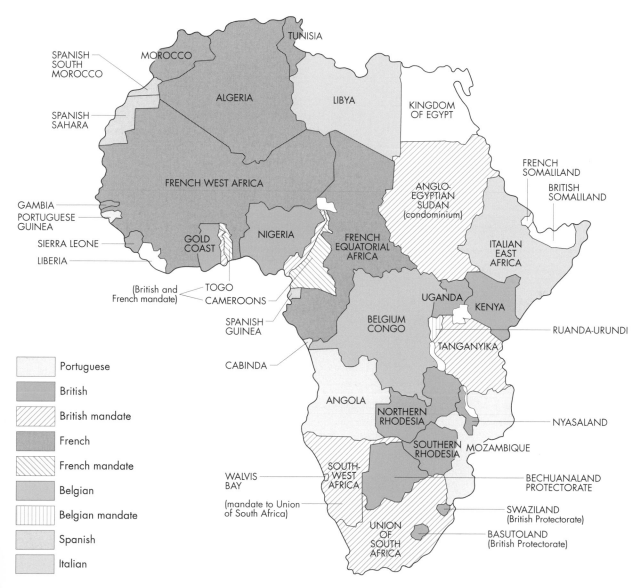

Figure 12.1 (a) *Africa in 1939, indicating areas controlled by European powers.*

expenditure to meet dwindling revenues. Expenditure on development and welfare was accordingly slashed, the salaries of Africans working for the colonial states were in many cases frozen and promotions for African clerks suspended. Britain's West African dependencies were instructed by London to introduce 'customs duties discriminating against Japanese textiles, which were beginning to invade markets hitherto dominated by Britain' (Wilson, 1994, p.33).

The international dimension must not be conceived narrowly in terms only of direction from a metropolitan power in Europe. Such powers responded to what they conceived to be the interests of powerful classes in their own society. Leaders of colonial states in Africa and India also were alive to the importance of these interests in shaping the character of their rule. For example, the Viceroy of India stated publicly in Calcutta in 1888 that he considered the

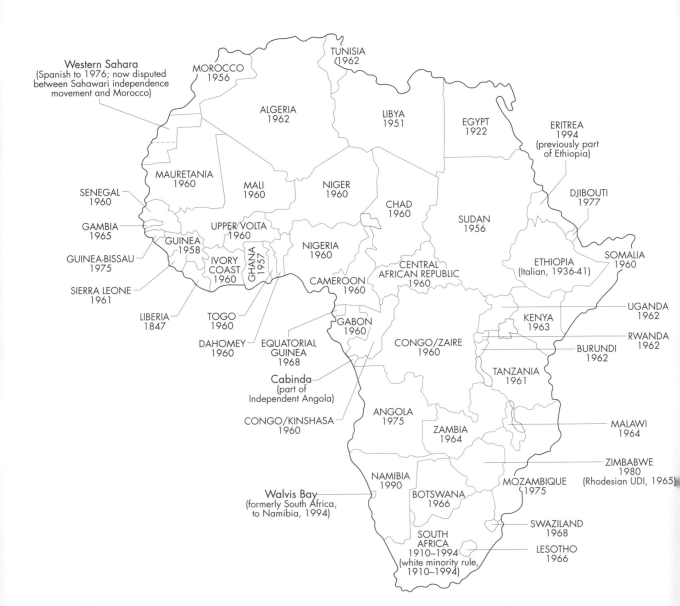

Figure 12.1   (b) The chronology of independence.

prime duty of his Government to be to watch 'over the enormous commercial interests of the mother country', and that 'it would be criminal to ignore the responsibility of the Government towards those who have...invested their capital in [India]' (cited in Misra, 1976, p.90).

Bearing in mind this international dimension, it is useful to see colonial rule as operating on different levels: the levels of the metropolitan power (e.g. London or Paris), the colonial government (e.g. Delhi or Nairobi), the provincial government (where colonies had provinces) and the local district or cercle (in French colonies) presided over by a District Officer. Complex relationships operated between levels. Subordinate levels could have considerable autonomy from time to time, and disagreements did occur between levels in this structure of rule. Normally, however, in important decisions to do with vital imperial interests the views of the metropolitan power prevailed.

Bureaucratic élitism and authoritarianism

Government organizations in colonial states in Africa and India were *bureaucratic*, at least from about the beginning of the twentieth century, in the sense that the army and the police and civilian departments of government were made up of large-scale organizations characterized by hierarchy, continuity, impersonality (in principle at least) and expertise (in the sense that most colonial officials had to have some qualification and/or minimal training). They were bureaucratic *élitist* in that most of the key positions in the bureaucracy at all levels of the state were reserved for a minuscule group of political administrators or police chiefs or military officers recruited in Europe. Most of the rest of the subordinate civil servants and policemen and soldiers/sailors were recruited from the indigenous populations of Africa and India (and Nepal). The European civilian **élites**, for example, were trusted agents of the metropolitan power placed in posts specially reserved for them in the districts and policy-making secretariats at a provincial headquarters (if there was one) and national headquarters of the colonial states. In the policy-making secretariats they were responsible for handling questions of policy arising in

the colony in a manner loosely consistent with the economic and strategic interests of the metropolitan power. In the districts, even while overseeing the routine work of subordinates, they were inevitably engaged in political work with local collaborators, chiefs and others, nursing support structures and moving for advantage in fluid situations while never losing sight of imperial aims and requirements (Potter, 1986). Each year a few young men (women were not allowed) were recruited in Europe to these superior civil services and sent out to the colony – only they had a clear career run to the key positions at the top of the colonial bureaucracy, commanding exceedingly handsome salaries most of the way. No wonder that British rule in India was referred to by a critic as a 'Rolls-Royce administration in a bullock-cart country' (Schiff, 1939, p.145).

> **Elite:** A small group within the state or other organization which has disproportionate power over important decisions.
>
> **Authoritarianism:** Non-existent or very limited participation in government decision-making by those being governed.

Political control by a bureaucratic élite under the broad rule of a foreign power is an instance of **authoritarianism** in that participation in government decision-making by those being governed was virtually non-existent. Colonial rule was marked by élitism and authoritarianism (Figure 12.2). In African colonies broadly speaking, a few foreigners 'enjoyed very wide powers without brakes from below' (Crowder, 1987, p.15). The Belgians allowed hardly any African participation in the Congo, the Portuguese none at all in Angola (similarly with the Italians in Libya), and 'even the more liberal systems such as those developed by the British in West Africa had allowed only limited participation in government, and this itself was confined to a small élite' (Gann & Duignan, 1967, p.331).

India was somewhat different. Towards the end of British rule more popular participation in government was allowed in India than in Africa, especially under the provisions of the

Figure 12.2   Elitist authoritarianism. Nineteenth-century wooden model of an Indian court, or cutcherry, with a British official in the chair.

Government of India Act, 1935. Popularly elected ministries (elected on a restricted franchise) governed during 1937–39 in the provinces of British India under the watchful eyes of the provincial Governors and the colonial Government of India.

Use of 'traditional' or 'customary' authority figures in colonial society

Political support for colonial rule from 'traditional' or 'customary' authority figures in colonial society is profoundly important to any explanation of how so few Europeans were able to hold down so many colonial peoples. I start with India's long association with Britain from the seventeenth century to 1947, then turn to Africa's comparatively short and late experience of colonialism from the end of the nineteenth century to the 1950s and 1960s.

When representatives of the British East India Company first arrived in India at the beginning of the seventeenth century to commence trading, they sought permission from Indian rulers to establish 'factories' at ports like Calcutta and Madras to hold and process goods in readiness for the arrival of the next ship from Europe. The survival of these tiny enclaves depended on the support of nearby Indian political and economic institutions which controlled the surrounding countryside. The character of British power in India was gradually transformed as a result of two main phases of territorial expansion by force of arms: between 1740 and 1760, and between 1792 and 1818 (for a general explanation of this transformation, see Bayly, 1989). The Company acquired vast tracts of populous and productive land, and land revenue began to replace trade as one of the most important sources of the Company's income. At first, the Company's officials in the mid-eighteenth century relied on the administrative organizations they inherited in India to collect the revenue for them and maintain a semblance of order in the countryside. In this, they were behaving roughly in accordance with Indian political tradition, where state power rarely implied direct territorial control. The normal mechanism of state formation in India in the past had usually been through the forging of alliances between a ruler and petty princes, priests, and other intermediaries with considerable power locally (Stein, 1998). The Company began to press down harder on the agrarian order in its endeavour to extract enough revenue to satisfy the directors in London and to pay for the insatiable demands of the Company's army.

The shift from rule by commercial enterprise to rule by a far-flung colonial bureaucracy coincided with Britain's industrial revolution. The Company lost its trade monopoly with India in 1813, lost its trading connections altogether in 1833, and was replaced in 1858 by a Government of India directly responsible to the Crown (i.e. the British Cabinet) in London. India was increasingly perceived 'as a financial asset of enormous potential value to Britain's industrial economy – a captive market for its manufacturers, a source of foodstuffs as well as of cotton, jute and other industrial raw materials, and, in its railways, plantations and public utilities a dependable recipient and multiplier of capital investment' (Arnold, 1986, p.12). To provide a favourable 'law and order' context for this 'enormous financial asset' became the principal purpose of the colonial state. The army was too crude an instrument for this purpose, so new police forces were set up in the provinces of British India, modelled on the authoritarian formation of the British police in nineteenth-century Ireland.

There was no way that the British could control their vast empire in India in the latter part of the nineteenth century (Figure 12.3) by using

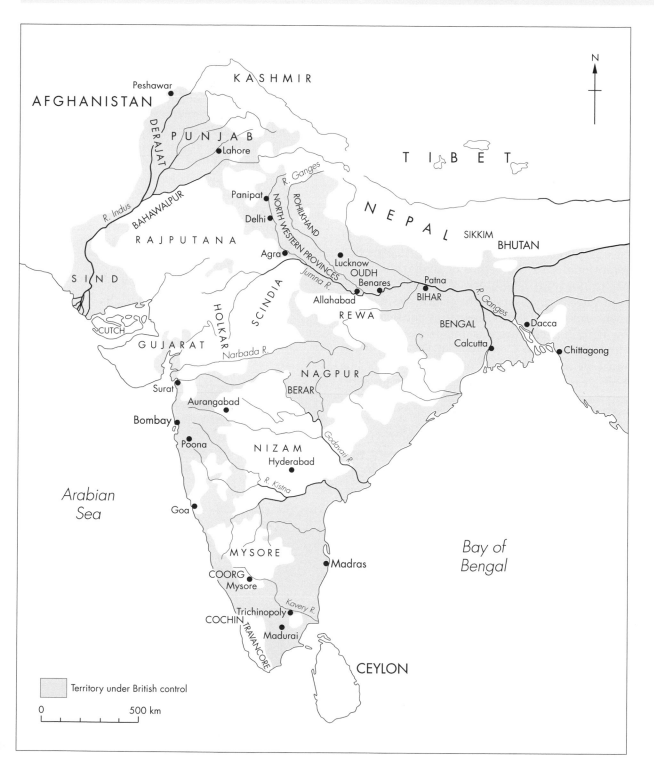

Figure 12.3   *India in 1857, indicating territorial acquisition by the British at that time.*

only the police and the army. No government lasts long on the basis of force alone. The British had to have 'traditional' authority figures in Indian society on whom they could rely for political support and who could bring to the new state the cloak of legitimacy. Where they could not find authority figures, they created them. Such 'traditional' political support came primarily from amongst princes in the princely states (occupying about 40% of the area of India from 1858 to 1947) and landlords or peasant proprietors in the provinces of British India.

To the extent that political legitimacy attached to any person in a princely state, it attached traditionally to the prince or maharaja. Since the prince controlled his people, and the British controlled and preserved the prince, the arrangement amounted to an important political asset for British rule. This was demonstrated during the Indian mutiny or revolt of 1857–58, when most princes remained at least neutral. The British rewarded them afterwards by preserving these princely states (or most of them) until 1947 (Figure 12.4).

In the provinces of British India, the *raj* (rule) rested on landlords or powerful peasant proprietors for the most part. For example, in the United Provinces (or 'North-western Provinces and Oudh') in North India in the mid-nineteenth century:

> "Government needed the support of those groups in the province that were powerful and therefore potentially dangerous. Over 80% of the provinces' population lived off the land, over 50% of its revenue came from the land; it was logical that government should seek the support of those with social and political power on the land: the landlords...[T]he policy of the British in the U.P. looked to the landlords as the main prop of their rule.
>
> Government's technique was simple. It doled out patronage, disbursed contracts, supported educational projects, bestowed a myriad of honours, consulted allies and did its best to make them strong."
>
> (Robinson, 1971, pp.10–12)

Similar connections with landed classes were forged and maintained in other provinces. The main reason why such connections with these traditional authority figures were so important was because their groups' 'influence over the entire agrarian base was strong...through

Figure 12.4   Preserving the Prince. Durbar procession of Akbar II, Emperor of Delhi, accompanied by the real rulers in top hats. Delhi school, c.1815.

influence over access to land, through provision of employment and credit opportunities, through traditional ideologies of deference, and through often extensive connections of caste and kinship' (Washbrook, 1981, p.688). The landed classes controlled much of the countryside and colonial officials nursed this political support structure while never losing sight of imperial aims and requirements.

One example of the usefulness of local landlords to colonial rulers and of the power they could exercise within their domain must suffice here. When Mohammed Raza was the Indian Civil Service collector of Larkhana District in Sind Province in the early 1940s, he found that the presence of the principal *jagirdar* (landlord) there 'was worth six police stations' because 'whenever my police were unable to trace an absconder and reported that he had moved to the Ghaidero Jagir [the *jagirdar's* estate], all that I had to do was to write a letter to the [*jagirdar*] and the absconder was handed over to us within 48 hours!' (Raza, undated). In due course, a knighthood was conferred on the *jagirdar* for his services in helping to maintain colonial rule.

Turning now to Africa, European powers already had a lot of experience of colonial rule by the time the scramble for colonies in Africa took place at the end of the nineteenth century. The emphasis in colonial thinking had become more conservative; power and maintaining law and order had become the paramount consideration. This was the overriding motivation in Africa from the outset. Although no colonial rule started with a 'clean slate' and therefore initial conditions varied a lot in different parts of Africa, it has been argued in an important recent book that the structure of the colonial state in Africa 'came to share certain fundamental features' because 'everywhere the organizations and reorganization of the colonial state was a response to a central and overriding dilemma: the native question. Briefly put, how can a tiny and foreign minority rule over an indigenous majority?' (Mamdani, 1996, p.16). In Africa there were two broad answers to this question: direct and indirect rule.

Direct rule came to be the usual way to control the cities. There was 'a single legal order, defined by the 'civilized' laws of Europe; no 'native' institution was recognized; 'natives' had to conform to European laws; only the 'civilized' would have access to European rights; and because the vast majority of 'natives' in the city were 'uncivilized' and therefore excluded from the rights of citizenship, direct rule signified an unmediated – centralized – despotism' (Mamdani, 1996, pp.16–17).

Indirect rule became the standard way to rule rural Africa where European settlers were not prominent; that is, it was the form of rule for most of Africa and most Africans. It relied fundamentally on what the colonial power came to regard and define as 'customary' in African society. The 'customary', in the first place, was *tribal* and the tribe was normally the basic unit of indirect rule. A 1930 *Native Administration Memorandum on Native Courts*, issued in Tanganyika, assumed it was stating the obvious when it said that 'every African belonged to a tribe, just as every European belonged to a nation', that tribes were cultural units 'possessing a common language, a single social system, and an established customary law', and that 'each tribe must be under a chief' (cited in Mamdani, 1996, p.79). However, where 'the tribes were in a very disorganized state', as in Northern Rhodesia when colonial rule was being established, then fresh tribal organizations were 'created' (Chanok, 1985, p.112). Where tribes did not exist, they were 'invented', as was the Ndebele in colonial Zimbabwe (Ranger, 1985).

What came to be 'customary' for a tribe in Africa was far more *comprehensive* in coverage than in other colonial rules, for it included *access to land*, on which African peasants depended for their livelihood. This meant that land could not be a private possession of landlords or peasants as in India but was defined as a communal holding of the tribe to which every peasant household in the tribe had access under 'customary' law. That law was defined and enforced by the Native Authority or 'chief' for the tribe. In effect, African peasants were subject to a comprehensive form of **patrimonial authority**.

> **Patrimonial authority:** A concept used by Max Weber to denote a type of authority found in small and traditional polities, in which 'an individual rules by dint of personal prestige and power; ordinary folk are treated as extensions of the 'big man's' household, with no rights or privileges other than those bestowed by the ruler; authority is entirely personalized, shaped by the ruler's preferences rather than any codified system of laws. The ruler ensures the political stability of the regime and personal political survival by providing a zone of security in an uncertain environment and by selectively distributing favours and material benefits to loyal followers who are not citizens of the polity so much as the ruler's clients' (Bratton & van de Walle, 1997, p.61).

The patrimonial chiefs were supervised, and if need be appointed, by the colonial power. In French West Africa (an area eight times the size of France), the rural population of around fifteen million was in the late 1930s administered by 118 French *cercle* commanders who supervised 48 000 village chiefs and 2200 canton chiefs; 'without the chiefs', admitted the former governor-general of 'overseas France' (Robert Delavignette), the French administration 'would have been helpless', not only because the chief 'represented his community in its dealings with the administration' but 'even more importantly', because he represented 'the administration vis-à-vis the community' (Delavignette, 1950, cited in Mamdani, 1996, p.82). If there were no chiefs in a colonial area, chiefs were created. Whenever a chief got out of control, he was replaced by another chief. Colonial officials may have occasionally interfered with, or replaced, chiefs but 'to the peasant', as Mamdani (1996, p.54) remarks, 'the person of the chief signified power that was total and absolute, unchecked and un-

restrained'. For example, in Nigeria in the 1930s:

> "The chief is the law, subject to only one higher authority, the white official stationed in his state as advisor. The chief hires his own police…[H]e is often the prosecutor and the judge combined and he employs the jailer to hold his victims in custody at his pleasure. No oriental despot ever had greater power than these black tyrants, thanks to the support which they receive from the white officials who quietly keep in the background."

(Padmore, 1936, cited in Mamdani, 1996, p.53)

White officials actually had to be repeatedly reminded about the importance of keeping in the background. The French governor of Senegal warned his field officers in 1910: 'let the Bour engage in whatever repression he judges necessary, but you will not accompany the Bour to Diohine when he goes there to punish his subjects' (cited in Mamdani, 1996, p.158). Such an instruction only makes sense within a context of indirect rule, of relying on a 'customary' patrimonial authority to rule subject peoples on behalf of the colonial power.

Use of force

The history of colonialism is one of extension of *political control by force of arms* and 'crushing' opposition. For example, British history is studded with the names of colonial wars – Maratha Wars, Sikh Wars, Burmese Wars, Afghan Wars, Zulu Wars, Ashanti Wars, Matabele Wars. And this list does not reflect the active resistance of countless groups whose names never reached the imperial history books. This resistance took many forms, ranging from hit-and-run tactics, kept up by the coastal forest people of Côte d'Ivoire (Ivory Coast) for almost 30 years, to the sophisticated and well-armed war waged by Samori Touré against the French in West Africa (Markowitz, 1977, pp.49–50). In many cases hostility was sustained over a period of years, but ultimately it foundered against the military superiority of the Europeans (Figure 12.5).

Later on, the military, having performed the task of conquest, retired to the background, to be used

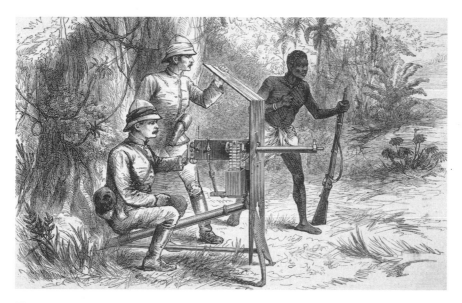

Figure 12.5 Military superiority. H. M. Stanley with the Maxim Automatic Machine Gun: the Emin Pasha relief expedition, 1887.

only in emergencies. Troops were too expensive to be used for maintaining law and order on a regular basis and they were rather inflexible as regards the degree of coercion used. Troops were also not well suited to guarding property or detecting and preventing crime. The civilian police in British India and in African cities were more suited to this work, although they always retained an exceptional capacity to use force through the development of sizeable armed and paramilitary units within their organizations.

Throughout Africa, it has been said that 'the colonial state was conceived in violence rather than by negotiation', and 'it was maintained by the free use of it' (Crowder, 1987, p.11). In the Native Authorities, Mamdani emphasizes that:

"African colonial experience was *marked by force to an unusual degree*. Where land was defined as a customary possession, the market could be only a partial construct. Beyond the market, there was only one way of driving land and labour out of the world of the customary: force. The day-to-day violence of the colonial system was embedded in customary Native Authorities in the local state, not in civil power at the centre. Yet we must not forget that customary

local authority was reinforced and backed up by central civil power. Colonial despotism was highly decentralized...Not only did the chief have the right to pass rules (by-laws) governing persons under his domain, he also executed all laws and was the administrator in 'his' area, in which he settled all disputes. The authority of the chief thus fused in a single person all moments of power: judicial, legislative, executive, and administrative. This authority was like a clenched fist, necessary because the chief stood at the intersection of the market economy and the non-market one. The administrative justice and the administrative coercion that were the sum and substance of his authority lay behind a regime of extra-economic coercion, a regime that breathed life into a whole range of compulsions: forced labour, forced crops, forced sales, forced contributions, and forced removals."

Mamdani (1996, pp. 22–3)

In India, colonial police establishments were formed to do much of the routine work of maintaining order. Two important features of colonial policing are brought out clearly in the standard work on the police in Madras Province (Arnold, 1986). First, force and violence were used extensively as a regular feature of police practice: 'a contempt for Indian lives (in marked contrast to the special protective role adopted towards Europeans) and a belief in the positive value of displaying and deploying armed force were basic and enduring elements in the psychology and practice of colonial control' and 'with repeated use, the frequent resort to high levels of state violence became sanctioned by departmental custom and entrenched in police procedures and mentality' (p.233). People in the towns on the receiving end of colonial policing were treated in a manner that would have been quite unacceptable in England. As for the villages, the Madras police (indeed all colonial police forces in India) were not large enough to provide a permanent police presence there, so when police intervention in a village came it tended to be 'abrupt, brutal and partisan' (p.114); invariably, it was landlords or other dominant villagers who called in the police, not the poor.

This last point relates to the second main feature of colonial policing in Madras Province – 'its close identification with the propertied classes…, both European and Indian' (Arnold, 1986, p.234). Such partisan policing served:

> "to frustrate or negate such coercive power as the rural and urban poor possessed and to enable employers, traders and landlords to resist demands for higher wages and lower prices to which they might otherwise have been obliged to succumb. While police intervention shielded the propertied classes from direct attack and left them secure in their pursuit of profit and the exploitation of wage labour, it also contributed to the brutalization of emerging class conflict in India."
>
> (Arnold, 1986, p.235)

Such partisan policing created a fund of bitterness against the police among ordinary people in urban and rural India.

Colonies may have differed in the extent to which the army or the police were used, but they were alike in not flinching from the widespread use of state violence and repression as a central characteristic of their rule.

Technological advantage

The use of force usually involved 'tools' and effective organization. Headrick (1988, pp.5–6) claims that a major reason why the conquest of Asia and especially Africa was so swift was the technological advantage of the Europeans. This included the continual improvement being made in the organized use of firearms: 'muskets and machine guns gave small European-led units an overwhelming advantage over their African and Asian enemies.' Another advantage was the discovery and efficient use of quinine as a prophylactic against malaria: the extremely high death rate among Europeans due to malaria was reduced, especially in West Africa. Two other technological achievements of major importance were telegraph cables and railroads. These tools made it easier for Europeans 'to control their newly acquired colonies efficiently.' The telegraph could (among other things) be used by local district officers to alert superiors to incipient revolt, and the railroads (or riverboats in places like lowland Bengal) could then be used to bring troops and armed police swiftly to the local area (Figure 12.6).

Figure 12.6   Technological advantage. French soldiers on the River Congo, 1914.

Railroads and steamships were not only used to advantage by the Europeans to police colonies. They also enabled bulky commodities and new materials to be transported from the colonies to feed the factories and breakfast tables of Europe.

The role of technology and organization in the expansion of Europe was not a simple one of cause and effect, with technologically more advanced societies inevitably overcoming more backward (and by implication 'inferior') ones. The relationship was circular rather than linear, in that the technological advance of Western Europe to some extent required and depended on the subjection of other societies to European control. Nevertheless, both the technological supremacy and the ideology of superiority which it helped to engender were important assets in the struggle to maintain colonial rule.

Statism

Colonial rule was **statist** in the sense that the colonial state intervened far more in economic life than the state did in Europe. The East India Company, for example, had monopoly control over many important areas of commerce. Later, even when British rule backed away from such monopoly control, the state nevertheless had exclusive control of most of the economic infrastructure. It owned the railways, controlled external trade, favoured foreign firms, and more generally imposed an array of laws and regulations which had the consequence of stifling industrial development in India to the advantage of industrialization in Britain. Even towards the end of the *raj*, from 1900 to 1939, 'the emergence of Indian entrepreneurship in most parts of India was systematically discouraged by the political, administrative and financial arrangements maintained by the British rulers' (Bagchi, 1972, p.423). The *raj* was statist not because the bureaucracy was gigantic (it was actually quite small in relation to the population) but because its command over the economy was fairly comprehensive.

Colonial rules generally were more or less statist, although there were a few exceptions, e.g. Hong Kong in the early 1990s. African colonial states

> **Statism:** Comprehensive (although not total) command over the economy by the state.

tended to be very statist. The usual colonial economic controls and state ownership obtained, but a special aspect of statism in Africa was the establishment of state monopoly control over the purchase and export of agricultural goods through various statutory marketing agencies or boards, which meant that the colonial state controlled the principal source of cash income in the economy (Bates, 1981).

Hegemonic ideology

Colonial rule relied to some extent on the acquiescence by colonial people in a belief system or ideology about the nature of the colonial state. Two clusters of ideas were central to the ideology of the *raj* in India for example. One was that the British were benevolent, just, and gradually 'modernizing' or developing India economically, socially and culturally. The second cluster of ideas centred on the belief that the colonial rulers were invincible, it was futile to oppose them, and that Indians were too weak and disunited to oppose them successfully. These principal ideas about the benevolence and invincibility of British rule were nurtured by the British, and to the extent that this ideology entered into the hearts and minds of Indian people it was an important asset for the British in their struggle to maintain their rule. Even during the heyday of the *raj* in the late nineteenth century, such ideas were never totally dominant, but they *were* the leading hegemonic ideas carefully promulgated and reproduced by the state. As with all **hegemonic ideologies**, at least as important as the main interconnected ideas *in* the ideology were the ideas that were organized *out*. This is the context for a remark by an Indian historian that 'a major objective of the hegemonic colonial ideology was to hide the face of the real enemy – colonialism – that is, to hide the primary contradiction between the interests of the Indian people and colonialism' (Chandra, 1989, p.501).

> **Hegemonic ideology:** The dominant or ruling set of ideas in a society which is reinforced regularly by the state as part of a process of legitimation supporting the continuation of the existing political regime.

The importance of ideology in the maintenance of the *raj* is perhaps underlined by the fact that Indian leaders in the Indian National Congress saw ideological work as the most important element in their political strategy for ending British rule. The idea that British rule was benevolent was repeatedly undermined by nationalist politicians in public statements forcefully demonstrating the fundamental contradiction in the colonial situation between the interests of the *raj* and the interests of the Indian people. The idea that British rule was invincible was challenged by the law-breaking mass movements led by Gandhi and others – movements whose basic objective was to show that British rule could be challenged and to build up confidence and courage among the people so that they could develop the capacity to struggle successfully against that rule.

Nationalist leaders in India, Africa and elsewhere were almost certainly right to see that building up confidence and courage was extremely important for people who had been for generations subject to colonial rule, the consequences of which had led to what has been referred to as widespread cultural and psychological dependency. Classic studies related mainly to Africa have addressed this idea. Worsley (1967, p.29) pointed out that it was 'the internalization and acceptance of the total superiority of European culture, not force alone, that was to lead the non-European in lengthy psychological subordination.' Frantz Fanon's (1963) *The Wretched of the Earth* focused on 'the colonization of the personality', and Mannoni (1956) in *Prospero and Caliban* suggested that colonial rule led to a 'dependence complex' – meaning that 'the colonized transfers to his colonizers feelings of dependence, the prototype of which is to be found in the effective bond

between father and son' (p.158). More generally, Ashis Nandy (1983) analysed what he calls the 'loss and recovery of self under colonialism'. Dhaouadi (1988) and others have argued that the colonial relationship tended to underdevelop the self-possessed resources and capacities of the dominated parties, such underdevelopment having not only socio-economic consequences (which Western scholars – both Marxists and liberals – have concentrated on) but also adverse cultural and psychological consequences (which Western scholars have largely ignored). To the extent that such dependency syndromes did obtain in colonial contexts, they provided another prop to the maintenance of colonial rule and help to explain why so few Europeans were able to rule so many colonial peoples.

12.2 Why did colonial rule end when it did?

Being aware of the seven political features of colonial rule identified in this chapter can help one to think cogently about how to approach another large and important question: why did colonial rule end when it did in India and in Africa (for the dates when colonial rule ended in Africa, see Figure 12.1b above). For example, in the case of India, it would be useful to examine at least the following set of factors in combination:

1 *The international political dimension.* There are several things here. For example, it was probably important that British rule in India ended in 1947, shortly after a Labour Government more sympathetic to Indian nationalist aspirations came to power in Britain. Secondly, the Second World War had just ended, a war which stretched to the limit the capacity of the British Government to continue to provide the colonial administrators and others needed to maintain the *raj*. Thirdly, reference can be made to the pressure of 'world public opinion' (more especially the US Government) at this time on the British Government to begin dismantling the empire (thereby opening up 'closed' colonial economies to US capitalist penetration).

2 *Use of 'traditional' authority figures.* The *raj* traditionally relied on the support of princes, *zamindars, jagirdars* and other 'big' landlords. By the end of the 1930s, it was becoming clear that the power of this rural class was fading as political workers in the Indian National Congress mobilized a successor class of smaller but more numerous peasant proprietors who had power locally. Colonial rule had come by the 1940s to rest precariously on a dying class, and because of the Congress the colonial state was now blocked from forging another alliance in the countryside.

3 *Use of force.* British power in India depended on the support of subordinate Indian personnel in the military, the police and the civilian bureaucracy. By 1946–47, this support (which had previously been unquestioned) began to crack. The British officials realized that they could no longer rely entirely on the police and others to respond to orders to use force to maintain British rule. It is significant, for example, that in the days immediately preceding the announcement on 19 February 1946 by the British Cabinet in London that a Cabinet mission would be going to India to discuss the transfer of power with the Indian political parties, there were clear indications of widespread disaffection in the police in Madras Province and there was a revolt by a section of the Royal Indian Navy in Bombay.

4 *Hegemonic ideology.* I have mentioned the decades of work by political leaders in the Indian National Congress to undermine the ideology of the colonial state as benevolent and invincible. By the end of the Second World War, the colonial ideology was no longer hegemonic; too many people had been educated to perceive the colonial state and its consequences for India rather differently. Also, many people no longer believed that the power of the colonial state was invincible.

Consideration of these four aspects does not constitute a full answer to why the variety of colonial rules in Africa and India ended when they did (Figure 12.7). Nevertheless, I suggest that in all the many unique cases of colonial rule

ending, the most useful places to start looking for an answer to this large question would be in the areas of: (1) What was happening internationally? (2) Could 'traditional' authority figures in the colony still be relied on? (3) Did the colonial state still have the capacity to use force? (4) Was the ideology of the colonial state still hegemonic?

Figure 12.7 Another colony becomes independent. Why? The Union Jack is lowered in colonial Bechuanaland at midnight, 30 September 1966, to make way for the blue, white and black tricolour of independent Botswana. Taking the salute is Sir Hugh Norman-Walker, whose term of office as Queen's Commissioner ended with the striking of the flag.

12.3 Legacies of colonial rule for post-colonial states and state-led development

Being aware of the seven political features of colonial rule discussed in this chapter helps us understand distinctive features of post-colonial states and state-led development. By way of illustration mention can be made of certain features in the context of Africa:

1 *International political dimension*. This feature of colonial rule, which was snapped at independence, left most African states acutely vulnerable to new forms of economic dependency on external forces. For example, changes in international commodity prices have had adverse effects on attempts at planned economic development.

2 *Statism*. The colonial state in Africa intervened profoundly in the economy for the benefit of the metropolitan economy in Europe, thereby discouraging the development of indigenous capitalist classes in Africa. As Diamond, Linz and Lipset suggest (1988, pp.7–8), 'both for its resonance with socialist and developmentalist ideologies and for its obvious utility in consolidating power and accumulating personal wealth, this legacy of statism was eagerly seized upon and rapidly enlarged by the emergent African political class after independence' and 'mushrooming state ownership and economic control, and the consequent emergence of the state as the primary basis of dominant class formations, was to have profound consequences' for the nature of African politics.

3 *Authoritarianism and the use of 'customary' authority figures in society*. All European powers with colonies in Africa set an example of authoritarian government where little or no popular participation was permitted until towards the end of colonial rule. Most Africans, therefore, had little experience of democratic government until independence in many cases was rather suddenly thrust upon them. African political élites, largely urban based, moved into the seats of power vacated by the departing

Europeans. They promulgated constitutions and established a range of rational-legal political institutions – bureaucracies, courts and chief executives accountable to legislatures. They also extended their rule to the countryside by appointing their own 'customary' chiefs in the Native Authorities. The post-colonial state was thus two-tiered (like its predecessor): bureaucratic and political institutions in the top tier, 'customary' patrimonial authorities in the lower tier. The anti-democratic character of post-independence politics in many African countries can be traced, at least in part, to the colonial legacy of authoritarianism.

By the end of the twentieth century African countries had moved along divergent and circuitous paths of political development, but all had evolved more or less hybrid forms of political regimes combining patrimonialism and rational-legal political institutions. These are now referred to as **neopatrimonial** regimes.

Neopatrimonialism: 'The right to rule in neopatrimonial regimes is ascribed to a person rather than an office, despite the official existence of a written constitution. One individual (the strongman, 'big man', or 'supremo'), often a president for life, dominates the state apparatus and stands above its laws. Relationships of loyalty and dependence pervade a formal political and administrative system, and officials occupy bureaucratic positions less to perform public service, their ostensible purpose, than to acquire personal wealth and status. Although state functionaries receive an official salary, they also enjoy access to various form of illicit rents, prebends, and petty corruption, which constitute a sometimes important entitlement of office. The chief executive and his inner circle undermine the effectiveness of the nominally modern state administration by using it for systematic patronage and client élitist practices in order to maintain political order' (Bratton & van de Walle, 1997, p.62).

There have been numerous examples of neopatrimonial 'big men' in African politics in the latter part of the twentieth century, e.g. Mobutu in Zaïre, Kaunda in Zambia, Amin in Uganda, Ahidjo in Cameroon, Sekou Touré in Guinea, Houphoet-Boigny in Côte d'Ivoire, Babangida in Nigeria. Hastings Banda bluntly stated his neopatrimonial position as President of Malawi this way in 1972: 'Nothing is not my business in this country: everything is my business, everything' (quoted in Jackson & Rosberg, 1982, p.165).

The prevalence of such neopatrimonial political regimes in Africa has posed problems for state-led development. Neopatrimonial strongmen have in practice made little distinction between public and private revenues. They amassed huge personal fortunes. Such activity by 'big men' and their supporters, in what amounted to institutionalized neopatrimonialism, was a major cause of endemic fiscal crises, inadequate public investment on infrastructure and diminished prospects generally for economic development.

This problem for development has been compounded by the retention of neopatrimonial chiefs. Rural development has been conceived as moving beyond the 'customary' and, since chiefly rule represented the 'customary', attempts at rural development have had to be engineered from 'above' or 'outside' the Native Authorities. Rural development, according to Mamdani (1996, p.288), has tended to 'become a top-down agenda enforced on the peasantry'; he gives numerous examples of 'enforced' attempts at rural development from Mozambique, Swaziland, Tanzania and Uganda (pp.170–9). Take Tanzania, one of the more progressive postcolonial states. Less than a year after independence from colonial rule, the Regional Commissioner of Tanga told his district commissioners at a meeting (in March 1962) that 'if the people failed to respond to persuasion and exhortation it might be necessary to resort to coercion.' The same year the Handeni District Council passed a resolution saying that 'any person not participating in development projects should be punished by six strokes.' By March 1967, 20 out of 58 district councils in Tanzania had promulgated by-laws 'requiring cultivation of one acre of a cash crop and one acre of a food crop.' And by August 1967 a government circular entitled 'enforcement of by-laws' for district councils aimed to 'step up the emphasis on coercion for development.' The significance of such coercion for development has varied to some extent from country to country, from time to time from the 1960s to the present, and between different social strata in a rural area. Rich peasants, for example, were far less affected by such coercion than poor peasants. Nevertheless, the use of 'customary' force has remained a prominent general feature of rural administration at the heart of African politics, and a problem hindering the success of state-led development.

world was politically independent from colonial rule, frequently after prolonged conflict between colonizers and colonized. The British did not leave India until intense and sustained opposition to their presence forced them out. Neither did they give up Kenya or Aden without taking military action against independence movements. Similarly, the French generated bitter confrontation in Algeria and Vietnam, and the Portuguese brutally suppressed opposition in Mozambique and Angola. Militarization in many former colonies has been a lasting legacy of colonialism.

Political sovereignty did not necessarily bring with it economic independence. This led some to question whether formal independence was indeed nothing more than a formality. Certainly the colonial experience (even in Latin America) resulted in ties with a world economic order that long outlived independence. Neocolonialism, as these inequitable ties became known, cannot be discounted, but there is more to it than that.

The post-war years to the late 1990s (the period under scrutiny in this chapter) have seen economic booms and slumps, wars and alliances, social transformation and political struggles, economic development and severe recession. Most of these have been mediated in some way by changes in the global economy.

Each country, region, community and individual has its own story to tell. We cannot convey this diversity in such a confined space. But it is possible to give it a context by examining the global changes that have influenced individual countries and regions. In this way, we will be able not only to place a certain coherence on diverse experiences but also to elaborate on a number of important ideas which have been used over the years by practitioners, politicians and academics to understand the term 'development' and its relation to the global economy. However, be warned: 'simple guidelines are not forthcoming from the bald statistics' (Toye, 1987, p.16); a global view helps our understanding but is not a substitute for detailed knowledge of specific situations. Other chapters in the book fill in some of the details.

Professor Hans Singer has this to say about the history of development since 1945:

> "Perhaps the story of development is more than just 'one damn thing after another': it is a story of unfolding, of one thing leading to another in a process which can be given some meaning. But the trouble seems to be one of time lags…[T]he development thinkers seem to base their action and thought on experiences of the last-but-one decade or a last-but-one phase, only to be overwhelmed by the inappropriateness of such action and thought in the face of new events and new problems. Is it perhaps a case of a problem for every solution, rather than a solution for every problem?
>
> This seems to come close to the truth. It can be presented pessimistically as always reacting too late and to an obsolete situation; or more optimistically as a learning process."
>
> (Singer, 1989, p.3)

In this chapter we are going to look at some of the proposed solutions to problems and to look at the new issues which emerged, through time, as an outcome of these 'solutions'. As you read, keep the following questions of events of the last 50 years in the back of your mind.

Q How has the meaning of development changed in fifty years?

Q Has development as an idea and as a set of diverse actions produced the goods? And if so, for whom?

Q In what ways has development failed?

Q Is the term 'development' still useful? Has it ever been useful?

The chapter is divided into five discrete chunks of time. Although I am not particularly concerned with the 'history of dates', the events of the last fifty years have some significant phases with their own characteristics and from which, as Singer pointed out above, subsequent lessons have been learned and solutions gleaned. So, the structure of the chapter is as follows:

1 Post-war restructuring   1945 to early 1950s
   and Bretton Woods

2 The 'Golden Years'   1950s and 1960s

3 Debt-led growth   1970s

4 The 'Lost Decade'   1980s

5 The end of   1990s
   development?

13.1 Post-war restructuring and Bretton Woods

By the end of the Second World War, the world economy was in disarray, caused first by the economic crisis of the 1930s and then by the war itself. During the 1930s, rising unemployment and heavy protectionism (see Chapter 2 and Box 13.2 below) resulted in a decline in world trade of 65% in value terms between 1929 and 1933. It was accompanied by a drastic fall in primary commodity prices, the major source of income for developing countries at that time.

This section will briefly examine the agreements initiated in July 1944 at Bretton Woods, New Hampshire, USA, and put in place in the following years. The Bretton Woods agreements are significant: (a) because they stayed intact as an international system until 1973; and (b) because even after this date right to the present, the major institutions it begat (the IMF, World Bank, the UN and GATT – now the WTO, see below) have considerable influence internationally.

The Marshall Plan for the restructuring of Europe and Japan in the aftermath of the Second World War was the model for setting up a more ambitious framework for economic stability. A new world system, supposedly based on large-scale international income transfers, was set up at Bretton Woods. The answer to capital scarcity and declining terms of trade was, in the view of the developed country contributors to Bretton Woods, quite simple: move from national-centred economic behaviour to internationally co-ordinated finance and trade.

Bretton Woods was a conference of 44 nations. It was dominated by the USA and Britain, while most of the developing countries present were from Latin America. In other words, it was scarcely an internationally representative conference.

The four Bretton Woods institutions will already be familiar names. The International Bank for Reconstruction and Development (IBRD) – later to become known as the World Bank – was to provide long-term finance for investment, while the International Monetary Fund (IMF) was to be a source of short-term finance to compensate for balance of payments deficits and exchange rate fluctuations. The United Nations (UN) was to be the forum through which international decisions were taken and the means by which international political and military stability was to be maintained. Finally, there was to be an organization that regulated international trade and stabilized world commodity prices. This role was taken on by the General Agreement on Tariffs and Trade (GATT) which later became the World Trade Organization (WTO).

Thus, through these institutions, the financial economic and political workings of the world were to be regulated and monitored. Perhaps not surprisingly, Bretton Woods was disproportionately favourable to the continued dominant position in the world economy of those developed countries which later formed the OECD (Box 13.1).

Box 13.1 OECD, G7 and G8

The OECD, formed in 1961, is the Organization for Economic Co-operation and Development. Its members are drawn from 25 developed countries, mainly from Western Europe and North America, but including Japan, Australia and New Zealand. Today the Group of Seven (G7; USA, Germany, UK, Canada, France, Italy and Japan) is the most powerful political and economic grouping within the OECD. The Group of Eight (G8) refers to the Group of 7 plus Russia).

The emergence of other political and economic groupings (such as the non-aligned movement, the Group of 77 and the campaign for a new international economic order) is discussed in detail in Chapter 16. They were a direct response to the inadequacies of the Bretton Woods system from the point of view of developing countries.

Despite statements to the contrary at the time, the restructuring of the world economy was predominantly arranged between the industrialized countries of the North. More truly international initiatives were thwarted by a combination of factors. First, there was only minority representation of developing countries at Bretton Woods; only 18 of the 44 present. Second, there was competition between the USA and UK for economic leadership in the capitalist world. Third, there was a struggle between conservative and liberal economists and politicians. Finally, there was divergence of interest over trade issues.

The representatives from developing countries saw commodity prices as the key trade issue. But no agreement could be reached with the USA. The latter, no doubt, was reluctant to forego its sources of cheap raw material easily. Most significantly, GATT did little to improve commodity price stabilization – one thing that might have helped developing countries to escape from their vulnerable position in the international economy.

Conservative US foreign policy objectives won the day. The developing countries might have achieved more favourable terms in these international agreements if it had not been for simultaneous changes in the US political climate. Immediately after the war, the 'Freedom from Want' ideals of the Roosevelt/Truman era and the liberal New Deal policies of the USA provided an auspicious context within the USA. But these were rapidly replaced by the harsher politics of the Cold War and the McCarthy era. The combined outcome was a system dominated by conservative US foreign policy objectives.

This domination also became evident in the United Nations in subsequent years. The setting up of the UN was an opportunity for developing countries to have a real say in the running of international affairs but any involvement of the UN in economic matters was opposed by developed countries. The UN's principal role was to be conflict resolution. This, role, however, was almost immediately undermined by Cold War rivalries. In its place, the OECD, dominated by the USA, became the arbiter of trade and dominance in the world. In the words of Hans Singer (1989, p.8) '...the Bretton Woods system which was meant to walk on four legs (UN, GATT, IMF and the World Bank) was hobbling along on the last two only.'

The United Nations, nevertheless, plays an important role in the international political arena, although since the optimism of the end of the Cold War, its role has become increasingly ambiguous (Chapters 8 and 9). The composition of the Security Council indicates who wields political power in the world. The last round of GATT multilateral trade negotiations, started in Uruguay and ending with the formation of the World Trade Organization in 1994, similarly indicated who calls the shots in world trade. During the 1980s, the World Bank and IMF redoubled their economic influence over the internal workings of many countries through programmes of structural adjustment (see Box 13.4 below).

Thus the institutions created by post-war restructuring are of continuing significance. Despite their limitations, they have provided an unprecedented continuity in the workings of the global economy. Bretton Woods sets the context for post-war international development. Let us now look to the events of subsequent decades and examine how the international economy fared under the new game rules set up at Bretton Woods.

13.2 The 'Golden Years' – 1950s and 1960s

The result of post-war restructuring was a boom in the developed countries, based on full employment and low inflation, which was to last for nearly 20 years. The two decades are often referred to as the 'Golden Years' for the USA, Western Europe and increasingly for Japan. How favourable was this new international climate to developing countries?

If nothing else, there was considerable optimism. The seeming success of the system for OECD countries led a number of economists to advocate a sure path to success for developing countries:

> "The process of development consisted...of moving from *traditional* society, which was taken as the polar opposite of the modern type, through a series of stages of development derived essentially from the history of Europe, North America and Japan – to *modernity*, that is, approximately the United States of the 1950s."
>
> (Toye, 1987, p.11, emphasis added)

The means by which 'modernity' was to be reached was economic *growth*. If an economy could achieve a certain critical rate of growth, the rest would all follow. The means to achieving growth varied. Some of the more influential theories included: savings and investment as the source of growth; development with surplus labour or rural labour as 'cannon fodder' for industrialization; stages of growth towards economic 'take off'; and the 'trickle down' effect where the spoils of growth would gradually filter through to the population at large. In all these, the emphasis was on capital accumulation, the primacy of investment and GNP growth rates as the key indicator of development. With the benefit of hindsight, it might be instructive to look at some aggregate growth rates over time.

Table 13.1 uses World Bank divisions of countries by income levels and by regional groups. The period 1965–73, or the latter part of the Golden Years, is the earliest for which consistent comparative international data are available. Growth rates from 1965–73 show two striking characteristics. First, both low- and middle-income economies averaged higher growth rates than high-income OECD countries. Second, there are strong regional differences in growth rates, with East Asia in particular averaging much faster growth than either South Asia or sub-Saharan Africa.

Optimism for growth gradually became dampened towards the end of the 1960s. Large-scale official flows of resources to enhance domestic savings and alleviate balance of payments difficulties (from the IMF and World Bank respectively) did not materialize. In their place there was a substantial increase in the flow of private capital in the form of direct foreign investment. Approximately 70% of capital flows into developing countries in the 1960s were from the investments of transnational corporations. This raised the question of how much of the observed economic growth was of an isolated type dependent on the location decisions of these corporations and how much it built up national capacity.

Table 13.1   GNP per capita 1980 and 1997, and growth rates 1965 to 1997

Country group	GNP per capita (US$)		Average annual growth of GNP per capita (%)			
	1980	1997	1965–73	1973–80	1980–86	1996–97
Low-income countries	320	350	3.6	2.4	4.0	2.8
Middle-income countries	1760	1890	4.6	2.4	0.1	3.8
Sub-Saharan Africa	570	500	3.0	0.1	-2.8	1.2
East Asia (including China)	420	970	5.4	4.4	6.6	5.6
South Asia	240	390	1.0	2.0	3.2	2.9
Latin America and Caribbean	2000	3800	4.1	2.4	-1.6'	2.7
High-income countries	10750	25700	3.5	2.2	1.9	2.2

Source: World Bank, *World Development Report* (1990, p.160; 1998, p.191), Oxford University Press, New York.

Finally, the **terms of trade** declined again from 1951 to 1965 by some 25% (Singer, 1989, p.13; refer back to Figure 7.4). This was at a time when 70–90% of exports from developing countries were primary commodities and 50–60% of imports were manufactures (Gwynne, 1990, p.41) As a result, balance of payments difficulties were unavoidable.

Or were they? The odds were stacked against the export of primary commodities (minerals, raw materials and agricultural goods such as sugar, cocoa, and coffee), so one solution was to diversify into manufacturing. The 1950s and 1960s was a period of rapid industrialization for many developing countries. It was the era of import substitution industrialization (Box 13.2; Figure 13.1).

ISI is often linked to the argument that new or 'infant' industries need time to develop, but whether such infants grow up or not was the subject of debate in the 1980s. Countries which have followed ISI strategies in a big way include China, India, Brazil, Argentina and Mexico.

Figure 13.1   Import substitution industrialization in Brazil.

Terms of trade: The relative prices of one group of commodities (generally those being sold) compared with those of another (those being bought). The terms of trade for a country is an index calculated by dividing the index of export prices by the index of import prices. The terms of trade deteriorate if import prices increase faster than export prices, or export prices fall faster than import prices. Similarly, the terms of trade for primary products (compared with manufacturing products) deteriorate if the prices of primary products fall relative to those of manufactured products.

Box 13.2   Import substitution industrialization in Brazil

Import substitution industrialization (ISI) is an inward-looking strategy which consists of setting up domestic industry to supply markets previously served by imports. This domestic industry may be locally owned (state or private) or foreign owned. The latter, direct foreign investment (DFI), will usually involve a series of incentives in order to attract foreign firms to set up production facilities within national boundaries. ISI is often contrasted with export oriented industrialization (EOI).

ISI policies will usually involve the use of relatively high import tariffs, quota restrictions on imports and controlled access to foreign exchange. Such protectionist measures to encourage domestic production are usually combined with disincentives to exporters. The typical pattern of ISI is to start with the production of consumer goods and move to intermediate goods (e.g. parts and components for consumer goods) and then to capital goods (e.g. machines to make parts and components). A major flaw in the strategy is that savings on imports are difficult to attain since substitution in one department (e.g. consumer durables) implies imports for another (e.g. intermediate and capital goods to produce the consumer goods).

Nevertheless, most developing countries (like developed countries before them) have employed some degree of import substitution.

Industrialization could not happen in a vacuum. The experience of some Latin American countries from the 1930s to the 1950s showed that, with little access to finance or to protected developed country markets, there was no choice but to look inwards. This generated what Singer called 'export pessimism' and forced countries to look to their internal markets as a means of accumulation.

Industrialization occurred at a different pace in different regions. The larger Latin American countries had begun to industrialize in the 1930s. By the 1960s they already had a substantial industrial base. Along with a considerable measure of direct foreign investment, Latin American industry looked towards internal markets. In contrast, the East Asian newly industrializing countries (NICs; South Korea, Taiwan, Hong Kong and Singapore) were building up industries based on the export of mass-produced consumer goods. India, strongly influenced by the Soviet development model (see Chapter 14), was developing industry with little direct foreign investment and substantial protection. The majority of African countries, with much smaller industrial bases, could not industrialize on a large scale, and could only begin to do so in the following decade when international conditions were very different. These patterns of industrialization reinforced the existing diversity of developing countries.

As with most aggregate international data, calculations of sectoral distribution of GDP vary. Thus Figure 13.2 should be treated as only an approximate measure of change. This said, between 1960 and 1997 there has been an unmistakable shift from agriculture to industry. The current structure of output has been quite stable since the 1970s. The overall statistics, however, conceal considerable variation. To give just one example, the extent to which manufacturing formed a significant share of GDP varied significantly between countries. In 1965 in India and China, manufacturing accounted for 24% of GDP, while in all low-

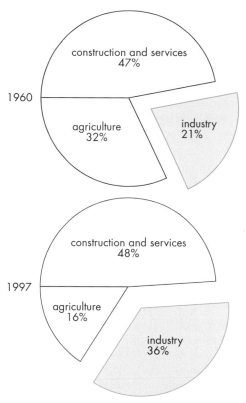

Figure 13.2   Sectoral breakdown of gross domestic product for low- and middle-income countries in 1960 and 1997.

income countries it accounted for 9% (World Bank, 1990, p.182).

While growth did occur in at least some developing countries, it became apparent towards the end of the period that by no means all countries were 'taking off' nor was the supposed 'trickle down' taking place. Even when growth did occur, it was not a sufficient condition to establish sustained social and economic development. In many cases, income distribution was not narrowing as predicted but widening. Emphasis on growth alone was limited. This was due to any number of reasons, most important of which were limits to ISI, the enclave nature of foreign investment with widespread repatriation of profits and little technological or economic linkages with the rest of the economy, and the neglect of agriculture resulting from an 'urban bias' and massive influxes of food aid (which, some argue, made governments even less inclined to invest in agriculture).

The disillusionment with modernization theories of development took two forms. Among development economists, there was a recognition that developing countries were not and probably never would be like the OECD countries. This was a radical departure from orthodoxy. Seers (1963) argued that OECD economies were a 'special case' rather than the norm and that a separate discipline had to be employed to understand the economics of developing countries. This was one of the earlier recognitions that developing countries showed great diversity and that there were no fixed models for economic development.

At the same time, an equally radical alternative explanation of the continued subordinate position of developing countries was emerging from developing countries themselves. In part, this was a criticism of the legacy of the colonial state in Africa and Asia. A more lasting criticism of orthodoxy came from Latin America based on the notion of *dependency* of developing countries (Cardoso & Faletto, 1979). Put simply, the dependency 'school' viewed 'underdevelopment not as a pristine condition of low productivity and poverty but an historical condition of blocked, distorted and dependent development' (Toye, 1987, p.12).

Dependency had two dimensions: political and economic. On the political side, the solution to the perceived negative implications of 'peripheral' status in the world were autonomy and delinking from the 'core' countries. This was associated with nationalist movements and the political cohesiveness that anti-colonial struggles produced. It was also linked to the examples of Cuba, China, Vietnam, Mozambique and other countries which had adopted a broadly socialist development path (see Chapter 14). Even in those countries firmly within the capitalist world, revolutionary movements of rural and industrial workers were widespread in the late 1960s.

The implications of the dependency school were also nationalist. Not only were the prevailing economic relations between developing and developed countries seen as unequal, but it was also perceived that the gap between the two was widening precisely because of this imbalance of economic power.

To sum up, it should be stressed that the so-called Golden Years gave grounds for both optimism and pessimism. Thus Toye suggests that they were:

"...neither the uncomplicated succession of economic take-offs which modernization theory predicted, nor the continuously growing gap in income and welfare between the rich countries and the poor countries prophesied by underdevelopment [dependency] theorists. Instead, there has been a combination of some take-offs, mainly in East Asia, and some severe cases of economic retrogression, mainly in Africa. Thus the polarization that has taken place has done so *within* the Third World, but not between the Third World taken as a group and the developed economies."

(Toye, 1987, p.15)

Thus, by the 1970s, the idea of international development both as an ideal and as an economic fact had become severely undermined.

13.3 Debt-led growth in the 1970s

The 1970s saw a shift away from growth-at-all-costs as the way forward in development thinking towards an emphasis on employment and redistribution with growth. It also saw a substantial increase in the indebtedness of developing countries which for some gave the illusion of development.

Redistribution with growth

In the early 1970s, the International Labour Organization (ILO) of the UN published a series of research reports on employment in different countries. This research was prompted by a substantial rural-to-urban migration resulting from the combination of neglect of agriculture in favour of industrial development and the failure of emerging industries to employ much of this labour. Going for growth alone was proving very costly in human terms. Unlike the modernization model where it was assumed industry would absorb surplus agricultural labour, another idea was put forward which contended that rural-to-urban migration would far outstrip the availability of urban employment (Box 13.3; Figure 13.3).

As a result, attention shifted to employment-intensive technologies which were seen as more 'appropriate' to situations of extreme labour surplus. Growth with employment was thought to be a means of attaining a more equitable income distribution, reducing poverty, minimizing the potential for political unrest, and so on. As a result of the employment missions, the ILO slogan at the time became 'from redistribution *from* growth to redistribution *with* growth'.

It took some time for academics and international organizations to realize that 'unemployment' was a misnomer since most of the world was hard at work (Chapter 5)! The 'informal sector' (those who were not in formal employment) became the focus of attention. There was a simultaneous 'discovery' that women are crucial in economic development. The 'household' (including differences within it) was recognized as a fruitful unit of analysis (see Chapters 5 and 18). Recognition of different patterns of labour utilization was an important step forward from the Keynesian notion of full (formal) employment. The ILO, rather than viewing the mass of people who were not in formal employment as a problem (of overcrowded cities of vagrants working on the margins of illegality), saw them as a resource, a view which resurfaced in the 1980s (Soto, 1989).

Subsequently, some argued that the informal sector, defined to include such a wide array of income-generating activities, was perhaps too broad a concept to be useful. Nevertheless, it seemed to be a step in the right direction that, at least, there was recognition that these economic activities were taking place.

Consideration of the 'basic needs' of the world's urban and rural poor puts a very different light on the meaning of development than that pre-

Figure 13.3   Dhaka: the problem of population concentration in urban areas.

viously linked to macro-economic growth. But the two cannot be separated too easily.

Debt-led growth

The suspension of the free convertibility of the US dollar to gold at fixed exchange rate occurred in 1971. This change was to have important financial ramifications for developing countries, particularly since it was linked to a growing structural crisis in the OECD (including growing protectionism breaching GATT agreements, increasing unemployment, etc.). The combination of the two threw the system of world trade into confusion.

The assertion of oil power by the oil-producing cartel OPEC (Organization of Petroleum Exporting Countries) in 1973, in the 'first oil crisis', radically changed the terms of trade (for the worse) of those dependent on oil imports.

Box 13.3 The urban explosion

There has been an urban explosion in the second half of the twentieth century. In the half century since 1950 the number of people living in cities has nearly quadrupled, increasing by 1.8 billion. In OECD countries, it doubled from 450 million to 900 million, and in developing countries it grew by a factor of six, from 285 million to 1.6 billion. Whilst urban population growth rates in industrial countries (1970–95) have been little over 1%, in developing countries they have been nearly 4%.

• In 1940 only one person in eight lived in an urban centre, and about one in a hundred lived in a city with a million or more inhabitants.

• In 1960 more than one person in five lived in an urban centre, and one in 16 in a city with a million or more.

• In 1995 nearly one in two people lived in an urban centre, and nearly one in five in a city with a million or more.

The league table of mega-cities (see chart below) has been taken over by the metropolises of the South for which expansion is projected to continue well into the next century. This rapid growth of urban populations is mainly due to in-migration. Thus, we get the astonishing example of a country like Brazil with a huge land mass where 87% of the population in 1995 was urban and, of these, 40% living in cities of over three-quarters of a million inhabitants.

(Source: UNDP, 1990, 1998a)

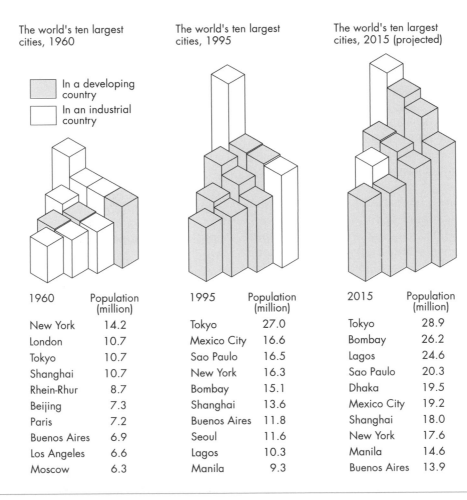

The world's ten largest cities, 1960

In a developing country

In an industrial country

1960	Population (million)
New York	14.2
London	10.7
Tokyo	10.7
Shanghai	10.7
Rhein-Rhur	8.7
Beijing	7.3
Paris	7.2
Buenos Aires	6.9
Los Angeles	6.6
Moscow	6.3

The world's ten largest cities, 1995

1995	Population (million)
Tokyo	27.0
Mexico City	16.6
Sao Paulo	16.5
New York	16.3
Bombay	15.1
Shanghai	13.6
Buenos Aires	11.8
Seoul	11.6
Lagos	10.3
Manila	9.3

The world's ten largest cities, 2015 (projected)

2015	Population (million)
Tokyo	28.9
Bombay	26.2
Lagos	24.6
Sao Paulo	20.3
Dhaka	19.5
Mexico City	19.2
Shanghai	18.0
New York	17.6
Manila	14.6
Buenos Aires	13.9

This can be seen from Figure 13.4. After the sharp oil price increase in 1973, oil prices stayed high for the following decade. This coincided with a long-term decline in other commodity prices, also shown in Figure 13.4. The combined impact was particularly serious for non-oil producing, primary commodity exporters, i.e. many developing countries. The terms of trade for primary commodities have continued to decline in the last ten years, with the exception of South Asia where there has been considerable improvement in aggregate terms (UNDP, 1998a, p.209).

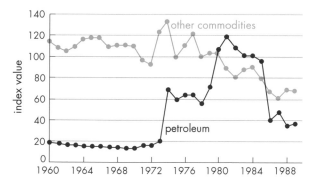

Figure 13.4   Weighted scale index of commodity prices (1979–81 = 100).

As OPEC savings surpluses grew from the increases in oil prices, large deposits were placed in the commercial banks. On account of the economic recession in OECD countries, partly brought about by the oil crisis, the demand for credit declined (something which in turn raised liquidity in the international banking system). Commercial banks began to turn their attention to other regions of the world and saw particularly good markets in the developing countries and, to a lesser extent, Eastern Europe. As a result, commercial and official lending to developing countries grew substantially (Figure 13.5).

OPEC made oil surpluses 'available' to developing countries through what was called the eurodollar market – oil dollars deposited in private European banks. After 1974 there was a rash of borrowing, encouraged by commercial banks which did not know what to do with so much cash. For a while it appeared that this was the flow of Marshall-type finance that had been deemed necessary at Bretton Woods. There was much talk of a New International Economic Order (NIEO) based on recycled oil money, but it remained only talk. The most comprehensive statement of this is to be found in *The Brandt Report* published in 1980 which generated controversy across the political spectrum (Brandt, 1980). Some considered this as an opportunity lost. Others saw it as a pipe dream or a thinly disguised strategy for developed countries to pull out of their own growing economic crises in the name of interdependence.

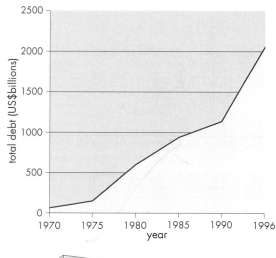

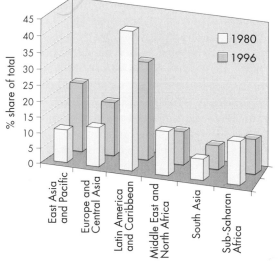

Figure 13.5   Growth and regional distribution of low- and middle-income country debt.

Nevertheless, at the time, recycled OPEC dollars were 'cheap money' (at low interest rates) which was hard for many developing countries (rapidly losing export markets and finding a mounting import bill) to resist. Then the 'debt trap' was sprung. By the late 1970s, the OECD began to adjust to the reality of recession. One outcome was continually rising interest rates which had serious consequences for large-scale borrowers and their debt repayments (Figure 13.6). As the 1980s opened, prospects for all but a few developing countries looked bleak.

Figure 13.6   The debt trap.

13.4 The 1980s – development in reverse?

The 1980s was the decade of neo-liberalism. Observers also talk about it as the 'Lost Decade' for developing countries. Many believed that up to the 1970s there was a measure of human progress in all parts of the world – however slow – which gave indications that it would continue. So what went wrong? And for whom was the decade lost? Some answers are proposed in Chapter 16, where global institutional changes are examined. In this section, we will discuss the economic and social reversals of the 1980s.

The debt crisis, as elaborated above, is crucial here. In attempts to reduce growing inflation, OECD countries slowed down their economies, thereby depressing prices and demand for commodities, and allowed interest rates to rise. For those developing countries which either relied on commodity exports or on borrowing as a source of foreign exchange, this turn-round by OECD countries had serious implications. For those countries which relied on commodity exports and borrowing, the consequences were dire. Thus, in the words of the South Commission: 'a large part of the cost of controlling inflation and introducing structural change in the North was borne by the South. Developing countries had to pay out more and more to service their debt while receiving less and less for their exports. As these contrasting movements aggravated their financial difficulties, commercial banks decided to stop lending them new money, and the result was the international debt crisis of the 1980s' (South Commission, 1990, p.56).

By 1983, OECD countries were making something of a recovery (by some indicators) although this was not on the scale of the 1960s. More significantly, and unlike the 1950s and 60s, the recovery did not generate improvements in the international economic environment for developing countries. This is shown by some of the dramatic reversals for many developing countries during the 1980s.

- *Debt repayments*. Continued high interest rates, combined with a decline in commercial bank lending, resulted in the paradox that developing countries were paying out more finance in service payments than they received as borrowing. In just five years from 1983, this amounted to some $160 billion (South Commission, 1990).

- *Direct foreign investment* declined by some two-thirds in the early 1980s, and there continued to be a net outflow of profits from developing countries (i.e. after taking into account new investment).

- *Non-oil commodity prices* continued to decline rapidly through the 1980s. Figure 13.4 above shows that the real price of the 18 main non-oil commodities fell by 25% from 1980 to 1988.

- *Growing protectionism* in the OECD further mitigated against other developing country exports, such as auto parts, steel, electronics, textiles, petrochemicals and agricultural products. This was perhaps the greatest irony for developing countries in the 1980s: while the neoliberal ideology of free markets took firm root, its proponents – OECD countries – were making their own economies more protected, not less. British readers in particular may recall repeatedly hearing the argument that cheap exports from the 'Third World' were threatening UK industry! The 'new' protectionism (so-called to distinguish it from previous versions such as in the 1930s or 1950s/1960s) was based on euphemisms such as 'voluntary export restraints' and 'orderly market arrangements', which meant little more than protectionism in favour of the OECD through a back door while the formal free trade decisions of GATT could remain intact.

• The 1980s saw an end to the very gradual increases in aid (measured as a percentage of donor GNP) which had been taking place since the 1960s. From the mid-1980s onwards, when the total averaged about 0.35% of GNP (well below the UN's 0.7% target), there was a gradual decline. In 1996, the figure was in the region of 0.25% (Eurostep, 1997, p.246).

Barring some significant examples (principally the East Asian NICs and, to some extent, China) the development reversals of the 1980s were either severe or very severe. In the former category falls much of Latin America while the latter includes much of sub-Saharan Africa.

For many developing countries, there was a combination of declining international demand, increasing protectionism in the OECD, deteriorating terms of trade, negative capital flows, continuing high interest rates, and unfavourable lending conditions. The signs of progress up to the 1970s ground to a halt and in many cases went into reverse. Per capita national incomes in Latin America and Africa declined, investment declined (resulting in the deterioration of infrastructure in transport, communications, education and health care), and unemployment and underemployment grew.

Least developed countries (LLDCs) grew in number from 31 to 42 countries in the 1980s. LLDCs are defined by the UN Development Programme as:

"A group of developing countries established by the United Nations General Assembly. Most of these countries suffer from one or more of the following constraints: a GNP per capita of around $300 or less, land-locked, remote insularity, desertification, and exposure to natural disasters."

(UNDP, 1990)

They were the most adversely affected since they are the most reliant on exports of primary commodities and on imports of basic inputs and capital goods to keep their economies going. Official development assistance to these countries has, nevertheless, been pitifully low. Despite a call by the UN in 1981 for assistance to reach 0.15% of donor GNP, the actual level in 1988 was only 0.09%.

Economic decline had social consequences. During the 1980s, conditions worsened on most, if not all, of the social indicators. Disaffection was compounded by recourse to oppression and military force which, in turn, added to loss of support and legitimacy for many governments.

Interventions by international financial agencies, particularly the World Bank and the IMF, became the universal panacea to crisis. Adjustments had to be recognized as necessary by many of the affected governments in order to claw their way out of crisis (Box 13.4). Nevertheless, the manner in which these adjustments were imposed has been criticized. The South Commission has been one of the more moderate critics in recent years. This is their view of the impacts of adjustment policies:

"…in the adjustment process of the 1980s, these needed reforms were frustrated by an unbalanced international approach towards structural adjustment and by the conditionality prescribed by the international financial institutions. The macro-economic policies – in particular fiscal and exchange rate policies – virtually forced upon developing countries as part of programs for stabilization and structural adjustment were geared to achieving a quick, short-term improvement in the balance of

---

Box 13.4   *Structural adjustment in a nutshell*

Structural adjustment programmes are driven by neoliberal thinking. Neoliberalism is concerned with universal laws of economic development. This school of thought posits that, in principle, the same rules of economic development can be applied across the board from the most developed country to the least developed.

The emphasis of neoliberal theory is on the individual and on the free play of market forces. While other development economists have tended to view development over the long term (often to the detriment of short-term considerations), neoliberals emphasize the short term in the belief that the long term will take care of itself. With its reliance on the market as the best arbiter of prices and efficiency, neoliberals recommend that the state should take a hands-off approach to development. Economic decision-making should be left to private individuals and the state should only provide those goods and services (such as infrastructure) which would not otherwise be provided by the private sector (Jenkins, 1992).

Structural adjustment packages are often imposed as conditions of financial assistance. Their main elements are summarized under the following headings:

• Price distortions produce inefficiencies. By letting the market determine prices, inefficiency is reduced. This is achieved through:

    removing price controls

    financial liberalization

    less intervention in labour markets.

• Trade liberalization (e.g. reducing protective tariffs) produces a more efficient economy. This is achieved through:

    removing import quotas

    reducing tariffs

    realistic exchange rates.

• Reduction of the direct role of the state in the economy. This is achieved through:

    privatization

    cutting government expenditure.

---

payments. Safeguarding the interests of international commercial banks even at the cost of a severe economic contraction thus became the primary concern of international strategy on debt management. Further, the programs for stabilization and adjustment pressed upon developing countries did not provide for sufficient external financial support to permit adjustment to occur and endure without choking their growth. The programs were based on unduly optimistic assumptions about the speed at which structural maladies could be corrected. In addition, they were generally shaped by a doctrinaire belief in the efficacy of market forces and monetarist policies. This combination of priorities and policies aggravated the developing counties' economic woes and social distress in a number of ways.

In particular, the complete disregard of equity in prescriptions for structural ad-

justment consisting in cuts in public spending and changes in relative prices [e.g. for basic foodstuffs] had devastating effects on vital public services like health and education, with especially harmful consequences for the most vulnerable social groups."

(South Commission, 1990, p.67)

By all accounts, such social belt-tightening (where most were already down to the last notch) had few visible positive economic outcomes. On the contrary, 'the application of such policies accentuated the maldistribution of income within developing countries, while in many cases their beneficial impact on public finances was negligible – and is certainly outweighed by their long-term economically detrimental effects' (South Commission, 1990, p.68) (Figure 13.7).

If the combined impacts of debt and inflation were at the heart of Latin America's troubles in the 1980s, in Africa a broader set of adverse circumstances resulted in a much deeper crisis.

Figure 13.7

- Fourteen of the *poorest 20 countries* in the world were in sub-Saharan Africa, many of which became poorer in the 1980s, with per capita GNPs below US$300 in 1987. Meanwhile debt increased dramatically. In absolute terms, the region's total external debt rose from US$6 billion in 1970 to US$134 billion in 1988, an amount equal to sub-Saharan Africa's total GNP or to 3.5 times its total export earnings.

- *Military spending* increased between 1972 and 1987 almost in direct relation to cuts in *social welfare* spending. War was commonplace. From 1945 to 1989 there were more than 30 wars in sub-Saharan Africa (see also Chapter 8).

- Many countries continued to rely on one *agricultural commodity* for more than 40% of export earnings. The real prices for these commodities dropped by more than 40% through the 1980s.

- *Desertification*: land degradation of 650 million square kilometres in the last 30 years is said to have affected the livelihoods of 60 million people, forcing at least 10 million to leave home as a result.

The experience of the 1980s in many regions of the world points to the accuracy of its description as a 'Lost Decade'. Nevertheless, there were glimmers of hope.

First, social and economic crisis was not universal. Some economies and regions, on a greater or more moderate scale, weathered the decade and even thrived. In particular, the South-east Asian countries prospered in economic (if not in political) terms (see Table 13.1). The economies of South Korea, Taiwan, Hong Kong and Singapore grew at a phenomenal rate, posing competitive threats to the USA and Europe. Even the so-called second-tier NICs (such as Thailand, Malaysia, the Philippines and Indonesia) registered remarkable economic growth through the 1980s. In short, macro-economic indicators hide a great and growing diversity among developing countries. This said, the economic crisis which hit the East and South-east Asian countries a decade later (see below) adds force to Hans Singer's thesis of 'a problem for every solution'.

Second, and still thinking back to the quotation from Hans Singer at the beginning of this chapter, the negative experiences of the 1970s and 1980s appear again to have engendered a reassessment of development thinking. In whichever area of development one cares to mention (rural development, aid, industrialization, employment, finance and so on) it has become difficult to stick to the dogmas of either decade. As Chambers points out, in the 1970s 'the solution to rural poverty was not less government but more' and in the 1980s 'the solution to the problems of development was not more government but less' (Chambers, 1989).

Chambers goes on to say that:

> "Both ideologies, and both sets of prescriptions, embody a planner's core, centre-outwards, top-down view of rural development. They start with economies not people; with the macro not the micro; with the view from the office not the view from the field; and in consequence their prescriptions tend to be uniform, standard and for universal application."
>
> (Chambers, 1989, p.6)

Even the World Bank was forced to rethink where it was going by the end of the decade. Its steadfast attachment to rigid policies such as market-led structural adjustment programmes throughout the 1980s weakened (but by no means disappeared). Its emphasis on poverty in the *1990 World Development Report* was, for the Bank, an unexpected shift of position. There continued to be substantial support in the Bank for policies of economic liberalization and the belief that development was best attained through support of the private sector in goods and service provision. Nevertheless, there was recognition at the end of the 1980s that liberalization alone was an inadequate response to the social and economic complexity of developing countries in particular. An emphasis on relieving poverty and improving education, nutrition and health care was a welcome step from such a powerful international institution.

13.5 The 1990s – The end of development?

In the early 1990s, Wolfgang Sachs wrote, 'The last 40 years can be called the age of development. This epoch is coming to an end. The time is ripe to write its obituary' (Sachs, 1992, p.1).

A combination of disillusionment with 'big ideas' (either the state or the market as panacea as noted by Chambers above) together with the legacy of the 'Lost Decade' generated a crisis of confidence in 'development' thinking. The very term 'development' came under close scrutiny. Sachs goes on from his comment above to say: 'The idea of development stands like a ruin in the intellectual landscape... It is time to dismantle this mental structure' (Sachs, 1992, p.1).

In both practitioner and academic circles, such statements shook up any complacency that development professionals might have slipped into. Development thinking had fallen into an impasse in the late 1980s with no viable alternative to the increasingly disreputable neoliberal policy. A spate of publications (such as the collections of articles in Schuurman, 1993; Booth, 1994; Crush, 1995b) brought some life back into the study and practice of development. As one of the authors puts it '...while accepting the importance of economic development, [recent critiques of development thinking] reject the adoption of

mindless modernity, calling instead for a creative synthesis of tradition and modernity, drawing on local knowledge and culture' (Parpart, 1995, p.254).

If the thinking about development was undergoing serious change at the start of the 1990s, events themselves were also not standing still. History has sprung several big surprises that continue to challenge the idea of development. Amongst these I would like to highlight just four:

- the collapse of the Soviet Union and the end of the Cold War;
- the partial demise of the dominance of neoliberal economic policies;
- the string of UN international conferences staged in the last decade and;
- the collapse of the East Asian economies.

Other events are of course significant, for example, the end of apartheid in South Africa (Figure 13.8), the proliferation of conflicts and refugees already mentioned, the enormous increases in private investment relative to aid disbursements internationally and the growing incidence of poverty worldwide, particularly in those parts of the world which are falling outside the reach of so-called globalization. My purpose is to indicate how certain key events have had a bearing on development thinking in the last ten years.

Figure 13.8   The new President of South Africa, Nelson Mandela, with the outgoing F. W. de Klerk at the swearing-in ceremony, May 1994.

The collapse of the Soviet Union

If the fifty-year period under scrutiny began with the politics of the Cold War as the determining factor in the directions of development – the Marshall Plan as a way of containing communism, subsequent aid to many countries determined more on geopolitical grounds than on the needs of particular populations and so on – then the collapse of the Soviet Union on the eve of the 1990s marked a significant turning point in development.

If nothing else, this event finally put to rest the idea of first, second and third worlds. In place of such old certainties (however misleading) we find fragmentation and diversity to be the key words in development. International aid disbursements are no longer determined by Cold War politics. Since the beginning of the decade, however, any hope for a 'peace dividend' has evaporated. Despite an estimated huge drop in military expenditure of US$500 000 million between 1987 and 1995, aid levels fell by 14% in real terms from 1992 to 1995. In 1996, aid fell by a further 4.2% to US$55 100 million. As a percentage of donor GNP, this figure was the lowest since records began in 1950 (Curtis, 1997, p.5).

The collapse of the Soviet Union is not to say that international divisions have disappeared, however. Despite some initial optimism, it appears to have led to greater insecurity in the world, as one of the editors to this volume states, 'a unipolar world would seem to provide less favourable conditions for dispute resolution than Cold War politics' (Allen, 1998b, p.2; see also Chapter 8). Thus, he observes, there has been an alarming proliferation of internal wars in this decade affecting about half the member states of the United Nations with devastating results for millions of individuals. In 1993, there were 18.2 million recognized refugees in the world with an additional 24 million people estimated to be internally displaced as a result of conflict. In the ensuing years these numbers have been on the increase (Allen, 1998b, p.2; see also Chapter 8). In short, greater insecurity and conflict than ever before seriously put into question the validity of the term 'development'.

The demise of the neoliberal agenda?

As intimated at the end of the last section, the neoliberal agenda of the 1980s began to soften in the 1990s. Strident faith in the market as the panacea of development became more nuanced as the decade proceeded. What in some circles (Robinson, 1993) has been labelled the New Policy Agenda (NPA), whilst still market driven, had a broader remit than the purely economic arguments of the 1980s. The NPA combines neoliberal economics with liberal democratic theory and creates the space '…for the centres of economic and political power in the North to 'market' (no pun intended!) the tenets of western liberal democracy as the only development path they are willing to finance in the countries of the South' (Hulme & Edwards, 1997). In the NPA, markets are still seen as the most efficient mechanism for economic growth and for service provision, whilst states play an 'enabling role' and NGOs provide welfare services to those that are not reached by markets. NGOs are also seen as appropriate vehicles for 'democratization' and strengthening 'civil society' (Hulme & Edwards, 1997, p.6). Two factors, I would argue, accounted for this slight change of emphasis in development assistance.

The first is linked to the declining influence of Conservative politics in the USA and Europe (particularly the UK). With this decline (or perhaps instigating it) was the view that free markets left to their own devices did not bring universal benefits. Second, whilst the economics of liberalization continued in many parts of the world driven by neoliberal ideas, questions of capacity building of institutions, governance and civil society crept into the formula. The language of development, once again, began to change in the 1990s.

In the UK, for example, the election of a Labour government in 1997 further consolidated these changes. The new Department for International Development's (DFID) White Paper published in November 1997, and rather grandly called 'Eliminating World Poverty: A Challenge for the 21st Century', was little more than a 'vision statement' but as such is significant in its intentions, which in brief are: to expand the UK aid budget from £2.3 billion in 1997 to £3 billion in 2001; to introduce 'policy coherence' where other UK policies do not run counter to DFID's programme including abolishing the Aid for Trade provision; introduce ethical trading and labour standards; introduce precise development targets (e.g. reduce by 50% those in poverty by 2010); substitute 'partnership' for 'conditionality'; have an overriding commitment to poverty alleviation.

So many words or a substantive change of direction? Only time will tell and, of course, we need to see precise actions attached to these statements of intent. The point is that the language of development in the UK at least has changed direction since the 1980s. This has given a shot in the arm to the debates about international development. There has been a spate of reactions – positive but critical in the main – to the publication of the White Paper (see, for example, contributions to Hewitt & Killick, 1998; JID, 1998).

International UN conferences

For all its inadequacies, the UN system has made an impact in the 1990s through the organization of several world conferences. These are not new but there has been a greater concentration of them in the 1990s than before, in part to mark the fiftieth anniversary of the UN (Table 13.2; Figure 13.9).

Figure 13.9   United Nations Conference on Women, Beijing, 1995.

Table 13.2 Major United Nations conferences in the 1990s

Conference title	Held in	Main themes
The World Summit for Children	UNICEF New York, May 1991	A plan of action for the Convention of the Rights of the Child (1990) attended by 71 Heads of State and Government
UN Conference on Environment and Development, the 'Earth Summit'	Rio de Janeiro June 1992	Attended by leaders from over 100 countries, the largest intergovernmental gathering in history, resulting in Agenda 21, a plan of action for sustainable development
The World Conference on Human Rights	Vienna May 1994	Commemorated the International Year for the World's Indigenous People (1993)
The International Conference on Population and Development	Cairo October 1994	Attended by representatives from 179 countries and addressed by 249 speakers. The Conference had population, sustained economic growth and sustainable development as its overall theme
The World Summit for Social Development	Copenhagen June 1995	One of the largest gatherings of world leaders in history met to renew the commitment to combating poverty, unemployment and social exclusion
The Fourth World Conference on Women	Beijing October 1995	To continue international efforts to advance the status of women world-wide

These have been huge gatherings of governmental and non-governmental representatives. They have been hailed as both international staging posts for global problems and as expensive talking shops for the international élites. Both positions hold an element of truth. A positive reading of the impact of these events in the last decade would include:

- mobilizing national and local governments and non-governmental organizations (NGOs) to take action on a major global problem;
- establishing international standards and guidelines for national policy;
- serving as a forum where new proposals can be debated and consensus sought;
- setting in motion a process whereby governments make commitments and report back regularly to the United Nations.

The United Nations is looking back over its fifty years of existence and grappling with how to reform the institution to make it of relevance to the next century (Singer, 1995). The global summits have put a marker on how it intends to engage with global social problems. It has little say in the international economic system – that role was barred at its birth – but it should be able to make a meaningful contribution to the myriad social issues which hamper social progress in international development.

The East Asian collapse and the implications of globalization for development

In the 1980s and 1990s, much of the economic debate about development hinged on the startling economic successes of the East Asian NICs – South Korea, Taiwan, Hong Kong and Singapore – and, in the wake, other economies of the region. These debates epitomize the positions of the ideological battle that has raged for at least three of the last five decades.

The East Asian 'miracle' – as the extraordinary spurt in economic growth has become known – has been explained (Kaplinsky, 1998) either as:

'governing the market' through guided credit, export support, co-ordination of investment and through picking winners; or as

'market efficiency' through building up human resources, infrastructure, hard work and entrepreneurship.

The sudden and unexpected financial crisis to hit these economies in 1998 appears to have made these debates redundant in one go. Both sides of the debate continue, however, to find explanations based either on the view that the East Asia model was fundamentally sound and the international banking system is to 'blame' or that the model was fundamentally flawed all along making the crisis only a matter of time.

It is also possible that this most recent crisis is part of a family of crises which belong to the phenomenon of globalization. Other family members would include: the Mexico debt crisis in 1982, other debt-related crises in Latin America during the 1980s, the European Monetary Union crisis in 1992 and Mexico again in 1994. The global economy now appears to have more force and impact than individual national economies, even the United States.

But globalization is a misleading label since it implies that all the globe is suddenly involved in integrated economic activity. Some authors have argued that globalization is not a new phenomenon at all but has been a feature of capitalism for all the period under scrutiny here and at least back to the turn of the century (Hirst & Thompson, 1996). Others have pointed out that the geographical reach of capitalism has receded in recent years – not extended. For example, the relative share in global trade of Latin America and Africa has declined (as has the share of foreign investments) since the colonial period.

The characteristics of globalization are more subtle than this. Hoogvelt (1997, p.120) argues that 'the shrinking of the world to a 'global village' amounts to a virtual annihilation of space through time'. Such space/time compression has important implications for global economic activity (Hoogvelt, 1997, p.121).

- Rather than a global market place which has existed for many decades, there has emerged a global market discipline which means that even goods produced for local markets must meet global market criteria of competitiveness.

- The compression of time through space has made the old three sector model – agriculture, industry and services – irrelevant to much global economic activity. So too is the more recent distinction between high and low value-added activities. Globalization means that division into 'real-time' and 'material' activities is a more useful distinction.

- Finally, money is now a real time resource with such rapid international mobility that decisions taken by financial speculators can have instant effects on whole regions. The case of East Asia touched on above is indicative of this. Thus, for example, whilst there was an inflow of $95bn to the Asian economies in 1996, there was a net outflow of $15bn just a year later in 1997 (Sachs, 1998).

13.6 Conclusion

What do all these 'developments' in the global economy have to do with development? Globalization, it appears, is exacerbating the exclusion of large parts of the world's population from any chance of economic development, whether these regions take up market-led development strategies or not. The growing strength of transnational corporations backed by international institutional agreements (for example, in the World Trade Organization) is just one example of the way things are going. The power of governments and of citizens is being subsumed by transnational economic interests where only those parts of the global economy that can keep up are included. The collapse of the negotiations for the Multilateral Agreement on Investment (MAI) (see Chapter 16), partly through pressure from NGOs and other lobbying groups, might appear to be a counter-example, but in general the rest, whether wishing to be included or not, are out of the picture.

The politics of development in the 1990s appears to be teetering between a real concern with poverty alleviation on the one hand and a containment of the effects of globalization and international exclusion on the other. So, to end on a point of hope and to answer at least one of my initial questions ('Has the idea of development ever been useful?'), it depends on what development means to you. I would go with the recent Nobel Prize winner, Amartya Sen, who sees development as the expansion of capabilities – increasing the possibilities for more people to realize their potentials as human beings through the expansion of their capabilities for functioning. According to Sen's 'capability approach', development should be about the enrichment of human lives – not in the sense of 'having more things' particularly, but rather that of having the freedom to choose between different ways of living (Sen, 1990b).

14

SOCIALIST MODELS OF DEVELOPMENT

ANDREW KILMISTER

Socialism has been one of the most influential movements of the post Second World War world. One of the main processes that has structured this world has been the attempt by a significant number of countries to follow a socialist path to, or model of, development. These attempts and their consequences are the subject of this chapter.

Q What are the basic tenets of socialist development?

Q What are the historical processes that shaped socialist development in the USSR? How has this model been adapted in China and how has it influenced development in other countries?

Q What future is there for a socialist model of development following the collapse of communism in Eastern Europe and the break up of the USSR?

14.1 Socialist development

Socialism as a system of ideas and as a political movement has taken a variety of forms, and the nature of a 'truly socialist' society is hotly debated. Despite this diversity the search for a socialist road to development resulted in a number of central features which united the different countries following this path. This analysis enables us to think of a distinctive model that can be described as a socialist model of develop-

ment. It is based on five economic characteristics and one political characteristic.

Economic

1   State ownership of large- and medium-scale industry, with relationships between individual enterprises governed by plans laid down from the centre rather than operating through the market. In particular, investment projects and the level of investment carried out in the economy are centrally planned.

2   Extensive state control over foreign trade and investment.

3   State intervention in the labour market and in the hiring and firing of labour by individual enterprises, often leading to virtual full employment in the economy.

4   State control over retail and wholesale prices, often associated with shortages of consumer goods at the ruling subsidized prices.

5   State intervention in agriculture and in the relationship between town and country, often taking the form of collectivization of farms and delivery of collective farm produce to state marketing agencies at fixed prices.

Political

6   In general, socialist societies are ruled by a single party, claiming to be a Marxist-Leninist party ruling in the name of the working class and peasantry and occupying a 'leading role' in the society. Organized political opposition is not tolerated.

You may want to think about what, if anything, has been left out of this list. Are there any important characteristics of socialist societies which have been ignored?

Clearly, the model of socialism outlined above diverges in several ways from the ideals of equality, solidarity, freedom from oppression, and so on, around which the socialist tradition was formed and has developed. Part of the purpose of this chapter is to explain how this divergence took place and to outline the various factors which led to the ideals of socialism being realized in this particular way rather than some other. This is not meant to imply that this model represents the only direction that socialist development might take in the future. Some writers have argued that the divergences between what has occurred in societies such as those outlined above and 'true socialism' is so sharp that these countries are not really socialist at all and should instead be described as 'centrally planned' or 'state socialist'. In this chapter I shall not attempt to judge this debate. I shall concentrate on analysing these societies as they have developed without prejudging whether this process lives up to any particular ideas or standards. However, it will be useful to keep in mind throughout this account what elements of socialism as a political goal have not been attained by these societies, and how failure to attain these elements has affected their pattern of development.

The model of socialism outlined above has, since the mid-1970s, been in a state of crisis. In the late 1980s and early 1990s this crisis became acute. Two socialist countries, East Germany and South Yemen were absorbed, through a process of national unification, into capitalist neighbours. It appears likely that a third, North Korea, may go the same way in the not too distant future. The former socialist countries in Central and Eastern Europe have opted to try to institute a capitalist market economy and have explicitly abandoned state socialism, though the extent to which this commitment has been carried out through fundamental economic changes varies from country to country. The largest socialist society in terms of land area, the USSR, has broken up into fifteen constituent republics, the majority of which have also committed themselves to the introduction of the market economy. The socialist society with the biggest population, China, along with other Asian socialist countries such as Vietnam, Laos and Cambodia, has instituted significant economic reforms, dismantling much of the centralized planning apparatus and strengthening market relations, particularly in the countryside. A number of these Asian socialist countries, including China, face profound political challenges.

However, these developments in no way diminish the importance of studying these societies and the socialist model that they embodied. It remains important to ask a number of questions about that model. Why did it develop in the way that it did? What lessons does it hold for other developing countries? What might the future bring for these societies? We have to ask these questions bearing in mind that the socialist model is now in a state of flux and that we are not analysing a static framework but something which is changing and developing.

14.2 The dilemmas and contradictions of Soviet socialist development

The concept of the socialist model of development would have seemed extremely strange to Marx, Engels and their immediate followers. The majority of socialists in the nineteenth century thought that socialism was something that would happen in countries with a significant degree of industrialization and a sizeable working class, and that the socialist revolution would be international. The idea of relatively poor countries undergoing a socialist revolution and then attempting to institute development policies within the framework of the nation state was not one which was widely considered prior to the Bolshevik revolution in Russia in 1917.

The most far-reaching attempt to consider these issues was the analysis developed by Trotsky in response to the 1905 Russian revolution. Trotsky argued that socialist revolution was not only possible in a country such as Russia, but was also necessary. In developing countries, dominated by imperialism, the working class were the only group in society that could carry out even basic democratic reforms and lay the basis for industrialization. For this to happen the revolution in such countries had to be 'permanent' in two senses.

First, each country's democratic revolution (the equivalent to the Civil War of the 1640s in England or the 1789 French revolution) would have to be transformed into a socialist revolution. Secondly, that nationally based socialist revolution would have to become international. Trotsky's analysis was combined by the Bolsheviks with Lenin's account of a world economy dominated by imperialism, an imperialism which distorted and suppressed national economic development in the non-imperialist and colonial countries. Together the two strands of thought provided the inspiration for the attempt to institute a socialist transformation in the USSR.

The 1917 revolution appeared to offer striking confirmation of Trotsky's analysis. The responsibility for industrializing and developing the USSR was now placed with the Soviet working class and the Bolshevik party. However, the revolution never became permanent in the second sense. It remained a national revolution and the Soviet state was forced to forge a new model of development in extremely beleaguered circumstances of civil war, foreign intervention, and comparatively low levels of economic development. The questions posed by this situation have marked all subsequent attempts at socialist development strategies. There were four interlinked questions which the Bolsheviks faced as they dealt with the heritage of the revolution.

1   What relationship would a socialist society such as the USSR have with a generally hostile and more developed outside world?

2   Where would the resources for industrialization and development come from?

3   What would be the relationship between the working class (in theory the main beneficiaries and leaders of a socialist project) and the most numerous group in the population, the peasantry?

4   What would be the role of the state and the government in building a socialist society?

The dilemma faced by the Bolsheviks was something like this. It was taken as a precondition for socialism that industrialization should take place. Yet who should finance this industrialization? In the absence of any significant group of capitalists or landowners in the USSR (these had all been expropriated) only three possibilities suggested themselves: resources could come from abroad, via foreign investment; from the working class; or from the peasantry. Yet foreign investment was unlikely to be forthcoming for political reasons. The working class was too small to provide the necessary resources, and anyway the contradiction of a workers' party financing industrialization on the backs of workers was too acute. This seemed to imply that the finance for industrialization would have to come from the peasantry. But this carried with it the risk that the Bolsheviks would alienate the peasantry, which was the largest group in the country and on which they depended for food and other agricultural products. The whole question thus arose of the extent to which a party and government based on the working class, which still constituted a minority of society, could intervene in the development process and shape that process, without undemocratic consequences. On the other hand, since the working class in the USSR only had political representation through party and state organs, party and state involvement in industrialization seemed essential if industrialization was to serve the interests of workers.

The Soviet industrialization debate
Initially, the policies of the Bolsheviks after 1917 were formulated very much in response to pressures from outside the party. Large-scale industry was nationalized in response to factory occupations by workers, while land was distributed to the peasants in response to land

occupations (Figure 14.1). Then in the civil war of 1918–21 during the period of 'war communism', the government established a system of total control over the economy of that part of the country which they still governed, as part of the mobilization of resources for the war effort. One current of opinion within the party, represented by Nikolai Bukharin and Evgeny Preobrazhensky, saw war communism as representing an opportunity for an immediate transition to a planned, moneyless socialist economy. However, by 1921 it became clear that the system was not workable in the long term. This was primarily because of severe peasant unrest over the requisitioning of grain. In 1921 Lenin instituted what was known as the New Economic Policy (NEP), the main features of which were state control of large and medium scale industry, finance and foreign trade, together with the restoration of market relations between town and country. After paying a tax in kind, peasants could market the rest of their output relatively freely. Politically the Bolsheviks emphasized the alliance or smychka between the working class and the peasantry.

Figure 14.1   Propaganda for the transformation of Soviet agriculture.

The immediate effect of the NEP was positive and allowed for the rebuilding of the shattered economy following the civil war. However, by the mid-1920s the question of how further industrialization was to be financed began to become critical. As the Soviet Union moved from reconstructing the old pre-war economy to new development, considerable resources were required. Various competing viewpoints emerged in a fascinating and wide-ranging debate (Erlich, 1960; Day, 1977). Ironically, Bukharin and Preobrazhensky now emerged on opposite sides in this debate.

Bukharin argued that industrialization was not possible without the consent of the peasantry. The peasantry could not be required to provide the resources for industrialization, and the pace of industrialization would have to be slowed to such a level that the growth of the economy generated enough resources for a steady industrial growth without placing a burden on the countryside. The state was extremely circumscribed in the role it could play and should not interfere with the equilibrium between town and country. Following the theory of 'socialism in one country', Bukharin believed that the USSR could maintain relatively self-sufficient development.

Preobrazhensky favoured taxing the peasantry in order to provide resources for a faster growth of industrial production and claimed that this would in turn benefit the countryside by increasing the flow of goods from town to country and thus boosting agriculture. The state and party were entitled and obliged to shape the path of industrialization. Following Trotsky and the Left Opposition within the party, he continued to see the outside world, despite its capitalist nature, as a possible source of resources for the development of the USSR and hoped for socialist revolution elsewhere before too long.

Other figures such as Groman and Bazarov attempted to steer a middle course between these two positions. In addition, Chayanov developed a distinct approach to the analysis of the peasantry, inspiring a school of writers who argued that the peasant economy had to be understood in its own terms and that using this understanding to further agricultural development was a precondition for progress in the USSR.

By 1928 the development of the USSR had run into several problems. It was not proving possible to provide sufficient incentives to the peasantry to produce enough grain to feed the towns. Consequently, industrial development was faltering. The problem appeared to have no easy solution. If the line of the Left Opposition were to be followed and the peasantry were to be taxed, they would be even less likely to support the industrialization effort. Yet without more resources industrialization could not proceed fast enough to modernize agriculture.

Stalinist collectivization and industrialization

The policies of Stalin in the early 1930s represented a response, an exceptionally brutal response, to the problems outlined at the end of the previous section. The difficulty of obtaining grain from the peasantry was met by forcible collectivization and grain extraction. It might appear that Stalinist development involved making the peasantry provide the resources for growth. For many years this was what people believed had happened; but recent research reveals a slightly more complex picture. The sheer weight of destruction of resources, particularly livestock, in the countryside which resulted from collectivization, and from peasant resistance to collectivization, was so great that the agricultural sector was not able to provide a surplus which would finance industrial growth. In fact, in the early 1930s the reconstruction of agriculture was more of a drain on the towns than before. What collectivization *did* provide was a massive flow of labour from the countryside to the towns, as rural society was shattered. This flow of labour helped to limit industrial wages even as the economy grew tremendously quickly. As the Soviet government quickened the pace of growth, often financing this by printing money, inflation rocketed and real wages fell dramatically. In this way Stalinist industrialization was financed not just by the peasantry, but, ironically, by the working class in whose name Stalin claimed to rule (Ellman 1975; for a dissenting view see Morrison, 1982; a classic analysis is Rakovsky, 1981, first written in 1930).

Collectivization in the countryside was matched by the growth of industrial planning, particularly the famous Five Year Plans, in the urban areas. The two together acted as a powerful means of cementing the dominance of the party and state over the rest of society. The planning system also acted as a means of mobilizing resources and directing them into priority areas for industrial growth. Under the banner of the doctrine of Socialism in One Country, foreign trade dwindled sharply. In this way the socialist model of development outlined at the opening of this chapter began to crystallize. While urban unemployment had been a major problem under NEP, the sheer pace of growth in the USSR in the 1930s led to virtual full employment by the end of the decade, and this was maintained during and after the Second World War. As the planning system became institutionalized, the role of money lessened to become purely a means of accounting for transactions, and goods were allocated to firms through the planning mechanism rather than the market. The planners gradually extended their control to the prices of final consumer goods, as well as industrial goods, and the distinctive model of socialist development became complete. This model answered the questions faced by the Bolsheviks in the 1920s starkly and clearly: the relationship of the USSR to the rest of the world was essentially hostile, and independence was a priority. The state and party were to shape the industrialization process in the name of the working class, and while nominally workers and poor peasants were in alliance against rich peasants (or kulaks), in reality the working class and peasantry together were to provide the resources for industrial development (Figure 14.2).

While it was tremendously harsh and wasteful, this model did allow for a dramatic industrialization effort in the USSR. The economy created was able to withstand Nazi Germany and, following the Second World War, to extend the framework created by Stalin to much of Eastern Europe. In this way the model of socialist development which had emerged from Stalinist industrialization became attractive, not only to communist parties outside Europe, but also to nationalist movements who saw it as the only

Figure 14.2   Two images of industrialization in the USSR: (top) an idealist image of Stalin at a new dam; (above) a grim reality 1931.

feasible path to industrial development and economic independence in a world dominated by imperialism.

14.3 The Chinese path to development under Mao

The first, and most important, test of the socialist model of development came with the Chinese revolution of 1949. Initially, the Chinese communist party followed a path very similar to the Soviet model, though with much less brutality and conflict. The first Chinese Five Year Plan was instituted in 1952, and collectivization was carried out in 1955–56. It is important to recognize the sheer scale of what the Chinese achieved in these years, including the largest land reform in history (a classic analysis is William Hinton's *Fanshen*, published in 1972). However, it quickly became clear that the Chinese case was significantly different from that of the USSR, and that the Soviet model of development could not simply be transposed to China. There were four main points of difference, described in Box 14.1.

As a result of these differences it was extremely difficult for the Chinese to carry out a similar process of industrialization to that which had occurred in the USSR. The Chinese party arose out of, was dependent for its support on, and was based in, rural society. Further, rural society and the countryside carried even more weight in terms of population and contribution to the economy in China than in the USSR in the 1920s. Industrialization based upon the break-up of rural society was not a feasible project in China. The working class in China was clearly too weak to provide the resources needed to industrialize the country. In the 1950s considerable assistance was forthcoming from abroad, from the USSR. But by the late 1950s it was becoming clear that the USSR would not and could not provide enough resources to guarantee industrialization in China, and also that such resources as it did provide might entail an unacceptable loss of national independence in decision-making for the Chinese. The Chinese party was thus faced with trying to initiate development in China within severe constraints, both political and material, and within a framework of little if any formal democracy, but a high degree of informal responsiveness to the views

---

Box 14.1   The characteristics of the Chinese revolution

1   Despite some areas of development, the Chinese economy in 1949 was even weaker than the economy inherited by the Bolsheviks in 1917, with less industrial development. (For a more detailed account see Riskin, 1988, ch.1.)

2   The Chinese revolution was essentially a peasant revolution in a way the Russian revolution was not. The Chinese communist party had begun, in 1921, as a predominantly urban party, on the Russian model. However, the vast majority of the urban cadres of the party had been massacred in 1927 by the Chinese nationalist movement, the Kuomintang, under Chiang Kaishek. After 1927 the leadership of the party had been based in the rural areas, under Mao Tsetung. By 1949 both leadership and membership of the party were mainly peasant in origin.

3   The Chinese revolution was very much a national revolution, arising in large part out of the struggle against Japanese invasion and coloni-

alism, and against imperialist domination from other large powers. During the nineteenth and early twentieth centuries Britain and France among others had forced trading treaties on the Chinese, including provision for the export of opium to China. China was still to a large extent not unified and under the sway of competing warlords when the Japanese invaded Manchuria in 1933, moving southwards in 1937.

4   The Chinese revolution arose out of a long period of war and civil war. When the Chinese communist party came to power it was in many ways a military organization with few formal democratic structures. On the other hand, because of long dependence on the rural population during wartime, it had achieved a considerable amount of sensitivity to changes in the mood of its supporters, while having few formal channels through which such changes could be expressed (Selden, 1971; Snow, 1972, is an eye-witness account).

---

of their supporters. In this context, development in China under Mao tended to take the form of a series of campaigns, the most important of which was the 'Great Leap Forward' of 1958–59, in which mass mobilization of the population acted as a substitute for formal political involvement, and was used as a way of trying to overcome the severe material constraints faced by the government (Maitan, 1976).

Collectivization in China and the problems encountered have been the subjects of lively debate, particularly in the light of the decollectivization which took place after 1978. There are disputed views about the extent to which collectivization seriously weakened communist support in the countryside (Nolan, 1976; Selden, 1984; Nolan, 1989). However, there is agreement that collectivization in China did not create adequate resources for industrial development. The Great Leap Forward was an attempt by Mao to solve this problem. It had two main features.

First, the problem of relations between town and country was to be solved by dissolving the

barrier between the two. Responsibility for production was to be decentralized radically to more or less self-sufficient territorial units ('people's communes') which would manage both industrial and agricultural production. There would be some agricultural production in urban areas and a great deal of small-scale industrial production in rural areas (for example, the famous 'backyard steel production'). In this way, through breaking down the division between town and country ('walking on two legs') the problem of financing industrialization would be overcome.

Secondly, the Great Leap Forward involved a massive mobilization of the population through propaganda and example, calling on the Chinese people to speed up development almost as an act of will (Figure 14.3).

The Great Leap Forward represented a distinctively different approach to socialist development from the Stalinist path, as it responded to China's particular problems. However, despite embodying many important ideas which have reappeared in China and elsewhere later, it was

Figure 14.3   Painting the peasants' vision of a better life in China.

unsuccessful. The quality of the industrial goods produced in the rural areas was not good enough, and much of the backyard steel production, for example, was unusable. Industrial output figures were hugely exaggerated. Agricultural disruption led to a calamitous famine in 1959–61. The rest of the party leadership abandoned the Great Leap and forced Mao into a 'backseat' role in economic policy, making him little more than a figurehead.

Following the abandonment of the Great Leap Forward, the Chinese reverted to a model of development which resembled much more closely the Soviet model. However, a lot more attention was paid to providing resources for the countryside and ensuring balanced growth between town and country than was the case in the USSR under Stalin. Despite the violent political upheavals of the late 1960s and the cultural revolution which followed, as Mao attempted to regain the power from which he had been ousted, economic policies remained remarkably constant until the mid-1970s. The Maoist faction which attained dominance in the cultural revolution did not succeed in implementing any significantly different model of development. It has been argued that the rebellion in 1971 by Lin Piao, the Minister of Defence and Mao's chosen successor, was aimed at giving a higher priority to industrial development, particularly electronics; however, this rebellion was crushed and development continued along the same path (Maitan, 1976, ch.14; Eckstein, 1977, pp.59–63).

14.4 The crisis of development in the USSR and China

In retrospect, the mid-1970s appear to be a turning point in both the USSR and China for different reasons. From 1975 onwards there was a decisive slowdown in the rate of growth in the USSR. The reasons for this are undoubtedly complex, but one central factor was widely seen as operating by observers both in the USSR and elsewhere. The Stalinist model of industrialization had proved effective as a means of mobilizing resources for the initial stages of industrialization. However, while it worked, although crudely, for 'extensive' industrialization, which was dependent on drawing new resources of both capital and labour (women, rural workers) into industry, it was much less well suited to 'intensive' industrialization which depended on technological development, increasing levels of skill and using existing resources more efficiently. By the mid-1970s there were few unused resources in the USSR for further extensive development, and intensive development had now become crucial. Further, as the population became urbanized and educated, the crude mechanisms of labour control and political repression became ineffective and labour productivity ceased to grow. This was accentuated by social problems, such as widespread alcohol abuse, and by the drain on resources caus ed by the stagnant agricultural sector. Finally, technological development appeared to require a greater openness to the West in terms both of foreign investment and imports of technology, with possible accompanying political changes. These issues provided the background for the changes which occurred in the USSR after the election of Mikhail Gorbachev as General Secretary of the Communist party in 1985 and the initiation of the policy of *perestroika* or reconstruction.

The policy of *perestroika* was intended to lead to the renewal of socialist development in the USSR through a combination of increased democracy, both within the party and within enterprises, through the election of managers, with the encouragement of market mechanisms. However, the result of the policy was the breakdown of the socialist model in both its political and economic aspects. Politically, demands for democratic reform increasingly challenged the 'leading role' of the party. Equally seriously the relaxation of political control allowed for the resurgence of nationalist movements in the various Soviet Republics, all of which had a non-Communist character. Economically, the combination of increased enterprise autonomy and the election of managers led to price and wage rises, and enterprise tax avoidance. As a result the government budget deficit rose dramatically and was financed by printing money. This led to a sharp rise in the inflation rate and the increasing collapse of what remained of the planning system.

From 1989 onwards the USSR became ever more polarized between those within the party who wished to halt the reform process and those reformers and nationalists who argued for further changes, even if this meant abandoning either the socialist model or the Soviet Union as a federation, or both. Gorbachev oscillated fruitlessly between these two positions. The failed August 1991 coup by hardliners within the Communist party provided a context for the latter group to gain ascendancy, and led to the break-up of the USSR and the explicit adoption of a market economy in the vast majority of the resulting independent republics, including the largest, the Russian Federation (Aslund, 1991; Kotz & Weir, 1997).

Whereas in the USSR the problems of the socialist model of development related to the fact that a measure of development had taken place and in turn had thrown up new problems, in China the problem was that the model had failed to ensure industrialization and development. By the time of Mao's death in 1976 industrial growth rates were falling significantly, and agricultural production was barely keeping pace with population growth. In addition, the situation of the poorest people in the countryside was such that Chinese official estimates in 1980 indicated that about 100 million peasants depended on state relief (McFarlane, 1984, p.25).

The response of the Chinese government to these problems was to institute a programme of

---

Box 14.2 Challenges facing the Chinese reform process

1   One major potential problem is growing inequality. Some who have done well out of the reforms have become exceptionally rich. By contrast, it has been argued that the narrowing of differentials between town and country which resulted from increased living standards in the country has reduced inequality in the country as a whole. This process, however, needs to be set against the regional inequality caused by the very rapid development of the Special Economic Zones in the South and their hinterland, as well as other coastal areas like the Shanghai region, and the relatively slower pace of growth in the North and East.

2   State-owned industries and enterprises continue to make substantial losses in money terms. The extent to which this actually reflects differences in productive efficiency remains controversial (Lo, 1997) but there has been a growing acknowledgement that further reform of this sector is necessary. The Chinese government pledged itself to this in 1997. However, this raises the probability of large-scale unemployment as enterprises are restructured or closed. In addition, the Chinese banking system is heavily indebted to loss-making state enterprises and is consequently fragile. Extensive closure of such enterprises might provoke a financial collapse.

3   A major problem for China over the last fifteen years has been inflation. Three times, at approximately five yearly intervals in the mid-1980s, late-1980s and mid-1990s, the government has had to act quickly to slow down growth in order to stop price rises getting out of control. This has caused considerable disruption to production. In addition, the combination of price controls in some areas of the economy where the old planning system still operates with inflation elsewhere provides opportunities for speculation and profiteering. These particularly arise for those with privileged access to goods at controlled prices, normally those with close party links or government positions. The resulting allegations of corruption are an important factor in eroding the legitimacy of the government with the population as a whole. In general, corruption is generally agreed to be a significant problem in the Chinese economy at a wide range of levels.

4   The rapid pace of growth in China has led to dramatic environmental problems (see also Chapter 7). During the last 40 years a third of Chinese cropland has been lost to soil erosion, desertification and to energy and construction projects. Of 500 Chinese cities, 300 are short of water and 108, including Beijing, have been described as 'acutely short'. The Agricultural Ministry reported that rural industrialization has polluted around 10 million hectares of farmland since the 1980s and that more than 100 000 people were poisoned by pesticides and fertilizers during 1992 and 1993. The Chinese National Environmental Agency reported in June 1995 that polluted air and respiratory disease is now the leading cause of death in urban areas. The government estimates that environmental losses amount to around US$12 billion annually. (See Smith, 1997, for a full account of China's environmental crisis.)

---

thorough economic reform. Initially the reform was centred in the countryside, and involved breaking up the communes, which were later abolished, and basing agriculture on small-scale family production. This 'production responsibility system' took several forms, but increasingly families came to act as *de facto* private peasant pro-ducers, leasing land and some equipment from the state. Small-scale rural industry was again encouraged, but now on the basis of production for the market. From 1984 onwards the pace of reform quickened in the urban industrial sector, with enterprises becoming linked much more through market relationships, and with responsibility for pricing and production decisions being decentralized to individual firms. China began to encourage foreign investment, particularly in 'Special Economic Zones' where incoming investors were to be attracted by cheap labour, freedom from taxes, and investment incentives.

The Chinese communists regarded these reforms as consistent with a socialist road to development. However, they had drastically changed their conception of the timescale required for such a road to be followed. They now saw a long-period of market-based industrialization as a necessary first step on the way towards a socialism which now lay decades into the future. The party leadership developed the concept of a 'socialist market economy' as a way of theorizing this process.

The record of the Chinese reforms has been a subject of great and continuing controversy. Over the last decade China has achieved growth rates of around 10% per annum, among the highest in the world. It is by far the single largest recipient of foreign direct investment in the developing world. China has so far escaped the currency and stock market crashes that swept across East and South-east Asia in 1997. However, a number of criticisms have been made of the effects of the reforms and potential challenges for the future noted. These are outlined in Box 14.2.

The relative success of the Chinese economy as compared with the record of Russia since 1991, where production has halved in seven years, has led a number of writers to contrast the 'gradualist' approach adopted there favourably with the rapid Russian reforms (Nolan, 1995). However, it is important to remember that the starting points for the two reform processes were very different. In the USSR the socialist model of development had in a sense achieved its object and outlived its usefulness, whereas in China this model had to be revised fundamentally as it failed to ensure industrialization and development. It is not clear that the methods adopted in China could have been transferred to the very different situation in Russia.

A more fundamental issue though in judging the Chinese reforms is that of their ultimate goal. Some observers see China as offering a revised socialist path to development which can overcome many of the problems of the traditional Stalinist approach, though with continuing challenges needing to be faced (Bowles & Dong, 1994). Others view the Chinese reforms favourably, but see their endpoint as being the establishment of a market economy, though they argue this is being done more successfully in China than elsewhere (Nolan, 1995). Critics of

the Chinese reforms claim that the reform process has now escaped party control and that an unequal and exploitative capitalist framework is being established in China, whatever the rhetoric espoused by the government (Smith, 1993). Clearly, the view taken on this issue has important implications for those who wish to apply the socialist model of development elsewhere in the world. In the next section we look at the record of attempts to do this as a prelude to exploring these implications.

14.5 Socialist development in a wider context

China was by no means the only country in the post-war world where socialist development proved a powerful attraction. There are three main groups of countries where the socialist model was either adopted or was a major influence on political and economic developments. I shall look at them in turn.

First, and least numerous, were those countries which had escaped formal colonization and which remained largely separated from the world economy, ruled by archaic monarchies or traditional regimes. In these societies there was no indigenous capitalist class which appeared able to initiate development and no sign of development occurring as a result of foreign penetration. The only agency that appeared capable of bringing about any development was the state. Consequently, socialist ideas, with their stress on state-sponsored industrialization, appeared attractive to groupings in the intelligentsia and the army. Examples here are Afghanistan (Halliday, 1978, 1980) and Ethiopia (Halliday & Molyneux, 1981). However, the record of such revolutions was not good. The parties or groupings which carried them out had insufficient social backing, particularly in the rural areas, and this was compounded by extensive social and cultural resistance to the idea of a unified interventionist state in these societies. Failure to respond adequately to the national question in Ethiopia, and to the issue of the role of religion in Afghanistan, coupled with ill-judged intervention by the USSR and foreign aid for rebel forces in the latter case, led to the downfall of both regimes. The oldest example of this kind of revolution, Mongolia, is now the most enthusiastic proponent of market-based liberalization.

The second grouping comprises those countries where socialist ideas became dominant in national liberation struggles against colonialism. This was particularly the case where decolonization was delayed and only achieved after fairly protracted guerrilla struggle (South Yemen) or prolonged war (Angola, Mozambique and the other Portuguese colonies in Africa). It was also the case where the decolonization process was blocked by foreign intervention and national division and partition (Korea, Vietnam). Related to this grouping, but slightly separate, are certain countries in the Caribbean and in Central America. Socialist ideas were able to gain predominance in popular national movements against weak national capitalist classes in Cuba and, in a different way, in Nicaragua. While these were not formally national liberation struggles against overtly colonial regimes, they had many of the characteristics of such struggles because of the overwhelming dominance of the USA in the political and economic life of these countries. This meant that the ruling groups there had a relatively small degree of real independence from the dominant imperial power in the region, the USA, and relatively weak roots in the society. The struggle against these ruling groups took on many of the characteristics of an anti-colonial struggle.

The record of socialist development in these countries has also encountered major problems, although in some cases it has been more successful than in the first group of countries. External hostility has taken the form both of military intervention and subversion and of denial of aid and investment, most graphically exhibited in the forty-year-long US embargo of Cuba. In some cases (e.g. Cuba and Vietnam), this led to considerable dependence on the USSR for material support and consequent difficulties when the Soviet Union collapsed. Relationships with the peasantry have not always been easy and there have been major reassessments of collectivization in Vietnam and Nicaragua.

Internal differences in Angola and Mozambique, fostered by external forces, have led to periods of protracted conflict. Most fundamentally, the extent of significant industrial development and growth of material living standards in these countries has been limited.

This grouping of countries has followed somewhat divergent trajectories in response to these challenges. Cuba and North Korea persist with a modified version of the socialist model, in conditions of great hardship. Both have opened up their economies to foreign investment. Vietnam and its neighbours in Indochina have embarked on a reform process which in many ways resembles that in China. Nicaragua, Angola and Mozambique have been forced to abandon a socialist approach, in large part through economic collapse, and have adopted a market system under the guidance of the IMF and other international institutions. As mentioned above, South Yemen has dissolved into North Yemen. None of these countries at present appears to offer a distinctive approach which might rejuvenate the socialist model of development.

In the third group of countries, external factors have also played a major role. Although socialist or communist parties did not come to power after decolonization, the nationalist movements which did so entered into loose alliances with socialists and appeared to adopt socialist policies. Such movements were often based around state employees: soldiers, teachers, doctors, or associated professional people such as lawyers, who shared the outlook that the state should be the prime motor of development. Emerging out of anti-colonial struggles, state control of the economy appeared to be a guarantee of national independence and unity in a hostile world. Consequently, these movements and governments adopted many of the formal trappings of the socialist model of development (five year plans, nationalization, control over finance and foreign trade) and in return received broad support from national communist parties, and from the USSR. Examples include Egypt under Nasser after the later 1950s, Iraq after the revolution of 1958, Indonesia in the 1950s under Sukarno, India under Nehru after independence, various forms of 'African socialism' and many others. The result of this has not been encouraging for proponents of socialist development. In these cases, almost without exception, the rhetoric of socialism has now been dropped and the countries in question have opted for capitalist development of one kind or another, involving free access for multinational capital and the institution of market relationships within the economy. In several cases denationalization and privatization are also on the agenda, or have already occurred. At best, communists and socialists have been marginalized, as in India, to relatively ineffective bases in regional government; at worst, as in Indonesia, they were massacred and the old nationalist government replaced by authoritarian government from the Right.

The reasons for this sorry story are many and complex. However, one central factor must be taken into account. With the increasing internationalization of the world economy it can now be questioned whether the kind of state-centred, nationally independent development which these countries attempted to initiate in the immediate post-war years is any longer possible. In particular, state-centred development runs up against two major disadvantages. First, the resources that individual nation states can put into industrialization now pale beside those of multinational companies. Secondly, individual countries' economic policies are now limited by an ever more developed international financial system which can direct and redirect monetary flows between countries with exceptional speed. In these circumstances, state-sponsored development appears increasingly unattractive, and even utopian, compared with opening up the country to a world economy which can dictate the allocation of incalculably more resources than relatively poor nation states.

For all these reasons, then, the socialist model of development, not just in Russia and China, but also elsewhere in the world, is in danger of appearing an unattractive and unviable model with little, if any, immediate future. The next section investigates the extent to which there do exist sources of renewal for socialist ideas and projects.

14.6 Prospects for the socialist model

The upheavals of the early 1990s have stimulated a wide-ranging debate about the future of the socialist model of development. A number of distinct, but not necessarily exclusive, viewpoints have emerged. These viewpoints can be divided into two main schools of thought.

First, there is the view that sees the main relevance of socialism as having shifted from the provision of a path for poor countries towards independence and development back towards the criticism and overthrow of developed capitalist systems. According to this view, socialist movements will once more have to become international in character, and will focus on transcending industrial capitalism (Arrighi, 1990; Halliday, 1990). The main support for such movements will thus come from the working class and other oppressed groups in the advanced capitalist countries.

It is not clear what role this approach leaves for socialism outside these countries. One possible answer to this question dovetails quite closely with the view taken by those sympathetic to the Chinese reform process. It can be argued that in developing countries the immediate, and even medium term, priority is the securing of economic growth and industrialization by whatever means possible, and that a socialist project can only arise subsequent to such development and the creation of a sizeable working class. Advocates of this view can point, for example, to the rise of militant trade unionism in countries like South Korea and Brazil in the 1980s, following lengthy years of repression (Beecham & Eidenham, 1987; Asia Labour Monitor, 1988).

In some ways this approach represents a return to the 'classical' conception of socialism in the works of Marx, Engels and their successors. As outlined above, this conception leaves relatively little room for a distinctive socialist model of development as such. It can be criticized on at least two points. First, it has been claimed that this view is both Eurocentric and excessively mechanistic, in that it is based on seeing all countries as necessarily passing through a common set of stages of development; those stages which have already been exhibited in the currently industrialized world. Secondly, this view remains vulnerable to Trotsky's argument that in a world divided by imperialism the option of successful capitalist development which will lead on to a later socialist stage is simply not open. The crises of 1997 and 1998 in some of the seemingly most successful 'late industrializers' in East and South-east Asia might be thought to lend credence to this view.

The second school of thought starts from a recognition of the interdependent nature of the world economy, as did Trotsky, but does not restrict the desired consequences of this to autonomous national development. Rather, it seeks to explore the possibilities for common political action around socialist ideals, linking the industrialized and developing countries. This broad current of activity is extremely heterogeneous. However, two main areas of concern can be isolated.

Firstly, there are struggles centred around particular movements in developing countries. The 1980s saw an upsurge in independent organization, particularly in those countries which had undergone a significant amount of industrialization, albeit highly uneven, precarious and exploitative. This organization differed sharply either from traditional communist parties or national liberation movements. The most salient difference was the role played by militant trade unionism, in countries like South Africa, Brazil and South Korea. Some would add Eastern European countries such as Poland to this list. During the 1990s the role of trade unionism in this context has declined for two main reasons. The worldwide ascendancy of neoliberal policies and the economic difficulties of many of these countries have weakened the position of workers there. In addition, the movements which emerged in the 1980s have largely failed to broaden their influence from the workplace to a wider political sphere. In South Africa the majority of trade unions have aligned themselves with the ANC-led government which, while it nominally pursues a policy of 'redistri-

bution through growth', largely operates within the framework of a conventional market economy. In Brazil the workers' party, the PT, founded by the trade unions among others, has failed to gain office at national level, and its regional initiatives are now threatened by economic austerity provoked by turmoil in the global currency markets. In Poland, Solidarity, weakened by the 1981 declaration of martial law, turned towards a free market programme and lost much of its support in the factories. In South Korea, the political opposition remained divided, allowing the old military regime to engineer a smooth succession despite the 1987 strike wave. While the unions remain combative, their situation has been transformed into a very defensive one, again owing to economic difficulties reflected through the financial markets.

The weakening of trade unionism in these countries has been paralleled, however, by the growth of social movements around a wide range of issues. In Mexico, the 'Zapatista' movement, the EZLN, has based itself largely on the struggles of the indigenous population, and attempts to combine a recovery of their political traditions with opposition to free market policies on a world scale (Figure 14.4). In Brazil, the movements of the landless have led to new alliances between the urban population and the rural poor. In a number of countries, notably in Latin America and Asia, environmental movements have been prominent, taking up issues like deforestation and water rights.

What is common to all these developments is the role of international solidarity between the industrialized world and those campaigning in the developing countries. This springs directly from a recognition that the situation in the developing world requires change both there and in the richer countries. The problems faced cannot be solved simply either by policies handed down from above or by action from below. An interaction between the two is required.

International solidarity is central to the second strand in this school of thought as well. This is based on the formation of networks linking activists around common projects which encom-

*Figure 14.4 (Top) Zapatista rebels in Mexico;
(above) activists trying to prevent tree clearing at the
Newbury bypass anti-road demonstrations in the UK.
These were two amongst many groups attending the
second 'encuentro' (encounter for humanity and
against neoliberalism) in Spain in 1997, reported
by the* Guardian *with the caption '…the struggle
may be different, but the principle is the same…'.*

pass both industrialized and developing countries (Waterman, 1998; Moody, 1997). Again,
trade unionism played an important initial role
here, through groupings like the Transnational
Information Exchange (TIE) and through co-
ordination of workers in particular multinational companies or industries. Again, however,
such networks have broadened to include movements based around gender, ecological questions
and a wide range of other issues. Faced with
particular concrete situations, such as labour
disputes or armed conflicts, such networks have
been able to play an important moral role in

calling for international solidarity among people rather than economic competition or divisive nationalism. This was so, for example, with
the international support movement for the
Merseyside dockers' strike from 1995 to 1998
and with the campaigns for workers' aid convoys to Bosnia-Herzegovina in the mid-1990s.
This approach also includes campaigns on a
more explicitly global basis. Coalitions including unions, NGOs, political organizations,
churches and others have taken up a variety of
issues, all of which have in common the aim of
limiting in some way the operation of the free
market on an international scale. Examples include demands for the cancellation of 'third
world' debt, for labour and environmental standards as a precondition for 'fair trade', and for
taxes on international financial speculation.
Again, what is characteristic of such campaigns
is joint involvement of activists from the industrialized and the developing world.

All these approaches have generated a number
of important initiatives and developments. It is
also the case that their ability to alter the dominance of market-based policies in the global
economy remains limited. Neither trade unionism and social movements in the developing
world, nor networks centred around local or
global campaigns, have been able to achieve
decisive breakthroughs. One reason for this is
that, despite having advanced beyond the traditional socialist model of development in a
number of areas, notably those involving democracy and participation, contemporary socialist
movements have not yet developed a coherent
view on the role of the state in achieving social
change.

The last decade, in particular the collapse of the
regimes in Eastern Europe and the USSR and
the Asian crisis of 1997, has stimulated a considerable amount of thinking on the role of the
state in development. The fact that the World
Bank recently devoted a world development report to this topic is an indication of the interest
in it (World Bank, 1997b). Discussion has centred both on the role of the state in limiting the
operation of the market where this proves harmful, and in structuring societies in such a way

that they can respond 'better' to market demands. It is noticeable that a distinctive socialist perspective has been absent from this debate.
In part this reflects prevailing political thinking. It can be argued that it also results from
the concerns which have recently dominated
discussion among socialists themselves. The
problems of the socialist model of development
and of its heritage in areas like the USSR and
Eastern Europe have understandably led to a
desire to shift socialist thought away from
excessive concern with the manipulation of state
power and towards alternative models of participation and activity. While this may well have
been a necessary shift in the light of previous
experience, it appears likely that further development of socialist practice will require a reconceptualization of the role of the state in social
transformation. It is unlikely, however, that such
a reconceptualization will reinstate pre-existing
socialist models of development. Rather, the
success of such a renewal of socialist ideas
appears to depend upon the ability to articulate
a convincing conception of the limits and
possibilities for nationally based movements in
the changed circumstances of the global
economy. This conception, if it arises, is likely
to depend on the emerging community of interests between workers in an interdependent
world.

Summary

The socialist model of development emerged out of a particular historical experience, that of the USSR following the Bolshevik revolution. However, the problems faced by the Bolsheviks were of a
general nature, and the industrialization achieved in the USSR
thus appeared to offer lessons for other countries attempting to
develop and industrialize. In part, this was true. But the model
proved to be of more limited applicability than had been hoped,
particularly in the Chinese case but also when applied elsewhere.
In addition, as the world economy has become more interdependent, the very concept of a nationally based socialist road to development has been called into question. That interdependence though,
and the global industrialization which accompanies it, has provided
the basis for movements which seek to renew the socialist model,
both through new movements in the industrializing world and
through networks linking activists in the industrialized and developing countries. In order to succeed in such renewal, however, such
movements will have to develop a convincing conception of the role
of the state in socialist development, which avoids the problems of
the traditional socialist model, but provides a basis for developing
a distinct alternative to market-based policies.

15

THE SECOND 'GREAT TRANSFORMATION'? CAPITALISM AT THE END OF THE TWENTIETH CENTURY

JOHN HARRISS

Stephen Jay Gould, the evolutionary theorist, writes that 'The history of life, as I read it, is a series of stable states punctuated at rare intervals by major events that occur with great rapidity and help to establish the next stable era' (quoted by Castells, 1996, p.29). A similar view is taken of the history of human society by some sociologists and historians, though there is wide agreement amongst them only over one such phase of social transformation in the course of more recent history. This is the view that the rise of 'modernity' – meaning, most simply, those 'modes of social life or organization which emerged in Europe from the seventeenth century onwards and which subsequently became more or less world-wide in their influence' (Giddens, 1991, p.1) – marked a fundamental change in the ways in which people live together in society. The conceptual opposition of 'tradition' and 'modernity' indeed, is as old as the discipline of sociology itself, for the early sociologists were all interested in understanding and explaining what they believed to be the fundamental differences between the societies of their own times and those that had gone before, or were still to be found elsewhere in the world. This sense of discontinuity, and of 'major events that occur with great rapidity', is reflected in the powerful language of the *Communist Manifesto*, written by Marx and Engels, and published first in 1848:

"Constant revolutionizing of production, uninterrupted disturbance of all social conditions, everlasting uncertainty and agitation distinguish the bourgeois epoch from all earlier ones...During its rule of scarce one hundred years the bourgeoisie has created more massive and more colossal social forces than have all preceding generations together...It has accomplished wonders far surpassing Egyptian pyramids, Roman aqueducts, and Gothic cathedrals...put an end to all feudal, patriarchal, idyllic relations [and] pitilessly torn asunder the motley feudal ties that bound man to his 'natural superiors'...[It has] drowned the most heavenly ecstasies of religious fervour, of chivalrous enthusiasm, of philistine sentimentalism in icy waves of egotistical calculation...created enormous cities...and rescued a considerable part of the population from the idiocy of rural life...[I]t draws all, even the most barbarian nations into civilization."

(Marks & Engels, 1992)

Marx and Engels associated the emergence of modern society above all with the development of capitalism; for Durkheim it was connected in particular with industrialization and the new social division of labour which this brought about; for Weber it had to do above all with the emergence of a distinctive way of thinking, the rational calculation which he associated with 'the Protestant Ethic' (more or less what Marx and Engels speak of in terms of those 'icy waves of egotistical calculation' – see Chapter 21). Together the works of these great 'classical sociologists' suggest what Giddens has recently described as a 'multi-dimensional view of the institutions of modernity' and which emphasizes not only capitalism and industrialism as key institutions of modernity, but also 'surveillance' (meaning 'control of information and social supervision') and 'military power' (control of the means of violence in the context of the industrialization of war). The latter pair are in particular functions of the state and, Giddens writes, 'If capitalism was one of the great institutional elements promoting the acceleration and expansion of modern institutions, the other was the nation-state' (1991, p.62).

In fact, a great deal of fine contemporary research has shown that the radical discontinuity between 'tradition' and 'modernity', emphasized by the classical sociologists, can easily be exaggerated. Christopher Fuller, for example, argues that anthropologists and historians of India have tended to build up a very misleading picture of pre-colonial India as a 'traditional society', one which seriously underestimates abundant historical evidence of the extent of the cash economy and of the development of ideas about private property well before the eighteenth century (Fuller, 1989). But there is still wide agreement with the view expressed by Giddens that, though there are important continuities, nonetheless 'The changes occurring over the past three or four centuries have been so dramatic and so comprehensive in their impact [that we have to recognize a major discontinuity]' (1991, p.5). The question, however, which I want to address in this chapter is:

> Q Can it sensibly be argued that, at the turn of the twenty-first century, we are experiencing a phase of 'social transformation', reflected in the emergence both of new ways of organizing capitalism, and of 'post-modernism' in the arts and in philosophy?

This is the view held by some leading contemporary thinkers, like Manuel Castells who writes:

'My starting point…is that at the end of the twentieth century we are living through one of those rare intervals in history. An interval characterized by the transformation of our 'material culture' by the works of a new technological paradigm organized around information technologies' (1996, p.29). My own aim here is to explore this idea, relating it to the contemporary history of capitalism. But it is necessary that I should first say a little more about the transformation described in terms of the rise of modernity.

15.1 Polanyi and the 'Great Transformation'

There are a number of ways of thinking through the social transformation which took place with the rise of 'modernity'. Amongst them, that of Karl Polanyi in *The Great Transformation*, which was first published in 1944, offers particular insights. The book provides an analysis of the dynamics of the political economy of the nineteenth and earlier twentieth centuries in terms of conflicts over the attempt to establish what Polanyi describes as the 'utopia' of the self-regulating market economy (markets in which prices 'regulate themselves' in response to the unhindered play of the forces of supply and demand).[1]

Polanyi argues that 'While history and ethnography know of various kinds of economies, most of them comprising the institution of markets, they know of no economy prior to our own, even approximately controlled and regulated by markets' (1944, p.44). Until the eighteenth century in the West economic systems were based on the principles of reciprocity or redistribution, or of (individual) house-holding, or some combination of the three; and: 'In this framework the orderly production and distribution of goods was secured

---

[1]Polanyi, it should be noted – in case of confusion – was not a Marxist, and was quite specifically critical of Marxist views in parts of *The Great Transformation*. There are, however, some strong similarities between Polanyi's arguments about the impact on society of attempts to establish self-regulating market economies, and Marx's on the significance of the 'cash nexus' for social relationships.

through a great variety of individual motives disciplined by general principles of behaviour. Among these motives gain was not prominent' (1944, p.55). 'The economy', in these circumstances, was actually 'submerged' (embedded) in social relationships; and, Polanyi says, '[Man] does not act so as to safeguard his individual interest in the possession of material goods; he acts so as to safeguard his social standing, his social claims, his social assets. He values material goods only in so far as they serve this end' (1944, p.46).

Then, 'the change from regulated to self-regulating markets at the end of the eighteenth century represented a complete transformation of the structure of society' (1944, p.71). If prices are to 'regulate themselves' there cannot be any kind of interference in the workings of the forces of supply and demand, which means in turn that narrowly economic considerations have to be separated out from other social concerns. The establishment of a 'self-regulating market economy' – which Polanyi saw as a critical condition for the development of industrialization (1944, pp.74–5) – requires, therefore, that the economy no longer be embedded in social relations, but rather the reverse: 'Instead of economy being embedded in social relations, social relations are embedded in the economic system' (1944, p.57). The economy has to be 'disembedded', or separated out from wider social relationships which – because they entail the existence of non-economic claims and commitments – would interfere with the operation of the market. This implies 'a change in the motive of action on the part of members of society; for the motive of subsistence that of gain must be substituted' (1944, p.41).

The idea of 'disembedding' is central in Polanyi's analysis of the 'Great Transformation'. It is one which has been developed subsequently by Giddens, in a comparable though distinct way, in his characterization of the discontinuity between tradition and modernity. In this, as he sees it, the disembedding of social systems – 'the 'lifting out' of social relations from local contexts of interaction and their restructuring across indefinite spans of time and space' (1991, p.21) –

is fundamental. Giddens also describes the 'reflexive ordering and reordering of social relations' as an intrinsic characteristic of modernity. This 'consists in the fact that social practices are constantly examined and reformed in the light of incoming information about those very practices, thus constitutively altering their character' (1991, p.38). Polanyi's account of the emergence of the self-regulating market economy demonstrates very clearly the importance of contemporary reflections upon late eighteenth century society – by thinkers such as Bentham and Burke, Godwin and Malthus, Ricardo and Marx, Robert Owen and John Stuart Mill – in the establishment of the philosophy of economic liberalism, which in turn brought about social change as it was sought to be put into practice in public policy. This is an important instance of what Giddens means by 'the reflexive reordering of social relations'.

The change to self-regulating markets required that people (as labour) and nature (as land), and money (a medium of exchange) be treated like any other commodities, produced to be bought and sold, their prices determined by the market. But they are only ever 'fictitious commodities', for they cannot by their very nature *really* be produced or exchanged like motor cars or bananas. Herein lies the core paradox of market economies as Polanyi saw it: markets can deliver good outcomes when they are restricted to typical products (like textiles, or steel, or motor cars) but tend to collapse when their influence is extended to those fictitious commodities which are also the three basic elements of economic life: labour (meaning people and human activity), land (which is really nature, not something which can be 'produced' like a cotton shirt), and money (which symbolizes value). The establishment of self-regulating markets, extending to the fictitious commodities, did not come about without a struggle. Polanyi takes the Enclosure Movement in England as a paradigm: as a contemporary writer observed, this set 'Habitation versus Improvement', or people's rights to homes and livelihoods against those of landowners to improve their properties and their profits. In practice the Tudor and Stuart monarchs used their power to slow down the process of 'improvement', in the wider social interest. It was not until the 1830s that the idea of a 'free market' in labour was finally established in England. Even then, the 'self-regulating market economy' remained an ideal rather than a reality, for:

"Although, undoubtedly, labour, land and money markets are essential to a market economy...no society could stand the effects of such a system of crude fictions even for the shortest stretch of time unless its human and natural substratum as well as its business organization was protected against the ravages of this satanic mill...Social history in the nineteenth century was thus the result of a double movement: the extension of market organization in respect of genuine commodities was accompanied by its restriction in respect of fictitious ones. While on the one hand markets spread all over the globe and the amount of goods involved grew to unbelievable proportions, on the other hand a network of measures and policies was integrated into powerful institutions designed to check the action of the market relative to labour, land and money."

(Polanyi, 1944, pp.73,76)

So 'Society protected itself against the perils inherent in a self-regulating market system' (Polanyi, 1944, p.76). For example: 'the labour market was allowed to retain its main function only on condition that wages and conditions of work, standards and regulations should be such as would safeguard the human character of the alleged commodity, labour' (1944, p.177). But 'protection' gave rise in the end to contradictions – because the market economy functions relatively poorly if there is extensive external regulation, while at the same time the conditions for self-regulation are ultimately unacceptable politically because of their consequences for people. These contradictions, Polanyi argued, underlay the economic and political crises of the first half of the twentieth century.

Polanyi's arguments, notably about the fictitiousness of labour as a commodity, have a remarkably contemporary ring. Much is being said and written at the turn of the twenty-first century about the virtues of 'flexibility' in labour markets, while the demand for mobility of labour was summed up trenchantly by Norman Tebbitt, then a member of Margaret Thatcher's Conservative government in the United Kingdom in the 1980s, when he said that people had to be ready 'to get on their bikes' to go to look for work. Polanyi wrote more than fifty years ago that: 'the employers' demand for mobility of labour and flexibility of wages means precisely what we described above as a market in which human labour is a commodity' (1944, p.177). Towards the end of the twentieth century, as in the nineteenth, according to Polanyi's account of it, one of the major fault lines of politics lies between the apostles of economic liberalism (who were very powerful in the regimes of Ronald Reagan and Margaret Thatcher, and in the World Bank, in the 1980s) and their advocacy of the 'self-regulating market' and, on the other side, those who favour intervention to 'protect society'. Latterly the proponents of protection have become more influential, once again. This is the substance of the so-called 'third way' which has come to be much talked of at the end of the 1990s. It stands in the place that was once occupied by socialists and it has brought together newly elected left-of-centre leaders in Europe – Tony Blair in Britain, Lionel Jospin in France and Gerhard Schroeder in Germany – with President Clinton in the United States.

Robert Reich, who served for four years as Clinton's Labour Secretary, writes:

"The central faith of the third way, is that the economic growth spurred by its free market policies can be widely shared if those who are initially hurt by them are given the means to adapt. Importantly, it is a moral precept as well as a policy idea: work is the core responsibility. If people are willing to work hard, they should have a job that pays enough for them to live on. In order to qualify for such a job, they should have access to adequate job skills. If that's not enough, *their wages should be subsidized*'." [emphasis added]

(from an article by Robert Reich in a special supplement of *New Statesman*, distributed with *The Guardian* on 1 May, 1999)

In other words 'labour' – and that means people's lives – cannot simply be left to market forces. Reich goes on to say, however, that the traditional Democratic constituencies in the United States 'have never accepted the basic premise – that education, retraining, wage subsidies and the rest of the mix, would compensate for the larger insecurities of a freer market' and that 'Elsewhere around the world, there is a growing backlash against open and deregulated markets.' Polanyi would not have been surprised.

15.2 Regimes of accumulation

Polanyi's analysis lays out for us an interpretation of the social transformation implied in the idea of 'modernity'. It also points up two major areas of recurring difficulty in capitalist economic systems. The first comes from the kind of anarchy which can arise as prices are determined by market forces, and which calls for some level of intervention to try to secure the stable growth of capitalism (we have only to think of responses to the Asian financial crisis

since 1997 in which arguments for the regulation of capital flows have figured prominently). The second concerns the problems that arise for capitalists in exerting sufficient control over that fictitious commodity of 'labour power' (which is really no other than the activity of human beings with all their different drives and aspirations) in order to guarantee the addition of value in production. 'Labour control' in this sense, entails 'some mix of repression, habituation, co-optation and co-operation, all of which have to be organized not only within the workplace but throughout society at large' (Harvey, 1989, p.123), and it is supported by the formation of dominant ideologies.

These crucial problems have been addressed in distinctive ways in different capitalist societies, and through history (as Polanyi, 1944, p.75, suggests). One way of understanding these differences is in terms of the idea of 'regimes of accumulation' and of their associated modes of social and political regulation. A *regime of accumulation*, it has been said, 'describes the stabilization over a long period of the allocation of the net product between the transformation of the conditions of both the conditions of production and the conditions of reproduction of wage-earners' (Harvey, 1989, p.121). Compare also what Boyer says (Box 15.1). A regime of accumulation implies the co-ordination of the activities of all sorts of social agents, or in other

---

Box 15.1 Regimes of accumulation

The term 'regime of accumulation' according to Boyer (1990) designates 'the set of regularities that ensure the general and relatively coherent progress of capital accumulation, that is, that allow for the resolution or postponement of the distortions and disequilibria to which the process continually gives rise' (Boyer, 1990, p.35). (Polanyi, of course, offers an analysis of the distortions which arose in the nineteenth century as a result of the attempt to establish 'self regulating markets'.) For Boyer the elements of a regime of accumulation are:

• the evolution of the *organization of production* and of the workers' relationship to the means of production;

• the *time horizon* for the valorization of capital, which offers a basis for the development of principles of management;

• a *distribution of value* that allows for the reproduction and development of the different social classes or groups;

• a composition of *social demand* that corresponds to tendencies in the development of productive capacity;

• a manner of *articulation* with non-capitalist economic forms, when they hold an essential place in the economic formation.

words institutionalization, in the form of 'norms, habits, laws, regulating networks and so on that ensure the unity of the process...[and]...This body of interiorized rules and social processes is [what is] called the *mode of regulation*' (Lipietz, quoted by Harvey 1989, p.122). What does all of this mean? I understand it to mean that there are historically specific correspondences between the way in which control is exercised over labour in the process of production, and wider economic management (which involves the allocation of resources between consumption and accumulation, in turn affecting 'the conditions of reproduction of wage earners', as well as being aimed at the creation of conditions for stable economic growth), and between both of these and political management.

Robert Boyer, one of the leading exponents of this approach – that of the so-called 'Regulation School' (see his exposition in Boyer, 1990) – has recently recast the argument in terms of what he and the sociologist Rogers Hollingsworth call 'social systems of production'. The broad thrusts of their argument recall Polanyi's. They point out that, in spite of the triumphalism at the end of the twentieth century about the virtues of the 'free market', in practice no economy is coordinated or regulated by the market alone – substantially because labour, nature and money are not simple commodities, and their integration into economic activity necessarily involves other institutions. Economies are then coordinated by historically varying combinations of institutions:

"the industrial relations system; the system of training of workers and managers; the internal structure of corporate firms; the structural relationships among firms in the same industry on the one hand, and on the other firms' relationships with their suppliers and customers; the financial markets of a society; the conceptions of fairness and justice held by capital and labour; the structure of the state and its policies;

and a society's idiosyncratic customs and traditions as well as norms, moral principles, rules, laws and recipes for action. All these institutions, organizations and social values tend to cohere with each other, although they vary in the degree to which they are tightly coupled with each other into a full-fledged system."

(Hollingsworth & Boyer, 1997, p.2)

This is what they refer to as a 'social system of production'. Such systems vary between states and regions, each of which has its own institutional logic. It makes sense to distinguish different 'varieties of capitalism' – 'Anglo-Saxon' or 'Anglo-American', 'German' or 'Japanese' (see, for a good example, the analysis of variation amongst East Asian capitalist 'social systems of production' by Hamilton & Biggart, 1988).

But it is also possible to distinguish broad variations across time; and it is suggested that the way of organizing industrial production which has been named after Henry Ford ('Fordism') was related systemically with particular forms of economic and political management, and that, with national variations, this 'regime' extended over much of the industrialized world in the second half of the twentieth century. It was indeed tremendously successful in the third quarter of the century. But thereafter its own characteristics gave rise increasingly to problems, described as 'rigidities' of various kinds, to which an answer seems to have been found in the restructuring of capitalism in what some describe as 'Post-Fordism', or others (like David Harvey) in terms of the regime of 'Flexible Accumulation', or 'Flexible Specialization'. This implies that systemic changes have taken place, connecting the organization of production and of labour, economic policy and political processes, and ideology (which both codifies and provides authority for 'norms, habits, laws, regulating networks and so on').

15.3 From 'Fordism' To 'Toyotism', or the rise of 'flexible accumulation'

It is appropriate, at least as a first approximation, to think about the organization of capitalism in the later twentieth century in terms of the ways in which motor cars, like Fords and Toyotas, are produced, for the motor car/automobile is the one product which more than any other marks out this epoch. It is *The Machine Which Changed The World* (the title of a major book on the automobile industry; Womack *et al.*, 1990); and the changing ways in which it has been produced seem also to mark out broad changes in the organization of capitalism. The recent history of capitalism is summed up in the phrase: From 'Fordism' to 'Toyotism'.

Henry Ford built on the principles of 'scientific management' developed by F. W. Taylor at the beginning of the twentieth century (and which were greatly admired, also, by Lenin). Taylor's view was that 'the absolute necessity for adequate management [is] the dictation to the worker of the precise manner in which work is to be performed' (quoted by Braverman, 1974), so that capital secures more or less the physiological maximum as a 'fair day's work' from the worker, thus realizing the potential of the 'labour power' which the capitalist purchases from people. In order to achieve this result, Taylor argued, it is necessary to dissociate the labour process as far as possible from the skills of the workers; this, in turn, requires the separation of 'conception' from 'execution' and the use by management of its monopoly over knowledge to control each step of the labour process and its mode of execution. The implementation of these precepts meant, in practice, highly detailed division of labour, and the use of time and motion studies to define very precise standards for the accomplishment of all the component tasks involved in a production process. The approach implies the 'deskilling' of labour: 'When [the process of separation of skill and knowledge] is completed, the worker is no longer a craftsman in any sense, but is an animated tool of the management' (Braverman, 1974). Ford really took over these principles, and added to them

the automated assembly line (introduced for the first time in 1913). The accent was on the mass production of homogeneous and standardized goods, for large and relatively stable markets, in a way which reduced the workers' responsibility as far as possible, and subjected them to hierarchical discipline.

But Ford's real genius was to have recognized that mass production required also mass consumption, and 'Fordism' means not just a way of organizing production, but also of consumption through the manipulation of mass markets by advertising. It was to a great extent for this reason that it took so long for 'Fordism' to become established. It was not until the long boom from 1945 to 1973, based on 'a certain set of labour control practices, technological mixes, consumption habits and configuration of political and economic power' (Harvey, 1989, p.124) that a distinctive regime can finally be distinguished. The establishment of Fordism before this time was constrained partly by worker resistance, and partly because 'A new mode of regulation had to be devised to match the requirements of Fordist production, and it took the shock of savage depression and near collapse of capitalism in the 1930s to push capitalist societies to some new conception of how state powers should be conceived of and deployed' (Harvey, 1989, p.128). This 'new conception' was primarily defined by Keynesian economics, which assigned an important role for the state, especially in managing demand and securing the conditions for mass consumption; and it was implemented by new welfare states, the establishment of which depended upon the achievement, after years of struggle, of a tense but still firm balance of power between the large-scale corporate sector, organized labour, and the state. This in turn came about only because of the effective defeat of working class power, notably in the last years of the 1940s, after the end of the Second World War. Thereafter 'bureaucratic trade union organizations were increasingly corralled (sometimes through the exercise of repressive state power [as when the Labour government in Britain in the 1940s turned out troops against striking workers: JH]) into the corner of swapping real wage gains for cooperation in disciplining workers to the Fordist production system' (Harvey, 1989, p.134). At the same time welfare statism was made fiscally viable, and the provision of collective goods was made possible, because of the continuous acceleration of the productivity of labour in the corporate sector.

(It might be argued that the idea of 'the defeat of working class power', in this account, is exaggerated, if not downright wrong, when we consider that some of the most important aspects of the Fordist regime in the third quarter of the century – shorter working hours, safety at work, education for children, access to health care – had all been fought for by the labour movement. Their realization represented real concessions on the part of capital, but in the context of a settlement which was achieved after the kind of repressive actions to which I have referred, and which effectively incorporated the trade union movement. The settlement made the interests of labour in the longer run subject to capital.)

A sharp recession, exacerbated by the steep rise in oil prices in 1973, seriously undermined the framework of Fordism, and initiated a difficult period of economic restructuring and of social and political adjustment which has crystallized at last, or so some scholars argue, in the formation of a radically new regime, which is even held by some, like Castells, to constitute a second 'great social transformation'. Even before the recession of 1973, the 'developed' capitalist economies of the West had started to show signs of crisis – one which Marxist economists believe they can explain in terms of the theory of overaccumulation and the long-run tendency of 'the falling rate of profit' (Harvey, 1982) – and which was reflected in the phenomenon of what was described at the time as 'stagflation' (the combination of inflation and low rates of economic growth). The internal weaknesses or contradictions of Fordism–Keynesianism had started to become apparent. They were to an important extent diseconomies of scale (additional costs associated with large scales of production, as opposed to economies), and they are well described, Harvey suggests, in terms of the single word, 'rigidity'. Fordist production involved massive and long-term investments in plant and in the design of goods, and assumed stable growth in consumer markets. It was, in this way, inflexible and presumed that it was possible to create mass demand for standardized products (rather than presupposing response to varying and rapidly changing demand). There was rigidity, too, in labour contracts and in labour allocation, which made it difficult to shift labour from one line of production to another; and rigidity in the commitments of states to the provision of welfare when rigidities in production restricted the expansion of the fiscal base.

Thus it is suggested that the restructuring of capitalism which has taken place since 1973 can most simply be described in terms of the idea of a shift to 'flexible accumulation', involving a change-over from mass production depending on economies of scale to production based rather on 'economies of scope', a term which refers to the capacity to adapt rapidly and to respond, flexibly, to diverse and rapidly changing markets: 'The economies of scale sought under Fordist mass-production have, it seems, been countered by an increasing capacity to manufacture a variety of goods cheaply in small batches' (Harvey, 1989, p.155) The change is associated, paradigmatically, with the approach to industrial organization developed by Toyota, in the production of cars in Japan, involving what appears, at least, to be a radically different approach to the organization of labour in the production process (see Table 15.1). Rather than the mass production of uniform and standardized goods 'Toyotism' is based on the production of small batches of a variety of product types, responding ('flexibly') to variations in demand in different market niches. It is, in this way, 'demand driven', rather than 'resource driven' (as was Fordism).

Toyotism depends, too, on the idea of *kaizen*, meaning 'continuous improvement', and referring in part to a distinctive approach to quality control, in which workers take responsibility for quality in the process of production rather than relying, as under Fordism, on testing quality ex-post (which involves relatively large numbers of rejects and considerable wastage). The prin-

Table 15.1   Contrasting regimes of accumulation: Fordism and Toyotism

Fordism	Flexible accumulation ('Toyotism')	
A: Production process		
Mass production of homogeneous goods	Batch production	
Uniformity and standardization	Flexible production of a variety of product types	} 'Just in time'
Large buffer stocks and inventory	No stocks	
Quality testing ex-post	Process quality control	'TQM'/*kaizen*
Rejects concealed in buffer stocks	Immediate reject of defectives	
Loss of production time because of long set-up times, defective parts, inventory bottlenecks, etc.	Reduction of lost time (diminishing ' the porosity of the working day')	
Resource driven	Demand driven	
Vertical (and sometimes) horizontal integration	(Quasi-) vertical integration; subcontracting	
B: Labour		
Single task performance by worker	Multiple tasks	
Payment per rate (based on job design)	Personal payment (detailed bonus system)	} Team working
High degree of job specialization	Elimination of job demarcation	
Little or no on-the-job training	Long on-the-job training	
Emphasis on diminishing workers' responsibility	Emphasis on workers' co-responsibility	
Limited job security	'Lifetime employment' for core workers; no job security and poor labour conditions for secondary workers	} 'Harmonious discipline'?
C: State		
Regulation, welfare state; collective bargaining	Deregulation; privatization	
D: Ideology		
Mass consumption of mass durables	Individualized consumption; 'yuppie' culture	
Modernism	Post-modernism	

Source: Harvey, D. (1989) *The Condition of Postmodernity*, Blackwell, Oxford (table 2.8, after Swyngedouw).

ciples of *kaizen* are sought to be realized partly through the participation of workers in Quality Control Circles. Toyotism also reduces inventory and stocks by means of the 'just-in-time' approach to the delivery of components (again, in marked contrast with Fordism, in which large amounts of capital were locked up in large buffer stocks and inventory). Both *kaizen* and 'just-in-time' symbolize and embody the flexibility of 'Toyotism' by contrast with the rigidities of Fordist methods; and they depend, it is argued, upon a radically different approach, as well, to the organization of labour in the production process. Rather than seeking to diminish the workers' responsibility, Toyotism – or so the advocates of this approach maintain – emphasizes the workers' co-responsibility, with management, and this is sought to be realized through horizontal labour organization, involving teamworking and the performance of multiple tasks by 'flexibly-skilled' workers. It was considered by some observers that this way of organizing labour would only work in the context of societies with cultural similarities with Japan, which was supposed to be characterized by a strong 'group orientation', an 'achievement oriented work ethic' and acceptance of authority (in contrast with, for example, the supposed 'bloody-mindedness' of English workers). (Probably the best statement of the cultural specificity of Japanese industrial organization is that of Ron Dore, 1987). But the success with which 'Japanese methods' have been transplanted into other societies, including Britain (Oliver & Wilkinson, 1988), has rather given the lie to this idea (which ignores, anyway, the recent history of the destruction of the militant labour movement in Japan after the Second World War, which plays at least some part in explaining 'acceptance of authority' by Japanese workers: see Clegg & Redding, 1990).

'Toyotism' is important in itself (though the recent recovery of the United States automotive industry has shown that Toyota has not had the last word on the attainment of higher levels of productivity and performance), and it very neatly exemplifies a 'flexible' alternative to Fordist 'rigidity' in the production system. But there are other modes of flexible specialization, too. One is the 'industrial district' model first recognized in studies of north-central Italy, where there are concentrations of small firms in particular industries (such as machine tools and small appliances in Bologna, or textiles and footwear in Tuscan and Venetian towns):

"when demand has been differentiated, markets have been volatile, and/or technology has changed rapidly [in contrast, therefore, to the conditions which make mass production in large vertically integrated firms advantageous], then firms have chosen flexible strategies – flexible machines, labour, and/or marketing. More specialized firms must constantly innovate. Being relatively small, however, they require a host of services that individual firms lack the capacity to provide: sophisticated training facilities in order to develop a highly skilled labour force, a continuing supply of credit, and complex marketing capacity. In response to these needs, producers in some areas [certain 'in-

dustrial districts'] have engaged with other firms – sometimes competitors, sometimes firms in complementary industries – to produce collective goods."

(Hollingsworth & Boyer, 1997, p.25)

Here independent small firms are integrated into 'a social system of flexible production' (Hollingsworth & Boyer, 1997), involving extensive networking and collective institutions which bring about a balance of co-operation and competition. The same principles, of 'network organization', seem to inform and underlie the restructuring of corporations which has been taking place rather widely:

"The corporation has itself changed its organizational model, to adapt to the conditions of unpredictability ushered in by rapid economic and technological change. The main shift can be characterized as the shift from vertical bureaucracies [characteristic of Fordism] to the horizontal corporation. The horizontal corporation seems to be characterized by seven main trends:
* organization around process, not task
* a flat hierarchy
* team management
* measuring performance by customer satisfaction
* rewards based on team performance
* maximization of contacts with suppliers and customers
* information, training and re-training of employees at all levels."

(Castells, 1996, p.164)

But the idea of 'flexible accumulation' or of 'flexible specialization' implies, too, labour mobility, and flexibility in labour markets, which have allowed employers to exercise stronger control over labour. This has meant, in practice 'relatively high levels of 'structural' unemployment [in contrast to the full employment of the boom years of Fordism between 1945 and 1973], rapid destruction and reconstruction of skills, modest (if any) gains in the real wage [again in marked contrast to the years of the Fordist boom] and the roll-back of union power' (Harvey, 1989, p.150). The latter was marked in Britain above all – and the symbolic significance of this can hardly be overstated – by the defeat of the National Union of Mineworkers, historically the vanguard of union power, at the hands of the Thatcher Government in 1985. At the same time there were – not just in Britain – cut-backs in welfare provision by states, in the interests of fiscal adjustment and stability.

There have taken place, indeed, really massive changes in patterns of employment and in the structure of labour markets, throughout the world (richly documented by Castells, 1996, chapter 4). Fordism was characterized by the so-called 'segmentation' of labour markets, in which there was both a clear distinction in terms of employment conditions, job security and remuneration between 'primary' or 'core' jobs in the public and large-scale corporate sectors, and other jobs, and powerful social constraints, involving race and ethnicity, on access to those 'good' jobs, which were held mainly by white men (Gordon *et al.*, 1982). In many industries the 'core' has subsequently been radically reduced, though the decreased power of the white male workers in the 'core' segment of the labour market has not meant that the power of those previously excluded from it has been enhanced. There has been a huge increase in the incidence of subcontracting, often involving the displacement of work to smaller firms with poorer wages and conditions of employment, and associated, too, with a resurgence of 'sweat shops', of artisanal and of patriarchally organized firms, and of home-working in the major industrial economies. There has been a huge increase, too, in the incidence of part-time working and of temporary jobs, partly associated with increased employment of women. There are relatively many fewer jobs in manufacturing and many more in the diverse service industries, in many of which employment is very unstable. These changes clearly make for much greater 'flexibility' for employers – they can take on and lay off workers much more easily than before, and switch them between activities. But the consequences have usually been quite negative for workers. While trends in financial markets (as I discuss below) have led to globalization and concentration of capital, 'Labour is dis-

aggregated in its performance, fragmented in its organization, diversified in its existence, divided in its collective action' (Castells, 1996, p.475). Perhaps the most important change of all has been the challenge to the whole idea of a 'career' and of what Giddens describes as 'reflexive life-planning', and the experience by most (both in 'advanced industrialized countries' and 'developing countries') of much higher levels of risk and insecurity in their working lives.

Flexible accumulation has been associated, too, with a 'new international division of labour' as firms have sought to maximize profits by (re)locating to take advantage of lower labour costs and lower taxation, or of new markets, or of the existence of particular expertise (as in the software industry). Many production processes, both of goods and services, are now thoroughly international, with different parts of the process taking place in different countries – though with much more manufacturing than before taking place in certain of the (erstwhile) 'developing countries'. This is one aspect of economic globalization. It is important to emphasize, however, that the relocation of manufacturing industry, associated in the last decade with the surge in foreign direct investment, which has come to dwarf official aid flows, has embraced a relatively small number of 'developing countries'. There has been an accentuation of uneven development. The economic historian David Landes concludes his eloquent survey of economic history, *The Wealth and Poverty of Nations*, by arguing that, contrary to the arguments of many economists that 'International competition is a positive-sum game [and] everyone benefits', the historical record shows rather that 'The gains from trade are unequal...some countries will do much better than others. The primary reason is that comparative advantage is not the same for all, and that some activities are more lucrative and productive than others'. He goes on to note (shades of Polanyi) that 'The export and import of jobs is not the same as trade in commodities. The two may be fungible [interconvertible] in theory, but the human impact is very different'. And he argues finally that 'the current pattern of technological diffusion and catch-up development will press hard on the haves, especially the individual victims of economic regrouping, while bringing 'goodies' and some hope to some of the have-nots, and despair, disappointment and anger to many of the others' (this and the preceding quotations, Landes, 1998, p.522).

These changes have been greatly facilitated, latterly, by policies of economic liberalization, and especially by the opening up (deregulation) of financial markets across the world. Economic globalization refers to 'much freer trade in goods and services combined with free capital movements' (Samuel Brittan, writing in the *Financial Times*); and global capitalism is now structured to a large extent around networks of massive financial flows: 'The formation of a global stock market, of global commodity (even debt) futures markets, of currency and interest rate swaps, together with an accelerated geographical mobility of funds, meant, for the first time, the formation of a single world market for money and credit supply' (Harvey, 1989, p.161). Rather than there being an 'international capitalist class', there is now – Castells argues – 'a faceless collective capitalist made up of financial flows operated by electronic networks' (1996, p.474); and the world's financial system eludes collective control even by the most powerful states. It remains to be seen whether the regulatory moves stimulated by the Asian crisis of 1997 will change this situation.

'Flexible accumulation' also depends significantly upon control over and the ability to process, rapidly, large amounts of information (concerning, for example, the requirements in a particular production process for different quantities of large numbers of components at very specific times – as in 'just-in-time' or 'lean production', or concerning markets). Accurate and up-to-date information is now a highly valued commodity. The restructuring of capitalism which has taken place since 1973 has thus depended in part on the new information technology (micro-electronics, computing, telecommunications and optoelectronics) which started to emerge also in the 1970s and was increasingly widely available by the 1980s (Figure 15.1). Capi-

talist restructuring was neither caused by the new IT, nor led to its development, but the two are intimately related and it is doubtful whether the critical new flexibility and adaptability of capitalism would have been realized without IT. Castells argues that what he calls 'informationalism' 'is linked to the expansion and rejuvenation of capitalism, as industrialism was linked to its constitution as a mode of production' (1996, p.19). What Castells actually argues, therefore, in *The Rise of the Network Society* (1996), is rather different from what might seem to be implied in the statement which I quoted above, that the social transformation of the end of the twentieth century is 'characterized by the transformation of our 'material culture' by the works of a new technological paradigm organized around information technologies.'

The changes which have been taking place in the organization of capitalism, globally, have also been associated, of course, with major changes in economic management and in politics, and in social and cultural life. The shift from Fordism to flexible accumulation was accompanied in the 1980s by the aggressive neocon-servatism championed by Reagan in the United States and by Margaret Thatcher in Britain (and finally hardly less aggressively by a socialist President, Mitterrand, in France). The World Bank exemplified the resurgence of nineteenth century doctrines of economic liberalism which, Polanyi argued, presupposed the 'utopia' of the 'self-regulating market economy'. It is not surprising, therefore, to find that there are passages in *The Great Transformation* in which Polanyi is talking about events early in the century, but which might well have been written by critics of economic liberalization in the 1980s or 1990s. For example: 'The repayment of foreign loans and the return to stable currencies were recognized as the touchstones of rationality in politics; and no private suffering, no infringement of sovereignty was deemed too great a sacrifice for the recovery of monetary integrity. The privations of the unemployed made jobless by deflation; the destitution of public servants dismissed without a pittance; even the

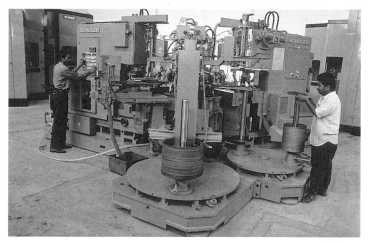

Figure 15.1   An example where IT as a production technology is becoming vital to the economy of a low-income country is found around Bangalore, India's 'silicon valley': (top) workers at an electronics factory; (above) young women receiving training in using a circuit board.

relinquishment of national rights and the loss of constitutional liberties were judged a fair price to pay for the fulfillment of the requirement of sound budgets and sound currencies, those *a priori* of economic liberalism' (Polanyi, 1944, p.142). Africa in the era of structural adjustment?

The 1980s (into the 1990s) was the decade of cutting back public expenditure (though in spite of much rhetoric it was rarely achieved in practice: in Britain, by 1997 when the Conservative party left office the share of the national income taken by the state was still only just below 40%, little changed from the ratio which the party had inherited when it entered government in 1979),

of 'rolling back the state' (though in practice governments which were committed ideologically to non-intervention were often forced by events to be more, not less interventionist), of privatization, and of deregulating financial markets, labour markets and commodity markets. There was a decisive rupture with the economic policies and with the mode of political regulation of the years of the long boom after 1945, but the conditions for it were laid in the fiscal crisis of Fordism–Keynesianism at the beginning of the 1970s. As Harvey suggests, the withdrawal of support for the welfare state and the attack on the real wage and on union power began as an economic necessity in the crisis of 1973–75, when slackening growth inevitably meant trouble for the welfare state and the social wage, and they were 'simply turned by the neoconservatives into a governmental virtue' (1989, p.168). But neoconservatism also encouraged and gave legitimacy to an ethos of competitive individualism in western societies, pushing out the adherence to collective values which had been quite strong in the 1950s and 1960s, whilst also – in apparent contradiction – reasserting the 'basics' (as Margaret Thatcher's sometime acolyte, and her successor as the British Prime Minister, John Major, described them) of family and religion, in the interests of social stability. But this was ever the contradiction to which the attempt to realize the utopia of the self-regulating market gave rise, as Polanyi showed in his discussion of nineteenth and early twentieth century history: 'it is at such times [of rampant individualism and] of fragmentation and economic insecurity [which follows when labour, notably, is treated as a commodity] that the desire for stable values leads to a heightened emphasis upon the authority of basic institutions – the family, religion and the state' (Harvey, 1989, p.171).

15.4 Much has changed but does it amount to a 'Great Transformation'?

There is no doubt that there have been widely ramifying and radical changes in the organization of capitalism in the last quarter of the twentieth century, or that these changes have entailed sweeping changes also in politics, in social relationships and in ways of life. But can they be said to constitute such a radical discontinuity as to warrant the claim that Castells makes and which does indeed suggest that we are living through a 'great social transformation'?[2]

There are many reasons for questioning Castells' argument. Notably, perhaps, recognizing that

[2]Compare the title of Harvey's concluding chapter: 'Flexible accumulation – solid transformation or temporary fix?' (1989, p.189)

both 'Fordism' and 'flexible systems of production' are ideal types of contrasting organizational principles which are in fact complementary to one another, we should also recognize that actual 'social systems of production' include all sorts of hybrid forms, and that 'flexible production' itself really predates Fordism historically. Sabel & Zeitlin (1985), notably, and others 'have demonstrated that flexible social systems of production existed in a number of nineteenth century industrial districts of Europe and Great Britain, from Lyon to Sheffield, as well as in parts of the United States' (Hollingsworth & Boyer, 1997, p.21). This helps to make the point that capitalism as a mode of production is all the time being reconstructed in different but specific ways as people, individually and collectively, respond to changing circumstances and the contradictions and distortions to which the processes of capital accumulation give rise (people 'making their own history though not in circumstances of their own choosing', exactly as Marx argued), and that there have always been tendencies towards realizing 'economies of scale', on the one hand, and 'economies of scope', on the other. 'Flexible accumulation' still reflects, Harvey argues, the underlying logic of capitalism, and can be seen simply as a recombination of the basic strategies which Marx defined for securing profits:

"The first, termed *absolute* surplus value, rests on the extension of the working day relative to the wage needed to guarantee working class reproduction at a given standard of living. The shift towards longer working hours coupled with an overall reduction in the standard of living either by erosion of the real wage or by the shift of corporate capital from high-wage to low-wage regions captures one facet of flexible capital accumulation...Under the second strategy, termed *relative* surplus value, organizational and technological change is set in motion to gain temporary profits for innovative firms and more generalized profits as costs of goods that define the standard of living of labour are reduced. Here, too, the proliferating violence of investments, which cut employment and labour costs in every industry from coal mining and steel production to banking and financial services, has been a highly visible aspect of capital accumulation in the 1980s."

(Harvey, 1989, p.186)

So, Harvey suggests, the shift from Fordism to flexible accumulation can be seen 'as a rather traditional response to crisis. The devaluation of labour power has always been the instinctive response of capitalists to falling profits' (1989, p.192). So it should not be regarded, either, as irreversible.

Similarly, others who have studied 'Toyotism' in practice argue that it rests ultimately upon the refinement of Fordist or Taylorist principles rather than on their replacement. Certainly it involves the determination of rigorous standards (through time-and-motion studies) for the fulfilment of very precisely defined tasks – standards which are sought to be improved upon over time according to the principles of *kaizen*. This means that workers are subjected to the same discipline as under Taylorism–Fordism, though the way in which workers are organized in the production process means that this discipline is more self-imposed. Some argue, therefore, that workers are subjected to even more intense pressures under Toyotism and that the changes that have taken place represent a 'reinforcement of the domination of capital over labour rather than the development of individual autonomy and the blossoming of the individual at work' (Boyer & Durand, 1997, p.67).[3]

Yet none of these writers denies that great changes have taken place. Harvey thinks that several other commentators have underestimated the extent of change from the workers' own perspective; and he suggests that 'the financial system has achieved a degree of autonomy from real production unprecedented in capitalism's history' (1989, p.194) – a conclusion which,

arguably, was confirmed by the Asian financial crisis in 1997. Durand, while questioning whether we can speak of 'rupture' or discontinuity, still argues that Toyotism has brought about a kind of 'intellectualization of production work' which is very distinct (Boyer & Durand, 1997, p.144).

So, finally, Castells' argument in support of his view that the end of the twentieth century *is* a rare period of social transformation rests on his assessment that the present restructuring of capitalism, which he describes in *The Rise of the Network Society* (1996) in much the same way as Harvey in *The Condition of Postmodernity* (1989, Part II), has dissolved the principal social institutions of industrial society. As he sees it there are three areas of quite fundamental change (discussed in *The Power of Identity*, 1997):

- the redefinition of personal relationships, with the decline of patriarchy (associated with the much more extensive participation of women in the labour force), and the emphasis on self-realization or personal fulfilment (paradoxically, as it might seem, in the context of that 'decline of reflexive life planning' and personal insecurity which Giddens describes, and which is associated with the weakening of labour in relation to capital);

- the crisis of legitimacy of political systems (reflected in sharply declining participation in politics) which has followed from privatization and the crisis of the welfare state (or of Fordism–Keynesianism) in industrial societies, and the apparent redundancy of political ideologies as politics itself has come increasingly to be formed by media representations;

- the weakening of the characteristic social movement of industrial society, the labour movement, which had a positive project of social change, and its progressive replacement by the so-called 'new social movements' – localist, nationalist, religious, environmental, feminist – which mobilize resistance to some aspects of the restructuring that is taking place, but which, in the main, lack a coherent vision of social change.

---

[3]Arguments about how different Toyotism really is are found in *The Machine That Changed The World* (Womack *et al.*, 1990); and in Kenney & Florida (1988). Harriss (1995) describes the application of Toyotism in Indonesia, concluding that it represents refinement rather than replacement of Taylorist–Fordist principles.

Most important, for Castells, and in a sense underlying all these three areas of change, is the fact that, as he puts it 'People increasingly organize their meaning not around what they do but on the basis of what they believe they are', regrouping around 'primary identities' of ethnicity, variously defined, and cultural nationalism (Chapter 23). What he is suggesting is that 'Fordism' represented the culmination of capitalist, industrial society. It consolidated patriarchy and a strongly gendered division of labour but it also defined relatively stable 'careers' and ways of life for individuals which also gave rise to quite a strong sense of class identity, and to well-defined patterns of class politics. The restructuring of capitalism which has been taking place has changed all this irrevocably.

Certain privileged groups of people/workers, those able to control information, have been empowered, but many more both within individual societies, and as between nation-states, have been progressively marginalized (a process partly reflected in the very sharp increases in inequality in the United States and the United Kingdom over the last fifteen years, and in the expansion of a distinct 'underclass'). 'What they do' has become increasingly variable and uncertain and their ways of life have become increasingly insecure. Robert Kearney shows this in the case of the erstwhile 'peasantry' of Mexico. Mexican *campesinos* now depend on varying combinations of informal urban employment and migrant labour, and less and less on agricultural pursuits, though these are still carried on. They are, he suggests, 'polybians', moving between different forms of employment and ways of life, much as 'amphibians' move between aquatic and terrestrial environments. In these circumstances personal meanings and politics are given much more by ethnic identity than by class positions (Kearney, 1996).

Such people are more disempowered than ever they were. For the very many in these circumstances the old 'class politics' are unpersuasive (or, perhaps more accurately, 'even less persuasive than ever') and both the ways in which they construct their own identities, and the politics which make sense to them, are given rather by a sense of 'community', defined in terms of religion, or language or nationhood.[4] The argument is put with panache and lucidity by Perry Anderson, in a discussion of the social bases of 'postmodernity':

> "Late capitalism remained a class society, but no class within it was quite the same as before. The immediate vector of postmodern culture was certainly to be found in the stratum of newly affluent employees and professionals created by the growth of the service and the speculative sectors of the developed capitalist societies. Above this brittle yuppie layer loomed the massive structures of multinational corporations themselves – vast servomechanisms of production and power, whose operations criss-cross the global economy, and determine its representations... Below, as an older industrial order is churned up, traditional class formations have weakened, while segmented identities and localised groups, typically based on ethnic or sexual differences, multiply. On a world scale...no stable class structure, comparable to that of an earlier capitalism, has yet crystallised. Those above have the coherence of privilege, those below lack unity and solidarity."
>
> (Anderson, 1998, p.62)

What was presumed by earlier generations of sociologists to be the trajectory of social change in capitalist, industrial societies has clearly not come to be.

This is the broad context of the rise of 'postmodernism' in the arts, philosophy and the human sciences, a diverse movement of ideas which entails a critique of scientific epistemology and of the notion of 'progress' which has been inherent in Western thought since the Enlightenment. There is not space enough in this chap-

[4]A similar case has been put nicely by the American historian Arthur Schlesinger: 'The more people feel themselves adrift in a vast anonymous sea the more desperately they swim towards any familiar life raft. The more, in other words, they crave the politics of identity' (quoted by Philip Stephens in the *Financial Times* of 7 May 1999).

ter to discuss these ideas in anything like sufficient depth. In relation to the theme of social transformation, however, it is important to note that a critical question concerns the extent to which they can best be understood as deriving from the pursuit of Enlightenment thinking, and thus seen as representing a 'radicalization of modernity' rather than a wholly new way of thinking. (See Giddens, 1991, pp 45–53; and Anderson, 1998, especially chapter 4.)

Of course, the question of whether or not a 'great social transformation' is taking place is a matter of judgement, not of fact. Personally, I remain agnostic, though I do believe that great changes are taking place. From the point of view of development in the twenty-first century perhaps the most significant trends of change, deriving from the restructuring of capitalism which has taken place – in the latest phase of the continuing struggle to manage the contradictions of the 'self-regulated market economy' – have to do with the accentuation of the unevenness of economic and social development. This is reflected in the vast and growing disparities between nations – and the progressive marginalization of many of them, notably in Africa – and in the increasing inequality within societies. Both the United Kingdom and the United States are characterized at the end of the twentieth century by greater inequality than at any time, so far as is known, in their histories. As Landes (1998) argues in his survey of modern economic history 'the greatest single problem and danger facing the world of the Third Millennium…is the gap in wealth and health that separates rich and poor'. This is one result of the relatively even greater weakness of labour in relation to capital at the turn of this century than at that of the last.

Acknowledgements

This chapter is an exposition of parts of the work of three contemporary scholars, Manuel Castells, Anthony Giddens and David Harvey, who have all written powerful interpretations of our world. It will be clear that my indebtedness to them extends far beyond attributed quotations. I have sought to establish connections, too, with the analysis of a great scholar of a previous generation, Karl Polanyi, stimulated in this partly by a reading of some of the work of Robert Boyer (see Boyer & Drache, 1996; Hollingsworth & Boyer, 1997).

I thank the editors of this book for their help and encouragement, and my friend James Putzel for incisive comments on an earlier version of this chapter, to some of which I have not responded. James bears no responsibility, therefore, for the final result.

Summary

1   There are rare but important phases of rapid change and discontinuity in human history that can be described as 'social transformations'. One of these is that of the rise of modernity – meaning, most simply, ways of life characteristic of the West – from the eighteenth century, which has been analysed in different ways by major social theorists – Marx, Durkheim, Weber, and Karl Polanyi.

2   Polanyi's conception of the 'Great Transformation' (the title of his book) was in terms of the attempt to establish a 'self-regulating market economy', and its consequences. This entailed the 'disembedding' of the narrowly economic aspects of human activity from their context in wider social relationships.

3   Polanyi argues, however, that the 'self-regulating market economy' can only ever be an ideal because the key elements of

economic activity, labour (which is nothing other than human activity), land and natural resources (which is nature itself) and money (a symbol of value), can never be true commodities (manufactured for sale).

4   The history of capitalism, therefore, has been one of struggle between economic liberalism, committed to the realization of the ideal of the 'self-regulating market', and the defenders of 'society' who have sought to regulate the way in which labour is employed by capital, the exploitation of nature, and the money market. This struggle is still going on, as is shown in debates today over the virtues of 'flexible' labour markets and the threats which they pose to livelihoods.

5   Polanyi's arguments concerning the difficulty, especially, of treating labour as a commodity, are reflected in the idea that the history of capitalism shows that there have been different 'regimes of accumulation', referring to different ways in which control is exercised over labour and their relations with wider economic management.

6   In the second half of the twentieth century one such regime, labelled as 'Fordism', involving large-scale mass production, automated assembly lines and hierarchically organized firms, in which labour is tightly disciplined, together with mass consumption, secured by welfare states, has been hugely successful.

7   In the context of the recession of the early 1970s, however, 'Fordism' began to be undermined, and capitalism has come to be restructured in such a way as to make for much greater flexibility in circumstances of rapidly changing markets. The restructuring has given rise to new ways of organizing the control of labour, through self-disciplining teams, and to new forms of industrial organization, which can loosely be described as those of 'Toyot(a)ism', or 'flexible accumulation'.

8   This new 'regime', associated with the development of global capital markets, a new international division of labour, and the rise of the ideology of neoliberalism, has also been immensely successful from the point of view of capital, but it has made for much greater insecurity for labour, and brought about the sharp accentuation of inequality both within and between nations – which is now 'the greatest single problem and danger facing the world of the Third Millennium' (David Landes).

9   The restructuring of capitalism, which is still in process at the turn of the twenty-first century, is bringing about great social changes, associated especially with the weakening of traditional class formations and the multiplication of different sorts of ethnic identities, and with the rise of 'post-modernism'. Do these changes constitute, however, a second 'great transformation', as Manuel Castells argues? Or should they be seen, rather, as a reworking of the dynamics of capitalism?

UNDERSTANDING DEVELOPMENT NOW

16

SUSTAINABLE GLOBALIZATION? THE GLOBAL POLITICS OF DEVELOPMENT AND EXCLUSION IN THE NEW WORLD ORDER

ANTHONY McGREW

Figure 16.1   Mr Salamet, a rickshaw owner in a town east of Jakarta, has a hard life made more so by the Asian crisis.

In the autumn of 1997 the Tiger economies of East Asia succumbed to their worst economic crisis since the 1930s depression – likely to be remembered as the Second Great Crash of the twentieth century. Talk of the 'Pacific Century' and expectations of continued rising affluence gave way to the crushing realities of bankruptcy, financial turmoil, downsizing, unemployment and rising poverty as the crisis cascaded through the region. In the five decades since the end of the Second World War most peoples in the region had experienced rising living standards, on a wave of unprecedented economic growth, but almost 'in the blink of an eye' poverty and unemployment returned to levels not witnessed in at least two generations. The human and social consequences of the crisis have been dire. For Mr Salamet (Figure 16.1), a rickshaw owner in Mojokerto (400 miles East of Jakarta), the Asian crisis meant the collapse of his livelihood, witnessing his mother's agonizing death because he was unable to afford the prescribed painkillers, and watching his children go hungry (Kristof & Wyatt, 1999). What went wrong?

The causes of the East Asian crash are hotly disputed. But almost all accounts acknowledge that, notwithstanding the role of domestic factors, 'On balance, most causes for the Crash are to be found in the recent monetary and financial history of Asia faced with globalization' (Godement, 1999, p.21). In particular, as these countries became more integrated into the global economy they also became more vulnerable to world financial markets and the ebb and flow of investor confidence. Few countries today, even the largest economies, can withstand concerted speculative attacks on their currencies when trade on the world's foreign exchange markets, at $1.5 trillion per day, dwarfs national foreign exchange reserves. Moreover, the globalization of finance, production and trade ensures that a crisis in one economy is speedily transmitted to others. In East Asia this so-called 'contagion effect' amplified the crash. Economic difficulties in Thailand provoked foreign banks and investors, fearing bad times ahead, to withdraw their money from other economies, causing massive currency devaluations and stock markets to crash. In just a few months the fallout of the crash had also engulfed other emerging economies, such as South Africa, Russia, and Brazil, precipitating what the then US President Clinton noted was 'the most serious [global] financial crisis in half a century' (Kristof & Wyatt, 1999). In so doing the Asian crash provoked a great debate about the benefits of unfettered global markets, the regulation of global finance and the prospects for sustainable development in a globalized economy.

For some commentators the crash signalled the end of the East Asian development experiment – the developmental state – which had appealed to many other developing states: in other words, the Asian tigers had been tamed by global finance. Moreover, contrary to many predictions of the 1980s – that the rise of East Asia signified the demise of the Third World as a geopolitical bloc in world politics – some argued that the crash would reinvigorate Third World solidarity since it reinforced the growing perception that globalization was simply a new expression of Western imperialism (Burbach *et al.*, 1997). In contrast, others argued that the very existence of a global contagion effect from the crash demonstrated just how fundamentally globalization had transformed the world – for the fortunes of core and periphery, in an epoch of instantaneous global finance, have become deeply entwined.

Globalization invites a fundamental questioning of the prospects for developing economies and the world's poorest peoples in an era marked by powerful forces of world-wide economic, political and cultural interconnectedness, over which they have little direct political control. Indeed, contemporary patterns of globalization even throw 'into question the possibilities of a national development strategy' (Dickson, 1997, p.155). Exploring and critically assessing the implications of globalization for patterns of global inequality and the prospects for sustainable development is the central task of this chapter. This involves addressing a number of key issues but in particular:

Q What exactly is globalization and what is driving it? Is it simply a new form of Western imperialism and global hegemony?

Q To what extent does globalization create new winners and losers in the global economy? How far is it transforming the pattern of North–South relations and the conditions for sustainable national development?

Q How have developing countries and the world's poorest peoples responded to globalization? Can globalization be tamed?

16.1 What is globalization?

As the East Asian crash demonstrated, today developments in one region of the world can come to have profound consequences for the life chances of individuals or communities in distant parts of the globe. Globalization refers to this growing sense of interconnectedness. It also tends to be associated with a perception of powerlessness and chronic insecurity in that the speed and scale of contemporary global social and economic change – as in the East Asian crisis of 1997–98 – appear to overwhelm governments, politicians and communities. The unevenness of globalization compounds such insecurities since 'it would appear that the strong are becoming stronger and the weak weaker' as the benefits of globalization accrue to a relatively small proportion of the world's population whilst global poverty and social exclusion continue to increase (Dickson, 1997; UNDP, 1997b).

Not surprisingly, therefore, the notion of globalization is the subject of charged public and academic debate. But the rhetoric of controversy often conceals more than it reveals. Indeed, the very idea of globalization tends, if at all, to be ill defined in such debates. Yet globalization, as a concept, is deceptively simple: it refers to the ways in which developments in one region can rapidly come to have significant consequences for the security and well-being of communities in quite distant regions of the globe. As Alan Greenspan, head of the US Federal Reserve at the height of the East Asian crisis, succinctly put it: 'there can be no 'islands of prosperity' in an ocean of economic instability.' In this sense globalization expresses the widening scope, deepening impact and speeding up of interregional flows and networks of interaction within all realms of social activity from the cultural to the criminal (Box 16.1).

Of course globalization involves much more than simply interconnectedness or a shrinking world, for it captures a sense that world-wide connectivity is very much a permanent or 'institutionalized' feature of modern existence. In this regard it signifies the *deepening enmeshment* of societies in a web of world-wide flows of capital, goods, migrants, ideas, images, weapons, criminal activity and pollution, amongst other things. Neither is it simply an economic phenomenon. On the contrary, it is evident in all the key arenas of modern life: the economic, political, legal, cultural, military, and the ecological. Accordingly, it has to be understood as a highly differentiated process in so far as distinctive patterns of globalization exist in each of these arenas. Nor, as Frank reminds us, is globaliz-

> ### Box 16.1 The four dimensions of globalization
>
> Globalization is characterized by four types of change.
>
> 1   It involves a stretching of social, political and economic activities across political frontiers, regions and continents.
>
> 2   It suggests the intensification, or the growing magnitude, of interconnectedness, i.e. flows of trade, investment, finance, migration, culture, etc.
>
> 3   The growing extensity and intensity of global interconnectedness can be linked to a speeding up of global interactions and processes, as the evolution of world-wide systems of transport and communication increases the velocity of the diffusion of ideas, goods, information, capital and people.
>
> 4   The growing extensity, intensity and velocity of global interactions is associated with their deepening impact such that the effects of distant events can be highly significant elsewhere and even the most local developments may come to have enormous global consequences. In this sense, the boundaries between domestic matters and global affairs become increasingly blurred.

ation a new phenomenon, for 'we live in one world, and have done so for a long time' (Frank, 1998, p.29). But over time globalization has been organized and institutionalized in quite different ways, from the global empires of the nineteenth century to the present when world empires have given way to the 'freedoms' of the global market, laissez-faire economics, and multinational capital. In this sense contemporary globalization is organized and reproduced through distinctive mechanisms and infrastructures of control, from the International Monetary Fund (IMF), the World Trade Organization (WTO), to the Internet, global corporations and non-government organizations.

To this extent contemporary **globalization** generates constraints upon what governments and communities can do whilst simultaneously opening up new opportunities and possibilities. But some are more constrained than others and some have greater resources than others to exploit these opportunities since globalization is a highly uneven process: it results in clear winners and losers, not just between countries but within and across them. For the most affluent it may very well entail a shrinking world – jet travel, global TV and the World Wide Web – but for the majority of people it tends to be associated with a profound sense of disempowerment as their fate is sealed by deliberations and decision-making in chancelleries, boardrooms, and bureaucracies many thousands of miles away. As the East Asian crisis of 1997–98 demonstrated, key sites of global power, such as the International Monetary Fund and the World Bank, are quite literally oceans apart from the communities whose destiny they shape. To this extent globalization nurtures a sense of alienation that 'Power is elsewhere, untouchable' (Walker, 1988, p.134; Box 16.2).

Globalization: A process (or set of processes) which embodies a transformation in the spatial organization of social relations and transactions – assessed in terms of their extensity, intensity, velocity and impact – generating transcontinental or interregional flows and networks of activity, interaction, and the exercise of power.

For these reasons globalization has to be understood as a process which both unites and divides peoples and communities; it does not automatically follow that humanity is becoming a single global community of fate. Indeed, there is much evidence to suggest that its consequences are much less benign. Conceived as a process of 'creative destruction', globalization arguably engenders a more 'unruly world' and a more unequal one (UNDP, 1997b; Herod *et al.*, 1998). But the consequences of globalization remain hotly disputed.

> ## Box 16.2   What's driving globalization?
>
> Globalization today is driven by a confluence of forces:
>
> 1   Economic shifts. The natural tendency of capitalism to expand is expressed increasingly in the information age in the need of business, large and small, to compete in regional and global markets.
>
> 2   Technological shifts. The move towards post-industrial economies and the informatics revolution greatly facilitates globalization in every domain from the economic to the criminal.
>
> 3   Political shifts. The last two decades have witnessed a dramatic shift away from state intervention to the market as the emphasis upon deregulation, privatization and economic liberalization continue to make economies and societies more open to the world.
>
> 4   Cultural shifts. Fuelled by the above developments, an awareness has grown among national élites and many citizens' groups or social movements (such as the global environmental movement represented by, for example, Greenpeace) that the fate of nations and communities is increasingly bound up with the dynamics of the global economy and the global environment.

16.2 Globalization, inequality and world order

There are broadly, within the existing literature, three distinct accounts of how globalization conditions patterns of global inequality and world order. The *neoliberal school* tends to view economic globalization as a benign force for change which, through free trade and capital mobility, is creating a global market civilization in which prosperity, wealth, power and liberal democracy are being diffused around the globe. In the process a new liberal world order is being constructed in which peace and an enduring harmony of interests will win out in the long term. In contrast, the *radical school* tends to conceive these very same developments as nothing more than an expression of Western – largely American – imperialism in which corporate empires and global markets have come to replace the world empires of the industrial era. Rather than prefiguring peace and an emerging harmony of interests, the radical account suggests the world is becoming ever more fragmented and unruly as the gap between the increasingly affluent North and increasingly impoverished South escalates. Finally, the *transformationalist school* suggests both these accounts overlook the ways in which contemporary globalization is reordering the relations between rich and poor, North and South, dominant and subordinate states in the global system. As a consequence neither of the other schools offers a convincing analysis of the changing architecture of world order and thereby the changing context of development in the twenty-first century. Let us explore these three accounts a little more fully. A summary is given in Table 16.2 at the end of the section.

The neoliberal analysis

For neoliberals, contemporary globalization defines a new epoch in human history in which market capitalism, following the collapse of state socialism in Eastern Europe and the Soviet Union, has triumphed across the globe such that there is no longer a viable alternative development path. This is a conception of globalization which reflects an economic interpretation and celebrates the emergence of a single global market and the principles of free trade, capital mobility, and global competition as the harbingers of modernization and development. Pointing to the East Asian economic miracle and the Latin American experience of the 1990s, the neoliberals emphasize that successful development issues from openness to global capital and competitive forces and closer integration within the global economy. For as globalization brings about a progressive denationalization of economies, through the establishment of trans-

national networks of production, trade and finance, governments have to adopt more market-friendly policies to attract much needed foreign capital. In this 'borderless' global economy governments are relegated to little more than transmission belts for global capitalism or catalysts for nurturing the competitive advantages of their national economies.

This vision of a 'global market civilization' has been reinforced by the policies of the major institutions of global economic governance, namely the IMF, World Bank and the G7 – at least up to the mid 1990s. Underlying their structural adjustment programmes has been a neoliberal development strategy – referred to as the Washington consensus – which prioritizes the opening up of national economies to global market forces and the requirement for limited government intervention in the management of the economy. The combination of structural adjustment programmes and the discipline of global market forces effectively constrains the development strategies which states may pursue. In this regard globalization significantly erodes the sovereignty and autonomy of states. National governments, in this view, are thus fast becoming 'a transitional mode of organization for managing economic affairs' (Ohmae, 1995).

Within this analysis there is a recognition that the dynamics of global market forces generates losers as well as winners. Nevertheless, in general, the analysis points to the growing diffusion of wealth and affluence in the world economy – the trickle-down effect. By historical standards global poverty, it is argued, has fallen more in the last 50 years than in the past 500, and the welfare of people in almost all regions has improved significantly over the last few decades. Rather than the old North–South fracture, a new world-wide division of labour is said to be replacing the traditional core–periphery model of global economic relations. As a result, what was called the 'third world' is becoming increasingly differentiated: embracing newly industrialized, emerging, least developed and 'fourth world' economies. South Korea is now a member of the OECD, the Western club of 'rich' nations, whilst many other 'third world' states are actively seeking membership. In addition, in the 'affluent' North, the transition economies of the former state socialist bloc define a new grouping of states having much more in common with many newly industrializing economies than the post-industrial economies of the Atlantic area. Accordingly, the notion of the 'third world', or North and South, as coherent geopolitical groupings or analytical categories has become decidedly misleading. To this extent globalization is associated with the 'end of the Third World' and growing global affluence.

The radical analysis

By comparison many radical accounts conclude that core and periphery – 'first world' and 'third world' – remain very much a fundamental reality of the contemporary world order. This is especially so today as most of the world's population and the majority of developing economies are becoming increasingly excluded from global affluence. Rather than globalization creating 'one world', the radical analysis suggests it has been accompanied by deepening global inequality and the marginalization of most 'third world' economies as trade and investment flows amongst OECD economies intensify to the exclusion of much of the rest of the globe (Figure 16.2). In comparison with the late nineteenth century some argue that the world economy has become considerably less, rather than more, 'global', as developing economies have become less important to its functioning (Gordon, 1988; Burbach *et al.*, 1997). Rather than the 'end of the Third World', and a fundamentally new international division of labour, the radical account points to a deepening North–South divide as a consequence of uneven globalization.

Central to this account is a conception of contemporary globalization as nothing less than a new mode of Western imperialism in which multinational capital has come to replace military power as the primary instrument of domination. In this 'new world order' the triumph of global capitalism, reinforced by the institutions of global economic governance such as the IMF

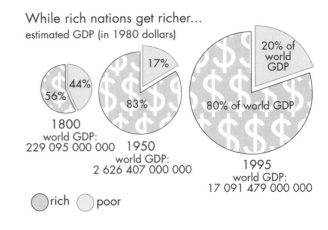

While rich nations get richer...
estimated GDP (in 1980 dollars)

1800
world GDP:
229 095 000 000

1950
world GDP:
2 626 407 000 000

1995
world GDP:
17 091 479 000 000

○ rich ○ poor

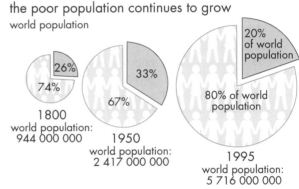

the poor population continues to grow
world population

1800
world population:
944 000 000

1950
world population:
2 417 000 000

1995
world population:
5 716 000 000

Figure 16.2 An example of the presentation of global data to make a radical case.

and the G7, has intensified the exploitation of the 'third world'. Today half of the world's population and two-thirds of its governments are subject to the disciplines of the IMF or the World Bank either through formal IMF economic stabilization programmes, as in the case of some East Asian economies following the Great Crash, or through World Bank lending (Pieper & Taylor, 1998). As the East Asian crisis demonstrated, even the strongest developing states are 'at the mercy of global economic forces that serve the interests of the dominant capitalist powers' (Burbach *et al.*, 1997, p.77). With the failure of state socialism too, no alternative development path exists. Globalization thus reinforces historical patterns of dominance and dependence such that the possibilities for real development remain effectively blocked. This is evident in the growing polarization between rich and poor in the global economy and the increasing immiseration of the poorest peoples in the world who bear the brunt, as the East Asian crash highlighted, of the 'boom and bust' logic of modern global capitalism. This 'new world order' is an 'unruly' one as poverty increases, the conflict between North and South deepens, and the affluent West, through various mechanisms from NATO to the World Bank, resorts to a kind of 'global riot control' to consolidate its power and secure its economic fortunes. Contemporary globalization, in the radical view, is thus implicated in the intensification of global poverty, deprivation, conflict and violence: in effect the consolidation, rather than the demise, of the Third World.

The transformationalist analysis

Rejecting both the proposition that contemporary globalization is simply a new Western imperialism and that it is a path to a single global market civilization, the transformationalist argument emphasizes its historically unique characteristics. In particular, transformationalists point to the unprecedented intensity and geographical embrace of contemporary processes of globalization, not just in the economic domain but within all aspects of social life from the cultural, security, and environmental, to the criminal, legal, and political. As Nierop puts it, 'Virtually all countries in the world, if not all parts of their territory and all segments of their society, are now functionally part of that larger [global] system in one or more respects' (Nierop, 1994, p.171). Yet it is also recognized that globalization is highly uneven in its embrace and its effects.

Contemporary globalization, in this analysis, is associated with a shift in the *configuration* of global power relations; that is, more complex and dynamic patterns of global hierarchy and stratification. Developing countries now account for a significant proportion of global exports, and through integration into transnational production networks have become extensions of, as well as competitors to, business in metropolitan economies. The role of 'maquiladores' – offshore production plants – in boosting Mexico's exports to the US is a case in point. The old North–South

hierarchy is arguably giving way to a new global division of labour in which the 'familiar pyramid of the core–periphery hierarchy is no longer a geographic but a social division of the world economy' (Hoogvelt, 1997). To talk of North and South, or First World and Third World, is to overlook the ways in which globalization is transforming old hierarchies by forging new patterns of inclusion and exclusion which cut into and reach across all the countries and regions of the world. This is not to deny that the world remains highly unequal. On the contrary, it acknowledges that instead of core–periphery, a more accurate analogy for this globalizing world might be a nested arrangement of four concentric circles – each cutting across all regions and societies – and constituted by the world's élites, the affluent middle-class, the marginalized and the dispossessed respectively (Hoogvelt, 1997). North and South, First World/Third World are no longer 'out there' but nestled together 'right here' in all the world's urban areas.

While inequalities of power and differential access to resources between states and societies remain considerable, they no longer mirror (not that they ever did) a crude North–South geopolitical division of the world. Such a crude division conceals the reality of very significant regional concentrations of wealth and military power in the 'South' alongside the enormous growth of poverty and social exclusion in the 'North'. Moreover, as the financial contagion effects of the East Asian crash showed, under conditions of contemporary globalization, economic prosperity in the North cannot be insulated from the consequences of national economic policy choices on the so-called periphery. Accordingly, globalization has transformed the context of national development in two ways. Firstly, in an interconnected world order, development is no longer just a third world matter but has become 'increasingly applicable to other parts of the world...The question of development is thus a shared one' (Dickson, 1997, p.154). Secondly, there is no longer a clear separation between domestic and international matters, so that governments have had to rethink how best to achieve national goals in an interconnected world. In response, a new development consensus is emerging – often referred to as the post-Washington or Geneva consensus – which recognizes development as a shared global challenge and responsibility amongst states and societies, North or South, industrializing as well as post-industrial.

Whether globalization is creating the political preconditions for a 'global New Deal' between rich and poor in the world economy remains to be seen. For the recognition of a shared fate does not necessarily lead to enhanced global solidarity or co-operation; on the contrary, it may engender greater competition, rivalry and conflict between states and peoples. Moreover, to the extent that globalization enmeshes states – North and South – in a plethora of transnational networks and systems, from the financial to the ecological, which are beyond their immediate control, it may make it more difficult for them to achieve their domestic and development policy objectives. The growth of cross-border problems too, combined with the expanding jurisdiction of institutions of global and regional governance, further alters the context of domestic governance and politics for rich and poor states alike, although in quite different ways.

This does not mean that states are becoming less important or less powerful. On the contrary, their roles and functions are changing as they seek coherent strategies for engaging with a globalizing world and an emerging framework of multi-layered governance, in which governments share the political stage with a host of other public and private agencies, domestic and transnational, from Greenpeace and the World Development Movement to General Motors and the World Health Organization (Table 16.1). As such, over the coming decades, 'we can expect to see more and more of a different kind of state taking shape in the world arena, one that is reconstituting its power at the centre of alliances formed either within or outside the nation-state' (Weiss, 1998). In this respect globalization is held to be transforming state power and with it the global context of development.

Table 16.1 State and corporate power, 1994

Country or corporation	Total GDP or corporate sales (US$ billions)
Indonesia	174.6
General Motors	168.8
Turkey	149.8
Denmark	146.1
Ford	137.1
South Africa	123.3
Toyota	111.1
Exxon	110.0
Royal Dutch/Shell	109.8
Norway	109.6
Poland	92.8
Portugal	91.6
IBM	72.0
Malaysia	68.5
Venezuela	59.0
Pakistan	57.1
Unilever	49.7
Nestlé	47.8
Sony	47.6
Egypt	43.9
Nigeria	30.4
Top five corporations	871.4
Least developed countries	76.6
South Asia	451.3
Sub-Saharan Africa	246.8

Source: UNDP (1997) *Human Development Report 1997*, Oxford University Press, Oxford, p.92.

Table 16.2 Globalization and development: summary of three accounts

	Neoliberal	Radical	Transformationalist
What's new?	A global market civilization	The empire strikes back	Development as a shared concern
Power of national governments	Declining both North and South	Expanding (North) and declining (South)	Reconfiguration of state power North and South
Driving forces of globalization	Capitalism and technology	G7 states and transnational capital	Modernity
North–South relations	Erosion of North–South differences	Increasing immiseration and marginalization of the Third World	New patterns of inclusion and exclusion; erosion of North–South hierarchy
Prospects for global solidarity	Spreading affluence	Erosion of global and national solidarity	New forms of transnational solidarity

16.3 One world of development or many?

Each of the above analyses of globalization (summarized in Table 16.2) expresses distinctive positions on several contentious issues:

1 whether the very idea of the Third World as a geopolitical or analytical category 'has become an anachronism' (Stallings, 1995, p.349);

2 the capacity of governments to realize sustainable national development strategies in a globalizing world; and

3 the architecture of the 'new world order' and its implications for the global politics of development.

This section will explore these issues further, reflecting upon which, if any, of the above analyses offers a convincing account of the global context of development today.

The 'end of the Third World' and the globalization of poverty

The phrase 'the end of the Third World' is used in several quite different ways. It may refer to the growing differentiation between the economic fortunes of countries in the South, or to the demise of a coherent geopolitical coalition of developing states, or to the reordering of the old North–South hierarchy in world politics. Except for the most ardent champions of neoliberal economics, people rarely take the phrase to refer to the ending of global poverty. Indeed, whilst the relationship between globalization and world poverty is enormously complicated, there is general acknowledgement that globalization is strongly associated with an intensification of global inequality (Bradshaw & Wallace, 1996; Castells, 1996; Dickson, 1997; Hoogvelt, 1997; UNDP, 1997b; Birdsall, 1998).

The evidence also indicates that growing poverty is no longer confined to the South (the 'third world'), but is on the rise in the affluent North. Globalization is generating new patterns of inclusion and exclusion in the global political economy which transcend the North–South divide but which nevertheless result in widening disparities in life chances across the globe. Paradoxically, contemporary patterns of globalization are associated both with a more affluent world and with growing global inequality.

Although in the last fifty years poverty has declined 'more than in the previous 500', that decline has been highly uneven (UNDP, 1997b, p.2). Three related global patterns are evident: the growing *polarization* between the richest and poorest in the world economy; the *segmentation* of the global workforce into the winners

world order dominated by the Great Contest between capitalism and state socialism: the USA and the Soviet Union respectively. Using its political muscle as a voting majority within the UN, the G77 sought successfully to make development and the eradication of global inequality a key priority of the UN and its specialized agencies, such as the World Health Organization, UNICEF, and the International Labour Organization (ILO) amongst others. This issued from a singular political strategy, often referred to as 'Tiersmondisme' (or Thirdworldism), which sought to contest and overturn the terms of economic engagement between North and South.

At its zenith 'Tiersmondisme' realized some significant achievements, from the creation of UNCTAD, a key forum within which deliberations on North–South issues and negotiated reforms could be progressed, to an agreed system of generalized trade preferences to provide developing economies with preferential access to Western markets. These initial successes also fuelled the demands for a more radical restructuring of North–South relations. In 1974, exploiting the potential vulnerability of the industrialized economies to the new-found commodity power so dramatically deployed by OPEC in its quadrupling of the price of oil in 1973, the G77 and NAM proposed a radical agenda for change. Agreed at the Sixth Special Session of the UN General Assembly in 1974, the Declaration on the Establishment of a New International Economic Order (NIEO) called for fundamental changes to the governance and rules of the global economic order to prioritize social justice over global market forces. There followed a period of intensifying diplomatic confrontation between North and South. But no significant advance was made in fundamentally altering the terms of economic engagement between the developed and developing world. As Halliday observes, 'The campaign for a NIEO...achieved none of its stated goals and was, by the early 1980s...in practice as dead as the League of Nations' (Halliday, 1989, p.21). Since then 'Tiersmondisme', faced with accelerating global-

ization and growing diversity within the G77 and NAM, has been in full retreat.

In part the failure of 'Tiersmondisme' was also significantly due to the major G7 countries, most especially the United States, refusing to implement a number of agreed reforms, and their growing preference for bilateral or regional dialogues – as opposed to the multilateralism of UN fora in which they were in a permanent minority. But, by the 1990s, the G7's desire to make progress with global trade liberalization, and the dismantling of barriers to global capital, gave renewed impetus to multilateralism as the primary vehicle for rule-making and governance of a rapidly globalizing world economy. At the same time, accelerating globalization and the impact of structural adjustment programmes had intensified the enmeshment of most developing countries within global economic networks such that the ideology of delinking and import substitution growth, so dominant during the campaign for a NIEO, came to lack political credibility. In particular, for those industrializing economies increasingly reliant on trade the fear of losing an effective voice in the Uruguay round of trade negotiations – which sought to establish new rules and arrangements for governing global trade matters in the form of the World Trade Organization – encouraged a reluctant return to multilateralism. Underlying this shift was a perception, amongst both the G7 and many developing states, that globalization was altering the terms of engagement between rich and poor states in the global economy.

By the early 1990s there was growing recognition that the globalization of trade, finance and production had significant consequences for economies in both North and South. With the increasing mobility of capital, a new global division of labour began to emerge as manufacturing production in Europe, Japan and the US moved offshore. By the late 1990s, according to ILO estimates, almost 50% of manufacturing jobs were located in developing economies whilst over 60% of developing country exports to the industrialized world were manufactured goods, a twelvefold increase in less than four decades (UNDP, 1998b, p.17). For the G7 governments, globalization brought not only increased competition between their own economies but also increased competition from newly industrializing economies in Asia and Latin America.

The intensification of global trade and the expanding reach of global production networks links the fate of workers and economies North and South more closely together. Similarly, the globalization of finance, as the 1997 East Asian crisis so graphically demonstrated, brings with it a sense of shared fates since loan defaults or currency speculation on the periphery can so readily trigger financial instability and turmoil across the globe. This is not to ignore the very different degrees of vulnerability between rich and poor states to these developments or their differential capacities to deflect or manage them. Nevertheless this reconfiguration of the terms of North–South economic engagement has begun to transform the politics of development.

Reinforcing this reconfiguration is a broadening agenda of global issues which cut across traditional North–South constituencies. As Ravenhill asserts, 'The changing global agenda...offers a growing number of issues on which there are mutual interests between North and South and on which the co-operation of the Southern countries will be necessary if the industrialized countries are to attain their goals' (Ravenhill, 1990). Many environmental issues, from global warming to the trade in hazardous waste, have generated a 'new power dynamics between developed and developing countries' (Miller, 1998, p.175). In so far as collective action, or adherence to common rules, is required for effective policy responses to such problems, developing states have acquired 'the potential to deny the industrialized countries their environmental objectives' (ibid., p.177). The global ban on exports of hazardous waste from North to South and the Global Environmental Facility are indicative of 'hard-fought victories for Third World states' (ibid., p.187).

On a range of issues, from the proliferation of weapons of mass destruction, humanitarian emergencies, money laundering, labour standards, genetic engineering, agricultural subsidies and debt issues, to the reform of the international financial architecture, the old North–South hierarchy is giving way to a more complex configuration of interests and power in the determination of global policy outcomes. On agricultural trade matters, for instance, many poorer states have found themselves allied to the US in WTO deliberations in pressing the EU to reduce barriers to 'free trade' on agricultural products. Moreover, where issues cut across different institutional jurisdictions, as with trade (WTO) and labour standards (ILO), the complexities of global rule-making multiply. In these circumstances those with the most power on one issue may find themselves forced to compromise because of the need to make trade-offs on other issues in a different arena. Under conditions of contemporary globalization effective global governance and compliance with global rules 'requires the co-operation of the so-called 'have-nots'. This cannot be achieved through the hierarchical arrangements of old' (Woods, 1999, p.21).

Furthermore, as the decisions of both public and private global agencies, such as the WTO or Standard and Poor (the international credit rating agency), touch more directly upon the welfare, values or interests of peoples around the globe this has triggered a corresponding globalization of political activity. Whilst governments and intergovernmental bodies, from WHO to UNEP, may be the primary locus of political authority in the world order they are not necessarily the most powerful or the sole participants in global rule-making. On the contrary they share the global political arena with a plethora of private associations constituting an emerging transnational civil society, embracing amongst others citizen groups, corporations, trade unions, employers organizations, professional organizations, industrial organizations, social movements, NGOs and international pressure groups of all kinds. As the scope and arrangement appeared to 'conform to many Ugandans' expectation of how 'government by the people' should work', according to survey data on democratic attitudes in Uganda (Ottemoeller, 1998). Museveni won the 1996 election in a landslide (70% of the vote), defeating an opposition candidate representing two old (defunct) political parties. But Kasfir (1998a, p.62) argued that although Museveni and the NRM 'have made fundamental contributions to improving life in Uganda', it seems unlikely that this particular form of democracy will last when Museveni has gone.

Democratization

Despite such variations, liberal democracy, with its limitations, is still the standard model of a democratic regime used in the huge literature on patterns of **democratization** in the modern world. Describing actual examples of democratization using these patterns involves making rough judgements regarding various complexities. Such movements may, for example, be quick on one or two dimensions of change, less quick or stagnant (or going into reverse) on the others; an instance is South Korea which 'jumped' to competitive elections in 1987–88 while authoritarian restrictions on civil and political rights hardly moved at all in a democratic direction. Rough judgements are also required when trying to assign any one country to one of the three 'ideal' types of regime, as is done in Table 17.2 below.

Democratization: Political change moving in a democratic direction from less accountable to more accountable government, from less competitive (or non-existent) elections to fuller and fairer competitive elections, from severely restricted to better protected civil and political rights, from weak (or non-existent) autonomous associations to more autonomous and more numerous associations in civil society.

Table 17.2 categorizes 147 countries in 1975 and 164 countries in 1995 throughout the world as either a liberal democracy, partial democracy or authoritarian regime. The summary totals are broken down in terms of major regions of the world.

The data in Table 17.2 show that patterns of democratization (moving in a democratic direction) between 1975 and 1995 were different in different regions of the world. There was virtually no regime change in Western Europe and North America and Australasia (apart from Spain and Portugal moving to liberal democracy), the main democratrization stories having occurred before 1975. The data show striking democratization in Latin America over the period, with 68% of regimes being authoritarian in 1975, and only 10% in 1995. In sub-Saharan Africa, authoritarianism was the overwhelmingly dominant regime type in 1975, whereas in 1995 67% of the countries were classified as either partial or liberal democracies. The data for Eastern Europe and the USSR/former USSR reflect the momentous political changes that occurred there during the period; all nine regimes were authoritarian in 1975 but by 1995 the Soviet Union had broken up (also Yugoslavia and Czechoslovakia), the number of regimes in the region had nearly tripled, and democratization was under way in 81% of them. The data show less regime change in Asia from authoritarian rule toward democracy between 1975 and 1995 and no change in the Middle East and North Africa.

These data catch what was referred to by Huntington (1991) and others as the 'third wave' of democratization (the 'first long wave' having occurred from 1828 to 1926, and the 'second short wave' after the Second World War). One of the things about waves is that they roll back; and, indeed, a number of the newly democratic regimes in Africa and elsewhere by 1999 had failed to consolidate their new liberal democracy, or looked increasingly fragile or had reverted to authoritarianism. An academic literature began to appear attempting to classify and explain this 'third reverse wave' (e.g. Burnell, 1998). Also,

Table 17.2 Global patterns of democratization, 1975–95

	1975			1995		
	Authoritarian	Partial democracy	Liberal democracy	Authoritarian	Partial democracy	Liberal democracy
Western Europe, North America and Australia	2	0	22	0	0	24
Latin America	15	2	5	2	5	15
Sub-Saharan Africa	43	2	3	12	16	20
Eastern Europe and the USSR/ former USSR	9	0	0	5	14	8
Asia	18	4	3	11	4	10
Middle East and North Africa	14	3	2	13	3	2
TOTALS	101	11	35	43	42	79
1975 (N = 147)	68.7%	7.5%	23.8%			
1995 (N = 164)				26.2%	25.6%	48.2%

Source: Potter (1997, p.9; for the names of all the countries behind the data, pp.37–8).

there is no doubt that many of the countries classified in Table 17.2 as liberal democracies in 1995 were compromised. For example, in the Philippines the President and the bicameral legislature had been elected since 1986 in what were perhaps the freest and fairest elections in Southeast Asia. But the literature on the subject makes abundantly clear that the elections were largely irrelevant to the lives of the poor, the overwhelming majority of the electorate (e.g. Anderson, 1996; Kerkvliet, 1996). In the 1992 Philippines Congress all but 17 of the 195 members were millionaires, one of many indicators that led Neher & Marlay (1995, p.65, p.72) to conclude that in the Philippines 'formal democratic appearances have triumphed over meaningful citizen participation'. Papua New Guinea certainly had had competitive electoral politics since it was granted independence from Australian colonial rule in 1975, with a high turnover of MPs and changes of government produced by regular elections with competitive party activity and high voter turnout (Lipset, 1989); but

the effect of a first-past-the-post electoral system operating in one of the world's most heterogeneous societies (over 800 different languages spoken by several thousand 'clan' or tribe groupings) had resulted by the mid 1990s in increasingly unstable and unaccountable governments (Reilly, 1997).

Granted that there can be problems in classifying countries as either liberal or partial democracies, there is no denying that the global totals in Table 17.2 indicate extraordinary political regime changes throughout most of the world during a 20-year period – historically a very short time. The data show that for all of Asia, Latin America, sub-Saharan Africa and Eastern Europe and the former USSR, 82% of the 104 countries classified for 1975 were authoritarian regimes; yet in 1995 only 25% of the 122 countries classified for those same regions were authoritarian, all the rest having moved to some form of partial or liberal democracy. Identifying the phenomenon is one thing, explaining it is another.

369

Explaining democratization

All explanations of political phenomena combine elements of *agency* and *structure* (see Chapter 9). Part of an explanation involves some agency – the actions, choices and initiatives of persons or groups causing the phenomena. And part of an explanation involves some structure – a set of physical and social constraints, a set of opportunities, a set of norms and values that shape or determine the content of the actions, choices and initiatives. How agency and structure are combined, and the weighting assigned to one or the other, are matters on which the various explanations of democratization disagree. Some explanations give more weight to structural factors like the dominant mode of economic production and the class structure related to it. Others emphasize instead the importance of agency factors like political leadership and the demands of particular groups. There are literally hundreds of different explanations of democratization in the vast literature on the subject, and this is not the place to try to summarize the main types. Brief attention can be drawn, however, to seven *explanatory factors* to which such explanations refer, but in different ways. An explanatory factor is a process, action, condition or structure that an explanation suggests is associated with, or causes, democratization.

Socio-economic development

All explanations of democratization refer to this. For Lipset (1960), Diamond (1992) and many others using a modernization approach, positive correlations between development (defined in terms of rising per capita income, growing per capita energy consumption, etc.) and democratization are profoundly significant. For Moore (1966), Therborn (1978), Rueschemeyer *et al.* (1992), and numerous others using a more structural approach, economic development is more exactly capitalist development which structures fundamentally the historical route that countries take toward liberal democracy or some other form of political regime. For Rustow (1970), O'Donnell *et al.* (1986), Di Palma (1990), Linz & Stepan (1996) and many others who approach the explanation of democratization in

terms primarily of agency and transition processes, socio-economic development helps to trigger the actions of competing élites busy crafting the democratic compromise. The different approaches also recognize that economic crises can destroy liberal democracy and that severe economic underdevelopment, as in many parts of sub-Saharan Africa, has not been a promising context for democratization. The relationship between democratization and socio-economic development is explored later in this chapter.

Social divisions

Capitalist development produces changing *class* divisions in society (divisions based on wealth and life chances). Changing class structures are a central feature of structural explanations of democratization. For Rueschemeyer *et al.* (1992), the rise of the working class (employed manual labour outside agriculture) has been historically the most important economic interest pushing for extensions of the suffrage and other aspects of democratic development; by comparison, the peasantry have tended to be disorganized and relatively weak in this regard; large landlords as a class, when powerful and closely allied to the authoritarian state, have been a major obstacle to democratization; the bourgeoisie (owners of and employers in enterprises engaged in industry, trade and commerce) has rarely pushed for democratization but their position has varied depending on the alignment of other classes; and the position of the 'middle classes' similarly has varied depending on other alignments – for example, where the working class has been weak the 'middle classes' have tended to push for democratization to improve their position, and where the working class has been strong the 'middle classes' may or may not have been as energetic. Capitalist development has the structural consequences of weakening large landowners and strengthening the bourgeoisie and labour. More particularly for labour, 'capitalist development enlarges the working class at the expense of agricultural labourers and small farmers; it thus shifts members of subordinate classes from an environment extremely unfavourable to collective action to one much more favourable, from geographical isolation and immobility to high concentrations of people with similar class interests' (Rueschemeyer *et al.*, 1992, p.58). However, there are numerous obstacles, internal conflicts and inconsistencies that weaken the potential 'force' of the workers engaged in 'collective action' for larger political objectives like democratization. An example is the well-known tension between such a large political project and the typical 'trade union consciousness' focused more narrowly on the struggle for better wages and working conditions. Generally, the working class has been too weak in most developing countries to achieve by itself democratic rights for the subordinate classes and therefore has had to form alliances with other classes and groups.

Divisions between political élites are vital in transition explanations of democratization. In such explanations it is the action of élites – what they do when, where and how – that drives democratization forward. In the early stages of a democratic transition from authoritarian rule, various political élites get involved. These include 'hardliners' and 'softliners' within the authoritarian coalition, and 'opportunists', 'moderates' and 'extremists' within the opposition (see Table 17.3). Certain scenarios involving particular links between some of the five categories and divisions between others are more favourable to a turn towards democracy than others. For example, comparative evidence from Latin America suggests that transitions are more likely to be successful if they are controlled by a coalition of 'softliners' and 'moderates', with 'radicals' kept out. During later stages of democratic transitions the consolidation of liberal or partial democracy involves historical paths that are complex and uncertain, but here again the character of the political élites involved is critical to success.

Explanations of democratization also refer to social divisions based on gender, ethnicity, race, tribe, language, religion and other cultural criteria. For example, transition theorists have argued that 'artificial' state boundaries were imposed on African society by colonialists resulting in either centralized or dispersed ethnic divisions in those countries. Where social conflict between two or several major ethnic groupings is a constant theme of politics nationally (as in Nigeria), the sense of shared political identity can be undermined, leading to democratic instability or breakdown. Where there are dispersed ethnic divisions, with a multiplicity of cultural groups (as in India), inter-ethnic cooperation is more likely and can be a force for political pluralism and democratization.

Historical legacies
For example, the legacies of colonial rule are frequently referred to in discussions of the problems of democratization in sub-Saharan Africa (see Section 12.3 in Chapter 12 on 'Legacies of colonial rule for post-colonial states and state-led development'). In Asia, modernization theorists (e.g. Diamond *et al.*, 1989) have argued

Table 17.3 Political élites during transitions

| Within the authoritarian coalition: | | Within the opposition: | | |
'hardliners'	'softliners'	'opportunists'	'moderates'	'radicals'
Firmly committed to maintaining authoritarian rule	Willing to negotiate with the opposition about possible political liberalization or democratization	Former regime supporters with no serious commitment to democratization but hoping to gain something from it	In favour of democratization while respecting the position of traditional élites (including the military)	Demand major democratic transformation, and unwilling to compromise with the authoritarian coalition

Source: Potter, D. (1997, p.15) 'Exploring democratization', in Potter, D. *et al.*, *Democratization*, Polity Press, Cambridge.

that the 'democratic prospect' has varied significantly with the historical and cultural legacies of the colonial experience. For example, they say that India's success with democracy owes something to the British colonial legacy – the establishment of the rule of law as a constraint on arbitrary government, the provision of a system of representation and election during the 1930s that gave educated élites some experience of government, an educational system that taught and praised British democratic concepts and values. By contrast, Japanese colonial rule in Korea strengthened the already centralized and autocratic character of traditional authority there, leaving Korea at the end of the Second World War with no countervailing institutions able to balance state power.

State power and political institutions

A very powerful and almost entirely autonomous state in relation to dependent social classes or to a weak civil society has provided a most uncongenial setting for democratization. This has been so especially where the military and the police have been strong within the state apparatus. A very weak state is also a problem, because a state must have some autonomy and power in relation to dominant classes or other social forces so that it can act against dominant interests when responding to subordinate class demands for democratization. Democratization has had more chance of success in the middle ground between too much and not enough state power.

State, class and civil society are very generalized explanatory factors and are of limited value in explaining variations in democratization experiences in countries with similar state–class–civil society relationships. For this reason, intermediate-level political institutions are also important explanatory factors, e.g. different types of legislatures, federal or unitary governmental relationships, different relationships between government departments in the state bureaucracies, different political party systems, and strong or weak trade unions. For example, democratization is difficult where party systems are weak and fragmented. Effective party systems can both mobilize the vote and mediate democratization pressures from subordinate classes in a manner that does not fundamentally threaten dominant class interests. Rueschemeyer *et al.* (1992) have argued that dominant classes are more likely to accommodate liberal democracy where the party system includes a strong party of the right; where such a party is lacking or no longer able to protect their interests, such conservative classes have been more ready to appeal to the military to end democratic rule.

Figure 17.2 'Howling for freedom' in South Africa. Jubilant inhabitants of Soweto gather on 11 February 1990 to celebrate the release of Nelson Mandela.

Civil society

There is lively debate about the significance of civil society for democratization in Latin America (e.g. Oxhorn, 1995) as distinct from Africa (e.g. Kasfir, 1998b) and elsewhere. Clearly, democratization has been stimulated by the growth of pro-democracy social movements. In sub-Saharan Africa, for example, there were such movements nearly everywhere by 1990, leading Dr Roger Chongwe (Chairman of the African Bar Association) to exclaim, rather wildly: 'There is a [new] wind of change blowing across this continent. It howls for freedom. Whether African leaders like it or not, they cannot stand against it' (*The Guardian*, 11 September 1990, p.19) (Figure 17.2). The growing proliferation of autonomous groups – students, women, trade unions, church members, consumers, the environmentally concerned, farmers, lawyers and other professionals – can also strengthen democratization prospects. This can involve the growth of independent media capable of bringing pressure to bear on authoritarian states. However, a state can also shape civil society for its own purpose by co-opting groups and associations. It is also important to appreciate that groups and associations in civil society can be hostile to democratization.

Political culture and ideas

There is more dispute about the significance of this as an explanatory factor than about the others. It may seem obvious that democratization is more likely in countries where political cultures – peoples' values, attitudes and beliefs – are pro-democratic. For many structural theorists, however, democratic political cultures (whatever they are) are likely to be primarily a consequence of democratization, not a cause. Others say that culture is not an explanatory concept but rather a context in which social action takes place (Chapter 21). There has been more widespread acceptance of the political importance of values, attitudes and beliefs that are institutionally grounded, the main example being organized religions. Even here, however, there has been debate. For example, some explanations of the comparative lack of democratization in the Middle East and North Africa during 1975–95 were based on the fact that this is the land of Islam, while others found no evidence to support this explanation. Bromley (1997), for example, has argued that democratization in Islamic Turkey suggests that authoritarianism in the Middle East has been caused primarily by factors other than religion (Figure 17.3).

Figure 17.3   Democratization in Islamic Turkey. A supporter of Turkey's Islamist Welfare Party prays for his party's success during a campaign rally for nation-wide elections in December 1995.

Transnational and international power

Democratization cannot be explained only in terms of structures and forces within a country. Processes of transnational globalization are increasingly important (Chapter 16). The effects of transnational economic and financial processes, the global division of labour, global communications and so on can be positive or negative for democratization. For example, transnational economic processes linking advanced capitalist countries and dependent Latin American countries delayed industrialization in the latter and kept the industrial working class small, thereby weakening pro-democracy forces between 1930 and 1980 (Cammack, 1997). Export-led growth based on primary products from plantations can provide a setting for the political organization of workers, but such growth can also strengthen large (anti-democratic) landowners. However, global ideological and cultural flows can enhance the democratic prospect, and liberal democracy as a 'good idea' has through improved communications networks percolated everywhere, even into societies dominated by repressive states and reactionary classes.

International power involves government-to-government relations such as military alliances, international war, the work of government aid agencies and intergovernmental institutions like the United Nations, the World Bank and so on. For example, it has suited the economic interests of the US government and the World Bank since the early 1990s to try to attach democratic conditionalities to aid packages for authoritarian regimes (after noticeably failing to do so in previous decades). The relaxation of international tension and the end of the 'cold war' may also have assisted the 'third wave' of democratization. The relation between international war and democratization, however, has varied depending on other factors. The national mobilization of men, and especially women, for war or in the face of external threat has historically led to extensions of the franchise and other democratic advance, yet war also can strengthen the military in society and the power of the state, and in the absence of other countervailing forces can severely threaten the prospects of democratization. Massive military aid to fragile liberal democracies can also strengthen the state apparatus unduly in relation to civil society and the balance of class forces.

Explanatory factors

Two general observations. The first is that any consideration of one factor always involves others. For example, a simple structural explan-

ation of democratization could go like this: *capitalist socio-economic development* and the *historical legacy* of the growth of social (nationalist) movements under *international* colonial rule leading to the creation of an incipient *civil society* strengthened the subordinate classes in post-colonial society thereby changing the balance of *class power*, such growth in due course encouraging the development of democratic ideas in the *political culture* and providing an important counterweight to the excessively powerful post-colonial *state apparatus*. The statement draws on all seven of the explanatory factors discussed here. A fuller explanation of democratization would link together in more complex ways many more such factors.

The other point is that there are clearly different and, to some extent, competing explanations drawing on these seven factors in different ways. The differences hinge at least in part on whether an explanation pays more attention to agency or to structure. It is worth noting, however, that some scholars towards the end of the 1990s were trying to move beyond this division. Bratton & van de Walle (1997, p.45), for example, in their study of democratization in Africa, say 'we resist making a forced, dichotomous choice' between structure and agency and 'insist on having the best of both worlds', an 'approach that is neither overly deterministic or excessively voluntaristic'. They call it 'a structured contingency' approach. No doubt the best explanations do combine structures and contingency (agency), but this does not end all argument between different explanations.

17.2 Democratization and development

Given this extraordinary burst of democratization in the latter part of the twentieth century, what impact has it had, or will it have, on poverty and development? It will come as no surprise to learn that there is no definitive answer to this question. From the huge literature on this subject in the 1990s four different positions can perhaps be identified to illustrate the character of the debates that went on.

Democratization stimulates development

This position was widespread in official Western aid circles and amongst their academic support. It was referred to, not very accurately, as the 'Washington consensus' (Gills & Philip, 1996). Essentially, the view was that a combination of liberal market capitalism in an international context and liberal democracy and 'good governance' domestically were mutually reinforcing (a 'virtuous cycle') and provided core elements of a comprehensive strategy for development success equally valid for all types of society. The position had important policy consequences. Aid agencies like the World Bank and others tried to stimulate development by attaching liberal democratic conditionalities to aid packages and supporting initiatives to encourage 'good governance' (discussed later). Aid agencies also tried to insist (for example, in the former socialist countries of Eastern Europe) that 'free' markets were the only suitable economic mechanism for substantial development within global capitalism.

The position was buttressed by numerous academic studies attempting to demonstrate its essential correctness. One of the most impressive was by Surjit Bhalla (1997), For Bhalla, democracy is strongly associated with greater freedom; and he asked the question: does greater freedom lead to improved economic growth and social development? He analysed the question using data for over 90 countries during the period 1973–90. Two concepts of freedom were used – political and civil rights as measured annually in Gastil/Freedom House surveys (e.g. Gastil, 1987) and economic freedom measured in terms of openness to (a) the international capital market, (b) the international goods market and (c) the domestic capital market. Economic growth and social development were measured by per capita income growth (in terms of both constant US dollars and purchasing power parity), total factor productivity growth, growth in secondary school enrolments and decline in infant mortality.

Having analysed these data, Bhalla reached a straightforward and robust conclusion: 'more freedom is unambiguously good for both growth and social development'; and he went on:

> "...the results suggest that economic development is likely to be successful if countries follow the right economic and political policies... The right policies provide maximum freedom to individuals. Economic policies should ensure that domestic tradable prices are close to international tradable prices, investors should be allowed freedom, and exchange rates should be allowed to move freely. The right political policies provide a free press and a 'free-wheeling' democracy. In conclusion, free markets and a free society are the important ingredients to rapid economic development... Growth and freedom can indeed be locked into a virtuous cycle."
>
> (Bhalla, 1987, p.228)

One of the unusual features of Bhalla's analysis was the incorporation in his framework of both economic and political freedoms. This enabled him to try to cope with a well-known anomaly levelled against the 'democratization stimulates development' position: India, a liberal democratic country for all but two years between 1960 and 1987, grew at a rate of only 1.9% per capita whereas three authoritarian regimes in Pacific Asia – South Korea, Taiwan, Singapore – grew during the same period at a rate of about 6.4% per capita. Authoritarian China also recorded spectacular growth rates during the 1980s and 1990s. Bhalla claims that 'India with high political freedom' grew slowly because of 'low economic freedom' and 'the East Asian economies with low political freedom grew considerably faster' because of 'high economic freedom' (Bhalla, 1987, p.196).

Critics contended that this coped with the anomaly only partially. They did not say that market forces or democratic values were irrelevant to development, but they did object to the idea that there was one neoliberal formula of 'right' economic and political policies as taught by the apostles of advanced industrial capitalism that could uniformly stimulate development at almost any stage in the development process of any society.

Democratization can impede development in poor societies

This position was popular among some leaders in various partially democratic and authoritarian regimes. Singapore's Lee Kwan Yew (1992) told an audience in the Philippines: 'I do not believe that democracy necessarily leads to development. I believe that what a country needs to develop is discipline more than democracy. The exuberance of democracy leads to indiscipline and disorderly conduct which are inimical to development.' The position was supported by dispassionate academic analysis. Leftwich (1993) examined the relation between liberal democracy and development and reached what he found to be an 'uncomfortable' conclusion: 'if eliminating the continuing offence of poverty and misery is the *real* target, then unlimited liberal democracy and unrestrained economic liberty may be the last thing the developing world needs as it whirls towards the 21st century' (p.621) (Figure 17.4).

The argument has many aspects. Perhaps the most important concerns the 'conservative' nature of liberal democracy and the radical character of development. When a liberal democratic constitution is established in a country, what amounts to a 'political settlement' is agreed between the major conservative and progressive interests in society. The settlement provides reasonable guarantees that, although governments may change due to competitive elections, the major interests in society will not be adversely affected in a major way. As Leftwich (1993, p.616) pungently puts it, 'no group will commit itself to the democratic process if it feels that losing an election will mean it will be wiped out.' The consequence, he says in a later study (Leftwich, 1998, p.56), is that 'both the decision-making processes and policy output in consolidated democracies are generally 'conservative' in that they normally involve inter-élite accommodation, compromise, consensus, and incrementalism, and seldom entail much popular participation.' Development, on the other hand 'is both by definition and in practice a radical and commonly turbulent process which is concerned with often far-reaching and rapid change in the use and distribution of resources, and which – if successful – must transform the fundamental structures of economic and social life, thereby generating new political interests and challenging established ones.' The contradiction is that 'the rules and hence practices of stable democratic politics will tend to restrict policy to incremental and accommodationist (hence conservative) options'; whereas 'developmental requirements (whether liberal or radical) will be likely to pull policy in the direction

Figure 17.4   The real target: schooling for children in rural Uganda.

Figure 17.5   Voting too blunt an instrument? The poor queue to vote in a village in South India.

of quite sharp change affecting the economic and social structure of the society and hence important interests within it.'

India provides an example of how this contradiction can impede development for the poor. At the end of the twentieth century, India had the largest number of desperately poor people in the world – between 370 and 390 million or about 40% of India's total population. Most of the rural poor were landless peasants, and landlessness was a major cause of their poverty. India had been a liberal democracy for 50 years, with political leaders like Nehru and others publicly committed to eradicating poverty. Efforts at land reform to benefit the poor were attempted, but liberal democratic political processes enabled powerful, landed (conservative) élites to ensure that land reform legislation in the states of India did not radically affect their interests. Liberal democracy also enabled the poor to vote, but periodic elections were too blunt an instrument to affect the power of the landed élites (Figure 17.5); Dube's (1998) memoirs of a landless peasant family in Uttar Pradesh during these 50 years of liberal democracy provides a moving account of this development failure. Sainath (1998) reached a similar conclusion based on discussions in the mid 1990s with hundreds of poor families in various parts of rural India.

Authoritarian regimes are better than liberal democracies at stimulating economic development in poor countries

This view was fairly prominent in US government and academic circles during the 'cold war'. De Schweinitz (1959) claimed that if poor countries 'are to grow economically, they must limit democratic participation in political affairs' because, as Galenson (1959, p.3) observed, 'the more democratic a government is,…the greater the diversion of resources from investment to consumption.' Huntington & Nelson (1976, p.23) argued that 'political participation must be held down, at least temporarily, in order to promote economic development.'

This view was contested at the time and by the 1990s was no longer widely accepted. The work of Przeworski *et al.* (1996) was important here. They counted the 'instances of survival and death of political regimes in 135 countries observed annually between 1950, or the year of independence, or the first year when economic data are available ('entry year')' and 1990 or the last year for which data were available to them ('exit year') and 'found 224 regimes, of which

101 were democracies and 123 dictatorships, observing 40 transitions to dictatorship and 50 to democracy'. They used a minimalist definition of democracy as 'regimes that hold elections in which the opposition has some chance of winning and taking office', treating everything else as dictatorship. This is in keeping with standard definitions of liberal democracy/democratization and therefore useful for the discussions here. They defined development as an increase in per capita income. They found the following:

> "Dictatorships are no more likely to generate economic growth than democracies. Indeed, the 56 dictatorships with annual per-capita income of less than $1,000 when we first observed them simply failed to develop. By the exit year, only 18 of them had made it (whether under democracy or continued dictatorship) to $1,000, only 6 to $2,000, and only 3 to more than $3,000. South Korea and Taiwan are exceptional: they are the only two dictatorships that started under $1,000 in 1950 and had annual per-capita income exceeding $5,000 by 1990. If we consider as 'initially poor' those countries with less than $2,000, we find that among 98 dictatorships first observed below this level, by the exit year only 26 had made it to $2,000, 15 to $3,000, 7 to $4,000, and 4 to $5,000. These figures should be enough to dispel any notion that dictatorship somehow promotes economic growth in poor countries."

> (Przeworski *et al.*, 1996, p.40)

One of the reasons why South Korea and Taiwan were 'exceptional dictatorships' (in Przeworski *et al.*'s terms) during the period of study was because they were outstanding examples of authoritarian *developmental states* (see Chapter 9), whose features were said to include '(a) a dedicated developmental élite; (b) relative autonomy of the state apparatus; (c) a complex and insulated economic bureaucracy; (d) a weak and subordinated civil society; (e) the capacity to manage effectively local and foreign economic interests; (f) a varying balance of repression, legitimacy and performance which appear to succeed by offering a trade-off between

such repression as may exist and the delivery of regular improvements in material circumstances' (Leftwich, 1998, pp.62–3). Some argued on the basis of the South Korean and Taiwanese experiences that such authoritarian states generally were better than liberal democracies at stimulating development in poor countries, while others contended that such states were peculiar, for a transitional period, to only a few countries in Pacific Asia within a special set of historical circumstances not found elsewhere. I say more about the developmental state below.

Democratization in poor countries is unrelated to subsequent economic growth

A number of statistical studies in the 1990s reached this conclusion. Helliwell (1994, p.246), for example, considered cross-sectional and pooled data for 125 countries over the period 1960 to 1985 and found that the evidence 'pours cold water on the notion that introducing democracy is likely to accelerate subsequent growth'. His data showed no significant relationship between the two. He did find, however, that democratization appeared positively to affect subsequent education and investment, both of which tended to increase economic growth. He also conceded that 'there may be country-specific or culture-specific factors that influence the linkages between democracy and economic growth, and which may be obscured in a study based on a large sample of countries' (p.245).

Przeworski and Limongi (1993), using the same data set for 135 countries summarized earlier, found that 'economic miracles' occurred in both democracies and dictatorships and that 'while Latin American democracies suffered economic disasters during the 1980s, the world is also replete with authoritarian regimes that are dismal failures from the economic point of view. Hence, it does not seem to be democracy or authoritarianism *per se* that makes the difference but something else' (p.65). They were unable to say from the data what that something else might be. They concluded that 'social scientists know surprisingly little: our guess is that political institutions do matter for growth, but thinking in terms of regimes does not seem to capture the relevant differences' (p.51).

Figure 17.6   A broader concept of development should incorporate some basic political freedoms? A woman casts her vote, Botswana, 15 October 1994.

One of the main problems with these analyses is that they use a narrow definition of development as an increase in per capita income. As Bardhan (1993, p.47) points out, 'if one takes a broader concept of development to incorporate general well-being of the population at large, including some basic civil and political freedoms, a democracy which ensures these freedoms is, almost by definition, more conducive to development on these counts than a non-democratic regime' (Figure 17.6).

Another version of this fourth position about the irrelevance of different types of political regimes to explanations of economic development in poor countries was summed up many years ago by Alexander Pope:

> "For forms of government let fools contest; whate'er is best administered is best."

A late twentieth-century rendering of Pope's eighteenth-century couplet would be that what matters for development is not liberal democracy or authoritarianism but 'good governance'. For example, Jeffries (1993, p.28) argued that whether or not there is multi-party democracy in Africa is irrelevant 'relative to the importance of, first, improving the capacity, commitment and quality of government administration, of developing an effective developmental state.'

17.3 'Good governance'

The governance features of authoritarian developmental states were indicated earlier as an aspect of a 'cold war' argument that 'authoritarian regimes are better at stimulating development than liberal democracy.' The classic examples of developmental states usually cited were South Korea and Taiwan in the 1970s and early 1980s. By the 1990s, however, the developmental state had been yoked to the 'virtuous cycle' of liberal democracy, 'free' market and 'good governance', as mentioned earlier in the discussion of the 'democracy stimulates development' position. In this final short section I want to elaborate on the idea of 'good governance', the most recent feature of the 'virtuous cycle', and to locate it within current discussion of the democratic developmental state.

The World Bank (1992) defined governance as 'the means in which power is exercised in the management of a country's economic and social resource for development' and 'good governance' as 'synonymous with sound development management' (p.1). In the elaboration of the Bank's definition in Box 17.1, four areas of governance are stated, together with indications of what they believe is 'sound' management in each area. For example, under 'legal framework for development', they say that 'legal reforms, however urgent, may come to naught if new laws are not enforced consistently' and 'efforts to develop privatized production and encourage market-led growth may not succeed unless investors face clear rules and instructions that reduce uncertainty about future government action' (1992, p.1). More broadly, 'good governance is

Box 17.1 'Good governance'

The World Bank (1992, p.1) defined 'good governance' as 'synonymous with sound development management' in four areas (as summarized by Turner & Hulme, 1997, p.231):

1 *Public sector management* Government must manage its financial and personnel resources effectively through appropriate budgeting, accounting and reporting systems and by rooting out inefficiency, particularly in the parastatal sector.

2 *Accountability* Public officials must be held responsible for their actions. This involves effective accounting and auditing, decentralization, 'micro-level accountability' to consumers and a role for non-governmental organizations.

3 *The legal framework for development* There must be a set of rules known in advance, these must be enforced, conflicts must be resolved by independent judicial bodies and there must be mechanisms for amending rules when they no longer serve their purpose.

4 *Information and transparency* There are three main areas for improvement, (a) information on economic efficiency; (b) transparency as a means of preventing corruption; and (c) publicly available information for policy analysis and debate.

Leftwich (1993, pp.610–11) says that 'good governance' for the World Bank involved 'an efficient public service, an independent judicial system and legal framework to enforce contracts; the accountable administration of public funds; an independent public auditor, responsible to a representative legislature; respect for the law and human rights at all levels of government; a pluralistic institutional structure, and a free press.' He identifies three strands of 'good' governance: (a) systemic (governance is broader than government, involving 'the distribution of both internal and external political and economic power'); (b) political (governance refers to 'a state enjoying both legitimacy and authority, derived from a democratic mandate'); and (c) administrative (governance involves 'an efficient, open, accountable and audited public service which has the bureaucratic competence to help design and implement appropriate policies and manage whatever public sector there is').

The UK's Overseas Development Administration (ODA, 1993, as summarized in Turner & Hulme, 1997, p.231) identified four components of 'good governance':

1 The *legitimacy* of government, which depends on the existence of participatory processes and the consent of those who are governed;

2 The *accountability* of both the political and official elements of government for their actions, depending on the availability of information, freedom of the media, transparency of decision-making and the existence of mechanisms to call individuals and institutions to account;

3 The *competence* of governments to formulate appropriate policies, make timely decisions, implement them effectively and deliver services;

4 Respect for *human rights and rule of law*, to guarantee individual and group rights and security, to provide a framework for economic and social activity and to allow and encourage all individuals to participate.

Kofi Annan (1998, p.123), Secretary General of the United Nations, said: 'UN programs now target virtually all the key elements of good governance: safeguarding the rule of law; verifying elections; training police; monitoring human rights; fostering investment; and promoting accountable administration. Without good governance…, no amount of funding, no amount of charity will set the developing world on the path to prosperity. Member states have increasingly recognized that good governance is indispensable for building peaceful, prosperous and democratic societies.'

central to creating and sustaining an environment which fosters strong and equitable development, and is an essential complement of sound economic policies.' Such 'sound' policies include governments playing 'a key role' in establishing 'the rules that make markets work efficiently' and that 'correct for market failure' (1992, p.1). (For a more general analysis of governance, as distinct from government, see Rhodes, 1997.)

The underlying assumption that runs through the World Bank's position is that for development to succeed in any country there must be sound development management, a well-run market economy and an effective liberal democratic political regime. The connection between 'good governance' and liberal democracy is more explicit in the definitions in Box 17.1 by the Overseas Development Association and the UN, and also Leftwich's summary of the Bank's definition. The whole package came to dominate official western development thinking in the aid agencies and elsewhere in the early 1990s. At the core of the package was the belief that 'good governance' and liberal democracy 'are not simply desirable but *essential conditions for development in all societies*' (Leftwich, 1993, p.605). The neoliberalism of the World Bank's position appeared to relax somewhat in the latter part of the 1990s, for example in their report *The State in a Changing World* (1997) (especially the chapter on 'Bringing the state closer to people'), but they continued generally to advocate 'good governance' within a liberal democratic developmental state.

There were, of course, numerous critics of this 'virtuous cycle' of liberal democratic democratization and 'good governance' as essential for development any time, anywhere. This is clear from the discussion earlier in this chapter summarizing debates over the relation between democratization and development. A central part of the critique was the recognition that there were many different development paths and no single (western) formula for development was likely to work in disparate circumstances. For example, how appropriate was it for foreign donors to insist on 'traditional' government

bureaucracies converting quickly to 'good governance' in the 1990s while conflict and internal war were escalating (Chapter 8) in increasing numbers of countries in Latin America, Asia and Africa? When Julius Jayewardene, a former President of Sri Lanka, was asked by a western consultant why he had failed to bring about civil service reform, he is reported to have replied (Turner & Hulme, 1997, pp 235–6): 'with an ethnic civil war in the North, a youth uprising in the South, my neighbour [India] rattling her sabre, and plummeting commodity prices, do you think I need to set the civil service on fire?' Others asked: Didn't South Korea, Taiwan, Indonesia and Malaysia achieve high levels of economic growth and a developing capacity to meet the welfare needs of increasing numbers of their people when they had public sectors marked by poor or non-existent democratic accountability, 'old fashioned' public administration by public bureaucracies, low levels of transparency and considerable corruption?

By the end of the 1990s, the idea of insisting on a single model of 'good governance' within a liberal democratic developmental state was increasingly being questioned. No one was in favour of 'bad governance', but 'good governance' could have different properties depending on the particular institutional context concerned. Luckham (1998), for example, urged consideration of various 'alternatives to liberal democracy' in poor societies (as in Uganda) within the discourse of good governance and the democratic developmental state; and Gordon White (1998), in one of his last essays, suggested that attention be given to the crafting of various types of developmental states with a more 'social democratic' (rather than liberal democratic) orientation, an enterprise that would need fresh examination of the institutional design of the state, the character of political society (especially the party system) and the character and role of civil society. It seemed likely that at the beginning of the new millennium such considerations would be prominent in the continuing debates about the relationships between democratization, 'good governance' and development.

Summary

Here again are the large questions posed at the beginning of the chapter and brief suggestions as to how to approach the challenge of trying to cope with them.

1 What is democratization? Why has it occurred? In liberal democratic terms, democratization is political movement from less accountable to more accountable government, from less competitive (or non-existent) elections to fuller and fairer elections, from severely restricted to better protected civil and political rights, from weak (or non-existent) autonomous associations to more autonomous and more numerous associations in civil society. There are different theoretical approaches to explaining why democratization occurs. Some give more attention to agency, others to structure. They all tend to refer to seven broad explanatory factors but in different ways: levels and rates of socio-economic development; social divisions of class, élites, ethnicity etc.; historical legacies; the relative power of the state and political institutions within society; the character of civil society; the nature of political cultures and ideas; transnational and international power relationships.

2 Does democratization stimulate development? Not necessarily. In the 1990s the idea that democratization stimulates development was the 'mainstream' view (popular in the World Bank and other aid agencies); democratization, market capitalism and 'good governance' provided a 'virtuous cycle' of core elements in a strategy for development valid for all types of countries. Others argued that democratization can impede development in poor societies due in part to certain limitations in (liberal democratic) democratization which allows powerful conservative interests to thwart egalitarian development initiatives. Yet others have claimed that authoritarian regimes with effective developmental states are better than liberal democracies at stimulating development in poor countries, while still others attempt to demonstrate with evidence that there is actually no direct or systematic causal connection between democratization and development. One important reason why there are such different views is that different definitions of development are being employed.

3 What is 'good governance'? How does it relate to debates about the relation between democratization and development? 'Good governance' is sound management of a country's economic and social resources for development. What is 'sound' for the World Bank and others holding the 'democratization stimulates development' view is a range of management techniques that are believed to work well within a standardized liberal democratic model. Critics contend that there are and ought to be different paths for development; they are not opposed to the idea of 'good governance' but urge that various alternatives to liberal democracy may be desirable for development in poor countries which each have different institutional contexts requiring a different or at least more flexible conception of governance.

18

RETHINKING GENDER MATTERS IN DEVELOPMENT

RUTH PEARSON

We are now some twenty five years on since the birth of 'gender' in the mid 1970s. Since that time the aspirations of the 'new wave' generation of feminists, who were finding their way into international development institutions and agencies as well as finding a voice to insist that women should be 'integrated into the development process', have resulted in an increasingly high profile given to women's issues and gender issues within development policies, programmes and projects. These women have been joined by the new generations of educated and activist women from Southern countries for whom development activity – be it in government departments, NGOs or community organizations, often externally financed by the development agencies based in the North – has become at one time both their labour market and their arena of political activism (Figure 18.1). What can we make of all this?

It is widely accepted in these times that development must be informed by gender analysis and that particular attention must be paid to the needs of poor women – so much so that such positions have become commonplace rather than radical; indeed, many would argue that the ways in which gender matters have been integrated into development thinking and practice indicate a high degree of co-option of politicized feminist objectives rather than their success in transforming the development agenda. Furthermore, feminist theory has taken a distinctly post-modern turn over the last few decades, rejecting the comfortable universal sisterhood of the 1970s for a

Figure 18.1   Tzotzile Indian women at a mass commemorating the 21 women among 45 people killed in the Acteal massacre of 22 December 1997, as part of the International Women's Day activities in the Southern Mexican state of Chiapas, 8 March 1999.

much more complex acknowledgement of social identities and political interests which encompass women's and men's class, age, ethnicity, location, etc. rather than taking gender as a universal reference point for analysis and action. If sisterhood is no longer global what can we make of this enthusiasm for privileging gender in development analysis and policy?

This chapter argues that gender is still a central part of the understanding, and the objective, of development, providing a unique lens with which to deconstruct social institutions and processes, and a never-ending new take on old issues, which has given birth to new aspects of development understanding and international policy. Far from seeing an end to notions of international women's solidarity, gender has provided the building blocks for comprehending the reality of women's lives and the gendered nature of economic, social and political processes.

The chapter is concerned mainly with the following question:

Q How can gender analysis be applied to development?

The first section, however, discusses the relationship between feminism and development co-operation and how that has changed over time. ('Development co-operation' indicates that international institutions and funding are involved in development interventions, often working with government agencies and non-governmental organizations.)

The chapter then traces the dominant approaches to gender and development as a reflection of the changing paradigms of feminist orthodoxy and development analysis. We will see how over the last thirty years there has been a shift from an emphasis on *women* in development (WID) to a broader use of gender analysis: *gender* and development (GAD).

The bulk of the chapter is then taken up with explaining the difference between an emphasis on women (WID) and a broader gender analysis (GAD). This is done by examining some current policy issues in development from a gender perspective, tracing the change from WID to GAD in each case and showing how gender provides a central window on development. To do this Sections 18.3 to 18.5 in turn examine:

- environmental conservation and sustainable development;
- macro-economic policy (structural adjustment);

- work, employment and household subsistence in the context of micro-credit for women and empowerment.

The chapter concludes by reviewing the current enthusiasm for mainstreaming gender in development policies and institutions in terms of whether this represents a genuine integration of gender analysis in development co-operation, or, as some critics have argued, a co-option and neutralization of a politically radical agenda. It also looks at demands to extend the arena of gender analysis of development to men and issues of masculinity in order to tease out the possible future directions of gender and development for the twenty-first century.

18.1 Women and gender: feminism and development institutions

As development co-operation has grown in the decades of the twentieth century, so has the realization that women should be key participants in and beneficiaries of policies, programmes and projects concerned with both poverty eradication and the achievement of social and political improvements in people's lives. The last few decades have seen four World UN Conferences on Women (in Mexico City in 1975, in Copenhagen in 1980, in Nairobi in 1985 and in Beijing in 1995). Far-reaching blueprints have been produced for eliminating discrimination against women (CEDAW) and for ensuring that women's interests and needs are reflected across the whole gamut of the development issues – not just in traditional 'women's' areas of health, family planning and education. Other major international development conferences – including the UN Conference on Environment and Development (UNCED) in Rio (1992), the International Human Rights conference in Vienna (1993), the Population and Development conference in Cairo (1994), the Social Summit in Copenhagen in 1995, Habitat in Ankara (1996) (see Chapter 13) – have been watershed events in terms of the extent to which women's voices were not just heard but incorporated into the final outcomes of these scene-setting events. The major development agencies – multilaterals such as the UN agencies and the European Union and the bilaterals such as DFID (Department for International Development in the UK), CIDA (in Canada) and DANIDA (in Denmark) – include mandatory frameworks for all activities to check that gender is considered even in seemingly neutral projects such as civil engineering works or famine relief. The World Bank – the high denizen of development orthodoxy – has recently accepted a women's monitoring committee to keep 'Women's Eyes on the Bank'.

In many ways then, we could argue that 'gender', in terms of ensuring that women do not get left out of the development process, has triumphed in development. Both development analysis, and the policies that spring from it, are now fully gender balanced, rather than being male biased as in previous decades.

But some critics are sceptical of such claims; they argue that development activity has co-opted gender issues and internalized them into mainstream development activity rather than allowing them fundamentally to challenge ideas and institutions. Others argue that gender as a universalizing framework and reference point has become another manifestation of the ways in which Western (Northern, ex-colonial) priorities and discourses have dominated development activity, a kind of neocolonial imposition on communities and countries where there are other priorities and other understandings of gender difference and gender roles.

So, to understand the extent to which gender really matters in development we need to go back to the underlying questions of gender analysis as it has been applied to development, and the ways in which these ideas have been taken up and operationalized.

Sex and gender

'Gender' rather than 'sex' is the key concept here because we are concerned with the social roles and interactions of men and women rather than their biological characteristics. Gender relations are part of social relations, referring to the ways in which the social categories of men and women,

male and female, relate over the whole range of social organization, not just to interactions between individual men and women in the sphere of personal relationships, or in terms of biological reproduction. In all aspects of social activity, including access to resources for production, rewards or remuneration for work, distribution of consumption, income or goods, exercise of authority and power, and participation in cultural, political and religious activity, gender is important in establishing people's behaviour and the outcome of any social interaction.

As well as interactions between individual men and women, gender relations describe the social meaning of being male and female, and thus what is considered appropriate behaviour or activity for men and women. What is considered male or female work or male or female attributes, behaviour or characteristics, varies considerably between different societies and different historical periods. But it is also important to realize that notions of gender identity, and thus what is fitting for men and women to do or to be, may have a strong ideological context, and one which is very susceptible to changes in dominant political ideology. For instance, in Britain in 1979, with nearly 50% of women of working age in the labour force, Patrick Jenkin, (Conservative) Minister of State for Social Services, claimed: 'Quite frankly, I don't think mothers have the same right to work as fathers do. If the Good Lord had intended equal rights to go out to work, he would not have created men and women. *These are biological facts*' (emphasis added).

However, by the late 1990s, when the ideology of welfare entitlement had changed and the emphasis was on the working poor, mothers, and even single parents with young children, were being urged to work as the following quotation from the then Secretary of State for Social Services, Harriet Harman, demonstrates:

> "Lone mothers say that work is about more than money, though that is important. Work for them means that they do not have to depend on benefits…They want to work so that they can set an example for their children and can bring them up to

understand that life is about work and not just about claiming benefits. They want to work to provide a positive role so that their children can see that work brings independence and self esteem...There is no intention that the New Deal should drive lone mothers with young children out to work...Work and opportunity are at the heart of the Government's approach, and that extends to lone parents..."

(Hansard, 10 December 1997)

In the rural sectors of many low-income countries both men and women often report to census enumerators and researchers that women do not do any productive agricultural work, or they are just involved as family helpers or they carry out only domestic work. In fact, most rural women spend the majority of their waking hours on a diverse series of activities including weeding and harvesting, collecting animal fodder, water and fuel wood, food processing and marketing of agricultural produce (Chapter 5), all of which make a direct economic contribution to the household income as well as to the local agrarian economy.

Because notions of gender roles and activities have such a strong ideological content, policy reflects normative or prescriptive versions of female and male roles rather than the diversity of what men and women actually do. But the real contribution of women as well as men to production and reproduction must be accurately recorded and recognized if development analysis and policies are to become genuinely gender equitable.

However, in spite of the analysis given above, in which it is clear that gender represents a more holistic and socially grounded category than the biological category of sex, the terms have not been accepted without dispute. This was very evident at the 1995 Beijing World Conference on Women, where governments with a well-recognized conservative approach towards maintaining traditional boundaries between men's and women's place and responsibilities in society contested the text of the 'Platform for Action' (Box 18.1).

18.2 From WID to GAD (women or gender): using gender to analyse development

In the 1970s the birth of 'gender' in development was very much influenced by the 'new wave' of feminism in the West which had emerged in the wake of the civil rights and anti-colonial struggles of the 1960s. That decade had also seen the first large-scale expansion of women in higher education, particularly in the USA where many of the international development agencies were located and managed. A logical consequence of this was that now women, and in particular feminist women, were able to obtain employment in the development agencies and apply a feminist critique of economics and other social sciences to the design and practice of development co-operation.

Not all gender advocates within development agencies and organizations would call themselves 'feminists'. Nevertheless they have largely adopted the 1970s feminist notion that, in spite of the fact that women and men are also differentiated by other elements of social identity, including class, race, ethnicity, geographical positioning in the global economy, age, etc., it is useful to employ gender as a major axis of identity and to build policy and analysis on the basis that there are significant commonalities in women's experience. Many of the models for gender planning in development assume that it is quite unproblematic to use women as an analytical category and to integrate gender into development planning and practice by careful, even contextual interpretation of 'women's needs' (Moser, 1993).

Whilst there has been endless debate about whether in practice it is possible to separate 'strategic' from 'practical' interests (Box 18.2), this division does throw some light on the last decade of gender and development practice. For instance, many would argue that policies focused on making it more feasible for women to carry out their gendered responsibilities for the health and welfare of their families, as well as their reproductive activities to do with fertility and childbearing – e.g. improved cooking

Box 18.1   The bracketing of gender in the Platform for Action at Beijing, 1995

'We have to try and neutralize the tremendous amount of gender, gender perspectives, which are going to go directly against our families and against our children' (Speaker on a panel of conservative women at the Fourth UN Conference on Women, Beijing, fringe meeting September 1995).

The Platform for Action which was agreed in September 1995 at the Fourth UN Conference on Women in Beijing was a more highly contested text than any of the other international statements agreed at international conferences – at one point two paragraphs of text alone had generated 31 pages of amendments. Unlike any of these other agreements, debate over the Platform for Action was unique in calling into question the conceptual foundation and subject matter of the conference itself – the concept of gender, and with it notions of the injustice and mutability of gender relations. Was the conference to be about 'sex' or 'gender'? At the first Preparatory meeting in March 1995 in New York, divergent views on this question emerged as country delegations took their last opportunity to signal their reservations over parts of the text prior to the Beijing meeting. Most dramatically, the representative from Honduras, backed by representatives from other Catholic countries, proposed the 'bracketing' of the word 'gender' throughout the text. (This would follow the practice whereby parts of the text of international agreements under negotiation are placed in square brackets – 'bracketed' – to indicate that they are not yet agreed.) A working group eventually resolved on an acceptably broad definition of the term, but the tremendous anxieties over the meaning and implications of the 'gender perspective' illuminate an unexpected politicization of the concept of 'gender' which expressed, in part, aspects of backlash reaction to contemporary feminism. The debates over the word 'gender' also shine light on some contradictions and inconsistencies in feminist theoretical and political distinctions between sex and gender.

It may be that the conservative opposition to the concept expressed second-wind reaction after the failure to prevent agreement at the International Conference on Population and Development in Cairo in 1994 on a broad definition of women's health rights. Other factors explaining the conservative fixation on gender may include the perceived greater influence and presence of feminist NGOs, the greater visibility of lesbians in NGOs and the inclusion, for the first time in the UN series of Conferences on Women, of very open language on sexual and reproductive rights.

The issue of the perceived influence of feminist NGOs became a particularly important target for conservative concern...The conservative challenge to the concept of 'gender' raises central issues for feminist epistemology and politics. How is the body constituted in gendered identity formation? What is the relation between gender identities and political subjectivities? Does sensitivity to gender reveal a concern for equality or a celebration of difference? Does a concern for equity risk assimilating women to the masculine mean? Would a celebration of difference play into the hands of a tradition which has used notions of 'biology is destiny' to explain and justify inequality?

(Baden & Goetz, 1998, p.26)

stoves, supply of domestic water and sanitation, family planning and primary health facilities – are really responding to women's practical interests.

Alternatively, there are policies which address changing gender relations between men and women in developing countries and making it easier for women to challenge traditional and contemporary structures and practices of subordination – such as violence against women and/or discriminatory political structures and regulations. The increasing interest of development agencies in the issue of violence against women can be seen as responding to women's strategic gender interests. It reflects not just the concerns of Northern feminists – who have since the 1970s sought both to make spousal violence and sexual and child abuse matters of public policy debate and priority – but also the aspirations of Southern women to achieve quality and dignity in their domestic lives as well as safety and respect on the streets or in the community (Box 18.3; Figure 18.2).

Box 18.2   Deriving women's strategic and practical needs from an analysis of gender interests

'Planning for low-income women must be based on their interests – in other words, their prioritized concerns. When identifying interests it is useful to differentiate between 'women's interests', strategic gender interests and practical gender interests.' Molyneux (1985) makes the distinction between 'women's interests' and gender interests. The concept of women's interests assumes compatibility of interests based on [the fact of being women]. In reality the position of women in society depends on a variety of different criteria such as class and ethnicity as well as gender. Consequently the interests they have in common may be determined as much by their class position or their ethnic identity as by their biological similarity as women. Women may have general interests in common. But these should be referred to as 'gender interests' to differentiate them from the false homogeneity imposed by the notion of 'women's interests': 'Gender interests are those that women (or men for that matter) may develop by virtue of their social positioning through gender attributes. Gender interests can either be strategic or practical, each being derived in a different way and each involving differing implications for women's subjectivity' (Molyneux, 1985, p.232).

Molyneux's distinction between strategic and practical gender interests is of theoretical significance for gender analysis. For gender planning it is the distinction between strategic and practical gender needs that is important. It is this that provides gender planning with one of its most fundamental planning tools.

Strategic gender needs

Strategic gender needs are the needs women identify because of their subordinate position to men in their society. Strategic gender needs vary according to particular contexts. They relate to gender divisions of labour, power and control and may include such issues as legal rights, domestic violence, equal wages and women's control over their bodies. Meeting strategic gender needs helps women to achieve a greater equality. It also changes existing roles and therefore challenges women's subordinate position.

Strategic gender needs may include all or some of the following:

The abolition of the sexual division of labour; the alleviation of the burden of domestic labour and childcare; the removal of institutionalized forms of discrimination such as rights to own land or property, or access to credit; the establishment of political equality; freedom of choice over childbearing; and the adoption of adequate measures against male violence and control over women (Molyneux, 1985, p.223).

Practical gender needs

Practical gender needs are the needs women identify in their socially accepted roles in society. Practical gender needs do not challenge the gender divisions of labour or women's subordinate position in society although arising out of them. Practical gender needs are a response to immediate perceived necessity, identified within a specific context. They are practical in nature and are often concerned with inadequacies of living conditions such as water provision, health care and employment.

Practical gender needs are those formulated from the concrete conditions women experience [and are] usually a response to an immediate perceived necessity. Because the gender division of labour within the household gives women primary responsibility, not only for domestic work involving child care, family health and food provision, but also for the community managing of housing and basic services, along with the capacity to earn an income through productive work, therefore in planning terms, policies to meet practical gender needs have to focus on the domestic arena, on income-earning activities, and also on community-level requirements of housing and basic services. In reality, basic needs such as food, shelter and water are required by all the family, particularly children. Yet they are identified specifically as the practical gender needs of women [arising out of women's gendered responsibilities for their families and communities].

(Edited extracts from Moser, 1993, pp.35–40)

Box 18.3   Examples of development agencies' interest in violence against women

UNIFEM organizes videoconference to focus world attention on violence against women

"On International Women's Day March 8 1999 a global videoconference was held on the theme 'A World free from Violence against Women' linking UN headquarters to sites in Nairobi, New Delhi, Mexico City and [the] EU parliament in Strasbourg. In New York over two thousand people gathered in the UN General Assembly Hall, including heads and members of UN agencies, and representatives from media, NGOs, governments and the general public. And on every continent across the world, the innovative use of technology helped bring the videoconference to thousands of universities, community centers and other viewing sites, via satellite and internet. The videoconference represents part of a wider inter-agency initiative to highlight the issue of violence against women, and complements regional campaigns in Latin America and the Caribbean, Africa and Pacific Asia. UNIFEM (the UN Development Programme for Women) is now spearheading a follow-up strategy with agency partners to ensure that the heightened awareness is channeled into concrete actions to work towards a world free of gender-based violence."

(UNDP: *Gender Beat*, 12 March 1999, gidp@undp.org)

From a press report of British Prime Minister Tony Blair's visit to South Africa, January 1999

"In the afternoon Mr. Blair and his wife, Cherie, left the capital to visit the Alexandra township near Johannesburg, a black settlement dominated by breeze blocks, barbed wire and a high crime rate. They spent 90 minutes visiting a clinic that houses the National Network on Violence against Women.

One of the women told Mr. Blair that South Africa was the 'rape capital of the world' and Alexandra had one of the worst records in the country, with an estimated 80 per cent of its women having been raped. 'South Africa is the first and third world in one country' she said.

The clinic, which Mr. Blair first visited two years ago, provides counselling for victims. He announced £1.9 million in aid for the women's organization and a related project called Soul City, a television production company that produces a soap opera that carries anti-violence messages…

As he left to return to Pretoria he passed a slogan saying: 'Women of Africa won't be beaten'.

(*The Guardian*, Friday January 8, 1999)

Figure 18.2   British Prime Minister Tony Blair and his wife with the manager and co-ordinator of a local NGO which deals with abused women and children, during a visit to a clinic in Alexandra Township, South Africa, 7 January 1999.

In the words of women's groups participating in struggles for the restoration of civilian rule in the last years of the military dictatorship in Chile in the late 1980s: 'Democracía en el país y en la casa' (Democracy in the home as well as in the country).

The term 'Women in Development' (WID) came out of a Washington-based network of women development professionals, which began to challenge 'trickledown' theories of development, arguing that modernization was impacting differently on men and women. Instead of improving women's rights and status, the development process was at best bypassing them and at worst contributing to a deterioration in women's position in developing countries. Hence WID lobbied for the 1973 Percy Amendment to the US Foreign Assistance Act which required development aid from the USA to help 'integrate women into the national economies of foreign countries, thus improving their status and assisting the development effort.'

The early and successful efforts to 'integrate women into the development process' (Boserup, 1970) were based on an analysis which was concerned that women were being excluded from the development process. This approach, although motivated by an analysis which acknowledged women's subordination, tended to concentrate on 'women's lack of access to resources as the key to their subordination without raising questions about the role of gender relations in restricting [that] access in the first place' (Razavi & Miller, 1995a, p.12).

However, through the 1980s and 1990s the WID approach has been criticized and broadened, in two stages. First, the 'women and development' position (known as WAD) arose in the 1970s from a questioning (led by Southern feminists) of the WID notion that it was the *exclusion* of women from the development process rather than the *process* which was the problem. The international network Development Alternatives for Women in a New Era (DAWN) had made a critique of development policy which ignored the structural constraints faced by low- and middle-income countries. This was extended to an analysis which argued that unless the very models of development themselves were transformed into a more holistic and equitable approach there could be no justice or equality for Southern women (Sen & Grown, 1988).

Second, the distinction between (biological) sex, and gender (which had a social and cultural origin) was increasingly being put into operation to challenge the existing social norms and positioning of women and men. This has led to the problematizing of gender relations and the ways in which they impact on development initiatives and the gendered processes of development policies themselves. This approach, known as GAD (gender and development) has been taken forward and applied to a range of development policies and practices. The following sections illustrate the shift from WID to GAD in a number of policy areas.

18.3 Policy case study A: Environmental conservation[a]

A major concern of development policy and analysis in the 1990s was the issues raised by environmental degradation. Like gender and development, environment has also become a 'cross cutting issue' in development discourses. Mainly (and over-narrowly) it has focused on natural (renewable) resources and the tension between exploitation for commercial use or subsistence livelihoods and future conservation of quality and stock of resources over time. There has been relatively little concern to date with issues of pollution, public health, and the urban environment.

Because of the focus on natural resources, there has been a link between women and nature, in both a spiritual and a conceptual sense. Initially of Northern origin, ecofeminism has an increasingly vocal international presence –

[a] Edited extracts in this section are from Green, C., Joekes, S. & Leach, M. (1998) 'Questionable links: approaches to gender in environmental research and policy', in Jackson, C. & Pearson, R. (eds), *Feminist Visions of Development: gender analysis and policy*, pp.271–8, Routledge, London.

for example, through the work of Indian writer Vandana Shiva. Ecofeminism has developed a critique of the:

> "dominant model of development which is perceived as a male construct which has promoted economic development in ways which have been harmful both to women and to the environment by trampling alternative, local knowledge, especially women's knowledge, associated with organic conceptions of people and nature as interconnected; by disregarding the spiritual and sacred in people's attitudes to their environment and women's special role therein; and by overriding holistic and harmonious practices. [Ecofeminists] insist that the feminine principle is not quite extinct in the environmental context but still manifest in a residual, near instinctual wisdom which some women have been able to retain in the face of developmental pressures…'[T]hird world women' are portrayed as the last bastion of feminine environmental wisdom and they provide the key to its retrieval."

> (Green *et al.*, 1998, p.273)

Ecofeminist arguments exclude analysis of gender or of men, whilst bringing to the foreground the importance to social survival of women's provisioning activities for household sustenance and survival. As unpaid reproductive labour rather than productive activities these are ascribed high spiritual value as feminine nurturing and caring activities. These views are widely reflected in the positions and documents of many environmentalist movements in both the North and the South and in the preambles of many donor and NGO documents as justification for special women's projects. In policy terms 'ecofeminist' recommendations are similar to those drawing from the idea of 'women as environmental managers' or 'women, environment and development' (WED). Policy-makers are urged to identify women and the prime agents of environmental conservation, and to prioritize women-only projects (Green *et al.*, 1998, pp.273–4).

> "Community and joint forest management [have been widely promoted]…as a way to build up local people's incentives for sustainable forestry. Many such programmes continue to ignore women, focusing on an 'undifferentiated' community. In others women and women's groups have become a special target group and institutional focus for activities in woodlot planting, rehabilitation or protection…[S]ocial or community forestry projects have highlighted the importance of secure tenure in creating incentives for planting or conservation, specifically the rights of women to land and trees, and donor policy documents now commonly echo this concern. Related to this is an attempt to increase women's incentives for participating in social forestry by improving their access to extension services, to technical forestry training and to markets for forest products…i.e. to put incentives to make conservation a 'rational choice' for women."

> (Green *et al.*, 1998, p.262)

This was a recognition of the role of trees and forest products in the household economy, the role of women in their collection and the specific knowledge they have – and a welcome advance on women's complete invisibility in forestry activities. But it was very much the WID approach – to mobilize women's labour input into forestry projects and benefit from their specific management skills and knowledge about forestry projects. There is little concern with the time, energy expenditure and other opportunity costs of women's involvement in such projects – women's labour is simply seen as a flexible input into, for example, community woodlots, ignoring the fact that this may mean that women switch time and effort, perhaps from independent crops which might offer them independent income. At the same time women are rarely involved in project planning or management at higher level and their interests are rarely heard. For example, in India and Ethiopia in recent years authorities have frequently closed off newly forested areas to allow regeneration of trees, cutting women off from their major sources of firewood either for domestic production or for subsistence income.

The WED approach highlights the specific relationship women have with the environment as the main 'users' and 'managers' of natural resources at the local level. It starts with an acceptance of gender roles and gender division of labour and focuses on women who are hewers of fuelwood and haulers of water and who play a major (if unacknowledged) role as cultivators (Green *et al.*, p.271). Like WID itself WED focuses on women, rather than on gender relations and men's gendered resource-related activities. It pays no attention to class and other differences between women. However, the emphasis of WED discussions has shifted over time. In the early 1980s women were commonly portrayed as the primary victims of environmental degradation, bearing the brunt of pollution and deforestation and the major responsibility for coping with problems such as drought. Natural resource degradation was seen as undermining women's ability to perform their sustenance roles and imposing increasing costs in terms of time and energy. In the late 1980s women came to be seen less as 'victims' and more as efficient environmental managers and conservers of natural resources. There was evidence that women were heavily engaged world-wide, according to the terms of local agro-ecological practices in environmental protection and rehabilitation; building conservation terraces, planting trees and dealing with seeds and wild plants to safeguard biodiversity. However, this is rather a universalizing picture and such conceptual simplifications lead to simplistic policy proposals: for example, that women are to be incorporated into programme activities; and that women's community groups are the appropriate vehicles for community environmental actions.

The WED approach has been taken up by the World Bank and others and assimilated into the literature on community-based approaches to sustainable development which is widely advocated by NGOs and donors. But clearly this approach is not concerned with intrahousehold gendered negotiation over labour inputs, or control and distribution of outputs, or the complex gendered relations of tenure and access to forested land and the ways in which major donors have advocated privatization of previously commonly held property.

A GAD analysis, however, draws back from the essentialist view that women have a particular and unchanging relationship with nature or a constant gendered responsibility for natural environmental and resource conservation. Instead it focuses on the ways in which women's and men's relationship with the environment are seen to emerge from the dynamic social context of gender relations.

If certain women are closely involved with natural resources, this may reflect gender-derived roles and lack of any other economic opportunity, rather than any inherent caring relationships; for instance, women may gather tree food products from communally managed land partly because they lack access to income from trees on private holdings. Moreover, women may, because they are locked into environmental resource dependence and deprived of access to more lucrative activities, have little incentive for environmental sustainability or improvement. Their preference may be to move into other areas of production, as they see men do.

Feminist environmentalism challenges the implication that women and men are homogeneous groups and acknowledges that different groups of women have different relationships (e.g. to firewood or water collection) depending on whether or not they are the ones with primary responsibility for collecting it. It extends the concern about gender division of activities to gendered relations of tenure and property. It is control over resources, products and decision-making which shapes people's interaction with environmental resources. A GAD analysis also points to the danger for women of policies which divert women's effort without remuneration to 'community' environmental conservation activities, which can reduce their own access to income and production and exacerbate existing gendered differences in time and work patterns within households.

18.4 Policy case study B: Gender analysis of structural adjustment – from vulnerable groups to male bias

In 1987 UNICEF published an important critique of the macro-economic policies which were being advocated by the Washington institutions (the World Bank and the IMF) as the route for indebted countries to reorientate themselves to the current parameters of the global market (see Chapter 13).

UNICEF's critique (Cornia *et al.* 1987), published under the title of *Adjustment with a Human Face*, was based on the observation that these policies required factors of production, including labour, to respond to changes in market incentives by relocating their sphere of activity to more efficient and profitable activities. UNICEF noted that there were certain groups in society which were less able or totally unable to respond effectively to changed market incentives. These groups were vulnerable not only because they were unable to sustain an adequate livelihood, despite the reorientation of the economy to more productive activities to meet their basic needs, but also because the new policies of imposing user charges for basic services, especially health and education, meant that they were being forced to cover a larger share of the costs of their reproduction than in the pre-adjustment era, when these services, although limited, had been available free. In other words they were suffering not just from income poverty but from exclusion from basic necessary services.

Given the concern about the feminization of poverty and the preponderance of women and female-headed households amongst poorest groups (see Section 18.4 below), not surprisingly UNICEF identified women, or rather mothers and young children, as the groups most vulnerable to economic adjustment programmes. It was argued that these were necessary in broad macro-economic terms, but must be given a 'human face' to protect the vulnerable:

"Can poor countries afford to be concerned with human welfare when their economic resources are so constrained?…There are three reasons for not postponing attention to human needs. In the first place, the basic health, nutritional and educational needs of the most vulnerable groups – the under 5s, pregnant women and nursing mothers – are urgent and compelling. If neglected they can set back the health and welfare of the whole future generation of a country, in addition to adding to present human and economic miseries. Secondly there is considerable evidence that there are positive economic returns to interventions supporting basic nutrition, health and education…And thirdly human welfare and progress is the ultimate end of all development policy."

(Cornia *et al.*, 1987, p.6)

Underlining the challenge this view offered to current orthodoxy which assumed that benefits of economic growth would trickle down to people at the lowest end of the income distribution, the authors comment that 'It takes a particular form of economic abstraction to believe that this goal [of achieving basic needs and human welfare for all] is achieved in the long run without specific attention to the human issues in the short run' (ibid.).

The UNICEF view is congruent with the WID view in seeing the vulnerability of women to adjustment in terms of the gendered roles and responsibilities of poor women, particularly in the reproductive and child-caring years. Moreover, as the report argued, to protect women and mothers of small children would be to make an investment in a country's human capital and thus in its economic future.

The policy response to this analysis was the suggestion of specific adjustment loans to provide special safety nets for those population groups which were unable to respond to the necessary structural changes in the economies. This included provision of basic health and literacy programmes and income safety net support delivered through food for work or other parallel labour markets. This is still the approach taken by the multilateral agencies (Chu & Gupta, 1998). The UNICEF position can be read as arguing that the economic policies themselves are gender neutral, but the impact of these policies is likely to have a greater effect on women, because of their gendered position as mothers and nurturers.

The GAD approach was more complicated. This approach started from a gender critique of the assumptions behind the economic models underlying structural adjustment policies (SAPs), arguing that far from being gender neutral they are in fact male biased, because of the gendered nature of the assumptions in the models, and the way in which gender relations are embedded in the economic processes which result from the policies:

> "[T]hree kinds of male bias are at work: male bias concerning the sexual division of labour, male bias concerning the unpaid domestic work necessary for producing and maintaining human resources and male bias concerning the social institution which is the source of the supply of labour – the household."
>
> (Elson, 1995, p.168)

Unravelled these three accusations of bias present a cogent case against the gendered nature of SAPs. The first relates to rigidities in the sexual division of labour. These include not only the pattern of work allocation between women and men that can be empirically observed at any moment of time but also the social practices that constitute some sorts of work as suitable for women but unsuitable for men, and other sorts of work as unsuitable for women but suitable for men (Elson, 1995, p.168). These give rise to obstacles to switching labour, particularly women's labour, from subsistence to commodity and exportable production. For example, although there has been very high growth of women's employment in the nontraditional export of fruits and vegetables from sub-Saharan Africa, the availability of women for such work is also constrained by their responsibilities for child care and other family duties. Moreover, women's productivity and willingness to work in such activities is also partly determined by the extent to which they, rather than male heads of households, have control over the income generated by such production. This is an issue which has beleaguered attempts to increase agricultural exports in many countries in the region (Dolan, 1999).

The second issue is the implication of adjustment for women's unpaid domestic and reproductive work. If commodity prices were increased by withdrawal of subsidies on basic goods, if state and community health and education services were cut back and access restricted by user charges, if progress on providing potable water or adequate sanitation and drainage is curtailed by ceilings on public expenditure – what are the implications of these changes for women's unpaid work for the family? Although UNICEF may acknowledge that protection of the young is investment in human capital they fail to point out that human capital does not grow itself. There is now extensive evidence that cutbacks in health expenditure, for example, have had a specific gendered impact. Not only have the services which women relied on to support them in their biological reproduction work – child clinics, prenatal and maternity care, etc. – been reduced, resulting in women having to travel further and pay more to get treatment for themselves and their families, but women also have to supplement the publicly provided services with their own labour – in nursing care, feeding the sick and disabled. Furthermore the asymmetry of power within household decision-making means that women's health needs do not have priority in terms of allocation of time and income, which are resources in short supply. Inadequacies in the supply of clean water and sanitation lead to more domestic work for women in trying to shield their families and themselves from potential diseases. As food prices soar women substitute their own time and energy into buying unprocessed food for home processing, buying cheaper foodstuffs such as coarse grains and root crops and generally economizing on household expenditure by replacing it with their own time and energy. (Soon after the Mexican peso was massively devalued in 1995, the PRI ruling party issued a pamphlet aimed at housewives urging them to economize by making nutritional meals from cheap ingredients; recipes were provided, reminiscent of war-time Britain.) By treating women's time as if it was infinitely elastic, SAPs assume implicitly if not explicitly that women's time and energy will serve as a buffer to maintain human capital and ensure survival of vulnerable households by stretching their unpaid work and effort to compensate for deteriorating economic conditions. But as Moser's studies on Ecuador illustrate, the process of re-allocating labour under adjustment polices places severe stress on women's ability to cope with the process of human resource production and maintenance, something that macro-models assume can safely be taken for granted: 'Not all women can cope under crisis and it is necessary to stop romanticizing their infinite capacity to do so' (cited in Elson, 1995, p.180).

The third issue concerns gender bias in the household. The problem here stems from the inability of conventional policies to understand the gendered nature of negotiation and exchange within households. Although the UNICEF study complains that SAPs rarely were informed by household-based data and analysis, in fact, by treating the household as an homogeneous – and closed – unit, erroneous assumptions are made about the ways in which economic policies affect poor people. For instance, the changes in the supply of agricultural labour discussed above are very much affected by the fact that in many sub-Saharan African communities income is not pooled between all members of the family and men and women's earnings are channelled to different kinds of expenditure. Women normally have responsibility for daily consumption items such as food; men may take responsibility for more durable items such as clothing, household equipment, or even school fees. In addition there is extensive evidence that 'women's income is almost exclusively used to meet household needs, whereas men tend to retain a considerable portion of their income for personal spending' (Elson, 1995, p.183). So economic incentive

– such as agricultural wage levels in export sectors for example – will be mediated by what happens to such income within the household. Moreover, in conditions in which household real income is being squeezed by the various elements of adjustment polices, there may be very different perceptions of priorities for expenditure from reduced household income. It is not just that women tend to prioritize maintaining adequate levels of food, clothing, schooling materials and household maintenance. Men's and women's perceptions of what is an adequate level or even what the maintenance of such levels actually costs can differ considerably. Such conflicts can result in increased stress, intrahousehold conflict and even violence, and women are generally those who suffer most from such situations.

The GAD approach went on to suggest that the response to these three forms of male bias should be to challenge the division between the paid (productive) economy and the unpaid (reproductive) economy and to insist that economic models should take into account the interaction between them. Adjustments if necessary could be gender aware; specific public expenditure reviews should be made in the knowledge of how changes in public expenditure would affect men and women in terms of employment and access to services, and the implications for the reproductive burden of women and their ability and that of men to enter into or extend their productive roles.

The GAD approach also stimulated other gendered reviews of macro-economic policies – e.g. the different implications of taxation and subsidies for men and women and the different allocations of income paid to women and men in terms of wages and salaries and transfer payments. It has long been recognized that women have a higher propensity to spend income on goods and services which enhance family welfare, whereas there is a higher 'leakage' from men's earnings into non-family expenditure (including alcohol and entertainment). This information has influenced the campaign in the UK to prevent child benefit payments being changed from being paid directly to the adult carer (usually the mother) to being integrated into a tax credit or money benefit to the working parent (often the father) (Women's Budget Group, 1998). The information has also been used to argue that women and men also may have a different marginal propensity to import so that redistribution of income between men and women can also affect the balance of payments of a country's economy (Catagny *et al.*, 1995).

Gender analysis of structural adjustment has had two outcomes. First, it has forced the leading institutions such as the World Bank to acknowledge the importance of understanding how gender relations will affect the efficacy of the implementation of SAPs. This applies to intrahousehold gender relations affecting decision-making and transfers, as well as to gendered patterns of labour demand and supply in the wider sphere of production of goods and services (World Bank, 1993). Secondly, it has also been an important factor in the shift of the Washington consensus away from a narrowly short-term production efficiency view of macro-economic adjustment. There is now greater understanding of the importance of human capital in long-term development and the centrality of non-marketable activities, including health, education and shelter. These are now recognized as important not only in terms of the reproduction of labour as a factor of production but also in their direct impact on the overall welfare of people as the result of the development process.

This kind of analysis leaves open a re-appraisal of the domestic division of labour as well as gender segregation in the paid labour force and the differences in money remuneration for male and female labour in the wider economy. It has also led to a wide-ranging international debate about the ways in which national accounting could be reformulated to reflect the value of women's unpaid domestic and other work for the whole economy. As a result there is a demand for the production of satellite accounts which not only reveal the negative effect of certain kinds of economic activity which cause pollution or disease but also show the positive contribution of reproductive work hitherto excluded from the notion of the economic (Waylen, 1997).

18.5 Policy case study C: Gender analysis of micro-credit and women's empowerment

Micro-credit has become a very popular tool of poverty alleviation in the 1990s and is our third example about the widespread adoption of a WID approach to gender and development, and the different and more complicated picture given by applying a gender analysis approach.

Delivery of credit to small-scale farmers in many developing countries has long been subsidized by development agencies, but such subsidized interventions were heavily criticized in the 1980s when market-based solutions became the dominant orthodoxy in development policy. However, in recent years there has been a strong revival in the use of micro-enterprise credit as a key anti-poverty strategy. The argument has been that money markets are distorted by a range of exploitative social relationships and that making small amounts of credit available to poor people will provide the 'missing link' in enabling them to build up petty trading and allied businesses and cover their subsistence needs (McKee, 1989).

The Grameen Bank model is perhaps one of the best known examples of micro-credit targeted at poor households. It is a fast-growing rural bank, which has diversified into a range of other financial services and business support activities. Grameen, in Bangladesh, pioneered the group collateral model which has been widely replicated and adapted in countries of the North as well as the South (Pearson, 1998).

Grameen, like other micro-credit programmes in developing countries, has long acknowledged that the majority of its borrowers are women. Although not specifically designed as a women-targeted policy, access to credit has come to be identified by donors, project designers and implementors alike as an approach which is able to empower women at the same time as facilitating women's productive economic activities.

Professor Yunus of the Grameen Bank claims:

"Credit has the capacity to create self employment for both men and women instantaneously. It brings a woman into the income stream without the usual sacrifices required under a wage-employment situation. She does not have to leave her habitat and her children. She does not have to learn a new skill to adapt herself to a new job. She can do whatever she does best and earn money for it. Credit frees both poor men and poor women, but does so more dramatically for women than for men."

(Yunus, 1992, cited in Mayoux, 1998)

Many observers maintain that the prominence of women in micro-credit projects derives from the fact that

"women as a group are consistently better in promptness and reliability of repayment. Targeting women as clients of Microcredit programmes has also been a very effective method of ensuring that the benefits of increased income accrue to the general welfare of the family, particularly the children. At the same time women themselves benefit from the higher status they achieve when they are able to provide new income."

(Results, 1997, cited in Mayoux, 1998)

The rationale for targeting micro-credit programmes towards women – because they are likely to be more reliable as borrowers, because increased income is more likely to accrue to the family and especially children, and because income generation carried out by women is likely to enhance their status in the family and community – is essentially a WID position. It parallels the arguments around women as nurturers of the environment and women as a vulnerable group in adjustment programmes set out above. This position focuses on resources and policies targeted at women and proceeds to analyse them not in terms of improving women's gendered position or transforming gender relations but in terms of the ways in which credit might successfully allow concerned donors to provide appropriate resources to poor households. Such an analysis by ignoring gender relations ignores the opportunity costs for women of additional work in income-generating activities alongside the necessity to maintain other domestic and productive work. It ignores the implications for

women of potential conflict within the household as the result of changes in women's access to financial resources and income-earning opportunities. It ignores the possibility that women's dependence on men is increased rather than diminished because of their responsibility for additional debts and repayment burdens (Rogaly, 1996).

In fact, the implications for women of becoming the 'beneficiaries' of targeted micro-credit programmes are complicated and vary according to the context and nature of prevailing gender relations in the community and wider society. In the case of South Asia some authors have argued that giving credit to women does not diminish intrahousehold gender conflict or increase women's autonomy over economic activities. On the contrary, their research indicates that most of the credit ends up in activities controlled by male household members and women retain just the actual social and moral responsibility of repayment (Goetz & Gupta, 1996). Other researchers take a more long-term view, arguing that domestic violence tends to diminish over time for women whose experience of economic activity and more prominent and visible contribution to household income gives them more authority and assertiveness in their domestic roles (Schuler et al., 1996). Kabeer (1998) disputes the conclusions of earlier research, arguing that credit-supported enterprises in Bangladesh increase women's voice in intrahousehold decision-making and improve the quality of intrahousehold spousal relationships, resulting in a diminution of family violence. She argues that many women value the ability to work on their home-based enterprises rather than as casual waged labour in the homes or fields of more wealthy people.

These analytical approaches, whilst not reaching a unified conclusion, set out to analyse the implications of micro-credit for women through the lens of gender. They problematize, rather than take for granted, the impact of such policy interventions on women's position. Firstly they discuss the personal sense of self-worth resulting from women's increased economic participation and visible contributions to household income. Secondly they posit a change in women's favour in the balance between co-operation, obligation and dependency within intra-household relationships and networks which can improve women's bargaining power in financial as well as social terms. Thirdly they throw open the possibility for changes in the ways in which poor women relate to the rest of the community (Figure 18.3), manifested in the ability to find alternatives to the deeply class-subordinating and dependent relationships implied in having no alternative but to seek survival wages from the casual work of 'superior' households. Such analyses of micro-credit reflect the relational approach of GAD to micro-credit; they also warn against simplistic assumptions which conflate gender and poverty approaches and analyses, an issue which is taken up in the next section.

18.6 Meeting women's practical and strategic needs – mainstreaming or co-option of gender in development

There was much discussion in the 1990s about the need to distinguish between the *needs* of poor women, in terms of their gendered responsibili-

ties for household survival and reproduction, and the *issues* surrounding the importance of supporting women to challenge gender relations (meaning that women and girls have less access than men and boys to the scarce resources and services available to the poor in developing countries). This distinction was referred to earlier as the difference between practical and strategic gender interests and needs, and is useful for understanding the kinds of policy appropriate for improving women's position *vis à vis* men and in improving their material conditions.

This distinction has often been lost in discussions of anti-poverty strategies, which have tended to focus on the concentration of women amongst the poorest groups in society at the expense of applying a gender analysis to the causes of poverty and the effectiveness of poverty elimination strategies. Whilst development is still very largely and rightly seen in terms of international structural and political inequalities and the ways in which these are reflected in people's lives, the fact is that gender is an important predictor of whether a person is 'poor' (however that is measured – see Chapter 1). But this welcome recognition of the 'feminization of poverty' (that women tend to be disproportionately represented among the lowest income groups of whatever

Figure 18.3   A women's group from the League for Education and Development, India, a women's micro-finance initiative. LEAD's mission is 'To create a fair, just and gender sensitive society by people's own initiative'.

economy or society, or indeed that 'the poorer the family the more likely it is to be headed by a woman'; World Bank, 1989, cited in Jackson, 1998) should not blind us to the fact that although most of the poor are women, structures of gender subordination cannot be reduced to poverty, nor can poverty analysis and policy be focused only on women. Both require an analysis based on the dynamic social processes of gender relations.

The 'feminization of poverty' represents the WID analysis of gender and poverty and its associated focus on women-headed households. Applying a GAD approach reveals several problems with this.

For example, one measure of poverty in many countries is whether individuals achieve certain levels of food consumption. However, measures and policies are both frequently organized on a household basis, which ignore intrahousehold gender inequalities of food access and distribution. The apparently increasing masculine population ratios in South Asian countries reflect a widespread son preference, which includes in many communities systematic discrimination in the allocation of food, health care and other scarce resources (Box 18.4). Of course such differences endanger girls significantly more the poorer the household is, and thus the more crucial the marginal differences in boy/girl food allocation. All the more reason, therefore, for poverty-focused food security programmes to understand and work with a detailed knowledge of the dynamics of intrahousehold food allocations rather than with undifferentiated notions of household and intrahousehold entitlements. Also, if the gendered needs of poor women are conceptualized only in terms of material provision of food, other causes of excess female mortality and morbidity (such as (non) accidental injury, differential access to health care, and prioritizing of food for male infants and children over their sisters) may be ignored.

Box 18.4 Sex ratios of population

It is commonplace to say that women are half the population, but on a world-wide basis women constitute more than 50% of the population. This is because of a variety of factors: although 'naturally' more male infants are born in any population, they have a higher rate of perinatal mortality, are prone to higher wastage in young adulthood, and are susceptible to fatal diseases. So in spite of women's propensity to suffer high rates of morbidity and mortality related to reproduction, including maternal mortality, demographic statistics indicate that in most countries women form the majority of any given population. The UN figures record that 'natural' sex ratios are about 106 females per 100 males. Any significant deviation from this, particularly population sex ratios which indicate majority of males in the population, is considered to indicate social practices which cause excess female mortality, which can be related to specific age cohorts recorded. But in much of South and West Asia such sex ratios have long been recorded. The Indian picture is particularly interesting. Census figures indicate that the sex ratio of the population became increasingly masculine. In 1929 there were 1029 males per thousand females. By 1981 there were 1073, a slight fall from the 1971 figures. However, in spite of expectations that the trend was finally falling the 1991 Census indicated another rise to 1080. The increase in masculinization was particularly significant in the 0–6 years age cohort, indicating a range of practices including son preference, and sex-selective foetal and perinatal mortality associated with falling fertility levels.

The Indian story is complicated – there are differences between the sex ratios of northern and southern states; there are various arguments about the significance of women's economic participation, education, prosperity, ethnic status, etc. But what is interesting to note is that a rise in per capital income which has certainly been the case in India over the last 80 years has not led to a more balanced population sex ratio. And that should alert us to the fact that gender equity is not simply a matter of economic change and modernization. Deeply entrenched cultural practices linked to religious, social and economic issues mean that for many women, not just in India, biology is indeed still destiny.

(Data from Harriss & Watson, 1987; Basu, 1999)

Such practices may be the result of discriminatory cultural practices but it should be recognized that patterns of gender difference in food distribution are widespread and socially enforced by both men and women. The issue is not about blaming men for masculine advantage, or indeed blaming women as mothers and wives for enforcing unequal distribution of food or other resources. The problem is to understand the ways in which gender norms and roles are reinforced and perpetuated and what opportunities exist for changing these practices and the inequitable outcomes they lead to.

Gender mainstreaming

The widespread enthusiasm for applying gender analysis to all aspects of development, rather than just to women or women's issues, has been termed 'gender mainstreaming'. It was a response to the slow progress of 'integrating women into the development process' achieved by women-targeted policies and projects and the gender machinery of ministries for women's affairs and women's bureaux since the 1970s. Such policies, which were responding to a WID agenda, had created 'gender ghettos' and it was decided that a new strategy of integration was required.

The new strategy was to mainstream gender into general development policies, programmes and projects in order to counteract the tendency for women's concerns and gender issues to become marginalized, underfunded and ignored by the 'real' development experts and activities. Instead of separate agencies or ministries, many development organizations set up WID focal points, departments or units which were mandated with institutionalizing gender issues in the organization's work. Indeed it became a commonplace assertion that to have earmarked funds or offices for women's concerns was old-fashioned and ineffective and that gender issues were to be taken into account across the whole gamut of an organization's activity. Nevertheless, in many development organizations, as well as academic courses and analysis, the gendered culture of organizations has resisted the attempt to move gender issues from the margin to the centre (Razavi & Miller, 1995b).

In this section, mainstreaming refers to the insistence that gender issues, often meaning women's issues, should be placed at the heart of all development policies and practices. But another way in which we can understand 'mainstreaming' is to de-link the exclusive association of gender with women, whether from a WID or a GAD perspective, and concentrate on the 'other' gender. And this means talking about men.

Gender matters: women or men, women and men

With the – albeit contested – success in integrating gender issues in development, there has been increasing concern that gender should reflect the perspectives of men as well as women. It is argued that the concentration on women and the neglect of men and masculinity has impoverished gender analysis and diminished its radical and transformatory potential in development. In recent years social scientists have turned their attention to problematizing men and masculinity in advanced countries in the face of seemingly intractable problems including: high unemployment, low labour and educational attainment of young men, an increase in irresponsible social behaviour including drug-taking, criminality and sexual irresponsibility, and the breakdown of the traditional family.

Gender and development analysts have also challenged the particular roles and interests of men in the development process. Rather than simply seeing a generic notion of men and masculinity as the root cause of women's subordination, researchers have begun to focus on the problematic and multiple roles of men (as biological fathers, economic providers, social parents and community representatives), and the ways in which changes in men's ability and desire to fulfil these roles pose challenges for men themselves as well as for women. New thinking about men's roles and responsibilities in family planning and family nurturing, about burdens of time and work for subsistence and survival, and about domestic violence and community safety, has demanded the contribution of men as being part of the solution as well as part of

> **Box 18.5 'Missing masculinity: bringing men into gender and development'**
>
> One of the most obvious gaps in gender and development studies, where new tools and new approaches are needed, is in relation to men. Old-style feminist theory dealt with them at a stroke: men were classed as the problem, those who stood in the way of positive change. And while feminist activism stressed change in attitudes and behavior on the part of women in coming forward to claim their rights, it offered little more to men than a serious of negative images of masculinity. Only by abandoning those attributes which are culturally valued and associated with masculinity could men reprieve themselves. It is hardly any wonder that many men found this difficult. Not only were they told that they should give up position which put them at an advantage, they were left without anything to value about being men...
>
> [It has been argued that] although there are many ways of being a man, some are valued more than others and men experience social pressure to conform to dominant ideas about being a man. They termed this 'hegemonic masculinity'. [This concept] is most valuable in showing that it is not men per se but certain ways of being and behaving that are associated with dominance and power. In each cultural
>
> context, the way in which masculinity is associated with power varies...[And] in each cultural context there is a range of available models of masculinity and femininity. Not all men benefit from and subscribe to dominant values. 'Hegemonic masculinity' can be just as oppressive for those men who refuse, or fail to conform. Yet these men are often implicitly excluded from being part of processes of changing and confronting gender inequality because they are male...
>
> If gender is to be everybody's issue then we need to find constructive ways of working with men as well as with women to build the confidence to do things differently...it is time to move behind the old fixed ideas about gender roles and about universal male domination. Time to find ways of thinking about and analysing gender that make sense of the complexity of people's lives...Taking complexity seriously does not mean that we need to abandon completely fundamental feminist concerns with women's rights. where we do need to be careful is in confusing strategic arguments about women or men in general with the everyday experiences of real women and men.
>
> (Extracted from Cornwall, 1997)

the problem. Interestingly, whilst most of these 'male' issues in development revolve around biological and social reproduction, there is little response from mainstream development analysis and thinking which tends still to focus on the 'economic' (and thus productive rather than reproductive) development activities. But this discussion has raised, both for development theory and practice, the need to replace an overweening notion of 'hegemonic masculinities' with an understanding that it is not men per se but certain ways of being and behaving that are associated with dominance and power, and that these will vary with cultural, economic and social context (Cornwall, 1997; Box 18.5).

18.7 Conclusion

It may have appeared that underneath the debate about the significance and priority of ad-

dressing gender policy to women's practical or strategic needs is an argument that practical issues, based on material needs of poor women, are in some ways less 'feminist' than those that address underlying inequalities between men and women, regardless of the priorities articulated by Southern women themselves. However, most commentators now acknowledge that this is rather a sterile debate since both kinds of activities are linked and often inseparable (Molyneux, 1998). It remains important to stress that the initial political motivation for insisting that women's perspectives and priorities are included in development policy and practice was related to a commitment to seeking equity and empowerment for women as well as the necessity of meeting the basic needs of poor women.

At the beginning of the twenty-first century, the central place of gender issues and gender analysis at the heart of development policy and practice is no longer disputed. The prime importance of understanding gender relations and the ways in which they intersect with markets, with civil society, with organizations, with state structures and state services, with anti-poverty strategies and with resource management and conservation has been amply demonstrated as the examples in this chapter illustrate. What is still contested is the extent to which this very success has led, and will lead, to a de-politicization of the fierce feminist passion which propelled gender matters into the centre of the development stage. Will gender analysis be left to contribute to the technical efficacy of policy interventions rather than the emancipatory transformation of the development agenda itself?

Summary

1   Gender analysis has become widely accepted as part of development thinking and practice. Here 'gender' rather than 'sex' is the key concept, indicating concern with the social interactions of women and men rather than their biological characteristics.

2   An important (though not clear-cut) distinction is made between women's practical gender interests and strategic gender interests (or needs). The former relate to the needs of women within their gendered roles; the latter to their interest in changing structures or practices of gender subordination and discrimination.

3   In the 1970s there was a successful attempt to integrate a focus on women into development policies (the Women in Development 'WID' approach). From the 1980s the WID approach has been criticized for dealing only with women's practical gender needs and a broader approach has been suggested based on a gender analysis of development policies and processes as well as challenging existing gender roles (the Gender and Development 'GAD' approach).

4   The implications of a shift from WID to GAD are illustrated in three policy areas: environmental conservation, structural adjustment, and micro-credit and women's empowerment. In each case WID focuses on women – as traditional environmental managers, as peculiarly vulnerable to the negative impacts of adjustment, and as appropriate targets for micro-credit interventions because of being more reliable repayers and more likely to spend increased income on family welfare. By contrast GAD focuses on gender relations and treats policy interventions themselves as requiring a gender analysis in order to assess their likely impact.

5   'Mainstreaming' gender into development policies has tended to mean anti-poverty strategies which focus on poor women (a WID approach). There is a need for a broader, critical (GAD) approach addressing strategic gender interests and analysing the causes of gender inequality. However, this should not be seen as a polarized debate since both approaches are needed. Also it is crucial to include the roles of men as well as of women both in any analysis and in any proposed solutions.

19

TECHNOLOGY, POVERTY AND DEVELOPMENT

GORDON WILSON AND RICHARD HEEKS

Try to think of human life without technology. It's impossible. Technology is an essential aspect of human activity – and, hence, of development.

A few examples serve to illustrate this obvious point. Take our basic needs of physical survival – water, food and shelter – and try to imagine these without some form of technological input, however 'simple' or 'sophisticated'. How do we harness the water that falls from the sky, plough the land or provide the materials for our homes? Think of the millions of poor people who make their livelihoods in low-income countries in small-scale enterprises, and again try to imagine these without a technological input. At a different level, think of what facilitates the processes of globalization you read about in Chapter 16. The answer is firstly information technology, with its fast, reliable communication, and secondly transport, which has grown ever cheaper with technological development. Finally, for all human activity we have to harness energy – as heat, light, sound, electricity and to make things move – which many argue is the most fundamental technological activity of all.

But what is **technology**? Implied in the above opening paragraphs are two dimensions:

- it is a purposeful practical activity;
- the activity involves an interaction of tools or machines (which we can collectively refer to as hardware) and human beings.

To these, we can identify a third and a fourth dimension. A fundamental aspect of the human input concerns our *knowledge*; which we apply in order to engage in the practical activity. But if the activity is to be purposeful, the interaction of humans and their knowledge with hardware has also to be *organized*. This leads to a composite definition, not far removed from that which used to be provided in the Open University foundation course in technology:

> **Technology:** A purposeful, practical activity that involves the application of knowledge by organizations of human beings and their interaction with hardware.

All human activity, whether we describe it as being technological or not, has a strong social content where good questions to ask are:

- What is the purpose of the activity?
- Who is undertaking the activity, and on behalf of whom?
- What is done with the result of the activity and by whom?

The answers to these questions are inextricably bound up in issues of power relations between groups in a given society (between rich and poor, men and women, high caste and low caste, ethnic group A and ethnic group B, to name just four). Meanwhile, reminding ourselves that this book is about poverty and development, we are led to our chapter question:

Q How can technology serve the poor in development?

A simple question? Yes. But a simple answer? The following sections engage with the question:

- to examine different views of how technology's role in development has been, and is currently, understood;

- to seek to understand further the importance of human knowledge in technology development, including different forms of knowledge and how we value them, how we develop existing knowledge and acquire new knowledge, and how knowledge itself is a social product;

- to analyse the claims of a technology that is supposed specifically to facilitate the use and acquisition of knowledge, namely information technology (IT);

- to explore the options for a pro-poor technology development.

In undertaking these tasks, the chapter will focus primarily on technology in the context of small and micro enterprises, because it is in such enterprises, usually operating in the informal sector, that the majority of the world's poor gain their livelihoods.

19.1 Some views on technology and development

Technology as the solution

More or less synonymous with the post Second World War 'Golden Age' (see Chapter 13) was the view that technology represented the solution to development, almost to the extent that technology became development and development became technology. This applied to the old industrial economies and also to those countries that had newly gained their independence from colonial rule. Thus, in the 1950s, for example, it was widely claimed in the industrialized countries that nuclear power, then in its infancy, would one day become so cheap that electricity would be given away.

During these decades, the dominant motif for development among the newly independent countries was *modernization*. This has been discussed in Chapters 2 and 13, but modernization also has a strong technological dimension, equivalent again to equating technology with development. Thus, according to Smelser, modernization consists of various interrelated technical, economic and ecological processes involving:

> "…in the realm of technology, the change *from* simple and traditionalized techniques *towards* the application of scientific knowledge."
>
> (Smelser, 1968, p.126)

This idea of technology as solution and therefore as development can be seen in the vast sums of official development aid that was poured during the 'Golden Age' into various infrastructure projects in what was called the 'third world'. Only relatively recently have development institutions, such as the World Bank, begun to appraise critically some of their work during this era, including some serious criticisms of these most visual and symbolic of infrastructure projects: the huge dams that were constructed to supply clean drinking water, water for irrigation and therefore food, and water for hydro-electric power.

Of course there was a reaction to the 'technology as solution' view. It would be wrong, however, to suggest that it has even today been superseded. Every new, generic technological development always seems to bring with it the same grand claim. Chapter 22 examines this claim in the context of biotechnology and agriculture. Later in this chapter we examine the same claim made for information technology.

Technology as the problem

It is dangerous to allocate ideological views to particular time slots in history and, in a real sense, the view of technology as solution has always competed with the reaction – technology as problem. As David Dickson observed:

> "Throughout history man has been warned that he was creating forces he would be unable to control, that machines would eventually take over the planet and demand total obedience of the human race…that to place one's faith in science and technology was to make a pact, like Faust, with the devil."
>
> (Dickson, 1974, p.15)

Having said that, one cannot but notice the proliferation of books and articles that appeared in the 1970s (David Dickson's included) at least questioning and frequently damning the association of technology with progress. Reviewing radical critics of technology of his era, Langdon Winner commented:

> "[For the radical critics],…whether by an inherent property or by an incidental set of circumstances, technology looms as an oppressive force that poses a direct threat to human freedom."
>
> (Winner, 1977, p.3)

Far-reaching criticisms of technology were made in similar vein in *Small is Beautiful*, the influential book written by the unorthodox British economist E. F. Schumacher (1973). Although subtitled *A study of economics as if people mattered*, the book could just as easily have substituted the word 'technology' for 'economics'. Schumacher's view of modern technology was no less forceful than those of other critics:

> "…we can say that the modern world has been shaped by technology. It tumbles from crisis to crisis; on all sides there are prophesies of disaster and, indeed, visible signs of breakdown."
>
> (Schumacher, 1973, p.122)

But *Small is Beautiful* was also a call to action and from his fundamental critique stemmed Schumacher's enquiry into 'whether it is possible to have something better – a technology with a human face' (ibid.).

Much of this enquiry was applied to the 'third world' and to the central concern of the current book – poverty. Arguing that the poor should be enabled to help themselves, Schumacher insisted that this could only come about by:

> "making available to them a technology that recognizes the economic boundaries and limitations of poverty – *an intermediate technology*."
>
> (Schumacher, 1973, p.158, our emphasis)

Schumacher not only wrote the extraordinary polemic of *Small is Beautiful*, he founded too what we know today as the developmental non-government organization called Intermediate Technology Development Group (ITDG). Meanwhile, the 1970s spawned several descriptors for this different approach to technology: *alternative technology* and *appropriate technology* to name two. Although there were different nuances in the use of these terms, they generally shared a 'people-centred' view of development (Chapters 2 and 7), seeing as *appropriate* that which gives control to individuals and communities at a local level, rather than to technocrats of either states or capitalist firms (Figure 19.1).

Technology as embedded in social, cultural and economic relations

The contribution of Schumacher and the notion of appropriate or intermediate technology was to tell us that choices could be made. Indeed, as suggested above, there could even be choices for a pro-poor technology which would have a profound effect on society.

The movement went so far as to create a set of criteria by which one could test a technology's appropriateness in any given situation. One such list is given in Box 19.1. It has a strongly normative feel, with either a 'should' or a 'must' in every item, but ultimately the list represents what is known as a *technical fix* because it suggests that all that has to be done to

Figure 19.1 'Appropriate' alternatives to big engineering projects? (top) Small-scale power station in Bhutan; (above) building a 'bund' or small dam in Maharasthra, India.

establish a pro-poor technology is to choose the 'correct' hardware according to the criteria. Life, however, is never as simple as the exhortations in Box 19.1 imply, as soon became apparent in practice as appropriate technology failed to catch on society-wide, being largely confined to specific donor-driven projects.

During the 1980s, therefore, a view gathered force that explained technology as a *social process*, where technology is embedded in social, cultural and economic relations of particular societies. In this view, technology both reflects and influences the society that produces it. Moreover, although an important influence in shaping society, technology is only one among several.

This view was well exemplified by Anderson (1985) who argued that when technology is transferred from one society to another, it reflects the 'social values, institutional forms and culture' of the transferring party (p.57). She then illustrated some of the issues and dilemmas by

Box 19.1   The criteria of a technology's appropriateness

Appropriate technology should be compatible with local cultural and economic conditions, i.e. the human, material and cultural resources of the community.

The tools and processes should be under the maintenance and operational control of the population.

Appropriate technology, wherever possible, should use locally available resources.

If imported resources and technology are used, some control must be made available to the community.

Appropriate technology should wherever possible use local energy sources.

It should be ecologically and environmentally sound.

It should minimize cultural disruptions.

It should be flexible in order that a community should not lock itself into systems which later prove inefficient and unsuitable.

Research and policy action should be integrated and locally operated wherever possible in order to ensure the relevance of the research to the welfare of the local population, the maximization of local creativity, the participation of local inhabitants in technological developments and the synchronization of research with field activities.

(Brace Research Institute, quoted in Lawand *et al.*, 1976, p.132)

Notes:

1 Appropriateness for women and taking account of gender relations would now be added to this list.

2 A weakness in the list is the poorly defined notion of 'community'.

examining the gender consequences of adopting new technologies. Thus, commenting on a study conducted for the United Nations on the impact of scientific and technological progress on employment and work conditions in various trades, she wrote:

"In every case where machinery was introduced in activities traditionally done by women, men either completely replaced women or the activity became subdivided and men took over the tasks that used the technology and required greater skill while women were relegated to less skilled, menial tasks. These shifts were accompanied by loss of income-earning opportunities or marginalization and lower income for women...

In Java, when rice mills were introduced, women who had traditionally earned their only monetary income from hand milling were displaced as men assumed the positions in the factories. In Korea, when the government installed rice mills, men in the mills did jobs previously done by women."

(Anderson, 1985, p.61)

Anderson was warning against technology transfer or choice of technology becoming 'gender blind' by ignoring the gender relations within societies (see Chapter 18). Later in her chapter, she also wrote of this gender blindness in relation to technologies intended to make life easier for women, two examples being solar stoves that obviate the need for collecting firewood, and pipes from distant water pumps which obviate the need for carrying water:

"Women have traditionally used the time of long walks to fetch water and firewood for social organization, conversation and interchange. Technologies which alter these functions eliminate these opportunities so that other social forms have to be found."

(ibid., p.66)

On the other hand, she argued, the consequences of technological development are not necessarily negative, precisely because they do disrupt cultural norms (Figure 19.2):

"Technologies which gather women in certain areas, such as grain mills, can facilitate social activity and opportunities for

Figure 19.2   Mothers in rural Uganda, waiting for their children to be immunized, are given a talk on health education.

education. For example, women in Asia have received literacy training while they wait for their rice to be ground at mills and women in Africa have received nutrition training while waiting in line at clinics."

(ibid., p.66)

The message from Anderson and others on technological action for development was that one must always take account of the social, cultural and economic contexts in which it is to operate. And these contexts vary enormously, whether at a 'macro' level, that is between countries and regions, or at a 'micro' level, say between rural and urban parts of the same country, or even between two cities or two villages. This has led in recent years to a *systemic* view which recognizes that one can never exert total control over technology, but that it can be managed or steered while recognizing its embeddedness in other relations. This view sees action for development as taking place within a system of inter-related arenas (the social, economic, cultural and technological arenas) where action in one arena has an impact in each of the others. It has given rise in low-income countries to what are known as integrated development projects, where one tries to act in concert in several arenas at once. Even where technology is central, as in enterprise development, one attempts to steer a course that recognizes the interactions with the other arenas.

Steering is a dynamic image. It recognizes that things are forever changing and that navigation is a hazardous business! If we take the obvious analogy with driving a car, we might see an obstruction in the road ahead and we take corrective action in order to get round it. In other words, we have received some *data* (e.g. the sight of something in the road ahead), turned that into *information* (interpreted the sight as an obstruction to be avoided) and taken *action*. We can say too that we have *knowledge*, which is why we are able to interpret the raw data correctly, and that we are able to *learn* from this incident (we are careful for the next few kilometres as the road might be prone to similar obstacles).

Steering technology is the same. It requires knowledge and the ability to learn. There is a two-way relationship between the two, in that we learn because of our knowledge of a situation, but we also increase our knowledge by learning. In order to learn and improve our knowledge, however, we need information. It is to these issues that we now turn.

19.2 Technology and knowledge

The importance of knowledge is a dominant concern in development at the turn of the century. The World Bank, for example, devoted all of its 1998/99 *World Development Report* to the subject. To quote from its Foreword:

"This year's *World Development Report*... begins with the realization that economies are built not merely through the accumulation of physical capital and human skill, but on a foundation of information, learning and adaptation. Because knowledge matters, understanding how people and societies acquire and use knowledge – and why they sometimes fail to do so – is essential to improving people's lives, especially the lives of the poorest."

(World Bank, 1999, p.iii)

And the Overview immediately reinforced the link between knowledge and poverty:

"Poor countries – and poor people – differ from rich ones not only because they have less capital but because they have less knowledge."

(World Bank, 1999, p.1)

The *Report* went on to say that knowledge is costly to create. Unfortunately, the *Report*'s 158 pages then tended to deal with its creation as a technical matter, both in terms of the decisions to allocate resources to the task, and of the processes involved. But we can ask similar questions to those that we asked of technological activity earlier:

- Who owns knowledge and why?

- For what purpose do they use their knowledge?

These kinds of question are at the heart of debates, for example, on protecting the biodiversity of tropical rainforests for commercial ends. Who owns the knowledge about the properties of different plant species in the forest? Local people who may have been using, say, medicinal products from the plants for a very long time, where the plants have been considered to be common property resources? Or a large pharmaceuticals company based in a rich country, which 'discovers' the properties and patents the knowledge as 'theirs'? Chapter 22 on biotechnology delves into this debate more deeply, but the point is that knowledge is very much related to economic and social power.

One can also become involved in a circular argument. The *World Development Report* about knowledge is largely premised on the view that people are poor because they lack knowledge, but one could easily reverse the causality hypothesis by suggesting that people lack knowledge because they are poor, or, more fundamentally, that the knowledge poor people do possess is undervalued because they lack economic and social power.

This opposite causality is claimed by Appleton (1995) with respect to the gendered aspects of technological knowledge. Introducing a book of case studies on women and technical innovation, Appleton argues:

"Compared to men, women in all the studies were disadvantaged in the amount of control that they had over their lives: they had less time available and less disposable income, had received less education, participated less in political decision-making, were less able to move about, interact with other technology users and obtain information. All these factors helped to constrain women's access to technological information and to new technologies. They also contributed to a lower self-image for women, which meant that neither women nor men regarded women as producers and users of technology or as having valuable technical skills and knowledge."

(Appleton, 1995, p.8)

Appleton also identifies one of the factors that contributes to the relative invisibility of women's technical knowledge as 'the cultural perception of what is 'technical' and what is 'domestic''. Thus, women may carry out a large number of technically related activities, often within a single day – farming, processing crops and food, weaving, sewing, collecting wood and water, cooking, fishing, tending animals, and caring for the sick and children. They tend to be classed as domestic, rather than as technical, activities, however, and domestic work is rarely regarded by outsiders, or by women themselves, as requiring technical skills and knowledge (ibid., p.7).

Types of knowledge

The World Bank's 1998/99 *World Development Report* (p.1) focused on two types of knowledge which it claimed are critical for developing countries:

> "*Knowledge about technology*, which we also call technical knowledge, or simply know-how. Examples are nutrition, birth control, software engineering and accountancy...
>
> *Knowledge about attributes*, such as the quality of a product, the diligence of a worker, or the creditworthiness of a firm..."

Clarifying different facets of knowledge in this way is a good start if we want not only to explore how it can be acquired, but also how it can be used as part of technological development for the poor. There are rather more, however, that are relevant to technology than the two given above. The following is our list, followed by a few comments on each: know-how and know-why; knowledge of quality; knowledge of social, cultural and economic context; knowing how to learn; knowing how to marshal and organize knowledge.

Know-how and know-why

Know-how corresponds to the first of the *World Development Report*'s knowledge types. But knowing *how* something works is, by itself, underdeveloped knowledge. Of equal importance, if one is to make informed choices about technology, is knowing *why* it works. This then enables users of the technology to adapt it to, say, local conditions, or to go beyond it and develop something else that does the job better. This is what Quingrui and Xiaobo (1991) call the process of moving from learning by mastering acquired technology to understanding by engaging in its adaptation.

Knowledge of quality

This relates partly to the second of the World Bank categories – knowledge about attributes – and applies to both technological processes and products.

A common stereotypical image in many low-income countries is of many small-scale entrepreneurs within the same, small geographical area making and selling exactly the same product. One of them may have had the original idea, and the others have simply copied. The result is usually an oversupply of the same product where nobody is able to make a proper return on their investment and consequently nobody is able to develop the product further, or make adaptations for particular niches in the market. Equally important is the lack of a discriminating market that might demand better quality at the right price and hence be a pressure for innovation.

There are inter-related issues here of supply and demand, both of which are connected to knowledge about quality. With respect to the latter, Wilson (1996), for example, compared manufacturing at two small worker co-operatives in Zimbabwe. One – all-male – was engaged in bread production, was based in a medium-sized town, and competed quite fiercely with two other bakeries. It placed a premium on quality in order to stay in the market and had quality control mechanisms in place. The other – all-women – was engaged principally in making school uniforms for local children in a rural area. It had little direct competition, customers were undiscerning, and quality of the product (and of the processes used to produce it) stagnated. Customers were also poor, which certainly contributed to their failure to demand a better product quality.

With respect to supply, attention has been directed to design capabilities among enterprises and especially how they might move beyond copying each other. Forbes and Wield (1999), for example, have suggested that, given that enterprises in poor countries cannot be 'technology leaders', they should make the most of their position as 'technology followers'. They thus should generate, absorb and adapt knowledge to push the limits of design with what they have.

Knowledge of social, cultural and economic contexts

As argued earlier, technology is embedded within these contexts, is influenced by them and in turn cannot move without disturbing them. The explicit generation of this kind of knowledge is especially important, therefore, for any intervention that is intended to benefit particular groups, such as the poor, including interventions that aim to develop technology. Examining the social and cultural influences on technological learning, Platt (1999), for example, has compared interventions aimed at developing food processing technologies among small-scale enterprises in two regions in Sri Lanka. Significantly, the enterprises are performing better in one district than the other. A key factor in the better performing district is that the intervention is based on making confectionery, which has a long history in the area, and where there is a good deal of tacit knowledge – for example, confectionery is made in the home for special occasions. Therefore the interventions do not represent a major intrusion on the overall context. In the lower performing district, however, food processing technologies (this time in fruit and vegetable preservation) are being introduced in an agricultural area where hitherto they were largely non-existent; markets also did not exist and the overall context is not conducive to absorbing the technologies.

Knowing how to learn
It is often said that most poor people working in small-scale enterprises in low-income countries learn by 'doing' – that is, while working, on the job – rather than by formal methods, such as training. This may be true, but a common feature of doing and training is that they generate information which needs to be assimilated by a process of learning into the stock of knowledge.

Whereas learning is usually the intended output of training (although training's efficacy in this regard is often contested), it is far more haphazard when it arises from doing. This is pretty much a statement of the obvious because we 'learn' informally from our experiences of what is good and bad, what works and what doesn't, all the time as part of life. There have, however, been increasing attempts to make learning on the job explicit and more systematic, and to use the knowledge generated to develop technologies further.

Action-learning is one label given to this formalized learning from doing and it is based on the idea of a *feedback* loop. Figure 19.3 illustrates it

in a generalized form. Note that the crucial elements of receiving data and converting it into information are what we would formalize as *monitoring and evaluation*. This conversion of raw data into information is usually achieved by comparing it with some ideal of technological performance (i.e. what should be happening) or by comparison of your product with that of, say, a competitor. In fact, a key aspect of learning, whether it arises from training or from doing, explicitly or implicitly, is that it involves comparison with what you know already, with what should be the case, or with what you have found out by other means.

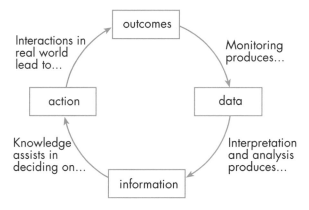

Figure 19.3   Action-learning as a feedback loop.

Knowing how to marshal and organize knowledge
We have distinguished above between several 'types' of knowledge. In practice, of course, they do not separate neatly. And anyway, having knowledge is one thing, knowing what to do with it is another. Thus knowing how to marshal and organize, or manage, the different 'types' of knowledge for technological development is another key area, one which usually goes under the name of **technological capability**.

Technological capability: The ability to manage the technological function of an enterprise (Trindade, 1991, pp.ix–x).

There are different levels of knowing how to manage knowledge for technological development. Wilson (1996) distinguishes between 'management as coping' on a day-to-day basis, which equates with an enterprise's routine production capability, and strategic management, which is the ability to make strategic choices about the enterprise function. This distinction, while useful, should, however, be considered as representing opposite ends of a technological capability spectrum for enterprises in low-income countries, with a range of capabilities at different levels in between (see Box 19.2).

Most enterprises within the informal sector of low-income countries are stuck at the initial levels of capability identified in Box 19.2, i.e. they rarely move beyond a production or coping capability (Platt & Wilson, 1999). Enabling them to move towards higher levels is one of the key challenges facing pro-poor interventions for technology development. This is a challenge, moreover, that has to recognize that the major source of learning among such enterprises is 'by doing' or by various informal mechanisms, such as from previous employment, a family member or a friend.

19.3   Information technology and development

Receiving and applying information are central aspects of the acquisition and generation of knowledge. Also, in turn, knowledge generates information. Reflecting a powerful global belief in its transformatory potential, a whole generic technology has grown around information, on which hundreds of billions of dollars are spent each year. In this section, we will therefore look at this pervasive new technology, using it as a specific example to illustrate the technology–development relationship.

For multinational corporations, certainly, information technology (IT) has become essential. Globalization demands such great flows of information and processing of information that they simply could not take place without IT. But what about a more direct relationship between IT and development? What, for example, does IT have to offer the poor? Some clearly believe it has a lot to offer:

Box 19.2   From 'day-to day coping' to 'strategic management'

Production (or *coping*) *capability*: routine management of production, i.e. the ability of an enterprise to produce and sell products at the given levels of efficiency and given inputs, including the ability to operate hardware, manage finances, and organizational management.

Formal and informal linkage capability: the ability of the enterprise to manage interactions and information sharing between enterprises, suppliers and contractors, buyers and sellers, and service providers (such as maintenance and repair) and other support institutions.

Minor (small) change capability: the ability of the enterprise to adapt and improve products and processes, including small changes to existing production processes, products and markets and marketing strategy.

Major (big) change capability: the ability of the enterprise to implement new or different production processes and/or products and markets or marketing strategy, or make significant changes to them.

Strategic management capability: refers to the stock of capabilities of an enterprise which results in the ability to gather and respond to information, to use existing resources and invest in new resources (internal and external) to make major or minor changes to the enterprise function (products, production processes, markets and marketing strategy).

(Platt & Wilson, 1999)

"This new technology greatly facilitates the acquisition and absorption of knowledge, offering developing countries unprecedented opportunities to enhance educational systems, improve policy formation and execution, and widen the range of opportunities for business and the poor."

(World Bank, 1999, p.9)

"Governments, donors and development organizations are rushing to realize the benefits that Internet access promises in the fight against poverty."

(Panos, 1998a, p.1)

There are opportunities for applying the new technology in supplying health, educational and agricultural information. In this section, though, we will focus on the scope for IT in small enterprises since these have a direct and growing relationship to poverty alleviation.

Understanding IT and small enterprise through systemic models

As we saw earlier in this chapter, we need to take a systemic, contextual view of technology in order to understand it. The same is also true of small enterprises, and so we will now present systemic models of each.

Information technology

We can define information technology as 'electronic means of capturing, processing, storing, and communicating information'. IT (also known as ICT: information and communication technology) is based on digital information held as 1s and 0s, and comprises computer hardware, software and networks. This will be the main focus of the section, but it is not the only technology that deals with information. Others include:

- 'Intermediate' technology, based largely on analogue information held as electromagnetic waves such as radio, television and telephone.
- 'Literate' technology, based on information held as the written word such as books and newspapers.
- 'Organic' technology, based solely on the human body, such as the brain and sound waves.

In building up a model of IT, we can already see two separate elements: the technology itself and the information on which it operates. In order to make this useful, we add in two further components: processes of purposeful activity and people to undertake those processes. All of these together now make up an 'information system', such as a support system that helps members of an NGO team share information using electronic mail. But this information system cannot sit in a vacuum. It exists within an environment of institutions (organizations, groups, markets) and of influencing factors (political, economic, socio-cultural, technical and legal). Putting all this together, we arrive at the model shown in Figure 19.4.

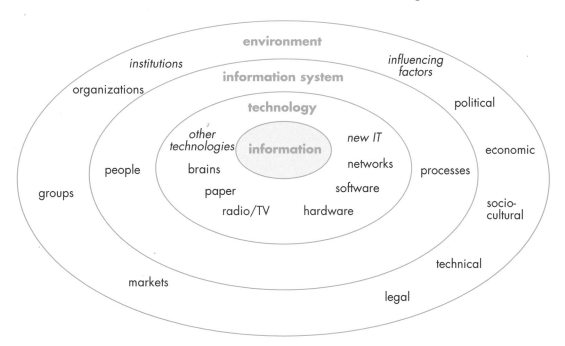

Figure 19.4   A model of information technology.

Both description and diagram are a reminder that information technology cannot be understood unless you also understand (a) information and its role, and (b) the institutional and factoral environment.

Small enterprise
We can build a similar systemic model for the operation of a small enterprise (Figure 19.5).

From Figures 19.4 and 19.5 and our earlier definition, we can identify four main potential roles for IT:

- As an *output* and as a *production technology*. Some enterprises produce either tangible (computers, networks, components) or intangible (software, Web pages) IT as an output. Other enterprises, such as designers and publishers, produce heavily information-based outputs. Both use IT as a production technology, and both form part of a nation's 'information economy'. Such enterprises are becoming increasingly vital to low-income countries, and represent a beneficial application of IT in terms of income, skill and export generation. However, thanks to scale economies and input barriers, these areas have traditionally been the preserve of large and/or highly skilled, capital-intensive firms. Barriers are coming down but these enterprises still remain at one step removed from 'mainstream' poverty alleviation, and will not be our focus here.

- As an *information processing technology*. All enterprises need to process the information that arises from both inside and outside the enterprise. However, the processing requirement of most small enterprises for processing formal information is relatively limited, and it can frequently be met by paper-based methods. Also, given the relatively high IT costs and low labour costs in developing countries, IT can easily raise rather than lower processing costs. Again, this will therefore not be our focus here.

- As an *information communication technology*. Small enterprises do have a significant need for both receipt and provision of information. Add in the fact that IT normally lowers communication costs substantially, and this can be seen as the main potential area for IT

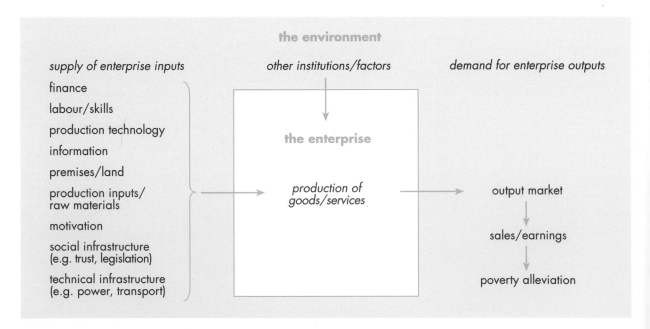

the environment

supply of enterprise inputs

finance

labour/skills

production technology

information

premises/land

production inputs/
raw materials

motivation

social infrastructure
(e.g. trust, legislation)

technical infrastructure
(e.g. power, transport)

other institutions/factors

the enterprise

production of
goods/services

demand for enterprise outputs

output market

sales/earnings

poverty alleviation

Figure 19.5   Systemic model of a small enterprise.

application for small enterprises in low-income countries. We will now look at its role in relation to both receipt and transmission of information.

The poor as information recipients

As noted, IT cannot be understood without understanding information, and developing a small enterprise requires information about several different things. It needs information relating to *supply*, such as the availability and sources of finance, labour, technology, raw materials, and other enterprise inputs. It needs information about *demand*, including market opportunities and characteristics of this market demand such as location, price, size, and quality. It also needs information about *other environmental factors*, such as competitors and laws.

Turning raw data into this kind of usable information is a staged process (the 'information chain') for which we will use a '4 As' model (Figure 19.6).

In order for the information chain to function, environmental components must be present that we will now investigate. These include *overt resources* (money, skills, technical infrastructure), *embedded/social resources* (trust, motivation, knowledge, power) and *relevant raw data*.

Overt resource inequalities for access

"New communications technologies are revolutionizing access to information – but the revolution is likely to reach everyone but the poor."

(Panos, 1998b)

Accessing IT-carried information requires a lot of overt resources including a telecommunications infrastructure to provide network access, an electrical infrastructure to make the IT work, a skills infrastructure to keep all the technology working, money to buy or access the IT, usage skills to use the IT, and literacy skills to read the content.

The poor simply do not have these resources. In a world where 80% of the world's population has no access to reliable telecommunications, and one-third have no access to electricity (Panos, 1998a), it is hardly surprising that the Internet reaches few poor people: there are more account holders in London than in the whole of Africa and many of the latter are affluent, white, urban South Africans. Likewise, more than half of the low-income countries' population is illiterate, with a far greater proportion unable to read English, the language that dominates digitized information (UNDP, 1998c).

Governments and donor agencies are working to provide the overt resources, but realistically the poor will not own the IT, and the poor will be very unlikely to control the IT or to use it hands-on in any significant numbers for the foreseeable future. The main strategy has therefore been to provide IT to intermediary institutions such as government agencies, NGOs and community-based organizations.

The most popular model is the community 'telecentre' with an Internet-linked computer providing a multi-function resource (Talero & Guadette, 1995). Only a few exist so far in low-income countries. Bringing them to poor communities would be a massive operation requiring huge diversion of investments and taking at least a generation. Most would also require large on-going subsidies to sustain them in the midst of poverty. But even this would not be enough.

Social resource inequalities for assessment and application
Poor entrepreneurs need more than money, skills and infrastructure in order to make use

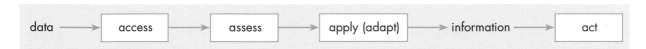

Figure 19.6 'Four As' model of the information chain.

of the data delivered by IT. They need other resources to interact with sources outside their own community, including (Panos, 1998b; World Bank, 1999):

- *'Source proximity'* The creation of data takes place within a particular context and retains embedded characteristics of that context: it contains what its creators do know and do feel is important and misses out what they do not know or do not feel is important; it reflects their political and economic beliefs; it reflects their culture. Unless poor entrepreneurs come from the same context as the sources creating information, problems of miscommunication and misunderstanding can arise.

- *Trust* Before they will accept data, recipients must trust both the source and communication channel of the data. For most entrepreneurs, sufficient trust to justify business decisions can only be created through personal contact, through interaction and, ideally, through shared context/proximity.

- *Knowledge* Information creates knowledge, but knowledge is also needed to create information. It is knowledge that helps us to access information, by knowing where to find and how to use information sources. It is knowledge that helps us to assess information, by judging whether it is truth or lies, of value or not. It is knowledge that helps us to apply information, by adapting it to our particular needs and circumstance. For the poor, such knowledge is frequently limited to their local context.

- *Confidence and security* In order to use new communication channels, recipients must have confidence and feel motivated to take a certain amount of risk. In general, because of their social circumstance and experience, the poor lack confidence and are risk averse.

None of these represents insuperable barriers and they should not be seen as excuses for inaction. However, they do all add to the problems of using IT, particularly because the poor lack the power to access or demand further social and overt resources.

Resource inequalities for action
Information supplied via IT (or via any other means) has no value unless it informs decision-making and action. Yet action implies resource endowments that have nothing to do with IT. Information received about a new technology supplier is of no value if the entrepreneur does not trust the supplier. Information about a new market is of no value if the entrepreneur cannot increase production to supply that market, through lack of capacity or aversion to risk. Information about new government tax rules is of no value if the entrepreneur cannot afford to pay tax. Inequality in endowment of both overt and social resources for action therefore keeps poor entrepreneurs poor regardless of whether information is supplied to them via IT.

We can see that information (and, hence, information technology) is only one resource amongst many that are required for successful development of a small enterprise. Put another way, information is a necessary resource for poverty alleviation but it is by no means a sufficient one. Equally – indeed more – important are factors such as financial credit, skills, production technology, demand for outputs, plus other social resources. All of these have to be borne in mind when assessing the relative priority to give to IT in the development process.

Lack of relevant data
As has been argued in the previous section, poor entrepreneurs get their most valuable information via informal information systems from those around them and like them. Unfortunately, the information from such systems can be inaccurate and is certainly incomplete. Formal information sources however, can be just as bad in meeting needs as they are increasingly dominated by commercially inspired data or trivia. The Web, for instance, mainly provides the information-thirsty poor with a flood of 'noise': digitized, Westernized irrelevance.

Markets therefore fail poor entrepreneurs not just in terms of information chain processes but also in terms of input: they do not provide enough relevant raw data for the poor (especially not in digitized form) about everything from materials suppliers to market prices to government regulations. In part, this is due to the inability of the poor to voice their demand for information and their inability to pay for supply of that information.

Where markets fail, national and global institutions may – and do – step in. UN bodies provide data about technology suppliers; governments provide data about market prices and regulations. Yet there are many problems here, in part because such interventions tend to be rather haphazard and frequently unsustainable. There can also be data problems. The provision of data is rarely in digitized form, making it suitable only for non-IT-based media, and it is often driven by the objectives of the source rather than the needs of the recipient (see Box 19.3). Lastly, unless the provider is a community-based institution, there remains a lack of proximity between such sources and poor entrepreneurs as recipients.

The poor as information sources

There is a general assumption within much writing about IT that the poor are merely recipients: of technology, of information, of knowledge. Of course, this is not correct. Poor countries now all produce at least some information technology, in the form of customized software systems. Poor communities all produce their own information and knowledge. IT can play a positive role, as in Alexandra (see Box 19.3), by allowing that information and knowledge to be more widely disseminated.

IT could be used to transmit information from poor entrepreneurs to donor and government agencies. The main use for IT, though, has been to transmit marketing information about small enterprise products and services to potential customers; typically via the Web to Western export markets (World Bank, 1999; Hegener, 1998). However, there are far more rose-tinted vignettes of claimed success with IT than there are long-term analytical studies by independent researchers.

Box 19.3 Failure and success in South Africa

In 1995, a project was begun by the Office of the Premier in North-West Province to provide information to six rural communities through touch-screen computer kiosks. The kiosks provided general demographic and economic information about the province, details of main government programmes, and speeches by the Premier and by Nelson Mandela. This did not meet community needs and it became apparent that this had been more a public relations exercise than a development initiative. The project was scrapped in 1997.

In 1995, a project was begun by the local government in Alexandra township (near Johannesburg) to create a database of local resources. All township organizations were asked to provide details, a process often organized by school children as homework. The database was made accessible over the Internet. Not only did the database provide information about local capabilities to community members, it also enabled community enterprises to win contracts from larger firms in Johannesburg.

(Adapted from Benjamin, 1999)

We can see, once again, that IT is neither universally necessary nor a sufficient condition for giving voice to poor entrepreneurs. In the first case, there are many other – potentially more appropriate – mechanisms to assist the poor, from face-to-face meetings to telephone conversations to newsletters and even radio/TV programmes. On the second point, technology only affects part of a much broader social process. Poor entrepreneurs must also have the capacity to generate information about themselves, and to access and use the IT. Frequently they do not, and they will again have to rely on intermediaries. At the other end of the transmission chain, someone must also be listening and able to act on what they hear. Panos (1998a), for example, describes the termination of a Web service selling products from low-income countries to Western consumers due to lack of use.

Examining the contemporary IT fetish

So far in this section, we have analysed the opportunities, challenges and problems for poor people that are posed by IT in relation to small enterprise. However, such analysis is rare, for, like any new generic technology, IT lends itself to sweeping statements about what it can do for development. If the poor are considered overtly at all, the feeling is that they must gain eventually from adopting the technology because the technology *is* development. This dominant 'technology-as-solution' view has its challengers, of course, including the authors of this chapter, and we will seek to place different views into perspective through the use of a framework of viewpoints about IT.

Such a framework about IT (or any other technology) can be constructed from two continua (see Figure 19.7). First, a continuum of *technology impacts*, from optimism to pessimism. Some people – optimists – associate IT with largely positive impacts like wealth creation and improvements in service quality. Others – pessimists – associate IT with largely negative impacts like unemployment and alienation.

Second, a continuum of *impact causes*, from technological determinism to social determinism. Some people – technological determinists – believe that it is mainly inherent features of the technology that determine impacts of introducing IT; for example, that computers cause job losses. Others – social determinists – believe

that it is mainly human choices within social structures that determine impacts of introducing IT; for example, that any job losses from computerization arise when managers decide to exploit employees.

Each continuum has a midpoint of, respectively, neutrality about impacts and contingency about the causes of those impacts.

Such a framework necessarily simplifies a complex reality, but we can use it to understand differing positions on technology and development. For example, the analysis presented so far in this IT section can be classified as roughly neutral to positive about the impact of IT, and contingent to socially determinist about the causes of those impacts. Our position on causes is supported by earlier discussion in the chapter, but the position on impacts should be rather more balanced since we have downplayed two things.

We have downplayed failure, yet estimates suggest that the majority of IT-based initiatives end in *total failure* of a system that never works; *partial failure* in which major goals are unattained or in which there are significant undesirable outcomes; *sustainability failure* that succeeds initially but then fails after a year or so; or *replication failure* of a pilot scheme that cannot be reproduced (Heeks & Davies, 1999).

We have also downplayed negative impacts. Yet, as well as reducing costs and improving

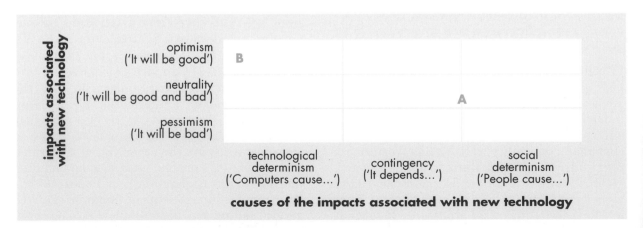

Figure 19.7   Framework for analysing different views about IT and its impacts.

processing and communication of information, IT has also been associated in some cases with negative impacts. These have included job losses, increased stress, reduced flexibility, centralized control and surveillance, and impoverished communications (Heeks, 1998). Our overall analytical viewpoint therefore lies around position A in the framework diagram.

However, this is not the viewpoint adopted by many of those involved in setting the current development agenda. Two sample quotes were provided at the start of the section, and there are many more which give a pervading sense that the new technologies' impact will be positive, and that the technology itself is the cause of that impact. Much of the development discussion therefore lies firmly in position B in the diagram. It is driven on by hype from IT vendors and the media that makes IT an icon for modern development, turning use of IT within development into an end in itself rather than a means of achieving other development goals. The main development objective becomes bringing as much IT to as many people as quickly as possible so that they can obtain the benefits it provides. The main development problem becomes inequality of access to IT.

But is there anything really wrong with the position B view? After all, we could do with a bit of good news and optimism about development, couldn't we?

There seem to be a number of things wrong with position B. In the first place, there are *development opportunity costs* of the investments this position promotes. Panos (1998a) recounts more than 50 major initiatives aimed at increasing Internet connectivity in Africa alone. Add in other IT expenditure and other low-income countries and we see significant investment by donors and by governments in this area. All of this comes with an opportunity cost since there are finite amounts of money, time and attention. Investing these in IT means explicitly not investing them in other development areas. Yet the 'IT fetishists' have so far been unable to demonstrate how IT-based information represents a more

important resource than water, food, land, power, production technology, money and skills in the development process.

There are also more specific *information system and technology opportunity costs*. 'Radio covers approximately 75 per cent of Africa's population and television 40 per cent. The Internet's 0.1 per cent shows just how marginal a medium it still is' (Panos, 1998a, p.2). Radio, television and newspapers have all been used to disseminate agricultural, educational and business information to the poor. These technologies have capacity, interactivity and ownership limitations the new IT does not. However, in access and coverage terms they beat it hands-down now and for the foreseeable future. The trouble is they are just not 'sexy' enough to capture decision-makers' attention. Even telephones have slipped down the visibility league tables because of this.

Likewise, a focus on IT and IT-based information means that 'organic information systems' and 'indigenous knowledge' – the systems and knowledge which arise from within poor communities – are being systematically ignored and overridden. These provide, respectively, the best communication channel and best information source for the poor. Yet, again, they cannot match up to the sales pitch and glitz of the new technology, and even poor communities come to devalue their own resources and to overvalue new technology.

Lastly, there are *factoral opportunity costs*. This approach to development means that attention switches to the technical factors underlying development and, since attention is finite, away from the political, the economic and the social factors underlying development. Experience suggests that, where this happens, 'development' allows those with political, economic and social power to reinforce their position at the expense of those without such power.

Development priorities for information and IT
Given the opportunity costs and other issues identified above, where should the main priorities lie for the development agenda? What are

the implications of our analytical position? We conclude that:

- *The poor need knowledge to access, assess and apply existing information and need resources for action more than they need access to new information.* Information deficits are certainly an issue for poor entrepreneurs, but a more important part of the total picture – and a prerequisite for making use of information – are resources like skills, knowledge and money.

- *The poor need access to new locally contextualized information more than access to existing information from an alien context. The information needs of the poor will be met more by informal, 'organic' information systems than by formal, IT-based information systems.* The poor lack, and need, information relevant to their local context. This may come more from interaction between communities and community members rather than from the typical IT-based pattern of data transfer from North to South. Based on both overt and social resourcing, such new information will best be delivered to them by organic information systems that arise from within their community. Failing that, because of access issues, information may be better delivered by literate or intermediate technologies – such as telephones – than by new IT. Where IT is used, it should provide a supplement to, not substitute for, existing information systems.

- *The poor need IT more to give them 'voice' than to give them 'hands', 'brains' or 'ears'.* IT can play a limited enabling role in the alleviation of poverty, but will be of greatest value as a technology to provide information from and about the poor. It will also, given the resourcing and data points made above, be of value in helping community members interact, though only where it beats face-to-face or phone interaction. This is only likely to occur via electronic mail with members based in distant potential markets either at home or overseas.

- *The poor need 'intelligent intermediaries' to use IT.* These intermediaries are needed to bridge both the overt and the social resource endowment gaps between what the poor have and what they would need in order to use IT. Indeed, IT currently has a far greater enabling value in building capacity within intermediary institutions – in 'helping the helpers' – than in directly affecting the poor. IT has enabled NGOs to share experiences about – and thereby improve – their microcredit programmes and has assisted 'those campaigning for greater democracy, social equality and protection of the environment' (Panos 1998a, p.2; World Bank, 1998). There are also individual examples of IT assisting government agencies, universities, and hospitals, some of which – albeit often indirectly and imperfectly – can serve the poor (Talero & Guadette, 1995).

- *The poor need 'community intermediaries' to use IT.* The identity of IT-using intermediaries is critical. Following the discussion of proximity, trust and knowledge (including the ability to combine 'techknowledge' about IT with 'context knowledge' about the environment within which it is used), we can see that the best intermediaries will be drawn from within poor communities, as they were in the Alexandra case. Poor communities with the highest 'social capital' of effective community institutions will therefore be the most effective users of IT. Initiatives in which technical and contextual knowledge are disconnected, with intermediaries and control located outside the community, are more likely to fail, as in the North-West Province case (see Box 19.3).

- *The poor will only reap the fullest benefits of IT when they own and control both the technology and its related know-how.* Intermediaries are a currently necessary mechanism. Yet their presence reduces the ability of the poor to have direct control over definition of information problems, design of new information systems, and ownership and operation of those systems. As we will see in the next section, this is essential to effective management and steering of the new technology. However, the current resource and contextual barriers to this are massive: an order of magnitude greater than those for connecting up intermediaries.

19.4 Pro-poor technology development

We end this chapter by examining briefly three broad strategies for technology development in low-income countries and the various claims that are made regarding their impacts on the poor. These are: opening up the development process; strategies of the poor themselves; and institutions for technological development.

Opening up the development process

This is the conventional wisdom, advocated by the World Bank among others. By 'opening up the development process' they mean encouraging greater competition among producers which in turn forces them to try and do things better. Hence, producers innovate and develop technologically. At country level, 'opening up' means allowing exposure to foreign goods and services under a free trading regime. It also means allowing foreign companies and technology to 'show the way', via direct investment or foreign companies granting use under licence of their technology to indigenous firms.

The argument against this approach has been that opening up the development process in this way is likely to destroy indigenous knowledge and technology in low-income countries as local firms are unable to compete with foreign ones who are using the more advanced technologies. Far from reducing poverty, it is argued, such a process is likely to increase it. Thus, in the past, the need for 'infant industry' protection has equally been emphasized by many, which has led to less open trading regimes and various restrictions on foreign investment.

To be fair, no agency today advocates open trading and foreign investment as the sole solution to technological development, and much has

changed since the early 1990s in this respect. Thus, in its 1998/99 *World Development Report*, the World Bank called for both open trading and developing indigenous capability:

> "*Acquiring knowledge* involves tapping and adapting knowledge available elsewhere in the world – for example, through an open trading regime, foreign investment and licensing agreements – as well as creating knowledge locally through research and development, and building on indigenous knowledge."
>
> (World Bank, 1999, p.2)

Strategies of the poor themselves

An important dimension of being poor is that one survives in a risky environment, and certainly one's sources of livelihood are continually at risk. Thus, strategies operated by poor people themselves are often aimed at reducing risk. This might mean that they have many livelihood sources (so if one fails, there are still others). It also means that the poor are often averse to taking part in risky ventures. Their acceptance or rejection of a new technology, therefore, is often a matter of a finely balanced calculation between the possible promises of a better livelihood by adopting it and of the risk of it failing to deliver.

Risk aversion, therefore, can be an impediment to technological development among poor people. Platt (1999) argues that this also extends to small-scale entrepreneurs sharing and developing their knowledge together. In her Sri Lanka studies she found that many small firms were unwilling to share for fear of another entrepreneur taking opportunistic action with the knowledge gained. This finding runs counter to ideas prevalent in high-income countries of 'networks of learning', where knowledge is shared between firms.

Risk averse strategies suggest that rather than being poor because they lack knowledge, poor people usually have an excellent grasp (and hence knowledge) of the risks and opportunities presented to them. However, their risk aversity may impede further knowledge acquisition and therefore technological development. Having said that, it must be stressed that the poor do adapt to changing opportunities. Thus, in agriculture, Woodhouse (1992, p.181) has reported how rural people in sub-Saharan Africa have, over the years, adopted new cash crops such as cocoa and maize and new technologies in pursuit of changing economic opportunities. Usually, however, *adaptation* of new technologies to local conditions and contexts goes hand-in-hand with their adoption and it is this process that strikes the balance between risk and opportunity. A good example is the 'Green Revolution' in India that started in the 1950s and eventually made the country self-sufficient in grain. It is now generally agreed that the Green Revolution was dependent on local people adapting the new seed varieties that had been developed in research stations originally situated in Mexico. Pacey (1990) elaborates the point:

> "...it was experiment and innovation by ordinary farmers which ensured the success of the new [Green Revolution crops in India] on the poorer soils. Sometimes, indeed, the farmers chose to use crop varieties which had been rejected by official research. One rice variety developed by the plant breeders and then discarded was known as IR 24. Farmers who got hold of this liked it and multiplied the seed themselves, selecting plants that did well in local conditions. The result has been rice which is more resistant to a local insect pest than are any of the varieties approved by the scientists."

> (Pacey, 1990, pp.192–3)

Institutions for technology development

By institutions we mean more than 'big' organizations. We also mean accepted ways of doing things. To give a simple example, the family in high-income countries is an institution. Families are organizations of a kind, but they also represent certain accepted ways of doing things, even if the practice rarely meets the ideal.

For the purposes of this chapter, we intend briefly to review three types of institution which relate to technological development at different levels: research and development (R&D); networks; participatory technology development.

Research and development

R&D conjures up images of discrete departments of large corporations in high-income countries containing scientists in white coats, working on new processes and products. It is an image of relative affluence. It would be a mistake, however, to think that R&D cannot take place among lower-income countries, although its focus should probably be different. We have referred earlier to the work of Forbes and Wield (1999) on 'technology followers', and it is worth quoting from their conclusion, although it must be noted that, with the exception of India, their examples concern medium-income countries, specifically newly industrializing countries (NICs) such as Brazil:

> "The role of R&D firms in technology followers involves solving shop-floor problems, functioning as the firm's formal learning unit, and providing a nucleus for organizational change. The role of R&D will rarely involve research as an activity aimed at generating new technological or scientific knowledge. This technology-following role of R&D requires that it be organized to maximize communication with the rest of the firm, and to function as both gatekeeper for outside knowledge and storehouse of in-house knowledge. As firms try to add more value to their activity, product innovation becomes increasingly key, and the role of R&D includes building an independent design capacity for the firm. The crucial distinction is between the design and technology frontiers – it is possible for firms to push out the design frontier without pushing out the technology frontier."

> (Forbes & Wield, 1999)

Emphasizing the key role of design, Forbes and Wield conclude from this that 'catching up with technology-leaders is a game of long-slog rather than leap-frog' and that 'ultimately the role of R&D in a technology follower is not one of Research and Development, but one of Development and Design'.

Networks

Some R&D in low-income countries is provided by Government-backed institutions, or even by aid agencies. One problem is poor co-ordination between these various agencies, resulting in fragmentation of effort. The problem has become particularly acute in low-income countries, all of which have undergone some form of 'structural adjustment' (see Chapter 13) since the 1990s, resulting in a proliferation of agencies. Thus, reporting on Tanzania, Hewitt and Wield (1997) state that the former co-ordination of industrial development by the state was replaced during the 1990s by more diffuse action from a multiplicity of public and private agents. They believe that a way forward might lie in a network approach, and refer to the work of the Economic and Social Research Foundation in Tanzania as playing an important co-ordinating role in bringing together interests from the public, private and non-governmental sectors.

Other work has been done on networks that are created organically, often by firms in the same sector forming concentrated 'clusters' of related activity in cities, and at least sharing some information and technologies. One issue in such settings, and also implied during the discussion of risk-averse strategies of the poor above, is that of trust between entrepreneurs. The result is that networking takes place among those where mutual trust exists, which often means relatives and close friends. It has been argued by Schmitz (1995), however, that such 'ascribed' networks are relatively closed and are therefore quite limiting in the quality and quantity of shared knowledge that they generate.

Participatory technology development (PTD)

PTD has been promoted in recent years by the Intermediate Technology Development Group (ITDG), and draws heavily on the general arguments in favour of participatory approaches to development interventions. Arguments in favour are often strongly normative, claiming that participatory approaches are empowering for the supposed beneficiaries (who are usually poor people) in that it gives them a say in, and hence ownership of, the planning and implementation of the intervention. There is not space here to enter into the various debates about this claim, but a second argument in favour is more utilitarian: by involving the participation of poor people in technology development, one learns crucially about the social, cultural and economic contexts, and this makes any interventions more effective. It also enables technology interventions to build on what is already there (and hence encourages the adaptive behaviour argued for above), rather than introduce something completely new.

Platt and Wilson (1999) agree that PTD is promising, but argue that a main issue is how to institutionalize it as a set of agreed ways of going about technology development. This, among other things, requires teachers of technology to become learners themselves – in order to discover what is already there and about context. Such behavioural and institutional changes represent a considerable challenge for those who work in R&D or other agencies that promote technology development.

Summary

1   There has always been a tension between 'technology-as-solution' and 'technology-as-problem' views. More recently, systemic views suggest that technology development can be managed or steered while recognizing its embeddedness in economic, social and cultural relations.

2   Knowledge is considered to be at the core of technology development. Several kinds of knowledge are required, including technical knowledge, knowledge about attributes (especially quality), knowledge about context, knowing how to learn, and knowing how to marshal knowledge. Knowledge, however, is not neutral. It is socially constructed and often knowledge held by poor people, and especially poor women, is undervalued. Poor people also face further constraints on its further acquisition and their ability to use it.

3   Great claims are being made for the role of information technology (IT) in poverty alleviation and development generally. These claims should be considered with caution. Not only may the benefits be exaggerated, but IT development takes away resources that may be better placed elsewhere.

4   Various strategies are promoted for pro-poor technology development:

- Strategies that simply advocate open trading and foreign investment in low-income countries have now been superseded by ones that take a more balanced view, recognizing the need also to maintain and enhance indigenous capability and to understand the strategies of the poor themselves.

- It is argued that the notion of Research and Development should be replaced in poorer countries by Design and Development, and that this is more appropriate for technological development in these countries.

- Fragmentation of technology support agencies in low-income countries in the 1990s has led to interest in co-ordinated networks of learning. Networking among small-scale enterprises, however, can be hampered by limited trust between them, this being itself a function of risk aversity among poor entrepreneurs.

- Finally, participatory technology development (PTD) is considered to hold considerable potential, although it presents equally considerable institutional challenges.

20

LIFE IN THE CITIES

JO BEALL

It is generally agreed that the early twenty-first century will see more urban inhabitants than rural dwellers world-wide (UNCHS, 1996, p.12). In 1800 only 3% of the world's population lived in urban centres, about 25 million people. By 1985 the proportion of urban dwellers was 40% (1.8 billion people) of a much larger total. It is predicted that by 2020 the world's population is likely to have doubled again, with over 90% of this increase occurring in countries of Africa, Asia and Latin America. Cities of the South will soon be host to the majority of the world's absolute poor and as a result, urban poverty is one of the most pressing social issues to be addressed in the 2000s.

Cities have long been symbols of civilization and material and scientific progress. Writers as diverse as Adam Smith and Karl Marx have seen urban centres as engines of national economic growth, while Jane Jacobs (1969) famously characterized cities as catalysts for technological innovation and economic advancement, generating surpluses and investment in their surrounding areas. Others such as Cronon (1991) and Rees (1992) have recognized that cities are also nodes of vast consumption, creating what Rees calls 'ecological footprints' through the extraction of resources from immense areas beyond their boundaries. In social terms, urban centres have been characterized as magnets attracting a heterogeneous mix of human creativity, encouraging new forms of individual interaction and collective association. Equally,

urban centres have been seen as the sites of pernicious social relations and institutions exhibiting the cheek-by-jowl manifestations of extreme wealth and grinding poverty, of ostentatious power and anonymous survival (Figure 20.1).

In looking at urban development and life in the cities of the South it is useful to keep in mind two key questions:

Q Are cities simply social and environmental negatives or are they centres of opportunity for millions of people for whom rural livelihood systems are no longer possible, desirable or a reality?

Q Are cities the end product of a linear journey towards economic growth, social sophistication and organizational possibility? What do we need to know about cities to understand them more as spatial congregations of diverse people and activities?

These questions will be addressed against a background which traces processes of urban development especially in countries of Africa, Asia and Latin America and points up the challenges posed by the growth of urban poverty. The conclusion drawn is that whether in the North or the South, cities are places of possibility for millions of resourceful people but they also have their dark side – the sweatshops and waste dumps alongside the skyscrapers and heaving markets. How you characterize the

Figure 20.1   Two worlds in one city, Nairobi, Kenya.

development of cities, and how heavily you come down on one side of the debate or the other, will ultimately depend on your view of development. It may also depend on whether you are thinking of Dhaka, Los Angeles, Calcutta or Stockholm at the time.

"There is a steady, manic beat to the market, and one must learn how to fall in with the crush of humanity and with the din of street cries, whistles, catcalls, and beggars' laments. Today...I was caught unaware by a hand attached to a long, thin arm that tugged at my skirt. It was a tall, skinny, sallow-faced boy with eye rims and fingernails that were morbidly white. 'Dona Nanci', he rasped in an eerie, faraway voice, *'estou morendo* [I'm dying]'. He repeated this several times with no other intent than announcing his obvious condition."

(Scheper-Hughes, 1992, p.9)

"The megacity is popularly depicted as being overcrowded with dense slums, squatter settlements, and pavement-dwellers whose access to the most elementary services is negligible and who frequently fall victim to epidemics and disease...What is omitted in these popular images is that the slums and crowded spaces of megacities are also productive areas...So there is an enormous potential among the large, desperately poor populations of megacities. We must find ways of harnessing this energy to make cities more productive and to ensure a better life for these workers and their children."

(Sassen & Patel, 1996, p.1)

20.1 Making sense of the urban experience

Earlier chapters explored what Polanyi (1957) called 'the great transformation' in Western Europe, the rise of industrial capitalism from the late eighteenth century and its impact on a wider world. An enduring legacy of the 'great transformation' was the growth of urban centres, a change in the character of cities and in their relationship with the world beyond them. The well-known geographer, David Harvey (1973) later employed Polanyi's (1968) three distinctive modes of economic integration – reciprocity, redistribution and market exchange – as a means for understanding the changing relationship between society and urban form. For Polanyi, where there is accumulation of surplus, and where hierarchical societies predominate, redistribution occurs, involving a flow of goods or rights over production to support the activities of an élite. According to Harvey this process has a spatial centre and so a transition to urbanism becomes possible, although not automatic.

Whereas previously **urbanism** had been understood as a way of life associated with residence in an urban area (Wirth, 1938), in *Social Justice and the City,* Harvey (1973) defined urbanism not simply as a 'thing in itself' but as 'relationally defined'. In other words, he fundamentally rethought the relationship between power, space and urban form, revealing cities to be anything but neutral spaces. Instead he saw them as spatial expressions, as concrete manifestations of social relations based on power, particularly economic power. Harvey's analysis had a tremendous impact on geographers and non-geographers alike. His influence was to demonstrate irrevocably that social relations do not play themselves out on 'the head of a pin' but within contested space.

Urbanism: A term originally coined by the Chicago School sociologist Louis Wirth (1938), who used it to refer to a way of life associated with living in an urban area. It is sometimes associated with social dislocation and the decline of community but more generally refers to the extent to which a given population conforms to what is deemed to be an urban lifestyle.

Nevertheless, Harvey has not been without his critics. In *Social Justice and the City* he articulated a linear view of progress familiar to modernization and Marxist theorists alike and he has been challenged, for example, for focusing on relationships founded on economic inequality, to the exclusion of other social relationships (Beall, 1997a; Massey, 1994). Particularly important for the analysis of cities in the South are Harvey's conclusions regarding reciprocity. This he understood as the transfer of goods, favours and services among individuals in a given group, for example the collusive practices of business associates or the mutual support found at neighbourhood level. According to Harvey, reciprocity exists in a residual form in urban society but economies dominated by reciprocity rather than simply accommodating it cannot sustain urbanism. However, more recent interpretations of cities point to the flourishing of reciprocal relationships in a number of crucial spheres, be they commercial networks (Fukuyama, 1996; Geertz, 1979), ties of identity (Cohen, 1969) or relationships of mutual support (Beall, 1995; Gonzalez de la Rocha, 1994).

More fundamentally, Ira Katznelson (1996) has observed that Polanyi was not just the materialist historian of economic exchange deployed by Harvey. For Harvey urbanism '*necessarily arises* with the emergence of a market exchange mode of economic integration with its concomitants – social stratification and differential access to the means of production' (Harvey, 1973, p.239; emphasis in the original). Thus the city becomes a place for disposing of surplus and the urban economy the site in which the circulation of surplus takes place. However, as Katznelson (1996) points out, in *The Great Transformation* Polanyi was also concerned with the political origins of modern liberalism, its doctrines and institutions.

> "A full Polanyian analysis of housing and spatial segregation, rather than the partial one Harvey provides, perforce would contain a more multiple account of the origins and reproduction of housing markets, more attention to the politics of spatial contest...more notice of group pluralism in more than the single dimension of class...and more of an orientation to the mutual impact of institutions, political norms, and patterns of identity and agency...considering 'the worker' at home, at work and as a citizen."
>
> (Katznelson, 1996, p.61)

This chapter considers the urban dweller at work, at home and as a citizen. It takes its cue from Harvey in that cities are seen as being built on material foundations and as being relationally defined. However, it equally subscribes to the critique that urbanism is about more than the economy. Other social relations mediate the dynamics of power as well as class, such as those based on gender, ethnicity, location or length of residence in the city. All in turn infuse the social and political institutions of cities.

20.2 Poverty, urbanization and the growth of mega-cities

Many countries in the South have experienced an unprecedented growth in their national populations. Although fertility rates are generally lower in urban centres compared with rural areas, natural increase is the single most important factor in **urban growth**. Nevertheless, rural-to-urban migration remains a significant factor in many Southern contexts, not least of all because it has ensured that urban populations are overwhelmingly youthful, contributing in turn to natural increase in cities.

There are important regional differences in global patterns of **urbanization**. At the beginning of the twentieth century only Britain had an urban population that exceeded the number of rural inhabitants, although over the course of the century this became a feature of all industrialized countries. By the 1980s, most people in Latin America, the Caribbean, the Middle East and East Asia also lived in urban centres. Even in poorer parts of the world, urbanization has proceeded apace; although Africa is presently the least urbanized continent, it is urbanizing fastest. Two-thirds or more of the population remain rural in China, India and Indonesia. However, in absolute terms the number of urban dwellers in these populous countries is huge.

Urban growth: The growth in the absolute numbers of people living in urban areas. It usually results from natural increase (the excess of births over deaths) within urban centres but can also be the result of migration into urban centres.

Urbanization: The proportion of a national population living in urban centres. An increase in the level of urbanization can result from rural–urban migration but usually results from rural settlements growing to a size where they are reclassified as urban, or boundaries of cities or metropolitan areas being extended to incorporate areas which were previously classified as rural. The urbanization process refers not only to changes in population size and distribution but also involves an analysis of the related economic, social and political changes.

Mega-cities: Very large cities, defined by their population size. The United Nations defines mega-cities as those with populations exceeding 8 million. By 1990, 14 mega-cities were located in countries of the South as compared with 6 in the industrialized countries.

The growth of mega-cities

These demographic trends have seen the ascendancy of large cities, particularly **mega-cities**, which are simply very large cities by virtue of their population size. Table 20.1 shows the world's largest urban agglomerations in 1990. Despite the growth of large cities, it is important to guard against the panic provoked by alarmist projections portending urban explosion and catastrophe in cities of unmanageable size.

Table 20.1 The world's largest urban agglomerations in 1990

Urban agglomeration	Population (thousands)	Comments
Tokyo	25 013	Population would be c.31.6 million if Greater Tokyo Metropolitan Area was taken
New York	16 056	19.3 million in the CMSA[a] in 1990
Mexico City	15 085	Would be several million larger if considered as a polynucleated metropolitan region
Sao Paulo	14 847	Population is for the large metropolitan region
Shanghai	13 452	Population within the large metropolitan region
Bombay	12 223	One reason for rapid growth is expansion of boundaries
Los Angeles	11 456	14.53 million in the CMSA in 1990
Beijing	10 872	Population of metropolitan region; core city much smaller
Calcutta	10 741	Urban agglomeration
Buenos Aires	10 623	Urban agglomeration
Seoul	10 558	
Osaka	10 482	Would be larger if 36 cities around Osaka were included
Rio de Janeiro	9515	Metropolitan Area
Paris	9334	Urban agglomeration
Tianjin	9253	Metropolitan region – core city has half this population
Jakarta	9250	Population of wider metropolitan region is double this
Moscow	9048	Urban agglomeration
Cairo	8633	Population of 'Greater Cairo' is several million larger
Delhi	8171	Urban agglomeration
Manila	7968	Urban agglomeration
Karachi	7965	Some local estimates suggest this is rather low
Lagos	7742	This appears high in comparison with the 1991 census
London	7335	The population could be 12.5 million within a metropolitan regional boundary
Chicago	6792	8 240 000 in the wider CMSA
Istanbul	6507	Urban agglomeration
Lima	6475	Lima–Callao metropolitan area
Essen	6353	Urban agglomeration
Teheran	6351	Urban agglomeration
Bangkok	5894	This is for Bangkok Metropolitan Area; Greater Bangkok or the metropolitan region has several million more
Dhaka	5877	Statistical metropolitan area

[a] CMSA, Consolidated Metropolitan Statistical Area.

Source: Satterthwaite, D. (1996) 'The scale and nature of urban change in the South', unpublished mimeo of the Human Settlements Programme, International Institute for Environment and Development, London, June.

A much faster rate of urban growth was predicted than actually occurred in the 1980s and some of the world's largest cities have in fact grown quite slowly over the last twenty years. For example, it was predicted that São Paulo would top 20 million people but, in fact, it was under 15 million in 1990; and whereas it had been predicted that Bombay would have a population of 18 million, there were just over 12 million in 1990 (UNCHS, 1996). It is also important to bear in mind that not all urban dwellers live in cities, let alone mega-cities. Rapid population growth rates can be more often observed among relatively small cities (Hardoy & Satterthwaite, 1986). This said, it is also the case that the larger the city the greater the increment in population has to be for the rate of urbanization to increase.

When the population of big cities increases dramatically it is often due to changing boundaries. For example, Bombay added 400 000 people to its population annually during the 1980s due to boundary changes between censuses (UNCHS, 1996, p.18). Therefore, care must be taken with international comparisons, given the different ways that **cities** and **urban centres** are defined. 'The proportion of the world's population currently living in urban centres is best considered not as a precise percentage (i.e. 45.2 per cent in 1995) but as being between 40 and 55 per cent, depending on the criteria used to define what is an 'urban centre'' (UNCHS, 1996, p.14).

Although cities have grown dramatically in size, their locations have changed much less. More than two-thirds of the world's 'million cities' in 1990 were already important cities 200 years ago, while around a quarter have been important cities for at least 500 years (UNCHS, 1996, p.14). Nevertheless, the last fifty years have undoubtedly brought great changes to the nature of human settlements – cities, towns and villages. Structural changes within and around cities and the fact that the international economy is becoming ever more integrated has served to reorder the relative importance of cities around the world and has led to economic,

World cities (or **global cities**): Defined and differentiated from other large cities by virtue of the functions they perform, functions which drive the global economy such as providing financial or transport and communications infrastructure and services. Most are in the advanced industrialized countries but Rio de Janeiro is considered to be a world city and Cairo and Johannesburg are thought to be on their way.

Cities: As defined by the UN, 'cities' are over 100 000, 'million cities' are over a million and 'big cities' are over 5 million in size.

Urban centres: According to the UN, these are settlements of over 20 000 people. However, there are different national definitions of cities, towns and urban centres. These are not only based on population size but may describe administrative areas.

social and political upheavals within them. Some cities have become particularly significant by virtue of the functions they perform in the new global economy and they are known as **world cities**.

Urban poverty

According to modernization theory and neoclassical economics, urban poverty should be a temporary phenomenon, which will disappear over time as urban consumption matches production and migrants become integrated into city life. However, the experience, recognized from the 1970s onwards, was of burgeoning squatter settlements and an expanding informal sector, showing little sign of the 'trickle down' economy reaching the vast majority of urban populations. Studies in the 1980s showed that the incidence of poverty rose in cities (Moser & Satterthwaite, 1985) and this has been confirmed by studies of

Figure 20.2 Modern high-rise buildings and shacks co-exist in all Brazilian cities.

the urban impact of structural adjustment policies since then (Chant, 1991, 1996; Kanji, 1995; Moser, 1996).

Urban poverty has been addressed with greater long-term consistency within industrialized countries than in the development literature. In the latter area the debate has largely concerned the rural poor, and the notion of urban bias (Lipton, 1977) has until recently been the mainstream view. This holds that cities have taken the lion's share of national investment while the greatest number of poor live in rural areas. This has indeed been the case, although a demographic shift is currently taking place so that before long the majority of the absolute poor will live in cities and towns. More important is the need to recognize that many poor people live in cities, often very unequal cities (Figure 20.2). They may have greater proximity to facilities and services than poor people in the countryside, but this does not mean they can necessar-

ily afford or access them. For example, poor women can be denied appointments at clinics or children from discriminated minorities be refused entry to schools (Beall, 1997b).

Moreover, Ellen Wratten (1995) has argued that it is not helpful to conceptualize urban poverty and rural poverty as separate definitional categories; they are in fact arbitrary and run the risk of a dualistic spatial classification that in turn confines solutions to the local level when they may be better sought at national or regional level. Nevertheless, poverty in urban areas has particular characteristics which warrant specific focus and attention. First, urban livelihood systems, discussed in the following section, are different from those pursued in the countryside. Urban labour markets and the position of the poor within them provide the single most important determinant of poverty in urban areas (Amis, 1995), and the poorest are found among the unemployed and casually employed.

Second, the urban poor pay more for their goods and services and are often more vulnerable than the rural poor to changes in market conditions, price increases and a decline in real wages because they live in an almost entirely monetized economy. The operation of the urban land market is a particular feature of urban areas which adversely affects the poor, who are squeezed off valuable land and are forced into peripheral or marginal locations. Insecurity of tenure is compounded by insecure living conditions brought about by crime and a lack of public safety. The poor are disproportionately affected, not least of all because they often have an ambiguous relationship with the police. Urban societies can also be very violent societies and violence is a frequent accompaniment to urban poverty (Table 20.2).

But if anything distinguishes the day-to-day life of poor urban dwellers from their rural counter-parts, it is their relationship with the built environment. Poor living conditions, such as appalling overcrowding, contaminated water, poor or absent sanitation, lack of services and the constant threat of floods, landslides or industrial pollution, all mean that the urban poor are exposed to severe environmental health risks (Box 20.1). There is a substantial literature on the impact of poor environments on the health and well-being of low-income urban dwellers (Bradley *et al.*, 1991; Douglass, 1992; Hardoy *et al.*, 1990, 1992; Satterthwaite, 1993). Indeed, in their book *Cities of Hunger*, Pryer and Crook (1990) have argued that the combination of increasing poverty, deteriorating physical environments, inadequate shelter and declining investment in urban infrastructure and services has meant that health conditions are deteriorating faster in cities of the South than in the surrounding rural areas.

Table 20.2 Perceptions of inner-city residents in Kingston, Jamaica, on types of violence in their communities

Type of violence (%)	Greenland, Kingston	Campbell Town, Kingston
Political	3	10
Drugs	8	10
Gang:	32	30
gang war	5	
war over guns	16	20
knives/bottles/stones	11	10
Economic	11	20
Inter-personal	38	10
rape	11	10
other	27	
Domestic:	8	20
male–female	8	10
adult–child		10
Total	100	100

Source: Moser, C. & Holland, J. (1997) *Urban Poverty and Violence in Jamaica*, The World Bank, Washington DC.

Box 20.1 Effects of housing on health

Features of the housing environment that can affect the health of the occupants:

• structure of the shelter (protection from extremes of heat, cold, insulation against noise, dust, insects and rodents);

• provision of adequate water supply (both quality and quantity);

• effective disposal of liquid (sewage) and solid (garbage) waste;

• quality of the housing site (for example, drainage);

• consequences of overcrowding (e.g. household accidents and airborne infections);

• indoor pollution associated with cooking and heating fuels;

• food safety and adequate storage to protect food from spoilage and contamination;

• vectors and hosts of disease associated with the domestic environment;

• the home as a workplace where occupational health questions need consideration.

(UNCHS, 1996, p.133)

20.3 Urban livelihoods in a world economy

Over the last quarter of the twentieth century the world economy has changed drastically, deeply affecting cities of the South. The debt crisis of the early 1980s that emerged among resource-exporting countries and the structural reforms that followed had a profound impact. Clearly not all cities were equally affected and nor did they respond in identical ways to the very uniform policies that constituted the structural adjustment packages of the 'Washington Consensus'. However, there is significant evidence to suggest that in most places the urban poor have been disproportionately affected by structural adjustment through price increases, wage restraints and the reduction in food, housing and transport subsidies. Moreover, the shift in emphasis from non-tradeables to tradeables saw the bulk of investment moving to rural areas. The World Bank itself in its 'new urban agenda' stated that 'By the late 1980s, urban per capita incomes in some countries had reverted to 1970 levels and in some countries to 1960s levels' (World Bank, 1991, p.45).

Cities in a global economy

Some Southern cities have found a niche for themselves in the global economy. For example, Bangalore as the 'Silicon Valley' of India has developed a world reputation as a computer software centre of growing importance. For many cities their global niche is to provide a manufacturing base, often founded on low labour costs in export-oriented activities. The nimble fingers of Asian women turn faxed and e-mailed text from all over the world into perfect typed documents, in what are essentially global typing pools. Other cities have attached free trade zones (FTZs) where often the requirements are for a cheap, passive and usually female labour force. In some countries of Asia, the issue of comparative advantage based on the exploitation of child labour has become a political hot potato in international trade negotiations.

The changes that have taken place in the world economy have been characterized as globalization (Chapter 16), the physical manifestation of which James Mittelman (1994, p.427) has defined as 'the spatial reorganization of production, the interpenetration of industries across borders, the spread of financial markets, the diffusion of identical consumer goods to distant countries.' This, he argues, is accompanied by massive transfers of people, with 'resultant conflicts between immigrant and established communities in formerly tight knit neighbourhoods.' In this context, many cities are still seeking a viable place in an increasingly unequal world. Among the regions that are lumped together as the 'South', Africa has been the region most adversely affected by processes of globalization, leading Carole Rakodi (1998) to conclude that no 'world city' as yet exists on the continent.

It is generally agreed that there is a high correlation between increased urbanization and strong and diversified economies. So why have so many large Southern cities failed to flourish? One reason is that they maintain relatively weak positions within world markets and are bypassed by the digital highways that connect the older major cities. The latter have a number of advantages as outlined by Saskia Sassen in *The Global City* (1991, pp.3–4):

"Beyond their long history as centers for international trade and banking, these cities now function in four new ways: first, as highly concentrated command points in the organization of the world economy; second, as key locations for finance and for specialized service firms, which have replaced manufacturing as the leading economic sectors; third, as sites of production, including the production of innovations, in these leading industries; and fourth, as markets for the products and innovations produced... Thus a new type of city has appeared. It is the global city. Leading examples now are New York, London and Tokyo."

The question we have to ask ourselves is what effect do these processes have on the lives of ordinary people in cities of the South? One thing we know for sure is that the struggle for livelihoods is an increasingly precarious one (Box 20.2).

Box 20.2   The garment factories of Dhaka

In 1996 people began to suggest that the Bangladesh garments industry may have seen its best times. The phasing out of the Multi-Fibre Arrangement over the period 1995–2005 removes the quota advantage it once held and leaves Bangladesh at the mercy of the free market and competition from other garment producers. In such an event the industry may be tempted to manipulate its remaining comparative advantage and reduce the wages of the young single women who make up its labour force.

Dhaka is part of a global putting-out system and these young women workers are among the most exploited in the world. Because the factories are relatively new their working conditions compare fairly well to those of workers in other places but they are still cramped and the work is intensive, often leading to physical problems such as poor eyesight, respiratory disease and damage to the spine. It is hard but there is often nothing else for these young women and the families they help support. They do not know that they are in competition with workers in Indonesia, Thailand, India or Vietnam when they 'pour forth from the slums of Dhaka each morning to labour on garments that we unthinkingly buy' (Seabrook, 1996, p.130).

Making a living

A powerful obstacle to sustainable urban development and urban poverty reduction is the inability to provide employment for a growing labour force. This constitutes one of the most intractable problems facing national and local governments. Most urban jobs are concentrated in the public, manufacturing and service sectors with the latter increasing in relative importance as public sector jobs are in decline and manufacturing employment becomes more insecure. For the majority of people who cannot find work in the formal waged sector, their only choice is to seek a livelihood in the informal economy (Chapter 5).

The conventional view of the informal sector is that it is relatively easy to enter, it operates on a smaller scale than the formal sector and often with indigenous resources and adapted technology. The work done within it is said to be labour intensive, using skills acquired outside the formal school system and involving minimal capital investment and maximum use of family labour (Figure 20.3). Much of this is true but simple categorizations are always problematic. For example, research has shown that sometimes entry into the informal economy can be difficult as there is gate-keeping by those who already have access to customers, skills, sites or markets. Sometimes informal operations are large scale, capital intensive and use imported technology. While many of the poorest urban dwellers are workers in the informal economy, many informal traders and producers themselves can make reasonable and even handsome livings. What is always the case is that the informal economy is unregulated and characterized by competition. However, it is problematic to lump together as 'the informal sector' such a broad range of unaccountable activities as self-employment, casual work and home-based production as well as illegal pursuits (Bromley & Gerry, 1979; de Soto, 1989; Gilbert & Gugler, 1992; Thomas, 1995).

Moreover, the dichotomy between a 'formal' and 'informal' economy is increasingly oversimplistic, given the spatial reorganization of production within the global economy and the rise of subcontracting and home-working. A related problem associated both with defining and measuring the informal economy centres on what is often a fuzzy boundary between income-generating and other areas of work, particularly among women. For example, a high percentage of women work in the informal sector but combine these activities with reproductive responsibilities such as making cooked food for sale while feeding their families, engaging in street trading close to home or looking after the children of others along with their own.

Figure 20.3   Children scavenging in Asia's garbage heaps have replaced adult workers on the production line as the leitmotif of the struggle for urban livelihoods.

Coping under economic stress

The struggle for urban livelihoods involves not only production but consumption as well. Declining real per capita incomes have put increasing pressure on urban households, and particularly women within them, not only to generate income but to engage in multiple strategies for survival and betterment. The literature on structural adjustment policies is rich in examples which demonstrate the impact on families of liberalization and of cuts in social sector spending and subsidies. City level studies have revealed that the social response to economic crisis and austerity has produced a variety of changes at the household level. These include increased labour force participation by women and income earning on the part of children and the elderly. However, they also extend to changing expenditure patterns, reduced overall consumption, changes in family diet, increased indebtedness and a rise in self-production of food, shelter, child care and health care (Chant, 1991, 1996; Kanji, 1995; Moser, 1996).

There are often important rural–urban linkages in the livelihood systems of urban households. On the one hand people migrate to cities in search of employment and urban workers send remittances to family members in rural areas. On the other, they can equally rely on relatives in the countryside during stringent times, for example for agricultural produce, medicines, family labour or extended periods of child care (Beall & Kanji, 1999). There is also evidence on increased income transfers within families and the growing importance of social networks and informal social security at household or community level as a resource for poor urban dwellers (Gonzalez de la Rocha, 1994). What this points to is the fact that the pursuit of livelihoods can include a swathe of responses ranging from labour market involvement to changing patterns of consumption, social networking and the rearrangement of household responsibilities. These responses are put under severe strain during periods of economic stress and as welfare services, however inadequate, are replaced by reliance on the caring capacity of families and communities (Beall, 1995; Moser, 1996).

20.4 Poverty, housing and the urban environment

The importance of safe, secure and adequately serviced housing for health, well-being and the pursuit of livelihoods is crucial to people living and working in cities. Yet David Satterthwaite (1997) estimated in 1990 that there were at least 600 million people in the urban areas of Latin America, Africa and Asia who were still living in housing of such poor quality and with such inadequacies in water, sanitation and drainage provision that their health and lives were under constant threat. He goes on to argue that:

"If these 600 million urban dwellers are considered 'poor' – for it is largely their lack of income (and assets) that makes them unable to afford better quality housing and basic services – it greatly increases the scale of urban poverty when compared to conventional income based poverty lines. Although the literature on poverty often refers to people 'living in poverty', it often gives little consideration to their living conditions."

(Satterthwaite, 1997, p.12)

In the last section we looked at urban livelihoods and focused on productive and reproductive activities at an individual or household level. Here we look at what Castells (1983) has called the production, distribution and management of 'collective consumption', being the goods and services needed for the reproduction of the urban workforce on a day-to-day and generational basis. They include, for example, land, housing, a safe water supply and sanitation, health, education and urban transport. The main illustrative examples used below are those of housing and urban basic services, notably water supply and sanitation. The lens through which they are examined is a policy lens, thus introducing into our considerations the perspective of urban policy makers and planners who have to make hard decisions in the context of rising need and limited resources.

Meeting the housing challenge

In the early 1950s and 1960s there was a general belief that the state could and should be responsible for the provision of housing and services, and governments attempted to deliver low-cost but conventional housing to growing urban populations. However, by the 1970s it was becoming increasingly clear that this strategy was failing to provide anything like a sufficient number of units to meet housing needs; nor were these units affordable to the majority of the urban poor. What they were doing, instead, was building their own homes in slums and informal settlements. This led to burgeoning informal land and housing markets, parallel to and unregulated by the formal system. As UNCHS (Habitat) (1996, p.199) has acknowledged: 'It is a well known fact that between 30 and 60 per cent of the housing units in most cities in the South are illegal in that either they contravene land ownership laws or they contravene building and planning laws or codes. Many contravene both sets of laws.'

A common response to rapid urbanization and employment and housing deficits was to try to discourage people from moving into cities in the first place and to remove those who either had no job or were living in temporary informal settlements. Such strategies were most blatant in apartheid South Africa where there was an underlying racial subtext to the policy of forced removals. However, they have been used in many other countries, albeit in a less systematic way. Even today, when urban development has generally seen bulldozers exchanged for more positive responses to urbanization, evictions continue. They often involve collusion between property developers or other powerful interest groups, including elements of the state.

The most important response to urbanization over the last half century has been investment in rural areas, not only to address rural poverty but to provide incentives for people to stay in the countryside rather than migrating to the

---

Box 20.3   International policy on housing and human settlements

The importance of providing adequate shelter was underscored by the United Nations Conference on Human Settlements (UNCHS (Habitat)), which was held in Vancouver, Canada in 1976 and became known as Habitat I. This was the era of welfare and state-led urban development.

Ten years later Habitat produced the *Global Report on Human Settlements*, which was more circumspect about being able to provide public housing. The emphasis instead was on 'enabling settlement strategies' which should contain a response to two main challenges: 'how to deal with problems posed by very large numbers of poor people and how to provide for effective autonomy of community-based groups' (UNCHS,

1986, p.196). This was the era of efficiency and community participation in urban projects.

In June, 1996, The Habitat II or 'City Summit' conference was held in Istanbul which had as its two key themes *shelter for all* and *sustainable human development in an urbanizing world* (UNCHS, 1996). One of the critical issues to infuse Habitat II was the debate on housing rights. It was ultimately agreed that everyone had a basic right to shelter but that governments did not have a responsibility to provide land and housing which also have a market value. This was a conference promoting public–private–community partnership in an era of cost recovery and institutional reform.

---

cities (Lipton, 1977). However, whether based on realistic assessments of opportunities provided by cities or not, people have continued to migrate (Todaro, 1976) and city governments have had to provide shelter and services for ever-growing urban populations. A number of policy alternatives were tried between the 1960s and 1980s (Box 20.3). These can be characterized as policies to reduce costs, reduce standards and reduce housing provision.

Efforts to reduce costs were made during the 1960s and 1970s through the promotion of self-help housing. The idea was that it would lower labour costs by formally involving people themselves in cheaper building processes than those they were already employing themselves informally (Turner, 1972, 1976). However, there were a number of problems with self-help housing (Ward, 1982). It was still expensive as management costs did not go down at the same time as labour costs. (In fact they often increased, as good workers often made bad builders.) Moreover, local politicians did not like self-help housing schemes as they could not offer housing as an incentive or reward for political support. *Reducing standards* was another method used during the 1970s to make urban housing more affordable. This involved the use of cheaper building materials and designs and was influ-

enced by intermediate technology and 'small is beautiful' approaches to development. For example, people were provided with starter or core houses, perhaps a single room which they could later add on to when they could afford it. In practice this rarely happened because even the core housing was more than many people could afford.

The next phase can be characterized as one of *reducing state housing provision* with a shift to what became known as 'enabling shelter strategies'. At first this involved the promotion of 'sites and services' schemes by governments and international donors such as the World Bank. Here serviced plots were provided on which people could build or have their own homes built when time and resources allowed. A major problem was land, which often turned out to be marginal or on the periphery of cities, far from jobs, amenities and all but the most basic services. Not surprisingly there was little take up from poor people although larger plots were often bought up (although not necessarily occupied) by middle and upper income people for investment purposes. The promotion of sites and services schemes gave way to 'upgrading' of informal settlements based on the premise that it was cheaper and easier to provide people with basic services than to move them against their will.

This so-called 'enabling approach' to shelter provision has not fundamentally changed since the mid-1980s, although there are differences in operational emphasis, such as a focus on upgrading of services, the provision of accessible housing finance or the involvement of informal sector builders in housing schemes promoting skills or small enterprise development.

Nevertheless, successive approaches have failed to keep pace with demand in many cities and this has resulted in inflated land and housing costs, making shelter a very costly item for the urban poor. Increasingly rental housing is being recognized as a solution to low-cost housing (Gilbert & Varley, 1990) as even low-income landlords rent out rooms or floor space to even poorer tenants (Kumar, 1996). Another response is to delay the formation of new households. This has led to a rise in the average size of urban households in many cities. Current housing strategies are said to provide the urban poor with a choice. But the choice is constrained to allocating a huge proportion of their incomes to housing and basic services or to living in poor quality accommodation without adequate services to reduce their housing costs.

Access to urban services

The known health impact of poor urban environmental conditions, and the recognition by urban élites that 'germs do not carry passports', means there is more of a consensus over the need to provide urban services such as water supply, sanitation and drainage to poor households and settlements than there is over seeing housing as a basic right. Housing not only gives shelter but is an economic asset and it is believed by many that the issue of house values and private land markets, whether formal or informal, complicates matters. However, the situation for services is also complicated. For example, it is asserted that upgrading informal settlements through the provision of services not only attends to environmental health but serves to legitimate what are often illegal settlements and to raise the value of their land and structures.

As a result, the widely held view that an adequate water supply and sanitation provision is a basic need or right has not necessarily translated into the majority of the urban poor in cities of the South receiving adequate services (Jarman, 1997). The environmental health risks of the urban poor are commonly addressed through the urban basic services approach, which identifies lack of access to services such as water and sanitation as both a cause and symptom of poverty in low-income settlements. More recent examples are of an integrated urban basic services approach which includes health, education and enterprise development components as well. There are two main problems with area-based approaches. First, they often fail to deal adequately with the practical difficulties of linking area-based services to city level services. For example, the NGO Orangi Pilot Project (OPP) in Karachi assists local communities in providing their own sanitation. The focus of their work is to lower the cost of sanitary latrines and sewerage lines so that residents can afford to pay for them and indeed, their systems are a fraction of the cost of the charges levied by the local authority. Renowned internationally for their success in participatory, community-level sanitation provision, OPP has nevertheless experienced inordinate difficulty in getting the metropolitan authorities to co-operate in connecting neighbourhood-based sanitation to the city's main sewers.

A second problem is that area-based approaches fail to deal with the more fundamental issue of inequalities at a city-wide level. In many instances, a piped water supply and sewerage connections only reach a minority of urban dwellers, invariably those concentrated in better off and high income areas. Moreover, investment and subsidies, whether socially or politically motivated, are often channelled at existing services. As a result, governments have tended to favour urban élites in service provision. This is compounded by the fact that area-based investment in urban services in low income areas is nowadays invariably accompanied by cost recovery (i.e. requiring those who benefit from public services to pay a fee which contributes to the cost of providing the services). The justification is that cost recovery is often less than what the poor already pay, for example for water from private vendors (Figure 20.4). Others argue that the answer is not universally free services, as no local authority in the South could deliver these successfully in any case. Rather there are alternatives through cross-subsidization at the city level, between those who can afford to pay for connections and those who cannot. Caroline Stephens (1996) makes the point starkly:

"There are inequalities, for example, in access to water and sanitation facilities or education opportunities between groups in cities – these may lead to health *inequalities*, often in incidence and prevalence of infectious diseases … the urban poor often have least access to piped water and are forced to pay more than the wealthy for poor quality and limited quantities of water from vendors. This becomes a double regressive taxation in which one group is doubly disbenefited (in health and economic terms) while another doubly gains. Put bluntly, the poor pay more for their cholera."

(Stephens, 1996, p.13)

The imperative for improving urban services at a city wide level can be argued for in two ways. At worst it can be said that the urban health risks involved constitute a social and environmental time bomb for cities of the South. At best it can be argued that they reduce the productivity of urban dwellers. For poor people themselves, ill health and the loss of adult breadwinners through ill health constitutes one of the main factors plunging families into poverty (Harriss, 1989) and efforts to improve urban services affect their survival as much as their efficiency.

Figure 20.4   In many cities the poor pay far more for water purchased from private water vendors than the better off pay for a piped water supply. Water vendor in Karachi, Pakistan.

20.5 Conclusion: cities of citizens

This chapter started by saying that cities are places where people assemble and engage in multiple and intense activities (Massey *et al.*, 1999). It has shown how they are spatial arenas in which who gets what in the city is determined by the collusion and collision of contested social relationships and identities (Beall, 1997a; Box 20.4). It has examined urban people at work and at home and in this final section it looks at urban dwellers as citizens and, more particularly, as organized citizens.

There are two broad perspectives on collective action in the city. First, there is the view that cities have given rise to innovative forms of social organization and politics. Even in the context of scarcity, it has been shown that people in urban communities, and particularly women, engage in a range of mutual support and self-help activities (Gonzalez de la Rocha,

1984) represented, for example, by the well-known soup kitchens of Lima, Peru, or the struggle for urban services in Gyuayaquil, Ecuador (Moser & Peake, 1987). These initiatives are often presented as evidence that communities are imbued with 'social assets' that can be identified and helpfully engaged with in policy terms (Moser, 1998).

Such initiatives are also characterized as collective action, which Manuel Castells (1983) has argued is a necessary although insufficient condition for the formation of urban social movements. According to Castells, urban social movements, which are built on co-operative activities at community or neighbourhood level, emerge in the absence of effective channels for social change and are the political manifestations of urban poverty, which in turn are only successful if they achieve structural change, notably a shift in the balance of power between social classes in a city.

Box 20.4 Bombay (Mumbai)

Any international visitor to Bombay is struck by the drive into South Bombay from Sahar International Airport, through the slums of Dharavi, Mahim and Parel where people live in shelters made from plastic, cardboard, tin and cloth, lined in rows along pavements, under bridges, in pipes and beside rail tracks. Over half the city's residents live in slums. An estimated 300 newcomers stream into Bombay each day and the problem of inadequate housing is compounded by physical constraints. Bombay was originally a group of seven islands linked by land reclamation. As a result land supply is limited and Bombay has one of the highest population densities of any city in the world – 160 000 people per square mile. The physical qualities of urban life for slum dwellers – the square footage of a person's shelter, whether they have clean drinking water or privacy – are unbearably hard but the possibility of a job necessarily outweighs the quest for home comforts.

Alongside this world is the Bombay of commerce, manufacture, finance capital and 'Bollywood', India's lucrative and prolific film industry. In the areas where the wealthy live, often in high rise buildings in the high- spots of the city, real estate prices are among the highest in the world. In their book *Bombay: The Cities Within* (1995) Sharada Dwivedi and Rahul Mehrotra describe the way these two worlds co-exist in space which they share, understand and use in different ways. There is a symbiotic relationship between these two worlds; just as the poor need to be close to their jobs, so the wealthy want ready access to cheap and willing labour. Thus the slums of Bombay are not transitory. Some residents have lived on a particular patch of pavement for twenty or thirty years. Communities form and mature. They struggle for services, start businesses, form neighbourhood associations. Adults hold down multiple jobs and children go to school. They suffer ill health and have short lives.

Some believe that things can only get worse as the government steps back from trying to provide amenities or improve the quality of life. Others believe that the future of Bombay lies in the heroic dignity of its thrifty, hard-working and energetic slum dwellers.

The second standpoint offers a more pessimistic view of human nature and the potential for collective action on any significant scale. It is represented here by Nancy Scheper-Hughes (1992) who says of the people in the town she studied over many years:

> "Their daily lives are circumscribed by an immensely powerful state and by local economic and political interests that are openly hostile to them...It is too much to expect the people of the Alto to organize collectively when chronic scarcity makes individually negotiated relations of dependency on myriad political and personal bosses in town a necessary survival tactic...Staying alive in the shantytown demands a certain 'selfishness' that pits individuals against each other and that rewards those who take advantage of those even weaker."
>
> (Scheper-Hughes, 1992, pp.472–3)

This is a bleak perspective but one that helps explain, perhaps, why the shantytowns of Latin America did not produce the revolutionary urban proletariat anticipated by the early Castells. Recently a more subdued Castells (1996) has characterized the urban proletariat not as active organized protesters but as pacified individual consumers or would-be consumers in a global market place, subordinate to the global culture of McDonalds and to structures of international power that have penetrated their local worlds in multiple ways. Popular resistance is represented, therefore, as cowed and weak.

An alternative and more integrated view of social organization and collective action in cities is presented by Friedmann and Douglass (1998, p.1) who focus on the local level, 'local not in the sense of being closed off from global influences, but as the effective terrain for engagement in civic life beyond the household and in relation to the state and the corporate economy.' Eschewing the concepts of 'people', 'proletariat' or even 'community', they embrace the concept of citizenship.

> "Citizenship is political and thus a concept in the public sphere. It pertains to only a segment of social life which itself is deeply rooted in what we call, for want of a better term, civil society. Civil society is that part of social life which lies beyond the immediate reach of the state and which, we would argue, must exist for a democratic state to flower. It is the society of households, family networks, civic and religious organizations, and communities that are bound to each other primarily by shared histories, collective memories and cultural norms of reciprocity."
>
> (Friedmann & Douglass, 1998, pp.1–2)

This view of the relationship between civil society organizations and the state in cities of citizens is closer to Katznelson's (1996) reading of Polanyi's 'great transformation' than it is to Harvey's (1973) original application. It is also closer to Harvey's more recent thinking on the urban environment and local level action (1996). Viewing cities as places of citizens rather than simply of inhabitants presents two key challenges for urban governance. The first is for cities to have enough political and financial autonomy to respond to the needs and demands of their citizens without financial responsibility devolving exclusively to the local level. This would lead to unfunded mandates and increased local level responsibilities not matched by adequate resources or fund-raising capacity. The second challenge is to ensure that civil society is allowed to flourish because, as Friedmann and Douglass (1998) argue, it is that part of social life that is essential if responsive urban planning, inclusive urban politics and a democratic city are to exist.

Summary

This chapter argues that because of rapid urbanization and the fact that cities of the South will soon be home to most of the world's absolute poor, urban poverty is one of the most pressing social issues to be addressed in the 2000s. Against a background of some of the critical debates on the character and role of cities, the chapter examines what life is like for low-income urban dwellers in cities of Africa, Asia and Latin America. The key problematic addressed in the chapter is whether cities are places of possibility or simply enduring poverty and grind for the millions of resourceful people that grow up in them and flock to them. The implications for urban development are explored through a discussion of urban livelihood systems and the challenge of ensuring adequate shelter and living environments for growing numbers of urban dwellers. The importance for responsive planning and democratic governance of recognizing urban dwellers as active citizens is highlighted.

21

TAKING CULTURE SERIOUSLY

TIM ALLEN

It may seem obvious that culture must be taken seriously when investigating issues of development, but unfortunately this often does not happen. Sometimes culture is treated as relatively unimportant, and sometimes culture is taken into account but in a muddled or simplistic way. Both result in highly misleading analyses. These pitfalls are discussed at some length here, partly because they have a considerable influence on policy-making, and partly because recognizing them helps to explain how the concept of culture might be used more effectively. Thus, the main question which the chapter attempts to answer is:

Q How can the concept of culture best be used to help us understand development processes?

21.1 The problem of conceptualizing culture

If you ask most British people what they think culture is, they might tell you that it is literature, art and music, and they would perhaps be thinking particularly of Victorian novels, paintings by Turner and music by Elgar. These are the things 'cultured' people enjoy. Those who are not 'cultured' eat fish and chips, go to football matches or bingo, drink beer, watch soap operas on television, and read the tabloid newspapers. On the other hand, and here is where everything starts to become muddled, these 'uncultured' folk might be classified as enjoying 'popular culture', something that may be thought of as better than the 'high-brow' culture of those who go to the opera. Additional complications arise if you ask a question like: 'What is the difference between French culture and English culture?' Your answer might then include some of the following: international languages, frogs' legs, snails, garlic, making love, sense of humour, the Royal Family, tweed jackets, crimes of passion, tea, 'stiff upper lips', and the Battle of Waterloo. In fact 'culture' is one of those words which is used without any exact shared understanding of what it means.

In 1952, two American anthropologists, Alfred Kroeber and Clyde Kluckhohn, asserted in a much quoted publication that the 'idea of culture, in the technical anthropological sense, is one of the key notions in contemporary thought.' They then proceeded to survey no less than 164 definitions of culture and civilization (which they regarded as a 'near-synonym'). Their own definition was that 'culture consists of patterns, explicit and implicit, of and for behaviour acquired and transmitted by symbols.' They also added that 'the essential core of culture consists of traditional…ideas and especially their attached values' (Kroeber & Kluckhohn, 1952, p.181, quoted in Kuper, 1999, p.58). Used in this sense, they asserted that culture is as important as 'such categories as gravity in physics, disease in medicine, evolution in biology' (Kroeber & Kluckhohn, 1952, p.3). But in fact the meanings of culture have not cohered exclusively around their definition, even amongst anthropologists, nor does it seem as precise and scientific a conception as it did to them, and a quarter of a century later, the influential British socialist thinker Raymond Williams could describe culture as: 'one of the most complicated words in the English language' (Williams, 1976, p.87).

Williams was one of the founding figures of 'cultural studies', which has become firmly established as a new academic subject area. For Williams, the term 'culture' could be useful because it 'more conveniently indicates a total human order' than the word 'society' (Williams, 1979, p.154). However, he also complained that he sometimes wished that he had never heard of the 'damned word', and that he had become ever more aware of its difficulties (ibid.).

In recent years the situation has been further complicated within academia, not only by the continued rise of cultural studies, but by the so-called 'cultural turn' in geography, the growth of media studies, and a resurgence of literature theory and of cultural anthropology (see for example the overviews in Jackson, 1989; Jenks, 1993; During, 1993; Nugent & Shore, 1997; Crang, 1998; Kuper, 1999). More and more books and articles elaborate insights into what culture might mean, with debates even within particular disciplines, let alone between them, sometimes indulging 'in purely definitional argy-bargy' (Baumann, 1996, p.11), and some of them couched in the kind of obscure jargon that is incomprehensible to the uninitiated. In addition there has been an increased tendency for economists, political scientists, journalists and politicians to invoke culture as a deterministic explanation for everything from market transaction costs, to civil war, to the 'spirit of capitalism' (see Box 21.1) – often without being at all exact about what they think the term actually means.

One extreme example of this is Samuel Huntington's *The Clash of Civilizations and the*

Box 21.1   The spirit of capitalism as a cultural prerequisite for development

Max Weber's book *The Protestant Ethic and the Spirit of Capitalism* is often cited as a powerful argument that a certain kind of culture is essential for development. Published in German in 1904–5, it first appeared in English in 1930. Weber shared Karl Marx's concern with the role of material factors in influencing the course of history, but he was also fascinated with religion, values and ethics. For Weber, the economic conditions that Marx believed determined the development and future transformation of capitalism were embedded within a unique way of behaving. He sought to identify the emergence of this 'ethos' or 'spirit' of modern Western Capitalism.

Weber took care to separate capitalistic enterprise from the pursuit of gain as such. 'Capitalism', he maintained, had existed for a long time in the shape of mercantile operations. But only in the West, and in relatively recent times, had capitalistic activity become associated with the rational organization of formally free labour – i.e. labour routinized by calculated administration within continuously functioning enterprises. This required two things: a disciplined labour force and regularized investment of capital. Workers had to be prevented from stopping work when they had met their needs, while those with wealth needed to do more than just consume it themselves. Thus, modern capitalism required the regular reproduction of capital, involving its continued investment and reinvestment for the end of economic efficiency – or, to put it another way, the continuous accumulation of wealth for its own sake. For Weber, this was the essence of the spirit of capitalism. He then posed the question: why did it first occur in Europe?

His explanation involved seven factors (not just one, as is sometimes suggested).

These were the following:

1   The separation of productive enterprise from the household.

2   The development of the European cities, with their political autonomy and bourgeois society.

3   The inherited tradition of Roman law, which provided an integrated and developed rationalization of juridical practice.

4   The emergence of the nation state, administered by full-time bureaucratic officials (this provided a rational-legal system which served as a framework within which capitalist enterprise could occur, and also a model for the organization of the enterprises themselves).

5   The introduction of double entry book keeping.

6   The series of historical processes which Marx had also emphasized, preparing the way for the formation of a 'free' mass of wage-labourers, whose livelihoods depended upon the sale of labour power in the market.

7   The emergence of Protestantism, and particularly the 'this worldly asceticism of Puritanism', as focused through the concept of the calling.

According to Weber, the concept of the calling did not exist in Antiquity or in Catholic theology. It refers to the idea that the highest form of moral obligation of the individual is to fulfil duty in worldly affairs. Weber linked this particularly with the teaching of Calvin on predestination. Success in a calling was seen as a sign of being among the elect, and the accumulation of wealth was morally sanctioned in so far as it was combined with a sober, industrious career.

Weber was not suggesting that all capitalists had to be Puritans. He argued that, once established, industrial capitalism eradicated the specifically religious elements in the ethic which helped to produce it: '...victorious capitalism, since it rests on mechanical foundations, needs its support no longer...[T]he idea of duty in one's calling prowls about in our lives like the ghost of dead religious beliefs.'

For the ultimately pessimistic Weber, Puritanism played a part in creating the 'iron cage' in which 'modern man' exists – an increasingly bureaucratic order from which the spontaneous enjoyment of life is ruthlessly expunged. 'The Puritan', Weber concluded, 'wanted to work in a calling; we are forced to do so.'

There are several criticisms that can be made of Weber's thesis.

1   Weber was wrong in some of his claims about Protestant theology.

2   The spirit of capitalism was present in earlier periods. Some historians have in fact argued that the Reformation was a reaction against the capitalistic tendencies of late medieval Catholicism.

3   It has been shown that Weber's empirical data about the specific economic activities of Protestantism is highly questionable.

4   The causal links he suggests are impossible to prove.

However, perhaps the most common criticisms are based on misconceptions. Weber was not arguing that Calvinism was the cause of capitalism, or that capitalism could not subsequently develop elsewhere.

Remaking of the World Order (1997). Here it is argued that, in the post Cold War world, the most important distinctions between people are cultural. This means that they 'define themselves in terms of ancestry, religion, language, history, values, customs and institutions', and that they identify with cultural groups, which 'at the broadest level' are 'civilizations' (Huntington, 1997, p 21).

Huntington's views are discussed in Chapter 23, but here it is worth highlighting that, on the one hand, he includes a huge array of things under his category of culture while, on the other, he distinguishes the 'cultural' from things that are 'ideological, political, or economic'. But how can politics be separated from values, customs and institutions, or ideology be divorced from religion, language and history? Culture for Huntington is something so general as to encompass virtually all aspects of being human, and at the same time is taken to refer to something quite specific.

A reason for the confusion is that culture cannot be thought of in isolation. As we have seen, it may be connected with the notion of 'society', or with the idea of 'civilization', or it may indicate 'a total human order'. At the same time it may refer to particular aesthetic judgements, or to refined ways of behaving, or to codes of ethics and morals. It is inherently ambiguous and suggestive. On the one hand, this seems like a good reason not to become too obsessed with a search for the word's 'real' meaning, but to accept that it has multiple associations. On the other hand, if the notion of culture is going to be employed for analytical purposes, it requires thought and care. Thus it is not a problem that Huntington uses the word 'culture' to draw attention to a range of issues he wants to investigate. The problem lies in the fact that he uses it in a vague way, and yet makes it the primary conceptual building block of his argument.

Perhaps the best way of unpacking culture is to focus on its etymology, because culture is a word with a history. Its origins are linked to 'cultivate' and 'cultivation', and a list of definitions given in *The Concise Oxford Dictionary* begins with: 'Tillage of the soil; rearing, production (of bees, oysters, fish, silk, bacteria); quality of bacteria thus produced.' During the seventeenth century this meaning was extended in a metaphorical way, to refer to the growth of individuals or of human society. Coleridge (1772–1834) wrote about the 'good' of human cultivation, and suggested the formation of a special group within society charged with upholding the necessary ideal of culture. Some thinkers, notably Herder (1744–1803) in Germany, also started to use the word culture in the plural, to refer to a number of separate and distinct entities, each with its own way of life or habits. This was an important introduction, because it was adopted by the German-born Franz Boas (1858–1942), perhaps the most important 'founding father' of American cultural anthropology.

By the turn of the twentieth century, 'culture' was already a concept with a complex of overlapping but potentially different kinds of meanings. Three of these have proved particularly significant in the social sciences and humanities.

The broadest related to debates about the theory of evolution – debates which continue up to the present. This is the argument about the extent to which human behaviour is determined by biology. For those who maintain that humans are not just another primate, the crucial difference between humans and animals is culture. Here culture refers to 'learned, adapted symbolic behaviour, based on a full-fledged language, associated with technical inventiveness, a complex of skills that in turn depends on a capacity to organize exchange relationships between communities' (Kuper, 1994, p.90).

A second meaning of culture was more overtly value laden. Culture was again conceptualized as singular, but it was viewed as less pervasive. It was what 'a person ought to acquire in order to become a fully worthwhile moral agent' (Barnard & Spencer, 1996, p.136). Some people (e.g. well-educated English gentlemen) and some human products (e.g. classical music), were understood as having more culture than others. This meaning still has a wide currency, although it is not usually expressed in such extreme terms, and is often implicit. It informs debates about aesthetic quality (for example of novels or films), and it is recognized in everyday conversation that a cultured person is unlikely to spit on the floor or pick her nose in public.

In contrast, a third usage was plural. It indicated that each distinct population group or society had its own values, norms, moral codes, customs and modes of thinking which were passed from one generation to the next. Building on the work of Franz Boas, this became a common approach in anthropology, especially in the United States. One recent encyclopaedia of social and cultural anthropology even calls it the 'anthropological sense', and explains that it:

"…is plural and relativistic. The world is divided into different cultures, each worthwhile in its way. Any particular person is the product of the particular culture in which he or she has lived, and the differences between human beings are to be explained (but not judged) by differences in their culture (rather than their race)."

(Barnard & Spencer, 1996, p.136)

Although they are very different, these three conceptions have rarely been kept completely separate. In popular discourse about culture, and in academic writing, there has usually been a shifting between them. In practice this has also been the case among anthropologists. Those who normally use the word in the plural, will revert to the singular when discussing human behaviour generally, and it is interesting to note how the definition of culture adopted by Kroeber and Kluckhohn in 1952 seems to have been an amalgamation of both singular and plural connotations. More insidiously, the élitist sense of culture also creeps in. It is only quite recently that anthropologists have refrained from referring to 'primitive' or 'savage' culture, and the more neutral terms nowadays employed cannot readily escape similar derogatory connotations. There is the suggestion in expressions like 'other cultures', 'traditional cultures' or 'local cultures' that there is something lacking in that 'they' are not like 'us'. Anthropologists have tried to side-step the problem, usually by emphasizing their relativism (i.e. their unwillingness to make judgements about which ways of life are better than others). However, this does little to challenge 'Western-centric' thinking, which can be hegemonic enough to appropriate what fits from anthropological studies, and leave aside what does not. Whatever the concerns of the authors, anthropological studies may be interpreted as representing people from 'other cultures' as trapped in their own ignorance, fixed in time and needy of 'help' to develop and to emulate the successful 'West'.

Anthropologists are acutely aware of these ambiguities in the concept of culture. In fact, there has been a line of thought in the British academic tradition of social anthropology that culture should be treated as something ephemeral, which has to be seen through in order to observe social structures underneath. At one time this led to some acrimonious debates with American cultural anthropologists, about what was proper anthropology. These arguments can seem a bit silly these days, but the thorough interrogation of concepts which they provoked has had a significant legacy. Contemporary anthropologists tend to be resistant both to the idea that culture can be scientifically observed in the way that Kroeber and Kluckhohn had in mind, and to the notion that 'a culture' can be understood as the shared values of 'a society'. Some go further, suggesting that it is better to avoid referring to culture as much as possible, and instead to make clear what aspects of the human condition are being discussed (e.g. religious beliefs, codes of morality, cognition, forms of economic exchange, kinship, art). However, most would also take the view that the fact that culture carries a variety of meanings should not lead us to sacrifice 'a good, if complicated word altogether' (Baumann, 1996, p.11). Essentially this is because it draws attention to the context in which social life occurs, and to the connections between activities which are often treated as distinct.

I will return to anthropological approaches towards the end of the chapter, because they have important implications for taking culture seriously in the study of development. But having indicated some of the complexities of culture as a concept, I will now turn to the dangers of ignoring it and of treating it too simplistically.

21.2 Setting culture aside

In this section I discuss the danger of treating culture as something relatively unimportant. I do so with reference to developments in Iran during the late 1970s and early 1980s. I try to explain why a political economist writing just before the revolution underestimated religion, and I indicate ways in which the specific nature of Iranian Islam had a fundamentally important bearing on what happened in the country. It is not my intention to suggest that political economy is misleading compared with other approaches. My point is more general: the assumption that society operates according to economic principles is a partial perspective, and one that can readily lead to flawed interpretations.

The following extracts are taken from a book on Iran by Fred Halliday. They refer to the activities of religious scholars, known as 'mollahs', and their leaders, known as 'ayatollahs'. The book was published in 1979 just before the Ayatollah Khomeini swept to power, and established an Islamic state (Figure 21.1).

"The role of the mollahs and their associates, the merchants of the bazaar, is of especial interest, given their apparent obscurity in the years prior to 1978 and then their major role in the events of that year. There has no doubt been a revival of religious sentiment in Iran in recent years, but it would be misleading to analyse the events of 1978 in purely religious terms or to accept the concept of an 'Islamic revolution' as propounded by the religious leaders. Both this characterization, and the Shah's references to his opponents as 'religious fanatics', obscure the deep material, i.e. social and economic factors, underlying this movement and the specific nature of the class alliance present within it...The ayatollahs and mollahs on their own can probably not sustain and channel the popular upsurge...It is quite possible that before too long the Iranian people will chase the Pahlavi dictator and his associates from power, will surmount the obstacles in its way, and build a prosperous and socialist Iran."

(Halliday, 1979, pp.216, 299, 309)

Three short quotes of this kind cannot do justice to a detailed study, which has much that is insightful to say about Iranian politics. Furthermore, what Halliday tells us here and in other parts of his book about the Islamic element in the resistance movement seemed reasonable to many people at the time he was writing. Certainly it would have been a mistake to analyse events in 'purely religious terms'. There was undoubtedly much more going on. In Iran, for example, mollahs have the right to collect taxes on trading profits (the khums) and on wealth (the zakat). Thus their association with the merchants of the bazaar is underpinned by an economic relationship, and religious rhetoric has often been used to protect traders' incomes. In the 1890s, the mollahs succeeded in mobilizing a national protest against the tobacco monopoly granted by the government to an Englishman,

Figure 21.1 'No one expected the Hidden Imam to arrive in a Jumbo Jet': Khomeini returns to Iran from exile, 1979.

and in 1905–6 similar pressures forced through constitutional reforms aimed at protecting the business community from foreign competition. The mollahs and merchants can thus be seen as powerful elements in a faction which has persistently sought to promote its own class interests, and which became increasingly antagonistic to the Shah's government from the mid 1970s, because attempts to introduce a one-party state led to attacks on the economic privileges of the religious establishment and to an 'anti-profiteering' campaign.

However, the fact that there were class interests of this kind at work in Iran does not explain how and why religion could so readily be harnessed as the language of political dissent. By setting up as a straw target the idea that

Islam was the primary influence on what was happening, Halliday ends up deflecting attention away from religion as a key factor. Notice how he makes a distinction between 'religious sentiment' and 'deep material, i.e. social and economic factors'. He thus implies that a study of changing Iran can largely exclude certain kinds of beliefs and values. A consequence of this approach is that the book as a whole persistently sets aside or devalues the role of Islam in Iranian politics. Khomeini's influence is characterized as ill-defined and ambiguous, and treated only in passing. Far more attention is focused on the secular resistance movements, which for Halliday appear to be crucially significant for the country's future. In the light of subsequent events, this seems remarkably misconceived.

It is always easy to be wise after the event, and it should be stressed that Halliday was not the only one to underestimate the religious element. Khomeini would never have come to power had he not been a shrewd and manipulative politician. He carefully avoided direct criticism of the Left, and argued for the restoration of the 1906 constitution right up until he came to power. He would probably have failed to establish an Islamic state had it not been for the active support of a broad range of opposition groups during the crucial months of takeover, including secular-minded intellectuals and the Marxist guerrillas (the Fedayeen). Many viewed Khomeini as no more than a useful figurehead, and would never have supported him had they recognized his ambitions and his capacity to achieve them. In retrospect it seems there were a lot of people with their heads in the sand.

Yet for those with the eyes to see, the writing had been on the wall for some time. In 1972 Hamid Algar had remarked:

> "Iranian national consciousness still remains wedded to Shi'i Islam, and when the integrity of the nation is held to be threatened by internal autocracy and foreign hegemony, protest in religious terms will continue to be voiced, and the appeals of men such as the Ayatullah Khumayni to be widely heeded."
>
> (Algar, 1972, p.255)

There was good reason for thinking this. Khomeini's own views had been clearly laid out in 1970, when he gave a series of lectures to young mollahs in Iraq, which were then published as *Hukumat-i Islami* (The Islamic Government) in 1971. He explained that mollahs would be the nucleus of the revolutionary vanguard under the leadership of the ayatollahs, with the 'virtuous faqih' (himself) at the head. These same clerics would then rule the post-revolutionary Iranian state. Halliday and others seem to have dismissed this manifesto as the deluded musings of a frustrated old man. But there were characteristics of Iranian Islam and political philosophy which might have prompted a closer investigation of Khomeini's assertions. Indeed, one author has gone so far as to claim that the main lines of development for the Iranian revolution had been laid down in the sixteenth century (Ruthven, 1984, p.219).

The population of Iran is predominantly made up of adherents of the main sect of the Shiite branch of Islam. They are sometimes called 'Twelvers', because they venerate twelve descendants of the Prophet Muhammad as his spiritual heirs. These descendants are known as the imams, the first being Ali, the cousin and son-in-law of Muhammad. The Twelfth Imam was Muhammad al Muntazar, who is believed not to have died, but to have disappeared in 940. He has become the Hidden Imam, and will eventually return as the Mahdi (Messiah), 'to fill the earth with equity and justice just as it was filled with oppression and tyranny' (Ruthven, 1984, p.204).

Iranian Shiites, together with other Shiite groups, comprise about 10% of all Muslims in the world. In most respects, their practices and traditions are similar to those of the majority of Muslims, known as Sunnis, but in interpretations of history and in political philosophy there are some important differences.

The schism between Sunni and Shiite Islam is linked to events in the mid seventh century. For the Shiites, everything went wrong when Ali's rightful claim to the caliphate of the Arab empire was usurped by Uthman of the Umayyad clan. They curse Uthman as the perpetrator of

By the end of the fifteenth century there were significant Shiite groups in Iran, but it was the rise of the Safavid dynasty from 1501 which turned the sect into the official, Iranian, state ideology. With the help of a forged genealogy, Isma'il I claimed descent from the Seventh Imam, asserted his right to rule on behalf of the Hidden Imam, and empowered Shiite mollahs to promote religious conformity. In due course, ideological uniformity cemented territorial unity. The modern Iranian nation came into being (Ruthven, 1984, p.222).

When Safavid fortunes declined during the eighteenth century, the Iranian mollahs began to draw upon the anti-statist connotations of Shiite political philosophy to assert an independent authority. With the end of the dynasty in 1722, some of them argued that, in the absence of the Hidden Imam from whom their authority came, they had the right to make individual interpretations of law on his behalf. This view was eventually accepted, largely because none of Iran's later rulers was able to lay claim to spiritual authority, and tended to rely heavily on the mollahs to provide some ideological underpinning of their rule. By the nineteenth century, the mollahs were in a strong enough position to resist attempts to abolish their rights, notably their right to give sanctuary in holy places even to the Shah's enemies. It had become firmly established in the popular, national consciousness that the only truly legitimate rule was that of the Hidden Imam. Governments were to be tolerated until the Hidden Imam's return, but the clergy, as the Hidden Imam's representatives, were the protectors of the faithful.

It took no great leap of imagination on Khomeini's behalf to tap into these notions. He could claim that a pragmatic accommodation with the Pahlavi state was impossible, because the Shah had relinquished part of Iranian sovereignty to foreigners, had barred the influence of Islam on public life, and had even made use of pagan symbols (derived from ancient Persia), like the title 'Light of the Aryans'. It was also quite natural for the clergy to be called upon to be the vanguard of resistance. They had already played this part on several occasions in the past.

Furthermore, while Khomeini did try to emphasize that he was not imbued with the Hidden Imam's spiritual powers, he nevertheless allowed followers to call him Imam (and adopted the title 'Vicar of the Hidden Imam' after coming to power). Comparison was therefore invited between Khomeini and the Mahdi, and the huge demonstration at the time of his triumphant return highlighted how widely messianic expectations had been aroused.

It is worth repeating that the characteristics of Iranian Islam do not in themselves explain Khomeini's success. Nevertheless, they were undoubtedly of considerable importance. So why did Halliday largely overlook them?

Part of the answer is probably that, like many others who were concerned about Iran's future in the 1970s, he had a tendency to indulge in 'wish fulfilment'. But there was an additional theoretical reason. Halliday did not deal with culture seriously because he thought it was relatively unimportant. His book is an example of taking materialism too far. Materialism is a way of thinking about the world that asserts the primacy of material things (as opposed to ideas or beliefs) in determining human behaviour. Until very recently it has been a premise of much of the scholarly writing on development issues. Unfortunately, it has been common for it to be applied simplistically (or 'mechanistically'), thereby giving an excessive emphasis to narrowly defined notions of politics and economics. Some writers have called this tendency economism (Sahlins, 1976; Geertz, 1984; Gramsci, 1988), not because it is a fault of economics, but because it assumes the theoretical separation of economic factors and forces from other aspects of human life, and in effect reduces these other aspects to economic causes.

Many writers influenced by Marxist ideas (like Halliday in the 1970s) have emphasized social stratification in terms of class structures at the expense of almost everything else. Indeed, it has not been rare to find academics and political activists stating that social forms are determined by class relations as if there was a straightforward correlation. Meanwhile, some of those of more conventional persuasions (such as neoclassical economists) have habitually utilized an even more reductive methodology. Numerical statistics are compared using sophisticated mathematical models. Both modes of analysis end up treating culture as a kind of residual factor. Shared values, which conflict with what the author perceives as objective realities, are readily interpreted as 'false consciousness', and phenomena such as religion dismissed as the consequence of superstition, ignorance and poverty. Or alternatively, culture becomes a set of variables which impinge upon 'rational' economic behaviour, and therefore have to be allowed for in equations. Either way, culture is treated as something separate from the business of production. The implicit assumption is that society runs on what the anthropologist Clifford Geertz has called 'the energies of want'.

In a review of the debates about social change in rural Java, Geertz takes gleeful pleasure in demolishing the arguments of scholars, obsessed with numbers, who divorce agricultural activities from the rest of daily life, and is equally mocking of those Marxist scholars who have vainly tried to explain inconvenient findings like the absence of an established landlord class. He concludes with the following observation:

"Whatever one may think of omega point models of social change, in which everyone ends up as a class warrior or a utility maximizer (and I, obviously, think very little of them), there is no chance of analysing change effectively if one pushes aside as so much incidental music what it is that in fact is changing: the moral substance of a sort of existence. The Renaissance, the Reformation, the Enlightenment and the Romantic Reaction made the modern world as much as trade, science, bureaucracy and the Industrial Revolution; and, indeed, vast changes of social mind, they made it together. Whatever happens in Asia, Africa, and Latin America…it will…involve comparable passages, comparably vast."

(Geertz, 1984, p.524)

This ought to be self-evident. The study of development, or indeed the study of human life generally, necessitates the study of shared values of all kinds, and the examination of their multifaceted transformations. Religion and kinship are just as significant as economic transactions and the political life of nation states, and in fact these things are not really separable or comparable. They do not exist in isolation from one another. The current interest in culture suggests that this is now being more widely recognized by social scientists, including economists. So called 'new institutional' economists, for example, lay great stress on connections between different aspects of life.

Douglas North, one of the leading figures of this school of thought (and a recent recipient of the Nobel Prize for economics), has argued that it is necessary to understand the structures and processes that make some paths relatively easy to follow, and others almost impossible:

"We cannot understand today's choices (and define them in the modelling of economic performance) without tracing the incremental evolution of institutions… Informal constraints matter. We need to know much more about culturally derived norms of behaviour and how they interact with formal rules to get better answers to such issues. We are just beginning the serious study of institutions."

(North, 1990, quoted in Putnam, 1993, p.181)

Yet, as North himself implies, economism retains a currency among analysts of economic change. Why is this so? Reasons include such things as ideological dogmatism, academic overspecialization, and the constraints of the aid business (in which numerical economics can still sometimes dominate development planning). But there is another factor which needs to be discussed at some length. It is the difficulty of writing about peoples' beliefs and moral codes and ways of life in such a way as to make explanatory generalizations useful. A tendency among scholars who have attempted it is to resort to simplistic models of human behaviour which lay undue emphasis on the social effects of cognition. They replace economism or simplistic materialism with its opposite – a kind of culturalism based on idealism (the view that mental phenomena, or 'ideas', are the basis of what people do in the world). Such an approach can be especially dangerous in development studies because it leads to the assumption that thought processes are the primary factor which facilitates or hinders progress. The poor may therefore end up being blamed for their own poverty: it is the consequence of the way they see the world, because if they thought 'correctly' they would become more affluent.

This form of culturalism underpinned colonial notions of European superiority, and retains a hold on the popular imagination in many rich countries, as well as among educated élites elsewhere. It is also implicit in some of the policy prescriptions of international aid agencies, particularly when programmes involve 'educating' a target population. I will discuss some of the implications in the following section. Here it is important to note that the materialism of some academic writing on development issues has partly been a reaction to idealist explanations of poverty. To an extent this is quite healthy. The problem is that the baby is thrown out with the bath water, and analysts simply ignore crucial issues, like religion and kinship, in the apparent hope that they will just go away. The trick is to find the balance.

21.3   Getting culture wrong

I have pointed out that in spite of the materialism of some development analysts, an idealist variety of culturalism is by no means something only to be associated with the past. There are many academics, aid workers and politicians who continue to assert the primacy of ways of thinking and local customs in interpreting processes of development. This is perhaps most striking in interpretations of contemporary civil wars which explain horrific violence in terms of the expression of 'ethnic' identities (see Chapter 8 and Chapter 23), but it can also be found in accounts of things as diverse as farming practices, enterprise management and hygiene behaviour. By and large, it would seem that the more peculiar the lifestyle of the people being

commented on looks to the outsider, the more likely it is that the way those people see the world is taken to be an explanation of what they do (or do not do). The arguments presented can be subtle and insightful, particularly if they are linked to an understanding of the structural constraints on people's lives. It is certainly useful to examine how different populations see things, and how they make decisions and engage in their own social circumstances. Deprivation is not something that is simply imposed. Oppressed groups will participate in their own oppression. But such arguments can often be misunderstood, and there is always a danger of slipping into unhelpful determinism.

Numerous models have been proposed for analysing or conceptualizing the mechanisms in which certain sets of behaviours linked to ways of thinking can act as a prerequisite or a block to (what is perceived to be) positive social change. Amongst the former are those who refer to some kind of variation of Weber's 'Protestant ethic' (see Box 21.1), and also many of those who make use of the notion of 'social capital' (Chapters 2 and 24) – defined by Robert Putnam as features of social organization, such as networks, norms and trust, that facilitate coordination and co-operation for mutual benefit (Putnam, 1993). Amongst the latter are social analysts who draw on a wide range of models of behaviour, including 'agricultural involution', 'amoral familism', 'cognitive maps', 'culture of poverty', 'limited good' and 'cattle complex'. Here I will focus particularly on the idea of a cattle complex. The other concepts are explained in Box 21.2.

'Cattle complex' was a term first coined by the American cultural anthropologist Melville Herskovits (a student of Franz Boas). It has been interpreted to mean that some groups of pastoralists are so obsessed with their livestock that they are unable to respond to new opportunities, and is sometimes given as a reason why African pastoralists are materially poor, why their soils become eroded, and why regional or even national economies fail to grow. Alternatively 'cattle complex' may be viewed as something worth preserving, because it indicates that

Box 21.2   Models of culture as a barrier to progress

Agricultural involution

This was an idea put forward by Clifford Geertz in a book on Java published in 1963. He argued that the pattern of ecological pressures in rural areas had the effect of making families work wet-rice plots ever more intensively, absorbing continuously increasing numbers of cultivators, and evolving ever more complex and introspective methods of organizing livelihood strategies. For some, he seemed to be suggesting that the Javanese 'involuted' value system was their main obstacle to development. In fact in this book Geertz was, if anything, more ecologically deterministic than culturally deterministic, but in some of his other works he certainly did adopt an 'idealist' point of view. With reference to the Balinese he made the categorical but unverifiable assertion that they 'share the same general beliefs, the same overall world-view, the same broad ideas about how their society is or should be arranged' (Geertz & Geertz, 1975, p.2, quoted in Leach, 1982, p.43). It is therefore not altogether surprising that some readers should have assumed that he meant 'involution' to refer to a kind of cognition which blocked progress.

Amoral familism

In *The Moral Basis in a Backward Society* (1958), Edward Banfield used the term amoral familism to describe the attitudes of peasants in southern Italy. He defined it as the belief that each person should maximize the material, short-term advantage of the nuclear family and should assume that all others will do likewise. A consequence was that social life outside the household lacked moral constraints. Amoral familism was thus almost the opposite of Putnam's 'social capital', and Putnam openly acknowledges a debt to Banfield's work. The idea was also developed in an African context by Goran Hyden, who argued that:

> "the peasant mode of production gives rise to an 'invisible' economy of affection that provides opportunities for social action outside of the framework of state control. These ties are personalized and very difficult to change, short of an effective transformation of the economic structures that support them."
>
> (Hyden, 1983, p.28)

Cognitive maps

This is an idea that has been used by several social analysts, including some of the new institutional economic theorists mentioned above. It was originally developed in the 1960s, notably by F. G. Bailey in his work on rural people in India. He explained that there are many near synonyms for 'cognitive map', such as 'ethos, world view, collective representations, beliefs and values, ideology and – most inclusive – culture'. He argued that the metaphor of a map is appropriate because it suggests a guide for action, and that cognitive maps consist of a set of value directives and existential propositions which together help to shape social interaction. In one article he concluded:

> "Cognitive maps do change; but for the most part they do so slowly as the result of experience. As the flow of water can change the course of a river, so experience can erode received ideas and allow others to settle in their place. With this most modernizers must be content…[T]he least effective use of their resources is to plan directly that the peasants shall have a change of heart. The cultural themes which I have been discussing here are like swamps and rocky mountains; the modernizers should plan to make a detour."
>
> (Bailey, 1987, p.297)

Culture of poverty

The expression 'culture of poverty' is sometimes invoked in a general manner, but was originally coined by O. Lewis in the 1960s with reference to peasant peoples in urban contexts (Lewis, 1965b). It suggested that poverty generated its own way of life with its own features of strategy and order. It was particularly developed in situations of rapid social change, but once in existence had considerable stability and was passed on from generation to generation. It was composed of a mixture of economic, social and sociopsychological factors. Prominent symptoms were a lack of participation by the poor in major social institutions, distinctive patterns of family life, and apathetic and resigned attitudes.

Limited good

The notion of 'limited good' was also developed in the 1960s, and in many respects was a kind of rural counterpart of the culture of poverty theory. The term was introduced by George Foster in the 1960s, who argued that a reason why Mexican peasants apparently lacked interest in new opportunities was because they perceived their world as a competitive game in which there were only a limited number of good things, and one person gained at the expense of another. This was one reason why, according to Foster, co-operatives did not work. Although there was a complex web of relationships based on various types of exchange, there always existed a high degree of distrust and envy between the parties to the relationships, and a constantly shifting pattern of alignment.

these people are unaffected by the corrupting impact of capitalism and are living in harmony with nature. The logical conclusion of the second line of argument ought to be that development should occur in such a way as to leave the pastoralists alone. However, as we shall see, the two views are often, in practice, combined (Figure 21.3).

David Turton, himself an anthropologist who works on African pastoralism, has made these observations about such views:

"Until recently it was widely assumed among development planners, and probably still is among administrators and politicians, that the chief obstacle to the development of pastoralists lay in their 'irrational' preoccupation with the accumulation of stock as an end in itself and their predilection for a wandering way of life. One of the authorities most frequently cited as responsible for this view is the anthropologist Melville Herskovits who coined the term 'cattle complex' to refer to a collection of cultural traits (such as the identification of individuals with 'favourite' beasts, the use of cattle in sacrifice and bride wealth and preferences for certain skin colours and patterns and horn shapes) which are widely distributed among cattle-keeping people in East Africa. Neither Herskovits, nor those anthropologists who subsequently wrote detailed monographs about particular pastoral peoples, argued that pastoralists were economically irrational. But, by concentrating on the social and cultural elaboration of cattle at the expense of analysing pastoral production systems…they did help to give an exaggerated impression of the uniqueness of the 'pastoral way of life' and of its isolation from regional and national economic and political processes. They must therefore take some of the blame for the fact that the term 'cattle complex' came to be used by others in a Freudian sense, never intended by Herskovits, to mean a sentimental and obsessive attachment to cattle and for the stereotype of the proud, aggressive and conservative pastoralist which became part of the conventional wisdom of pastoral development."

(Turton, 1988, p.138)

Some of Turton's observations about cattle complex can also be applied to the other models of culture as a barrier to progress too. Whatever the original intentions of their authors, there has been a tendency to interpret them as if they encapsulated the qualities of a particular kind of 'local culture'. They seem to imply the existence of closed and static social systems. Critics of 'limited good' and 'agricultural involution', for example, have pointed out that Foster's view of the life of Mexican peasants largely ignored social inequalities and rural/urban linkages, while Geertz' work on Java treated social stratification as little more than instances of religious affiliation. It has also been suggested that these kinds of models are basically just an elaboration of some informants' views. It is not altogether surprising that impoverished groups should become somewhat resigned to their circumstances, and resistant to the interventions of philanthropists or government officials. Moreover, it is always very difficult to demonstrate causality. It may be that many people in urban slums or cattle camps behave in a manner which aid workers view as detrimental to their own well-being but, leaving aside the issue as to whether or not the behaviours are as

Figure 21.3 Romanticized and abused: Somalia's pastoralists.

counter-productive as they seem, it cannot be proved that such activities emanate from 'cognitive maps' or ways of thinking. It is possible to highlight links, not to demonstrate causes.

In the rest of this section I show how a 'culture as barrier to progress' approach can lead to profoundly flawed assertions. I focus on the issue of Somali pastoralism. Whereas in the last section I showed how Iranian politics cannot be properly understood without locating discussion in a context of what might be termed 'Iranian culture', here I will argue that Somali 'culture' cannot be properly comprehended without analysing Somali political economy.

The following passage is taken from an article by Robert Mister, describing the kinds of problems facing aid workers in Somalia during the early 1980s.

> "Somalia is one of the world's poorest countries, with a stagnating economy which is frequently close to collapse. Many of its people live at a level of absolute poverty. Since nomads form the bulk of the population, their pastoral lifestyle pervades almost all aspects of life. The economy is very dependent on the export of nomads' livestock, which accounts for some 80% of export earnings. The nomad way of life is slow, people act individually, outlooks tend to be conservative, and the nomad struggle for survival has tended to produce a society that exploits and damages the long-term environment.
>
> The Somalis are Muslims who adhere to Koranic law when it does not conflict with local customary law. They have strong sentiments of national esteem, but tend to guard the secrets of their culture and only share them on their own terms. And they are proudly independent, aggressive and wary of outside influences. As in many traditional societies, the people of Somalia are also fatalistic..."
>
> (Mister, 1988, p.127)

We are presented with a grim picture of the Somali economy, and it is clear that the author intends us to draw the conclusion that the basic problem is the Somali people themselves. Their culture may be worthy of respect, but it has disastrous consequences. It seems to me that this is a shockingly misinformed view, and reveals a dangerous mixture of romantic and derogatory notions about ostensibly exotic ways of life. The fact that it appears in a book which purports to provide a local-level, grassroots perspective on implementing development projects, reveals how deeply ingrained such attitudes remain.

There is no doubt that in the early 1980s Somalia was in trouble, but only a decade or so previously it had been self-sufficient in grain production as well as being a significant livestock and livestock produce exporter (it was one of the world's major suppliers of high-quality sheepskins). It may have been the case that the national economy had been weak, but it was a combination of factors during the 1970s which led to the situation Mister confronted. Drought, oil price increases, inflation, war with Ethiopia over the Ogaden (1977–78), an influx of thousands of refugees, and a disastrous attempt by the government to regulate the marketing system as a step towards 'scientific socialism' all contributed. To make matters even worse, in 1983 an embargo was placed on Somali livestock exports due to a rinderpest epidemic. The country's main market in Saudi Arabia was lost, and catastrophe was only avoided by an Egyptian agreement to accept imports.

By this time, economic difficulties and a dissatisfaction with the USSR as an arms and aid supplier had prompted an ideological shift towards the USA and a loan agreement with the IMF. In 1982 the World Bank had put together a 'structural adjustment' package, and although the Ministry of Planning had stated in 1983 that self-sufficiency in food was a remote possibility, Somalia was again in grain surplus by 1989. The apparent improvement was partly due to the enormous quantities of food relief which the country secured from the United Nations' World Food Programme by exaggerating the numbers of refugees, but also due to the introduction of maize production in irrigation schemes. These schemes seem to have benefited the relatively affluent rather than the very poor, and the economic upturn has been reversed in recent years due to the civil war. Nevertheless, there are indications that Somalia is far from being a hopeless case.

The purpose of this brief sketch is to emphasize that the difficulties of Somalia in the 1980s were not something that had been inevitable. Mister himself goes on to explain in his article how the refugee influx played a part in the country's problems, but the economy was also not as stagnant as he thought, and certainly was not in a mess as a consequence of the immutable characteristics he ascribes to the Somali people. It is undoubtedly the case that groups living in Somalia hold certain values very dear, and over some issues will resist change. But to exaggerate this conservatism, to suggest that the Somalis 'guard the secrets of their culture' (whatever that means), to accuse them of fatalism, and to claim that 'the nomad struggle for survival…exploits and damages the long-term environment' contradicts the evidence.

It is true that, at the time Mister was writing, some 55% of the country's population had what might loosely be called a pastoral lifestyle, but 45% did not. Some 20% were almost exclusively engaged in agriculture (bananas are the second most important export), while the remainder lived in the towns or worked abroad. Moreover, for generations Somalis have been renowned for their entrepreneurial skills and eagerness for paid employment. Back in the 1930s, the British Member of Parliament representing the Tiger Bay area of Cardiff was known as the 'MP for Somaliland' because of the large number of Somali sailors and their families residing in his constituency, and it was not so long ago that there were two Somali cafes in Salford near the docks to serve the Somali seamen. Throughout East Africa, it is more often than not Somalis who drive the long-distance trucking routes, and in Muslim areas it is often Somalis who are the butchers. In addition, until recently, there were some 500 000 Somalis working in the oil-producing states in the Gulf, whose repatriated salaries and 'gifts' have been critical to the economy for many years (something which does not necessarily appear in official statistics).

But Mister had not just overlooked these things, he was also fundamentally mistaken about pastoralism. The Somali pastoral sector may be thought of as comprising two main sections:

1 various groups living in 'traditional' ways, herding camels, cattle, sheep and goats, who may be termed 'nomadic' in that they move their animals along established routes between water points and grazing land (but it should be stressed that there is in fact nothing aimless about their movements);

2 sedentary groups of 'nomadic' origin who retain their herds.

Sedentarization of pastoralists is something that has happened for generations. Particularly at times of drought or war, groups from the north and centre of the country have migrated to the arable south, and taken up farming. Often they have tried to rebuild lost herds at the same time, but over the years have given this up and become permanently settled, retaining only a few animals. The number of these sedentary pastoralists in the south has grown rapidly since 1974, when a drought provided the then Soviet-backed government with the opportunity to 'modernize' the rural economy. A spectacular programme of enforced settlement of 'nomads' was launched, modelled on the schemes imposed on the pastoralists of the southern Soviet republics. In 1975, 110 000 'nomads' were forcibly located at three agricultural and three fishery projects, far removed from their home areas. They were organized as production co-operatives, and were subject to rigid state controls. Not surprisingly, the enterprise was a fiasco. Ten years later the projects were still being supplied with relief food by the World Food Programme, and most of the men had left for the towns, the Gulf, or tried to mix farming with herding (something which sometimes leads to an excessive concentration of animals in one place).

Since the 1960s, there has also been increased sedentarization in other parts of the country. This has been due to a shift towards a more commercialized way of life among 'nomadic' pastoralists in the arid zones. From colonial times, governmental posts, new wells providing permanent watering places, and facilities like schools and shops attracted ever larger settlements. Some family members began to reside permanently in such places, and this process has accelerated since the 1974–75 drought. Settlement was also greatly encouraged by the construction of a tarmac road running through the centre and north. It is in these places that the effects of overgrazing were most severe.

Where there is evidence of long-term damage being done to the environment, it is almost always where pastoralists have become settled but have retained some or all of their herds. Even in these instances the evidence may be far from conclusive. But the point is that where soil erosion is found, it is not the consequence of 'the nomad struggle for survival'. On the contrary it is precisely because of the enforced or encouraged abandoning of the old ways that the problem has arisen. Far from being a consequence of conservatism, it is the direct result of inappropriate development.

Nevertheless, in spite of almost continuous drought during the 1970s and 80s, repeated interference by the government, and all the upheavals of the 1990s, there remain a large number of 'nomadic' pastoralists in Somalia. There are perhaps as many as two million, and with good reason. In 1986 a study of the Somali 'nomadic' production system by an adviser to the Ministry of Livestock observed (in the understated language of a semi-official document) that it is 'quite efficient'. Recognizing ecological constraints, and that 'the pastoralists have perfect knowledge of their production system including pasture and water management', the adviser concluded that development in the arid zones of Somalia will involve neither the promotion of agriculture nor the teaching of better stock-raising methods. The existing livestock system 'has proven its efficacy and steadiness under normal climatic and drought conditions over many years', and rearing practices are well adapted to the prevailing climate conditions. With the proviso that Somalia's 'nomadic' pastoralists have additionally demonstrated extraordinary adaptability and deep political skills (they have had to in order to survive), it seems reasonable to agree with the study's conclusion. If the government succeeded in providing the necessary moderate support (i.e. water, animal health, marketing), the pastoralists would probably continue generating a great deal of the country's protein and foreign currency for the indefinite future (Hübi, 1986, pp.62–3,72).

The wonder is that anyone should be taken aback by these insights. The life of Somali pastoralists is far from being a closed and secretive world. There is a readily available literature on them, much of it published in English (De Lancey *et al.*, 1988). Furthermore, during the 1980s and early 1990s, the Somali Academy of Sciences and Arts in Mogadishu published a series of excellent working papers entitled *Camel Forum* which investigated a wide variety of aspects of camel husbandry in the country. Virtually all these studies concurred that livestock production among the pastoralists is both economically efficient and ecologically sound.

Why is it that so many people who really should know better persist in the belief that progress for pastoralists means settling them down in one place and 'educating' them to be farmers? Why do schemes which promote or enforce sedentarization continue to be implemented (and by no means only in Somalia)? Why has there been so little interest in the difficulties which pastoral peoples themselves worry about and try to cope with? What is it about pastoralists that so often causes them to be deemed as the problem?

Some of the answers to these questions are fairly obvious. Defining pastoralists as the problem may be cynical or deliberate. It may underpin a policy of integrating pastoral groups into the national economy – to secure resources from them and (ideally) provide them with modern services. Or it may simply be the excuse for imposing governmental controls, particularly if the pastoralists in question have managed to secure automatic rifles (as they have in several parts of north-east Africa). But such political motivation does not explain why even those wishing to assist pastoralists or to comment objectively on development issues may lack a basic understanding of pastoral ways of life. In these instances wrong-headedness seems to have more to do with innocent ignorance, unconscious ethnocentrism (i.e. the belief that ultimately 'our' way of doing things is better than 'theirs'), and, perhaps above all, a muddle about culture.

Mister clearly considered the shared values and customs of the Somali as extremely important, but his conception of how these relate to behaviour was unhelpful. Notice his use of the expression 'local society and culture'. He conceptualized a group of people he found strange as a society with a specific culture. The society was the product of the culture, and vice versa. In effect, the society and the culture were so interwoven as to amount to the same thing: Somali society is like this…Somali culture is like that…He wrote about the Somali as if their thinking, and their corresponding way of behaving, exists within a closed system – one with its own logic and rules. Such an approach makes it possible to describe a functional and ideally stable way of life, and also makes change seem like an exception or an aberration. Consequently, certain kinds of things are noticed and over-emphasized, while others are largely ignored.

21.4 Approaching culture sensibly

The critique of economism presented in Section 21.2 and the models of culture-as-obstacle discussed in Section 21.3 are both largely based on insights from anthropological research. This emphasis on anthropology is not surprising. As was explained in Section 21.1, 'non-Western' or 'other' culture has often been regarded as the anthropologist's subject. It is usually assumed that anthropologists have hoped to protect or preserve cultural forms by recording them. In fact, there are numerous schools of thought within anthropology, some of which have been more economistic than most economists. Marvin Harris, for example, went so far as to argue that ideology and social organization can be explained in terms of 'adaptive responses to techno-economic conditions' (Harris, 1969, p.240). Nevertheless, it is true that anthropology has been especially associated with the promotion of the concept of culture in social research, and even those anthropologists who bemoan the fact have still been more interested in the significance of different shared values, customs, and ways of seeing the world than most of their colleagues from other disciplines. In fact their very method of doing fieldwork requires it (Box 21.3).

Box 21.3 Ethnographic research

Both the British tradition of social anthropology and the American tradition of cultural anthropology lay great stress on ethnographic research. This can involve a mixture of methodologies, but is particularly associated with so-called 'participant observation', which requires the anthropologist to try to learn the language of the people being studied, to live with them for a long period, and to see things from their point of view.

There are tremendous strengths with this approach, not the least of which is that it makes it possible to look at the interconnections between things. Thus, I. M. Lewis has revealed in fascinating detail how kinship, poetry, livestock, sexual desires, lines of authority, attitudes to exchange and markets, and a host of other things are interwoven in the fabric of the daily life of Somalis whom he came to know very well (Lewis, 1965a, 1975, 1985). In the 1990s he used this knowledge to present a critique of the high-profile humanitarian intervention in Somalia (see Box 8.2 in Chapter 8), arguing that its poor design and execution indicated the mis-match between high-tech operations and 'local social and cultural conditions', and in particular the failure of outsiders to understand the nature of Somali clan and lineage alliances (Lewis, 1997, pp.197–8).

However, the traditional methodology of anthropologists like Lewis also has limitations.

1   It generates extremely complex micro-level information. In the past this was conventionally coped with by conceptualizing the people being studied as comprising a separate, usually small, autonomous unit. The problem was that, like so many other social models, the artificiality of the construct was often forgotten, and ideas and values exchanged between units, as well as wider political and economic linkages, were played down or overlooked. The world was sometimes described as if it is full of sociocultural islands. This is a criticism that can be made of the models discussed in Box 21.2.

2   Because anthropologists wanted to undermine Western-centric views of exotic ways of life, and therefore concentrated on the logic of ostensibly odd behaviour and thinking (like witchcraft beliefs), they often tended to explain how things worked, rather than how things were changing. Indeed, in some of the older anthropological studies, change seems to be only accounted for by external interference, and is depicted as something upsetting to the social equilibrium.

3   The tendency not to examine processes of change was also a consequence of basing knowledge on observation and participation. It is difficult to examine long-term processes of change using this method alone, unless fieldwork is carried out over many years (something which has rarely possible).

4   Making a virtue of necessity, many anthropologists responded by taking an ahistorical approach to theoretical analysis, arguing that it was possible to understand aspects of human life by comparing the characteristics of one society with those of another. They might, for example, compare different conceptions of gender, or the symbolic meanings of rituals and myths found in different parts of the world. Often such studies were sophisticated and interesting, but in separating beliefs from their social context, there was a tendency towards idealism which could be amplified when comparative anthropological work was simplified or summarized. In effect, it was suggested that different ways of life are comprehensible as though they are systems of thought.

These difficulties have been issues of debate within anthropology at least since the 1950s. For example, in *The Political Systems of Highland Burma* (1954), Edmund Leach showed how complex were the connections between political action and ideal models of society, when examined regionally and through time. He noted, amongst other things, that people adopted different collective identities when moving from one village to another.

Most anthropologists would now accept that it is misleading to write about 'other' societies as if they are discrete objects or bounded units with their own distinct cultures, and are very aware of the fact that anthropology itself has been bound up with Western ways of creating the world. For Marilyn Strathern, it is absurd for scholars trained in the Western tradition to imagine that others will be engaged in solving the problems of Western thought. Why should they be expected to focus their philosophical energies on such issues as the relationship between society and the individual? (Strathern, 1988, pp.3–4).

Many anthropologists have tried to come up with more subtle ways of writing, often involving interactive and historically embedded conceptions of culture. However, the continued commitment to the production of anthropological knowledge through ethnographic research means that problems associated with participant observation cannot be resolved with any finality. Rather they have to be continuously grappled with. This is a reason why reflecting on the nature of perception, and especially the bearing that different ways of thinking and communicating (or 'discourses') have on social action, has become a major focus of anthropological theory.

This emphasis on cultural variety has often been the source of tension with other traditions of scholarship, notably the study of development, which has similarly tended to focus on the 'non-Western' word, but has explicitly conceptualized it as 'less developed' or even 'underdeveloped'. For many anthropologists the very term 'development' implies a disturbing homogenization of human experience, and also evokes uncomfortable associations with anthropology's own origins in Victorian theories of social evolution and its links with European colonialism. As one anthropologist, James Ferguson, has put it, development and anthropology are like 'evil twins' locked in a strange dance:

> "Anthropology resents its twin fiercely (hence the oft-noted distaste of mainstream anthropology for 'development' work), even as it must recognize a certain intimacy with it, and a disturbing inverted resemblance. Like an unwanted ghost, or an uninvited relative, 'development' haunts the house of anthropology. Fundamentally disliked by a discipline that at heart loves all those things that development intends to destroy, anthropology's evil twin remains too close a relative to be simply kicked out."

> (Ferguson, 1996, p.160)

The entrenched antipathy has certainly not helped encourage a sensible approach to culture amongst development analysts. But there are signs that things are now changing, partly because students of development are less confident about what they think they know than they used to be, and partly because more anthropologists are entering into debates about development – not least because the aid business offers opportunities for employment. The increased engagement has helped create a much larger space in policy-making for understandings of different realities and knowledges. This has had great significance for the design and implementation of grassroots projects, while, at a more theoretical level, it has contributed towards the emergence of the radical group of thinkers, often referred to as the 'post development' school (Ferguson, 1990; Sachs, 1992; Crush, 1995b; Escobar, 1995; Rahnema & Bawtree, 1997; Tucker, 1997).

Several of the most important post-development theorists have, like Ferguson, been trained as anthropologists. They emphasize the potential variety of human experience, and tend to view development strategies as a mechanism for imposing cultural uniformity. Some go so far as to argue that the whole notion of development is counterproductive – a kind of race-track, pointing in the wrong direction. It is a dream that turned into a nightmare, a historically produced discourse, imbued with culturally imperialist assumptions, which inflicts cultural alienation on those that it targets. It grew out of the subjugation of the rest of the world by European colonialism and evolved as an aspect of Western-centric visions of modernization. It has become a hegemonic way of seeing, which causes many people to perceive themselves as 'underdeveloped' and inadequate, such that 'the 'uprooted'…are…set adrift, in many cases without ever being able to find new roots for themselves' (Ki-Zerbo et al., 1997, p.159).

The post-development school is by no means tightly integrated. Although grouped together in books like *The Post Development Reader*

(Rahnema & Bawtree, 1997), the approaches of, for example, Ferguson and Arturo Escobar are not without important differences.

In the *Anti-Politics Machine,* Ferguson (1990) uses discourse theory, derived from an anthropological reading of the work of Michel Foucault, to analyse a specific situation in Lesotho. He shows how the World Bank employs a particular gaze, which depoliticizes all that it comes into contact with, pushing political realities out of sight, and at the same time surreptitiously expanding its own power and ability to keep political control. Here is how he introduces his book:

> "It is true that many ideas about Lesotho generated by the 'development' problematic are indeed false, and it will be necessary from time to time in the discussion to point this out; but the main thrust of this study is not to show that the 'development' problematic is wrong, but to show that the institutionalized production of certain kinds of ideas about Lesotho has important effects, and that the production of such ideas plays an important role in the production of certain sorts of structural change."
>
> (Ferguson, 1990, p.xv)

He seems to view himself as a social observer, an anthropologist who looks at development in the way that an anthropologist might in other circumstances look at a set of religious beliefs. As he has made explicit more recently, his project is as much about the nature of anthropology as it is about the study of development:

> "…the extraordinarily tenacious vision of a world divided into the more and less 'developed' has been, and in many ways continues to be, definitive of the anthropological domain of study. It may even be suggested that the idea of 'development' (and its lack) is so intimately intertwined with the idea of anthropology that to be critical of the concept of 'development' requires, at the same time, a critical re-evaluation of the constitution of the discipline of anthropology itself."
>
> (Ferguson, 1996, p.160)

Escobar also uses discourse theory, and is similarly concerned about the regrettable 'absence of anthropologists from discussions of development as a regime of representation' (Escobar, 1995, p.15). Like Ferguson he views development as a powerful, historically compromised conception, bent on destroying alternative worlds. Both authors view discourse and policy as virtually indistinct. Cognition and action cannot be separated. We can only 'bid farewell to the Third World', Escobar asserts, if we can 'unmake development', and that will 'depend on the social invention of new narratives, new ways of thinking and doing' (Escobar, 1995, p.20). But Escobar goes on to take the argument much further than Ferguson, adopting a more overtly aggressive and far-reaching stance. In *Encountering Development*, he sets out parameters for a new grand theory, which he really thinks might change the world. Here is how he introduces the book:

> "…the approach is discursive, in the sense that it stems from the recognition of the importance of the dynamics of discourse and power to the study of culture. But there is much more than an analysis of discourse and practice; I also attempt to contribute to the development of a framework for the cultural critique of economics as the foundation structure of modernity, including the formulation of a culture-based political economy."
>
> (Escobar, 1995, p.vii)

Clearly there are significant limitations and problems with the post-development school. As another anthropologist, Raymond Apthorpe, has pointed out, Escobar in particular is prone to both over-ambition and misplaced ambition. Social science cannot be 'usurpatory of political power' (Apthorpe, 1996, p.171). Moreover, poverty does not disappear when we recognize that development can be analysed as a kind of discourse linked to Western values. There is also a mixture of ecological mysticism and ethno-romanticism in some post-development writing which strikes me as unhelpful. However, the way in which Ferguson and Escobar have placed culture and power at the centre of their analysis seems to be a positive and significant contribution. Among other things, it has enabled them to avoid the trap of deterministic culturalism which has ensnared other analysts, such as Samuel Huntington (1997) in *The Clash of Civilizations*, with its crude representations of world cultures as Western, Confucian, Japanese, Islamic, Hindu, Orthodox, Latin American, African and Buddhist (see Chapter 23).

The acclaim in some circles for Huntington's thesis (Henry Kissinger has called it one of the most important books to have emerged since the end of the Cold War), the growing influence of new institutional economics, the interest in social capital and indigenous knowledges, and the considerable impact of the post-development school, all suggest that culture is moving into the mainstream of debates about development. This is at least partly to do with a struggle to

Figure 21.4   No model, or hypothesis, or theory of social life is worth much if it simply omits most aspects of human behaviour, and makes no reference at all to what people think and feel. (top) A resident makes her voice heard as council workers, guarded by riot police, bulldoze shacks in a Cape Town squatter camp during April 1990. (above) Celebrating the setting up of an ANC branch for west Johannesburg.

find modes of explanation for social action following the end of Cold War certainties and the erosion of post-Cold-War optimism. The world seems to have become more difficult to understand, or at least more difficult to fit into simple paradigms. Turning to culture is probably less an enthusiastic recognition of an overlooked way of seeing things than an aspect of the crisis of confidence. Nevertheless, it does offer grounds for hoping that some of the reductive and misleading simplifications of so much development thinking may be in the process, at last, of being questioned. But we need to avoid the temptation of replacing one all-embracing 'meta-narrative' with another.

There is no point in trying to 'police' usage of the word 'culture'. It is always going to mean a range of different things in different contexts. However, it seems to me that taking culture seriously in the study of development requires avoiding determinisms of whatever variety, and accepting the complexity of life, even rejoicing in it. Social analysts will always have to construct models, because it is necessary to set some issues aside in order to comment on others. But they should never lose sight of what they are doing and conflate the model with reality. Moreover, no model, or hypothesis, or theory of social life is worth much if it simply omits most aspects of human behaviour, and makes no reference at all to what people think and feel (Figure 21.4). While recognizing the dangers of using culture as an analytical category, it can direct our gaze to social life as a whole, to the connections between things. It is not that culture is more important than politics or economics, but rather that it is useful to conceptualize culture as the context in which political, economic and other activities occur. As Peter Worsley has put it, the 'cultural' should not be thought of as causally secondary, or as a separate sphere. It makes most sense to think of it as 'the realm of those crucial institutions in which the ideas we live by are produced and through which they are communicated' (Worsley, 1984, p.60).

Summary

Culture is a complex and ambiguous concept. Often it is not at all clear what it means. This is partly because it cannot be thought of in isolation. It is bound up with the ways in which human activity is to be generally understood. At the turn of the twentieth century, it was already a term with a variety of meanings and associations.

At the broadest level it encapsulated most of those things which distinguish human beings from other animals, and in particular referred to symbolic behaviour based on a fully fledged language. A second meaning was more overtly value laden. It was what a person ought to have in order to become a fully worthwhile moral agent. In contrast, a third meaning was relativistic, and used the word in the plural. Each culture was viewed as worth while in its way. Often all three perspectives were interwoven in analyses, and all three have continued to influence the way that culture is conceptualized, notably within anthropology.

This suggests that we should not become too obsessed with the search for the 'real' meaning of culture, but accept that it has multiple associations. It also highlights the dangers of trying to employ the idea of culture as an analytical tool. If the word is going to be used at all, it requires thought and care. Often it is better to resort to more precise terms, like religion, or art.

Nevertheless, retaining a conception of culture can be valuable if it directs our attention at the interconnections between things. This is important in that it helps to avoid too narrow a focus. There is not much point in studying development if this is simply reduced to economic growth, or class formation. A broad notion of culture also helps us avoid misleading prognoses, such as the under-estimating of the significance of Shiite Islam in Iran by some scholars during the 1970s.

However, use of culture in this way should not lead us to the view that the shared values of a particular group determine behaviour within it. This is misleading in that it makes us see the world as if it was made up of socio-cultural islands, and it can suggest that thought processes are the primary factor which facilitates or hinders social change. It is, for example, ludicrous to suggest that Somalia is impoverished because Somalis exist in some kind of closed social system, and are imbued with 'fatalistic' tendencies.

In the past, the study of development was dominated by economistic perspectives. The fact that this has been changing in recent years must be viewed as something positive. But we must be cautious about the current fashion for cultural explanations. If culture is understood to be the general context in which social action occurs, then all human behaviour which is not biological can be viewed as being cultural, including political and economic behaviour. Culture therefore explains everything, and nothing in particular. Yet it is still a very useful idea if it makes us ask about how market trans-actions relate to changing attitudes to moral probity and conceptions of individuality, or how forms of government are related to systems of kinship and beliefs about what happens after death. Such questions help us avoid the simplistic determinisms which have afflicted so much social analysis, and which have caused so much of what has been written about development to simply miss the point.

THE FUTURE OF DEVELOPMENT

22

GENETIC ENGINEERING OF DEVELOPMENT? MYTHS AND POSSIBILITIES

JOANNA CHATAWAY, LES LEVIDOW AND SUSAN CARR

For some, biotechnology holds the promise of dramatic breakthroughs in overcoming hunger. For others it is a potentially damaging red herring, misleading because the alleviation of hunger cannot be solved with science and technology. This chapter looks at the debate around new biotechnologies and agriculture.

First, some definitions. A common and broad understanding of **biotechnology** is 'the application of biological science to the manipulation and use of living things for human ends' (Walgate, 1990). Some recent biotechnologies derive from discoveries made centuries ago, such as some fermentation techniques and some biofertilizers and biocontrol agents. However, most of the more high profile innovations (**genetic engineering** or **genetic modification**) involve intervention at the molecular, cellular or tissue level and result from laboratory research. Recent developments include mo-

lecular intervention, notably isolation, characterization, modification and transfer of genes, and the isolation and characterization of DNA probes for use as genetic markers in plant and animal breeding (Bunders *et al.*, 1996, p.132).

The debate about the technology reaches far beyond the direct consequences of splicing genes and touches on fundamental aspects of the economics and politics of development. The two main questions of this chapter, therefore, are:

Q How can we understand the debate about biotechnology?

Q Could biotechnology help in reducing world hunger?

22.1 Visions of progress and development

Biotechnology inspires a set of different reactions and visions about the future construction of agriculture. For some the technology is an incontrovertibly positive set of techniques which will contribute to resolving the world's hunger problem. An extract from an advertisement from a company producing agricultural biotechnology says, for instance:

> "...scientists hope to develop crops that fight off disease. Survive an extended drought or severe frost. Withstand extreme temperature changes. In short, crops that can grow where they never could before."
> (Monsanto Company advertisement, 1998)

Biotechnology: 'The application of biological science to the manipulation and use of living things for human ends' (Walgate, 1990).

Genetically engineered (GE) or **genetically modified (GM) crops:** New strains of crops developed through laboratory research involving molecular, cellular or tissue level interventions.

This view tends to define the problem of world hunger as a product of inadequate inputs into agriculture. New technology, combined with conducive production methods, can overcome the problem. The claims made for biotechnology from this quarter are often based on analysis which points to falling world food production. The statistics used in the following quotation have been collected and compiled by UN agencies and do, indeed, point to falling output per capita and a slow down in yield improvements.

"In 26 of the 40 low-income countries listed by the World Bank, and in 26 of the 50 reporting countries in the middle and higher income category, per capita food output sank in the period from 1979 to 1991. In most African countries south of the Sahara and in the Middle East the degree of self-sufficiency in grains, the most important staples of these regions, decreased.

Annual growth rates in yields per hectare of rice and wheat fell off in some of the most productive areas of cultivation in Asia, mainly those where very intensive agriculture was practised over many years. In the opinion of FAO...this trend will continue well into the 21st century. The FAO anticipates that by 2010 many developing countries that were hitherto net exporters will have become net importers of agricultural products – and this in the face of continuing precarious shortages of foreign exchange."
(Novartis Foundation, 1998, p.2)

A 'pro-biotechnology' argument has it that the new technology can play a major role in increasing food production and is particularly important for poorer countries. Box 22.1 contains an extract from a report written by the Chair of the Board of Directors of the International Service for the Acquisition of Agri-Biotech Applications (ISAAA), an organization which works to promote co-operation amongst biotechnology producers for the benefit of developing countries. In the extract, Clive James outlines three reasons why biotechnology is strategically important for poorer countries.

In contrast, some non-governmental organizations oppose the technology, pointing to its risky nature and the possibly negative social and economic consequences of its use (Box 22.2).

Box 22.1 A pro-biotechnology perspective

Firstly, developing countries have potentially more to gain from transgenic crops than industrial countries because the areas of almost all crops is far greater in developing countries than in the USA and Canada, where adoption has been the highest to date. For example, there are 145 times more rice, five times more cotton, three times more maize and wheat and as much soybean grown in the developing countries as compared with the USA and Canada. This excludes important staples such as cassava and sweet potato that are grown almost exclusively in developing countries and have the potential to benefit significantly from biotechnology.

Secondly, yields of almost all crops are significantly lower in developing than industrial countries; for example, there is almost a threefold difference in maize yields between the USA and developing countries for many reasons but one of the principal causes is that crops in developing countries suffer much more from biotic stresses, due to pests, weeds and diseases, for which current transgenic crops already offer improved protection. Thus, the potential gain for developing countries from improved control of biotic stresses is relatively greater than for industrial countries.

Thirdly, and most importantly, it is in the developing countries, not the industrial countries, where 800 million people suffer from malnutrition today and where transgenic crops could increase crop productivity and contribute to the alleviation of hunger and poverty which are inextricably linked...Denial of the new technologies to the poor is synonymous to condemning them to continued suffering from malnutrition which eventually may deny the poorest of the poor their right to survival.

(James, 1998, p.v)

One conclusion which could be drawn from the quotations in Boxes 22.1 and 22.2 is that the differences in viewpoint over biotechnology amount to fundamentally opposed objectives between commercial and non-profit organizations (Figure 22.1). Another way to look at this would be to see the debate as between those who produce inputs for large modern farmers and those who are concerned about poor smallholders. However, the debate is not that straightforward. Many UN agencies and national research institutes are working on biotechnology with

Figure 22.1   Fundamental opposition? A Greenpeace activist holding stalks of genetically modified corn during a protest action, Bourg-en-Bresse, France, September 1998.

Box 22.2   An anti-biotechnology perspective

'Biotechnology companies claim that their research will lead to new crops that will 'feed the world' and that they need patents to protect their investment in such research. Feeding the world is an attractive claim. However, complex social, political and economic forces are the real causes of hunger and malnourishment suffered by people in developing countries and GE crops will not address them…Genetic engineering and patenting may actually be a threat to world food security by damaging farmers' livelihoods and reducing the diversity of food crops world-wide. The GE crops being developed are particularly suited to a monoculture system. Their use would therefore lead to further erosion of agricultural biodiversity – the varieties on which we all rely for our food' (Five Year Freeze Leaflet, February 1999).

'For 25 years Action Aid has been listening to the world's poor farmers and supporting their efforts to maintain sustainable farming. Even though the world's population is growing we know that the world produces enough food for all – food mountains are evidence of this. It is inequitable distribution of food which is keeping millions of people hungry' (Open letter to *The Observer* from Salil Shetty, Director of ActionAid, 5 August, 1998).

'[Terminator seeds which produce for one harvest only] Designed to produce but not reproduce, these seeds are a direct challenge to traditional agriculture where the farmers harvest and store their seed for replanting. Not only would farmers lose the freedom of independent crop breeding and seed exchange; they would have to purchase expensive seeds from the biotech companies. Such controls would further marginalize poorer farmers, leading to increased homogenisation of crops and consolidation of land' (Joan Ruddock, *The Independent on Sunday,* 14 February 1999).

development objectives in mind; they also consider the new technology to be an important ally in the war against hunger. A number of important agricultural NGOs in the South have supported the development of various aspects of biotechnology and are exploring innovative ways to adapt new technologies to small farmers' needs (Bunders *et al.*, 1996). For these NGOs, the problem is that there are two agricultural systems and two research systems which need to be bridged.

A group of researchers interested in looking at the potential for new biotechnological techniques for poorer farmers defined two types of agriculture as low-external-input agriculture (LEIA) and high-external-input agriculture (HEIA) (Bunders *et al.*, 1996). Practitioners of HEIA concentrate on the specialized production of few commodities and use genetically homogeneous seeds. The production environment is controlled using fertilizers, pesticides and other systems which reduce the variability of natural conditions. This type of agriculture is capital intensive and tends to be highly mechanized. It is possible only where ecological conditions are relatively uniform and can be controlled (for example, irrigated systems) and where delivery, extension, marketing and transport systems are good. On the other hand, some 1.4 billion farmers are estimated to rely on LEIA farming for their livelihoods (Bunders *et al.*, 1996). And the area is growing; under structural adjustment programmes external inputs have become more expensive and fewer farmers can afford them. In order to survive many farmers in LEIA systems are exploiting the land beyond its carrying capacity. This leads to accelerated deforestation, soil degradation and vulnerability to pest attacks and extreme weather conditions.

Two research systems correspond to the types of farming. The research generated through the 'formal' research system (composed of national and international research centres) has mostly benefited HEIA farmers and has been much less successful in reaching poor farmers. This is widely acknowledged by researchers themselves and efforts have been made to make institutes and researchers more focused on the poor. En-

couraging participation by poor farmers, particularly at the stage where they could influence the design of new technologies, has proved immensely difficult, however. The logic of scientific progress and laboratory-based research is very different from the approach that would value farmers' tacit knowledge and would take an interdisciplinary approach to the development of new techniques (Pretty, 1995).

Outside the formal research and development system, NGOs began working more intensively with poor farmers directly. Bunders *et al.* write:

> "In the mid 1980s, disappointed by the performance of the formal system,…NGOs began working more intensively with farmers at village level, concentrating on LEIA areas. The knowledge and technologies of these farmers became the starting point for informal research and development, using methods such as trial and error and learning by observation. In contrast to the formal system, technologies were to be developed and improved by the people who actually used them. Other farmers, rather than researchers, were seen as the main source of innovations. While criticising the formal system, which was seen as largely irrelevant, indigenous knowledge was revalued…This approach soon showed that it too had its limitations. The improvements brought were too small to deal with the immense problems afflicting some LEIA systems, which needed more radical change. Although it could strengthen the self-respect of the rural community, the informal system was too introspective, its practitioners often remaining unaware of the goods and services offered by the formal research and development system."

(Bunders *et al.*, 1996, p.6)

Technology and in particular biotechnology may hold enormous promise in the eyes of these authors and some NGOs. But a necessary prerequisite for Bunders *et al.* would be a new set of methodologies and institutional responsiveness which would build bridges between the two different types of agriculture and research.

What could biotechnology actually offer?

The previous section identified a key issue: while food output might grow as a result of new technology in industrially developed countries, it is not clear what benefits the populations of poorer countries would derive from this (Figure 22.2). In one author's words:

> "So much is certain: food security in the developing countries must not come to depend on surpluses from the industrialised countries or, worse, food aid. For a number of political, economic and ecological reasons this would not make sense. [Priority] must be given to the future nutritional need of their people and to ways and means of meeting those needs locally."
>
> (Novartis Foundation, 1998, p.2)

The enormous scope for biotechnology to impact on agriculture and food production systems makes it difficult to describe fully how the technology could lead to specific improvements. One way to begin is to separate out the technical possibilities and other various issues involved. This section tries to flesh out some of the ways in which the technology might contribute to various types of farming.

Biotechnology does have the potential to impact in beneficial ways on both HEIA and LEIA systems. Kumar and Siddharthan (1997) summarize contributions which biotechnology could make. In terms of increased food security, they include the following:

- Improvements in agricultural productivity could be achieved through enhancement of the efficiency of photosynthesis and by bridging the gap between actual and potential yields by accelerating the pace of plant breeding (tissue culture techniques, for instance). Gains in yield have already been reported in different parts of the world. These have resulted from the application of tissue culture in oil palm, coconut, banana, tubers, and other plants. Techniques like embryo rescue, protoplast fusion and the use of DNA vectors enable plant breeders to overcome the barriers of sexual incompatibility in transferring desirable traits.

"Run for your lives, it's Monsanta!"

Figure 22.2   Gifts for all? Cartoon from Private Eye, *January 1999.*

- Reclamation of poor soils and wastelands could be attempted. In South Asia and Southeast Asia alone about 86.5 million hectares of land can be made productive with rice varieties tolerant to salinity and alkalinity. In India, biotechnology is being used to create mustard plants with increased salinity tolerance. Adaptation of cereal crops to drought-prone areas could be valuable to sub-Saharan Africa in particular.

- Pest resistance and disease resistance could be particularly useful to LEIA farmers. Additionally, biological nitrogen fixation offers a great potential for increasing the agricultural yield in developing countries without increasing their dependence on chemical fertilizers.

- Biotechnological techniques provide the possibility for ecological sustainability of high yields by reducing risks from pests, pathogens and weeds and promoting conservation of genetic resources. This could contribute substantially to long-term food security.

- The potential spectrum of biological pesticides occurring naturally or in the form of genetically restructured organisms that are specifically pathogenic to important pests, parasites, or weeds is enormous and remains largely unexplored.

There are serious constraints to the creation of biotechnology-based products which could meet local needs in poor countries, particularly those related to LEIA. The next section looks more closely at issues which complicate the technical possibilities and which influence the pace and direction of innovation.

22.2   Feeding the world – or the market?

"Worrying about starving future generations won't feed them. Food biotechnology will."

(Monsanto advertisement, *The Observer*, 2 August 1998)

As sketched at the start of this chapter, proponents claim that GM crops will help to avoid world hunger, while many critics argue that biotechnology does not address – or may even aggravate – the real source of the problem. The debate could be summarized by asking: Are GM crops being designed mainly to feed the world or the market? Or is it possible to achieve both aims at once? The answer in practice will depend upon many variables: the types of crops to be cultivated, the people to be fed, the form of markets, and the institutions which influence the agro-food chain.

To explore such issues, this section examines three of the more contentious aspects relevant to development issues: links between GM crops and the Green Revolution; the role of GM crops in world food markets; and the 'biopiracy' debate over patent rights.

The Green Revolution: a contentious reference point

In many respects the biotechnology debate extends earlier arguments about the Green Revolution, begun long before GM crops existed. The term 'Green Revolution' refers to the develop-ment of high-yielding varieties (HYVs) in the 1960s. These are also called 'high-response varieties' because their higher yield depends upon the use of agrochemicals, irrigation and other purchased inputs. Their use substantially increased grain yields of wheat and rice, especially in the Punjab district of India. Once distributed, some of the grain helped to avoid local shortages.

At the same time, that yield increase involved a loss of some other benefits. Higher grain yield meant less straw, used locally as animal feed. Previously many farmers had practised intercropping using a combination of crops (e.g. sorghum and wheat with pulses) the combination of which helped to renew soil fertility. That yield was lost in the switch to HYVs. More generally, land use shifted away from cultivating oilseeds and pulses; the latter are 'the poor person's meat' – i.e. a cheap source of protein (Spitz, 1987). Eventually this switch led to a shortage of oilseeds and pulses in India, which had to be obtained through imports.

According to proponents, the Green Revolution was essential to increase food production: the main alternatives were either to risk famine or to cultivate more scarce land, or even more land than was potentially available. According to critics, the HYVs favoured those farmers who could obtain loans for the purchased inputs. Financial dependency and market competition drove many into debt, even out of business, leading some to commit suicide. Landless peasants became wage-labourers for the successful farmers or migrated to cities (Conway, 1998).

Moreover, argue critics, the intensive methods degraded agricultural resources. Chemical fertilizers exhausted the soil's fertility, making it dependent on such treatments. Crop monocultures became susceptible to pests and disease, while farmers lost access to traditional cultivars. The higher yielding varieties required more water, which resulted in lower water tables and salinization. For these reasons critics argue that yield benefits cannot be extended or even sustained (e.g. Shiva, 1991). As an alternative system, one critic advocates integrated pest management: 'input use can be cut substantially if farmers substitute knowledge, labour and management skills. Yields can be maintained or even slightly improved' (Pretty, 1995, p.211).

Many people liken the potential impacts of GM crops to those of the Green Revolution. Proponents may see the Green Revolution as an achievement to be extended whilst opponents may refer to mistakes to be avoided, or at least negative lessons to be learned. Such arguments can be illustrated by the following debate in a specialist magazine, *Biotechnology and Development Monitor*.

To a proponent of both the Green Revolution and biotechnology, millions of small farmers' livelihoods have benefited from the productivity and hardiness of modern HYVs: 'Science has prevented an environmental disaster of truly global proportions, and science must do so with more vigour in the future. The demography and technology gaps must be closed if agriculture is again to become part of an environmentally stable system' (van Loesch, 1996).

According to a critic of both innovations, however, they are founded upon Malthusian models, which attribute poverty to the excessive procreation of the poor exhausting the means of subsistence: such models obscure 'how the poor were deprived of those means in the first place'. Its advocates have evaded the question of whether land was really scarce or just unequally distributed. Contemporary arguments for technical solutions perpetuate that model (Ross, 1996).

According to another critic of the Green Revolution, it offered standard solutions from a far-off institute, oblivious to local needs and conditions. Given that the high yields depended upon prescriptive inputs, farmers had to be persuaded to apply 'often inappropriate innovations', e.g. pesticides and irrigation. By contrast, the Biotechnology Revolution could thrive only in a different culture, by integrating top-down and bottom-up interactions. Moreover, 'biotechnology research could provide tailor-made answers

to local problems in local processes' (van de Sande, 1994).

This argument suggests an important distinction between the two 'revolutions'. Genetic modification techniques have greater flexibility, being available for redesigning a crop for various purposes, not just for the chemical-intensive methods of the Green Revolution. In some countries, national institutes are developing GM crops which require no more purchased inputs, except for the seeds, and whose produce would remain in local markets. For example, cyanide-free cassava would spare women the labour of detoxifying the crop, while virus-resistant cassava could avoid crop damage for which no pesticides are available (Walgate, 1990).

As another distinction, however, GM seeds have been developed mainly by multinational companies, though often with substantial public subsidy. They have initially targeted their R&D at bulk commodity crops for high-input farming, whose products compete on the world food market. Proponents emphasize that GM crops open up new market opportunities for farmers, e.g. in developing countries. Critics warn that competitive pressures could lead yet more farmers to shift land use away from crops for local consumption, and towards intensive monocultural methods, with consequent problems of new pests and lowered soil fertility.

Moreover, GM crops give a new meaning to the phrase 'high-input' agriculture. The seed itself is being further commoditized to ensure that farmers pay for new seed each season. The various means include hybrids (which cannot breed true), licence conditions which forbid farmers to save seed for resowing, and genetic inserts which render the progeny infertile.

GM crops in the world food market

"Increasingly, we're looking...at creating value throughout the chain, running from seed and inputs all the way through to consumers."

(Bob Shapiro, Monsanto Chief Executive Officer, *1997 Annual Report*)

In the debate over GM crops, a common statement is that they are being designed mainly for cultivation in industrialized countries. Although this is generally true, it is important to examine the uses for which the crops are designed (e.g. for types of farming, trade and markets) in order to anticipate potential effects on different social groups, both within and across countries.

One way of categorizing the main types of GM crops, entering or approaching the commercial stage, is as follows:

1 'Commodity' crops, mixed at source, sold in bulk quantities, and used for purposes such as animal feed and edible oil. These include soybean, maize, oilseed rape, fodderbeet, cotton. These crops are being genetically modified for new crop-protection methods (e.g. herbicide tolerance, insect resistance), which reduce chemical inputs and may increase yields. Herbicide-tolerant crops are designed to encourage sales of the herbicide; often both are sold by the same company.

2 Import substitution, e.g. through commodity crops which are genetically modified to substitute for speciality items currently imported from developing countries.

3 High-value crops (e.g. tropical fruits), already being exported from developing countries, genetically modified for pest resistance, among other traits.

By examining the impacts of some of these crops in more detail, we begin to explore different interpretations of how the new technology will affect farmers' livelihoods and whether or not they are likely to deliver food security for hungry people.

Soybeans in Argentina

Bulk commodity crops such as soybeans and maize are being widely exported, especially to Europe for use mainly in processed food or animal feed. Soybeans are grown in several countries, including USA, Argentina and Brazil, which compete for export sales. Farmers in those three countries were the initial target market for Monsanto's Roundup-Ready™ soybean, which is genetically modified to tolerate the company's own herbicide, glyphosate. Many farmers in the USA and Argentina have bought these seeds for their promise of higher yields and lower herbicide costs.

Monsanto's soybean has been widely adopted in Argentina, alongside a government–industry commitment to make exports more competitive. According to James (1998, pp.16–17), this change was stimulated by government policy, which eliminated export taxes on agricultural exports, as well as privatizing grain elevators, railroads and ports. Many Western companies have invested heavily in silo storage, oilseed crushing mills, processing plants and waterways to lower freight costs.

Changes could mean more efficient production, and thus more intense international competition between Argentina and USA for soya exports. European consumer and retailer boycotts of GM soya in the late 1990s, however, confronted farmers with a difficult choice: grow either GM soya for the domestic market or non-GM soya for export to Europe. In this unpredictable competition, it is difficult to be sure precisely who will win and who will lose. However, by the nature of the farming system to which these innovations apply it is clear that it is larger HEIA farmers who will be affected by the new products.

Bt cotton in India

GM crops became a greater political issue in India in summer 1998, when a broad coalition launched an opposition campaign. The immediate focus was Monsanto's Bollgard cotton, which had an inserted insecticidal gene known as Bt. Protesters such as the Karnataka State Farmers Association (KRRS) 'cremated' field trials at many sites. For them, Monsanto's cotton seeds represented a real threat: corporate control over the seed supply, linked with seed sterility and high-value crops.

For many years Indian farmers have been buying hybrid seeds, which must be purchased anew each season. Farmers have become more dependent upon private companies for the crop processing and marketing too. In some places, rice production has been partly replaced by sunflower farms, and potato and bean cultivation has been replaced by soybean cultivation to supply the oil industry (Pandry, 1994). Thus new market opportunities, for companies and some farmers, have served to reduce production of traditional foodstuffs.

To resist such changes, some organizations have campaigned against hybrid seeds. In addition the KRRS has established its own seed research centre, to promote the free exchange of seeds among farmers internationally. From their experience, activist farmers regarded Monsanto's Bt cotton as a further step towards privatizing seeds.

Others took a different view and found it hard to understand the antipathy. According to some observers, the farmers mistakenly thought that the Bollgard crop contained a 'Terminator' technology, which renders seeds sterile (RAFI, 1999). Several public bodies supported the field trials, partly on the grounds that crop losses plus pesticide costs amount to $186 million annually (*Agrow*, 29 January 1999, p.20). By using Bollgard seeds, US farmers were already reducing pesticide use and increasing yields (James, 1998, p.14). For these benefits, however, farmers pay the seed supplier a 'technology licensing fee', i.e. a premium price, and are forbidden to resow seeds.

High-value substances and interchangeability
Some GM crops are designed to produce high-value substances which are presently imported from developing countries. For example, an oilseed rape high in lauric acid has been designed to produce oils to substitute for coconut palm oil, presently exported from the Philippines and Kerala in India in particular. Such varieties are already in commercial use in the USA and are being field tested in Europe. Similar substitutions are being designed for products of small-scale farmers, e.g. vanilla (a major export of Mozambique), quinoa (a high-protein export of Bolivia) and cocoa butter (an export of West Africa).

If technical advances make these substitutions economically feasible, then the GM crops could drive down world prices or even eliminate some suppliers. Such a scenario would repeat the earlier cases of conventionally bred high-fructose maize and sugarbeet, which undermined developing-country exports of cane sugar. As an NGO notes, 'even if no GM crops are actually grown in developing countries, the technology could still have a significant adverse effect on their national economies' (Panos, 1998c).

Some tropical fruits have been genetically modified for pest resistance, among other traits. If technically successful, these products would help increase yields and reduce pesticide usage. However, greater productivity could intensify competition and drive down world prices – while perhaps encouraging changes in land use away from local food production towards more lucrative exports, possibly affecting people's livelihoods and food security.

More generally, GM crops intersect with broader political–economic changes in the world food market system. Under the 1994 GATT/WTO agreement (GATT, 1994), as well as the IMF's structural adjustment criteria, most developing countries have been forced to reduce their agricultural subsidies. Such reductions are advocated by biotechnology companies and grain traders. According to one analyst, 'By reducing price supports, the corporations maximize their ability to structure comparative advantages in the world market, sourcing their inputs from the varieties of producing regions' (McMichael, 1998, p.106).

Critics view the trends in biotechnology as a further step in the industrialization of agriculture. 'Biotechnology makes food production more and more like an assembly industry. Crops as such are no longer agricultural commodities, but their molecular components increasingly are... Interchangeability of crops also means interchangeability of producers' (Hobbelink, 1991, p.95; Hobbelink, 1995).

From this perspective, the grain industry aims to find more interchangeable or cheaper sources of its raw materials. As a result, the agro-food chain becomes more global and more insecure for the producers.

'Biopiracy': what patent rights?

"...legal protection of intellectual property serves the public interest by stimulating continued investment in technological innovation."

(John Duesing, Ciba-Geigy
(later Novartis), 1989)

As mentioned earlier, GM crops mark a new stage in the commoditization of seeds (Figure 22.3), partly through extended patent rights. In this context, 'biopiracy' has become a common term for the theft of genetic resources, though it has two opposite meanings. For advocates of greater patent rights, 'biopiracy' means violating those rights, e.g. by using patented materials without a licence agreement or without paying royalties. For opponents of such rights, 'biopiracy' means the patents themselves, on the grounds that plant material should remain freely reproducible as a common resource.

Underlying that dispute lies not only an economic conflict between companies and farmers, but also a conceptual issue about the inserted genes and germplasm of GM crops. For advocates of greater patent rights, such genes are

inventions, involving a significant contribution by scientists. For opponents, such genes are discoveries (or simulations) of common resources which have been already selected and cultivated by farmers over generations.

These concepts have legal significance because patent rules require the applicant to have contributed an 'inventive step'. Interpreting that criterion loosely, the US Patent Office has accepted broad patent claims (for example, on substances derived from plants traditionally cultivated in developing countries such as those from the neem tree) on genes inserted into GM plants, and even on all GM cotton. Large companies have bought up smaller ones which hold such patents.

The US government has sought to extend its patent criteria to other countries, by using the TRIPS (Trade-Related Aspects of Intellectual Property Rights) rules under the WTO. Even some non-GM seeds have been subjected to royalty payments by farmers; GM seeds provide a stronger basis to identify the source of the seed and thus to enforce such payments. If such attempts are successful, farmers could be required to pay royalties on some seeds even if they were not bought from the company holding the patent. Among other countries, India has had a protracted internal debate over whether to accept such demands.

The breadth of patent rights has also been the subject of an on-going dispute in Europe. The 1973 European Patent Convention prohibits patents on 'animal or plant varieties'. This criterion has been widely interpreted to prohibit patents on material or progeny propagated from a plant.

Nevertheless the recent EC Patent Directive allows broad patents on 'biotechnological inventions', such as GM crops, 'even if they comprise new varieties of plants' (EC, 1998). The final draft excludes an amendment passed by the European Parliament guaranteeing a farmer's privilege to resow seed, regardless of any patented gene. The Patent Directive has since been challenged at the European Court of Justice by the Netherlands and Italy.

Figure 22.3   Commoditization of plant life? Cartoon from El Mundo, *March 1999.*

The EC Directive followed a ten-year-long debate which still continues. Opponents demand 'No Patents on Life!' (e.g. Corner House, 1997; Global 2000, 1997). According to an NGO lobby group, 'The Directive now legalizes biopiracy.' According to opponents, plant patents provide an incentive for companies to use GM techniques rather than other methods of improving seeds, while the mere prospect of litigation may deter breeders from using the germplasm.

Biotechnology companies claim that they need plant patents as an incentive and reward for improving crops: they should be able to benefit from the progeny of GM crops or restrict their use. According to a European lobby group,

> "Seed companies contribute to the objectives of the Biodiversity Convention through maintaining and improving biodiversity through the maintenance of genebanks and by using genetic resources for the benefit of mankind. They are creating a new biodiversity by recombining genomes through traditional crossing and adding new attributes via genetic engineering. For this it is of utmost importance to be able to patent inventions in the kingdom of plants."

> (FEBC, 1997)

22.3 Alternative visions of the future

This chapter has highlighted a number of different interpretations of the nature and impact of the new biotechnologies. The variety of views can be linked to an underlying analysis of 'progress' and how development can be achieved. This concluding section draws out three perspectives and their limitations.

The previous section posed the question, 'feeding the world – or the market?' As we have seen, the practical question is more complex, depending upon which people and markets are meant. Moreover, government influences the type of market which exists, e.g. by subsidizing some innovations rather than others, by reducing ag-

ricultural subsidies in some countries more than in others, by extending patent rights to seeds, or by setting standards for acceptable environmental effects. Those regulatory activities can influence the types of biotechnological innovations which become products, which products find significant markets, who benefits from their use, how the agro-food chain is globalized, and thus the direction of development. Within the debate over the appropriate regulation, some advocate the 'free market', which really means some types of regulation rather than others.

The free market vision

This vision encompasses the view that current debates over 'new' biotechnology reflect fear of the unknown and that once the benefits of the technology are demonstrated, current concerns will fade into the background. This is the view held by many managers in companies involved in biotechnology innovation and a number of analysts.

The free market vision rests on two principal arguments about how industrializing countries need to engage with market forces and the power of biotechnology to help them do this.

First, it is argued, responding to market signals is a necessity. Developing countries need to compete in a global market place. Once the competitive advantages of using new genetically manipulated crops become clear, all countries will follow the market and adopt the technologies. The increase in production which will result from adopting new technologies will be a significant contributor to the reduction of global food shortages.

Second, the market is the best way of delivering choice. New genetically modified crops may be more efficient, but for religious, political and ethical reasons some consumers and farmers will choose not to use them. Market demand will ensure that other options are available and those who worry that biotechnology will preclude other options are worrying without good reason. This argument also applies to concerns about farmers who do not wish or are unable to buy seeds and make royalty payments every year; if there is sufficient demand the market will ensure that alternatives are available for those who wish to use non-GM crops.

Two principal objections to these arguments are as follows. The first is that many of the countries which have chronic food shortages and are the least competitive have very underdeveloped market structures. There is an assumption in the free market vision that hypothetical demand seamlessly creates efficient and smoothly functioning markets. In fact, delivery mechanisms, storage problems, marketing structures, information deficits, corruption and other factors mean that the institutional basis upon which markets operate is weak. The free market argument ignores the complexity of market structures and the difficulties of establishing market-based institutions in very poor environments. Second, the market may deliver food production increases in commodity crops, but low value crops which are nevertheless essential to many poorer people are not the targets for biotechnology innovators. If the current situation continues, with R&D dominated by the private sector and transnational corporations, what is likely to happen is that increases in output will be limited to commodity crops in specific locations.

The regulated development vision

The vast majority of free trade advocates would acknowledge the need for risk regulation. However, for them it should focus on narrowly defined scientific and technical data. This approach has been called into question by policymakers and academics pushing for a more 'pro-active' or precautionary approach. Assessing risk on the basis of damage done and established harmful effects is not adequate; the aim should be to prevent damage. Risk, here, becomes a much more subjective category as perception of future risks (necessarily subjective) is involved. This more precautionary approach has been attempted within the European Union. It has, however, been difficult to reach international consensus on the regulatory criteria and thus on the types of evidence deemed relevant. The difficulty arises partly from divergent accounts of the 'risk' to be regulated. There

are disagreements over the types of potential effects which must be prevented, the burden of evidence for demonstrating risk or safety, the extent of the food chain which must be evaluated, and the appropriate types of legal liability.

Those issues are controversial within each country, as well as among them. Governments adopt criteria which may be difficult to reconcile with each other and which may change in response to political pressures. In general, risk regulation is the only statutory procedure for guaranteeing public information and for evaluating undesirable effects of products, so this procedure often becomes burdened by all the issues arising in the wider public debate.

Many more GM crops have gained regulatory approval and entered commercial use in the USA than in most other countries. Sometimes their approval by the EU has been delayed on grounds that safety data are inadequate, i.e. on grounds of plausible risk rather than documented harm. The US government has threatened to challenge such delays as an unjustified trade barrier to its GM exports through the World Trade Organization.

The conflicts can be illustrated by two high-profile efforts at harmonizing regulatory criteria: an international 'biosafety protocol', and a European 'internal market'. Both cases illustrate how official language is interpreted differently and contested vis à vis development issues, at least implicitly.

Biosafety Protocol: what biodiversity?

The proposal for a Biosafety Protocol originated in the Convention on Biological Diversity, as adopted at the 1992 Rio Summit. A 1995 follow-up meeting mandated a protocol focusing on transboundary movement of any 'living modified organism (LMO) resulting from biotechnology that may have an adverse effect on the conservation and sustainable use of biological diversity'. That original mandate has been interpreted in quite different ways in negotiating the agreement. Some major exporters of commodity crops – e.g. USA, Canada, Australia as well as Argentina – have sought to restrict the Protocol to an information-sharing role.

In principle there has been an international consensus to guarantee 'advance informed agreement (AIA)', whereby the exporter would provide risk-assessment information to the importing country. Many developing countries have sought a stronger Protocol, for example because they are likely to be importers of GM seeds or produce, or because they are centres of diversity for the traditional crops on which the GM crops are based. Many demand that the AIA assesses socio-economic effects, e.g. on grounds that GM crops may undermine traditional agricultural systems and/or may substitute for their exports. Most Western countries want the risk assessment limited to direct biological effects, as in their own regulatory procedures, and want the Protocol limited to seeds intended for cultivation. Many developing countries demand that the Protocol encompass bulk commodity shipments too, e.g. on grounds that DNA from GM grains may be transferred to other organisms. Some propose that the AIA should impose more strict requirements upon national regulatory procedures as well as upon transboundary trade.

Although the USA has not signed the Convention on Biological Diversity or the 1995 agreement, it has played a leading role in opposing these demands, thus serving to delay any final Biosafety Protocol. The USA has proposed an exemption for LMOs 'which are not likely to cause harm', as if this were a straightforward scientific issue instead of one involving value judgements. It has also proposed that the Protocol be subordinated to the WTO rules, in any case involving trade disputes, so that the WTO could invalidate an import ban. The Protocol was due to be finalized at a meeting in Carthagena in February 1999 but no final agreement emerged.

The 1995 mandate emphasized the need to protect 'biological diversity', but various countries disagreed about its meaning, especially regarding its 'sustainable use'. In disagreements about the appropriate breadth of risk-assessment information, there are underlying issues of GM crops as development choices – or even as threats to development.

EU internal market

As a means to harmonize risk regulation, the European Community adopted Directive 90/220 on the Deliberate Release of Genetically Modified Organisms (GMOs). This established an EC-wide procedure for approving GM products for commercial use, so as to establish an 'internal market'. Nevertheless, more and more member states have objected to market approval, or even imposed restrictions on products which already gained approval in the European Union (incorporating the European Community in 1995).

On the surface, the regulatory disputes concern how to define 'adverse effects'. Under the Directive, member states must ensure that GMOs do not cause 'adverse effects', but the term is undefined. Some member states have defined it broadly, e.g. including the selection pressure for insects resistant to an in-built insecticide; the inadvertent flow of herbicide-tolerant genes to weedy relatives, which may thereby jeopardize the corresponding herbicide as a future option; and the increased use of broad-spectrum herbicides on GM crops tolerant to them. Other member states have dismissed these concerns as 'agricultural effects', not relevant to the risk of the GM crop (Levidow *et al.*, 1996).

Such conflicts arise from deeper issues of intensive agriculture and sustainable development. For example, Denmark has demanded that the risk assessment encompass the overall herbicide implications of herbicide-tolerant crops, given its national policy of reducing pesticide use and thus maintaining the safety of groundwater for drinking purposes. More recently the UK too has emphasized the herbicide implications, for somewhat different reasons: broad-spectrum herbicides could harm wildlife habitats, yet it has a biodiversity policy to reduce pesticide usage in ways that enhance wildlife. Austria's assessment accepts no product involving pesticide use, e.g. herbicide-tolerant crops, because it compares effects of GM crops to a baseline of organic agriculture, which the government has been promoting. Italian regulators have come under national pressure to oppose approval of GM crops; the Italian Parliament foresees such products threatening agricultural biodiversity and has allocated subsidies to promote local crop varieties.

In various ways, then, public debate has linked environmental risk with agricultural strategy, e.g. how GM crops are designed to favour particular agricultural practices. The prospect of more 'efficient' methods can be regarded as either a benefit or threat, depending on one's viewpoint. The risk debate becomes an informal Technology Assessment on how future agricultural options may be opened up, favoured or precluded by GM crops. These pressures lead to different, changeable accounts of the 'risks' to be regulated.

Although the risk debate may have facilitated learning among national regulatory systems, harmonization has not been possible within Europe – much less internationally via the Biosafety Protocol. In both industrialized and developing countries, GM crops have been evaluated according to development criteria, be it favourably or negatively. We may ask: On what basis should GM products be permitted to circulate in international trade? How could the development issues be incorporated into regulatory criteria?

The partnership and networking vision

In this vision researchers and producers in industrialized countries and developing countries share information, knowledge and experience. The focus here is on capacity building. An emphasis on partnerships and networks is common both in development and business literature and the associated focus on the importance of knowledge is clearly related to profound changes wrought by the revolution in information technology and changes in industrial structure. Numerous studies and authors have noted that in many industrial sectors and contexts individual firms are no longer able to operate as independent units. Increasingly firms and research centres need to operate in partnerships and networks (Castells, 1996; Mytelka, 1998; World Bank, 1998).

This phenomenon is a particular feature of biotechnology innovation. Inclusion or exclusion from networks and partnerships becomes an important issue; exclusion is dangerous because knowledge is built up and shared amongst groups of actors, and those outside the 'knowledge circle' risk falling further behind.

A number of studies on attempts in developing countries to build capabilities in biotechnology have stressed the need for linkages between different actors and the need to build networks and partnerships (Komen & Persley, 1993; Kumar & Siddharthen, 1997). In particular, studies have stressed the need to involve the private sector. However, network building and the construction of effective partnerships are far from easy. Success is thought by some analysts to derive largely from trust and careful attention to the durability of the institutional basis upon which partnerships and networks are constructed.

Some examples of partnerships between researchers and producers in different parts of the world are as follows:

- A programme of co-operation between the Mexican public agricultural research institute, the Centre of Research and Advanced Studies (CINVESTAV) and Monsanto on the transfer of gene technology for virus resistance in potatoes. The programme had some notable successes in creating modified varieties especially popular with small farmers. The experience gave CINVESTAV scientists not only technical insight but also new skills in dealing with regulatory matters, risk assessment practice and biosafety regulations (Nature Biotechnology, 1999).

- An agreement between Zeneca and research institutes in South-east Asia which allows the research institutes to use Zeneca's delayed ripening technology in papaya. The agreement releases the research institutes from royalty payments while the technology is being used in domestic markets. The agreement also involves co-operation in building regulatory and monitoring capabilities in South-east Asia.

- In the late 1980s, SIME Darby, a Malaysian company, and the US firm International Plant

Research jointly created the Association of South East Asian Nations (ASEAN) biotechnology corporation. Based in Malaysia the corporation undertakes research into the application of genetic engineering techniques to perennial plants (Mytelka, 1998, p.13).

- Empresar La Moderna (ELM, Mexico City) is a seed and fresh product company, a world leader in the vegetable seed market. To widen its access to biotechnology in 1996, ELM acquired a US company, DNA Plant Technology. This company owned more than 40 biotechnology patents. It also collaborates with Monsanto in developing herbicide-resistant vegetables (Nature Biotechnology, 1999).

- In Argentina, the Instituto Nacional de Tecnología Agropecuaria adopted a new policy that permits the institute to enter into joint ventures with private agricultural firms. The institute also facilitates linkages between other private and public sector actors, as does Fundacion Chile. A specific organization mentioned earlier, the International Service for the Acquisition of Agri-Biotech Applications (ISAAA) is designed to promote technology transfer to developing countries.

There are plenty of other examples of increased networking and partnership. The powerful agricultural-based research organization, the Consultative Group on International Agricultural Research (CGIAR) has set up a 'Private Sector Committee' to explore opportunities for greater CGIAR–private sector collaboration in agricultural research. The CGIAR has, however, chosen to be selective in terms of the technology it will work with. It has, for example, recommended that its 16 member institutes ban use of 'terminator' technology in their crop-improvement projects.

Incentives for large multinational corporations (MNCs) to engage in networks and partnerships include the desire to build markets for the future and the desire to enhance the image of biotechnology. In relation to the second point, firms which have often referred to the capacity of biotechnology to feed hungry people are looking for

success stories to prove their point. MNCs will therefore create technological co-operation agreements and 'donate' patent-protected technology in cases where market opportunities would not interest them or would become a threat to them. These agreements may extend into the infrastructure needed to undertake biotechnology research and plant GM crops; for example, it is also in a firm's interest that regulatory structures prevent catastrophes which could undermine the technology's image.

Some of the types of networks and partnerships which might be established around biotechnology are as follows:

- farmer and innovator networks which seek to improve relevance and efficacy of new products;
- partnerships and networks between firms and research institutes in the South aimed at targeting smaller niche markets in developing countries;
- North/South private sector partnerships where firms in the South acquire new technologies for use in local and regional markets;
- North/South multi-party partnerships involving private sector organizations and research institutes aimed at creating new technologies and opening up new markets;
- bioconservation/development networks as a response to the need to implement the principles of conservation and equity in the use of genetic resources from the South.

The extent to which these partnerships and networks can assist in building capabilities is yet to be seen. For some, new information and knowledge based production and research webs will be the basis of future political and economic orders. Manuel Castells puts it as follows:

"...as a historical trend, dominant functions and processes in the information age are increasingly organised around networks. Networks constitute the new social morphology of our societies, and the diffusion of networking logic substantially modifies the operation and outcomes in processes of production, experience, power and culture...I would argue that this networking logic induces a social determination of a higher level than that of the specific social interests expressed through the networks: the power of flows takes precedence over the flows of power. Presence or absence in the network and the dynamics of each network vis-à-vis others are critical sources of domination and change in our society: a society that, therefore, we may properly call the network society..."

(Castells, 1996, p.469)

New models of research and partnering hold out the promise of access to knowledge and expertise which could enable a narrowing of the gap in capabilities between richer and poorer countries. And domestically based networks could begin to develop advanced biotechnology inputs into crops grown by local poor farmers. The agreements mentioned earlier are perhaps examples of this. It seems possible that in this way networking and partnering arrangements could overcome the divide between HEIA- and LEIA-based research systems, but the question of who will be included is key.

22.4 Conclusion

The debate about biotechnology is more than a technical discussion about spliced genes. People disagree about the impact the technology will have because they differ in their analysis of the causes of hunger and poverty and because they have different visions of the future.

It is possible but unlikely that calls for a complete freeze will result in a halt to biotechnology development. It is more likely that the different visions of development outlined in the previous section will continue to be played out. Economic and political control will continue to be contested. The impact which the technology will have on poverty and hunger depends very much on the ability of players to shape applications so that they meet the needs of the poorest.

Summary

This chapter has looked at the possibilities and constraints in using agriculture and food related biotechnology for development. The following are some of the main points:

1   There is a diversity of views about how biotechnology will impact on development. These are closely linked to different stakeholders' perceptions of the root causes of hunger and poverty.

2   Whilst technical possibilities exist, the institutional framework within which the technology is being developed constrains the extent to which the technology will reach the poorest, at least in the short term.

3   Both the free market and regulated market visions of the future are problematic and the extent to which they can provide sustainable institutional structures to facilitate pro-poor development of the technology is questionable. There is a possibility that new networks and partnerships will facilitate products and techniques which will reach beyond richer consumers, but *who* will be included in these new networks is the key factor.

23

THE NEW POLITICS OF IDENTITY

TIM ALLEN AND JOHN EADE

Figure 23.1 'Why did the lights go out in Sarajevo?': a refugee from Bosnia & Herzegovina reaches Croatia in 1992, and holds up a newspaper with the headline, 'Through Terror to Greater Serbia'.

Chapter 21 has noted that, in the course of the 1990s it became fashionable to explain events in terms of culture. Here we explore one of the reasons why this has occurred: the alarming spread of a 'culture-based' politics of identity. At the start of the 1990s, the US Senator and former Harvard professor Daniel Patrick Moynihan warned us of its coming. Like several other commentators he believed that the age of totalitarianism had ended, and he

speculated on what would happen next. At first he predicted that the United States would play a leading role in 'a New World Order based on old legal principles' (Moynihan, 1993, p.9). But by 1991 he had recognized that 'the argument was incomplete. It did not deal with the yet larger question: Why did the lights go out in Sarajevo?' (ibid.; Figure 23.1). His answer was that ethnicity (or ethnic-nationalism) had struck:

Box 23.1   Nationalities and European colonialism

The emergence of ideologies of state nationalism in Europe created contradictions with respect to colonial territories. Across the British Empire, for example, a confused situation prevailed. Colonial subjects owed their loyalty not just to the representative institutions of their particular colony, but to the Crown and the person of the Queen-Empress/King-Emperor. As the Empire rapidly expanded during the late nineteenth century and the Dominions (Canada, Australia, New Zealand and South Africa) asserted their distinctiveness, so the confusions of nationality law across the empire became more obvious. In 1914 an attempt was made:

"to formulate a common category of belonging that would…enable Britain and the dominions to restrict entry into their territories by people from other parts of the Empire, notably the native populations of colonies in Africa and Asia."

(Cesarani, 1996, p.63)

Those living in the Dominions and colonies were defined by the Act as subjects of the British crown, but not all these British subjects enjoyed the right of entry into a particular dominion or colony.

The tensions between colonialism and nationality have not been fully resolved by the unravelling of the European empires. Notions of racial superiority which influenced colonial policies have also informed post-colonial definitions of citizenship, and have shaped immigration controls. Another important development is that popular memory about colonial history is rapidly fading in western Europe, and this amnesia is encouraged by politicians who deny the relevance of their country's colonial experience to current debates. For example, in 1999 a controversial book about the exploitative policies pursued in the name of the Belgian King Leopold II in the Congo during the nineteenth century was dismissed as irrelevant to contemporary Belgian society by the Prime Minister, Jean-Luc Dehaene.

were prepared to die for its cause is a matter of debate. It seems to have been the product of a variety of factors, including the spread of print media, the expansion of formal education, increased literacy, the promotion of idealized sets of values linked to state citizenship by European colonial powers (see Box 23.1), and the mobilization of entire populations for military purposes, notably during the First World War.

It also took on different qualities in different states. During the 1930s and 1940s, extremely militant nationalism was shown to be an extraordinarily effective means of promoting social integration in Germany and Japan. In these countries powerful mythologies of common origin coincided with state structures. Hitler could claim that the state was the living organism of a nationality, and most Germans understood what he meant, even if they disagreed with him. Elsewhere, such as in Britain and the United States, belief about common origins were much less widely accepted or absent altogether. Here state nationalism was not something which

emanated from a mythical, 'racial' core, but something which fostered the sense of actively choosing to be identified with an idealized, moral community ('the Land of the Free'). In striking contrast to German nationalism, a quality of nationalism in the USA was (and to a large extent still is) a pride in being part of a nation of immigrants.

The muddling up of 'nation' with 'state', and 'nationalism' with 'state patriotism', helps explain what now seem to have been serious inadequacies in social analysis. Walker Connor drew attention to this problem at the end of the 1970s. Referring to a standard dictionary of international relations he pointed out a widespread conceptual contradiction. After carefully noting that 'a nation may comprise part of a state, or extend beyond the borders of a single state', the dictionary elsewhere explained that nationalism 'makes the state the ultimate focus of the individual's loyalty.' It also stated that nationalism 'as a mass emotion is the most powerful political force operative in the world.' Connor observed:

"Few would disagree with this assessment of the power of nationalism, *and this is precisely the problem. Impressed with the force of nationalism, and assuming it to be in the service of the state, the scholar of political development has been pre-programmed to assume that the new states of Africa and Asia would naturally become the foci of their inhabitants' loyalties*. Nationalism, here as elsewhere, would prove irresistible, and alternative foci of loyalty would therefore lose the competition to that political structure alternately called the nation, the state, or the nation-state. Contrary to its nomenclature, the 'nation-building' school has in fact been dedicated to building viable states. And with a very few exceptions, the greatest barrier to state unity has been the fact that the states each contain more than one nation, and sometimes hundreds."

(Connor, 1994 [1978], pp.97–8; italics in the
original)

A prime fact about the world, Connor argued, is that 'it is *not* largely composed of nation-states' (ibid., p.39). According to a survey of the 132 states in the world in 1971, only 12 could justifiably be described as nation-states in the strict sense, including Germany and Japan. For Connor these were exceptions, and making generalizations about all states as if they were the norm was misleading:

"German and Japanese nationalism were more prophetic auguries of the growth of concepts such as, inter alia, Ibo, Bengali, Kikuyu, Naga, Karen, Bahutu, Kurd, and Baganda, than they were auguries of the growth of concepts such as Nigeria, Pakistan, Kenya, India, Burma, Thailand, Rwanda, Iraq and Uganda."

(ibid., p.43)

Reviewing the literature at the time, Connor found little reflection on how the psychological bonds that tied segments of a state's population were to be supplanted by loyalty to a state-structure. It seemed that the assumption that nationalism was in the service of the state made the difficult investigation of 'those abstract ties that identify the true nation' unnecessary (Figure 23.3).

Figure 23.3   Promoting loyalty to a state-structure: in China, formal education is emphasized as a means of communicating the Communist Party's national ideology.

There was surely another factor at work here too.

"The great social theorists like Weber and Marx often treated nationalism, and the vision of human cultural difference on which it is based, as a self-evident feature of the world, whereas other kinds of collective category, like class, received endless theoretical scrutiny. Their followers in sociology, history and political science usually followed suit so that nationalism, despite its pervasive effects on twentieth-century world history, was the great forgotten topic of the human sciences."

(Spencer, 1996, pp.391–2)

It was not in fact until Walker Connor and others directed attention to the issue in the 1970s that nationalism really began to be investigated, and not until the 1980s that it became a major focus of social research (Box 23.2).

Box 23.2 Theories of nationalism

Much of the academic debate about nationalism has centred on the connections between nationalism and modernity. Some see nationalism and the nation-state as a typically modern phenomenon created through the development of political institutions such as a mass electorate, political parties and government bureaucracies, the emergence of urban, industrialized communities and notions of citizenship and national sovereignty. Others draw attention to the pre-modern character of modern nationalism and nation-states revealed in beliefs about the historical origins of a particular nation, the cultural traditions of its people and the importance of social ties based upon family and kinship. In the second approach nationalism is closely allied (or often muddled up) with the related concept of ethnicity. Three particularly influential thinkers on nationalism have been Ernest Gellner, Benedict Anderson and Anthony Smith. Each takes a different position on this relationship between nationalism and modernity.

In *Nations and Nationalism*, Ernest Gellner claims that:

"Nationalism is not the awakening and assertion of mythical, supposedly natural and given units…It is, on the contrary, the crystallization of new units, suitable for the conditions now prevailing, though admittedly using as their raw material the cultural, historical and other inheritances from the pre-nationalist world."

(Gellner, 1983, p.49)

Industrialized society requires cultural homogeneity. In practice this means that the state takes over control of cultural reproduction, through the institution of mass schooling. Nationalism should therefore be seen as an argument for the political pre-eminence of culturally homogeneous units, which is deployed in the context of the transition from 'agro-literate' to industrialized societies. In this sense it is unquestionably modern.

Benedict Anderson in *Imagined Communities* (1983) also views nationalism as something modern, but directs attention to its conceptual power. For him, it is an artefact of political imagination, which could be studied in much the same way as, for example, religion. Distinctive nationalisms are not so much consciously fabricated (as Gellner, amongst others, implies), but are part of ways of thinking, which should be understood in terms of the institutions which make that thinking possible. The most important of these institutions, he suggests, is 'print capitalism'. He argues that 'the convergence of capitalism and print technology on the fatal diversity of human language created the possibility of a new form of imagined community, which in its basic morphology set the stage for the modern nation.' It resulted in the emergence of newspapers and novels, which portrayed the nation as a sociological community moving along 'homogeneous, empty time'. An especially interesting element in Anderson's work is his emphasis on the New World origins of nationalism. In the Americas from the 1760s, he argues, neither economic interest, Liberalism nor Enlightenment could, or did, create in themselves the kind, or shape, of imagined community to be defended from Madrid, Lisbon and London. None provided the framework of 'a new consciousness'. 'In accomplishing this specific task, pilgrim creole functionaries and provincial creole printmen played the decisive role' (Anderson, 1983, p.65).

The approaches of both Anderson and Gellner are partly countered by Anthony Smith's view, put forward in several books, including *The Ethnic Origin of Nations* (1986). Smith accepts that the modern state has had a pivotal role in the promotion of nationalism, but thinks that the problem of legitimacy is more far-reaching, in that nationalism arises out of a pervasive moral crisis of 'dual organization', where divine authority is challenged by secular state power. Alternative solutions to this crisis are conducive to different forms of nationalism. The two commonest bases of a nation are a 'political community' (usually a territorial state) and a 'community of culture'. In the first case, that of territorial nationalism, the leaders of the political community or new state aim to create a culturally homogeneous population with a sense of unique 'ethnic' ties. The second case, that of 'ethnic' nationalism, relies first and foremost on the existence of 'an identifiable community of culture'. In these cases, the nationalists come to believe that their cultural communities are, or can become, nations.

A key component of Smith's analysis, is his use of the concept of 'ethnic communities'. Anderson and Gellner both avoid this issue. Anderson's emphasis on the idea of an imagined community, and especially on the relational boundaries between imagined communities, is applicable to other kinds of collective identity, and this has meant that his work has been of interest to scholars working on ethnicity, but the overlap is not something he explores himself (indeed, neither 'ethnic' nor 'ethnicity' appear in the index of his book). For Gellner, 'nationalisms are simply those tribalisms, or for that matter any other kind of groups, which through luck, effort or circumstance succeed in becoming an effective force under modern circumstances' (1983, p.87). In contrast, Smith makes use of a concept of ethnic cores, which he terms *ethnie*, and argues that these existed in pre-modern times and can be linked to the origins of many contemporary nationalisms.

Ethnicity

A consequence of the pre-empting of 'nation' and 'nationalism' by the state was potential confusion when the same terms were used for 'subnational' groupings – such as the one hundred and twenty-five officially registered 'nationalities' of the USSR (Russian, Ukrainian, Azerbaijani, Armenian, Moldavian, Lithuanian, Georgian, etc.), or the non-Spanish 'nationalities' of Spain (i.e. Basques, Catalans and Galicians), or the various immigrant nationalities of the USA (Italian, Irish, Greek, etc.). There was a need for other words to describe these kinds of collective identities, and more generally to indicate all those identities associated with ideas about a common origin that existed within states (or, in some cases, across state boundaries). In some parts of the world, specific alternative terms became well established. In Europe, until quite recently, the word 'race' was sometimes employed (e.g. 'the Scottish race'), while in much of Africa many collective identities were commonly labelled as 'tribes'. But one concept has become especially prevalent since the 1970s as a broad categorization: ethnicity.

The terms 'ethnic group' and 'ethnicity' are derived from two Greek words, *ethnos*, which cor-

responds with the Latin word *natio*, and *ethnikos*, which can be translated as 'heathen'. When the word ethnic appeared in the English language during the fourteenth century, it combined both these meanings. It was used to refer to pagan populations. By the mid-nineteenth century it had taken on overtly racial connotations, and could be used to indicate populations who were not 'highly civilized' Europeans. However, the more neutral meaning of a group claiming common descent also survived. Both these associations have influenced the usage of the concept in modern times.

Although some thinkers, including Weber, had used the term 'ethnic group' in their work, its introduction as a key concept in the social sciences only occurred during the 1960s and 1970s. Walker Connor, amongst others, promoted its use as a specific term for groups with a subjective belief in their common descent. For Connor, an ethnic group was not necessarily a nation, because a nation was a community which aspired towards political autonomy, but some forms of nationalism could be highly ethnic in character (or 'ethno-nationalist'). However, by the time that Connor was writing, 'ethnicity' had also taken on different connotations (much to his irritation), and in fact most of the academic discussion of it was curiously divorced from the notion of nationalism.

Ethnicity as social instrument

The book which probably did more than any other to establish ethnicity as an analytical construct was first published in 1963. It was called *Beyond the Melting Pot: the Negroes, Puerto Ricans, Jews, Italians and Irish of New York City*. Here Nathan Glazer and Daniel Patrick Moynihan, at the time both professors of education at Harvard, tried to explain why people in New York who were descended from immigrants continued to assert their separate ethnic identity, even though they did not live their lives in a way that was similar to that of their African, Puerto Rican or European ancestors.

Essentially Glazer and Moynihan argued that people recognized that asserting an ethnic identity was a means of obtaining jobs and resources. They maintained that 'the ethnic group in American society became not a survival from the age of mass immigration but a new social form' (1970, p.16). The members of an ethnic group are connected by ties of family and friendship, but they are also interest groups, and this is 'perhaps the single most important fact about ethnic groups in New York City' (1970, p.17). Thus the idea that ethnicity is some kind of constant, essential core which binds together a population over the generations was rejected. Rather, ethnicity was viewed as a phenomenon that had emerged out of living in modern America.

This was a highly instrumentalist conception (which contrasts markedly with Moynihan's more recent views). It also could be read as implying that an ethnic group was a subgroup of a larger society (otherwise the Anglo-Saxons of New York should have been included). This had already become a well-established popular usage of 'ethnic' in the US by the mid twentieth century, and it was in this form that the concept appeared in standard American sociological dictionaries and encyclopaedias from the late 1960s. As we shall see, it later informed the design of so-called 'multicultural' public policies

in several Western countries. However, it was the more general idea that ethnicity related to new kinds of collective identities which seized the imagination of social scientists then researching in Africa.

Several anthropologists had been researching among urban Africans, and had found that identities were forged in the towns that had little to do with the so-called 'tribal' relations of rural areas. This work had demonstrated the inadequacies of analysing African populations as if they belonged to separate, relatively static tribal groups. Drawing on the work being carried out in the USA, Africanist anthropologists started using the expression 'ethnic group' for the new identities of 'modern' Africans living in the towns and cities. But quite quickly that application was broadened. Several scholars pointed out that ostensibly traditional rural 'tribal' identities were also recent introductions, in many cases having initially been created for administrative purposes by European colonial administrations. 'Ethnic group' began to be used as the preferred label for all population categories formerly called tribes, and by the end of the decade, a corresponding substitution was often additionally being made between 'tribalism' and 'ethnicity'.

Apart from its focus on the newness of what often appeared to be old identities, the position of Glazer and Moynihan was appealing in that it offered a powerful counter-argument to prevalent patronizing and misleading views about Africans. Far from being trapped by static customs and incapable of sustained entrepreneurial activity, when the right opportunities were available they would eagerly seize them. Sometimes they would do so by asserting particular identities. Abner Cohen, for example, in *Custom and Politics in Urban Africa* (1969) argued that Hausa traders in the Nigerian city of Ibadan used what he termed 'political ethnicity' to control the market in cola nuts and cattle. In later works he developed this position into a general theoretical analysis, arguing that ethnicity must have a practical function in order to be viable. For him, ethnicity is a particular form of informal political organization that invokes cultural values for essentially material reasons. He even went so far as to suggest that London stock-brokers may be said to constitute an ethnic group in that they tend to marry into their own class and have a shared identity (Cohen, 1974).

Ethnicity as relational boundary

However, for other scholars, this kind of pure instrumentalism was not entirely convincing. While accepting that it could help explain certain forms of ethnicity, they also drew attention to less overtly rational qualities of identity. Many anthropologists came to view ethnicity as an aspect of social relations, linked to the maintenance of boundaries. This approach is commonly traced back to a book edited by Frederik Barth (Barth, 1969).The crux of the argument was that study of ethnicity should primarily focus on the way in which ethnic boundaries are constructed and maintained. Ethnic groups do not exist independently, but are made in relation to one another. Thus ethnicity is not so much the character or quality of an ethnic group, but 'essentially an aspect of a relationship' (Eriksen, 1993, p.12). An implication of this line of argument is that ethnicity cannot really act as a causal explanation for something, but is rather a way of describing a social situation.

It is striking that, although relationalists and instrumentalists could sometimes end up with different points of view on particular situations, they shared an antipathy to interpretations of collective identity which took at face value the claims of groups being studied to be naturally or inevitably distinctive. They recognized, of course, that once the mythologized constructions of ethnic identity are sealed in bloodshed, to all intents and purposes they become objective social phenomena (Figure 23.4). To show, for example, that many African tribal identities were partially or wholly created under European rule, and that they were adapted and changed after independence, is no consolation to a man who has watched his wife and daughters being raped and killed because they were 'Hutu', or 'Acholi', or 'Dinka'. Nevertheless, such groupings were in fact quite recently forged subjective realities. In effect they were a kind of false consciousness, which might shape behaviour, but which was always changing and open to manipulation by political élites.

Figure 23.4   Once the mythologized constructions of ethnic identity are sealed in bloodshed, to all intents and purposes they become objective social phenomena: Rwandan refugee from Burundi, 1993.

Ethnicity as primal essence

One reason for so vigorously rejecting what are sometimes called primordialist or essentialist conceptions of collective identities has already been given. In former European colonies it was a reaction against views that non-Western ways of life were static, backward and resistant to progress. It can also be linked to a shift in academic analysis, away from older models of social life which suggested that populations existed in functional and culturally separate systems, toward interpretations which gave greater emphasis to processes of change and to human agency. In addition, it became an aspect of an anti-racist stance. Indeed, in the 1970s and 1980s, 'primordialist' came close to a term of abuse amongst many Western social scientists. Anyone who argued that collective identities could emanate from deep, primal, subconscious traits (whether biologically determined or historically formed and culturally embedded) could be dismissed as, at best, rather reactionary.

There were, however, important exceptions. Socio-biologists were prepared to consider the possibility that there might be a genetic basis to group affiliation, and some sociological theories of nationalism, notably those of Anthony Smith (see Box 23.2), suggested that nationalist movements could be motivated by an historically constituted ethnic essence. However, in retrospect, perhaps the most significant exception of all was the school of thought known as 'ethnos theory' which was promoted from the late 1960s under the auspices of Yulian Bromley in Moscow. Bromley and his colleagues argued that ethnicity had a stable core (the 'ethnos'), and that this resulted in specific cultural forms persisting through long-term processes of social evolution (see Box 23.3). For Western scholars, reading these ideas in translation during the 1970s and 1980s was discomforting. But in fact somewhat similar ideas were emerging outside academic circles in their own countries, as ethnicity became incorporated into discourses about multiculturalism.

Multiculturalism and the new racism

Multiculturalism refers to both a body of theories about society, and policies designed to change group relations within society. It emerged as a distinct movement in the 1970s, although it obviously drew on much earlier ideas about cultural difference, particularly the perception that there were numerous cultures in the world, each with a degree of internal coherence. From the start, multiculturalism was not a unitary view. There was a shared perception of ethnic pluralism, and all versions of multiculturalism challenged models of the nation-state which assume a homogeneous culture expressed, for example, through language. However, there was a vigorous debate about what kinds of social policies this implied. Some radicals promoted outright separatism, while those of more liberal persuasions maintained that respect of cultural differences could be incorporated into strategies for encouraging a new kind of pluralistic social integration. In the US context, multiculturalism can be seen as an inversion of the 'melting pot' thesis that Glazer and Moynihan had so forcefully critiqued. It was, in effect, an ideology of anti-assimilation.

> "The multiculturalist rejects the view that the immigrant should assimilate to the American mainstream, that all proper Americans share the same ideals and aspirations. On the contrary, the America of the multiculturalists is culturally fragmented. They do not regard this as a problem in itself. The trouble is not that differences exist, but that they are treated with disdain, as deviations from the norm."
>
> (Kuper, 1999, p.233)

The use of ethnicity as a popular term, outside academic analysis, was linked with these developments. In Britain, for example, multicultural policies played a key part in efforts to promote the integration, as opposed to assimilation, of immigrant groups in the 1970s and 1980s. School materials on the 'cultural traditions' of ethnic groups were introduced, and Ethnic Minority Units were set up within local councils to help facilitate mutual understanding and tolerance. In many respects, this proved to be a successful strategy. Britain has become a multicultural society in a way that would have been hard to imagine in the 1960s. However, in

Box 23.3 Ethnos theory

Ethnos theory began to be promoted by Yulian Bromley, the director of the Institute of Ethnography at the Soviet Academy of Science in Moscow, from the late 1960s. Bromley proposed that ethnicity has a stable core, for which he used the Greek word 'ethnos'. This is not an eternal thing, but persists through the various evolutionary stages of history (like other Soviet scholars, Bromley held a Marxist view of history in which societies evolved from primitive communism through slave-ownership, feudalism and capitalism to socialism). He defined the ethnos as 'a historically formed community of people characterized by common, relatively stable cultural features, certain distinctive cultural traits, and the consciousness of their unity as distinguished from other similar communities' (1974, p.66, cited in Banks, 1996, p.19). From this starting point, the problem was to determine how the characteristics of ethnos manifested in overt cultural forms (such as language, costumes, and folklore) were integrated as a system. The theory was taken a stage further by some of Bromley's colleagues, who suggested that ethnos was at least in part a biological (not just an historical) phenomenon.

Within the Soviet Union and its satellite countries, variations of the ethnos thesis had a considerable influence. On the one hand it provided an explanation of why cultural distinctiveness had failed to wither away in the face of rational socialist planning. On the other hand, ethnos theory did not contradict official views about 'ethnogenesis' based on the Leninist theory of the national question – in which the nation is defined as the highest type of ethnic community, and is treated as an archetypal form of social grouping which legitimizes the state. This latter point was important because discussion about the characteristics of the different Soviet populations had become highly regulated under Stalin, and remained sensitive in the 1970s and 1980s.

Until recently, Soviet ethnos theory has generally been overlooked in the West. This is now changing, partly due to the opening up of eastern Europe following the collapse of the Soviet Union, but also because of the upheavals occurring in the region. Soviet ethnos theory was shaped by, and has contributed towards, ethno-nationalist ideologies. As elsewhere, protagonists in contemporary wars themselves offer ethnically essentialist explanations, and these have readily been picked up by Western journalists and political analysts. The phrase 'ethnic cleansing', for example, has been employed by all parties in the Bosnian conflict, and has rapidly progressed from being a shocking new term requiring a definition for a British audience to being an accepted fact. Sometimes such ideas have deliberately been given a conceptual sophistication and credibility by local academics.

(Adapted from Allen & Eade, 1999, pp.18–20)

Britain, as elsewhere, multiculturalism also had adverse consequences. While it played a central role in resisting and reducing discrimination, stripped of that commitment, the 'right to be different' took on very different overtones.

'Ethnic' increasingly became a term which was used for black minorities. In effect, ethnicity became a term which could act as an alternative to the word 'race', and was often viewed as preferable because it was apparently less divisive and more neutral. It also became associated with what were presented as different cultures. A danger here was that racism based upon myths of biological difference was replaced with racism based on cultural difference. From the 1970s,

what has been called the New Right adopted the language of ethnic diversity, and actively promoted the preservation of supposedly separate cultures. Already by the early 1980s, concerns were being expressed that this had allowed racism to be modernized and made respectable (Barker, 1982).

Unlike the European racisms of the colonial period, this new form of racism rarely made claims that one 'race' was biologically superior. On the contrary, it conceded that the concept of 'race' as an isolatable biological unit is flawed. Racial identity was recognized to be the product of contingent historical circumstances. A race was, in effect, the same as 'a culture', or 'an ethnic group'. There was also no attempt to assert that ethnic or cultural diversity should be eradicated. Instead the new racism stressed the need to respect these differences, and sometimes would even use the term 'racist' for those who wanted to deny or erode cultural distinctions. On this basis, it was argued that creating a multicultural or 'multiracial' society was a threat to British or French or Belgian or German national cultures. As one right-wing French intellectual put it:

"In keeping with the core of the right to difference doctrine, we must reject multiracial society and envisage, together with the immigrants themselves, their return to their country of origin."

(Guillaume Faye, *Elements*, no.48, Winter 1983/4, quoted in Hildyard, 1999, p.11)

In response to these developments, some political activists and scholars in Western Europe and North America became disillusioned with the multicultural perspective. They stressed, for example, the ways in which collective identities change and influence each other. In Britain there was a focus on 'new ethnicities' which had been formed out of interaction, while the idea of cultural hybridity became part of more general debates about the effects of globalization. However, these discussions were somewhat remote from the mainstream of popular debate. Ethnicity had escaped from academic discourse, and could not readily be recaptured.

23.2 Ethnicity at the end of the millennium

During the decades following the publication of Glazer and Moynihan's book on New York City, scholarly analysis of ethnic identity took a variety of directions. By the turn of the 1990s, it was sometimes used as an all-encompassing concept, which included within it the notion of nationalism. Nationalism from this point of view was a kind of ethnicity with territorial aspirations, or it was simply a kind of ethnicity that was accepted by a relatively large group. Ethnicity was also sometimes used more specifically as a term which suggested ideas about common

origin, in much the same way as the original idea of the nation. From this point of view there might be some nationalisms (like Serbian nationalism in the 1980s and 1990s) which were overtly ethnic (or ethno-nationalist), and others which were not (like US nationalism). Alternatively, analysis of ethnicity from this point of view could be influenced by Benedict Anderson's discussion of nationalism (see Box 23.2), which itself was influenced by anthropological discussion of ethnicity. Thus some commentators have explained that ethnicity is grounded in social imagination and produces 'imagined communities'.

In addition, ethnicity could be used to refer primarily to the relations between population groups, rather than the specific cultural qualities of the groups themselves, or it could refer to new kinds of collective identities, adopted for mainly material purposes, usually by people caught up in processes of rapid social transition. At the same time, in Western countries ethnicity was often associated only with minorities, and sometimes only with 'racialized' minorities. In other words, ethnicity could be a euphemism for 'race'.

It would be fair to state that academic discussion of collective identity had become increasingly sophisticated. This could cause confusion, with terms often being used in different ways, and analysts talking past each other. But this is often true of expanding areas of study, and there were also many insightful contributions. However, as Moynihan put it in 1993: 'We were heard and yet not heard'. It might be that there was considerable interest in some aspects of ethnicity amongst policy-makers 'at home' in the US or Britain, but particularly in the field of international relations, issues of identity associated with cultural similarity or mythologies of common origin were largely being ignored. Political scientists too remained more concerned about other things, such as class and social structure. Ethnicity and nationalism were still mainly viewed as the preserve of anthropologists, some social historians, and sociologists working on immigrant groups. They were the subject matter of those who studied the past or the passing, whereas the future, as Francis Fukuyama famously proclaimed in 1989, was 'the end of history'.

It seems extraordinary nowadays that Francis Fukuyama could have seriously believed that ideological visions would be absent in the post Cold War world, and that things were going to become much more mundane now that liberal democracy and market economics were unchallenged (Fukuyama, 1989). However, he was not the only one to predict an easing of tensions. Here is the closing passage of *Nations and Nationalism since 1780*, published in 1990 by the British historian Eric Hobsbawm:

> "It is not impossible that nationalism will decline with the decline of the nation state…It would be absurd to claim that this day is already near. However, I hope it can at least be envisaged. After all, the very fact that historians are at last beginning to make some progress in the study and analysis of nations and nationalism suggests that, as so often, the phenomenon is past its peak. The owl of minerva which brings wisdom, said Hegel, flies out at dusk. It is a good sign that it is now circling round nations and nationalism."
>
> (Hobsbawm, 1990, p.192)

The turning point was events in Yugoslavia. War in the heart of Europe did more than anything to undermine post Cold War assumptions (Figure 23.5). In *Pandaemonium: Ethnicity in International Politics* (1993), Moynihan who, as we have already seen, had been one of the initiators of academic discussion of ethnicity back in the 1960s and 1970s, seems to have taken some pleasure in saying 'I told you so'. He had become a US Senator, and includes in the book several statements he had made in the Senate and elsewhere during the 1980s, predicting the break-up of the Soviet Union along ethnic lines. Apparently Henry Kissinger wrote to him in 1992, stating 'I stand corrected. Your crystal ball was better than mine' (Moynihan, 1993, p.xiii).

He cannot be blamed for gloating a little. However, what is perhaps most interesting about his views in the early 1990s is not so much their similarity with the arguments he had presented thirty years previously, but their difference. *Beyond the Melting Pot* (1963) was an instrumentalist interpretation of ethnicity, which focused on specific ethnic subgroups existing within the USA. In *Pandaemonium*, ethnicity is treated more broadly, deliberately conflated with the notion of nationalism, and viewed as being primordial. Moynihan makes his new

Figure 23.5   War in the heart of Europe: refugees from Bosnia & Herzegovina arrive in Croatia, 1995.

For many commentators, deep psychological urges had been brought into play. This begged the question: by what?

Two of the most forceful and influential answers to this question have been provided by Samuel Huntington in *The Clash of Civilizations and the Remaking of World Order* (1997), and Manuel Castells in *The Power of Identity* (1997). In the next subsection we comment on the similarities and differences between their arguments, and especially on the ways in which they describe collective identity.

Theorists of the new politics of identity

In *Pandaemonium*, Moynihan seems to take the view that the 1990s have been marked by the re-emergence of something old. Warren Christopher, John Keegan and others have agreed. In many respects, Huntington and Castells agree too (the former called it 'A brilliant essay…on perhaps the central issue of our time'), but their views have been especially influential because they have added an additional aspect. In very different ways, they stress that it is the interaction between post Cold War international relations and long-standing cultural systems which characterizes the modern or 'post-modern' era. In other words, the apparent violence of ethnic expression is not so much 'a regression from civilized order' and a throw-back to a primitive past, as the symptom of new kind of global politics (Figure 23.7).

The Clash of Civilizations

In *The Clash of Civilizations*, Huntington suggests that victory of the USA in the Cold War is no reason for apathy. The country is under threat, with the very core of its national integrity in danger of being destroyed. As discussed in Chapter 21, he detects the arrival of a new world order where global politics has become 'multipolar and multicivilizational' (1996, p.21) and where identity politics plays a central role. Different civilizations are engaged in cultural struggles where:

> "Peoples and nations are attempting to answer the most basic question humans can face: Who are we? And they are answering that question in the traditional way human beings have answered it, by reference to the things that mean most to

Figure 23.7   Is this a new kind of global politics? Refugee mother and child, forcibly removed from Kosovo in 1999.

them. People define themselves in terms of ancestry, religion, language, history, values, customs and institutions. They identify with cultural groups: tribes, ethnic groups, religious communities, nations and, at the broadest level, civilizations. People use politics not just to advance their interests but also to define their identity."

(Huntington, 1996, p.21)

Thus, for Huntington,

"a civilization is a culture writ large. They both involve the 'values, norms, institutions and modes of thinking in which successive generations in a given society have attached primary importance'."

(ibid. p.41, quoting from A. Bozeman, 1975, 'Civilizations Under Stress', Virginia *Quarterly Review*, 51, pp.1–18)

In the post Cold War world, according to Huntington, there are seven or eight major civilizations. Cultural commonalities within these and differences between them shape the interests, antagonisms, and associations of states. Local conflicts most likely to escalate into broader wars are those between groups and states from different civilizations, and this is potentially very dangerous, because the most important countries in the world come overwhelmingly from different civilizations.

Although Huntington stresses that the world contains several important civilizations, he believes that the central fault-line lies between 'a Western one and a non-Western many' (Huntington, 1996, p.36). He also argues that power is shifting from the long predominant West to non-Western civilizations. However, although the influence of Western civilization may have declined since the early twentieth century, the trend can be reversed and its leading role across the globe reasserted. Above all, this must involve dealing with 'problems of moral decline, cultural suicide, and political disunity in the West' (ibid., p.304).

In the USA such a reversal of fortunes depends on resisting the multiculturalist assault on national identity by 'a small but influential number of intellectuals and publicists' (ibid., p.305). This minority has 'attacked the identification of the United States with Western civilization, denied the existence of a common American culture, and promoted racial, ethnic, and other subnational cultural identities and groupings' (ibid.). In Huntington's view, during the 1990s, the leaders of the US have not only allowed the country to become a tangle of squabbling nationalities, but have assiduously promoted the diversity rather than the unity of the people they govern (ibid., p.306). National revival requires a vigorous rejection of such things.

In Huntington's scheme we are presented with a form of cultural determinism. He is clearly deeply concerned about the ways in which politics has become ethnicized both within the USA and across the world, and he recognizes that these identities have often been asserted for instrumentalist purposes by political élites. But, rather than stressing countervailing processes, such as knowledge flows and other factors associated with globalization, his vision is of a mighty civilizational struggle. Indeed, supposedly discrete sets of cultural traditions are made the building blocks of his own analysis. When it comes to global politics, other civilizations or cultures should be left to their own devices. 'We' should relate to 'them' in ways which accept the fundamental differences between us, and this is what 'they' want to do with 'us'. After all, Huntington emphasizes:

"The West won the world not by the superiority of its ideas or religion (to which few members of other civilizations were converted) but rather by its superiority in applying organized violence. Westerners often forget this fact, non-Westerners never do."

(ibid., p.51)

The desire to be separate is manifested very clearly in the rise of religious movements, including fundamentalism. Modernity has disrupted long-standing systems of authority. People need new sources of identity, new forms of stable community, and new sets of moral precepts to provide them with a meaning and purpose. The religious resurgence throughout the world should therefore be viewed as 'a reaction against secularism, moral relativism, and self-indulgence, and reaffirmation of the values of order, discipline, work, mutual help, and human solidarity' (ibid., p.98). It also must be recognized that, whatever universalistic goals they may have, 'religions give people identity by positing a basic distinction between believers and non-believers, between a superior in-group and a different and inferior out-group' (ibid., p.97). According to Huntington:

> "[T]he revival of non-Western religions is the most powerful manifestation of anti-Westernism in non-Western societies. That revival is not a rejection of modernity, it is a rejection of the West and of the secular, relativistic, degenerate culture associated with the West. It is a rejection of what has been termed 'Westoxification' of non-Western societies. It is a declaration of cultural independence from the West, a proud statement that 'We will be modern but we won't be you'."

(ibid., p.101)

Huntington's thesis leads him to the conclusion that:

> "Western intervention in the affairs of other civilizations is probably the single most dangerous source of instability and potential global conflict in a multi-civilizational world."

(ibid., p.312)

It seems that he wants some form of international apartheid. His views are an example of the New Right position discussed above, which turns positive aspects of multiculturalism on their head, and are not incompatible with a 'new racist' agenda. He does not maintain that cultural, tribal, ethnic, national, religious or civilizational groups are biologically distinct (although he does occasionally imply that this might be a factor). But the fact that the West is not based on natural distinctiveness makes it more fragile, and all the more in need of protection from adverse pressures and influences. Multiculturalism at home should be stamped out, not because it is wrong to think that cul-

tures should be kept separate from one another, but because if they are not, US culture (and therefore Western culture) will cease to be distinctive.

Certainly the popularity of the book cannot be explained outside the context of widespread fears among Western hegemonic groups about the growth of civil rights, equal opportunities, anti-racism, the movements of refugees and the settlement of migrant workers, as well as a growing sense that some parts of the world (particularly in Africa) are so barbaric that they should be abandoned to their fate. Interestingly (and disturbingly), Henry Kissinger, who wrote so humbly to Moynihan at the start of the 1990s, has described Huntington's contribution as 'one of the most important... to have emerged since the end of the Cold War' (Huntington, 1997, back cover). Francis Fukuyama is also an admirer, although with certain reservations (see Box 23.5).

The power of identity

Manuel Castells' starting point is very different. His work can be located within the tradition of radical political economy. He has developed his thesis in three volumes on the 'information age', including *The Power of Identity* (1997), as well as through his collaborative analysis of the relationship between local and global in the context of global cities (Borja & Castells, 1997). For him, a key feature of contemporary society is the ways in which power and wealth are determined not by the industrial production of goods but by access to information. In the information society 'the global moulds the local, and electronic flows shape the economy through relations between units that are far away from each other in terms of space' (Borja & Castells,1997, p.1). Recent technological transformations in the ways in which information, ideas and images are transmitted around the globe by transnational corporations have crucial effects on nation-states and cultural formations.

Identity politics, therefore, has to be explained not in terms of a civilizational struggle between the West and the rest of the world, but as an

Box 23.5 Francis Fukuyama on social virtues

In his more recent work, Francis Fukuyama has moved a long way from the argument of *The End of History and the Last Man* (1992). How could he not have done so given the events of the 1990s? In *Trust: the Social Virtues and the Creation of Prosperity* (1995) he reveals that he has come to share some of the same concerns as Huntington:

"Huntington is clearly correct that cultural differences will loom larger from now on and that all societies will have to pay more attention to culture as they deal not only with internal problems but with the outside world…[I]t is now vitally important to develop a deeper understanding of what makes…cultures distinctive and functional, since the issues surrounding international competition, political and economic, increasingly will be cast in cultural terms."

(Fukuyama, 1995, pp.5–6)

But Fukuyama avoids some of Huntington's extremism. He rejects the assumption that 'cultural differences will necessarily be the source of conflict'. On the contrary, he asserts, 'rivalry arising from the interaction of different cultures can frequently lead to creative change' (ibid., p.6). The amazing success of Japanese capitalism is a case in point. Its origins can be traced to the Japanese response to the arrival of American warships in 1853. The key issue, for Fukuyama, is not so much cultural integrity, but trust. In the new world order, he maintains, economic prosperity is generated not just by hard work, competition and free markets but also by networks of accountability and a shared 'language of good and evil' (ibid., p.270). These phenomena are grounded in a particular population's 'social capital' and, ultimately, in family structures and group loyalties.

Fukuyama warns his fellow Americans about the inadequacies of the situation in the USA, notably the excessive individualism, competition and fragmentation. While capitalism has triumphed over its global communist adversary, these tendencies could lead to disaster. In this situation, again like Huntington, he sees well-intentioned, multiculturalist social policies as highly counterproductive:

"[I]t is clearly necessary to learn to tolerate differences among people. It is quite another thing, however, to argue either that the United States never had a dominant culture of its own or that as a matter of principle it *ought not to have* a dominant culture to which diverse groups can assimilate…Diversity surely can bring real economic benefits, but past a certain point it erects new barriers to communication and cooperation with potentially devastating economic and political consequences."

(ibid., p.270)

At the same time help is at hand because America also enjoys another (less publicized) tradition of hierarchical corporate organization and collective action (ibid., p.270). Americans, Fukuyama explains, have historically been far less individualistic than they think they have. If Americans were really so headstrong and unco-operative, they could never have built so many lasting private institutions. Thus, the divisions opened up by identity politics across the USA must be healed by building on indigenous collectivism and by learning about how social capital works in other societies.

expression of local resistance to the global flows of capital, technology, images and information:

"Along with the technological revolution, the transformation of capitalism, and the demise of statism, we have experienced in the last quarter of the century the widespread surge of powerful expressions of collective identity that challenge global-

ization and cosmopolitanism on behalf of cultural singularity and people's control over their own lives and environment. These expressions are multiple, highly diversified, following the contours of each culture, and of historical sources of formation of each identity. They include proactive movements, aiming at transforming human relationships at their most fundamental level, such as feminism and environmentalism. But they also include a whole array of reactive movements that build trenches of resistance on behalf of God, nation, ethnicity, family, locality, that is, the fundamental categories of millennial existence, now threatened under the combined contradictory assault of techno-economic forces and transformative social movements."

(Castells, 1997, p.2)

Castells places his general discussion of local/global dynamics and multiculturalism within the context of the debates about nationalism and the nation-state which we have reviewed earlier in this chapter. In a rather muddled section, he conflates the work of Gellner and Hobsbawm with Anderson's 'influential notion of imagined communities', and then dismisses this conceptualization as 'either obvious or empirically inadequate' (1997, p.29). He accepts the argument that nations are 'cultural communes constructed in people's minds and collective memory by the sharing of history and political projects' (ibid., p.51). But he emphasizes the distinction between nations and states, and argues that,

"because contemporary nationalism is more reactive than proactive, it tends to be more cultural than political, and thus more orientated towards the defence of an already institutionalized culture than towards the construction or defence of a state."

(ibid., p.31)

Hence,

"nationalism as a source of identity cannot be reduced to a particular historical period and the exclusive workings of the modern nation-state. To reduce nations and nationalisms to the process of the nation-state makes it impossible to explain the simultaneous rise of postmodern nationalism and the decline of the modern state."

(ibid., p.31)

Although he is sometimes vague about the specific meanings he ascribes to concepts, he seems to come close to Smith's position, with its notion of ethnie (see Box 23.2). For Castells, ethnicity is 'a fundamental feature of our societies, especially as a source of discrimination and stigma', but it 'may not induce communes on its own. Rather it is likely to be processed by religion, nation, and locality, whose specificity it tends to reinforce' (ibid., p.65). Thus, what for him distinguishes religious fundamentalism, whether it be Christian of Moslem, is that it acts as 'a most important source of constructing identity in the network society' (ibid., p.12). With respect to nationalism he contends that Japan and America, for example, possess a:

"shared history and a shared project, and their historical narratives build upon an experience socially, ethnically, territorially and genderly diversified, but common to the people of each country on many grounds. Other nations and nationalisms did not reach modern nation-statehood (for example, Scotland, Catalonia, Quebec, Kurdistan, Palestine), and yet they display, and some have displayed for several centuries, a strong cultural/territorial identity that expresses itself as a national character."

(ibid., p.29)

Thus, according to Castells, identity politics in the 1990s expresses the dynamic interplay between global and local processes within 'postmodern' nations and declining state institutions. Yet this is a politics which fails to provide:

"the basis for communal heavens in the network society, because it is based on primary bonds that lose significance, when cut from their historical context, as a basis for reconstruction of meaning in a world of flows and networks, of recombination of images, and reassignment of meaning. Ethnic materials are integrated into cultural communes that are more powerful, and more broadly defined than ethnicity, such as religion or nationalism, as statements of cultural autonomy in a world of symbols. Or else, ethnicity becomes the foundation for defensive trenches, then territorialized in local communities, or even gangs, defending their turf."

(ibid., p.59)

When attempts are made to define meaning in terms of identity alone by asserting the value of an ethnicity (or 'race') as a thing of value in itself, the consequence can be marginalization, which makes it increasingly impossible to sustain in the context of globalization. This explains the:

"yearning for a lost community that is emerging in black America in the 1990s – because perhaps the deepest wound inflicted on African-Americans in the past decade has been the gradual loss of collective identity, leading to individual drifting while still bearing a collective stigma…In the ghetto trenches, and in the corporate boardrooms, historical African-American identity is being fragmented, and individualized, without yet being integrated into a multiracial, open society."

(ibid., p.59)

In contrast to Huntington, who offers us a world of civilizational struggle with multiculturalism as the enemy within, Castells sympathizes with the expression of ethnic, 'racial' and national identities as a defensive local reaction to globalization, but proposes as a more progressive strategy a move towards a more democratic and just society led by revived state institutions. He makes this clear in *Local and Global: Management of Cities in the Information Age*, where he suggests that:

"We need to look beyond the local responses to global flows which result in the fragmentation and exclusivism of identity politics and create a reformed, dynamic nation-state relationship through the reconstruction of a flexible, dynamic state, articulated through all its different levels."

(Borja & Castells, 1997, p.1)

23.3 Conclusion

What is so striking about Huntington and Castells is how they share certain assumptions about the politics of identity, despite the considerable theoretical differences between them. They both have concerns about the decline of state institutions and prevalence of identity politics, and they also think this dramatically expresses the fundamental transformations associated with the new world (dis)order. They are also both critical of the paths which identity politics have taken in the country where they are domiciled – the USA – even if their remedies differ considerably.

Whatever we may think of their very different political views, they both offer a useful lesson in that they highlight the importance of placing events within the context of longer term processes. But at the same time we need to remember that these processes cannot be fully contained within the few big ideas they so urgently proclaim. Indeed, when we look more carefully at what they are saying we can see that they are, in fact, recontextualizing what some analysts had already been telling us. The points that they both make about religious fundamentalism, for example, have been a subject of debate for many years, especially since the Iranian revolution of 1979. Also, as we have seen, many of their arguments about the artificiality of state nationalism, and about the prevalence of subnational nationalities or ethnic identities, have been made before. Walker Connor drew attention to the rise of ethno-nationalism back in the 1970s, and debates about multiculturalism were intense in some quarters during the 1980s. In many respects, the various insights of scholars like Gellner, Anderson, Cohen, Barth, and Barker (or, for that matter, Moynihan in his earlier instrumentalist manifestation), have been more subtle and penetrating.

We also need to be aware of how the similarities between contemporary analysts indicate the remarkable influence of primordialism during the 1990s. It is no longer enough, it seems, for political projects based on various identities to be explained in terms of instrumental strategies, social construction or group relations. They are perceived as drawing on, or as being informed by, unconscious and essential attachments. In a variety of ways, views are being expressed here about communal action that would have been considered provocative to many scholars in the 1970s. It seems that the concern to reverse colonial ideas about the nature of subject peoples, which informed the initial enthusiasm for studying ethnicity, has been abandoned. Ethnic primordialism, far from being a term of abuse, has become an almost unquestioned social fact. There may be positive aspects to this development if it opens up areas for debate which have been closed off for 'politically correct' motives. But its main effect so far seems to have been the opposite, in that it has allowed ethnicity to be seen as something which explains a huge variety of different sorts of social action, rather than a phenomenon which itself requires explanation.

It is not difficult to find reasons for this shift in approach. Three have been particularly significant. First, the end of the Cold War had made redundant many of the conventional simplifications of international events put forward by politicians and journalists. There was a need for a new shorthand to describe events. Huntington explicitly recognizes this, and makes no bones about offering his 'clash of civilizations' as an alternative framework for policymakers. Second, the rise of multicultural theories and policies in the1980s, not so much in academia, but in the arena of public policy in Western countries, had led to a situation in which it had become part of popular discourse to describe social action in terms of discrete cultural value systems. This created a ready audience for big theories of global politics which were based on such a perception. Third, the horrors occurring in Yugoslavia, the Transcaucasus, Somalia, Rwanda and elsewhere were experienced vividly through televised images, which made instrumentalist or relationalist interpretations seem inadequate. As Michael Ignatieff has put it, it is not really that the world is becoming more chaotic and violent, it is our failure to understand and act that makes it seem

so, and television makes it harder to sustain indifference or ignorance (Ignatieff, 1998, p.8).

But this still begs the question: Is identity politics more important now than it was in the past; and will it be a driving force for social action in the twenty-first century? One response would be that this is not really a very helpful way of thinking about things, because identity politics of one form or another has obviously always been crucial for human beings, and always will be. In this respect it is undoubtedly important that kinds of collective identity which have long been overlooked by social analysts should have become a major focus of inquiry. However, if primordial psychology is going to be given as the reason why the behaviour of human groups occurs in particular ways, at the very least we need to know much more about crowd mentality than we do at present. A better way forward, perhaps, is to be less ambitious, and to take a less comprehensive and more conventional approach. After all, the careful reader of this book will already be able to offer interpretations of contemporary identity politics without reference to millenarian visions of pandemonium, characterized by mass identities on the move.

Chapter 9, for example, comments on the weakness of many states. This fact was often overlooked, because ways of seeing were so powerfully affected by the rhetorics of state nationalism, reified through the international system put in place in the mid 1940s. With the demise of the Cold War gaze, it has become easier to see things that some scholars had been pointing out all along. The reach of states has never been as extensive as has sometimes been supposed, and the institutions of statehood have been in on-going crisis in some regions from the moment of their inception. A striking illustration of this can be found in Chapter 8. Figure 8.3 reveals that increasing numbers of governments have been drawn into the use of military force against their own 'national' populations since the 1950s. Chapter 8 also provides several reasons for the awfulness of modern wars and for what appears to be their especially 'ethnic' character.

We have traced here the evolution of analytical models of nationalism and ethnicity from the 1960s, when they were a relatively marginal aspect of academic debates about development, to a point where they threaten to dominate our perceptions in almost any social situation we choose to study. The terminological chaos which Walker Connor bemoaned remains a problem, but at least discussion of the two terms is no longer being kept artificially separate, and ideological assertions about the cultural integrity of nation-states are no longer taken at face value. The scales have fallen from our eyes at last, and the multifaceted dimensions of identity politics have appeared before us in all their variety and complexity.

Responding to this by resorting to new overarching simplifications seems a shame. Of course we need to recognize that globalized changes are happening, such as the proliferation of information technologies. But this is not grounds for assuming that everything is being transformed in the same way all at once, and for replacing one misleading paradigm of bipolar opposition with another based on crude models of primordial attachment. 'Culture-based' collective identities have not suddenly become more important, but have always adapted to and affected historical processes. They are a fundamental aspect of social agency. Why and how particular identities are formed and in what circumstances seems to us to be a much more interesting line of inquiry than recourse to far-reaching but superficial (and in fact ideological) theories. Identity for us is grounded in the specific and requires investigation: it is not something to be evoked as a way of papering over the cracks in our understandings.

Summary

At the turn of the millennium there is a widespread perception that 'culture-based' collective identity is subverting established state structures, and threatening international stability. For many this is linked to the lifting of controls following the end of the Cold War and the re-emergence of primal ethnic loyalties. This chapter has challenged such a view, mainly by tracing the evolution of notions of nationality and ethnicity, and showing how these concepts have shaped ways of seeing.

Section 23.1 starts by commenting on the links between the ideas of 'nation' and 'state', and between 'nationalism' and 'state patriotism'. It is pointed out that very few states have ever been genuine nation-states in the full sense of the term. Discussion then turns to the issue of 'subnational' nationalisms, and to the concept of ethnicity. 'Ethnic' has sometimes been used to refer to a group with a subjective belief in its common origin (hence the term ethno-nationalism). However, the way in which ethnicity emerged as a concept in the modern social sciences initially separated it from discussion of nationalism. It was used either to refer to minorities within a larger group, or to refer to identities in a very general sense (such that all people had ethnicity). Both of the two main applications of the term were influenced by theories which can be classified as instrumentalist, relationalist and primordialist. Until the 1990s, most Western scholars distanced themselves from a primordialist approach, partly because it had underpinned assertions of European superiority in colonial times. However, primordialist ideas about ethnicity became incorporated into discussions about multiculturalism, and to a large extent it was in this form that ethnicity emerged as a popular term in Western Europe and North America in the 1970s and 1980s. This a reason why multiculturalism, which was often promoted for the best of reasons, could end up providing conceptual support for 'new racism'.

Section 23.2 reviews ideas during the 1990s. It describes the shift in perspective following the end of the Cold War. Important aspects of this shift were the linking together of ethnicity and nationalism (or ethno-nationalism), and widespread recourse to crude primordialist explanations. The latter part of the section discusses the influential theories of Huntington and Castells, noting that both strongly emphasize the growing significance of primal identities. It is argued in this section and in the conclusion that such invocation of ethnic primordialism is misleading in several respects. The main thrust of the criticism is that these identities themselves need to be investigated in their specific contexts, rather than used as a social given, and employed as a component of big theories which aim to replace the old comfortable certainties of the Cold War era with new simplifications.

24

INDUSTRIALIZATION AND DEVELOPMENT: PROSPECTS AND DILEMMAS

JOANNA CHATAWAY AND TIM ALLEN

Figure 24.1   Petro-chemical plant on the South Korean coast.

Industrialization has frequently been mentioned in this book, and attempts at promoting it discussed. However, debates about it have not been tackled in any depth. To do so would have required a review of a large number of models and theories, many of which have been based on the kinds of economistic presuppositions critiqued in Chapter 21. To have fully engaged with this literature here would have narrowed the focus of the book (it is taken up in some detail in another volume in this series – see Hewitt *et al.*, 1992). It is also arguable that current understandings of poverty and development have shifted away from the obsession with industrial growth, which characterized both development studies and development policy from the 1950s.

Nevertheless, it is implicit in much of what has been written in the preceding chapters that rethinking industrialization remains a major challenge. Indeed, many analysts would still regard it to be *the* fundamental issue. It therefore seems appropriate to end by posing the following questions.

> **Q** Is industrialization essential for development?

> **Q** Are some forms of industrialization less destructive in terms of social development than others?

In the next section, we present the case for the conventional wisdom that industrialization is essential. We then elaborate and comment on this view. In the second part of the chapter, we explore problems with this thesis, and review some current perspectives, which suggest that there may be alternative paths or forms of industrialization from those that were pioneered by the older industrialized states.

24.1 The necessity to industrialize

Modernization, development and industrialization have sometimes been treated as synonymous concepts. This is not to suggest that the benefits of heavy industry have been universally applauded. There has in fact been a long tradition of trying to improve living standards by other means, such as by improved agricultural production and alternative technology. Recently these efforts have been encouraged by the decline of heavy industry in some countries, such as Britain, and by an increased recognition of the appalling environmental effects of rapid industrialization in, for example, the USSR and India. Nevertheless, the view that development is impossible without industrialization remains a potent one, linking together Marxist and classical economic theory with most neoclassical and development economics. Compelling statements of this argument have been made by various authors including Gavin Kitching and the great German-born American economist, Albert Hirschman. This conventional wisdom contrasts with those who look at the world through rose-tinted spectacles. Economic development and the eradication of poverty tend to be connected inextricably with industrialization. It is a long-term process of structural change, which poses awesome moral and political dilemmas. To confront these dilemmas adequately requires hard and informed thinking and, for the policy-makers themselves, considerable courage and self-discipline.

Hirschman's defence of industrialization

Albert Hirschman's general argument is that many of the general and broad-brush criticisms of industrialization have not been valid. In an article in the influential journal *World Development*, Hirschman takes an historical and a con-temporary view, revisiting concerns about industrialization in the late nineteenth and early twentieth century and looking at some of the recent concerns about industrialization in Latin America and Central and Eastern Europe. He also builds on arguments that he himself started to make forty years ago. A passage from an article written then about early German critics of industrialization lays the foundation for his more recent reflections:

> "German writers took a certain delight in showing that the industrial countries were digging their own grave through the export of machinery and industrial techniques…These numerous prophecies of doom do not teach us so much about the real nature of industrialization, capitalism, and competition as about the state of mind of their intellectual authors, ill at ease in the industrial age, and therefore inordinately fertile in finding proofs for its inevitable dissolution."
>
> (Hirschman, 1952, p.281, quoted in Hirschman, 1992, p.1228)

Hirschman carries this train of thought through to contemporary anxiety about industrialization in the former Soviet Union and Latin America. In both cases, he suggests, this anxiety is indicative of broader sociological and political concerns. So, in the former Soviet Union, the infamous disregard for consumers and consumer goods was not an inherent product of industrialization; rather it resulted from the particular political and economic context in which industrialization took place. In Latin America, the anxiety is in some respects the opposite to that in the former Soviet Union. Industrialization has only produced more consumer goods and has not improved the underlying productive capacity of regional economies. Its roots, however, are also buried in underlying socio-political mindsets. According to Hirschman, 'industrialization [in Latin America] was widely criticized as 'inferior', 'unintegrated', 'incomplete', 'mutilated', 'truncated', 'fragile', and so on.' But, he goes on, difficulties in industrialization, and the different form it took from early industrializers in Europe and North America, "[do] not mean that industrialization in Latin America was totally misguided and deserves that contempt with which it has been met on the part of many Latin American economists and commentators of the most diverse political orientation...I believe that this attitude has historical and cultural roots...[T]he contempt for what local industry there is expresses a hidden nostalgia for the good old days of 'belle epoque' at which time Argentina's role in the world economy...was felt as both brilliant and nature-given. In other cases, the critical attitude toward industrialization can be traced to half-nationalist and half-Marxist images of what a 'true' or 'complete' or 'integrated' industrialization should look like."

(Hirschman, 1992, p.1230)

Concluding, Hirschman says that he hopes:

"Latin American economists and intellectuals will learn something from the bitter experiences of East Europeans with their distorted pattern of industrialization. As a result, their attitude toward the industrialization of their own countries might become less negative than hitherto. Similarly, East Europeans should perhaps become acquainted with the Latin American critiques, for in this manner they might realize that their industrialization was not wholly misguided. A historical perspective and mutual knowledge of the mirror-image character of the two critiques might thus mitigate the widespread and dispiriting feeling on both sides that 'we have done everything wrong'."

(Hirschman, 1992, p.1231)

Hirschman's argument undoubtedly reinforces the idea that industrialization is the way forward and that efforts must be focused on creating solutions to problems within the framework of industrial growth. His plea is for one of tolerance to diversity within the framework and for acceptance that imperfect solutions do not necessarily represent fatal mistakes.

Lying behind his remarks is a powerful theoretical model, one that he assumes his readers will recognize without elaboration even if they are disturbed by it. In contrast, Gavin Kitching in his book *Development and Underdevelopment in Historical Perspective* (1982, 1989) presents an outright polemic against those who seek to ignore the model or do not understand it. He therefore sets out to explain it in detail.

Kitching's exposition of the conventional wisdom

Kitching makes his view clear from the start of his book. He accepts the established orthodoxy that 'if you want to develop you must industrialize'. He then proceeds to defend this contention by demonstrating that historically this is an incontrovertible fact, and by highlighting the inadequacies in alternative approaches, particularly those put forward by promoters of 'people-centred development', who he calls 'populists'.

In this view, populists promote a form of development which tries to respond to immediately perceived needs rather than empirically verified 'truths' about the development process. An important part of the argument is that people who suggest that development can be made more palatable by means of rural-oriented, grassroots strategies are not facing facts, and that there is simply no viable alternative to what he calls 'the old orthodoxy'. Thus Kitching's case for industrialization is also a critique of 'people-centred' approaches to development. His understanding of development itself falls clearly in the category of promoting progress, and he thinks that this will occur by increasing production and wealth. He accepts that, just because things have tended to happen in a certain way, this does not preclude the possibility that a viable alternative may emerge, but observes that if there is a lesson for poor countries to learn from the rich ones, it would seem to be that industrialization is the key to affluence. In countries where per capita incomes have risen, the importance of industry in their economies has usually increased, while the importance of agriculture has diminished (the point is well illustrated by the

Table 24.1   Share of agriculture and industry in the economies of selected developed and underdeveloped countries c.1800–1985 and 1997 and their per capita GNP in 1985 and 1997

Country	Share of agriculture (%)	Share of industry (%)	GNP per capita 1985 ($)	GNP per capita 1997 ($)
UK[a]				
1801	32	23		
1901	6	40	8460	
1995	2	32		20 710
France				
1835	50	25		
1962	9	52	9540	
1997	2	26		26 050
Germany				
1860	32	24		
1959	7	52	10 940	
1997	1	38[b]		28 260
USA[a]				
1869	20	33		
1963	4	43	16 690	
1995	2	26		28 740
Japan				
1878	63	16		
1962	26	49	11 300	
1997	2	38		37 850
Russia[c]				
1928	49	28		
1958	22	58	4550[d]	
1997	7	39		2740
Bangladesh				
1960	61	8		
1985	57	14	150	
1997	30	17		270
Kenya				
1960	38	18		
1985	41	20	290	
1997	29	17		330
Thailand				
1960	40	19		
1985	27	30	800	
1997	11	40		2800

Table 24.1 (continued)

Country	Share of agriculture (%)	Share of industry (%)	GNP per capita 1985 ($)	GNP per capita 1997 ($)
Bolivia				
1960	26	25		
1985	17	30	470	
1997	13	27		950
Côte d'Ivoire				
1960	43	14		
1985	21	26	660	
1997	27	21		690
Turkey				
1960	41	21		
1985	27	35	1080	
1997	17	28		3130

[a]Updated sectoral data for the UK and USA refer to 1995.

[b]'Share of industry' is for year 1993 and refers to the Federal Republic of Germany before the reunification (World Bank, 1995, *World Development Report 1995*, Oxford University Press, Oxford).

[c]The 1928 and 1958 data refer to the former USSR.

[d]1980 figure (from World Bank, 1982, *World Development Report 1982*, Oxford University Press, Oxford, table 1, p.111).

Original source: Kitching, G. (1989) using data from Kuznets, S. (1966) *Modern Economic Growth: rate, structure and spread*, Yale University Press, New Haven, table 3.1, pp.88–92; and World Bank (1987) *World Development Report 1987*, Oxford University Press, Oxford, tables 1,3, pp.202–7. Updated mainly from World Bank (1999) *World Development Report 1998/99*, Oxford University Press, Oxford.

data presented in Table 24.1, which updates data presented by Kitching in his book).

A standard theoretical argument suggesting that there is a limit to the levels of prosperity forthcoming from agricultural production alone is used to explain why industrialization is so closely connected with increased affluence. This requires the construction of an ideal model of a closed economy (that is, not open to foreign trade or investment, etc.), made up of small-scale farmers who do not export to or import from any other economy. Once this is done, certain evolutionary assumptions might be made.

At first the farmers will produce mainly for their own consumption, and will therefore grow a wide variety of food crops. Then they will begin to specialize in growing crops suited to their particular area. As their skills improve, they will

be able to produce ever more crops from the same total land area, possibly even with a decreasing input of labour. They will be able to exchange more and more food with their neighbours, which means that their individual incomes and their total income will grow along with their total output. But the process has a definite limit. Eventually, the requirements for food will no longer grow as fast as the capacity to produce and exchange it. Once this point has been reached, the farmers will want to exchange their surplus food for something else. They will want to obtain clothing, footwear, better housing and other manufactured goods. But this will only be possible if there is some sort of industry making these things.

A logical progression of this kind may also be interpreted as indicating that an agricultural surplus is a precondition for the emergence of producers of non-agricultural commodities.

> "[T]he emergence of such a surplus makes it possible for some people to give up subsistence agriculture entirely and trade non-agricultural products for food, and at the same time it enables an 'effective demand' for these goods to emerge, i.e. it creates a 'surplus' of food which can be exchanged for such goods (and indeed for non-material services such as are provided by priests or government officials)."

(Kitching, 1982, 1989, p.8)

The next step is to assess how far this logical model corresponds to the real world.

Refining the conventional wisdom

Kitching accepts that there are several important ways in which so crudely sketched an exposition of the conventional wisdom fails to correspond with what actually happens in practice, and this is accepted by those writing from the standpoint that industrialization is necessary. Kitching and others have made the model more subtle in order to incorporate apparent weaknesses. Here we highlight some of the queries that can be raised, and summarize responses to each of them in turn.

Agricultural production is not restricted to food

This is obviously true. Vegetable fibres, oil seeds, wool and cotton are agricultural products as well as being industrial raw materials. When non-agricultural production begins, it may produce an increased demand for such products, and this may replace the slowing demand for extra food. But these are not grounds for adopting non-industrial development strategies, because demand for agricultural raw materials implies the presence of industry (or at least of small-scale non-agricultural production).

Agricultural production can itself be industrialized, and this makes it problematic to separate the concepts of 'agriculture' and 'industry'

It is certainly the case that agriculture can be industrialized. It involves the enlargement of the scale of production on estates and plantations, the increased use of machinery, and the employment of wage labour by profit-maximizing enterprises. Nevertheless, it makes sense to maintain the distinction between 'industry' and 'agriculture', for reasons which have in fact been emphasized by agrarian populists themselves.

There are two major differences between agricultural and non-agricultural production.

> "First, the environment of agricultural production tends to be less controllable because of the variability of the weather and (to a lesser extent) of soils and pests. Second, a number of crucial operations in agriculture (particularly harvesting and weeding) tend to be technically difficult to mechanize effectively. As a result it is difficult to obtain the degree of 'capital intensity' of production in agriculture which can be obtained in a lot of industry."

(Kitching, 1982, 1989, p.13)

A consequence of these factors is that small-scale farming can sometimes compete effectively with industrialized agriculture, particularly when people are prepared to work very long hours for very low remuneration. Kitching provides the example of coffee, tea and pyrethrum production by Kenyan 'peasants'.

He therefore accepts that populists can be on firmer ground when arguing about the viability of smallholder agricultural production than they are when assessing the viability of small-scale non-agricultural production or 'cottage industries'. This needs to be recognized, but it does not add up to a general argument against industrialization. After all, the markets which allow peasant production to survive are to a large extent urban centred. Moreover, it is always possible that an innovation may break through the technical barrier, making peasant production uncompetitive. This happened in the late nineteenth century, when the introduction of the combine harvester in North America, along with other innovations in transportation, made a great deal of peasant wheat production in Europe non-viable.

Economies are not closed

The standard theoretical model about the need to industrialize assumes that the hypothetical economy made up of small-scale farmers is closed. But of course in the real world economies are not clearly separated and have trade links between them.

An implication of this is that an agricultural economy may grow by means of the export of food and/or agricultural raw materials to other economies. If the exports are raw materials for industry then there may be continually rising output and incomes in the agricultural economy as a result of continually rising demand in the industrialized or industrializing economies. Well-known examples are the economic development of Denmark, New Zealand and Australia in the late nineteenth century. In these countries economic growth was initially based on the export of meat and dairy products to the rapidly growing industrial economies of Europe. More recently, a similar situation has evolved in some parts of Africa and Asia, where development has mainly been based on the export of food and agricultural raw materials to the industrialized economies of the West. Thus, continuously rising output and income may occur in an agricultural economy provided that there are industrial (or at least non-agricultural) economies somewhere to provide continually expanding markets.

Refining the theoretical argument along these lines takes on board the possibility that development strategies might be oriented towards agriculture in some countries. But this rarely proves to be the case (even when smallholder agriculture remains an economically viable proposition), because there is an 'economo-political' logic which prompts the rulers of agricultural economies to adopt programmes of national industrialization. Global competition between states causes a conceptual linking of an industrial base with national independence. National economic policies therefore aim at decreasing dependence on foreign suppliers of industrial goods by encouraging manufacture within the country (this is one of the principles of import substituting industrialization, ISI).

Industry is something distinct from the small-scale production of non-agricultural commodities

The conventional theoretical argument about industrialization undoubtedly uses the term 'industry' in a misleadingly loose way. In effect, it is being used as a residual category, to refer to all kinds of non-agricultural production. Some scholars have argued that this side-steps an important issue: the difference between 'industry' and 'small-scale non-agricultural production' or 'cottage industries'. The distinction has commonly been ignored, but it was important for nineteenth-century thinkers, and remains useful because it concentrates attention on the ways in which small-scale production becomes large scale and capital intensive (it has recently become important again in debates about the significance of post-Fordist strategies, discussed below).

When Marx and others wrote about small-scale non-agricultural production, what they usually had in mind was a form of manufacturing with the machinery owned by its operators, and the labour being provided by the family. In contrast, the machinery and raw materials for industry were owned by a capitalist, work took place in a factory rather than the homes of producers, and the labourers depended on wages paid by the capitalist for their livelihood. The change from small-scale non-agricultural production to industry therefore involved fundamental shifts in social relations, as well as a change of scale. Industrial forms of non-agricultural commodity production required fixed capital (buildings and machinery) and the employment of much labour. It also meant the concentration of wealth in the hands of industrial capitalists, and the destruction of much of the earlier household production which was unable to compete. There was also a tendency for capital-intensive industries to become spatially concentrated in towns, and for peasants and former artisans to migrate to such towns to seek work as property-less proletarians.

The debate between those who hold with the conventional wisdom on industrialization and the populists is not about the need for small-scale non-agricultural production, but about industry. Nineteenth- century populism was no simplistic defence of agricultural development. It was a critique of the social and spatial concentration of production, income and power associated with industrialization. Against it was juxtaposed an ideal of a society of small-scale agricultural and non-agricultural producers living in villages or, at most, in small towns.

Similarly, modern populists tend to bemoan the effects of industrial growth, while promoting the development of non-agricultural production in conjunction with family farming. The issue is how to respond to the demand for non-agricultural commodities. On the one hand, those who think that industrialization is necessary for development point to 'economies of scale' (see below), and deny that small-scale production can transform income levels. On the other, populists question the benefits of industrial development. They argue for policies aimed at reversing or avoiding the industrialization process, and promoting social and economic equality. It is easy to feel sympathetic to their position. The trouble is that they cannot provide good examples of where their alternative schemes have worked. Success has been possible only for relatively short periods, in very particular locations, and usually with considerable amounts of outside support.

Bigger is not always better

'Economies of scale' is the basic idea behind the development of mass production. The term is used to indicate a situation where the long-run average costs of production fall, because the expansion of production causes total production costs to increase less than proportionally with output.

This has usually been viewed as crucial when an industrial process requires large amounts of fixed capital (plant and machinery).

"Up to a certain size of operation the volume of output from that fixed capital (we might think of an example such as the production of strip steel) grows proportionately with the size of the investment. But beyond a certain point, which varies with the technology being employed, the volume of output grows more than proportionately

to the capital investment required to produce it – hence the cost in terms of fixed capital of each unit of output falls. Since highly 'capital-intensive' industrial technologies tend also to reduce the amount of labour employed per unit of output as the scale of production grows, then, all other things being equal, the enterprise using such techniques stands to reduce all costs per unit of output and thus to gain more profit per unit of output as output rises, and hence more profit overall."

(Kitching, 1982, 1989, p.12)

The likelihood of 'economies of scale' occurring varies from one place to another, and from one product to another. It has already been noted that in some countries industrialized agriculture is less efficient than labour-intensive, peasant farming. Similarly, for some non-agricultural products small production units may be more efficient.

"If, for example, the industrial process involved is a very complex one in which it is technically difficult to design or utilize machinery to replace human labour, and if, in addition, there is for some reason an abundance of labour seeking employment and wages are low, then it may be more profitable for an enterprise to continue to operate in small units and to increase production by multiplying the units rather than by enlarging the scale of production in big plants. This has been the case in the production of electronic and optical equipment in Japan and other parts of Southeast Asia."

(ibid., pp.12–13)

But it cannot be concluded from this that the populist ideal of rural-based, small-scale, non-agricultural production is feasible as a general development model. Across a wide range of industries (and particularly heavy 'producer goods' industries like iron and steel, chemicals and cement manufacture) the world-wide tendency from the nineteenth century onwards has been towards a larger and larger scale of production. This has normally been the cheapest means of producing the commodities required for material affluence. At the same time there has been a tendency towards urbanization, with factories cutting costs by sharing essential public facilities (roads, sewerage, water and energy), and taking advantage of the large markets afforded by dense populations.

Facing the 'facts'

Defence of the conventional wisdom on industrialization does not simply dismiss 'populism' out of hand. It keeps coming back to the issue of what has actually happened where economic affluence has been achieved. In essence the contention is that, while industrialization is a grim business, there is no real alternative. Populist strategies are flawed by wishful thinking.

Arguments that industrialization is necessary may be summarized as follows:

- Empirical evidence indicates that high living standards are linked to industrialization.

- General and broad-brush critiques of industrialization are invalid and have their roots in underlying socio-political mindsets rather than comprehensive analysis.

- A widely accepted theoretical argument suggests that agricultural development will lead to a demand for manufactured products.

- While it is possible that manufactured products might be purchased from abroad by means of the export of agricultural produce (including non-food produce), this is only possible for some countries (with surplus farm land), and even in these cases various political and economic processes will eventually encourage the development of national industries.

- Although agriculture can be industrialized, it is difficult to obtain the degree of 'capital intensity' which can be obtained in a lot of industry. This means that small-scale farming can sometimes compete with industrialized agriculture.

- It is useful to make a distinction between 'industry' and small-scale non-agricultural production. This helps clarify the historical processes involved in industrialization: a shift in ownership of the means of production to capitalists, a concentration of capital-intensive production, the organization of labour in factories, and a socially transforming rise in output.

- Sometimes industries can be run viably in small units, but in many cases there is a tendency towards an ever larger scale of production (due to 'economies of scale'), as well as towards the urban concentration of production;

- Imperfect solutions within the industrialization framework do not necessarily represent fatal mistakes, and efforts should be made to identify corrective policies rather than attack industrialization in its entirety.

Kitching's attack on populism, together with his emphasis on the increasing scale and concentration of industry, has given some readers of his book the impression that he favours a Stalinist, heavy industry model of development. But in a postscript to the second edition, he states categorically that this is not so. He explains that his view is that industrialization strategies should be adapted to the particular context in which they are applied. What is appropriate depends on a host of factors:

"including the demographic and geographical size of the economy involved, its resource endowment (including its 'human capital' endowment) and its role in the world economy at the point at which industrialization is attempted. For small, resource-poor Third World countries a development sequence which begins with the expansion of primary product exports, moves to the manufacture of simple inputs and basic consumption goods for the primary producers (usually, though not always, peasant producers) and from there to the manufacture of labour-intensive consumer and producer goods for export and domestic consumption, is a particularly appropriate strategy. Certainly it is a more appropriate industrialization strategy for small peripheral economies than either 'crash' heavy industrialization under state auspices or luxury 'import substitution' industrialization undertaken under the auspices of multinational corporations. Such a strategy is particularly desirable in that it can accommodate forms of rural 'agro-industry' which can act as a counter-balance to over-rapid urbanization."

(ibid., p.192)

Nonetheless, even the most appropriate of industrialization strategies is going to involve difficult decisions. Kitching concludes:

"[D]evelopment is an awful process. It varies only, and importantly, in its awfulness. And that is why my most indulgent judgements are reserved for those, whether they be Marxist-Leninists, Korean generals, or IMF officials, who, whatever else they may do, recognize this and are prepared to accept its moral implications. My most critical reactions are reserved for those, whether they be western liberal-radicals or African bureaucratic elites, who do not, and therefore avoid or evade such implications and with them their own responsibilities."

(ibid., p.195)

24.2 Problems and new perspectives

We have examined arguments for industrialization at some length because it is a strong case, and because its ramifications are enormous. But there are grounds for questioning parts of it, and for asking if it is in fact going to be much help as an overarching, guiding prognosis for development in the coming years. In this section we raise a further set of problems with the conventional wisdom. It will be apparent that we have rather more sympathy with some forms of 'people-centred development' than Kitching does, and rather less sympathy with ruthless 'Marxist-Leninists, Korean generals, or IMF officials'. We also do not attempt to replace the conventional wisdom with a fully worked-out alternative. Rather we point to limitations in the kinds of arguments that Kitching, Hirschman and others have put forward, and indicate some of the current thinking about new industrialization strategies.

Fundamental problems with the conventional wisdom on industrialization

We begin with a series of fundamental reservations with the defence of the conventional wisdom.

Development is more than material affluence
The eighteenth and nineteenth century political economists (like Smith, Ricardo and Marx), who established the conventional wisdom on industrialization, thought that economic progress was occurring if the volume and value of output or production was continuously rising. This view was later incorporated into the mainstream of development planning. It is the underlying premise behind the use of economic growth data as indicators of whether or not development is occurring. It is also the definition of development adopted by Kitching, i.e. high and continuous growth of output and incomes.

In contrast, there has been a tradition of analysis that has been more concerned with distribution, and that has rejected the idea that the co-existence of great wealth with mass poverty can be regarded as progress in any sense. For Kitching this is an aspect of populism. It is not based upon a serious examination of the historical evidence, and is, at best, dangerously naïve.

However, it could be argued that it is not so much a question of the facts as the starting point. If development is defined narrowly in terms of growth, then certain conclusions follow almost inevitably. If, on the other hand, 'real' development is defined as the eradication of poverty, or as the amelioration of the effects of certain social processes, then it is possible that there could be industrialization without development, and possibly even some development without much industrialization.

The empirical evidence on the link between material affluence and industrialization is not so straightforward
As Table 24.1 above shows, per capita GNP is still used as a development indicator, and can be connected with a shift in the labour force out of agriculture and into industry. But, leaving

aside the ambiguities involved in contrasting 'agriculture' and 'industry' in this way, the use of GNP data can be very misleading.

In this particular context it needs to be borne in mind that GNP may reflect increased per capita income from industrial production more accurately than per capita income from agriculture, because non-agricultural commodities are more likely to be marketed through 'official' channels. Also, in recent years, it has become more obvious that the 'real' GNP figures for former 'second world' countries were far lower than had been estimated.

Such factors suggest that the empirical evidence needs to be examined more closely. It may be that the importance of industrialization appears overwhelming, partly because of the categories used for assessing it, and partly because its economic benefits have sometimes been exaggerated for political purposes. Furthermore, although a few developing countries certainly have increased material affluence through industrialization (e.g. Hong Kong, South Korea), there is considerable evidence that such cases are exceptional, and that their achievements will not be repeated elsewhere (Figure 24.2).

"Join us. It's only a step."

Figure 24.2

Development planning cannot simply be based on 'economies of scale'

If development ultimately means achieving and maintaining 'economies of scale', it could be argued that countries like Britain, the USA and the USSR, where capital-intensive manufacturing industry has been in relative decline, could be seen as 'not developing'.

A danger of taking such an approach is that a certain kind of economic development becomes a pre-ordained historical process, something which has to be harnessed or tapped into. Large-scale industrialization is both necessary and inevitable. The implication is that development policy and political struggle mean no more than facilitating a situation in which history can speed up. This is a very traditional North/South approach to looking at development. The focus is on how the South might 'catch up' with the North.

If we look at development (however it is defined) as a more complex and global set of events, then this conceptual framework appears rather limited. It is certainly Western-centric. Moreover, the grimly deterministic view could lead to a position that there is little point in doing anything directly to help the poor. It also suggests an anti-democratic, and end-justifies-the-means argument with respect to certain oppressive regimes committed to autonomous industrial growth, because they might be viewed as historical catalysts. For many concerned people this has to be resisted. It may be that there are powerful logical arguments lying behind elaborations of the conventional wisdom, but some of the premises are not acceptable.

If development is equated with nations industrializing, that is tantamount to saying it is impossible, given resource constraints

Kitching recognizes that industrialization need not always be attempted within national boundaries, but he argues that an 'economo-political' logic ensures that, in the long run, this is almost invariably what happens. When he outlines what he sees as the appropriate forms of industrialization for particular contexts, his particular contexts are all countries. Ideally each country should have its own thriving industrial sector and, it seems to be suggested, each should aspire towards the kinds of lifestyles associated with the West. But if this were possible, could the world afford it? Many years ago Gandhi observed:

> "God forbid that India should ever take to industrialization after the manner of the West. The economic imperialism of a single tiny island kingdom is today keeping the world in chains. If an entire nation of 300 million took to similar economic exploitation, it would strip the world bare like locusts."
>
> (Gandhi, 1928, p.422)

Of course Gandhi has not been the only one to highlight the environmental consequences of industrialization. Even some of those who would accept the main thrust of the conventional wisdom, like Albert Hirschman, have been very concerned about it. In the article discussed above, Hirschman recognizes that there are 'many warranted ecological concerns', for which there can be 'needed corrective policies' (Hirschman, 1992, p.1231).

New perspectives

In recent years, different ways of analysing development and looking at the evolution of capitalism have emerged. These have helped shift the debate. Here we briefly comment on six of these new perspectives, all of which have already been touched upon in other chapters of this book.

Ecologically sustainable industrialization

As discussed in Chapter 7, during the 1990s it became increasingly clear that something will have to be done about global pollution. The situation has become very serious. It is also incontrovertible that the brunt of the blame lies with the industrialized countries of the North (see Figure 24.3). The nature of industrialization, it seems, must be changed, and made more environmentally friendly everywhere.

One of many frameworks for a 'sustainable industrial economy' has been proposed by David Wallace, a senior policy analyst working for the International Energy Agency in Paris. He argues that some common elements have emerged from interactions between governments, academics and business, although there is no agreement on which are the most important (Wallace, 1996, p.11). They include the following:

Biodiversity Preservation and restoration of representative ecosystems; stable long-term goals for land given over to the built environment, intensive farming, wilderness areas, etc., based on scientifically determined environmental 'footprints' and social consensus on the balance between preservation and exploitation.

Pollutants Zero emissions of bio-accumulating toxins such as heavy metals; ecologically conservative critical load limits for all other pollutants such as acid emissions, ground-level ozone promoters and global warming gases.

Products and services A pervasive 'Design for the Environment' mentality including design for recycling, reuse and upgradability; focus on services for consumers instead of products, e.g. thermal comfort, 'easy-clean' clothes and public transport in place of natural gas, washing machines and cars.

Business processes Integration of environmental accounting systems (such as eco-audits), environmental management systems and environmental issues into financial accounting, corporate planning and board-level corporate strategy; involvement of employees, local communities and customers in decision-making.

Wallace is well aware that the industrial countries are the main producers of pollution. However, like a number of other influential analysts, he proposes that it is developing countries that must lead the way in reforms. He suggests that 'sustainable industrialization in developing countries can be achieved more easily than transformation of the industrial economies of the North' (Wallace, 1996, p.83), and argues that introducing sustainable industrialization in the South will overcome major flaws in the international community's current approach.

He points out that the 'follow-the-leader' model (embodied in recommendations of the 1992 Earth

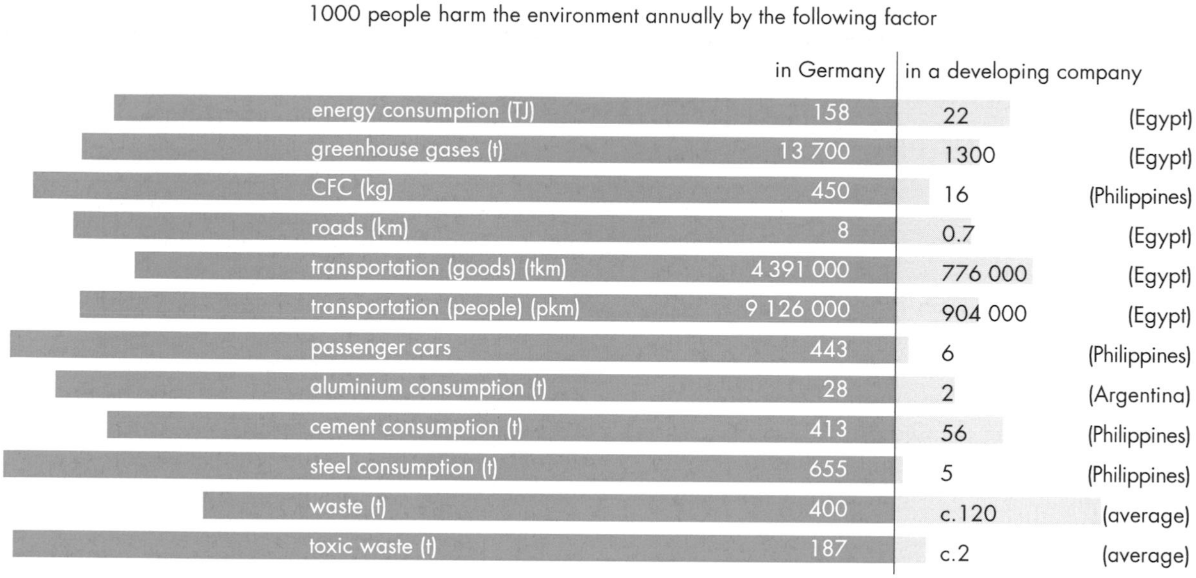

1000 people harm the environment annually by the following factor

	in Germany	in a developing company	
energy consumption (TJ)	158	22	(Egypt)
greenhouse gases (t)	13 700	1300	(Egypt)
CFC (kg)	450	16	(Philippines)
roads (km)	8	0.7	(Egypt)
transportation (goods) (tkm)	4 391 000	776 000	(Egypt)
transportation (people) (pkm)	9 126 000	904 000	(Egypt)
passenger cars	443	6	(Philippines)
aluminium consumption (t)	28	2	(Argentina)
cement consumption (t)	413	56	(Philippines)
steel consumption (t)	655	5	(Philippines)
waste (t)	400	c.120	(average)
toxic waste (t)	187	c.2	(average)

Figure 24.3 A North–South comparison of pollution and resource consumption.

Summit held in Rio) supposes that technological fixes (which in any case can only be a very partial element of any comprehensive plan) will be developed mainly in the industrialized countries and subsequently adopted by the South. He notes that it is envisaged that substantial aid will assist this technology transfer. This he says is not happening and there is increasing danger that industrialization taking place in developing countries continues to be modelled on old unsustainable Western models.

For Wallace, the need for financial resources and for the capacity and knowledge necessary to achieve ecological sustainability in modern societies points to a major role for multinational corporations in promoting sustainable industrialization in the South. Foreign direct investment is outstripping aid globally and makes up a significant share of the economy in some developing countries. Successful Western firms can be carriers of leading-edge managerial, organizational and technological expertise and of expertise in dealing with complex environmental issues. Free of the deep-rooted institutional barriers of the industrialized societies and faced with rapid growth prospects in a policy context which emphasizes sustainability, new environmental concepts and technologies would have

an opportunity to evolve further and become an integral part of the production system. New domestic firms and institutions emerging in rapidly growing economies could take this process further (Wallace, 1996, p.85).

Wallace raises some interesting points, which provide a good illustration of where discussions and international policy are heading. But it needs to be noted that his analysis raises at least as many questions as solutions. For example, why would MNCs engage in the way he envisions? It may be that policy incentives could be devised in countries where large markets attract foreign firms which might encourage better practice, but in poorer countries this is likely to be difficult. Additionally, why would developing countries adopt this agenda, when some of them feel understandably reluctant to bear the brunt of having to make drastic changes, when it is industrialized countries which have created the problem?

Nevertheless, there is little doubt that the problem will get worse. Industrialization continues to be fundamentally linked to development goals, and it is the aim of political élites in many developing countries to promote them as rapidly as possible, by whatever means are available. This may eventually create political pressures in richer countries to fund environmentally friendly industrialization in poorer ones. This has started to happen in some places, notably Western Europe, as indicated by the agreements reached at Kyoto, Japan, in 1997 (see Chapter 7).

Post-Fordism

For some, the distinction which Kitching and others have emphasized between, on the one hand, industrialization which favours 'economies of scale' and mass production (Figure 24.4) and, on the other, solutions which focus on small-scale production, is a false one. Since the late 1980s the differences in modes of industrialization have became of increasing interest to analysts and academics. New technologies and new forms of enterprise organization have opened up a range of alternative approaches, and indicated that smaller units of production might even be preferable on grounds of economic efficiency. Influential thinkers have claimed that global capitalism has entered into a new phase, characterized as 'disorganized' (Lash & Urry, 1987), and based on new principles of flexibility (Chapter 15). Whereas older styles of industrial

production were centred on mass manufacturing, new models rest on the ability to respond quickly and to sustain organizational forms which allow for rapid and on-going innovation. Indeed, some authors maintain that it is the extent to which the new forms of industrial production have been adopted which account for relative success and failure (Box 24.1).

A variety of forms are claimed by authors as constituting 'flexible production'. In Japan, for instance, supplier relations are central to manufacturing in what is sometimes called the Toyota system (Chapter 15). Tightly co-ordinated layers of formally independent subcontractors work with 'core' firms to enable 'just-in-time' production to manufacture and deliver goods when required rather than making large quantities of standard items which are stored until sold. This type of production system uses flexible technology which allows for more rapid changes in styles and models and a multi-skilled workforce in core firms, in many cases privileged with guarantees of long-term employment and often also characterized as flexible. Flexible has a dual meaning here.

Figure 24.4   Car factory, Shanghai, China.

Box 24.1 The 'New Competition'

In 1990, Michael Best, one of the early analysts of new forms of industrialization and the relative decline of Western Europe and United States, made the following points:

"The first cause of the deterioration is the emergence elsewhere of a 'New Competition' led by business enterprises based upon different production and organizational concepts. At the centre of the New Competition is the entrepreneurial firm, an enterprise that is organized from top to bottom to pursue continuous improvement in methods, products and processes. The pursuit of continuous improvement is a production-based strategy that has redefined the meaning of entrepreneurial activity from its traditional individualist approach to a collectivist concept. The entrepreneurial firm seeks a competitive edge by superior product design, which may or may not lead to lower costs, but it demands organizational flexibility which in turn requires organizational commitments to problem solving, a persistence to detail, and an integration of thinking and doing in work activities.

The New Competition is manifest in a variety of inter-firm complexes which range from groups of small Italian firms linked by co-operative associations for joint marketing, technological advance, and financial underwriting, to giant Japanese organizational structures coordinating trading companies, banks, and manufacturing enterprises. While Japan, Germany, and Sweden have led the way in the development of new manufacturing methods and strategies geared to continuous improvement, examples can also be found in South Korea, Taiwan, Hong Kong, Singapore, and specific regions and enterprises within Europe and the United States."

(Best, 1990)

"Flexible labour can refer both to the skills utilized by a small proportion of the workforce and to the extended division of the labour market into core and periphery. As regards the former, the Toyota system developed a core of multi-skilled workers able to undertake a number of tasks and whose shopfloor knowledge is utilized by management to promote continuous improvement in the production process. These core workers are therefore granted a job for life, are continuously trained, and are paid according to seniority."

(Kiely, 1998, p.147)

The cost of employing 'core' workers, however, means that there is an incentive to subcontract as much as possible. Workers in subcontracting positions are flexible in the sense that they often work on short-term contracts and are relatively poorly paid.

This dual meaning of 'flexibility' is at the root of many arguments about the merits and limitations of new flexible production and service delivery systems. By the 1990s and as we go into the next century, aspects of flexibility in the labour market, such as multi-skilling, continuous training and acceptance of contract-based working for many workers, have been widely accepted by policy-makers in some Western countries, particularly the United States and the United Kingdom but are heavily contested in other parts of the world. Critics say that the system relies heavily on cheap labour and believe 'flexibility' is often used as a justification for the further demise of trade unions. Thus, the model is much more closely related to 'Fordist' models and neoclassical economic models than some proponents would contend.

Another strongly contested feature of Japanese, South Korean, and to some extent other Southeast Asian late industrializers, is the role played by large conglomerates of firms. The work of authors such as Alice Amsden (1989) and Robert Wade (1990) has highlighted the role played by large industrial networks of firms called *chaebol* in South Korea and *keiretsu* in Japan. These large networks provide financial and a range of other services for member firms. Together with sophisticated industrial policy that did not slavishly follow market indicators and rules, the financial and industrial strength afforded by these conglomerates lies at the heart of Japanese and South Korean industrialization. Of course, this view is contested by those who blame the severe problems which South-east Asian economies ran into in 1998 on inefficiencies generated by the conglomerates and industrial policies which protected poorly performing firms. But those who maintain the centrality of *chaebol* have responded by arguing that the collapse indicated the wayward and uncontrolled nature of global finance rather than a serious indication of weakness in South-east Asian economies. The jury, it would be fair to say, is still out on this ussue.

Another much studied model of flexible production has emerged in the Emilia Romagna region of Italy, where over the last 25 years small firms have established a competitive position in world markets in shoes, leather goods, furniture, musical instruments and in the machinery used to make these products.

"The Italian experience of flexible specialization is based on the development of a cluster of small firms, spatially concentrated and sectorally specialized, develop-

ing forward and backward linkages such as exchange of goods, information and people, and supported by local government institutions."

(Kiely, 1998, p.148)

The fundamental idea is that clusters of mainly small and medium sized firms can gain economies of scale and economies of scope by increased flexibility and inter-firm co-operation. An example of inter-firm co-operation in the Italian case is the National Confederation of Artisans (Box 24.2). It is also apparent that other important institutions based on extensive co-operation, such as financial consortia which facilitate loans and technical consultancy and advisory service providers, underlie the success of the 'Third Italy' model. Many argue that these productive networks are crucial, but are also specific to this context.

Clearly, the extent to which such 'flexible production' models are really an alternative to the previously predominant model of large-scale manufacture in independent units is yet to be

---

Box 24.2 The Italian Confederation of Artisans

The Confederazione Nazionale dell'Artigianato (CNA) was created at a national conference of artisans in Rome in 1946. The CNA became, and remains, the biggest business association in Italy with 340,000 member firms, a staff of 7,000 and 2,300 offices throughout the country...By statute, every CNA chapter must be managed by elected directors (who must be artisans), an executive committee, and a council. At least 60 percent of the executive committees and the councils must be artisans who are actively engaged in business. The CNA is organized vertically into trade federations representing 27 sectors of the economy...

The province of Modena chapter of the CNA has 14,000 member firms, representing 39,000 persons (artisans and 'dependents'). The 14,000 firms are grouped into 11 sector federations, the largest of which are the federations of metalworking, clothing, construction, transport, woodworking, newspaper, food, and traditional artists, plus a category of non-classified. The CNA has 60 locations within the province for supplying administrative services to artisan firms...

In sum, the CNA is a confederation of trade associations that does more than lobby the government: it provides business services to member firms, particularly those services for which substantial economies of scale exist. While member companies pay an annual fee for membership of the CNA, as well as a fee for specific services, the relation between member firms and the CNA is neither a market nor a bureaucratic relation. Artisan firms do not seek the lowest cost provider of such services on the market nor do they find themselves in a subordinate relation to CNA officials as in a managerial enterprise. The relation is better described as a co-operative relationship in which information flows vertically from the apex to the base of a pyramid and vice-versa.

Membership of the CNA allows member firms to co-operate in the provision of collective services while remaining autonomous in areas of decision-making and finances. But the CNA can operate most effectively in partnership with other extra-firm agencies such as governments, trade unions, and universities.

(Best, 1990, pp.209–11)

seen. For one thing, it is not obvious to what extent these models are transferable. Something else to note is the role of new information technology in these systems. Technology cannot account for the emergence of diverse new networked and partnership-based economic organization, but without new automated production systems which can respond in rapid and sophisticated ways, and without the powerful new ways to share information which are emerging as the new millennium begins, the production systems which have developed in Japan and South Korea would not have been possible. And this is no less true for many of the firms involved in the Italian success story. The capacity to link with domestic and international suppliers using new information systems and to feed information on trends in demand, sometimes on a daily basis, has been key in the revival of industrial capacity in Italy (Best, 1990).

From our earlier discussion you may remember that Kitching calls into question the viability of a development and wealth creation strategy based on cottage industries. Post-Fordism highlights the role played by small-scale producers and the importance of flexibility rather than scale. There is no doubt that the new production philosophy and practice of manufacturing have revived small-scale production in some sectors and regions. However, it is important to note that small scale only forms part of the picture. As noted above, the success of smaller units often depends on high-tech links with large firms and mass producers both on the supplier and distributor sides. Much analysis of Post-Fordism suggests that the interaction between large and small scale is an integral part of the model.

Earlier in the chapter we discussed environmental constraints on industrialization. Some analysts view Post-Fordism and improved environmental management as compatible and even synergistic. Table 24.2 outlines the environmental implications of lean production in one firm.

However, studies suggest that only a very few firms are taking a strategic view of environmental management (Wallace, 1996). And there is

little reason to believe that firms by themselves will improve their environmental performance without changes in policy government and sets of appropriate incentives and disincentives which encourage them to do so.

The discussion of flexibility and different modes of capitalist development does make clear that there are many ways in which the state, the private sector and the multitude of other organizations which make up social and economic systems – often referred to as civil society – interact. Indeed, a broad spectrum of analysts and policy-makers believe that this interaction is at the root of understanding the rate and pattern of successful industrialization.

Trust and social capital
The Nobel prize winning economist Kenneth Arrow once said, 'It can plausibly be argued that much of economic backwardness in the world can be explained by the lack of mutual confidence' (quoted in Harriss, 1999). The model of perfectly competitive markets assumes that perfect information underlies markets. If one adopts this assumption, Arrow's statement does not make much sense.

"But in real world markets, economic transactions are influenced by the fact that (a) agents have 'bounded rationality' (they cannot have complete or 'perfect' information), and (b) (relatedly) that opportunism or 'malfeasance' (cheating) can occur. These features of real-world transacting give rise to costs…costs that are entailed in the activities of searching out information, of negotiating and securing contracts and then of monitoring compliance with them. But in the real world too – as opposed to the ideal world of the model of perfect competition – economic transactions generally involve wider social relationships (they don't just involve momentary contacts between completely anonymous people or agents). So it has come to be recognized…that if these social relationships generate some degree of trust, then transaction costs can be lowered, making for greater efficiency in the use of resources."
(Harriss, 1999)

Table 24.2 Environmental management implications of lean production for a UK cosmetics manufacturer

Strategic management priorities	Fordist paradigm	New paradigm	Implications for environmental management
Work organization			
Stock control and storage	New warehouse building for extra storage	Introduced just-in-time 'system'; reduced turnaround of stock to 1 week	Avoided greenfield site for building; reduced risk of fire. Gave opportunity to consider global view of JIT – road and transport issues
Efficiency gains in production process	Time and motion studies; 'scientific' management; new technology	Informal production 'cells' allowing communication at all levels	Allows for a rounded view of efficiency, including environmental performance, to be formed
		Closed loop water system with heat recovery	Elimination of need for water. Reduction in energy use cutting energy costs by 71%
Improve quality	Quality control system	Total quality management; flexible manufacturing; 48hr delivery service	Use of natural ingredients only in products. Short production runs when required minimize waste
Management organization			
Streamlined and flexible organization	Top-heavy management system	Flatter management hierarchy; manufacturing 'cells'; employee involvement	Improved communications, increased efficiency, less paper use
Product innovation	R&D	Production cells; rewarded suggestion schemes	
Inter-organizational relationship			
Reduce costs/improve image	Internal auditing and cutbacks	Collaborative schemes with other organizations	Energy savings – clean technology

Source: Wallace, D. (1996) *Sustainable Industrialization*, Energy and Environmental Programme, The Royal Institute of International Affairs, London, table 4.1.

Trust has a major part to play in constructing effective partnerships and networks. In turn, the ability of economic and social actors to co-operate and work together is at the root of a society's social capital.

The term *social capital* – 'the ability of people to work together in groups and organizations' (Coleman, 1988; see Chapter 2) – is now widely used at least partially to answer questions like why the north of Italy developed faster than the south (Putnam, 1993), and essentially requires trust between those involved in transactions. It is like physical capital (equipment) and human capital (skills) because it augments productivity. Lack of such trust breeds high transaction costs, leads to attempts by mafias or monopoly groups to control trade, inhibits development and reinforces poverty.

Trust and social capital have become key policy issues and the subject of considerable attention amongst academics. Fukuyama (1995) and Putnam both stress cultural predisposition towards trust. Others have looked at how trust is constructed and how it evolves and wanes in different contexts (Sabel, 1992; Humphrey & Schmitz, 1996; Harriss, 1999). These authors stress the role of policy and in particular the state in fostering trust and social capital. Previous studies suggest that certain institutional arrangements can play a part: conflict-resolution mechanisms which are seen to be legitimate by all parties; collective-choice arrangements which permit those affected by operational rules to participate in modifying them; and monitoring arrangements in which those doing the monitoring are either accountable to the resource appropriators, or are the appropriators. The broader institutional setting within which networks are constructed is also thought to be very important. Legal frameworks, funding mechanisms and, if public sector bodies are involved, the extent to which they can encourage participation, are all important factors (Harriss, 1999). The legitimacy of the state and local layers of government are fundamental in determining the success or failure of development efforts in general and the organization of the economic sphere in particular (Evans, 1996).

The importance of the trust/social capital debate in terms of industrialization theory is that it places the focus of enquiry and policy on the way in which culture, state and civil society interact rather than trying to pinpoint firm economic rules as development formulae. This line of thinking constitutes a more holistic approach to explaining why industrialization succeeds and fails in different environments. What some theorists of social capital and trust seem to suggest is that the most successful forms of industrialization will now be those that attempt to combine progress with respect for people's needs. This thinking can be related to Cowen and Shenton's (1996) definition of development (Chapter 2); it could be thought of as an effort to ameliorate the negative consequences of progress but on an on-going and immediate basis.

Clearly, however, there are many other variables at stake in explaining why some countries attain seemingly successful industrialization and others not. For example, as the world becomes more integrated and 'smaller', the issue of how opening to world financial systems and industrial markets affects developing countries is strongly contested.

Globalization

You will have read about globalization in Chapter 16. In terms of industrialization and the impact of globalization on it, policy-makers and analysts are in stark disagreement. We have already noted disagreements about financial collapse in South-east Asia. Simplifying arguments somewhat, one view is that internal economic and political structures were weak, fostering protection of inefficient industries; another is that the region fell victim to out-of-control global financial capitalism. Whatever the case, in this region as elsewhere there has been a fundamental questioning of the 'economo-political' logic which Kitching argues propels governments to adopt programmes of national industrialization.

Differences are reflected in the position of some of the major development institutions. For example, a newspaper report noted several differences in the 1997 reports from UNCTAD and the World Bank, reproduced in Table 24.3.

The term 'globalization' is sometimes used by bodies such as the World Bank to convey a smooth and universal inclusion of countries into a core economic system. It also implies that every country, apart from those choosing to pursue forms of autarky such as North Korea, has chosen industrialization as the course to pursue. 'To say that we live in an era of globalization is to say that nearly every society is now industrialized or embarked on industrialization' (Gray, 1998, p.55). Globalization implies that economies are networked throughout the world but it does not require that economic life throughout the world be equally integrated. John Gray, a Professor at the London School of Economics and author of a book about globalization, *False Dawn: the delusions of*

Table 24.3 Views from the UN and the World Bank

View from the UN	View from the World Bank
On globalization Increased global competition does not automatically bring faster growth and development	*On globalization* There is a positive link between freeing markets and trade and the eradication of poverty in the long term
On impact of trade on wages for unskilled workers In almost all developing countries that have undertaken rapid trade liberalization, unemployment has increased and wages have fallen for unskilled workers	*On impact of trade on wages for unskilled workers* There is no evidence to justify fears that free trade pushes down wages for unskilled workers in developing countries
On world growth Growth of the world economy this year will again be too slow to make a significant dent on poverty	*On world growth* The prospects for global economy are the most promising for many decades for growth and for poverty reduction in the developing countries
Trade and Development Report 1997, UNCTAD	*Global Economic Prospects 1997*, World Bank

Source: Denny, C. (1998) 'Rich–poor divide could cause popular backlash', *The Guardian*, 16 September.

global capitalism, argues powerfully that globalization does not offer a panacea for development's ills. The crux of his argument is that globalization will not create a universal model of capitalism. Rather, unless the complex and uneven effects of this historical trend are acknowledged and managed, it will exacerbate global political and economic tensions (Box 24.3).

The series of crises in Russia, South-east Asia and Japan and the fragile state of regional economies make it harder to argue that policies should rely on globalization to order national economies and create wealth. While countries obviously cannot ignore globalization, and in fact need to insert themselves in some way in the global economy, it is becoming clearer that institutional differences and local state policies are also important.

Information and knowledge flows

One of the writers who has been mentioned a number of times in this book is Manuel Castells. Castells (1996) writes about a new era of capitalist growth based around networks and partnerships. Information and knowledge are central to this new era. Is it possible that development will come increasingly to depend on knowledge rather than industrialization? Is it possible that knowledge, high technology and service-based economies will increasingly be at the heart of the new economic élite? The World Bank thinks to some extent this is already a reality and is worried that lack of knowledge rather than industry will pose a huge problem for poor countries. The 1998/99 World Bank report says that 'differences in some important measures of knowledge creation are far greater between rich and poor countries than the difference in income' (World Bank, 1999). Certainly, the decline of the manufacturing sector and rise of service and knowledge-based sectors in industrialized countries will pose new questions for development analysts and policy-makers in the future.

People-centred development

We have noted Kitching's admission that 'development is an awful process'. At several points in the book we have heard Cowen and Shenton's

Box 24.3 What globalization is not

'Globalization' can mean many things. On the one hand, it is the worldwide spread of modern technologies of industrial production and communication of all kinds across frontiers – in trade, capital, production and information. This increase in movement across frontiers is itself a consequence of the spread to hitherto pre-modern societies of new technologies. To say that we live in an era of globalization is to say that nearly every society is now industrialized or embarked on industrialization.

Globalization also implies that nearly all economies are networked with other economies throughout the world. There are a few countries, such as North Korea, which seek to cut their economies off from the rest of the world. They have succeeded in maintaining independence from world markets – but at great cost, both economic and human. Globalization is an historical process. It does not require that economic life throughout the world be equally and intensively integrated. As a seminal study of the subject has put it, 'Globalization is not a singular condition, a linear process or a final end-point of social change.'

Nor is globalization an end-state towards which all economies are converging. A universal state of equal integration in worldwide economic activity is precisely what globalization is *not*. On the contrary, the increased interconnection of economic activity throughout the world accentuates uneven development between different countries. It exaggerates the dependency of 'peripheral' developing states such as Mexico on investment from economies nearer the 'centre', such as the United States. Though one consequence of a more globalized economy is to overturn or weaken some hierarchical economic relationships between states – between western countries and China, for example – at the same time it strengthens some existing hierarchical relations and creates new ones.

Nor does the claim that we are undergoing a rapid advance in the further globalization of economic life necessarily mean that *every* aspect of economic activity in any one society is becoming significantly more sensitive to economic activity throughout the world. However

far globalization proceeds, it will always be true that some dimensions of a society's economic life are not affected by world markets, though these may shift over time.

Globalization – the spread of new, distance-abolishing technologies throughout the world – does not make western values universal. It makes a plural world irreversible. Growing interconnection between the world's economies does not signify the growth of a single economic civilization. It means that a *modus vivendi* will have to be found between economic cultures that will always remain different.

The task of transnational organizations should be to fashion a framework of regulation within which diverse market economies can flourish. At present they do the opposite. They seek to force a revolutionary make-over on the world's divergent economic cultures.[...]

History does not support the hope that global *laissez-faire* can easily be reformed. It took the disaster of the Great Depression and the experience of the Second World War to shake the hold of an earlier version of free market orthodoxies on western governments. We cannot expect feasible alternatives to global *laissez-faire* to emerge until there has been an economic crisis more far-reaching than that which we have experienced thus far. In all probability the Asian depression will spread throughout much of the world before the economic philosophy that supports the global free market is finally abandoned.

Without a fundamental shift in the policies of the United States all proposals for reform of global markets will be stillborn. At present the US combines an absolutist insistence on its own national sovereignty with universalist claim to worldwide jurisdiction. Such an approach is supremely ill-suited to the plural world which globalization has created.

The practical upshot of American policy can only be that other powers will act unilaterally when the instability of global markets becomes intolerable. At that point, the jerry-built edifice of global *laissez-faire* will begin to crumble.

(Gray, 1998, pp.55,235)

suggestion that development means 'ameliorating the disordered faults of progress'. To a large extent, as we have seen in this chapter, 'development' or 'progress', or at least material progress, are impossible without industrialization. We have also been looking at new perspectives which might indicate alternative forms of industrialization for the future whose faults might be lessened – 'ameliorated' in advance, so to speak.

But we also noted back in Chapter 1, and in Chapter 9, how much of the effort of development agencies these days goes not into finding ways of promoting alternative forms of industrialization but into ameliorating the problems of poverty, environmental degradation and social disorder much more directly. 'Development'

is often equated with programmes for the relief and welfare of poor communities or displaced populations.

The heirs to Kitching's 'populists', namely those promoting 'alternative development' or 'people-centred development' such as Robert Chambers or David Korten, do not generally concentrate on building utopian alternatives to industrialization at a village level. If pressed they might acknowledge that since the world is industrialized the question of local alternatives is irrelevant. The point is *how* poor communities are to be integrated into the global system (Figure 24.5). This is where Chambers, for example, would suggest a participative approach on the part of professionals working for development agencies, and one which goes beyond attempts

Figure 24.5   What chance is there of the consumer needs of rising populations being met with people-centred development?

to involve people in plans made for them, but is radical in its intention to empower them. Chambers has been largely responsible for promoting what is now a large global network or movement concerned with 'participative rural appraisal' (PRA) or 'participative learning and action' (PLA), including idealistic precepts such as 'handing over the stick' to poor communities to allow them to design and run their own development projects. In this book we have not been concentrating on policy or action. Other books in the series consider participation, empowerment, 'action from below', 'public action', and so on (Bernstein *et al.*, 1992; Wuyts *et al.*, 1992). The point of mentioning this here is that such 'development' work, whether or not it is 'people-centred', will perhaps be increasingly important as industrialization provides the material needs of the world as dictated by market demand, while excluding more people in the old industrialized world and failing to benefit many from less developed countries.

24.3 Conclusion

This chapter has explored some of the issues around industrialization, its relationship to development and the potential for different forms of industrialization to take root in different contexts. However, much has been left out. There is a great deal, for example, to be learned from careful scrutiny of particular cases. Why, for example, was South Korea able to industrialize so quickly, and to sustain such extraordinarily high growth rates for so long? Why did Brazil's industrialization strategies falter in the 1980s? What mix of policies are most successful? Does ISI always lead to inefficiency? Have the Post-Fordist approaches adopted in some parts of the world actually resulted in more environmentally sound forms of industrialization?

Moreover, as we head into the new millennium a host of other development dilemmas and possibilities will become apparent. In the next decade or so it may be that processes of globalization and the kinds of information flows that Castells and others have highlighted will not just raise questions about the conventional wisdom. They may make it increasingly redundant. It is already arguable that those countries that have industrialized most successfully in the 1990s, and in which the well-being of the population as a whole appears to have improved, are not those that have applied the old 'econopolitical' logic of adopting programmes of autonomous 'national' industrialization.

Nevertheless, many of Kitching's points about romantic populism remain pertinent. Self-reliant agrarian utopias, in which everyone works together as a community, are not a viable option. Manufactured commodities, from medicines and buses, to radios and fridges, will undoubtedly play a hugely important part in the eradication of poverty – and they will have to come from somewhere. Industrialization is surely not just another word for progress. Real development involves many other things. But the problem of mass manufacturing will not just go away.

Summary

Industrialization does seem to be essential for development. However, it is certainly not a panacea for all problems. Indeed, in important respects, although it creates wealth, it causes as many problems as it resolves. But as we enter the new century there may be room for more diversity with respect to models of industrialization.

Several new perspectives, including some discussed earlier in the book, have implications for new forms of industrialization: notably, ecologically sustainable industrialization; post-Fordism; globalization; trust and social capital; information and knowledge flows.

'Development', in this context, can mean promoting particular forms of industrialization. However, the work of many development agencies in practice is concerned with assisting the casualties of the modern world, or those excluded from the benefits of industrialization. While the 'populist' vision of a small-scale alternative to industrialization may be an impossible dream, in practice 'people-centred development' concentrates on promoting a participatory approach to development in this restricted sense.

References

African Rights (1994) *Humanitarianism Unbound? Current Dilemmas Facing Multi-Mandate Relief Operations in Political Emergencies*, African Rights, London.

Algar, H. (1972) 'The oppositional role of the Ulama in twentieth-century Iran', in Keddie, N. (ed.) *Scholars, Saints and Sufis*, University of California Press, Berkeley.

Allen, T. (1998a) 'From "informal sectors" to "real economies": changing conceptions of Africa's hidden livelihoods', *Contemporary Politics*, 4(4), pp.357–73.

Allen, T. (1998b) 'Internal wars and humanitarian intervention', in *TU872 Institutional Development: Conflicts, Values and Meanings* (Part 1 Readings), The Open University, Milton Keynes.

Allen, T. & Eade, J. (eds) (1999) *Divided Europeans: understanding ethnicities in conflict*, Kluwer International Law, London.

Allen, T. & Seaton, J. (eds) (1999) *The Media of Conflict: war reporting and representations of ethnic violence*, Zed Books, London.

Allen, T. & Thomas, A. (eds) (1992) *Poverty and Development in the 1990s*, Oxford University Press, Oxford/The Open University, Milton Keynes (first edition of Book 1 of this series).

Alvares, C. (1994) *Science, Development and Violence: the revolt against modernity*, Oxford University Press, Oxford and New Delhi.

Amin, S. (1976) *The Arab Nation*, Zed Books, London (2nd edn 1978).

Amin, S. (1997) *Capitalism in the Age of Globalization*, Zed Books, London.

Amis, P. (1995) 'Making sense of urban poverty', *Environment and Urbanization*, 7(1), pp.145–58.

Amsden, A. (1989) Asia's Next Giant, Oxford University Press, Oxford.

Anderson, B. (1983) Imagined Communities: *reflections on the origin and spread of nationalism*, Verso, London.

Anderson, B. R. (1996) 'Elections and participation in three Southeast Asian countries', in Taylor, R. H.(ed.) *The Politics of Elections in Southeast Asia*, pp.12–33, Cambridge University Press, Cambridge.

Anderson, M. B. (1985) 'Technology transfer: implications for women', in Overholt, C., Anderson, M. B., Cloud, K. & Austin, J. E. (eds) *Gender Roles in Development Projects: a casebook*, pp.60–8, Kumarian Press, West Hartford CT.

Anderson, P. (1998) *The Origins of Postmodernity*, Verso, London.

Annan, K. (1998) 'The quiet revolution', *Global Governance*, vol.4., pp.123–38.

Appleton, H. (1995) 'Introduction', in Appleton, H. (ed.) *Do It Herself: women and technical innovation*, In-termediate Technology Publications, London.

Apthorpe, R. (1996) 'Policy anthropology as expert witness: review article', *Social Anthropology*, 4(2), pp.163–79.

Archibugi, D., Held, D. & Kohler, M. (eds) (1998) *Reimagining Political Community: studies in cosmopolitan democracy,* Polity Press, Cambridge.

Arnold, D. (1986) *Police Power and Colonial Rule: Madras, 1859–1947*, Oxford University Press, Delhi.

Arrighi, G. (1990) 'Marxist century, American century: the making and remaking of the world labour movement', *New Left Review*, 179, pp.29–63.

Asia Labour Monitor (1988) *Min-Ju No-Jo: South Korea's new trade unions*, Asia Monitor Resource Centre, Hong Kong.

Aslund, A. (1991) *Gorbachev's Struggle for Economic Reform*, Pinter Publishers, London.

Atwood, J. (1997) 'Foreword', in Kumar, K. (ed.) *Rebuilding Societies After Civil War*, L.Rienner, Boulder.

Ayres, E. (1996) 'The expanding shadow economy', *World Watch*, 9(4), pp.10–23, July–August.

Azarya, V. (1988) 'Reordering state–society relations: incorporation and disengagement', in Rothchild, D. & Chazan, N. (eds) *The Precarious Balance: state and society in Africa*, pp.3–21, Westview Press, Boulder.

Baden, S. & Goetz, A.-M. (1998) 'Who needs [sex] when you can have [gender]: conflicting discourses on gender at Beijing', in Jackson, C. & Pearson, R. (eds), *Feminist Visions of Development: gender analysis and policy*, Routledge, London.

Bagchi, A. K. (1972) *Private Investment in India, 1900–1939*, Cambridge University Press, Cambridge.

Bagenda, D., Mmiro, F., Mirembe, C., Nakabito, C., Mugenyi, D. & Kukasa, L. (1995) 'HIV-1 prevalence rates in women attending antenatal clinics in Kampala, Uganda', Abstract MoC016, Ninth International Conference on AIDS and STDs in Africa, Kampala, Uganda, December 10–14, Institute of Public Health, Makerere University, Kampala, Uganda.

Bailey, F. G. (1987) 'The peasant view of the bad life', in Shanin, T. (ed.) *Peasants and Peasant Societies*, Blackwell, Oxford.

Bandarage, A. (1998) *Women, Population and Global Crisis: A Political Economic Analysis*, Zed Books, London.

Banfield, E. C. (1958) *The Moral Basis of a Backward Society*, Free Press, Glencoe.

Banks, M. (1996) *Ethnicity: anthropological constructions,* Routledge, London.

Banuri, T. (1990) 'Modernization and its discontents: a cultural perspective on the theories of development', in Marglin, F. & Marglin, S. (eds) *Dominating Knowledge*, Clarendon Press, Oxford.

Barbier, E. (1989) *Economics, Natural Resource Scarcity and Development: conventional and alternative views*, Earthscan, London.

Bardhan, P. (1993) 'Symposium on democracy and development', *Journal of Economic Perspectives*, 7(3), pp.45–9.

Barker, M. (1982) *The New Racism*, Junction Books, London.

Barnard, A. & Spencer, J. (1996) 'Culture', in *Encyclopaedia of Social and Cultural Anthropology*, Routledge, London.

Barratt Brown, M. (1963) *After Imperialism*, Heinemann, London.

Barth, F. (ed.) (1969) *Ethnic Groups and Boundaries*, Allen & Unwin, London.

Basu, A. M. (1999) 'Fertility decline and increasing gender imbalance in India, including a possible south Indian turnaround', *Development and Change*, 30(2), pp.218–35.

Bates, R. H. (1981) *Markets and States in Tropical Africa*, University of California Press, Berkeley.

Bauman, Z. (1999) 'The burning of popular fear', *New Internationalist*, no.310, pp.20–3.

Baumann, G. (1996) *Contesting Culture: discourses of multi-ethnic London*, Cambridge University Press, Cambridge.

Bayly, C. A. (1983) *Rulers, Townsmen and Bazaars*, Cambridge University Press, Cambridge.

Bayly, C. A. (1989) *Imperial Meridian: the British Empire and the World, 1780–1830*, Longman, London.

Beall, J. (1995) 'Social security and social networks among the urban poor in Pakistan', Habitat International, 19(4), pp.427–45.

Beall, J. (ed.) (1997a) *A City for All: valuing difference and working with diversity*, Zed Books, London.

Beall, J. (1997b) 'Assessing and responding to urban poverty: lessons from Pakistan', *IDS Bulletin*, 28(2), pp.58–67.

Beall, J. & Kanji, N. (1999) 'Households, livelihoods and urban poverty', background paper for the ESCOR Commissioned Research on Urban Development: Urban Governance, Partnership and Poverty.

Beecham, D. & Eidenham, A. (1987) 'Beyond the mass strike: class, party and trade union struggle in Brazil', *International Socialism*, Series 2, 36, pp.3–48.

Beneria, L. (1982) *Women and Development: the sexual division of labor in rural societies*, Praeger, New York.

Benjamin, P. (1999) 'Community development and democratization through information technology: building the new South Africa', in Heeks, R. B. (ed.) *Reinventing Government in the Information Age*, Routledge, London.

Benthall, J. (1993) *Disasters, Relief and the Media*, I.B. Tauris, London, New York.

Berman, M. (1997) 'Faust, the first developer', in Rahnema, M. & Bawtree, V. (eds) *The Post-development Reader*, Zed Books, London.

Bernier, F. (trans. Constable, A. & Smith, V., 1916) *Travels in the Mogul Empire 1656-1668*, Oxford University Press, Oxford.

Bernstein, H. (1983) 'Development', in Thomas, A. & Bernstein, H. (eds.) *The 'Third World' and 'Development'*, Block 1 of the Open University course U204 *Third World Studies*, The Open University, Milton Keynes.

Bernstein, H. (1988) 'Production and producers', in Crow, B. & Thorpe, M. (eds), *Survival and Change in the Third World*, Polity Press, Oxford.

Bernstein, H., Crow, C. & Johnson, H. (eds) (1992) *Rural Livelihoods: crises and responses*, Oxford University Press, Oxford. (Book 3 of this series)

Best, M. (1990) *The New Competition: institutions of industrial restructuring*, Polity Cambridge.

Bhalla, C. S.(1997) 'Freedom and economic growth: a virtuous cycle?', in Hadenius, A. (ed.), *Democracy's Victory and Crisis*, pp.195–241, Cambridge University Press, Cambridge.

Birdsall, N. (1998) 'Life is unfair: inequality in the world', *Foreign Policy*, 111, pp.76-93.

Blackburn, R. (1988) *The Overthrow of Colonial Slavery, 1776–1848*, Verso, London.

Booth, D. (ed.) (1994) *Rethinking Social Development: theory, research and practice*, Longman Scientific and Technical, Harlow.

Borja, J. & Castells, M. (with M. Belil & C. Benner) (1997) *Local and Global Management of Cities in the Information Age*, Earthscan, London.

Boserup, E. (1970) *Women's Role in Economic Development*, Allen & Unwin, London.

Boutros-Ghali, B. (1992) *An Agenda for Peace*, United Nations, New York.

Bowles, P. & Dong, X-Y. (1994) 'Current successes and future challenges in China's economic reforms', *New Left Review*, 208, pp.49–76.

Boyer, R. & Drache, D. (eds) (1996) *The Future of Nations and the Limits of Markets*, Routledge, London.

Boyer, R. & Durand, J-P. (1997) *After Fordism*, Macmillan, Houndmills and London.

Boyer, R. (1990) *The Regulation School: a critical introduction*, Columbia University Press, New York.

Bradley, C., Stephens, C., Harpham, T. & Cairncross, S. (1991) *A Review of Environmental Health Impacts in Developing Countries*, The World Bank, Washington DC.

Bradshaw, Y. W. & Wallace, M. (1996) *Global Inequalities*, Pine Forge Press – Sage, London.

Brandt, W. (1980) *North-South: A Programme for Survival*, Report of the Independent Commission on International Development (The Brandt Report), Pan Books, London.

Bratton, M. & van de Walle, N. (1997) *Democratic Experiments in Africa: regime transitions in comparative perspective*, Cambridge University Press, Cambridge.

Braverman, H. (1974) *Labor and Monopoly Capital*, Monthly Review Press, New York.

Brett, E. (1996) 'Rebuilding war-damaged communities in Uganda', in Allen, T. (ed.) *In Search of Cool Ground: war, flight and homecoming in Northeast Africa*, pp.203–19, James Currey, London.

Bromley, J. (1974) 'The term ethnos and its definition', in Bromley, Y. (ed.) *Soviet Ethnology and Anthropology Today*, Moulton, The Hague.

Bromley, R. J. & Gerry, C. (1979) *Casual Work and Poverty in Third World Cities*, John Wiley, Chichester.

Bromley, S. (1997) 'Middle East exceptionalism – myth or reality?', in Potter, D., Goldblatt, D., Kiloh, M. & Lewis, P. (eds), *Democratization*, Polity Press, Cambridge.

Brown, L. (1998) *The State of the World 1998*, World Resources Institute, Washington DC.

Brown, L. R. *et al.* (1998) *Beyond Malthus: Sixteen Dimensions of the Population Problem*, The Worldwatch Institute, 89, September, Worldwatch Paper 143.

Bruner, R. W. (1993) 'Economy: unreported business in Hungary spreads budgets red ink', *Christian Science Monitor*, 85(244), p.10.

Buchanan, A. (1982) *Food, Poverty and Power*, Spokesman, Nottingham.

Bunders, J., Haverkort, B. & Hiemstra, W. (1996) *Biotechnology: building on farmers' knowledge*, Macmillan Education Ltd., London, and Basingstoke.

Bundy, C. (1979) *The Rise and Fall of the South African Peasantry*, Heinemann, London.

Burbach, R. *et al.* (1997) *Globalization and its Discontents*, Pluto Press, London.

Burnell, P. (1998) 'Arrivals and departures: a preliminary classification of democratic failures and their explanation', *Journal of Commonwealth and Comparative Politics*, 16(3) (November), pp.1–29.

Burridge, K. (1969) *New Heaven, New Earth*, Blackwell, Oxford.

Caldwell, J. C. (1976) 'Towards a restatement of demographic transition theory', *Population and Development Review*, 3(4), pp.321–66.

Cammack, P. (1997) 'Democracy and dictatorship in Latin America, 1930–1980', in Potter, D., Goldblatt, D., Kiloh, M. & Lewis, P. (eds), *Democratization*, Polity Press, Cambridge.

Cardoso, F. & Faletto, E. (1979) *Dependency and Development in Latin America*, University of California Press.

Carnegie Commission (1997) *Preventing Deadly Conflict*, Carnegie Commission, Washington DC.

Carr, M., Chen, M. & Jhabvala, R. (eds) (1996) *Speaking Out: women's economic empowerment in South Asia*, IT Publications, London.

Carson, R. (1962) *Silent Spring*, Houghton Mifflin, Boston, Mass., and Penguin, Harmondsworth.

Cassen, R. & Bates, L. M. (1994) *Population policy: a new consensus*, Overseas Development Council, Washington DC.

Castells, M. (1983) *The City and Grassroots: a cross-cultural theory of urban social movements*, Arnold, London.

Castells, M. (1996) *The Rise of the Network Society* (Volume 1 of *The Information Age: economy society and culture*), Blackwell, Oxford.

Castells, M. (1997) *The Power of Identity* (Volume 2 of *The Information Age: economy society and culture*), Blackwell, Oxford.

Castells, M. (1998) *End of the Millennium*, Blackwell, Oxford.

Catagny, N., Elson, D. & Grown, C. (1995) 'Introduction: Special Issue on gender, adjustment and macroeconomics', *World Development*, 23(11), pp.1827–36.

Cesarani, D. (1996) 'The changing character of citizenship and nationality in Britain', in Cesarani, D. & Fulbrook, M. (eds), *Citizenship, Nationality and Migration in Europe*, Routledge, London.

Chambers, R. (1988) 'Sustainable rural livelihoods', in *The Greening of Aid: sustainable livelihoods in practice*, Earthscan, London.

Chambers, R. (1989) *The State and Rural Development: ideologies and an agenda for the 1990s*, IDS Discussion Paper 169, Institute of Development Studies, Brighton.

Chambers, R. (1997) *Whose Reality Counts? Putting the First Last*, Intermediate Technology Publications, London.

Chandavarkar, R. (1998) *Imperial Power and Popular Politics: class, resistance and the state in India, 1850–1950*, Cambridge University Press, Cambridge.

Chandra, B. *et al.* (1989) *India's Struggle for Independence*, Penguin, Harmondsworth.

Chanok, M. (1985) *Law, Custom and Social Order: the colonial experience in Malawi and Zambia*, Cambridge University Press, Cambridge.

Chant, S. (1991) *Women and Survival in Mexican Cities: perspectives on gender, labour markets and low-income households*, Manchester University Press, Manchester.

Chant, S. (1996) 'Women's roles in recession and economic restructuring in Mexico and the Philippines', *Geoforum*, 27(3), pp.297–337.

Chant, S. (1997) 'Single-parent families: choice or constraint? The formation of female-headed households in Mexican shanty towns', in Visvanathan, N. *et al.*, *The Women, Gender and Development Reader*, Zed Books, London.

Charlton, R. (1991) 'Bureaucrats and politicians in Botswana's policy-making process: a reinterpretation', *Journal of Commonwealth and Comparative Politics*, 29(3), pp.265–82.

Chen, R. S. (general ed.) (1990) *The Hunger Report*, The Alan Shawn Feinstein World Hunger Program, Brown University, Providence, Rhode Island.

Cheru, F. (1997) 'The silent revolution and the weapons of the weak: transformation and innovation from below', in Gill, S. & Mittelman, J. (eds) *Innovation and Transformation in International Studies*, Cambridge University Press, Cambridge.

Chu, Ke-young & Gupta, S. (eds) (1998) *Social Safety Nets: issues and recent experiences*, International Monetary Fund, Washington DC.

Clegg, S. & Redding, S. (eds) (1990) *Capitalism in Contrasting Cultures*, Walter de Gruyter, Berlin.

Clemens, J. D., Stanton, B. F., Chakraborty, J., Chowdhury, S., Rao, M. R., Ali, M., Zimicki, S. & Wojtyniak, B. (1988) 'Measles vaccination and childhood mortality in rural Bangladesh', *American Journal of Epidemiology*, pp.1330–9.

Cliffe, L. & Cunningham, G. L. (1973) 'Ideology, organization and the settlement experience in Tanzania', in Cliffe, L. & Saul, J. S. (eds) *Socialism in Tanzania*, vol.2, East African Publishing House, Nairobi.

Cohen, A. (1969) *Custom and Politics in Urban Africa: a study of Hausa migrants in Yoruba towns*, Routledge and Keegan Paul, London.

Cohen, A. (1974) *Two Dimensional Man*, Tavistock, London.

Coleman, J. (1988) 'Social capital in the creation of human capital', *American Journal of Sociology*, vol.94 (supplement), pp.5095–120.

Commonwealth Secretariat (1989) *Engendering adjustment for the 1990s*, Report of a Commonwealth Expert Group on Women and Structural Adjustment, London.

Connolly, B. & Anderson, R. (1988) *First Contact: New Guinea's Highlanders encounter the outside world*, Penguin Books, Harmondsworth.

Connor, W. (1994) *Ethnonationalism: the quest for understanding*, Princeton University Press, Princeton (first published 1978).

Conway, G. (1998) *The Doubly Green Revolution: food for all in the 21st century*, Penguin, Harmondsworth.

Corner House (1997) *No Patents on Life!*, Corner House, PO Box 3137, Sturminster Newton, Dorset DT10 1YJ; e-mail: cornerhouse@gn.apc.org; Internet url: http://www.icaap.org/cornerhouse

Cornia, G. A., Jolly, R. & Stewart, F. (1987) *Adjustment with a Human Face: protecting the vulnerable and promoting growth. A study by UNICEF*, Clarendon Press, Oxford.

Cornwall, A. (1997) 'Men, masculinity and 'gender in development", *Gender and Development*, 5(2), pp.8–13.

Corrêa, S. & Reichmann, R. (1994) *Population and Reproductive Rights: feminist perspectives from the South*, Zed Books, London.

Cowen, M. P. & Shenton, R. W. (1991a) 'The origin and course of Fabian Colonialism in Africa', *Journal of Historical Sociology*, 4(2).

Cowen, M. P. & Shenton, R. W. (1991b) 'Bankers, peasants and land in British West Africa', *Journal of Peasant Studies*, 19(1).

Cowen, M. P. & Shenton, R. W. (1996) *Doctrines of Development*, Routledge, London.

Crandon, L. (1983) 'Grass roots, herbs, promoters and preventions: a re-evaluation of contemporary international health care planning: the Bolivian case', *Social Science and Medicine*, 17, pp.1281–9.

Crang, M. (1998) *Cultural Geography*, Routledge, London.

Cranna, M. (ed.) (1994) *The True Cost of Conflict*, Earthscan, London.

Cronon, W. (1991) *Nature's Metropolis: Chicago and the Great West*, W.W. Norton, New York.

Crouch, H. (1996) *Government and Society in Malaysia*, Cornell University Press, Ithaca.

Crowder, M. (1968) *West Africa under Colonial Rule*, Hutchinson, London.

Crowder, M. (1987) 'Whose dream was it anyway? Twenty-five years of African independence', *African Affairs*, 86(342) (January), pp.7–24.

Crush, J. (1995a) 'Introduction: imagining development', in Crush, J. (ed.) *Power of Development*, Routledge, London and New York.

Crush, J. (ed.) (1995b) *Power of Development*, Routledge, London and New York.

Curtin, P. D. (1969) *The Atlantic Slave Trade*, University of Wisconsin Press, Wisconsin.

Curtis, M. (1997) 'Development cooperation in a changing world', in German, T. & Randel, J. (Eurostep/ICVA) (eds) *The Reality of Aid 1997/1998: an independent review of development cooperation*, Earthscan, London.

Dahl, R. (1989) *Democracy and Its Critics*, Yale University Press, New Haven.

Dasgupta, P. (1993) *An Enquiry into Well-Being and Destitution*, Clarendon Press, Oxford.

Davey, B. (1975) *The Economic Development of India*, Spokesman University Paperback 20, Nottingham.

Davidson, B. (1978) *Africa in Modern History*, Penguin, Harmondsworth.

Davis, S. H. (1988) 'Introduction: sowing the seeds of violence', in Carmack, R. (ed.) *Harvest of Violence: the Maya Indians and the Guatemalan crisis*, pp.3–36, University of Oklahoma Press, Norman.

Day, R. (1977) 'Trotsky and Preobrazhensky: the troubled unity of the Left Opposition', *Studies in Comparative Communism*, 10, pp.7–91.

De Lancey, M., Elliot, S., Green, D., Menkhaus, K., Moqtar, M. & Schraeder, P. (1988) *World Bibliographical Series: Somalia*, Clio Press, Oxford.

De Waal, A. (1990) 'A re-assessment of entitlement theory in the light of recent famines in Africa', *Development and Change*, 21, pp.469–90.

De Waal, A. (1994) 'Dangerous precedents? Famine relief in Somalia 1991–93', in Macrae, J. & Zwi, A. (eds) *War and Hunger*, Zed Books, London.

De Waal, A. (1997) *Famine Crimes: politics and the disaster relief industry in Africa*, James Currey, Oxford, and Indiana University Press, Bloomington.

de Haan, A. (1998) 'Social exclusion: an alternative concept for the study of deprivation?' *IDS Bulletin*, 29(1), p.10.

de Haan, A. & Maxwell, S. (1998) 'Poverty and social exclusion in North and South', *IDS Bulletin*, 29(1), pp.1–9.

de Schweinitz, K. (1959) 'Industrialization, labour controls and democracy', *Economic Development and Cultural Change*, vol.7, pp.385–404.

de Soto, H. (1989) *The Other Path: the invisible revolution in the Third World*, I.B. Taurus, London.

Delavignette, R. (1950) *Freedom and Authority in French West Africa*, Oxford University Press, London.

Denny, C. (1998) 'Rich–poor divide could cause popular backlash', *The Guardian*, 16 September.

Dessalegn Rahmato (1987) *Famine and Survival Strategies: a case study from Northeast Ethiopia*, Addis Ababa University, Institute of Development Studies, Addis Ababa. Food and Famine Monograph Series No 1.

Dhaouadi, M. (1988) 'An operational analysis of the phenomenon of the other underdevelopment in the Arab world and in the third world', *International Sociology*, 3(3) (September), pp.219–34.

Di Palma, G. (1990) *To Craft Democracies: an essay on democratic transitions*, University of California Press, Berkeley.

Diamond, L. (1992) 'Economic development and democracy reconsidered', *American Behavioral Scientist*, 35(4/5), pp.450–99.

Diamond, L., Linz, J. & Lipset, S. (eds) (1988) *Democracy in Developing Countries: Africa*, Adamantine Press, London.

Diamond, L., Linz, J. & Lipset, S. (eds) (1989) *Democracy in Developing Countries: Asia*, L.Rienner, Boulder/Adamantine Press, London.

Dickson, A. (1997) *Development and International Relations*, Polity Press, Cambridge.

Dickson, D. (1974) *Alternative Technology and the Politics of Technical Change*, Fontana/Collins, Glasgow.

Dolan, C. (1999) 'Conflict and compliance: Christianity and the occult in horticultural exporting', *Gender and Development*, 7(1), pp.23–30, Oxfam, Oxford.

Dore, R. (1987) *Taking Japan Seriously*, Stanford University Press, Stanford.

Douglass, M. (1992) 'The political economy of urban poverty and environmental management in Asia: access, empowerment and community based alternatives', *Environment and Urbanization*, 4 (2), 9–32.

Drèze, J. & Sen, A. (1989) *Hunger and Public Action*, Clarendon Press, Oxford.

Drèze, J. & Sen, A. (eds) (1991) *The Political Economy of Hunger: Vols I to III*, Clarendon Press, Oxford.

Dube, S. (1998) *In the Land of Poverty: memoires of an Indian family, 1947–1997*, Zed Books, London.

During, S. (ed.) (1993) *The Cultural Studies Reader*, Routledge, London.

Dwivedi, S. & Mehrotra, R. (1995) *Bombay: the cities within*, India Book House PVT Limited, Bombay.

Dyson, T. (1996) *Population and Food: Global Trends and Future Prospects*, Routledge, London.

EC (1998) Directive of the European Parliament and of the Council on Protection of Biotechnological Inventions, *Official Journal of the European Communities*, 30 July, L 213: 13.

Eckstein, A. (1977) *China's Economic Revolution*, Cambridge University Press, Cambridge.

Edwards, M. & Hulme, D. (eds) (1992) *Making a Difference: NGOs and development in a changing world*, Earthscan, London.

Edwards, M. & Hulme, D. (eds) (1995) *Non-Governmental Organizations: performance and accountability*, Earthscan, London.

Eisenstadt, S. (1966) *Modernization: Protest and Change*, Prentice-Hall, Englewood Cliffs, NJ.

Elazar, D. (1998) *Constitutionalizing Globalization*, Rowman and Littlefield, New York.

Ellman, M. (1975) 'Did the agricultural surplus provide the resources for the increase in investment in the USSR during the first Five Year Plan?', *Economic Journal*, 85, pp.84–63.

Elson, D. (1995) *Male Bias in the Development Process*, 2nd edn, Manchester University Press, Manchester.

Eriksen, T. (1993) *Ethnicity and Nationalism: anthropological perspectives*, Pluto Press, London.

Erlich, A. (1960) *The Soviet Industrialization Debate 1924–8*, Harvard University Press, Cambridge, Mass.

Erlich, P. (1968) *The Population Bomb*, Ballantine Books, New York.

Escobar, A. (1992) 'Planning', in Sachs, W. (ed.) *The Development Dictionary: a guide to knowledge as power*, pp.132–45, Zed Books, London.

Escobar, A. (1995) *Encountering Development*, Princeton University Press, Princeton.

Esteva, G. (1992) 'Development', in Sachs, W. (ed.) *The Development Dictionary: a guide to knowledge as power*, pp.6–25, Zed Books, London.

European Foundation (1995) *Public Welfare Services and Social Exclusion: the development of consumer oriented initiatives in the European Union*, European Foundation for the Improvement of Living and Working Conditions, Dublin.

Evans, P. (1995) *Embedded Autonomy: states and industrial transformation*, Princeton University Press, Princeton NJ.

Evans, P. (1996) 'Introduction: development strategies across the public–private divide', *World Development*, 24(6), pp.1033–7.

Fallers, L. (ed.) (1964) *The King's Men*, Oxford University Press, Oxford.

Fanon, F. (1961, 1963, 1967, 1969) *The Wretched of the Earth*, trans. C. Farrington, Penguin, Harmondsworth.

FAO (1996) *The Sixth World Food Survey*, UN Food and Agriculture Organization, Rome.

Fardon, R. (1999) 'Ethnic pervasion', in Allen, T. & Seaton, A. (eds) *The Media of Conflict: war reporting and representations of ethnic violence*, Zed Books, London.

Farooq, G. M. & DeGraaf, D. S. (1990) *Fertility and Development: an introduction to theory, empirical research and policy issues*, International Labour Office, Geneva. Training in Population, Human Resources and Development Planning 7.

Fawcett, L. & Hurrell, A. (eds) (1995) *Regionalism in World Politics: regional organization and international order*, Oxford University Press, Oxford.

FEBC (1997) Views on 'The Directive on the Legal Protection of Biotechnological Inventions', Forum for European Bioindustry Coordination, hosted by EuropaBio; Internet url: http://www.europa-bio.be/

Ferguson, J. (1990) *The Anti-Politics Machine: 'development', depoliticization and bureaucratic state power in Lesotho*, Cambridge University Press, Cambridge.

Ferguson, J. (1996) 'Development', in *Encyclopaedia of Social and Cultural Anthropology*, Routledge, London.

Forbes, N. & Wield, D. V. (1999) *Innovation in NICs: managing R&D in technology-followers*, DPP Working Paper, Development Policy and Practice Discipline, Open University, Milton Keynes.

Foster, G. (1965) 'Peasant society and the image of limited good', *American Anthropologist*, 67, pp.293–315.

Frank, A. G. (1998) *Re-Orient: global economy in the Asian age*, University of California Press, New York.

Franke, R. & Chasin, B. (1981) 'Peasants, peanuts, profits and pastoralists', *Ecologist*, 11, pp.156–68.

Frankel, S. & Lehmann, D. (1984) 'Oral rehydration therapy: combining anthropological and epidemiological approaches in the evaluation of a Papua New Guinea programme', *Journal of Tropical Medicine and Hygiene*, 87, pp.137–42.

Friedmann, J. & Douglass, M. (1998) 'Introduction', in Douglass, M. & Friedmann, J. (eds) *Cities for Citizens*, John Wiley, Chichester.

Fukuyama, F. (1989) 'The end of history?', *The Public Interest*, Summer.

Fukuyama, F. (1992) *The End of History and the Last Man*, Penguin, Harmondsworth.

Fukuyama, F. (1995, 1996) *Trust: the social virtues and the creation of prosperity*, Penguin, Harmondsworth; Zed Books, London.

Fuller, C. (1989) 'Misconceiving the grain heap: a critique of the concept of the Indian jajmani system', in Parry, J. & Bloch, M. (eds), *Money and the Morality of Exchange*, Cambridge University Press, Cambridge.

Galbraith, J. K. (1990) 'The price of world peace', paper prepared for 1990 Oslo conference sponsored by the Norwegian Nobel Peace Prize Committee and the Elie Wiesel Foundation for Humanity on the continuing issues of hate and conflict as the Cold War ends, reprinted in *The Guardian*, 8 September 1990.

Galenson, W. (1959) 'Introduction', in Galenson, W. (ed.), *Labor and Economic Development*, John Wiley, New York.

Gamble, A. & Payne, A. (1991) 'Conclusion: the new regionalism', in Gamble, A. & Payne, A. (eds) *Regionalism and World Order*, Macmillan, London.

Gandhi, M. K. (1920) 'The doctrine of the sword', *Young India*, 11 August.

Gandhi, M. K. (1928) *Young India*, Viking Press/Ganesan, London.

Gann, L. H. & Duignan, P. (1967), *Burden of Empire: an appraisal of Western Colonialism in Africa South of the Sahara*, Praeger, New York.

Gantzel, K. J. (1997) 'War in the post-World War II world: some empirical trends and a theoretical approach', in Turton, D. (ed.) *War and Ethnicity: global connections and local violence*, University of Rochester Press, New York.

Garrow, J. (1994) 'Diseases of diet in affluent societies', in Harriss-White, B. & Hoffenberg, R. (eds)

Food: multidisciplinary perspectives, Blackwell, Oxford.

Gastil, R. (1987) *Freedom in the World*, Freedom House Inc., New York.

GATT (1994) *The Results of the Uruguay Round of Multilateral Trade Negotiations: the legal texts*, General Agreement on Tariffs and Trade Secretariat, Geneva.

Geertz, C. (1963) *Agricultural Involution*, University of California Press, Berkeley.

Geertz, C. (1979) 'Suq: the bazaar economy in Sefrou', in Geertz, C. & Rosen, L. (eds) *Meaning and Order in Moroccan Society*, Cambridge University Press, Cambridge.

Geertz, C. (1984) 'Culture and social change: the Indonesian case', *Man*, 19, pp.511–32.

Geertz, H. & Geertz, C. (1975) *Kinship in Bali*, Chicago University Press, Chicago.

Gellner, E. (1983) *Nations and Nationalism*, Blackwell, Oxford.

George, S. (1976) *How the Other Half Dies*, Penguin, Harmondsworth.

Ghana VAST Study Team (1993) 'Vitamin A supplementation in northern Ghana: effects on clinic attendances, hospital admissions and child mortality', *The Lancet*, 342, pp.7–12.

Gheerbrant, A. (ed.) (1961) *The Incas*, Orion Press, New York (Avon Books, 1966).

Giddens, A. (1991) *The Consequences of Modernity*, Polity Press, Cambridge.

Gilbert, A. & Gugler, J. (1992) *Cities, Poverty and Development: urbanization in the Third World*, 2nd edn, Oxford University Press, Oxford.

Gilbert, A. & Varley, A. (1990) 'Renting a home in a Third World city: choice or constraint?', *International Journal of Urban and Regional Research*, 14(1), pp.89–108.

Gilbert, A. (1997) 'Employment and poverty during economic restructuring: the case of Bogotá, Colombia', *Urban Studies*, 34(7), pp.1047–70.

Gills, B. & Philip, G. (1996) 'Towards convergence in development policy? Challenging the "Washington consensus" and restoring the historicity of divergent development trajectories', *Third World Quarterly*, 17(4), pp.585–91.

Gilsenan, M. (1982) *Recognizing Islam*, Croom Helen, London.

Ginwala, F., Mackintosh, M. & Massey, D. (1991) *Gender and Economic Policy in a Democratic South Africa*, DPP Working Paper no.21, The Open University, Milton Keynes.

Glazer, N. & Moynihan, D. P. (1970) *Beyond the Melting Pot: the Negroes, Puerto Ricans, Jews, Italians and Irish of New York City*, Cambridge: MIT Press (first published 1963).

Global 2000 (1997) *No Patents on Life!*, Global 2000, Flurschützstraße 13, AT-1120 Wien, Austria.

Godement, F. (1999) *The Downsizing of Asia*, Routledge, London.

Goetz, A.-M. & Gupta, R. S. (1996) 'Who takes the credit? Gender, power and control over loan use in rural credit programmes in Bangladesh', *World Development*, 24(1), pp.45–63.

Goldsworthy, D. (1988) 'Thinking politically about development', *Development and Change*, 19(3) (July), pp.505–30.

Gonzalez de la Rocha, M. (1994) *The Resources of Poverty: women and survival in a Mexican city*, Blackwell Publishers, Oxford.

Gordon, D. (1988) 'The global economy: new edifice or crumbling foundations?' *New Left Review*, 168, pp.24–65.

Gordon, D. *et al.* (1982) *Segmented Work, Divided Workers*, Cambridge University Press, New York.

Gough, K. (1990) *Political Economy in Vietnam*, Folklore Institute, Berkeley.

Goulet, D. (1971) *The Cruel Choice: a new concept in the theory of development*, Atheneum, New York.

Governance, Commission on Global (1995) *Our Global Neighbourhood*, Oxford University Press, Oxford.

Gramsci, A. (1988) 'Some theoretical and practical aspects of 'economism'', in Forgacs, D. (ed.) *A Gramsci Reader*, Lawrence and Wishart, London.

Gray, J. (1998) *False Dawn: the delusions of global capitalism*, Granta Books, London.

Green, C., Joekes, S. & Leach, M. (1998) 'Questionable links: approaches to gender in environmental research and policy', in Jackson, C. & Pearson, R. (eds), *Feminist Visions of Development: gender analysis and policy*, Routledge, London.

Grosskurth, H., Mosha, F., Todd, J., Mwijarubi, E., Klokke, A., Senkoro, K., Mayaud, P., Changalucha, J., Nicoll, A., Ka-Gina, G., Newell, J., Mugeye, K., Mabey, D. & Hayes, R. (1995) 'Impact of improved treatment of sexually transmitted diseases on HIV infection in rural Tanzania: randomised controlled trial', *The Lancet*, 346(8974), pp.530–6.

Grugel, J. (1991) 'Latin America and the remaking of the Americas', in Gamble, A. & Payne, A. (eds) *Regionalism and World Order*, Macmillan, London.

Guha, R. (1989) *The Unquiet Woods: ecological change and peasant resistance in the Himalaya*, Oxford University Press, Delhi.

Gwynne, R. B. N. (1990) *New Horizons? Third World Industrialisation in an International Framework*, Longman Scientific and Technical, London.

Haass, R. N. & Liton, R. E. (1998) 'Globalization and its discontents', *Foreign Affairs*, (May/June).

Habib, I. (1969) 'Potentialities of capitalistic development in the economy of Mughal India', *Journal of Economic History*, 29, pp.32–78.

Habluetzel, A., Diallo, D. A., Esposito, F., Lamizana, L., Pagnoni, F., Lengeler, C., Traore, C. & Cousens, S. N. (1997) 'Do insecticide-treated curtains reduce all-cause child mortality in Burkina Faso?' *Tropical Medicine and International Health*, 2(9), pp.855–62.

Halliday, F. (1978) 'Revolution in Afghanistan', *New Left Review*, 112, pp.–44.

Halliday, F. (1979) *Iran: dictatorship and development*, Penguin, Harmondsworth.

Halliday, F. (1980) 'War and Revolution in Afghanistan', *New Left Review*, 119, pp.2–41.

Halliday, F. (1989) *Cold War, Third World*, Abacus, London.

Halliday, F. (1990) 'The End of Cold War', *New Left Review*, 180, pp.5–23.

Halliday, F. & Molyneux, M. (1981) *The Ethiopian Revolution*, Verso, London.

Hamilton, G. & Biggart, N. (1988) 'Markets, culture and authority: a comparative analysis of management and organization in the Far East', *American Journal of Sociology* (Supplement), 94, pp.S52–S94.

Hanlon, J. (1991) *Mozambique: who calls the shots?*, James Currey, London.

Hardoy, J. & Satterthwaite, D. (eds) (1986) *Small and Intermediate Urban Centres: their role in national and regional development in the Third World*, Hodder and Stoughton, London; Westview Press, Boulder.

Hardoy, J., Cairncross, S. & Satterthwaite, D. (1990) *The Poor Die Young: housing and health in Third World cities*, Earthscan, London.

Hardoy, J., Mitlin, D. & Satterthwaite, D. (1992) *Environmental Problems in Third World Cities*, Earthscan, London.

Harris, M. (1969) *The Rise of Anthropological Theory*, Routledge and Kegan Paul, London.

Harriss, B. & Watson, E. (1987) 'The sex ratio in South Asia', in Momsen, J. & Townsend, J. (eds), *The Geography of Gender in the Third World*, Hutchinson, London.

Harriss, B. (1991) 'The intra-family distribution of hunger', reproduced in Drèze, J., Sen, A. & Hussain, A. (eds) *The Political Economy of Hunger: selected essays*, Clarendon Press, Oxford.

Harriss, J. (1989) 'Urban poverty and urban poverty alleviation', *Cities*, August.

Harriss, J. (1995) "Japanisation' in the Indonesian automotive industry', *World Development*, 23(1).

Harriss, J. (1999) 'Working together: the principles and practice of co-operation and partnership', in Robinson, D., Hewitt, T. & Harriss, J. (eds) *Managing Development: understanding inter-organizational relationships*, Sage, London/The Open University, Milton Keynes.

Hartmann, B. (1987) *Reproductive Rights and Wrongs: the global politics of population control and contraceptive choice*, Harper & Row, New York.

Hartmann, B. (1995) 'The Cairo 'consensus': women's empowerment or business as usual?', *Geojournal*, 35(2), pp.205–6.

Harvey, D. (1973) *Social Justice and the City*, Blackwell, Oxford.

Harvey, D. (1982) *The Limits to Capital*, Blackwell, Oxford.

Harvey, D. (1989) *The Condition of Postmodernity*, Blackwell, Oxford.

Harvey, D. (1996) *Justice, Nature and the Geography of Difference*, Blackwell, Oxford.

Hayter, T. (1989) *Exploited Earth*, Earthscan, London.

Headrick, D. P. (1988) *The Tentacles of Progress: technology transfer in the Age of Imperialism, 1850–1940*, Oxford University Press, New York.

Heeks, R. (1998) *Management Information and Management Information Systems*, School of Oriental and African Studies, University of London, London.

Heeks, R. & Davies, A. (1999) 'Different approaches to information age reform', in Heeks, R. B. (ed.) *Reinventing Government in the Information Age*, Routledge, London.

Hegener, M. (1998) *The Use of Information and Communication Technologies in Agricultural and Rural Development in Developing Countries*. Technical Centre for Agricultural and Rural Cooperation, Wageningen, Netherlands. Also on Internet website: http://www.agricta.org/observat.htm

Heggenhougen, K. (1984) 'Will primary health care efforts be allowed to succeed?' *Social Science and Medicine*, 19(3), pp.217–24.

Held, D. (1995) *Democracy and Global Order*, Polity Press, Cambridge.

Held, D. (1996) *Models of Democracy*, 2nd edn, Polity Press, Cambridge.

Held, D., McGrew, A., Goldblatt, D. & Perraton, J. (1999) *Global Transformations: politics, economics and culture*, Polity Press, Cambridge.

Helliwell, J. (1994) 'Empirical linkages between democracy and economic growth', *British Journal of Political Science*, 24(2), pp.225–48.

Herod, A. *et al.* (eds) (1998) *Unruly World? Globalization, Governance and Geography*, Routledge, London.

Hewitt, A. & Killick, T. (1998) 'The 1975 and 1997 White papers compared: enriched vision, depleted policies?' *Journal of International Development*, 10(2), pp.185–94.

Hewitt, T. & Wield, D. (1997) 'Networks in Tanzanian industrialization', *Science and Public Policy*, 24(6), pp.393–405.

Hewitt, T., Johnson, H. & Wield, D. (eds) (1992) *Industrialization and Development*, Oxford University Press, Oxford/The Open University, Milton Keynes. (Book 2 of this series)

Hildyard, N. (1999) *Blood and Culture: ethnic conflict and the authoritarian right*, The Corner House, Sturminster Newton.

Hinton, W. (1972) *Fanshen*, Penguin, Harmondsworth.

Hirschman, A. (1992) 'Industrialization and its manifold discontents: West, East and South', *World Development*, 20(9), pp.1225–32.

Hirst, P. & Thomson, G. (1996) *Globalisation in Question?* Polity Press, London.

Hobbelink, H. (1991) *Biotechnology and the Future of World Agriculture*, Zed Books, London.

Hobbelink, H. (1995) 'Biotechnology and the future of world agriculture', in Shiva, V. & Moser, I. (eds), *Biopolitics: a feminist and ecological reader on biotechnology*, pp.226–33, Zed Books, London.

Hobsbawm, E. J. (1962) *The Age of Revolution 1789–1848*, Weidenfeld and Nicholson, London.

Hobsbawm, E. J. (1968) *Industry and Empire*, Penguin, Harmondsworth.

Hobsbawm, E. J. (1990) *Nations and Nationalism since 1780*, Cambridge University Press, Princeton NJ.

Hollingsworth, J. R. & Boyer, R. (eds) (1997) *Contemporary Capitalism: the embeddedness of institutions*, Cambridge University Press, Cambridge.

Hoogvelt, A. (1997) *Globalization and the Postcolonial World: the new political economy of development*, Macmillan, London.

Hooper, E. (1990) 'AIDS epidemic moves south through Africa', *New Scientist*, 7 July 1990, p.22.

Hübi, K. (1986) 'The nomadic livestock production system of Somalia', in Conze, P. & Labahn, T. (eds) *Somalia: agriculture in the winds of change*, Epi Verlag, Hamburg.

Hulme, D. & Edwards, M. (1997) 'NGOs, states and donors: an overview', in Hulme, D. & Edwards, M. (eds) *NGOs, States and Donors: Too Close for Comfort?*, Macmillan, London, in association with Save the Children.

Humphrey, J. & Schmitz, H. (1996) *Trust and Economic Development*, IDS Discussion Paper 355, Institute of Development Studies, Brighton.

Huntington, S. P. (1991) *The Third Wave: democratization in the late twentieth century*, University of Oklahoma Press, Norman.

Huntington, S. P. (1997) *The Clash of Civilizations and the Remaking of the World Order*, Touchstone, London.

Huntington, S. P. & Nelson, J. M. (1976) *No Easy Choice: political participation in developing countries*, Harvard University Press, Cambridge MA.

Hurrell, A. (1999) 'Security and inequality', in Hurrell, A. & Woods, N. (eds) *Globalization, Inequality and World Order*, Oxford University Press, Oxford.

Hyden, G. (1983) *No Shortcuts to Progress*, Heinemann, London.

Ignatieff, M. (1998) *The Warrior's Honor: ethnic war and the modern conscience*, Chatto & Windus, Random House, London.

Iliffe, J. (1979) *A Modern History of Tanganyika*, Cambridge University Press, Cambridge.

ILO (1997a) *Year Book of Labour Statistics 1997*, International Labour Organization, Geneva.

ILO (1997b) *IPEC Fact Sheet*, January, International Labour Organization, Geneva.

ILO (1989–90) *Labour Statistics*, International Labour Organization, Geneva.

Jackson, C. (1998) 'Rescuing poverty from the gender trap', in Jackson, C. & Pearson, R. (eds) *Feminist Visions of Development: gender analysis and policy*, Routledge, London.

Jackson, P. (1989) *Maps of Meaning*, Routledge, London.

Jackson, R. & Rosberg, C. (1982) 'Why Africa's weak states persist', *World Politics*, 35(1), 1–24.

Jackson, R. H. (1990) *Quasi-states: sovereignty, international relations and the Third World*, Cambridge University Press, Cambridge.

Jacobs, J. (1969) *The Economy of Cities*, Random House, New York.

James, C. (1998) *Global Review of Commercialized Transgenic Crops: 1998*, International Service for the Acquisition of Agri-Biotech Applications (ISAAA) Briefs, no.8, ISAAA, Ithaca, NY.

Jarman, J. (1997) 'Water supply and sanitation', in Beall, J. (ed.) *A City for All: valuing difference and working with diversity*, pp.182–93, Zed Books, London.

Jean, F. (1997) 'The plight of the world's refugees: at the crossroads of protection', in Médécins Sans Frontières (1997) *World in Crisis: the politics of survival at the end of the 20th century*, Routledge, London.

JEEAR (1996) *The International Response to Conflict and Genocide*: lessons from the Rwanda experience (5 volumes), Joint Evaluation of Emergency Assistance to Rwanda, Copenhagen.

Jeffries, R. (1993) 'The state, structural adjustment and good government in Africa', *Journal of Commonwealth and Comparative Politics*, 31(1), pp.20–35.

Jenkins, R. (1992) 'Theoretical perspectives', in Hewitt, T., Johnson, H. & Wield, D. (eds) *Industrialization and Development*, Oxford University Press, Oxford/Open University, Milton Keynes.

Jenks, C. (1993) *Culture*, Routledge, London.

Jesudason, J. (1995) 'Statist democracy and the limits of civil society in Malaysia', *Journal of Commonwealth and Comparative Politics*, 32(3) (November), pp.335–56.

JID (1988) 'Special issue on the UK Government's White Paper', *Journal of International Development*, 10(2).

Johnson, H. & Bernstein, H. (eds) (1982) *Third World Lives of Struggle*, Heinemann, London.

Johnson, R. W. (1972) 'French imperialism in Guinea', in Owen, E. R. J. & Sutcliffe, R. B. (eds) *Studies in the Theory of Imperialism*, Longman, London.

Johnson, Samuel (1810) *Dictionary of the English Language*, F. & C. Rivington, London.

Jordan, B. (1985) The State: authority and autonomy, Blackwell, Oxford.

Kabeer, N. (1991) Gender dimensions of rural poverty: analysis from Bangladesh, *Journal of Peasant Studies*, 18 (2 January), pp.241–62.

Kabeer, N. (1994) *Reversed Realities: gender hierarchies in development thought*, Verso, London.

Kabeer, N. (1998) *Money Can't Buy Me Love: re-evaluation of gender, credit and empowerment in rural Bangladesh*, IS and DS Discussion Paper no.363, Brighton, Sussex.

Kanji, N. (1995) 'Gender, poverty and economic adjustment in Harare, Zimbabwe', *Environment and Urbanization*, 7(1), pp.37–56.

Kaplinsky, R. (1998) 'If you want to get somewhere else, you must run at least twice as fast as that!', in *The Roots of the East Asian Crisis*, East Asia Conference, 13–14 July, Institute of Development Studies, Brighton.

Kasfir, N. (1998a), '"No-party democracy" in Uganda', *Journal of Democracy*, 9(2) (April), pp.49–63.

Kasfir, N. (1998b), 'Civil society, the state and democracy in Africa', *Journal of Commonwealth and Comparative Politics*, 36(2) (July), pp.123–49.

Kasongo Project Team (1981) 'Influence of measles vaccination on survival patterns of 7–35 month old children in Kasongo, Zaire', *The Lancet*, i: pp.764–7.

Katznelson, I. (1996) 'Social justice, liberalism and the city: considerations on David Harvey, John Rawls and Karl Polanyi', in Merrifield, A. & Swyngedouw, E. (eds) *The Urbanization of Injustice*, pp.45–64, Lawrence and Wishart, London.

Kearney, M. (1996) *Reconceptualizing the Peasantry*, Westview Press, Boulder.

Keegan, J. (1998) *War and Our World*, Hutchinson, London.

Keen, D. (1994) *The Benefits of Famine: a political economy of famine and relief in southwestern Sudan, 1983–89*, Princeton University Press, Princeton.

Kenney, M. & Florida, R. (1988) 'Beyond mass production and the labor process in Japan', *Politics and Society*, 16, pp.121–58.

Keohane, R. O. (1998) 'International institutions: can interdependence work?' *Foreign Policy*, (Spring), pp.82–96.

Kerkvliet, B. (1996) 'Contested meanings of elections in the Philippines', in Taylor, R. H.(ed.) *The Politics of Elections in Southeast Asia*, pp.136–63, Cambridge University Press, Cambridge.

Khan, A. (1990) *The impact of international labour migration on the rural 'Barani' areas of modern Pakistan*, PhD thesis, University of Sussex, Brighton.

Khomeini, R. (1971) *Hukumat-i Islami* (The Islamic Government), Nahzat-i Islami, Najaf.

Kiely, R. (1998) *Industrialization and Development: a comparative analysis*, UCL Press, London.

King, M. (1990) 'Health is a sustainable state', *The Lancet*, 336 (15 September).

Kitching, G. (1982) *Development and Underdevelopment in Historical Perspective*, Methuen, London.

Kitching, G. (1989) *Development and Underdevelopment in Historical Perspective*, Routledge, London (2nd revised edition).

Kloosterboer, W. (1960) *Involuntary Labour Since the Abolition of Slavery*, E.J. Brill, Leiden.

Kloppenburg, J. (1988) *First the Seed: the political economy of plant biotechnology, 1492–2000*, Cambridge University Press, Cambridge.

Komen, J. & Persley, G. (1993) *Agricultural Biotechnology in Developing Countries: a cross country review*, Research report no.2, Intermediary Biotechnology Service, ISNAR, The Hague.

Korten, D. (1990) *Getting to the Twenty-First Century: voluntary action and the global agenda*, Kumarian Press, West Hartford CT.

Korten, D. (1995a) *When Corporations Rule the World*, Kumarian Press, West Hartford CT and Berrett-Koehler, San Francisco.

Korten, D. (1995b) 'Steps toward people-centred development: vision and strategies', in Heyzer, N., Riker, J. V. & Quizon, A. B. (eds) *Government–NGO Relations in Asia: prospects and challenges for people-centred development*, pp.165–89.

Kotz, D. & Weir, F. (1997) *Revolution from Above: the demise of the Soviet system*, Routledge, London.

Krimsky, S. (1991) *Biotechnics and Society: the rise of industrial genetics*, Praeger, London.

Kristof, N. & Wyatt, E. (1999) 'Who sank, or swam, in choppy currents of a world cash ocean', *The New York Times*, 15 February 1999.

Kroeber, A. L. & Kluckhohn, C. (1952) *Culture: A Critical Review of Concepts and Definitions*, Cambridge, Mass.: Papers of the Peabody Museum, Harvard University, vol.47, no.1.

Kumar, N. & Siddharthan, N. S. (1997) *Technology, Market Structure and Internationalisation: issues and policies for developing countries*, UNU/INTECH studies in new technology and development, Routledge, London.

Kumar, S. (1996) 'Landlordism in Third World low income settlements: a case for further research', *Urban Studies*, 33(4/5), pp.753–82.

Kuper, A. (1994) *The Chosen Primate*, Harvard University Press, London.

Kuper, A. (1999) *Culture: the anthropologists' account*, Harvard University Press, Cambridge, Mass.

Landes, D. (1998) *The Wealth and Poverty of Nations*, Little, Brown and Company, London.

Lappé, F. M. & Schurman, R. (1988) *Taking Population Seriously*, Earthscan Publications, London.

Lash, S. & Urry, J. (1987) *The End of Organised Capitalism*, Polity Press, Cambridge.

Lassonde, L. (1997) *Coping with Population Challenges*, Earthscan Publications, London.

Lawand, T. A., Hvelplund, F., Alward, R., & Voss, J. (1976) 'Brace Research Institute's *Handbook of Appropriate Technology* (1975)', in Jequier, N. (ed.) *Appropriate Technology: problems and promises*, pp.124–36, OECD, Paris.

Lawrence, R. H. (1988) 'New applications of biotechnology in the food industry', in *Biotechnology and the Food Supply*, pp.19-45, National Academy Press, Washington, DC.

Leach, E. (1954) *The Political Systems of Highland Burma*, Cambridge University Press, Cambridge.

Leach, E. (1982) *Social Anthropology*, Oxford University Press, Oxford.

Lee Kwan Yew (1992) Statement to an audience in the Philippines, quoted in *The Economist*, 2 August 1994, p.17.

Leftwich, A. (1993) 'Governance, democracy and development in the Third World', *Third World Quarterly*, 14(3), pp.605–24.

Leftwich, A. (1994) 'Governance, the state and the politics of development', *Development and Change*, 25(2), pp.363–86.

Leftwich, A. (1998) 'Forms of the democratic developmental state: democratic practices and development capacity', in Robinson, M. & White, G. (eds) *The Democratic Developmental State: politics and institutional design*, ch.2, Oxford University Press, Oxford.

Lengeler, C. (1998) *Insecticide Treated Bednets and Curtains for Malaria Control* (Cochrane Review), The Cochrane Library, Issue 3, Update Software, Oxford.

Lenin, V. I (1939) *Imperialism: the Highest stage of capitalism, a popular outline*, English version, International Publishers, New York (first published in Moscow 1916).

Levidow, L., Carr, S., von Schomberg, R. & Wield, D. (1996) 'Regulating agricultural biotechnology in Europe: harmonization difficulties, opportunities, dilemmas', *Science & Public Policy*, 23 (3), pp.135–57.

Levidow, L., Carr, S. & Wield, D. (1999) 'Market-stage precautions: managing regulatory disharmonies for transgenic crops in Europe', *AgBiotechNet*, April; Internet url: http://agbio.cabweb.org

Lewis, I. (1965a) 'The northern pastoral Somali of the Horn', in Gibbs, J. (ed.) *Peoples of Africa*, Holt, Rinehart and Winston, New York.

Lewis, I. (1975) 'The dynamics of nomadism: prospect for sedentarization and social change', in Monod, T. (ed.) *Pastoralism in Tropical Africa*, Oxford University Press, Oxford.

Lewis, I. (1985) *Social Anthropology in Perspective*, Cambridge University Press, Cambridge.

Lewis, I. (1997) 'Clan conflict and ethnicity in Somalia', in Turton, D. (ed.) *War and Ethnicity*, University of Rochester Press, New York.

Lewis, O. (1965b) 'Further observations on the folk–urban continuum and urbanization with special reference to Mexico City', in Hauser, P. M. & Schnore, L. F. (eds) *The Study of Urbanization*, Wiley, New York.

Linz, J. & Stepan, A. (1996) *Problems of Democratic Transition and Consolidation*, Johns Hopkins University Press, London.

Lipset, D. M. (1989) 'Papua New Guinea: the Melanesian ethic and the spirit of capitalism, 1975–1986', in Diamond, L., Linz, J. & Lipset, S. (eds) *Democracy in Developing Countries: Asia*, L.Rienner, Boulder.

Lipset, S. M. (1960) *Political Man*, Heinemann, London.

Lipton, M. (1977) *Why Poor People Stay Poor: urban bias in world development*, Maurice Temple Smith, London.

Little, P. D. (1992) *The Elusive Granary: herder, farmer, and state in northern Kenya*, Cambridge University Press, Cambridge.

Lo, D. (1997) *Market and Institutional Regulation in Chinese Industrialization 1978–94*, Macmillan, Basingstoke.

Low, D. A. (1973) *Lion Rampant: essays on the study of British Imperialism*, Cass, London.

Luckham, R. (1998) 'Are there alternatives to liberal democracy?', in Robinson, M. & White, G. (eds) *The Democratic Developmental State: politics and institutional design*, ch.10, Oxford University Press, Oxford.

MacGaffey, J. (1991) *The Real Economy of Zaire: the contribution of smuggling and other unofficial activities to national wealth*, James Currey, London.

Maitan, L. (1976) *Party, Army and Masses in China*, New Left Books, London.

Maldonado, C. (1995) 'The informal sector: legalization or laissez-faire', *International Labour Review*, 134(6), pp.705-28.

Mallett, V. (1999) *The Trouble with Tigers*, Harper and Collins, London.

Mamdani, M. (1996) *Citizen and Subject: contemporary Africa and the legacy of late colonialism*, Princeton University Press, Princeton, NJ.

Mannoni, D. (trans. Powesland, P.) (1956) *Prospero and Caliban: the psychology of colonization*, Methuen, London.

Markowitz, I. L. (1977) *Power and Class in Africa*, Prentice-Hall, New Jersey.

Massey, D. (1994) *Space, Place, Gender*, Polity Press, Cambridge.

Massey, D., Allen, J. & Pile, S. (eds) (1999) *City Worlds*, Routledge, London, in association with The Open University Press, Buckingham.

Maxwell, S. (1999) 'The meaning and measurement of poverty; *ODI Poverty Briefing 3*, Overseas Development Institute, London.

Mayoux, L. (1998) *Women's Empowerment and Micro-finance Programmes: approaches, evidence and ways forward*, DPP Working Paper 41, Open University, Milton Keynes.

McFarlane, B. (1984) 'Political economy of class struggle and economic growth in China 1950–1982', in Maxwell, N. & McFarlane, B. (eds) *China's Changed Road to Development*, Pergamon, Oxford.

McGrew, A. (1999) 'The WTO: technocracy or banana republic?', in Thomas, C. & Taylor, A., *Global Trade and Global Social Issues*, Routledge, London.

McKee, K. (1989) 'Microlevel strategies for supporting livelihoods, employment, and income generation for poor women in the Third World: the challenge of significance', *World Development*, 17(7), pp.993–1006.

McKeown, T. (1979) *The Role of Medicine*, Basil Blackwell, Oxford.

McLelland, D. (1963) 'The achievement motive in economic growth', in Hoselitz, B.F. & Moore, W.E. (eds.) *Industrialization and Society*, UNESCO and Mouton, The Hague.

McMichael, P. (1998) 'Global food politics', *Monthly Review*, 50(3), pp.97–111.

McNeill, W. H. & Waldman, M. R. (1973) *The Islamic World*, Oxford University Press, New York.

Meadows, D. H., Meadows, D. L., Randers, J. & Behrens, W. III (1972) *The Limits to Growth*, Earth Island Ltd, London.

Messenger, C. (1995) *The Century of Warfare: worldwide conflict from 1900 to the present day*, Harper Collins, London.

Michaelson, K. L. (1981) *And the Poor Get Children: radical perspectives on population dynamics*, Monthly Review Press, New York.

Miller, M. A. (1998) 'Sovereignty reconfigured: environmental regimes and Third World states', in Litfin, K. T. (ed.) *The Greening of Sovereignty in World Politics*, MIT Press, Cambridge, MA.

Misra, B. B. (1976) *The Indian Political Parties: an historical analysis of political behaviour up to 1947*, Oxford University Press, Delhi.

Mister, R. (1988) 'Refugees and nomads: successes and failures in Somalia', in Poulton, R. & Harris, M. (eds) *Putting People First*, Macmillan, London.

Mittelman, J. H. (1994) 'The globalization challenge: surviving at the margins', *Third World Quarterly*, 15, pp.427–443.

Molyneux, M. (1985) 'Mobilization without emancipation? Women's interests, state and revolution in Nicaragua', *Feminist Studies*, vol.11, pp.227–34.

Molyneux, M. (1998) 'Analysing women's movements', in Jackson, C. & Pearson, R. (eds), *Feminist Visions of Development: gender analysis and policy*, Routledge, London.

Moody, K. (1997) *Workers in a Lean World: unions in the international economy*, Verso, London.

Moore, B. (1966, 1967,1987) *Social Origins of Dictatorship and Democracy: lord and peasant in the making of the modern world*, Beacon Press, Boston; Allen Lane, London; Penguin, Harmondsworth.

Moore, H. L. & Vaughan, M. (1994) *Cutting Down Trees: gender, nutrition, and agricultural change in the Northern Province of Zambia, 1890–1990*, James Currey, London.

Morrison, D. (1982) 'A critical examination of A. A. Barsov's empirical work on the balance of value exchanges between the town and the country', *Soviet Studies*, 34, pp.570-84.

Moser, C. (1993) *Gender Planning and Development: theory, practice and training*, Routledge, London.

Moser, C. (1996) *Confronting Crisis: a comparative study of household responses to poverty and vulnerability in four poor urban communities*, Environmentally Sustainable Development Studies and Monographs Series no.8, The World Bank, Washington DC.

Moser, C. (1998) 'The asset vulnerability framework: reassessing urban poverty reduction strategies', *World Development*, 26(1).

Moser, C. & Holland, J. (1997) *Urban Poverty and Violence in Jamaica*, The World Bank, Washington DC.

Moser, C. & Peake, L. (1987) *Women, Human Settlements and Housing*, Tavistock Publications, London.

Moser, C. & Satterthwaite, D. (1985) 'Characteristics and sociology of poor urban communities', unpublished mimeo, International Institute of Environment and Development, London.

Moynihan, D. P. (1993) *Pandaemonium: ethnicity in international politics*, Oxford University Press, Oxford.

MSF (Médécins Sans Frontières) (1997) *World in Crisis: the politics of survival at the end of the 20th century*, Routledge, London.

Muhilal, Permeisih, D., Idiradinata, Y., Muherdiyantiningsih & Karyadi, D. (1988) 'Vitamin A fortified monosodium glutamate and health, growth and survival of children', *American Journal of Clinical Nutrition*, 48, pp.1271–6.

Mulder, D., Nunn, A., Kamali, A. & Kengeya-Kayondon, J. (1995) 'Decreasing HIV-1 sero prevalence in young adults in a rural Uganda cohort', *British Medical Journal*, 333(30), pp.833–6.

Murphy, Y. & Murphy, R. F. (1974) *Women of the Forest*, Columbia University Press, New York.

Mytelka, L. (1998) 'New Trends in Biotechnology Networking', Paper presented to the UN Working Group on Science and Technology Partnerships and Networking for National Capacity-Building, Malta, 28–30 September.

Nandy, A. (1983) *The Intimate Enemy: loss and recovery of self under colonialism*, Oxford University Press, Delhi.

Nature Biotechnology (1999) *North-South Innovation Transfer*, vol.17, Supplement.

Neher, C. & Marlay, R. (1995) *Democracy and Development in Southeast Asia*, Westview Press, Boulder.

Nierop, T. (1994) *Systems and Regions in Global Politics*, John Wiley, London.

Nolan, P. (1976) 'Collectivization in China: some comparisons with the USSR', *Journal of Peasant Studies*, 3, pp.19–220.

Nolan, P. (1989) *The Political Economy of Collective Farms*, Blackwell, Oxford/Polity Press, Cambridge.

Nolan, P. (1995) *China's Rise, Russia's Fall: politics, economics and planning in the transition from Stalinism*, Macmillan, Basingstoke.

North, N. (1990) *Institutions, Institutional Change and Economic Performance*, Cambridge University Press, New York.

Norwegian Refugee Council (1998) *Internally Displaced People*, Earthscan, London.

Novartis Foundation (1998) *The Socio-political Impact of Biotechnology in Developing Countries*, Internet url: http://www.foundation.novartis.com/biotech.htm

Nugent, S. & Shore, C. (eds) (1997) *Anthropology and Cultural Studies*, Pluto Press, London.

Nzula, A. T., Potekhin, I. I. & Zusmanovich, A. Z. (1979) *Forced Labour in Colonial Africa*, Zed Books, London (first published in Moscow, 1933).

O'Donnell, G., Schmitter, P. & Whitehead, L. (eds) (1986) *Transitions from Authoritarian Rule* (4 vols), Johns Hopkins University Press, Baltimore.

ODA (1993) 'Good government', *Technical Note* no.10, Overseas Development Administration, London.

ODI (1988) *Commodity Prices: investing in decline?* Overseas Development Institute, London.

ODI (1998) 'The state of the international humanitarian system', *Overseas Development Briefing Paper*, 1, March.

OECD (1985) *Twenty-five Years of Development Co-operation: a review*, Organization for Economic Co-operation and Development, Paris.

OECD (1996) *OECD Economic Outlook*, OECD, Paris.

Ohmae, K. (1995) *The End of the Nation State*, Free Press, New York.

Okanjo, I. (1974) *British Administration in Nigeria: 1900–1950*, NOK Publishers, New York.

Oliver, N. & Wilkinson, B. (1988) *The Japanization of British Industry*, Blackwell, Oxford.

Oliver, R. & Fage, J. D. (1962) *A Short History of Africa*, Penguin, Harmondsworth.

Ottemoeller, D. (1998) 'Popular perceptions of democracy: elections and attitudes in Uganda', *Comparative Political Studies*, 31(1) (February), pp.98–124.

Oxhorn, P. (1995) 'From controlled inclusion to coerced marginalization: the struggle for civil society in Latin America', in J. Hall (ed.) *Civil Society: theory, history, comparison*, ch.11, Polity Press, Cambridge.

Pacey, A. (1990) *Technology in World Civilization*, Basic Blackwell, Oxford.

Pandry, B. (1994) 'Hybrid seed controversy in India', *Biotechnology and Development Monitor*, 19, pp.9–11.

Pankhurst, D. (1989) 'Review article: poverty and food: contemporary questions', *Journal of International Development*, 1(4), pp.508–13.

Panos (1998a) *The Internet and Poverty: real hope or real hype?* Panos, London.

Panos (1998b) *Information, Knowledge and Development*, Panos, London.

Panos (1998c) *Greed or Need?* Briefing no.30, Panos Institute, London.

Parpart, J. L. (1995) 'Post-Modernism, gender and development', in Crush, J. (ed.) *Power of Development*, Routledge, London and New York.

Payne, P. R. (1990) 'Measuring malnutrition', *IDS Bulletin*, 21(3).

Payne, P. (1994) 'Not enough food: malnutrition and famine', in Harriss-White, B. & Hoffenberg, R. (eds) *Food: multidisciplinary perspectives*, Blackwell, Oxford.

Pearson, R. (1998) 'Microcredit meets social exclusion: learning with difficulty from international experience', *Journal of International Development*, vol.10, pp.811–22.

Perham, M. & Simmons, J. (1948) *African Discovery*, Penguin, Harmondsworth.

Peters, P. E. (1994) *Dividing the Commons: politics, policy and culture in Botswana*, University Press of Virginia, Charlottesville.

Pieper, U. & Taylor, L. (1998) 'The revival of the liberal creed: the IMF, the World Bank, and inequality in a globalized economy', *Globalization and Progressive Economic Policy*, Cambridge University Press, Cambridge.

Platt, L. J. (1999) PhD thesis in prepration, Development, Policy and Practice Discipline, The Open University, Milton Keynes.

Platt, L. J. & Wilson, G. A. (1999) 'Technology development and the poor/marginalised: context, intervention and participation, *Technovation*, 19(6/7), pp.393–40.

Polanyi, K. (1944, 1957) *The Great Transformation: the political and economic origins of our time*, Beacon Press, Boston.

Polanyi, K. (1968) *Primitive, Archaic and Modern Economies. Essays of Karl Polanyi* (edited by G. Dalton), Beacon Press, Boston.

Post, C. (1982) 'The American road to capitalism', *New Left Review*, 133.

Posthuma, A. (1998) 'Liberalisation and labour market adjustment in Brazil: reconciling the challenges of employment and competitiveness'. Multidisciplinary Team, International Labour Organisation, Santiago, Chile, mimeo.

Potter, D. C. (1986) *India's Political Administrators: 1919–1983*, Clarendon Press, Oxford.

Potter, D. (1997) 'Explaining democratization', in Potter, D., Goldblatt, D., Kiloh, M. & Lewis, P. (eds), *Democratization*, ch.1, pp.1–40, Polity Press, Cambridge.

Pretty, J. (1995) *Regenerating Agriculture*, Earthscan, London.

Pryer, J. & Crook, N. (1990) *Cities of Hunger: urban malnutrition in developing countries* (revised edition), Oxfam, Oxford.

Przeworski, A. & Limongi, F. (1993) 'Political regimes and economic growth', *Journal of Economic Perspectives*, 7(3), pp.51–69.

Przeworski, A. *et al.* (1996) 'What makes democracies endure?', *Journal of Democracy*, 7(1), pp.39–55.

Putnam, R. D. (1993) *Making Democracy Work: civic traditions in modern Italy*, Princeton University Press, Princeton.

Quingrui & Xiaobo (1991) 'A model of the secondary innovation process', *Proceedings of the 1991 Portland International Conference on Management of Engineering and Technology*, pp.617–20.

Raffer, K. & Singer, H. (1996) *The Foreign Aid Business: economic assistance and development co-operation*, Edward Elgar, Cheltenham.

RAFI (1999) 'Traitor tech: the terminator's wider implications', Rural Advancement Foundation International Communique, Jan/Feb; Internet url: http://www.rafi.org

Rahmathullah, L., Underwood, B. A., Thulasiraj, R. D., Milton, R. C., Ramaswamy, K., Rahmathullah, R. & Babu, G. (1990) 'Reduced mortality among children in Southern India receiving a small weekly dose of vitamin A', *New England Journal of Medicine*, 323, pp.929–35.

Rahnema, M. (1992) 'Poverty', in Sachs, W. (ed.) *The Development Dictionary: a guide to knowledge as power*, Zed Books, London.

Rahnema, M. (1997) 'Towards post-development: searching for signposts, a new language and new paradigms', in Rahnema, M. & Bawtree, V. (eds) *The Post Development Reader*, pp.377–403, Zed Books, London.

Rahnema, M. & Bawtree, V. (eds) (1997) *The Post Development Reader*, Zed Books, London.

Rakodi, C. (1998) 'Globalization trends and sub-Saharan African cities', in Fu-Chen Lo and Yue-Man Yeung (eds), *Globalization and the World of Large Cities*, pp.314–51, United Nations University Press, Tokyo, New York, Paris.

Rakovsky, C. (1981) 'The Five Year Plan in crisis', *Critique*, 13, pp.5–54.

Randall, V. (ed.) (1988) *Political Parties in the Third World*, Sage, London.

Randel, J. & German, T. (EUROSTEP/ICVA) (eds) (1998) *The Reality of Aid 1998–1999: an independent review of poverty reduction and development assistance*, Earthscan, London.

Ranger, T. (1985) *The Invention of Tribalism in Colonial Zimbabwe*, Mento Press, Harare.

Ravenhill, J. (1990) 'The North–South balance of power', *International Affairs*, 66(4), pp.731–48.

Raza, S. H. (undated) Unpublished Papers, India Office Library, MSS, Eur. F.180/29.

Razavi, S. & Miller, C. (1995a) 'From WID to GAD: conceptual shifts in the women and development discourse', *Occasional Paper No 1, Beijing Conference*, UN Research Institute for Social Development, Geneva.

Razavi, S. & Miller, C. (1995b) 'Gender mainstreaming: a study of efforts by the UNDP, the World Bank and the ILO to institutionalize gender issues', *Occasional Paper No 4, Beijing Conference*, UN Research Institute for Social Development, Geneva.

Redclift, M. (1987) *Sustainable Development: exploring the contradictions*, Routledge, London.

Rees, W. (1992) 'Ecological footprints and appropriated carrying capacity: what urban economics leaves out', *Environment and Urbanization*, 4(2), pp.121–30.

Reilly, B. (1997) 'Preferential voting and political engineering: a comparative study', *Journal of Commonwealth and Comparative Politics*, 35(1), March, pp.1–19.

Results (1997) *Micro-Credit Summit, Feb 2–4 1997: declaration and plan of action*, Results, Washington.

Rhodes, R. (1997) *Understanding Governance: policy networks, governance, reflexivity and accountability*, The Open University Press, Buckingham.

Richards, M. (1997) 'Tragedy of the commons for community-based forest management in Latin America?' *Natural Resource Perspectives*, no.22, Overseas Development Institute, London.

Riskin, C. (1988) *China's Political Economy*, Oxford University Press, Oxford.

Robinson, F. C. R. (1971) 'Consultation and control: the United Provinces' government and its allies, 1860–1909', *Modern Asian Studies*, 5(11), pp.313–36.

Robinson, M. (1993) 'Governance, democracy and conditionality: NGOs and the new policy agenda', in Clayton, A. (ed.) *Governance, Democracy and Conditionality: what role for NGOs?*, INTRAC, Oxford.

Rodrik, D. (1997) *Has Globalization Gone Too Far?* Institute for International Economics, Washington DC.

Rogaly, B. (1996) 'Micro-finance evangelism, 'destitute women', and the hard selling of a new anti-poverty formula', *Development in Practice*, 6(2), pp.100–12.

Rogow, D. (1986) 'Quality care in international family planning: a feminist contribution', in IWHC (eds) *The Contraceptive Development Process and Quality of Care in Reproductive Health Services*, International Women and Health Coalition (with The Population Council) meeting, 8–9 October, IWHC, New York.

Rosenberg, M. (1998) 'Preparations for Cairo+5, Report on the UNFPA Meeting in Kamala', *Women's Global Network for Reproductive Rights*, 63.

Ross, E. (1996) 'Malthusianism and agricultural development: false premises, false promises', *Biotechnology and Development Monitor*, 26, p.24.

Ross, E. B. (1998) *The Malthus Factor: poverty, politics and population in capitalist development*, Zed Books, London.

Rotberg, R. I. (1983) 'Nutrition and history', in Rotberg, R. I., Rabb, T. K. & Boserup, E. (eds), *Hunger and History: the impact of changing food production and consumption patterns on society*, Cambridge University Press, Cambridge.

Rowlands, I. (1998) 'Mapping the prospects for regional cooperation in Southern Africa', *Third World Quarterly*, 19(5), pp.917–34.

Rueschemeyer, D., Stephens, E. & Stephens, J. (1992) *Capitalist Development and Democracy*, Polity Press, Cambridge.

Rungta, R. S. (1970) *The Rise of Business Corporations in India, 1851–1900*, Cambridge University Press, Cambridge.

Rustow, D. (1970) 'Transitions to democracy', *Comparative Politics*, vol.2, pp.337–63.

Ruthven, M. (1984) *Islam in the World*, Penguin, Harmondsworth.

Sabel, C. & Zeitlin, J. (1985) 'Historical alternatives to mass production: politics, markets and technology in nineteenth century industrialization', *Past and Present*, 108, pp.133–76.

Sabel, C. (1992) 'Studied trust: building new forms of co-operation in a volatile economy', in Sengenberger, W. & Pyke, F. (eds) *Industrial Districts and Local Economic Regeneration*, pp.215–50, International Institute for Labour Studies, Geneva.

Sachs, J. (1998) *The Observer*, 25 October 1998.

Sachs, W. (1992) 'Introduction', in Sachs, W. (ed.) *The Development Dictionary: a guide to knowledge as power*, Zed Books, London.

Sachs, W. (ed.) (1992) *The Development Dictionary: a guide to knowledge as power*, Zed Books, London.

Sahlins, M. (1976) *Culture and Practical Reason*, Aldine, Chicago.

Sahlins, M. (1997) 'The original affluent society', in Rahnema, M. & Bawtree, V. (eds) *The Post Development Reader*, pp.3–21, Zed Books, London.

Sainath, P. (1998) *Everybody Loves a Good Drought: stories from India's poorest villages*, Headline, London.

Sandbrook, R. (1992) 'From Stockholm to Rio', in *Earth Summit 1992*, Regency Press, London.

Sassen, S. & Patel, S. (1996) 'Cities today: a new frontier', *Urban Age*, 4(1).

Sassen, S. (1991) *The Global City: New York, London, Tokyo*, Princeton University Press, Princeton, N.J.

Satterthwaite, D. (1993) 'The impact on health of urban environments', *Environment and Urbanization*, 5(2), pp.87–111.

Satterthwaite, D. (1996) 'The scale and nature of urban change in the South', unpublished mimeo of the Human Settlements Programme, International Institute for Environment and Development, London, June.

Satterthwaite, D. (1997) 'Urban poverty, reconsidering its scale and nature', *IDS Bulletin*, 28(2), pp.9–23.

Scheper-Hughes, N. (1992) *Death Without Weeping: the violence of everyday life in Brazil*, University of California Press, Berkeley.

Schiff, L. M. (1939) *The Present Condition of India: a study in social relationships*, Quality Press, London.

Schmitz, H. (1995) 'Collective efficiency: growth path for small scale industry', *Journal of Development Studies*, 31(4), pp.529–66.

Schuler, S. R., Hashemi, S. M., Riley, A. P. & Akhter, S. (1996) 'Credit programs, patriarchy and men's violence against women in rural Bangladesh', *Social Science and Medicine*, 43(12), pp.1729–42.

Schumacher, E.F. (1973) *Small is Beautiful: a study of economics as if people mattered*, Blond and Briggs, London.

Schuurman, F. J. (ed.) (1993) *Beyond the Impasse: new directions in development theory*, Zed Books, London.

Seabrook, J. (1996) *In the Cities of the South: scenes from a developing world*, Verso Press, London.

Seers, D. (1969; 1979) 'The meaning of development', in Lehmann, D. (ed.) *Development Theory: four critical studies*, Frank Cass, London.

Seeth, H. T., Chachnov, S., Surinov, A. & Von Braun, J. (1998) 'Russian poverty: muddling through economic transition with garden plots', *World Development*, 26(9), pp.1611–24.

Selden, M. (1971) *The Yenan Way in Revolutionary China*, Harvard University Press, Cambridge, Mass.

Selden, M. (1984) 'The logic – and limits – of Chinese socialist development', in Maxwell, N. & McFarlane, B. (eds) *China's Changed Road to Development*, Pergamon, Oxford.

Sen, A. (1981) *Poverty and Famines: an essay on entitlement and deprivation*, Oxford University Press, Oxford.

Sen, A. (1983) 'Poor, relatively speaking', *Oxford Economic Papers 35*, reprinted in Sen, A. (1984) *Resources, Values and Development*, Blackwell, Oxford.

Sen, A. (1985) *Commodities and Capabilities*, North-Holland, Amsterdam.

Sen, A. (1990a) 'More than 100 million women are missing', *New York Review of Books*, (20 Dec. 1990), pp.61–6.

Sen, A. (1990b) 'Development as capability expansion', in Griffin, K. & Knight, J. (eds) *Human Development and the International Strategy for the 1990's*, Macmillan, London.

Sen, G. (1992) 'Social needs and public accountability: the case of Kerala', in Wuyts, M., Mackintosh, M. & Hewitt, T. (eds), *Development Policy and Public Action*, Oxford University Press, Oxford, with The Open University, Milton Keynes.

Sen, G. & Grown, K. (1988) *Development Crises and Alternative Visions: Third World women's perspectives*, Earthscan Publications, London.

Sen, G. & Snow, R. C. (eds) (1994) *Power and Decision: the social control of reproduction*, Harvard University Press, Boston.

Sen, G. et al. (eds) (1994a) *Population Policies Reconsidered: health, empowerment and rights*, Harvard University Press, Boston.

Sen,. G. et al. (eds) (1994b) 'Reconsidering population policies: ethics, development and strategies for change', in Sen, G. et al. (eds), *Population Policies Reconsidered: health, empowerment and rights*, Harvard University Press, Boston.

Sers, D. (1963) 'The limitations of the special case', *Bulletin of the Oxford Institute of Economics and Statistics*, 25(2).

Serwadda, D., Wawer, M., Sewankambo, N., Gray, R. J., Li, C-J., Kelly, R. & Lutalo, T. (1995) 'Trends in HIV incidence and prevalence in Rakai district, Uganda', Abstract MoC085, Ninth International Conference on AIDS and STDs in Africa, Kampala, Uganda. December 10-14, Institute of Public Health, Makerere University, Kampala, Uganda.

Shaban, M. A. (1971) *Islamic History: a new interpretation*, Cambridge University Press, Cambridge.

Shiva, V. (1991) *The Violence of the Green Revolution*, Third World Network, Penang.

Silverblatt, I. (1988) '"The Universe has turned inside out. There is no justice for us here." Andean women under Spanish rule', in Etienne, M. & Leacock, E. (eds) *Women and Civilization: anthropological perspectives*, Praeger, New York.

Simon, J. L. (1992) *Population and Development in Poor Countries: selected essays*, Princeton University Press, Princeton NJ.

Sindharan, K. (1998) 'G-15 and South–South Co-operation: promise and performance', *Third World Quarterly*, 19(3), pp.357–73.

Singer, H. (1989) *Lessons of Post-War Development Experience: 1945–1988*, Discussion Paper 260, April, Institute of Development Studies, Brighton.

Singer, H. (1995) 'Rethinking Bretton Woods: from an historical perspective', in Griesgraber, J. M. & Gunter, B. G. (eds) *Promoting Development: Effective Global Institutions for the Twenty-First Century*, Pluto Press, London.

Singh, J. S. (1998) *Creating a New Consensus on Population*, Earthscan Publications, London.

SIPRI (Stockholm International Peace Research Institute) (annual) *Yearbook*, Oxford University Press, Oxford.

Sivan, E. (1985) *Radical Islam: medieval theology and modern politics*, Yale University Press, New Haven.

Smelser, N. J. (1968) 'Towards a theory of modernization', in Smelser, N. J. (ed.) *Essays in Sociological Explanation*, Prentice-Hall, Englewood Cliffs, NJ.

Smith, A. (1986) *The Ethnic Origin of Nations*, Blackwell, Oxford.

Smith, R. (1993) 'The Chinese Road to Capitalism', *New Left Review*, 199, pp.5–99.

Smith, R. (1997) 'Creative destruction: capitalist development and China's environment', *New Left Review*, 222, pp.3-41.

Smyth, I. (1996) 'Gender analysis of family planning: beyond the feminist vs. population control debate', *Feminist Economics*, 2(2), 63–86.

Snow, E. (1972) *Red Star over China*, Penguin, Harmondsworth.

Snow, R. W., Bastos de Azevedo, I., Lowes, B. S. *et al.* (1994) 'Severe childhood malaria in two areas of markedly different falciparum transmission in east Africa', *Acta Tropica*, 57, pp.289–300.

Sommer, A., Tarwotjo, I., Djunaedi, E., West, K. P., Tilden, R. L., Loedin, A. A., Mele, L. and the Aceh Study Group (1986) 'Impact of vitamin A supplementation on childhood mortality: a randomised, controlled community trial', *The Lancet*, 1, pp.1169–73.

South Commission (1990) *The Challenge to the South: The Report of the South Commission*, Oxford University Press, Oxford.

Spencer, J. (1996) 'Nationalism', in Barnard, A. & Spencer, J. (eds) *Encyclopedia of Social and Cultural Anthropology*, Routledge, London.

Spitz, P. (1987) 'The Green Revolution re-examined in India', in Glaeser, B. (ed.), *The Green Revolution Revisited*, pp.56–76, Allen & Unwin, London.

Spoor, M. (1998) 'The Aral Sea Basin crisis: transition and environment in former Soviet Central Asia', *Development and Change*, 29(3), pp.409–15.

Stallings, B. (1995) 'The new international context of development', in Stallings, B. (ed.), *Global Change, Regional Response*, Cambridge University Press, Cambridge.

Stein, B. (1998) *A History of India*, Oxford, Blackwell.

Stephens, C. (1996) 'Healthy cities or unhealthy islands: the health and social implications of urban inequality', *Environment and Urbanization*, 8(2).

Stewart, F., Humphreys, F. & Leas, N. (1997) 'Civil conflict in developing countries over the last quarter of a century: an empirical overview of economic and social consequences', *Oxford Development Studies*, 25(1), February.

Stockton, N. (1998) 'In defence of humanitarianism', *Disasters*, 22(4), pp.352-60.

Strathern, M. (1988) *The Gender of the Gift*, University of California Press, London.

Swift, R. (1998) 'The Cocoa Chain', *New Internationalist*, August, pp.7–30.

Talero, E. & Guadette, P. (1995) 'Harnessing information for development: a proposal for a World Bank Group vision and strategy', *Information Technology for Development*, 6(3/4), pp.145–88.

Taylor, C. (1990) *Sources of the Self: the making of the modern identity*, Harvard University Press, Cambridge MA.

Thaiss, G. (1972) 'Religious symbolism and social change: the drama of Husain', in Keddie, N. (ed.) *Scholars, Saints and Sufis*, University of California Press, Berkeley.

Thelwell, M. (1982) 'Looking for work in Kingston', in Johnson, H. & Bernstein, H. (eds) *Third World Lives of Struggle*, Heinemann, London.

Therborn, G. (1978) 'The rule of capital and the rise of democracy', *New Left Review*, no.103 (May–June), pp.3–41.

Thomas, A. (1996) 'What is development management?', *Journal of International Development*, 8(1), pp.95–110.

Thomas, A. & Crow, B. (1994) *The Third World Atlas*, Open University Press, Buckingham.

Thomas, J. J. (1995) *Surviving in the City? The Urban Informal Sector in Latin America*, Pluto, London.

Tiffen, M. (1995) 'Population density, economic growth and societies in transition: Boserup reconsidered in a Kenyan case-study', *Development and Change*, 26(1), pp.31–65.

Tinker, H. (1974) *A New System of Slavery*, Oxford University Press, Oxford.

Todaro, M. (1976) *Internal Migration in Developing Countries*, International Labour Organization, Geneva.

Todaro, M. (1997) *Economic Development* (6th edn), Longman, Harlow.

Toole, M. J. & Waldman, R. J. (undated, *c.*1988) 'Mortality trends in refugee emergencies: an analysis of refugee populations in Thailand, Somalia and Sudan', Center for Disease Control, Atlanta, Georgia (manuscript).

Townsend, P. (1979) *Poverty in the United Kingdom*, Penguin, Harmondsworth.

Toye, J. (1987) *Dilemmas of Development*, Blackwell, Oxford.

Trape, J. F. & Rogier, C. (1996) 'Combating malaria morbidity and mortality by reducing transmission', *Parasitology Today*, 12, pp.236–40.

Trindade, S. (1991) in Bhalla, A. S. (ed.) *Small and Medium Enterprises: technology policies and options*, Intermediate Technology Publications, London.

Tripp, A. M. (1997) 'Deindustrialization and the growth of women's economic associations and networks in urban Tanzania', in Visvanathan, N. *et al. The Women, Gender and Development Reader*, Zed Books, London.

Troebst, S. (1997) 'An ethnic war that did not take place', in Turton, D. (ed.) *War and Ethnicity*, University of Rochester Press, New York.

Tucker, V. (ed.) (1997) *Cultural Perspectives on Development*, Frank Cass, London.

Turner, J. (1972) 'Housing as a verb', in Turner, J. & Fichter, R. (eds) *Freedom to Build*, pp.148–75, Macmillan, New York.

Turner, J. (1976) *Housing by People: towards autonomy in building environments*, Marion Boyars, London.

Turner, M. & Hulme, D. (1997) *Governance, Administration and Development: making the state work*, Macmillan Press, Basingstoke.

Turton, D. (1988) 'Anthropology and development', in Leeson, P. & Minougue, M. (eds) *Perspectives on Development*, Manchester University Press, Manchester.

Turton, D. (1994) 'Mursi political identity and warfare: the survival of an idea', in Fukui, K. & Markakis, J. (eds) *Ethnicity and Conflict in the Horn of Africa*, James Currey, London.

Turton, D. (ed.) (1997) *War and Ethnicity: global connections and local violence*, University of Rochester Press, New York.

UN (1989) *World Population Prospects 1988*, United Nations, New York.

UN (1996) *The Blue Helmets: a review of United Nations peace-keeping*, United Nations, New York.

UNAIDS (1998) *HIV and Infant Feeding: a review of HIV transmission through breastfeeding* (May), United Nations Programme on HIV/AIDS.

UNCHS (Habitat) (1986) *Global Report on Human Settlements 1986*, Oxford University Press, Oxford, for the United Nations Centre for Human Settlements (Habitat).

UNCHS (Habitat) (1996) *An Urbanizing World: global report on human settlements 1996*, Oxford University Press, Oxford, for the United Nations Centre for Human Settlements (Habitat).

UNCTAD (1998) *The Least Developed Countries: 1998 Report*, UN Conference on Trade and Development, Geneva.

UNDP (1990, 1994, 1997b, 1998a) *Human Development Report*, Oxford University Press, New York.

UNDP (1997a) *The Shrinking State*, United Nations Development Programme, New York.

UNDP (1998b) *Globalization and Liberalization*, United Nations Development Programme, New York.

UNDP (1998c) *Information and Communication Technologies for Development*, United Nations Development Programme, New York. Also on Internet website: http://www.undp.org/info21/

UNFPA (1989) *The State of the World Population 1989*, United Nations Fund for Population Activities, New York.

UNFPA (1990a) *Investing in Women: the focus of the '90s*, United Nations Fund for Population Activities, New York.

UNFPA (1990b) *Population Issues: a briefing kit*, New York, United Nations Fund for Population Activities, New York.

UNFPA (1998) *The State of the World Population 1998*, United Nations Fund for Population Activities, New York.

UNHCR (1995) *The State of the World's Refugees*, Oxford University Press, Oxford.

UNICEF (1995, 1996, 1997) *Annual Report*, UNICEF, Geneva.

UNICEF (1998) *The State of the World's Children 1997*, UNICEF, New York.

UNICEF (1999) *The State of the World's Children 1998–99*, UNICEF, New York.

United Nations (1998) *Demographic Yearbook 1996*, United Nations, New York.

United Nations (1998) *UN World Economic and Social Survey 1998*, United Nations, Geneva.

UNRISD (1993) *Rebuilding Wartorn Societies*, UN Research Institute for Social Development, Geneva.

UNRISD (1994) *The Challenge of Rebuilding War-Torn Societies*, UN Research Institute for Social Development, Geneva.

van de Sande, T. (1994) 'On the exposure of Trojan horses', *Biotechnology and Development Monitor*, 19, p.24.

van Loesch, H. (1996) 'The Green Revolution protects the environment', *Biotechnology and Development Monitor*, 29, p.24.

Vaughan, M. (1985) 'Famine analysis and family relations: 1949 in Nyasaland', *Past and Present*, 108 (August), pp.177–205.

Vijayaraghavan, K., Rameshwar Sarma, K. V., Rao, N. P. & Reddy, V. (1984) 'Impact of massive doses of vitamin A on incidence of nutritional blindness', *The Lancet*, 2, pp.149–51.

Vivian, J. (1994) 'NGOs and sustainable development in Zimbabwe: no magic bullets', *Development and Change*, 25(1), pp.167–93.

Wade, R. (1990) *Governing the Market*, Princeton University Press, Princeton NJ.

Walgate, R. (1990) *Miracle or Menace? Biotechnology and the Third World*, Panos, London.

Walker, R. B. J. (1988) *One World, Many Worlds: struggles for a just world peace*, L.Rienner, Boulder CO.

Wallace, D. (1996) *Sustainable Industrialization*, Earthscan; The Royal Institute of International Affairs, London.

Wallensteen, P. & Sollenberg, M. (1998) 'Armed conflict and regional conflict complexes, 1989–97', *Journal of Peace Research*, 35(5), pp.621–34.

Walsh, J. & Warren, K. (1979) 'Selective primary health care: an interim strategy for disease control in developing countries', *New England Journal of Medicine*, 301(18), pp.967–74.

Ward, P. (1982) *Self-Help Housing: a critique*, Mansell, London.

Warnock, J. W. (1988) *The Politics of Hunger*, Methuen, Toronto.

Washbrook, D. A. (1981) 'Law, state and agrarian society in colonial India', *Modern Asian Studies*, 15(3), pp.649–721.

Waterman, P. (1998) *Globalization, Social Movements, and the New Internationalisms*, Mansell/Cassell, London.

Watkins, K. (1995) *The Oxfam Poverty Report*, Oxfam (UK and Ireland), Oxford.

Watts, M. & Peet, R. (1996) 'Towards a theory of liberation ecology', in Peet, R. & Watts, M. (eds) *Liberation Ecologies: environment, development and social movements*, Routledge, London.

Waylen, G. (1997) 'Gender, feminism and political economy', *New Political Economy*, 2(2), pp.205–20.

WCED (1987) *Our Common Future* (The Brundtland Report), Oxford University Press, Oxford.

Weber, M. (1976 [1904–5]) *The Protestant Ethic and the Spirit of Capitalism*, 2nd edn, 1st translation 1930, George Allen and Unwin, London.

Wei Hu (1998) 'Mining liberalization, resource and environmental depletion in the fragile loess plateau, China', paper given at Workshop on 'Participatory Natural Resource Management', Mansfield College, Oxford, April 1998.

Weiss, L. (1998) *State Capacity: governing the economy in a global era*, Polity Press, Cambridge.

Werner, D. (1977) 'The village health worker – lackey or liberator?' Paper presented at the International Hospital Federation Congress, Tokyo, Japan, May 22–27.

Werner, D. (1983) 'Health care in Cuba: a model service or a means of social control – or both?', pp.17–38 in Morley, D., Rohde, J. & Williams, G. (eds) *Practising Health for All*, Oxford University Press, Oxford.

West, K. P., Pokhrel, R. P., Katz, J., LeClerq, S., Khatry, S. K., Tielsch, J. M., Pandey, M. R. & Sommer, A. (1991) 'Efficiency of vitamin A in reducing preschool child mortality: a randomised, double-masked community trial in Nepal', *The Lancet*, 338, pp.67–71.

Whitcombe, E. (1972) *Agrarian Conditions in Northern India*. Vol.1: *The United Provinces under British Rule, 1860–1900*, University of California Press, Berkeley.

White, G. (1996) 'Development and democratization in China', pp.209–29 in Leftwich, A. (ed.) *Democracy and Development*, Polity Press, Cambridge.

White, G. (1998) 'Constructing a democratic developmental state', in Robinson, M. & White, G. (eds) *The Democratic Developmental State: politics and institutional design*, ch.1, Oxford University Press, Oxford.

Whitehead, A. (1990) 'Food crisis and gender conflict in the African countryside', in Bernstein, H. *et al.* (eds) *The Food Question: profits versus people?*, Earthscan, London.

Whitehead, A. (1994) 'Food symbolism, gender power and family', in Harriss-White, B. & Hoffenberg, R. (eds) *Food: multidisciplinary perspectives*, Blackwell, Oxford.

Whiteside, A. (1998) 'A global pandemic', *The Health Exchange*, August, pp.4–5.

WHO (1998) *The World Health Report*, World Health Organization, Geneva.

Williams, R. (1958) *Culture and Society*, Pelican, Harmondsworth.

Williams, R. (1974) *Television: technology and cultural form*, Fontana, London.

Williams, R. (1976) *Keywords*, Fontana, London.

Williams, R. (1979) *Politics and Letters: interviews with New Left Review*, NLB, London.

Wilson, G. A. (1996) 'From day-to-day coping to strategic management: developing technological capability among small-scale enterprises in Zimbabwe, *International Journal of Technology Management*, pp.488–99.

Wilson, H. (1994) *African Decolonization*, Edward Arnold, London.

Winner, L. (1977) *Autonomous Technology: technics-out-of-control as a theme in political thought*, Massachusetts Institute of Technology Press, Cambridge, MA.

Wirth, L. (1938) 'Urbanism as a way of life', *American Journal of Sociology*, 44, pp.1–24.

Wittfogel, K. (1957) *Oriental Despotism*, Yale University Press, New Haven.

Womack, P. *et al.* (1990)*The Machine That Changed The World*, Macmillan, New York.

Women's Budget Group (1998) *The Purse or the Wallet*? Seminar report, Fawcett Society, London.

Woodhouse, P. (1992) 'Social and environmental change in sub-Saharan Africa', in Bernstein, H., Crow, B. & Johnson, H. (eds) *Rural Livelihoods: crises and responses*, Oxford University Press, Oxford, with The Open University, Milton Keynes.

Woods, N. (1999) 'Order, globalization and inequality in world politics', in Hurrell, A. & Woods, N. (eds) *Globalization, Inequality and World Order*, Oxford University Press, Oxford.

World Bank (1980, 1990) *World Development Report*, The World Bank, Washington DC.

World Bank (1983) *The Effect of Piped Water on Early Childhood Mortality in Urban Brazil, 1970–76*, Thomas Merrick, World Bank, Washington DC.

World Bank (1985) *Quantitative Studies of Mortality Decline in the Developing World*, Julie DaVanzo, Jean-Pierre Habicht, Ken Hill & Samuel Preston, World Bank, Washington DC.

World Bank (1986) *Poverty and Hunger*, World Bank, Washington DC.

World Bank (1993, 1996) *World Development Report*, Oxford University Press, New York.

World Bank (1991) *Urban Policy and Economic Development: an agenda for the 1990s*, World Bank, Washington DC.

World Bank (1992) *Governance and Development*, World Bank, Washington DC.

World Bank (1993b) *Paradigm Postponed: gender and economic adjustment in sub-Saharan Africa*, Technical Note (August), Human Resources and Poverty Division, Africa Region, World Bank, Washington DC.

World Bank (1995) *World Development Report: workers in an integrating world*, Oxford University Press, New York.

World Bank (1997a) *Confronting AIDS: public priorities in a global epidemic*, Oxford University Press, Oxford.

World Bank (1997b) *World Development Report: the state in a changing world*, Oxford University Press, New York.

World Bank (1998) *World Development Report 1998/99: knowledge for development*, Oxford University Press, New York.

World Bank (1999) *World Development Report 1999/2000: Entering the 21st century: the changing development landscape*, forthcoming September 1999 (pre-publication overview, summary and consultation on http://www.worldbank.org/wdr/2000/)

World of Work (no author) (1997), 'Africa undergoing economic revival: programme for Africa: jobs policy can ignite further growth', *World of Work*, no.22 (December), pp.25–7.

Worsley, P. (1967) *The Third World*, Weidenfeld and Nicolson, London.

Worsley, P. (1979) 'How many worlds?' *Third World Quarterly*, 1(2), pp.100–8.

Worsley, P. (1984) *The Three Worlds*, Weidenfield and Nicolson, London.

Wratten, E. (1995) 'Conceptualising urban poverty', *Environment and Urbanization*, 7(1), pp.11–36.

WTO (1998) *United States: Import Prohibition of Certain Shrimp and Shrimp Products*, World Trade Organization, Geneva.

Wuyts, M. (1992) 'Deprivation and public need', in Wuyts, M., Mackintosh, M. & Hewitt, T. (eds) *Development Policy and Public Action*, Oxford University Press, Oxford, with The Open University, Milton Keynes.

Wuyts, M., Mackintosh, M. & Hewitt, T. (eds) *Development Policy and Public Action*, Oxford University Press, Oxford/The Open University, Milton Keynes. (Book 4 in this series)

Xiong Lei (1998) 'Going against the flow in China', *Science*, 280, pp.24–6.

Acknowledgements

Grateful acknowledgement is made to the following sources for permission to reproduce material in this book:

Text

Box 1.5: Davies, N. (1998) 'There is nothing natural about poverty', *New Statesman*, 6 November 1998. Copyright © 1998 New Statesman; *Box 1.6:* Bellos, A. (1998) 'Seed of hope in Amazon's urban jungle', *The Guardian*, 4 December 1998. Copyright © 1998 Alex Bellos; *Box 6.1:* From *World Development Report 1990* by World Bank. Copyright © 1980 by the International Bank for Reconstruction and Development/The World Bank. Used by permission of Oxford University Press, Inc; *Box 13.3:* UNDP (1990 and 1998) *Human Development Report 1990* and *Human Development Report 1998*, United Nations Development Programme, Oxford University Press, Inc.; *Box 18.1:* Baden and S. Goetz, A. M.(1998) 'Who needs [sex] when you can have [gender]: conflicting discourses on gender at Beijing', in Jackson, C. and Pearson, R., *Feminist Visions of Development: gender analysis and policy*, Routledge; *Box 18.2:* Moser, C. O. N. (1993*) Gender Planning and Development: theory, Practice and training*, Routledge; *Box 18.3(right):* MacAskill, E. (1999) 'Blair left dazzled by Pretoria's shining light', *The Guardian*, 8th January 1999, © *The Guardian*.

Tables

Table 1.1: UNDP (1998) *Human Development Report 1998*, Oxford University Press, Inc.; *Table 3.1:* Sen, A. (1981) *Poverty and Famines: an essay on entitlement and deprivation*, p. 163. Copyright © 1981 International Labour Organization, Geneva. Published on behalf of the ILO by Oxford University Press, Oxford; *Table 3.2:* FAO (1996*) The Sixth World Food Survey*, Food and Agriculture Organization of the United Nations; *Tables 4.1, 4.2, 4.5, 4.9: The State of the World's Children 1997*, UNICEF, 1998; *Tables 4.3, 4.6:* WHO (1998) *The World Health Report*, World Health Organisation; *Table 4.4:* UN (1998) *Demographic Yearbook 1996.* The United Nations is the author of the original material; *Tables 4.7, 4.8:* Whiteside, A. (1998)

'A global pandemic', *The Health Exchange*, August 1998, International Health Exchange; *Table 5.4:* Sethuraman, S. U. (1981) *Urban Sector in Developing Countries*, Geneva, ILO. Copyright © International Labour Organization 1981; *Table 5.5:* Gilbert, A. (1997) 'Employment and poverty during economic restructuring: The case of Bogotà, Colombia, *Urban Studies*, 34(7) 1997, Taylor and Francis Ltd (Carfax Publishing Taylor and Francis Group); *Table 8.1:* Reprinted by permission of Sage Publications Ltd from Wallensteen, P. & Sollenberg, M. (1998) 'Armed conflict and regional conflict complexes 1989-97', *Journal of Peace Research*, vol. 35, no. 5. Copyright © 1998 Sage Publications Ltd; *Table 13.2:* from http://www.un.org/events/, The United Nations is the author of the original material; *Table 15.1:* Harvey, D. (1989) *The Condition of Postmodernity*, Blackwell Publishers Ltd; *Table 16.1:* UNDP (1997) *Human Development Report*, United Nations Development Programme; *Table 16.3:* adapted from Elazar; D. J. (1998) *Constitutionalizing Globalization*, Rowman and Littlefield Publishers Inc.; *Table 20.1:* Satterthwaite, D. (1996) 'The scale and nature of urban change in the South', Human Settlements Programme, International Institute for Environment and Development, June 1996; *Table 20.2:* Moser, C. and Holland, J. (1997) *Urban Poverty and Violence in Jamaica*, The World Bank; *Table 24.2:* Wallace, D. (1996) *Sustainable Industrialization*, Energy and Environment Programme, The Royal Institute of International Affairs, Earthscan Publications Ltd;

Cover/part title page photographs

Outer front cover: Background: © A.P.Photo/ David Guttenfelder; *Inset:* © UNHCR/ H.J.Davies; *Part title pages: Part I* (Ugandan children helping to build their own school): © Tim Allen; *Part II* (internally displaced person, Tuzla airbase, Bosnia & Herzegovina): © UNHCR/ 25105/08.1885/R.LeMoyne; *Part III* (Soviet miners): David King Collection; *Part IV* (sporting practice at 'China Little Heroes' private school, China): © Chris Stowers/Panos Pictures; *Part V* (Brazilian child with engine): © Jenny Matthews/ Oxfam.

Figures

Figure 1.1(above): © Associated Press; *Figure 1.1(below):* © Popperfoto; *Figure 1.2:* © Christopher Pillitz/Network Photographers; *Figure 2.1 and 2.6:* © R. K. Laxman in *The Times of India*; *Figure 2.2:* © Sharma Studio, New Delhi; *Figure 2.3:* © Rachid Ait-Kaci, Morocco, reproduced from Regan, C., Sinclair, S. and Turner, M. (1988) *Thin Black Lines*, Birmingham Education Development Centre; *Figure 2.4:* Reproduced from Regan, C., Sinclair, S. and Turner, M. (1988) *Thin Black Lines*, Birmingham Education Development Centre; *Figure 2.5:* © Pan-Asia Newspaper Alliance (PANA)/Fotomedia; *Figure 3.1:* © R. K. Laxman. Reproduced by courtesy of *New Internationalist*; *Figure 3.2(left):* © ICRC/Thierry Gassmann; *Figures 3.2(right), 3.7:* © ICRC/Halvor Fossum Lauritzen; *Figures 3.3, 3.4, 3.5:* © Mark Edwards/Still Pictures; *Figure 3.6:* © Mike Goldwater/Network; *Figure 3.8:* Reproduced by courtesy of *New Internationalist*; *Figure 3.9:* © UNHCR/A. Hollman; *Figures 4.1, 4.7:* © John and Penny Hubley; *Figure 4.2:* © Julio Etchart/PANOS Pictures; *Figure 4.8:* © Jenny Matthews/Oxfam; *Figures 4.9, 4.10:* UNAIDS (1997) *Aids: A Challenge for Government*, July 1997; *Figure 4.11(above):* © Sean Sprague/Panos Pictures; *Figure 4.11(below):* © Jeremy Horner/Panos Pictures; *Figure 4.13:* © Oxfam; *Figure 5.1(top left):* © Walter Holt/Oxfam; *Figure 5.1(top right)* © Maggie Murray/Format; *Figure 5.1(below left) and 5.6(above):* © Hartmut Schwarzbach/Still Pictures; *Figure 5.2:* © John and Penny Hubley; *Figure 5.3(above):* © Hjalte Tim/Still Pictures; *Figure 5.3(below) and 5.8:* © Mark Edward/Still Pictures; *Figure 5.4:* Castells, M. (1997) *The Power of Identity*, Blackwell Publishers Ltd. Copyright © Manuel Castells 1997; *Figure 5.5(both):* © Shahidal Alam/Oxfam; *Figure 5.6(below):* © Heine Pedersen/Still Pictures; *Figure 6.2:* © Oxfam; *Figure 6.3(left):* © Tom Hewitt/Ines Smyth; *Figure 6.4:* © Tom Hewitt; *Figure 6.5(right):* © International Planned Parenthood Federation; *Figure 6.5 top left:* © Maggie Murray/Format; *Figure 6.5 below left:* © Sally and Richard Greenhill; *Figure 7.1(above):* © Manchester City Art Galleries; *Figure 7.1(below):* © Sally and Richard Greenhill; *Figure 7.2:* © Associated Press/Greg Baker; *Figure 7.3:* © Associated Press/Gregory Bull; *Figure 7.5:* © Financial Times; *Figure 7.6(both):* © Nigel Dickinson/Leader Photos; *Figure 7.7(top):* © Mark Edwards/Still Pictures; *Figure 7.7(middle):* © Puttkamer/The Hutchison Library; *Figure 7.7(bottom):* © Popperfoto; *Figure 7.8:* © Bruce Petty. Reproduced from Regan, C., Sinclair, S. and Turner, M. (1988) *Thin Black Lines*, Birmingham Education Development Centre; *Figure 8.1:* © UNICEF/94-0883/Roger LeMoyne; *Figures 8.2, 8.3:* Gantzel, K. J. (1997) 'War in the post-World War II world: some empirical trends and a theoretical approach', in Turton, D. (ed.) *War and Ethnicity: Global Connections and Local Violence*, University of Rochester Press; *Figure 8.4:* This figure was prepared as a report to the Carnegie Commission on *Preventing Deadly Conflict* and appears here with the permission of the Commission. Copyright 1997 by Carnegie Corporation of New York. Reprinted 1998. To order this publication or other Commission reports, please contact the Commission at 1779 Massachusetts Avenue, NW, Washington, DC 20036-2103, or by e-mail at pdc@carnegie.org. Reports are also available on the Commission's Web site: www.ccpdc.org; *Figure 8.5:* © UNHCR/1994/B.Press; *Figure 8.7:* © UNHCR/1996/B.Press; *Figure 8.6:* Hampton, J. (ed.) *Internally Displaced People – A Global Survey*, Kogan Page Limited, London; *Figure 8.7:* © UNHCR/1996/B.Press; *Figure 8.8:* © UNICEF/94-0877/Roger LeMoyne; *Figure 8.9:* © UNICEF/HQ97-0718/Robert Grossman; *Figure 8.10(left):* © UNICEF/HQ97-0594/Roger LeMoyne; *Figure 8.10(right):* © Giacomo Pirozzi/Panos Pictures; *Figure 8.12:* © UNHCR/T. Moumtzis; *Figure 9.1:* © Sharma Studio, New Delhi; *Figure 9.2:* Reproduced from the work *The All-India Muslim League: from the late Nineteenth Century to 1919*, with due permission of the author, Muhammad Saleem Ahmad, Department of History and Pakistan Studies, Islamia University, Bahawalpur, Pakistan; *Figure 9.3:* Department of Public Information (1998) *Basic Facts About The United Nations*, United Nations, USA; *Figure 9.4:* © UNHCR/H. J. Davies; *Figure 9.5:* *The Reality of Aid 1998/1999*, Earthscan Publications Ltd; *Figure 9.6:* © UNCHR/24246/

07.1994/H. J. Davies; *Figure 9.7(above):* © Paul Smith/Panos Pictures; *Figure 9.7(below):* © Martin Godwin; *Figures 10.1, 10.6, 10.7:* © Mary Evans Picture Library; *Figure 10.2:* © Carlos Pasini, *Disappearing World*, Alan Hutchison Library; *Figure 10.3:* © Hulton Getty; *Figure 10.4:* © Popperfoto; *Figures 10.5, 10.6:* © Victoria & Albert Picture Library; *Figure 11.3:* © The National Museum of Denmark, Department of Ethnography. Photographer: Lennart Larsen; *Figure 11.4:* Reproduced from *Judy Magazine*, 28th January 1885; *Figure 11.5(left):* © Mary Evans Picture Library; *Figure 11.5(right):* Courtesy of Punch Ltd; *Figures 11.6, 11.7:* © Katz Pictures (Mansell Collection); *Figure 11.8:* © Murray Ball. Reproduced from Regan, C., Sinclair, S. and Turner, M. (1988) *Thin Black Lines*, Birmingham Development Education Centre; *Figure 11.9:* © Victoria & Albert Picture Library; *Figure 12.1(b):* Wilson, H. (1994) *African Decolonization*, Edward Arnold (Publishers) Limited; *Figure 12.2:* © Victoria & Albert Picture Library; *Figure 12.4:* By permission of The British Library; *Figure 12.5:* © Mary Evans Picture Library; *Figure 12.6:* © Roger-Viollet Collection; *Figure 12.7:* © Camera Press; *Figure 13.1:* © The Hutchison Library; *Figure 13.3:* © Walter Holt/Oxfam; *Figure 13.5:* Reprinted with permission of The World Bank, 1818 H Street, NW, Washington, DC 20433. *World Development Report*, 1998. Reproduced by permission of the publisher via Copyright Clearance Center, Inc.; *Figure 13.6:* unknown source; *Figure 13.7:* © Cartoon by Wasserman, USA. Reproduced from Regan, C., Sinclair, S. & Turner, M. (1988) *Thin Black Lines*, Birmingham Development Education Centre; *Figure 13.8:* © Mykel Nicolaou/Link; *Figure 13.9:* © Associated Press/Greg Baker; *Figures 14.1, 14.2(b):* © David King Collection; *Figure 14.3:* © Sally and Richard Greenhill; *Figure 14.4(above):* © AP Photo/Scott Sady; *Figure 14.4(below):* © Karen Robinson/Format; *Figure 15.1(above):* © Hartmut Schwarzbach/Still Pictures; *Figure 15.1(below):* © Jorgen Schytte/Still Pictures; *Figure 16.1:* © Stuart Isett/Sygma; *Figure 16.2:* Reprinted with permission from *Foreign Policy*, 111 (Summer 1998). Copyright by the Carnegie Endowment for International Peace; *Figure 16.3:* © Sally Wiener Grotta/The Stock Market; *Figure 16.4:* Held, D. and McGrew, A. *et al.* (1999) *Global Transformations: Politics, Economics and Culture*, Union of International Associations; *Figures 17.1, 17.2, 17.3 and 17.6:* © Popperfoto; *Figure 17.4 :* © Jenny Matthews/Oxfam; *Figure 17.5:* The Hindu, Chennai; *Figure 18.1:* © AP Photo/Eduardo Verdugo; *Figure 18.2:* © Popperfoto/Reuter; *Figure 18.3:* The Open Univeresity; *Figure 19.1(above) :* © Jorgen Schytte/Still Pictures; *Figure 19.1(below):* © Maggie Murray/Format; *Figure 19.2:* © G. G. Moreno/Oxfam; *Figures 20.1(both), 20.3, 20.4:* © Jo Beall; *Figure 20.2:* © Mike Goldwater/Oxfam; *Figure 21.1:* © Abbas/Magnum Photos; *Figure 21.2:* © Popperfoto; *Figure 21.3:* © Jeremy Hartley/Oxfam; *Figure 21.4(above):* every effort has been made to trace the copyright holder; *Figure 21.4(below):* © Maggie Murray/Format; *Figure 22.1:* © Popperfoto/Reuter; *Figure 22.2:* © Private Eye, Jan 1999/Goddard; *Figure 22.3:* © Sean Mackaoui/*El Mundo*; *Figure 23.1:* © UNHCR/22037/05.1992/A. Hollman; *Figure 23.2:* © Murray Ball. Reproduced from Regan, C., Sinclair, S. & Turner, M. (1988) *Thin Black Lines*, Birmingham Development Education Centre; *Figure 23.3:* © Gun Kessle/Tiofoto, Stockholm; *Figure 23.4:* © UNHCR/23076/11.1993/B. Press; *Figure 23.5:* © UNHCR/25116/08.1995/R. LeMoyne; *Figure 23.6:* © UNHCR/25139/09.1995/A. Kazinierakis; *Figure 23.7:* © Andrew Testa/*The Guardian*, 26th June 1999; *Figure 24.1:* © Tom Hanley; *Figure 24.2:* Cartoon reproduced from *South – The Third World Magazine*; *Figure 24.3:* Ernst Ulrich von Weizacker (1994) *Earth Politics*, Zed Books Ltd; *Figure 24.4:* © Hartmut Schwarzbach/Still Pictures; *Figure 24.5:* © S. Salgado/Network.

Every effort has been made to trace all copyright owners, but if any have been inadvertently overlooked, the publishers will be pleased to make the necessary arrangements at the first opportunity.

Acronyms, abbreviations and organizations

AIDS	acquired immune deficiency syndrome (or immunodeficiency)
ANC	African National Congress (South Africa)
ASEAN	Association of South East Asian Nations
BBC	British Broadcasting Corporation
CEDAW	Convention to Eliminate All Forms of Discrimination Against Women
CFCs	chlorofluorocarbons
CGIAR	Consultative Group on International Agricultural Research
CMR	crude mortality rate
CNN	Cable News Network
CSCE	Commission on Security and Cooperation in Europe
DFID	Department for International Development (UK)
DNA	deoxyribonucleic acid
EC	European Community (incorporated into the European Union in 1995)
ECOSOC	Economic and Social Council (United Nations)
EU	European Union
FAO	Food and Agriculture Organization of the United Nations
G7	Group of Seven (leading industrialized countries)
G77	Group of Seventy-Seven (political grouping of developing countries)
G8	Group of Eight (G7 plus Russia)
GAD	gender and development
GATT	General Agreement on Tariffs and Trade (succeeded by World Trade Organization)
GDP	gross domestic product
GM	genetically modified
GMO	genetically modified organism
GNP	gross national product
HDI	Human Development Index
HEIA	high-external-input agriculture
HIV	human immuno-deficiency virus
HPI	Human Poverty Index
HYV	high-yielding variety
IBRD	International Bank for Reconstruction and Development (the main part of the World Bank)
ICPD	International Conference on Population and Development
ICRC	International Committee of the Red Cross
IDA	International Development Association (soft loan window of the World Bank)
ILO	International Labour Organization
IMF	International Monetary Fund
IPCC	Intergovernmental Panel on Climate Change
ISI	import substitution industrialization
IT	information technology
LDCs	less developed countries
LEIA	low-external-input agriculture
LLDCs	least developed countries
LMO	living modified organism
MERCOSUR	South American Common Market
MNC	multinational corporation
MP	Member of Parliament (UK)

MSF	Médécins Sans Frontières
NAM	non-aligned movement
NASA	National Aeronautics and Space Administration (USA)
NATO	North Atlantic Treaty Organization
NEP	New Economic Policy (USSR, 1920s)
NGOs	non-governmental organizations
NICs	newly industrializing countries
NIEO	New International Economic Order
NRM	National Resistance Movement (Uganda)
ODA	official development assistance
OECD	Organization for Economic Co-operation and Development
OPEC	Organization of Petroleum Exporting Countries
PLA	participative learning and action
PNG	Papua New Guinea
PPP	purchasing power parity (dollars)
PRA	participative rural appraisal
PTD	participatory technology development
R&D	research and development
RPF	Rwanda Patriotic Front
SAP	structural adjustment policy
SIPRI	Stockholm International Peace Research Institute
SPLA	Sudan People's Liberation Army
TFR	total fertility rate
U5MR	under-five mortality rate
UK	United Kingdom
UN	United Nations
UNCHS	United Nations Conference on Human Settlements (Habitat)
UNCTAD	United Nations Conference on Trade and Development
UNDP	United Nations Development Programme
UNFPA	United Nations Population Fund
UNHCR	Office of the United Nations' High Commissioner for Refugees
UNICEF	United Nations (International) Children's (Emergency) Fund
USA	United States of America
USAID	United States Agency for International Development
USSR	Union of Soviet Socialist Republics
WED	women, environment and development
WFP	World Food Programme
WHO	World Health Organization
WID	women in development
WTO	World Trade Organization
WWF	World Wide Fund for Nature

Index

Page numbers in bold type indicate definition boxes in the text

accountability, and 'good governance' 380
accumulation 38
acid rain 143
action learning 411
advocacy, and development NGOs 210
Afghanistan
    land mines in 178, 179
    socialist regime in 319–20
    supply of weapons to 177–8
Africa
    cities 425
    colonialism in 242, 244, 245, 249, 264
    and the doctrines of development 267, 269
    economic activity rates 104, 105
    employment in 103
    and European capitalism 221
    famine prevention 73
    industrialization 295
    Islam in 236–7
    life expectancy 81
    malaria in 75
    mortality rates 77, 78, 81, 168–9
    pastoralists and cattle complex 454–7
    post-colonial states in 198–9
    pre-capitalist states in 226, 229, 236–7
    tribalism and ethnicity 492, 493
    undernourished people 66, 67
    unemployment in 101
    women 68, 69
    see also North Africa; South Africa; sub-Saharan Africa; West Africa
agencies
    and democratization 375
    development 40–1, 47–8, 189–216
    famine relief 64–5
    and population policies 137–8
    and violence against women 389
agency **189**
    and democratization 370
Agenda 21 161
agricultural development 31
    and biotechnology 469–84
    cash crop production 70–1
    and colonial rule 272–3
    and industrialization 511–14, 515, 517
    and Soviet collectivization 313
agricultural involution 455, 456
agricultural prices, effects of fall in 153, 154
agricultural protectionism 151–2

agricultural trade, and global politics 357
agricultural work 109, 117
AIDS (Acquired Immune Deficiency Syndrome) 89–95, 98
Akbar, Mogul emperor 239
Algar, Hamid 449
alternative development 28, 29, 32–6, 530
    analytical and normative aspects of 42
    and immanent development 36
    and 'mainstream' development 47–8
    see also people-centred development
alternative technology 405, 406
America
    colonization of 242, 245–7
    see also Latin America; United States
amoral familism 455
analytical aspects of development **42**
Anderson, Benedict, Imagined Communities 490, 491, 496, 504
Anderson, Perry 340
Annan, Kofi 380
anthropological approaches to culture 444, 446, 447, 460–5
appropriate technology 405
appropriation 38
Arab world, and Islam 233–5
Argentina
    biotechnology networks in 483
    genetically modified soybeans in 476
armed conflicts 165–6
arms trade 176–9
Arrow, Kenneth 525
ASEAN (Association of South East Asian Nations), biotechnology corporation 483
Asia
    child labour in 433
    cities 425
    colonialism in 242, 244, 265, 269
    and democratization 365, 371–2
    and the developmental state 196, 215
    and the doctrines of development 267
    economic activity rates 104, 105
    employment in 103
    forced labour regimes 258
    life expectancy 81
    mortality rates 77, 81
    socialist countries in 310

undernourished people in 66, 67, 74
unemployment in 101
see also Central Asia; East/South-east Asia; South Asia
Asian model of capitalism 359
asylum seekers 172
atmospheric pollution, global effects of 142–4
authoritarian regimes 365–6, 368, 369, 374, 375
    and economic development 377–8
authoritarianism
    and colonial rule **275**, 275–6, 285, 286, 288
    patrimonial authority **280**
    'traditional' authority figures 276–80
Aztec civilization 228

Bailey, F.G. 455
Bakongo, kingdom of the 226
'balance sheet' of human development 6, 7
Balla, Surjit 375
Banfield, Edward, The Moral Basis in a Backward Society 455
Bangladesh
    child workers in 102
    garment factories of Dhaka 434
    Grameen Bank 396–7
    making a living in 109–10
    war of independence 170
    women and food in 69
Barth, Frederik 493
Beijing World Conference on Women (1995) 384, 386
    Platform for Action 387
Berlin wall 12
Berman, Marshall 24
Bernier, François 220
Best, Michael, and the 'New Competition' 523
Bhutan, alternative technology in 406
biotechnology 409, **469**, 469–84
    anti-biotechnology perspective 471
    and Biosafety Protocol 480–1, 482
    free market vision of 479–80, 484
    and the Green Revolution 474–5
    partnership and networking vision of 482–4
    and patent rights 478–9
    pro-biotechnology perspective 470–1
    progress and development visions 469–74

regulated development vision of 480–2, 484
and the world food market 475–7
see also GM (genetically modified) crops
birth control 129, 136, **137**, 138
birth rates 126
    crude birth rate **126**
    and demographic transition theory 128
Bismarck, Count Otto von 486
Blair, Tony 328, 389
Boas, Franz 446
Bogatà, formal and informal employment 109
Bombay 430, 440
Bosnia & Herzegovina
    refugees from 485, 497
    war in 166, 173
Botswana 196, 285
Boyer, Robert 330, 334
Brandt Report 299
Brazil
    cities 431
    development of the Amazon 158, 159
    import substitution industrialization 294–5
    Mundurucu 'Indians' 222–6
    poverty in 15, 18
    and socialism 321, 322
    urban explosion in 298
    wealth, disease and public policy in 95–7
breastfeeding, and HIV transmission 94–5
Bretton Woods agreements (1944) 204, 291, 292, 299
Britain
    collective identities in 486
    and colonial rule in India 271, 272, 274–9, 281–2, 283, 284, 285, 290
    and colonial state development 267
    colonies 247, 248, 249, 251
    decline of heavy industry 510
    DFID (Department for International Development) 305–6, 385
    diseases in nineteenth-century 84–5
    multiculturalism in 494–5
    Overseas Development Administration 380
    poverty in 17
    and the slave trade 254, 255
British East India Company 220–1
Brittan, Samuel 336
Bromley, Yulian 494, 495

Brown, Lester, *The State of the World* 148
Brundtland Commission 34, 142, 144, 145, 158, 160
Buganda, kingdom of 221, 229
built environment, and urban poverty 432
Bukharin, Nikolai 312
bureaucracies
    and colonial rule 275–6
    and the state 191, 194–5
Bush, George 9
Byzantine empire 234

Cambodia 310
capitalism **242**, 325–42
    and colonialism 220–1, 240, 241–63, 270
    and communism 8, 10, 22
    and the dependency school 46
    and development 21, 22, 23, 24–9, 36, 42–7, 48
    development of 4
    dynamics of growth 37–9
    elements of global 27–8
    and flexible accumulation (Toyotism) 330, 332–9
    and Fordism 330, 331–2, 334–5, 337, 339, 340, 342
    and the 'great transformation' 220–1, 241, 244, 267, 289, 326–9, 338–41, 427, 428
    and historical process 36–7
    and imperialism 248–52, **250**
    industrial capitalism 32, 246, 248–52, 266, 267
    'industrial district' model of 334
    and interventionalism 26–8, 29, 43, 45–8
    in Japan 503
    and labour 242–3, 253–62
    liberal 9–10, 36
    and Marxism 45
    mercantile 220, 227, 233, 243, 246, 265–6
    and the Mogul empire 233
    monopoly capitalism 43, 246, 249, **250**
    and neoliberal views of development 42–5
    and postmodernity 340–1
    and primitive accumulation 243
    and regimes of accumulation **329**, 329–30
    spirit of 444–5
    and the state 190, 192–3
capitalist authoritarian regimes 366
carbon dioxide emissions 144–5
    reducing 146–7

selling rights 159
Caribbean
    colonialism 245, 247
    indentured labour 258
    slavery 255
    urban centres 428
Carson, Rachel, *Silent Spring* 142
cash crop production, and hunger 70–1
caste system in India 231, 238, 240
Castells, Manuel 326, 335, 336, 338, 339–40, 436, 440, 483–4, 500
    The Power of Identity 486, 502–5
cattle complex 454–7
Central Asia
    Aral Sea Basin 145
    economic activity rates 104
    employment in 103
    setbacks in development 6
CFCs (chlorofluorocarbons) 143
CGIAR (Consultative Group on International Agricultural Research) 483
Chad 198
Chambers, Robert 21, 530–1
child benefit payments 395–6
child mortality **78**, 98
    in Brazil 95
    and literacy 82
    and poverty 83–4
    and selective biomedical interventions 86, 87–8
    in Sri Lanka 95
    and undernutrition 83–4
    see also infant mortality
Child Survival Development Revolution 86
children
    and the 'balance sheet' of human development 7
    child labour 102, 134, 135, 433
    child soldiers 180
    famine and hunger 68
    with HIV 89, 91
Chile, women's groups in 390
China
    characteristics of the revolution 315
    and comprehensive primary health care 88–9
    economic growth 6, 375
    and economic reform 317–18
    and the end of the Cold War 8
    energy projects 146
    environmental problems 318
    famine in 62–3, 70
    hunger reduction 67–8
    indentured labour 258
    life expectancy 67–8, 88–9
    market socialism in 366
    Muslims in 235

empowerment 34, **35**, 41
  and micro-credit 396–8
enabling approach to shelter provision
    437–8
ENDA-Tiers-Monde 211
endowment approach to famine **60**, 74
energy consumption 145
energy projects 145–6, 147
enterprise management 28
entitlement approach to famine **60**, 61,
    62, 149
environment 8, 141–62
  and the 'balance sheet' of human
      development 7
  and ecofeminism 390–2
  ecological crisis 19
  environmental problems in China
      318
  global 47, 141–9
  and industrialization 510
  and livelihoods in the global
      economy 149–54
  and sustainable development 33, 34,
      154–62
environmental degradation 4, 36, 162,
    303, 530
  deforestation in Malaysia 154,
      156–7, 158
  in less industrialized countries
      144–9, 154
  in Niger 155
  and population 133
environmental management, and lean
    production systems 526
Eriksen, Thomas 498
Escobar, Arturo 20–1
  Encountering Development 463–4
ethic essentialism 175
Ethiopia
  famine in 55, 56–60, 61, 62, 64, 70
  socialist regime in 319
  women and the environment in 391–
      2
ethnic primordialism 494, 506, 507–8
ethnicity 491–4
  and gender 388
  meanings of 496
  and the politics of identity 485–6
  and race 495–6
  and theorists of the politics of
      identity 500–5
  and the war in Yugoslavia 497–9
ethnographic research 461–2
ethnos theory 494, 495
Europe
  and pre-capitalist societies 219–21,
      222, 240
  see also colonialism
European Community/Union 197

and globalization 357, 360, 362
  and GM crops 478–9, 481–2
European countries
  and carbon emission reduction 147
  life expectancy 81
  mortality rates 77, 81
evolution, and culture 446
exchange, and famine 58–60, **59**

families, male and female-headed
    110–11
family planning 129, 136, 137
famine **52**, 53–65
  approaches to analysing 60–2
  causes of 53
  and colonial rule 70, 71
  death in 52, 54–5
  debate on prevention and
      amelioration 71–3
  entitlement approach to famine **60**,
      61, 62, 149
  and exchange 58–60, **59**
  and gender relations 68–9
  humanitarian intervention dilemmas
      in 64–5
  and hunger 51–3, 74
  international coverage of 54, 72
  'man-made' and 'natural' 57–8
  and poverty 67, 71, 74
  pre-history of 56
  processes of 53–6, 71–2
  and production 58, **59**
  relief camps 54, 55, 72
  Sahelian 154, 155
  struggle against 62–4, 68
  and war 57, 58, 62, 73
  see also hunger
Fanon, Franz 7
  The Wretched of the Earth 8, 284
FAO (United Nations Food and
    Agriculture Organization) 203–4
  estimates of global hunger 65, 66,
      67
Fardon, Richard 499
feminism
  and development 383, 384, 386–90
  ecofeminism 390–2
Ferguson, James 462
  The Anti-Politics Machine 463
fertility **126**
  and mortality rates 127–9
  and population control 138
  rates **126**, 131
  TFR (total fertility rate) **126**
  and women 136–7
feudalism, crisis of 245–7
financial markets, deregulation of 336
First World War, and pre-capitalist
    states 251

flexible accumulation/production
    (Toyotism) 330, 332–9
food, and the 'balance sheet' of human
    development 7
food availability
  decline 60, 61
  national measures of 66
food markets, and GM crops 475–7
food shortages 52
  see also famine
forced labour
  and colonial economies 253–8, **254**,
      262
  indentured 254, 258, 262
  railway construction in the Belgian
      Congo 266
Fordism 330, 331–2, 334–5, 337, 339,
    340, 342
forest management 391–2
Foster, George 456
Foucault, M. 463
France, and nationalism 487
free press, and famine prevention 63,
    64, 73
FTZs (free trade zones) 433
Fukuyama, Francis 32, 37, 502
  on social virtues 503
  'The End of History' 9, 10, 496–7
  on trust 527

G22 Group 360
G77 (Group of Seventy-Seven) 7, 292,
    355–6, 358, 360
G7 (Group of Seven) 291, 349, 356,
    357, 358, 359, 363
G8 (Group of Eight) 291
GAD (gender and development) 384,
    390, 402
  and feminist environmentalism 392
  and gender mainstreaming 400
  and micro-credit 398
  and poverty 399–400
  and structural adjustment 394–6
Gandhi, Mahatma 271, 284, 520
GATT (General Agreement on Tariffs
    and Trade) 291, 292, 297, 301
  and GM crops 477
  Uruguay Round 152
GDP (gross domestic product) **11**
  and industrialization 31
  sectoral distribution of 295
Geertz, Clifford 453, 455, 456
Gellner, Ernest, *Nations and
    Nationalism* 490, 491, 504
gender
  analysis of micro-credit and
      women's empowerment 396–8
  analysis of structural adjustment
      393–6

and development issues 383–402
and environmental conservation 390–2
and food distribution 68–9, 400
and life expectancy 81–2
mainstreaming 400, 401
practical and strategic needs 386, 388, 398–401
relations 8, 385–6, 387
and sex 385–6
and technological knowledge 409
and technology 407–8
see also men; women
generalized commodity production 26, 27
genetic engineering **469**, 469–84
genetic modification **469**
Geneva Conventions, and war 174
Germany
and nationalism 486–7, 488, 489
reunification of 8
Ghana
cocoa production in 152, 153
and Islam 236, 237
Giddens, A. 326, 327, 335, 339
Glazer, Nathan 492, 494, 496
global cities **430**
global environment 47, 141–9
global environmental management 160–2
global threefold human crisis 6, 19, 47, 189
global warming 143, 147–8
globalization 197, 346–8, **348**
and the Asian financial crisis 346, 348
and capitalism 250, 335, 336
cities in a global economy 433–4
and democratization 373–4
and development 4, 307–8
and the developmental state 359–60
economic 336
forces driving 348
four dimensions of 347
global 'New Deal' 362–3
global politics 355–8
and industrialization 527–8, 529
inequality and world order 348–53, 363–4
and IT (information technology) 412
and neoliberalism 10, 26, 28, 29, 348–50, 353, 359, 364
of poverty 353–5
radical analysis of 349, 350–1, 364
regionalizing 361–2
regulating 360–2
resisting 362
and sustainable development 360–2, 364

and technology 403
and 'Tiersmondisme' 356, 358, 361, 364
of trade, finance and production 356–7
transformational analysis of 349, 351–3, 364
GM (genetically modified) crops **469**
and the Green Revolution 474–5
and patent rights 478–9
and world food markets 475–7
GMOs (Genetically Modified Organisms), and the EU internal market 481
GNP (gross national product) **11**
and development 30
growth rates 293
and industrialization 518–19
as a measure of poverty 12
selected countries 131
in Sri Lanka and Brazil 95, 96
'Golden Age' 292–6
and technology 404
'good change', and development 23, 48
'good governance' 365, 379–81, 382
Gorbachev, Mikhail 9, 317
Gould, Stephen Jay 325
Goulet, Denis 14
government, and the state 192
Grameen Bank, and micro-credit 396–7
Gray, John 527–8, 529
Great Transformation 220–1, 241, 244, 267, 289, 326–9, 338–41, 427, 428
Green Revolution 422
and GM (genetically modified) crops 474–5
greenhouse effect 143, 147
Greenpeace 471
Greenspan, Alan 347
Gulf War (1991) 8, 183

Halliday, Fred 447–9, 452
Harappa (ancient civilization) 230
Harman, Harriet 385–6
Harris, Marvin 460
Harvey, David 332, 333, 334, 337, 339
Social Justice and the City 427
HDI (Human Development Index) 16
and AIDS/HIV 91–2
health
and the 'balance sheet' of human development 7
comprehensive primary health care 88–9
and education 82–3
and housing 432
and mortality decline 127
and 'traditional doctors' 225

WHO definition of 75
see also disease
hegemonic ideologies 283–4, **284**, 285
hegemonic masculinities 401
HEIA (high-external-input agriculture) 472, 473, 484
Herder, J.G. 446
Herskovits, Melville 454, 456
Hinduism, and Islam 238–9, 240
Hirschmann, Albert, defence of industrialization 510–11, 518
historical legacies, and democratization 371–2
HIV (human immuno-deficiency virus) 89–95, 98
and breastfeeding 94–5
poverty and inequality 91–3
strategies for preventing transmission 93–5
transmission 90–1, 94
worldwide distribution of infection 89–90
Hobsbawm, Eric 497
Hollingsworth, R. 330, 334
Hong Kong 6
households, and gender bias 395
housing
in Bombay 440
in cities 436–8
effects on health 432
HPI (Human Poverty Index) 16, 19
Human Development Index *see* HDI
human rights, and 'good governance' 380
human-needs centred development 32–6, **34**
Hungary, Soviet invasion of (1956) 6
hunger 65–73
and cash crop production 70–1
chronic **52**, 53, 65–8, 74
crop yields and biotechnology 470, 472
estimate of global 65–7, 74
and famine 51–3
and gender relations 68–9
indirect measures of 52
and social change 70–1
undernutrition and disease 83–4
see also famine
Huntington, Samuel, *The Clash of Civilizations* 444–6, 464, 486, 500–2, 505
Hurricane Mitch 147–8
Husayn, Imam 450, 451
hygiene improvements, and disease 85

IBRD (International Bank for Reconstruction and Development) *see* World Bank

ICPD (International Conference on Population and Development) 125, 138–40
IDA (International Development Association) 205
idealism, and culture 454
identity, politics of 485–508
Ignatieff, Michael 506
IMF (International Monetary Fund) 40, 202, 204, 206–7, 209, 216, 291
    as a development agency 190
    and globalization 347, 348, 349, 350, 360
    and Somali pastoralists 458
    and structural adjustment programmes 292
    on tin mining 154
    and trusteeship 41
immanent development **25**, 36, 48
imperialism **250**
    and industrial capitalism 246, 248–52
    and pre-capitalist states 226–7
    see also colonialism
Incas (Peru) 227–8
inclusiveness, and people-centred development 33
income
    and the 'balance sheet' of human development 7
    in Brazil and Sri Lanka 96
    and capitalism 27
    disease patterns in low-income countries 79–84, 98
    gender allocation of 395–6
    measures of hunger 66
    measures of poverty and development 10–12
    micro-finance to increase women's 122
    and mortality rates 77–9
indentured labour 254, 258, 262
India
    alternative technology in 406
    Bangalore 'Silicon Valley' 433
    biotechnology in 473
    Bombay 430, 440
    caste system 231, 238, 240
    child workers in 102
    colonial rule in 271, 272, 274–9, 281–2, 283, 284, 285, 290
    colonialism in 248, 249
    democracy and development in 375, 377
    and democratization 372
    environmental peasant movements 160
    and European capitalism 220–1

family planning programmes 137
famine prevention 62–3, 64, 68
female economic activity rate 106–7
Gandhi-ism in 115
Green Revolution 422
    and hybrid cotton seeds 476–7
indentured labour 258
industrialization 295
Islam in 34, 237–9
markets 26
Mogul empire 230–3, 234, 235, 237–9, 239–40
and the non-aligned movement (NAM) 6
pre-colonial 326
rural people and cognitive maps 455
sex ratio of the population 399
and socialism 320, 321
the state in 191
urban and rural dwellers 428
women and the environment in 391–2
Indian National Congress 284, 285
individuals
    and alternative development 35, 36
    and capitalist growth 37–8
Indonesia
    capital authoritarian regime 366
    child workers 102
    cocoa production 152
    and socialism 320, 321
    urban and rural dwellers 428
industrial capitalism 32
    and development 267
    and imperialism 246, 248–52, 266
industrial revolution, and colonialism 244
industrialization 31, **32**
    and agriculture 511–14
    and alternative development 48
    in China 314, 318
    and the dependency school 46
    in developing countries 295
    and development 44, 509–32
    ecologically sustainable 520–2
    and economies of scale 516–17, 519
    and globalization 527–8, 529
    and hunger 71
    import substitution 294–5, 517–18
    information and knowledge flows 528
    and the market economy 327
    and material affluence 518–19
    necessity of 510–18
    and non-agricultural production 515–18
    and people-centred development 511, 528–31

    and populism 515–17, 531
    and post-Fordism 522–5
    and Soviet socialist development 311–14
    trust and social capital 525–7
industrialized countries
    and food supplies 52
    and the HPI (Human Poverty Index) 16
industry **31**
inequality
    and access to IT (information technology) 415–16
    and access to water and sanitation 439
    and capitalist growth 38
    disease and public policy 95–7
    and globalization 348–53, 363, 364
    and the globalization of poverty 353–5
    and HIV 91–3
    increase in 340, 341
    of wealth 4
infant mortality **78**
    by country 77, 79
    China 67, 68
    and life expectancy 77, 78
    rate **126**
    and selective biomedical interventions 87
    and undernutrition 84
    urban and rural 81
    see also child mortality
informal sector **107**, 108
information, and industrialization 528
information communication technology, and small enterprises 414–15
information processing technology, and small enterprises 414
information technology *see* IT (information technology)
information and transparency, and 'good governance' 380
integrated development projects 408
intentional development **25**, 36, 39, 41, 45, 48
    and the developmental state 195–6
international debt 4, 8
International Monetary Fund *see* IMF
international political dimension, of colonial rule 272–5, 284, 286
Internet 347
    and the poor 415
interventionalism, and capitalist development 26–8, 29, 43, 45–8
Iran, and Islam 447–52
Iraq 320

irrigation schemes 141
  in Somalia 458
ISI (import substitution
    industrialization) 294–5, 517–18
Islam
  and ancient African kingdoms
    236–7
  and democratization 373
  and Iran 447–52
  and Mogul India 237–9
  religion and society 235–6
  rise of 227, 233–5
  Sunni and Shiite 449–52
IT (information technology)
  and development 404, 412–21, 424
  development priorities for 419–20
  and flexible accumulation 336, 337
  impact of 418–19
  opportunity costs 419
  and the poor 415–17, 420–1
  systemic models of 413–15
  see also technology
Italian Confederation of Artisans 524
Italy
  and the 'industrial district' model
    334
  peasants and amoral familism 455
ITDG (Intermediate Technology
    Development Group) 405

Jacobs, Jane 425
Jamaica, violence and urban dwellers
    432
James, Clive 470
Japan 252
  capitalism in 503
  and the developmental state 359
  and flexible accumulation/
    production 333–4, 522, 523, 525
  and the 'Golden Years' (1950s and
    1960s) 292
  and nationalism 488, 489
Java, agricultural involution in 455, 456
Jayewardene, Julius 381
Jenkin, Patrick 385
Jospin, Lionel 328
Jubilee 2000 358
Judaism, and Islam 235
justice, and people-centred
    development 33

Katznelson, Ira 427–8
Kearney, Robert 340
Keegan, John 500
  'War and Our World' 164, 165, 173
Keynesian view of capitalist
    development 46, 331, 332, 337,
    339

Khomeini, Ayatollah 448, 449, 450,
    452
kinship, and the Mundurucu 'Indians'
    223–4, 226
Kissinger, Henry 9, 464, 497, 502
Kitching, Gavin, on industrialization
    and development 510, 511–18,
    519, 522
Kluckhohn, Clyde 443–4, 447
knowledge
  and industrialization 528
  and technology 408–12, 424
Korea, Japanese colonial rule in 372
Korten, David 32–3, 35, 36, 210, 530
  global threefold human crisis 6, 19,
    47
Kosovo 500
Kroeber, Alfred 443–4, 447
Kyoto Protocol 143–4, 146–7, 159, 161

labour
  and capitalism 242–3, 253–62
  child labour 102, 134, 135, 433
  and colonial economies 253–62,
    270
  and democratization 370–1
  deskilling of 331
  and flexible production 330, 332–9,
    523
  and Fordism 331–2, 334–5, 339,
    340, 342
  and market forces 328–9
  and proletarianization **261**, 261–2
  and semi-proletarianization 258–9,
    259, 261
  and urban livelihoods 435
  see also division of labour; forced
    labour; work
labour market
  casualization 113
  flexibility 328, 334, 335
labour movement 339
  see also trade unionism
labour productivity **113**, 116
  and capitalist growth 37, 38
land
  access to 120–1
  alienation 115
  and colonialism 263–4
  and population distribution 133–4
  urban land market 432
land mines 176, 178–9, 180
landed classes, and colonial rule 278–9
Landes, David, The Wealth and Poverty
    of Nations 335–6, 341
Laos 310
Latin America
  Aztec civilization 228

cities 425, 428, 441
colonialism in 244, 245, 263–4
debt bondage in 259
and democratization 365, 368, 369,
    371, 373, 374
and development reversals 301, 302
economic activity rates 104, 105
economic strategies 359
employment in 102–3
forced labour regimes in 256–8
and globalization 349
housing 436
and industrialization 295, 510–11
informal sector work 108
life expectancy 81
mortality rates 77, 81
primary commodity production 150
setbacks in development 6
slavery 255
undernourished people in 66, 67
unemployment in 101
women's groups in Chile 390
  see also Brazil; Mexico; Peru
LDCs (less developed countries),
    protectionism and pro-market
    forces in 40
Leach, Edmund, The Political Systems
    of Highland Burma 461
League of Nations, colonial mandates
    251, 252
Lee Kwan Yew 376
Leftwich 376, 380, 381
legal framework for development, and
    'good governance' 380
legitimation
  and global capitalism 28
  and the state 190
LEIA (low-external-input agriculture)
    472, 473–4, 484
Lenin, V.I.
  and the Bolshevik revolution 311
  Imperialism: the highest stage of
    capitalism 249–51
  and the NEP (New Economic
    Policy) 312
  and scientific management 331
Lewis, I.M. 461
Lewis, O. 455
liberal democracies 366–7, 368, 369,
    382
  and capitalist industrialization 32
  and development 376–7, 382
  and 'good governance' 379, 381,
    382
  and international power 374
  and socio-economic development
    370
  and the 'Washington consensus' 375

life expectancy **78**
  by country 77, 78–9
  China 67–8, 88–9
  and gender 81–2
  and HIV/AIDS 92
  and hunger reduction 67–8
  and infant mortality 77, 78
'limited good', notion of 455–6
Limits to Growth (Meadows *et al.*) 142
literacy
  and mortality rates 82
  in Sri Lanka and Brazil 96
  and women 82–3
LLDCs (least developed countries), in the 1980s 301
localization 197
lone mothers, and work 385–6

McKeown, Thomas, *The Role of Medicine* 85
McLelland, David 37
McNamara, Robert 206
MAI (Multilateral Agreement on Investment) 308, 362
Major, John 338
malaria 75, 86, 282
Malaysia
  deforestation in 154, 156–7, 158
  economic strategies 359
Malthus, Thomas, on population 125, 132
Mandela, Nelson 304, 372, 417
manufacturing
  and developing economies 356–7
  and primary commodity production 150–1
Mao Tse-tung 315, 316
market efficiency view of intervention 47
market socialism 365–6
markets
  and capitalist growth 37, 38
  free market vision of biotechnology 479–80, 484
  and the 'great transformation' 326–9
  and interventionalism 45
  and the New Policy Agenda (NPA) 305
  pro-market and protectionist movements 39–40, 44
  self-regulating 26, 27
Marshall Plan aid 204, 205, 291, 305
Marx, Karl 258, 259, 262, 310, 321, 325, 326, 338
  and cities 425
  and nationalism 490
  and non-agricultural production 515
  and Weber 444

Marxism 44, **45**, 46, 332
  and social change 453
material affluence, and industrialization 518–19
materialism, and culture 453–4
Mecca 234
media, coverage of wars 175–6
mega-cities 298, **428**, 429–30
men
  in the development process 400–1
  and economic activity 104–5
  and gender analysis of development 384
  and masculine population ratios 399
  Mundurucu 'Indians' 223–5, 226
mercantilism 220, 227, 233, 243, 246, 265–6
merchants, and colonial capitalism 247–8
MERCOSUR 362
Mexico
  changing work patterns 340
  forced labour 256
  peasants and 'limited good' 455–6
  Tzotzile Indian women 383
  women and structural adjustment 395
  'Zapatista' movement 322, 323
micro-credit 122, 396–8
middle class, and democratization 370
Middle East
  and democratization 373
  and imperialism 251–2
  urban centres 428
migration
  and famine 55–6, 72
  periodic labour migration 259, 262
  and population distribution 129
mining
  coal mining in China 146, 147
  in colonial territories 253
  in South Africa 260
  tin mining 154
Mister, Robert 457, 458, 460
MNCs (multinational corporations)
  and biotechnology partnerships 483
  and ecologically sustainable industrialization 521
modernity
  and economic growth 293, 296
  and nationalism 490
  and tradition 325–6, 327
modernization
  development as 30–2, 39
  and technology 404
Mogul empire 230–3, 234, 235, 239–40
  and Islam 237–9
Mongolia, socialist regime in 320

monopoly capitalism 43, 246, 249, **250**
Montreal Protocol 142, 143, 161
mortality rates **78**
  age structure of 80
  and armed conflict 166–7
  CMR (crude mortality rate) 56, 164, 168–9, 172, 187
  and demographic transition theory 128
  and disease 75, 76, 77–9
  and famine 52, 54, 55
  and fertility 127–9
  maternal 131
  selected countries 131
  and sex ratios of population 399
  urban and rural 80–1
  see also child mortality; infant mortality
Moynihan, Daniel Patrick 485–6, 492, 494, 496, 497–8, 500, 505
Mozambique, international NGOs in 182
Muhammad, Prophet 234, 235
multiculturalism, and the new racism 494–6, 502, 505
Mundurucu 'Indians' 222–6
Museveni, Yoweri 367, 368
Muslims *see* Islam

NAM (non-aligned movement) 6–7, 8, 355, 360
Nandy, Ashis 284
Narx, Karl 258
nation-states 197
  and ethnic pluralism 486–96
  and globalization 359–60
  and political regimes 365–8
nationalism 487–91
  theories of 490–1, 504, 507
nationalities, and European colonialism 488
nations
  and human-needs centred development 35
  and nationalism 487–91
neocolonialism 290
neoliberalism 8–10
  and development 42–5, 48, 300–4
  and flexible accumulation 336–8
  and globalization 10, 26, 28, 29, 348–50, 353, 359, 364
  partial demise of 304, 305–6
  and the state 196
  and sustainable development 158–9
neopatrimonialism **286**, 287–8
Nepal, NGOs in 213
'New Competition' 523
New Guinea 222

New Internationalist 70–1
New Malthusian views
    on environmental degradation 148,
      149
    on population 132–4, 138, 139
New Policy Agenda (NPA) 305
new social movements *see* social
    movements
new technology *see* IT (information
    technology)
newly industrializing countries *see*
    NICs
NGOs (non-governmental
    organizations)
    and agricultural biotechnology 472
    as development agencies 210–15,
      216
    and global politics 358
    and globalization 352
    growth of the sector 212–15
    international campaigning 211, 212
    and IT (information technology)
      415
    mutual benefit 211
    and the New Policy Agenda (NPA)
      305
    and people-centred development 34,
      35
    public benefit 211
    service-providing 211, 212
    and trusteeship 41
    in war-affected areas 181–3
    and women 387, 392
Nicaragua 320
NICs (newly industrializing countries)
    8, 295, 303
    and development reversals 301
    and protectionism 46
    R & D (research and development)
      in 422
    and relocation of multinational
      companies 113
NIEO (New International Economic
    Order) 299, 356, 360
Niger, groundnut cultivation and
    environmental degradation 155
Nigeria
    capital authoritarian regime 366
    ethnicity in 492–3
    malaria in 75
non-aligned movement *see* NAM
normative aspects of development **42**,
    44
North Africa
    and democratization 373
    states in 197–8
North, Douglas 453
North Korea 310, 320

Norwegian Refugee Council 170
NPA (New Policy Agenda) 305
nuclear power 404
nutrition
    and the 'balance sheet' of human
      development 7
    and disease 85
    measuring undernutrition 52, **53**
nutritional deprivation 52
Nyerere, Julius 269

Oceania
    economic activity rates 104
    employment in 103
    unemployment in 101
ODA (Official Development
    Assistance) 181, 182, **199**, 207–
      10, 216
    and NGOs 213–15
OECD countries 291, 292, 293, 296
    and globalization 349–50
    inequalities in 354
    and neoliberalism 301
    and structural crisis 297, 299, 300
    urban explosion 298
oil crisis (1973) 297, 299, 332, 356
output technology, and small
    enterprises 414
overpopulation 132–4
    and unemployment 99
Oxfam 211
Oxfam Poverty Report 163–4, 170, 186
ozone depletion 143

Papua New Guinea
    and democracy 369
    health programme 87–8
part-time employment 113
partial democracies 269, 366, 367
partnerships, in biotechnology 482–4
pastoralists
    and cattle complex 454–7
    sedentarization of 459
    Somali 457–60
patent rights, and biotechnology 478–9
patriarchy
    decline of 339
    and Fordism 340
patrimonial authority **280**
    and neopatrimonialism **286**, 286–7
people-centred development 28, 29, 30,
    32–6, 48
    and industrialization 511, 528–31
    and sustainable development 160
perestroika 317
Peru
    forced labour 256, 257
    Incas 227–8, 229

petty commodity production 259–60,
    260, 261, 262
Philippines, and democracy 369
PLA (participative learning and action)
    531
planning, and development 20–1
Poland 322
Polanyi, Karl 3, 4, 25, 36–7, 39–40, 44,
    242, 263
    and the 'great transformation' 241,
      326–9, 336, 427, 428
policing, colonial 281–2, 285
political culture, and democratization
    373
political organization
    in the Mogul empire 231–2
    and the Mundurucu 'Indians' 224
political parties, and the state 192, 194
political regimes
    and democracy 365–8
    and development 374–9
political shifts, and globalization 348
politics
    and the 'balance sheet' of human
      development 7
    and development 193–5
    global politics 355–8
    of identity 485–508
    and socialist development 309–10
poor countries, democracy and
    development 376–9
Pope, Alexander 379
popular culture 443
population control **137**, 137–40
population distribution **126**, 129
population growth 125–40
    and cities 425, 429–30
    in high and low-income countries
      126–7
    and HIV/AIDS 92
    New Malthusian view on 132–4,
      138, 139
    and population size 126–7
    rate **126**
    and resources 125
    selected countries 131
    social view on 134–6
    and unemployment 115
    urban 298
population sex ratios 399
populism, and industrialization 515–17,
    531
Portugal, and imperialism 251
Post, Charles 255–6
post-development school 5, 19, 20–1,
    22, 28, 29
    and cultural anthropology 462–4
Post-Fordism 330

and industrialization 522–5
postmodernism 340–1
    and feminism 383
poverty
    and the 'balance sheet' of human
        development 7
    in Brazil 18
    and child mortality 83–4
    and chronic hunger 67
    conceptions of 10–19
    culture of 455
    debate 13
    and development 3, 5, 34, 36
    and development agencies 216
    and disease 75–98
    and famine 67, 71, 74
    feminization of 393, 398–9
    global 349
    globalization of 353–5
    and GNP **12**
    and HIV 91–3
    and idealism 454
    income measures of 10–12
    and industrialization 510
    and inequality 4
    and interventionism 47
    and IT (information technology)
        412–13, 415–17
    and knowledge 409
    as part of the global 'crisis' 16–19
    and population growth 125, 134,
        138, 140
    in pre-industrial societies 20
    relative 12–14
    rural 148–9, 431
    and technology 403, 404, 405, 405–
        6, 421–3, 424
    in the UK 17
    urban 430–2, 436–42
    and urban services 438–9
'poverty line' 10–11
    in industrialized countries 13–14, 16
power
    of colonial states 271–88
    and globalization 351–2
    and the state 190, 194–5
    state power and democratization
        372
    and technology 403–4
PRA (participative rural appraisal) 531
pre-capitalist societies 219–40, 243
    and European colonization 220–1,
        222, 226–7, 228–9
    and the rise of Islam 233–9
    subsistence producers 221–6
pre-capitalist states 226–33
    Aztec civilization 228
    Bakongo kingdom 226
    and First World War 251

general characteristics of 229–30
    Inca empire 227–8, 229
    Mogul empire 230–3, 234, 235,
        237–9, 239–40
Preobrazhensky, Evgeny 312
prices
    in colonial Africa 273
    fall in commodity prices 151, 152–4
    and GM crops 477
primary commodity production 150–4
production 115–16, 124
    and capitalism 243
    commodity **118**, 118–19
    and economies of scale 516–17, 519
    and famine 58, **59**, 70–1
    flexible 522–5
    global 356–7
    non-agricultural 514–17
    in pre-capitalist states 229–30
    primary commodity production
        150–4
    and reproduction 116–18, **117**, 124
    subsistence **118**
    and work 111
progress **25**
proletarianization **261**, 261–2
protectionism **40**, 44, 46
    agricultural 151–2
    in OECD countries 300–1
PTD (participatory technology
    development) 423, 424
public sector management, and 'good
    governance' 380
Puritanism, and capitalism 445
Putnam, Robert 454

quality, and technical knowledge 410

R & D (research and development)
    422–3, 424
    and GM crops 480
race, and ethnicity 495–6
racism, and multiculturalism 494–6
Rahnema, Majid 21
rainforests
    destruction of 156–8
    technology and knowledge 409
Reagan, Ronald 328, 336
refugees
    and famine 54, 55–6
    from Bosnia & Herzegovina 485,
        497
    from Rwanda 56, 169, 186, 493
    numbers of 129
    and war 169–71, 186, 187
regimes of accumulation **329**, 329–30
regionalism 361–2
Reich, Robert 328–9
relative poverty 12–14

religion
    in colonial societies 264
    see also Christianity; Islam
religious fundamentalism 4, 501–2, 504
renewable resources 149
replacement level **126**
reproduction 116–18, **117**, 124
resources
    and primary commodity production
        150
    renewable and non-renewable 149
Rio Earth Summit (1992) 47, 143, 161,
    306, 520–1
risk adverse strategies, and pro-poor
    technology development 421–2
rural areas, investment in 436–7
rural development
    in China 314, 316
    in former colonial states 287
rural mortality rates 80, 81
rural people, and cognitive maps 455
rural poverty 431
    and environmental degradation
        148–9
rural women, and work 386
rural–urban linkages, and urban
    livelihoods 435–6
Russia
    capitalism development 45
    unemployment 112
Russian Revolution 311
Rwanda
    condom use in 93
    genocide in 184, 499
    Kibeho relief camp 72
    pre-colonial kingdom of 229
    refugees from 56, 169, 186, 493
    supply of weapons to 177

Sachs, Wolfgang 304
sanitation, access to 438–9
São Paulo 430
Sassen, Saskia, *The Global City* 433
Satterthwaite, David 436
scarcity, politics of 148
Scheper-Hughes, Nancy 441
Schroeder, Gerhard 328
Schumacher, E.F., *Small is Beautiful*
    35, 405
scientific management 331
Second World War
    and decolonization 265
    and the doctrines of development
        267
Seers, Dudley 33
selective biomedical interventions 86–
    8, 89
self-help housing 437
self-regulating markets 26, 27

semi-proletarianization 258–9, **259**, 260, 261, 262
Sen, Amartya 14, 51–2, 60–1, 308
Sen, Gita 72–3
sex, and gender 385–6
sexual division of labour 117–18
  and the Mundurucu 'Indians' 223–4
  and structural adjustment 394
Shiite Muslims 449–52
Shiva, Vandana 391
Sikhs 239
Singapore 6
  democracy and development 375, 376
Singer, Hans 290, 303
SIPRI (Stockholm International Peace Research Institute) 165, 166, 167, 168
slave trade 226, 236, 247, 255
slavery 253, 254–6
small enterprises, systemic models of IT (information technology) for 414–15
smallpox 85
Smith, Adam 37, 39, 43, 425
Smith, Anthony, *The Ethnic Origin of Nations* 490–1, 494, 504
social capital **37**, 196, 454
  and trust 525–7
social change
  and colonialism 264–5, 270
  competing views on development and 42–8
  and famine 53–6
  and hunger 70–1
social class
  and democratization 370–1
  and famine 60, **61**
  and gender 388
  and Marxism 45
social dislocation 4
social division of labour **116**
social exclusion **14**, 14–16, **121**, 121–2
  in OECD countries 354
social movements 323, 339
  and NGOs 214
social process, technology as 406–8
social reproduction 117
socialist development 309–24
  in China 6, 310, 314–16, 324
  and the 'classical' conception of socialism 321–2
  and colonialism 265
  crisis in 310, 317–19
  economic 309
  political 309–10
  prospects for 321–4
  Soviet 6, 8, 28, 310–14, 317, 319, 324

society
  and culture 445, 460
  and the state 190
socio-economic development, and democratization 370
Somali pastoralism 457–60
Somalia, humanitarian intervention in 184, 185–6
South Africa
  and democratization 372
  end of apartheid 304
  housing policies 436
  IT (information technology) in 417
  and micro-credit programmes 397
  mining 260
  trade unions 322
  unemployment in 115
  violence against women in 389
South Asia
  HIV infection in 90
  plantation economies 263
  undernourished people in 66, 67, 74
  women and children's claims to food 68, 69
  see also East/South-East Asia
South Commission, on structural adjustment programmes 301–2
South Korea 6, 321, 322, 349–50, 368
  as a developmental state 375, 378, 379
  and industrialization 523–4
South Yemen 310
Southern countries
  cities in 425, 428, 433–9
  and dependency thinking 46
  and land alienation 115
  paid employment in 102–3
  and social exclusion 16
  and state-led socialist development 6
  and women 383, 387, 389, 401
Southern Europe, and democratization 365
Soviet Union 252
  and the Cold War 6
  collapse of the 8, 44, 304, 305, 368
  and democratization 365, 369
  and ethnos theory 495
  and industrialization 510
  management of the Aral Sea Basin 145
  and *perestroika* 317
  and socialist development 6, 8, 28, 310–14, 317, 319, 324
  see also Russia
soybeans, genetically modified 476
Spain, Muslim influence in 235
Spice Islands 248
SPLA (Sudan People's Liberation Army) 179–80

Sri Lanka, wealth, disease and public policy in 95–7
Stalin, Joseph 314, 316
Standard and Poor 357
state institutions, decline of 175
state regulation, and capitalism 43–4
states
  as development agencies 189, 190–9
  and interventionalism 45, 47–8
  key features of 190–1
  and nationalism 487–91
  power of colonial 271–88
  power and democratization 372
  power and globalization 351–2
  pre-capitalist 226–33
  role in development 323–4
  and Sunni and Shiite Muslims 451
  weaknesses of 506
  see also developmental states
statism **283**, 286, 288
statist democracies 367
Stephens, Caroline 439
Stockton, Nicholas 73
strategic management capability 412
Strathern, Marilyn 461–2
structural adjustment 40, 301–4
  gender analysis of 393–6
  and technology 423
  urban impact of 431
  and urban livelihoods 435
structuralism, and capitalist development 26, 29, 42, 43, 44, 45, 48
structure **189**
  and democratization 370, 374
sub-Saharan Africa
  and AIDS/HIV 90, 92
  and biotechnology 470, 473
  colonial rule in 271, 272, 273–5, 279–81
  colonialism in 268
  and democratization 365, 368, 369, 371, 373
  and development reversals 301, 303
  famine in 64
  forced labour regimes 258
  and globalization 359
  informal sector work 108
  life expectancy and population growth 92
  neopatrimonialism in **286**, 286–7
  and new technologies 422
  overpopulation and underpopulation 130
  primary commodity production 150
  reduction in child mortality 86
  setbacks in development 6
  socialist regimes in 320, 321

Somali pastoralism 457–60
undernourished people in 66, 74
and women's employment 394
see also individual countries
subsistence production **118**
Sudan, war and famine in (1983–89)
62, 64
Suez crisis (1956) 6
Sunni Muslims 449, 451
supernatural beliefs, in pre-capitalist
societies 224–5, 229
surplus 38
sustainable development 33, 34, 154–
62, **158**
and ecofeminism 392
global environmental management
view of 160–2
and globalization 360–2, 364
neoliberal view of 158–9
people-centred development view
160

Taiwan 6
as a developmental state 375, 378,
379
Tanganyika Agricultural Corporation
265, 267–8
Tanzania
changing work practices in 111
proletarianization process in 115
refugees expelled from 172
rural development in 287
Social Research Foundation 423
taxation, in the Mogul empire 230
Taylor, F.W. 331
Tebbitt, Norman 328
technical change, and unemployment
113–15
technical division of labour 116
technological advantage, and colonial
rule 282–3
technological capability **411**, 411–12
technological change, and development
30–2
technological shifts, and globalization
348
technology **403**, 403–24
alternative 405, 406
appropriate 405
criteria of appropriateness 407
embedded in social, cultural and
economic relations 405–8,
410–11
from coping to strategic
management 411–12
and knowledge 408–12, 424
leaders and followers 410
learning about 411
and poverty 403, 404, 405

pro-poor technology development
404, 405–6, 421–3, 424
as problem 405, 424
PTD (participatory technology
development) 423, 424
and R & D (research and
development) 422–3, 424
as solution 404, 418, 424
see also biotechnology; IT
(information technology)
terms of trade **294**
TFR (total fertility rate) **126**
Thatcher, Margaret 328, 336, 338
third way 328–9
'Third World', end of the 353–5
TIE (Transnational Information
Exchange) 323
'Tiersmondisme' 356, 358, 360, 361,
364
tin mining 154
Townsend, Peter 12–13
Toyotism (flexible accumulation) 331,
332–8
trade
and colonialism 247–8
global 356–7
and India 238
and mercantilism 220, 227, 233
and pre-capitalist states 226, 227,
236, 237
and the rise of Islam 233–4, 237,
239
trade unionism 321, 322–3
and Fordism 331, 332, 334–5
transformational analysis of
globalization 349, 351–3, 364
transport technology, and colonial rule
282–3
tribute labour 254, 256
TRIPS (Trade-Related Aspects of
Intellectual Property Rights) 478
Trotsky, L. 311, 312, 322
Truman, Harry S. 5, 6
trust, and social capital 525–7
trusteeship, and development agencies
41, 48, 189, 190, 215, 266
tuberculosis (TB), and HIV 93
Turkey, democratization in 373
Turton, David 456

Uganda 221, 381
HIV in 93–4
political regime 367–8
UN (United Nations) 6, 199–204, 487
agencies and famine relief 65
and armed humanitarianism 182–7
budget 200
conferences on Women 384
and democratization 374

as a development agency 190
Economic and Social Council
(ECOSOC) 202, 204, 205, 212
First Development Decade 200
General Assembly 200
and globalization 528
international conferences in the
1990s 304, 306–7
International Court of Justice 200
and IT (information technology) 417
and post-war reconstruction 292
principle organs 201
programmes and specialized
agencies 203
Secretariat 200
Security Council 181, 202
specialist agencies 201
and trusteeship 41
Trusteeship Council 200
and war 163–4
World Commission on Environment
and Development *see* Brundtland
Commission
World Summit on Social
Development (1995) *see*
Copenhagen Summit
see also WHO (World Health
Organization)
UNCHS (United Nations Conference on
Human Settlements) 436, 437
UNCTAD (UN Conference on Trade
and Development) 200, 356, 363
underclass 340
underemployment **120**, 120–1
UNDP (United Nations Development
Programme) 16, 19, 203
Human Development Report 164,
172, 181, 200, 354, 499
The Shrinking State 192
unemployment 99–102 **100**
causes of 99, 112–15
crisis of 19
data on 101–2, 107, 123
and human-needs centred
development 34
in OECD countries 354
and paid work 100–1
and production 115–16
ratio 100
and social exclusion 15–16
and urban poverty 431
see also employment
UNFPA (United Nations Population
Fund) 127, 134, 136–7
UNHCR (United Nations High
Commissioner for Refugees) 164,
170, 182, 187, 202, 203, 210
UNICEF (United Nations Children's
Fund) 203

Adjustment with a Human Face
   393, 394
   and selective biomedical
      interventions 86
United Kingdom *see* Britain
United Nations *see* UN
United States
   carbon dioxide emissions 144–5,
      147
   and the Cold War 6, 8, 9
   employment in 103
   and ethnicity 492
   Food Stamps 67
   and global politics 357
   and the 'Golden Years' (1950s and
      1960s) 292
   and identity politics 503
   income poverty line 14
   informal sector work 108
   and multiculturalism 501
   and nationalism 488
   and post-war reconstruction 291,
      292
   slavery and the development of
      capitalism 255–6
   and socialist regimes 320
   total fertility rate 126
   and women in higher education
      386
urban centres **430**
urban explosion 298
urban growth **428**, 430
urban mortality rates 80–1
urban services, access to 438–9
urbanism **427**, 427–8
urbanization **428**
USAID (United States Agency for
   International Development) 40
USSR *see* Soviet Union
Uthman of the Umayyad 449–50

vaccination programmes 86
Vaughan, Meghan 68
Vietnam 310, 320
   political economy 366, 367
Vietnam War 173
   and displacement 170
   and overpopulation 132–3
violence
   against women 389
   and 'ethnic' identities 454
   and urban poverty 432
'virtuous cycle' of 'good governance'
   379, 381

WAD (women and development) 390
wages, disparity of 113
Wallace, David 520–1

war 163–88
   characteristics of contemporary
      172–80
   civil wars 170, 173–4, 187–8, 454
   colonial wars 280
   combat-related deaths 166–7, 187
   and ethnicity 506
   and famine 57, 58, 62, 73
   and forced displacement 169–72
   in former colonies 167–8
   and intermediate armed conflict 166
   and major armed conflict 165
   and military spending 303
   and minor armed conflict 166
   and prospects for 'human security'
      181–7
   scale of contemporary 164–72
   and Soviet communism 312
'Washington consensus' 40, 352, 363,
   375, 396, 433
water control 141
water pollution 142
water supplies
   access to 438–9
   clean water and disease prevention
      85
   in Sri Lanka and Brazil 96
wealth
   disease and public policy 95–7
   inequalities of 4
Weber, Max 280, 325–6
   and ethnicity 491
   and nationalism 490
   *The Protestant Ethic and the Spirit
      of Capitalism* 444–5, 454
WED (women, environment and
   development) 391, 392
welfare states
   and capitalist development 46–7
   crisis of 322, 337–8, 339
West Africa
   colonial economies 263, 274
   colonial rule 245, 275
   patrimonial authority in 280
   slave trading 255
Western Europe
   economic activity rates 104
   employment in 103
   and the 'Golden Years' (1950s and
      1960s) 292
   HIV in 90
   'nationality' movements in 197
   unemployment in 101
WHO (World Health Organization) 204
   definition of comprehensive
      primary health care 88
   definition of health 75
   and HIV 93, 95

WID (women in development) 384, 390,
   391, 392, 402
   and gender mainstreaming 400
   and micro-credit 396, 397
   and poverty 399
   and structural adjustment 393
Williams, Raymond 444
Winner, Langdon 405
Wirth, Louis 427
Wollo, famine in (1984–85) 56–60, 61,
   62
women
   and the 'balance sheet' of human
      development 7
   and biological reproduction 117
   and development 383–402
   and economic activity 104–7, 109,
      113
   famine and hunger 68–9
   feminism and development
      institutions 384–6
   and fertility 136–7
   and forced labour in Peru 256
   and HIV infection 91, 93
   life expectancy 81–2
   and literacy 82–3
   maternal mortality rates 131
   meeting practical and strategic needs
      of 398–401
   and micro-credit 122, 396–8
   Mundurucu 'Indians' 223–4, 225–6
   as a percentage of the population 399
   and the sexual division of labour
      117–18
   status and political participation 33,
      34
   and structural adjustment 393–6
   and technological knowledge 409
   and technology 407–8
   and underemployment 120
   Vietnamese 367
   violence against 389
   work and development 122–3
   see also feminism; gender
work **105**
   domestic 57, 58, 394–5
   examples of making a living 109–11
   improving ways of making a living
      120–3
   paid and unpaid 111, 119
   technical and domestic 409
   and underemployment **120**, 120–1
   and women 385–6, 394–5
   see also employment; labour
working class
   and democratization 370–1
   and Soviet socialist development
      311, 313

World Bank 40, 202, 204–7, 216, 291
  assessment of the state 196–7
  and conditionality **209**
  and democratization 374, 375, 382
  as a development agency 190
  development goals 4
  and globalization 348, 349, 350, 351, 361, 527, 528
  and 'good governance' 379–81, 382
  and IT (information technology) 412
  measures of poverty 10–11, 14, 16
  and neo-liberalism 42, 45, 328, 336
  and official aid programmes 207–10
  and pro-poor technology development 421
  and Somali pastoralists 458
  and the state in development 323
  and structural adjustment programmes 292, 301, 303–4, 396
  and technology 404, 408–9, 410
  and trusteeship 41
  and urban housing 437
  and women 385, 392
  World Development Report 10, 82, 88–9, 112, 138, 196, 304, 408–9, 410, 421
world cities **430**
World Wide Fund for Nature 159
Worsley, Peter 6, 8, 465
WPF (World Food Programme) 203

WTO (World Trade Organization) 291, 292, 308, 347, 356, 357, 358, 360, 361
  and GM crops 477, 480, 481

Yugoslavia
  'humanitarian' bombing of 187
  and the non-aligned movement (NAM) 6
  war in former 176, 497–9

Zaïre, Kasongo Project Team 88
Zimbabwe, development agencies 210

Indexing by Isobel McLean